D1199068

LINGUISTICS OF AMERICAN SIGN LANGUAGE

LINGUISTICS OF AMERICAN SIGN LANGUAGE

An Introduction

Third Edition

CLAYTON VALLI
CEIL LUCAS

Clerc Books
Gallaudet University Press
Washington, D.C.

Clerc Books
An imprint of Gallaudet University Press
Washington, DC 20002

First edition 1992
Third edition 2000
Printed in the United States of America

Library of Congress Cataloging-in-Publication Data

Valli, Clayton.
Linguistics of American Sign Language : an introduction / Clayton Valli, Ceil Lucas.—3rd ed.
p. cm.
Includes bibliographical references and index.
ISBN 1-56368-097-1
1. American Sign Language—Handbooks, manuals, etc.
I. Lucas, Ceil. II. Title.

HV2474 .V35 2001
419—dc21

00-064369

∞The paper used in this publication meets the minimum requirements of American National Standard for Information Sciences—Permanence of Paper for Printed Library Materials, ANSI Z39.48-1984.

For William C. Stokoe
and for our students

"In 1960, when *Sign Language Structure* and *The Calculus of Structure* were published . . . they argued that paying attention to sign language could only interfere with the students' proper education."

William C. Stokoe
May 1988

"The language [ASL] I finally discovered when I was 14 years old made me understand what's happening around me. For the first time, I understood what was happening and finally started to learn. Now my education brain is blossoming."

Gallaudet undergraduate
November 1990

Contents

Preface to the Third Edition

In the years since the publication of the first edition of *Linguistics of American Sign Language*, we have been fortunate to have had the opportunity to communicate with teachers and students who have used the book. During that same time period, we have been using the text in our classes and workshops. The changes in this edition reflect both our experience and the comments received from users.

In this new third edition, we set out to refine and clarify the existing text and, at the same time, make substantive changes that reflect the ever-developing linguistic thinking about ASL. Readers familiar with the first two editions will find a revised unit on the function of space in ASL and new supplementary readings. In addition, we have added a section on artistic uses of ASL. These changes have been made in order to provide students with a broader understanding of the linguistics of ASL.

It is our hope that the users of this text and its accompanying videotape will continue to find them to be useful tools in their exploration of ASL structure.

Acknowledgments

Many people participated in the preparation of these materials. We gratefully acknowledge our colleagues in the Department of ASL, Linguistics, and Interpretation at Gallaudet University: Scott K. Liddell for detailed feedback on major portions of the text, and Robert E. Johnson and Elizabeth Winston for their feedback and for using the text in their courses on ASL structure. We want to thank Holly Roth and Leslie Rach for using the text and for their valuable feedback, and Sandy Brown of Catonsville Community College for allowing us to field-test the materials in the college's Interpreter Training program. We also thank Ben Bahan, M. J. Bienvenu, Sandra Frankel, Barbara Kannapell, Arlene B. Kelly, Sue Mather, Paul Siegel, Sam Supalla, and Ted Supalla for reviewing the manuscript. We thank Paul Setzer of the Art Department of Gallaudet University for the sign drawings and his models: Steven Collins, Tiri Fellows, Byron Bridges, James Chien Min Chao, and Leslie Saline.

We are grateful to Val Dively for providing the snowmobile story for the videotape and to Robert Hahn for the voiceover. We thank Melanie Metzger, our colleague in the Department of ASL, Linguistics, and Interpretation, for updating the unit on discourse, and Rachel Turniansky and Cheryl Reinagel for preparing the original manuscript. We would like to acknowledge Ivey Pittle Wallace and Jill Hendricks of Gallaudet University Press for their work in the production of the materials.

Finally, we owe a significant debt of gratitude to our students and the many workshop participants who gave us their feedback—they played a central role in the development of the text.

Introduction

We developed *Linguistics of American Sign Language* because of the lack of materials on American Sign Language (ASL) structure at the undergraduate level. The text emerged over the years as we taught ASL structure to fluent users of the language. We had two basic goals in writing this text.

Our first goal is to teach the basic concepts of linguistics as they pertain to ASL structure. To this end, we introduce fundamental areas of linguistic inquiry—phonology, morphology, syntax, semantics, and the use of language—and discuss the phonological, morphological, syntactic, semantic, and sociolinguistic structure of ASL. Our discussion reflects the current state of research in these areas, including the work of individual researchers. We recognize that there is more than one perspective on some aspects of ASL structure. We have chosen to work within the theoretical framework developed by our colleagues in the Department of ASL, Linguistics, and Interpretation at Gallaudet University—Scott K. Liddell and Robert E. Johnson. We also recognize that perspectives on linguistic phenomena are often subject to rapid change, and our materials reflect some of the most significant changes in perspective. One of the most important concepts we want to convey is that linguistic inquiry is a dynamic and flexible undertaking, not a frozen or static one. In fact, even since the first publication of this book in 1992, perspectives on some aspects of sign language structure and its use have changed, and research in areas such as discourse and variation has increased dramatically.

Our second goal is to teach students to think critically about the structure of ASL and about claims that researchers make about that structure. We encourage students *not to memorize* linguistic facts, but rather to *think* about language structure. This text is designed for undergraduate-level students who already know how to sign ASL and who have skills in using the language. For that reason, we set aside the time for class discussions, during which students can think about and question the information being taught. We encourage students to use what they already know to learn about the linguistics of ASL.

Linguistics of American Sign Language consists of seven parts; six of these parts are divided into units. The first part, Basic Concepts, introduces fundamental ideas about languages as unique communication systems. We use this section to focus attention on the fact that ASL is a language. No one can really understand the structure of ASL without first knowing its basic components. The second part, Phonology, provides an introduction to the basic parts of signs and lays the groundwork for the examination of the different aspects of ASL morphology (part three), ASL syntax (part four), and ASL semantics (part five). Part six, Language in Use, deals with variation and historical change, discourse, bilingualism and language contact, and artistic uses of ASL, in other words, how signers *use* their language.

Part seven consists of supplemental readings. The readings are of three types: "classics," such as the articles by Battison and Stokoe, to provide historical background for the study of sign language linguistics; articles that represent current research on ASL; and readings that provide a foundation in general linguistics. Many of the readings cover, in detail, concepts that are explained in the text.

In addition, a two-part videotape accompanies the text. The first part of the videotape contains a short story in ASL. The story will be used for homework assignments. The second part of the videotape follows the text and provides examples of the signs discussed in the text and on the homework.

Because of our focus on the linguistic structure of ASL, we have not included information about Deaf culture or the Deaf community. Your teacher may choose to include such information in your course.

PART ONE

BASIC CONCEPTS

Basic Concepts

GOALS
To identify the basic characteristics of any language, spoken or signed; to understand why ASL is a language; to understand what linguistics is and what linguists do.

SUPPLEMENTAL READINGS
"Analyzing Signs," by Robbin Battison (1978); pp. 199–218

Files 4, 5, and 6 from *Language Files: Materials for an Introduction to Language,* by Monica Crabtree and Joyce Powers (1991); pp. 219–230

WHAT IS A LANGUAGE?

In this course, we will explore the structure of ASL. The scientific study of language is called linguistics. Linguists are interested in discovering and describing the rules that govern the communication system we call language. Linguists analyze many aspects of language (see p. 2 for a list of the major subfields of linguistics). We will begin with a discussion of the basic characteristics common to all languages, whether signed or spoken.

Language is a rule-governed communication system. A communication system is a system that people use to communicate information to each other. When a system is based on rules that its users know and follow, it is called a *rule-governed system.* Without these rules, people would not have a communication system, making communication impossible. Other rule-governed communication systems include Morse code, semaphore (the flag system used in the United States Navy), traffic signals, symbols used in public places, and the communication systems used by bees, birds, dolphins, and nonhuman primates. Both Morse code and semaphore use symbols to represent letters of the alphabet, numbers, and, in the case of Morse code, punctuation, so they are in essence "codes for codes," codes for a writ-

The Major Subfields of Linguistics

Listed below are some of the major subfields of linguistics and the aspect of language with which each is especially concerned.

ANTHROPOLOGICAL LINGUISTICS: the study of the inter-relationship between language and culture (particularly in the context of non-Western cultures and societies).

APPLIED LINGUISTICS: the application of the methods and results of linguistics to such areas as language teaching; national language policies; lexicography; translation; and language in politics, advertising, classrooms, courts, and the like.

HISTORICAL LINGUISTICS: the study of how languages change through time; the relationships of languages to each other.

MORPHOLOGY: the study of the way in which words are constructed out of smaller meaningful units.

NEUROLINGUISTICS: the study of the brain and how it functions in the production, perception and acquisition of language.

PHONETICS: the study of speech sounds; how they are articulated (articulatory phonetics); their physical properties (acoustic phonetics); how they are perceived (auditory/perceptual phonetics).

PHONOLOGY: the study of the sound system of language; how the particular sounds used in each language form an integrated system for encoding information and how such systems differ from one language to another.

PRAGMATICS: how the meaning conveyed by a word or sentence depends on aspects of the context in which it is used (such as time, place, social relationship between speaker and hearer, and speaker's assumptions about the hearer's beliefs).

PSYCHOLINGUISTICS: the study of the interrelationship of language and cognitive structures; the acquisition of language.

SEMANTICS: the study of meaning; how words and sentences are related to the (real or imaginary) objects they refer to and the situations they describe.

SOCIOLINGUISTICS: the study of the interrelationship of language and social structure; linguistic variation; attitudes toward language.

SYNTAX: the study of the way in which sentences are constructed; how sentences are related to each other.

Note: Reprinted by permission of the publisher, from M. Crabtree and J. Powers, compilers, *Language Files: Materials for an Introduction to Language* (1991):5. Columbus: Ohio State University Press.

ing system. Language shares some features with other communication systems, but is also distinguished from other communication systems by a number of features.

Features Shared by Language and Other Communication Systems

Language Is Composed of Symbols. Language, as other communication systems, is composed of symbols that its users manipulate to produce meaning. Different kinds of symbol systems exist to facilitate linguistic communication. English has a writing system that uses symbols to represent sounds or combinations of sounds. For example, the written letter *a* is a symbol for one sound in the English word *cat*, and the combination of written letters is a symbol for an entity in the real world; *cat* is a symbol for a small mammal having a tail, whiskers, etc. The spoken English word is a symbol, part of a different symbolic system separate from the written system, though not unrelated to it. The ASL sign CAT is also a linguistic symbol (see

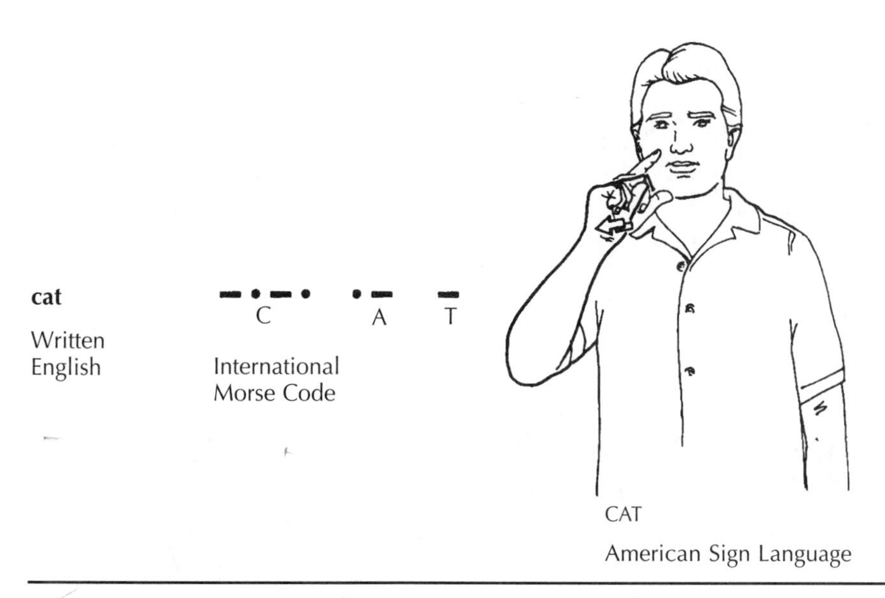

FIGURE 1. Symbolic representation of "cat."
Note: This is one of several variants of the sign CAT.

Figure 1). (Small capital letters are used for the English word that corresponds to the ASL sign. This is called a gloss and will be discussed at length in part two.)

Language Is a System; Symbols Are Organized and Used Systematically. Languages are rule-governed systems, and it is the job of linguists to discover what the rules are and how the system works, a job that is not always easy. The rule-governed nature of ASL can be explained, in part, by examining the conditions on the formation of ASL signs. These conditions were first described by Robbin Battison (1978) as a result of his observations about the structure of ASL signs. Battison proposed that sign formations were based on two conditions, which he called the Symmetry Condition and the Dominance Condition. The Symmetry Condition states that in a two-handed sign, if both hands move, then they will have the same handshape and type of movement. This is illustrated by the signs DRAMA and MAYBE. The Dominance Condition states that in a two-handed sign, if each hand has a different handshape, then only the active hand can move; the passive hand serves as a base and does not move. (For right-handed signers, the right hand is the active or dominant hand, while the left hand is the passive or base hand. The opposite is true for left-handed signers.) The Dominance Condition is illustrated by the signs WORD and MONEY.

When a two-handed sign has different handshapes, Battison reported that the passive hand tends to be one of seven basic handshapes—B, A, S, O, C, 1 (or G), or 5 (see Figure 2). From this information, it is clear that sign structure is not random. Signs can be grouped into different classes; for example, signs like DRAMA and MAYBE are systematically different from signs like WORD and MONEY.

Several observations can be made at this point.

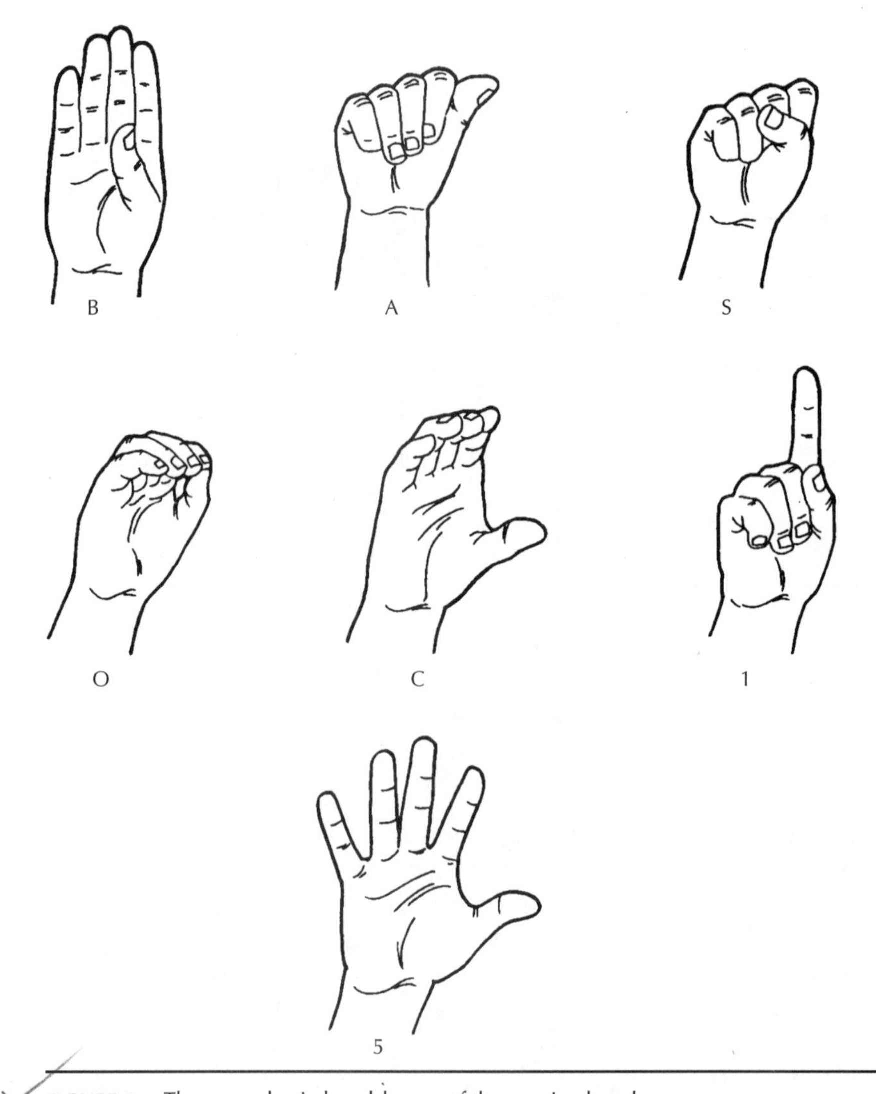

FIGURE 2. The seven basic handshapes of the passive hand.

1. ASL users can think of many examples of signs in both classes.
2. If both hands move in signs like WORD and MONEY, the sign looks odd and seems to break the rules.
3. The movement in DRAMA and MAYBE is alternating, meaning that the hands move in exactly opposite ways (that is, when the right hand is up, the left hand is down; when the left hand moves up, the right hand moves down). If the movement is not alternating, the signs look funny and seem to break the rules.

Not all two-handed signs where both hands move require alternating movement; some use simultaneous movement, as seen by the signs CAN (be able to) and PLAY. The point is that the signs DRAMA and MAYBE clearly illustrate some underlying structure or rules. It is also important to begin to notice and describe sign structure—How many hands does the sign DRAMA have? Are the handshapes the same or different? Is the movement of the hands alternating or simultaneous? Skilled users of ASL and some native users may never have noticed or articulated the rules that govern the structure of signs.

Symbol Forms May Be Arbitrary or Iconic. When talking about the forms of a communication system, *arbitrary* means that the actual form of the symbol does not reflect the form of the thing or activity it symbolizes. *Iconic* means that the form of the symbol is an icon or picture of some aspect of the thing or activity being symbolized. Examples of "folk explanations" of the origin of signs based on iconicity include the sign GIRL, which is made on the chin to represent bonnet ribbons; and the sign MAN, which depicts the brim of a hat.

All languages, spoken and signed, have examples of arbitrary forms and iconic forms. Liddell (1990) pointed out that this is not an either-or issue. All languages have iconic and arbitrary symbols. This recognition is especially important for the study of sign language structure because until recently, although researchers recognized the iconicity in ASL signs, they did not seem to know how this fit in the overall description of ASL structure. Furthermore, linguists had a definite sense that admitting the existence of iconicity in sign languages was admitting that sign languages were not "real" languages, certainly not as real as spoken languages whose forms were supposedly arbitrary. It was as though the arbitrary nature of ASL signs had to be emphasized to prove that ASL is a real language and not just a collection of "pictures in the air."

In many communication systems, the actual form of the symbols used may be arbitrary; that is, the fact that red traffic lights are red is of no importance. What is important is the constant relationship between the form, a red light, and its conventional meaning, stop. The actual *form* of the dance that bees do has no connection with the distance from the hive. Likewise, the actual number of dots and dashes in each Morse code signal or the actual design on a semaphore flag is arbitrary. What is important in each case is the relationship between the established form and the meaning. Likewise, in language, the actual forms that speakers or signers use may be arbitrary. We discussed the English word *cat*, which consists of three sounds, *k ae t*. The combination of those sounds and the resulting form is arbitrary; that is, the form of the linguistic symbol does not reflect the physical entity it symbolizes. Nothing about the word *cat* is reminiscent of an actual cat.

Not all words in spoken languages are completely arbitrary in their form. Linguists have described processes in spoken languages such as onomatopoeia and phonesthesia. Onomatopoeia in spoken languages occurs when the linguistic form of a word symbolizes the sound of the object or activity to which the form refers. For example, the sound that a rooster makes is called *cock-a-doodle-do* in English, *chi chi ri chi* (*ch* is pronounced as *k*) in Italian, and *kokekokko* in Japanese. Another example in English would be *choo choo*, referring to a train.

Phonesthesia describes groups of words that resemble each other and whose form seems to reflect their meaning. For example, Bolinger (1975) pointed out that English words that end in *-ump*, such as *rump, dump, hump, mump, lump, bump,* seem to share a meaning of heaviness and bluntness. Likewise, words such as *twirl, whirl, furl,* and *gnarl* seem to share a meaning of twisting. One problem with the linguistic analysis of such words is that *-ump* and *-irl* or *-url* cannot be isolated and described as meaningful units in the way that meaningful units (or morphemes) are traditionally isolated and described. Nevertheless, part of the linguistic form of the word seems to symbolize some aspect of the thing or activity that it represents, and that is what iconicity means: The linguistic form is an icon or picture of some aspect of an entity or activity.

It would appear, then, that all spoken languages have iconicity. And clearly, sign languages have iconicity as well. While the form of many signs, such as WRONG or LOUSY, is arbitrary, the form of many other signs reflects some physical aspect of the entities or activities they represent.

Sarah Taub (2000) speculated that iconic forms are created in ASL when a mental image associated with an original concept is selected (for example, a typical tree for the sign TREE). This image is then *schematized* so that it can be represented in the language. In this process, the essential features are kept and the unnecessary ones are dropped—using the example of the sign TREE, it doesn't matter exactly how many branches an actual tree has or how thick the trunk is. This image is then *encoded*, using the appropriate aspects of ASL, such as the forearm and the 5 handshape. The result is an iconic symbol that is a part of the vocabulary of the sign language.

Images are schematized differently in different sign languages. This can be seen in the different signs for STUDENT in ASL, Italian Sign Language (LIS), and Thai Sign Language (see Figure 3). So, simply because the forms of some signs reflect some physical aspect of the entity or activity to which they refer (i.e., are iconic) does not mean that there are no arbitrary forms in ASL or that ASL is a col-

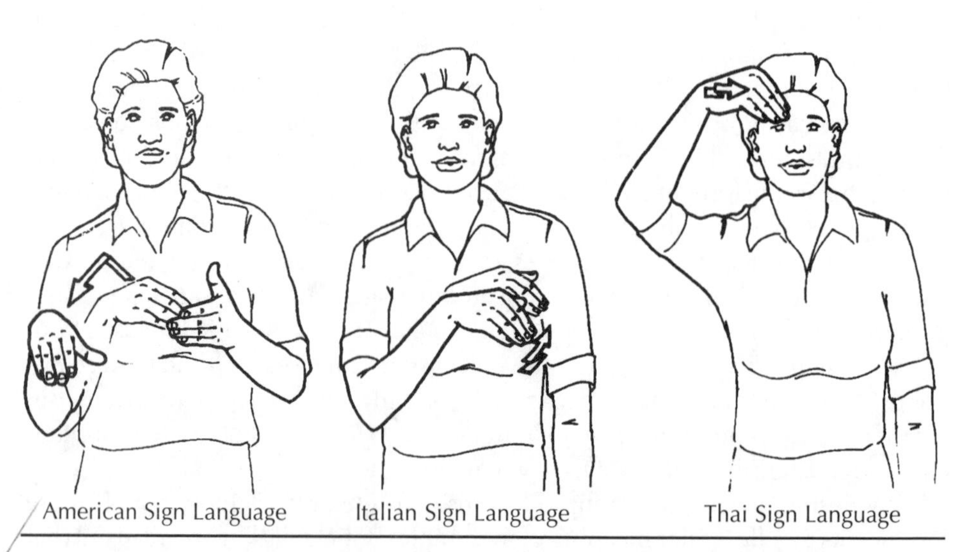

FIGURE 3. Signs for STUDENT in ASL, Italian Sign Language, and Thai Sign Language.

lection of pictures in the air with no grammatical structure. For example, it is probably true that the form of the sign SIT is an iconic representation of human legs sitting. However, other sign languages have different ways of symbolizing this concept; the actual way of iconically symbolizing in sign language is language specific. That is, as long as some physical aspect is symbolized, it doesn't matter which of several symbolizeable aspects is chosen, and different sign languages choose different aspects.

While the sign SIT may be iconic, focusing on its iconicity will not provide much insight into the interesting relationship between SIT and the noun CHAIR, and other noun-verb pairs like it. Nor will it help explain how the movement of the verb SIT can be modified to mean SIT-FOR-A-LONG-TIME (slow, circular movement) or SIT-ABRUPTLY (short, sharp movement). Finally, while the sign SIT may be iconic of human legs sitting, the sign for CAT SIT is made with two bent fingers, not four, even though most cats have four legs; the signs CAT SIT and BIRD SIT are made with the same two bent fingers, even though cats and birds have different kinds of legs. The point is that while signs may be iconic, iconicity does not mean a literal representation of the thing or activity. Sign are linguistic units; they are not pictures in the air. While the iconicity of signs is interesting and important, it is only one aspect of American Sign Language structure (see Figure 4).

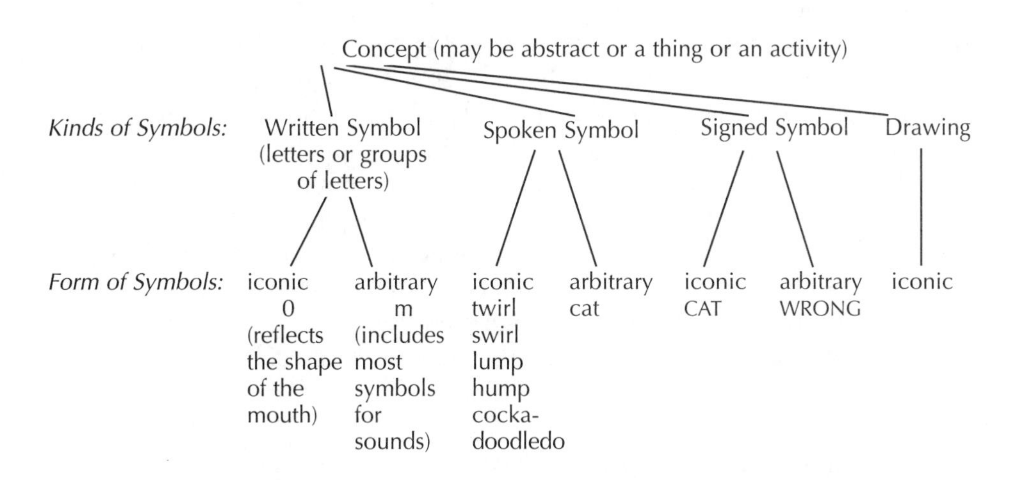

Arbitrary: The form of the symbol does *not* reflect the characteristics of the concept, thing, or activity it symbolizes.

Iconic: The form of the symbol *does* reflect some characteristic of the concept, thing, or activity it symbolizes.

Note: The form of the symbol may be arbitrary or iconic; the form cannot be predicted; what can be predicted is the *constant* relationship between a symbol (arbitrary or iconic) and a concept, to produce a meaning.

It is possible to have symbols for other symbols. For example, CAT is the written symbol for the ASL signed symbol (9 handshape on the cheek).

FIGURE 4. Arbitrary and iconic symbols.

Members of a Community Share the Same Communication System. Users of Morse code know how the system works; likewise, sailors who use semaphore share a knowledge of that system. Bees, dolphins, and birds share the rules of their respective communicative systems. And the same can be said for the users of communication systems that are known as languages. The concept of a community of users traditionally has been the source of debate in linguistics. Nevertheless, it is possible to define communities of users, often in terms of regional, ethnic, occupational, socioeconomic, or gender differences. That is, users of American Sign Language in one part of the country may have different signs from users in another part of the country; black signers may sign differently from white signers; particular occupational groups may have special signs for their work; although no research is yet available on this, it may be the case that middle-class, college-educated signers sign differently than working-class signers who completed high school; men and women may sign differently depending on the topic.

Many ASL signs have regional variants. Although this has not been studied extensively, there is evidence of its occurrence. It is not a question of a "wrong" sign or a "right" sign, but simply a question of different signs for the same concept.

Features That Make Language Unique

Language Is Productive; The Number of Sentences That Can Be Made Is Infinite; and New Messages on Any Topic Can Be Produced at Any Time. Other communication systems are limited in the number of messages that can be produced. Bees show limited productivity, while the calls that birds make show none. That is, there is a limit to the number of messages that birds and bees produce. Since semaphore and Morse code are codes for a written language, an infinite number of messages *could* be produced, but it would be impractical. Semaphore and Morse code are designed for the rapid communication of a limited number of messages. However, the number of sentences that can be produced with the symbols and signals of human language is infinite. It is impossible to even try to count how many sentences can be produced in a given language. Part of the very nature of language is that the number of sentences is infinite, that anything can be encoded.

Language Has Ways of Showing the Relationship Between Symbols. In other communication systems (e.g., Morse code, semaphore, and animal systems), the symbols occur sequentially, and the perceiver gets meaning from seeing or hearing the sequence of symbols. But other communication systems do not have ways of showing a relationship between symbols, while languages do. For example, in the English sentence *The boy sits on the couch,* the *-s* on the verb *sit* indicates that the subject of the verb is third person singular; that is, the *-s* shows a relationship between the verb and the subject noun. In the sentence *The boy drives carelessly,* the word that follows the verb is known as an adverb, and it describes the verb.

ASL also has ways of showing relationships between symbols. The verbs DRIVE and LOOK AT can be signed with the mouth in what is usually described as "mm," with the lips slightly protruded. This facial expression is a nonmanual signal that can be translated into English as "regularly, unexceptionally." This nonmanual signal is very different from "th," with the lips pouted and the tongue visibly positioned between the teeth. This can be translated into English as "carelessly." (See part three for further explanation of nonmanual adverbs.)

Languages have grammatical signals that are used to show the relationship between symbols. English has a class of words called *prepositions* that are used to show the relationship between other words. In the sentence, *The book is on the table*, the word *on* shows the relationship between the words *book* and *table*. ASL shows this relationship in a different way. The sentence could be translated as

```
_____________t    ____t
TABLE INDEX-right,  BOOK   CLASSIFIER-PREDICATE-for-BOOK ON TABLE
```

In ASL, the relationship between the table and the book is shown with the use of *classifier predicates*, not with a preposition. The classifier predicate in this sentence is the sign used to show the book being placed on the table. The *t* on top of the signs TABLE and BOOK indicates topicalization; in other words, by raising the eyebrows and tilting the head slightly, the signer can indicate the topic of the sentence. ASL has a way of showing the relationship between symbols, a way that is different from English.

Language Has Mechanisms for Introducing New Symbols. The set of symbols used in other communication systems is limited and set. New symbols cannot be introduced during the course of use. However, one of the most interesting facts about language is that it permits the constant introduction of new symbols by a variety of avenues. The sign MICROWAVE was introduced fairly recently, for example, through the process of compounding. Other examples of ASL compounds include HOME (EAT⁀SLEEP), BROTHER (BOY⁀SAME), AND RESEMBLE (LOOK⁀STRONG).

New signs are added to the language as a result of language contact. Many American signs for countries are now being abandoned in favor of the country's own sign (see Figure 5). The Deaf Way conference, an international meeting held

American Sign Language: ITALY

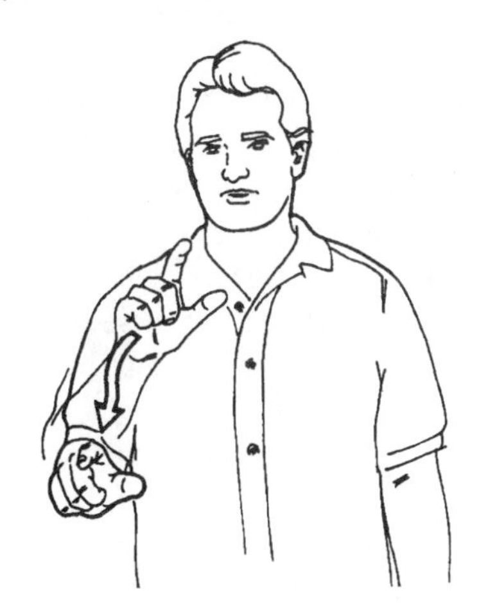

Italian Sign Language: ITALY

FIGURE 5. The ASL and Italian Sign Language signs for ITALY.

FIGURE 6. The Deaf Way sign for CLUB.

at Gallaudet University in July 1989, had the effect of introducing a number of new signs into ASL, such as the sign for CLUB (see Figure 6).

Language Can Be Used for an Unrestricted Number of Domains. The domains (topic areas) of other communication systems are generally restricted to essential survival or emergency management; this is not the case with a language. The communication systems that animals use are restricted to the domains of food, danger, and mating, while the domains of semaphore are restricted to navigational and emergency information. However, language can be used for any domain that humans need to express, from survival and emergencies to philosophy and art. Again, since semaphore and Morse code are codes for written language, it would be *possible* to discuss any topic, but highly impractical.

The Symbols Can Be Broken Down into Smaller Parts. In most other communication systems, each symbol is a discrete unit that does not seem to have internal structure that can be manipulated by its users. For example, there are different types of bee dances, but the units that make up the dances cannot be recombined to make new dances; some research evidence shows the existence of smaller parts in birdsong and primate calls; the design on a semaphore flag is constant and discrete, as is the number of beeps in a Morse code signal. However, a fascinating fact about language is that the symbols of which it is composed can be broken down into smaller parts. In linguistics, this fact is called *duality of patterning*. In language, meaningless units are combined to form arbitrary symbols, and these symbols can in turn be recombined to create larger meaningful units. This point can be illustrated by comparing the signs LOUSY, AWKWARD, and PREACH with the signs THREE-MONTHS, THREE-DOLLARS, and NINE-WEEKS. All six signs have internal structure: they each have a handshape, a location, a palm orientation, and movement. In ASL, the separate parts of some of the signs also have independent mean-

PREACH (handshape has no meaning)

NINE-MONTHS (handshape has specific meaning)

FIGURE 7. A comparison of signs in which handshape has no meaning and specific meaning.

ing. In the signs THREE-MONTHS, THREE-DOLLARS, and NINE-WEEKS, the handshape has specific meaning, such that the sign THREE-MONTHS is different from TWO-MONTHS, the sign THREE-DOLLARS is different from FIVE-DOLLARS, and NINE-WEEKS is different from SIX-WEEKS.

In other signs, all the parts together have one meaning. For example, in LOUSY, AWKWARD, and PREACH, the handshape has no meaning; all of the parts of the sign function together as a unit (see Figure 7).

More than One Meaning Can Be Conveyed by a Symbol or a Group of Symbols. In other communication systems, each symbol or group of symbols has one meaning. These systems are incapable of expressing irony, sarcasm, humor, or indirectness. Not so with language. A single ASL sentence can function as a request for information, a command, or a statement. In any language, a single symbol or group of symbols may have different functions and, conversely, a single function may be realized by different symbols. For example, the simple question in ASL,

$\overline{\text{HOME YOU}}^{\,q}$

meaning, "Are you going home?" can function either as a request for information or as a request for a ride home. [Note: the *q* above the line indicates a yes-no question, which entails raising the eyebrows and thrusting the head slightly forward (see Figure 8).] In linguistics, these differences have to do with *pragmatics*; that is, the meaning of a word or sentence depends upon aspects of the context in which it is used, such as time, place, relationship with the other person, and so forth. Related to this is the fact that we can also use language to lie or misrepresent a situation. While some birds do learn the calls of other bird species for the purposes of deception, it may be purely genetically determined behavior.

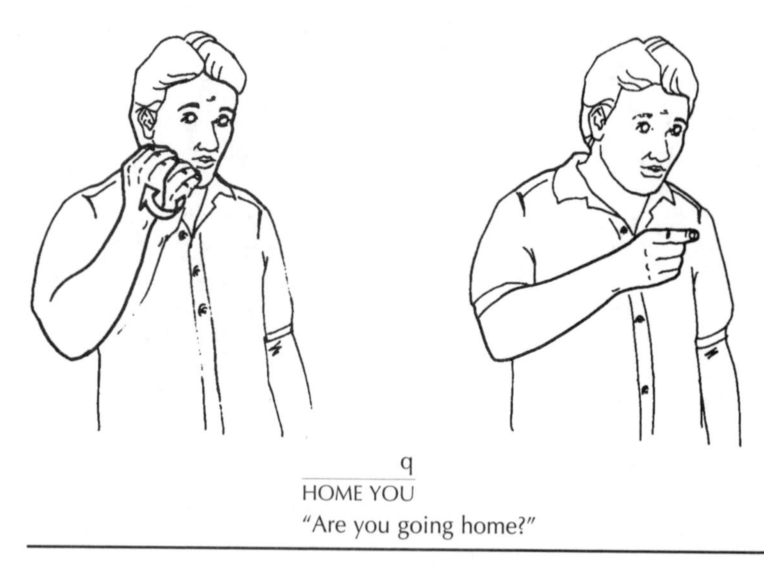

FIGURE 8. An example of raised eyebrows and head tilt with yes-no questions.

Language Can Refer to the Past, the Future, and Nonimmediate Situations; It Is Not Restricted to the Present and the Immediate. The feature of language that allows users to refer to different time periods is known as displacement. Other communication systems generally are restricted to present and immediate situations. It is true that the dance that bees perform may refer to a food source not in the immediate vicinity, but the reference is nonetheless to a fairly immediate entity. Birdsong shows no evidence of displacement. Language distinguishes itself by allowing references to events and entities not immediately present, and to past, future, and conditional events and entities. This concept is illustrated in the following ASL sentence:

> YESTERDAY PRO.3 TOLD-ME GO WILL PRO.3
> "Yesterday she told me she would go."

In this sentence, PRO.3 refers to a person who is not immediately present; the sign YESTERDAY refers to an event that happened prior to this particular sentence. (The structure and function of what is written as PRO.3 will be discussed in part three.)

Language Changes Across Time. A major difference between language and other communication systems is that language changes across time as the result of use and interaction among users. While other communication systems may change, change must be consciously introduced and is not the result of natural interaction and use. This is not so with language. New words or signs are added to a language to reflect new technology (for example, the sign COMPUTER). Existing signs change over time. You can see this by comparing your signs for COW, WILL, TOMATO, and HELP with the older forms of these signs illustrated on the videotape (see Figure 9). What changes do you see?

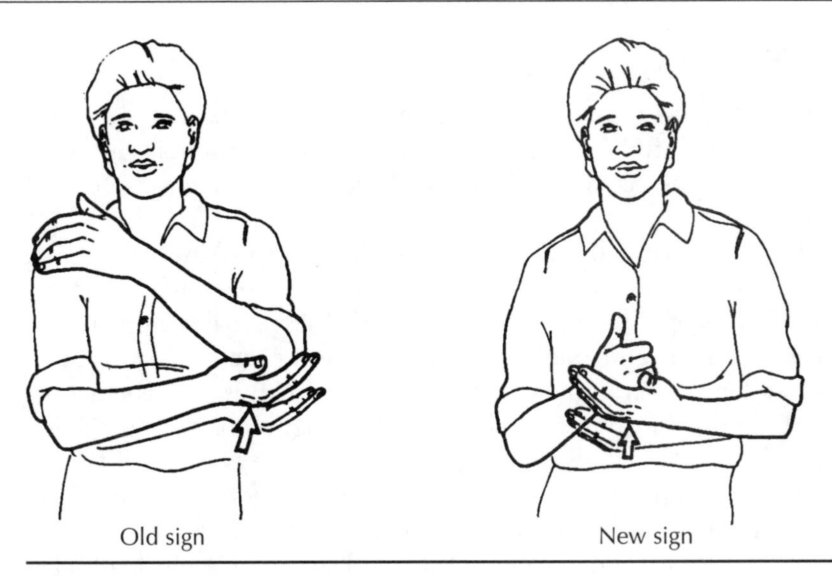

FIGURE 9. A comparison of old and new signs for HELP.

Language Can Be Used Interchangeably. All users of a language can send and receive messages. This is not true, though, of other animal communication systems. Birdsong, for example, is done only by males, and bee dancing is done only by the foragers, the bees who hunt for food.

Language Users Monitor Their Use. As people produce language, they listen to or watch themselves, and they also correct themselves if they think the production is faulty. If an ASL signer produces the wrong sign, he or she may erase the air or sign NO-I-MEAN and start over. Researchers don't know if birds and bees monitor their messages or not.

Parts of the System Must Be Learned from Other Users. A lot of research evidence indicates that humans are born with an innate capacity to learn and use language. Children must interact with adults and with other children to completely learn their language. Researchers think that this may be important for bee dancing and birdsong, but probably only to a limited extent.

Language Users Can Learn Other Variants of the Same Language. Clearly, users of ASL from New York can learn and use California signs that may differ from New York signs. And users of ASL can learn and use foreign sign languages. Research shows that this is simply not the case with bees, birds, and nonhuman primates—they seem to be restricted to using one variant.

Language Users Use the Language to Discuss the Language. Users of language write dictionaries, grammar books, and linguistics textbooks. They reflect upon their language, they think about it, and discuss it. This feature seems to be unique to the human species.

WHAT IS ASL? WHY IS ASL A LANGUAGE?

American Sign Language is a natural language used by members of the North American Deaf community. It is a language that has developed naturally over time among a community of users. ASL exhibits all of the features of language discussed in this section.

Not much is known about the deaf people who lived in North America before 1817, but some probably came from Great Britain or Europe and some were probably born here. Deaf people who came from other countries probably brought their sign languages with them, and other communities of deaf people living in America probably developed their own language. Because there was little contact between different communities, several kinds of sign language probably were used in America before 1817.

In 1817, Thomas Hopkins Gallaudet and Laurent Clerc established the Connecticut Asylum for the Education and Instruction of Deaf and Dumb Persons—now called the American School for the Deaf—in Hartford, Connecticut. Gallaudet had met Clerc when he travelled to Europe in search of a method for educating Alice Cogswell, the deaf daughter of his neighbor, Dr. Mason Cogswell (Lane, 1984). He had first gone to Great Britain to learn about the oral method used by the Braidwood Schools in Scotland and near London, but the directors of these schools refused to share their methods.

While in London, Gallaudet met a Frenchman by the name of Sicard, who was the director of the Royal Institution for the Deaf in Paris. Sicard was in London with two of his deaf students, Jean Massieu and Laurent Clerc, demonstrating the success of his teaching methods. The method used at the Royal Institution involved the use of French Sign Language along with a set of signs invented to represent parts of written and spoken French not found in French Sign Language. These so-called methodical signs were originally developed by Abbé de l'Epée, the founder and first director of the school in Paris. Sicard invited Gallaudet to the Royal Institution to learn French Sign Language and their teaching method. Gallaudet accepted Sicard's offer and spent several months in Paris. When he returned to the United States, he was accompanied by Laurent Clerc. Clerc came to the United States to help establish a school for deaf children in Connecticut. On the trip to the U.S., Clerc taught Gallaudet French Sign Language, and Gallaudet taught Clerc English.

Many deaf people and some hearing people came to Hartford to learn the method being used at the newly established school. Some of the deaf students who came to Hartford brought their own sign language with them, including those from Martha's Vineyard. They also learned the sign language being used at the school, which no doubt included some French signs. As students graduated, they became teachers in other schools, thus spreading sign language to states across the country.

ASL is very different from systems such as SEE or LOVE that were developed to represent English on the hands for use in deaf education. (These systems are also commonly known as Manually Coded English, or MCE.) ASL and other sign languages are also very distinct from the gestures found in many spoken languages. As

David McNeill (1992) explained, and as we will see as we explore the structure of ASL, one of the basic principles of languages is that parts combine to create larger wholes. In ASL, handshape, movement, and other grammatical features combine to form signs and sentences. In spoken languages, smaller gestures do not combine to form larger gestures, and gestures usually only occur while a person is speaking. In addition, units of language have standards of form (that is, a word or a sign is consistently produced the same way and that way is recognized by the community that uses it). Gestures do not have such standards of form. Each gesture is created at the moment of speaking and is not controlled by the structure of a linguistic system. ASL is such an autonomous linguistic system and it is independent of English. It has all of the features that make a language a unique communication system. ASL is a language.

REFERENCES

Battison, R. 1978. Analyzing signs. In *Lexical borrowing in American Sign Language*, 19–58. Silver Spring, MD: Linstok Press.

Bolinger, D. 1975. *Aspects of language*. 2d. ed. New York: Harcourt Brace Jovanovich.

Lane, H. 1984. *When the mind hears*. New York: Random House.

Liddell, S. 1990. Lexical imagery in American Sign Language. Paper presented at Theoretical Issues in Sign Language Research, III, May 17–19, Boston.

McNeill, D. 1992. *Hand and mind: What gestures reveal about thought*. Chicago: University of Chicago Press.

Taub, S. 2000. *Language and the body: Iconicity and metaphor in American Sign Language*. Cambridge: Cambridge University Press.

PART TWO

PHONOLOGY

UNIT 1

Signs Have Parts

GOAL

To introduce the concept that signs have parts, that signs have internal structure.

We know that one of the features that makes language unique is that the symbols that make up language can be broken down into smaller parts. Phonology is the study of the smallest contrastive units of language. For spoken languages, those contrastive units are sounds, and linguists study how the sounds in a language are structured and organized.

ANALYZING THE PARTS OF SIGNS

Sign language linguists use the term phonology to refer to the study of how signs are structured and organized. ASL signs have five basic parts—handshape, movement, location, orientation, and nonmanual signals (facial expression). These basic parts are also known as parameters. Signs can share one or more of the same parameters. For example, the sign FEEL has the same handshape as the sign SICK, the same movement as the sign HAPPY, and the same location as the sign COMPLAIN. SUMMER and DRY differ in location, RED and CUTE in handshape, SHORT and TRAIN in palm orientation, and SIT and CHAIR in movement. However, these pairs share three parameters: SUMMER and DRY share handshape, movement, and orientation; RED and CUTE share movement, orientation, and location; SHORT and TRAIN share handshape, location, and movement; and SIT and CHAIR share location, handshape, and orientation (see Figure 10). It is the difference in one parameter that is responsible for the difference in meaning.

We know that signs have parts, and we must identify those parts in order to know the meaning of a sign. We know from signs like SUMMER and DRY that location must be an important part because SUMMER and DRY have different meanings, yet the only difference between the two signs is the location. Likewise, we know from signs like SIT and CHAIR that movement must be an important part because

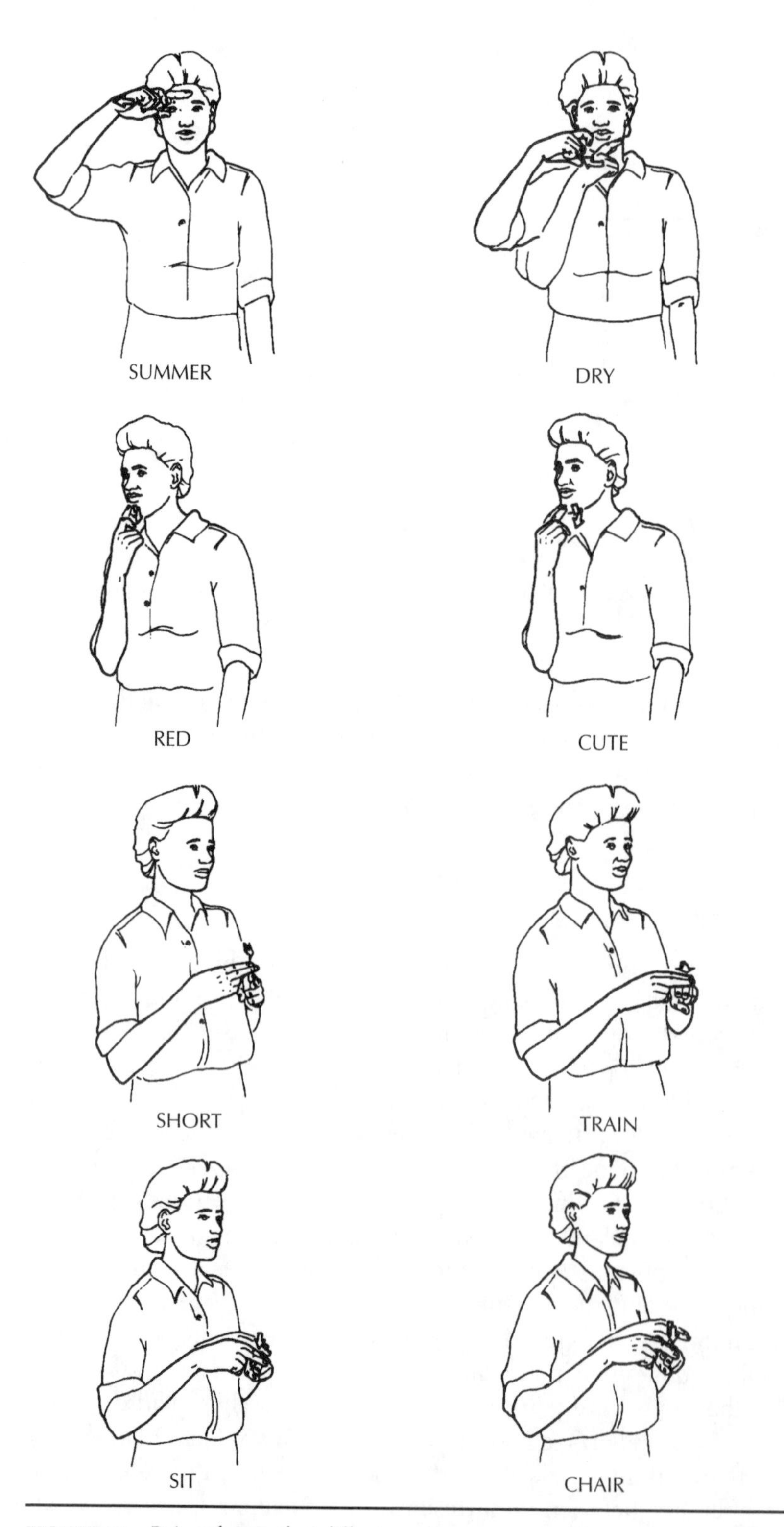

FIGURE 10. Pairs of signs that differ in only one parameter.

the only difference in the form of the two signs is the movement. The same is true of handshape for RED and CUTE and orientation for SHORT and TRAIN. The basic questions to be answered when analyzing pairs of signs are How do you know that pairs of signs have different meanings? and What part of the sign is responsible for the difference in meaning?

Nonmanual signals are the fifth basic part of signs. Many signs in ASL require a nonmanual signal in order to be produced correctly. Nonmanual signals are the facial expressions that accompany certain signs. For example, the sign NOT-YET is usually made with the mouth open and the tongue slightly out; the sign FINISH is made with the lips protruded. Without these nonmanual signals, the signs are not correct.

When analyzing the distinct parts of signs, it is helpful to remember the following three points:

1. Make sure that the parts are indeed the same and not just similar. For example, the handshape of RESPONSIBILITY is a Bent B, the same as the handshape in COMPARE, but only similar to the handshape in BOOK.
2. Sometimes two English words are represented by the same sign. For example, SHOULD may sometimes be glossed as NEED, but the form of the sign is identical.
3. There are items that look like ASL signs in that they have handshape, movement, location, and orientation, but neither their meaning nor their function is ASL. For example, the sign BECAUSE has the same movement as FORGET or the same location as SUMMER, but BECAUSE is not an ASL sign. It is the result of codes invented to represent English manually.

GLOSSING SIGNS

Glossing means choosing an appropriate English word for signs in order to write them down. Glossing is not the same as translating, but, like translating, it is sometimes a difficult task. A gloss of a signed story will be a series of English words, written in small capital letters, that correspond to the signs in the ASL story. Parts of English, such as plural markers, past-tense markers, and prepositions, do not appear in glossing unless they are produced in the specific story. The nonmanual features are indicated on a line above the sign glosses. Some basic conventions used for glossing are as follows:

1. Signs are represented with small capital letters in English; for example, CAT HOUSE, STUDENT.
2. Lexicalized fingerspelled words are written in small capital letters and preceded by the # symbol; for example, #DO.
3. Full fingerspelling is represented by dashes between small capital letters; for example, M-A-R-Y.
4. Nonmanual signals and eye-gaze are represented on a line above the sign glosses; for example:

   ______________t
   PRO.1 ONE STORY NEVER FORGET
   "There's one story I'll never forget."

Labelling Systems

In addition to glossing signs into English, linguists have seen the need to devise a system for describing the structure of signs. We will discuss two systems that have been developed for describing the handshapes, locations, and movements of signs—the Stokoe system and the Liddell and Johnson system. These systems will be explained in later units; however, as an introduction to the concept of labelling systems, it is important to know the following three points:

1. In order for linguists to describe the structure of signs, they need to agree on the symbols used for description. These agreed-upon symbols are known as *conventions*, and they provide linguists with a consistent and predictable tool for description. A labelling system is such a tool.
2. It is important that the labels used be as precise as possible. The particular label for a handshape, a movement, or a location and the arrangement of the labels in a particular way reveal something about the structure of signs.
3. The system chosen for labelling the parts of signs is a direct reflection of the researcher's perspective on the structure of signs. Labelling systems do not exist in a vacuum, independent of linguistic theory. This point will be returned to in detail in discussion of the Stokoe system and the Liddell and Johnson system.

Homework Assignment 1

1. For each sign listed below, find another sign that has the same parameters for handshape, movement, and location.

	Same Handshape	Same Movement	Same Location
Example: FEEL	SICK	HAPPY	MY

   a. RESPONSIBILITY
   b. FORGET
   c. CUTE
   d. ENJOY
   e. BICYCLE
   f. UGLY
   g. BEST
   h. WORSE
   i. MONKEY
   j. DISCUSS

2. What is the difference between the signs in each pair?
   a. SUMMER/DRY
   b. RED/CUTE
   c. SHORT/TRAIN
   d. SIT/CHAIR

3. What does each pair of signs have in common?
   a. SUMMER/DRY
   b. RED/CUTE
   c. SHORT/TRAIN
   d. SIT/CHAIR

4. List four signs that must have a nonmanual signal with them.

5. After viewing the story on the videotape, gloss the beginning 30 seconds of the story. The first sentence is glossed below. Keep a record of how long it takes to gloss this part of the story.

Example: PRO.1 ONE STORY NEVER FORGET (t over "PRO.1 ONE STORY")

Homework Assignment 2

1. Suppose you are the first linguist to describe ASL signs and you have to describe the handshape in each of the following signs. Pick a name for each handshape.

   Example: SHOE S handshape

   a. GIRL
   b. ELEVATOR
   c. SPAGHETTI
   d. AWKWARD
   e. TRAVEL
   f. PLAY
   g. LECTURE
   h. PREACH
   i. PEOPLE
   j. GIVE
   k. MATH
   l. PITY
   m. MOTHER
   n. ALWAYS
   o. PLATE (DISH)
   p. LOBSTER
   q. SHOULD
   r. MARRY

2. Pick a name for the location (place where the sign is made) of each of the following signs.

   Example: KNOW face

   a. PLAY
   b. NOT
   c. FEEL
   d. DOCTOR
   e. FACE
   f. YESTERDAY
   g. HOSPITAL
   h. TIME
   i. STRICT
   j. BROKE (NO MONEY)
   k. PUNISH
   l. DUTY

3. Pick a name for the movement in each of the signs listed below.

   Example: HELP upward

   a. OPPRESS
   b. BUSY
   c. KEY, LOCK
   d. BOIL
   e. RELATED
   f. MAYBE
   g. SELL
   h. YES
   i. COFFEE
   j. MISS (didn't see something)
   k. TRAVEL
   l. COMMUTE
   m. CLEAR
   n. APPROACH
   o. DIVIDE
   p. DIE
   q. FASCINATING
   r. CONTACT

4. Using the labels you have picked for handshape, location, and movement, describe the following signs.

   a. CHILDREN
   b. PLAY
   c. TRAIN
   d. UNDERSTAND
   e. DEAF
   f. GIVE

UNIT 2

The Stokoe System

GOAL
To explain Stokoe's system for describing signs.

SUPPLEMENTAL READINGS
"Signs Have Parts: A Simple Idea," by Robbin Battison (1980); pp. 231–242

"Introduction," from *A Dictionary of American Sign Language,* by William C. Stokoe (1965; 1976); pp. 243–258

In unit 1, we saw that ASL signs have internal structure; that is, that they can be broken down into smaller parts. Those parts include handshape, location, movement, palm orientation, and nonmanual signals. In this unit, we examine the first system devised for the formal description of signs. Homework Assignment 2 introduced you to labelling systems. In the first section, you described the handshape for each sign; in the second and third sections you described the location and the movement of signs. You have probably discovered that there may be different solutions to the same problem. For example, the handshape of PREACH can be described as a 9 or as an *F*; there are different signs for LOBSTER; both BUSY and COMMUTE can be described as having a back-and-forth movement.

The realization that emerges from the homework assignment is that there is a need for consistency and uniformity in a descriptive system. Arguments can be made for choosing either 9 or *F* as the label for the handshape in PREACH, but once a choice of label has been made, it must be used consistently. In addition to consistency, there is a need for precision, so that if the movement in both BUSY and COMMUTE can be described as *back and forth*, some way must be created to uniquely describe the movement in each sign. The movement in some signs, such as APPROACH or DIVIDE, may be difficult to describe, making the need for precision in descriptions even more important.

THE STOKOE SYSTEM

William C. Stokoe devised the first system for describing signs. Before Stokoe, signs were thought of as unanalyzable wholes, with no internal structure. Stokoe was the first to suggest that signs could be analyzed in the same way that the units of spoken language can be analyzed. In 1960, Stokoe proposed that signs have three parts (parameters) that combine simultaneously. The three parts are the location of the sign, which he called the *tabula* or *tab;* the handshape, which he called the *designator* or *dez;* and the movement, which he called the *signation* or *sig.* Palm orientation and nonmanual signals were dealt with indirectly in the Stokoe system.

Stokoe referred to the three parameters as *cheremes,* from the Greek word *cheir,* for hand. He saw cheremes as meaningless elements that combine to form all signs, in the same way that phonemes combine to form words in spoken languages. Each parameter has a set of members known as primes. For example, handshape primes include *A, B,* and *5;* location primes include face, nose, and trunk; movement primes include upward movement, downward movement, and movement away from the signer. Figures 11 and 12 show the symbols used for writing the signs of ASL, as they appear in *The Dictionary of American Sign Language* (1965) by William C. Stokoe, Dorothy C. Casterline, and Carl G. Croneberg. In Stokoe's system, cheremes were written down in a specific order—TD^{S}. That is, the location of the sign (tab) was written first, followed by the handshape (dez), and then the movement (sig). For example, the sign IDEA is written as follows:

∩ I ^

∩ indicates the forehead location, I represents the handshape, and ^ represents the upward movement. Stokoe's system allows for some variations on the basic TD^{S} representation of signs. Signs with two hands are represented as TDD^{S} (for example, WITH); signs with one movement and then another are shown as TD^{SS} (for example, MILLION).

Tab symbols

1. Ø zero, the neutral place where the hands move, in contrast with all places below
2. ⌓ face or whole head
3. ⌒ forehead or brow, upper face
4. △ mid-face, the eye and nose region
5. ∪ chin, lower face
6. ʒ cheek, temple, ear, side-face
7. Π neck
8. [] trunk, body from shoulders to hips
9. \ upper arm
10. √ elbow, forearm
11. ɑ wrist, arm in supinated position (on its back)
12. ɒ wrist, arm in pronated position (face down)

Dez symbols, some also used as tab

13. **A** compact hand, fist; may be like 'a', 's', or 't' of manual alphabet
14. **B** flat hand
15. **5** spread hand; fingers and thumb spread like '5' of manual numeration
16. **C** curved hand; may be like 'c' or more open
17. **E** contracted hand; like 'e' or more claw-like
18. **F** "three-ring" hand; from spread hand, thumb and index finger touch or cross
19. **G** index hand; like 'g' or sometimes like 'd'; index finger points from fist
20. **H** index and second finger, side by side, extended
21. **I** "pinkie" hand; little finger extended from compact hand
22. **K** like G except that thumb touches middle phalanx of second finger; like 'k' and 'p' of manual alphabet
23. **L** angle hand; thumb, index finger in right angle, other fingers usually bent into palm
24. **3** "cock" hand; thumb and first two fingers spread, like '3' of manual numeration
25. **O** tapered hand; fingers curved and squeezed together over thumb; may be like 'o' of manual alphabet
26. **R** "warding off" hand; second finger crossed over index finger, like 'r' of manual alphabet
27. **V** "victory" hand; index and second fingers extended and spread apart
28. **W** three-finger hand; thumb and little finger touch, others extended spread
29. **X** hook hand; index finger bent in hook from fist, thumb tip may touch fingertip
30. **Y** "horns" hand; thumb and little finger spread out extended from fist; or index finger and little finger extended, parallel
31. **ȣ** (allocheric variant of **Y**); second finger bent in from spread hand, thumb may touch fingertip

Sig symbols

No.	Symbol	Description	Group
32.	^	upward movement	vertical action
33.	v	downward movement	vertical action
34.	ᴺ	up-and-down movement	vertical action
35.	>	rightward movement	sideways action
36.	<	leftward movement	sideways action
37.	z	side to side movement	sideways action
38.	⊤	movement toward signer	horizontal action
39.	⊥	movement away from signer	horizontal action
40.	I	to-and-fro movement	horizontal action
41.	ɑ	supinating rotation (palm up)	rotary action
42.	ɒ	pronating rotation (palm down)	rotary action
43.	ω	twisting movement	rotary action
44.	ŋ	nodding or bending action	
45.	□	opening action (final dez configuration shown in brackets)	
46.	#	closing action (final dez configuration shown in brackets)	
47.	ꝗ	wiggling action of fingers	
48.	@	circular action	
49.	)(	convergent action, approach	interaction
50.	×	contactual action, touch	interaction
51.	⌶	linking action, grasp	interaction
52.	†	crossing action	interaction
53.	⊙	entering action	interaction
54.	÷	divergent action, separate	interaction
55.	ʻʼ	interchanging action	

FIGURE 11. Stokoe's symbols for writing the signs of American Sign Language.

Note: Reprinted by permission of the publisher, from W. C. Stokoe, D. C. Casterline, and C. G. Croneberg, *A Dictionary of American Sign Language* (rev.). (1976): x–xii, Silver Spring, MD: Linstok Press.

$_{\cup}R^{\times}$ — $^{\times>\times}$
(initial dez; tips of dez fingers touch lips or chin) $_{N}$ *restaurant*. In some localities sign may be used for 'doughnut'.

$_{\cup}R_{\perp}{}^{\times}$
(imit.; knuckles of dez touch tab so that fingers project outward)
$_{N}$ *cigar*.

$_{\cup}V_{T}{}^{@\cdot}$
$_{v}$ *read lips;* $_{N}$ *speech reading, lipreading, oralist;* $_{\times}$ *oral*. May also be extended 'speech' and 'the organs of speech'.
See also Π $V_{T\times}^{\wedge\cdot}$

$_{\cup}\ddot{V}_{D}{}^{@}_{\perp}$
(imit.: fangs; may also be made in high zero-tab with or without left **G**-hand touching dez elbow) $_{N}$ *snake, serpent*. See also synonym: $\underline{B}_{D}$ $\surd G^{@}_{\perp}$.

$_{\cup}V^{\times\cdot}$
(initial dez; index fingertip of dez touches chin) $_{N}$ *vinegar*.

$_{\cup}V_{\#T}{}^{\times\square}_{\wedge}$
(imit.; dez touches chin, moves up and snaps open to full **V** with or without touching forehead) $_{N}$ *goat*. In some regions used for 'cheese'. 'Goat' is also signed $_{\cup}A^{II}5^{\omega\cdot}_{\times}$

$_{\cup}W^{\times\cdot}$ — $^{\times Z}_{\perp}$
(initial dez) $_{N}$ *water*.
This sign serves as first element in several compounds:
—— ⁞ Ø $C_{D}C_{D}{}^{\vee\cdot}$ 'rain'
—— ⁞ Ø $5_{DQ}5_{D\perp}^{\&}$ 'river'
—— ⁞ Ø $BB^{Z}_{\perp}$ 'stream'
—— ⁞ Ø $\surd 5_{D9}\surd 5_{D\perp}^{N}$ 'ocean'
—— ⁞ $V_{D}V_{D}{}^{\times\cdot}$ ⁞ Ø $\surd 5_{D9}\surd 5_{D\perp}^{N}$ 'salt sea'

All these are imitative of the flowing, meandering, or undulating nature of the referent. However, these signs are seldom used except for such uses as signing a poem when nonce compounds too are acceptable, e.g. 'water' plus 'quiet' for 'pond'.

Usually signers spell the names of lakes, beaches, rivers, and oceans. On the east coast *a-c* 'Atlantic City' and *o-c* 'Ocean City'.

FIGURE 12. Examples of Stokoe's transcription system.

Note: Reprinted by permission of the publisher, from W. C. Stokoe, D. C. Casterline, and C. G. Croneberg, A *Dictionary of American Sign Language* (rev.). (1976): 168, Silver Spring, MD: Linstok Press.

Homework Assignment 3

1. Using the Stokoe symbols for movement, location, and handshape, transcribe the following signs:

   a. ENJOY
   b. BEGIN
   c. BROKE (no money)
   d. BUSY
   e. SUNDAY
   f. EVERY SATURDAY
   g. KNOW
   h. NOT

UNIT 3

The Concept of Sequentiality in the Description of Signs

GOAL

To explain why sequentiality is a key concept in the description of signs.

SUPPLEMENTAL READINGS

Files 20 and 30 from *Language Files: Materials for an Introduction to Language,* by M. Crabtree and J. Powers (1991); pp. 259–266

In unit 2, we discussed the system devised by William Stokoe for describing ASL signs. Stokoe's work clearly represents the beginning of linguistic analysis of sign language structure. In this unit, we will focus on two issues relating to sign language structure that emerge from Stokoe's system—the level of detail needed to describe ASL signs, and the representation of sequence in ASL signs.

DETAIL IN THE DESCRIPTION OF ASL SIGNS

According to Stokoe's system, the location for the signs HEAVEN, SIGN, and CHILDREN is described as Ø, or "the neutral place where the hands move," in contrast with other specific locations on the body such as nose, neck, or arm. Similarly, the handshape for GIVE, NUMBER, and NOTHING is described as O. In the case of the location, the description Ø does not show that the signs HEAVEN, SIGN, and CHILDREN are in fact produced at distinctly different levels (see Figure 13). To produce the sign HEAVEN at the level at which SIGN is produced would be unacceptable; likewise, to produce the sign CHILDREN at the level at which HEAVEN is produced would be unacceptable. The description of the location for each sign needs to be more specific. The description Ø is not specific enough. And while the handshape of GIVE and NUMBER may look the same, the handshape for NOTHING is quite distinct. The description of O for the handshape of these three signs is not specific enough (see Figure 14).

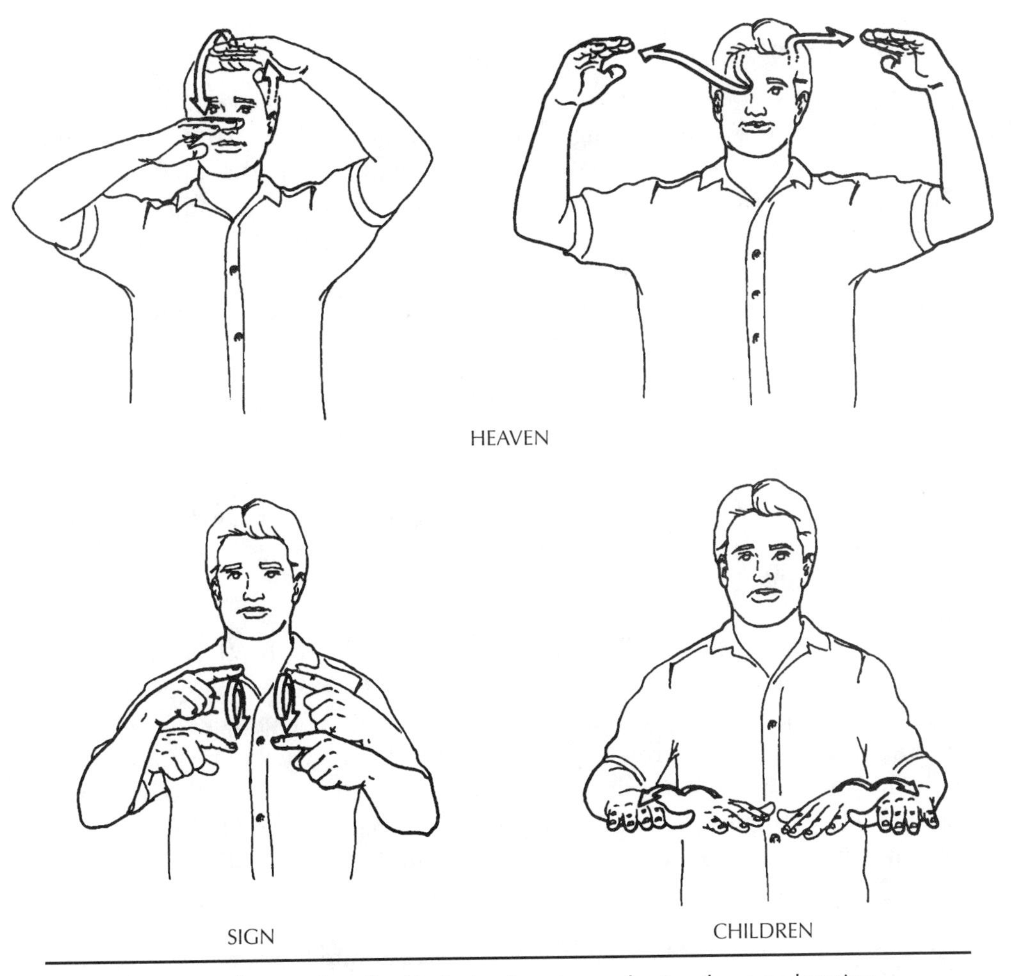

FIGURE 13. Signs that are described in Stokoe's system as having the same location.

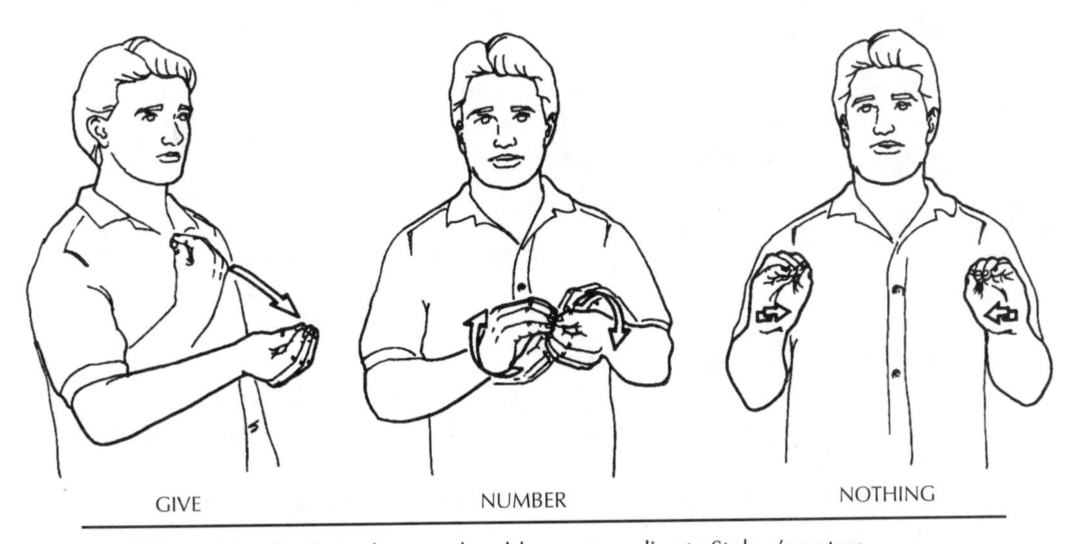

FIGURE 14. Signs that have the same handshape, according to Stokoe's system.

THE REPRESENTATION OF SEQUENCE IN ASL SIGNS

Some ASL signs have only one handshape, one movement, one location, one palm orientation, or one nonmanual signal. For example, the sign MOTHER has only one handshape; the sign UNDERSTAND has one location; the sign COLOR has one handshape and one location; and the sign MAYBE has one palm orientation. However, many ASL signs have more than one handshape, location, palm orientation, or nonmanual signal. That is, many ASL signs have a sequence of hand-shapes, locations, palm orientations, or nonmanual signals. Examples of such sequences are as follows:

handshape:	UNDERSTAND	X →1
location:	DEAF	ear → chin
palm orientation:	DIE (1-handed)	palm down →palm up
nonmanual signals:	FINALLY	closed lips →mouth open

In the Stokoe system, a sequence of two movements is shown in the movement part of the transcription. The sign MILLION would be written as follows:

MILLION BɑB̈ẋ⊥ẋ

This notation means that the Bent **B** handshape of the active hand (**B**) contacts the base hand (palm up, **Bɑ**) once in a sharp movement (ẋ) and then moves away from the signer (⊥) and repeats the contacting movement (x). The sequence of movements, then, is represented as ẋ⊥ẋ. In the Stokoe system, when there is a sequence of handshapes, orientations, or locations, the change is shown in the movement portion. For example, UNDERSTAND has two handshapes, **X** and **G** (in the Stokoe system), and the second handshape is shown with the movement

∩X⊤□ [G]

This notation means that the handshape **X** moves toward the signer (⊤) at the forehead (∩) and that there is an opening action (□) that results in the handshape **G**.

The sequence of orientation in the sign DIE is shown in the movement

BᴅBɑ ɑ/ᴅ

This notation means that one hand begins with the palm down (**Bᴅ**) and the other hand begins with the palm up (**Bɑ**). In the course of producing the sign, the orientation of each hand changes so that ᴅ becomes ɑ and ɑ becomes ᴅ.

In one variant of the sign DEAF, the **G** handshape moves upward (∧), contacts the face (x) and then moves toward the signer (⊤) and contacts the face again. The sign is represented as follows:

∪G∧x⊤x

So the sequence of locations is shown by x⊤x.

It is not that the Stokoe system ignores sequences of handshapes, locations, and orientations. These sequences are seen as a function of the movement component. It is essential to understand that in Stokoe's system these sequences are seen as unimportant in the description of signs. What this means is that he proposed a structure for sign language that is different from the structure of spoken language at its most basic level. To clarify this point, we must examine one of the most basic concepts in the phonology of any language, that is, the concept of contrast.

In English, we are able to isolate and describe the basic parts of English phonology *(phonemes)* because of word pairs that are called minimal pairs. An example of a minimal pair are the words *pat* and *bat.* These words are contrastive in meaning (that is, they mean different things), and they are identical in all segments (parts that occur in sequence) except one. Furthermore, the two segments that contrast, *p* and *b,* differ in only one feature: *b* is produced with vibration of the vocal cords and is called a voiced sound, while *p* has no vibration and is voiceless. The following diagram analyzes the segments of the minimal pair *pat* and *bat* (æ is the symbol used to represent the vowel):

	p	æ	t	b	æ	t
place of articulation:	bilabial		alveolar	bilabial		alveolar
manner of articulation:	stop		stop	stop		stop
voiced or voiceless:	voiceless		voiceless	voiced		voiceless

The features that are listed under each sound are referred to as a bundle of articulatory features. *P* and *b* differ in only one feature in the bundle, in the feature of voicing. We know that *p* and *b* must be contrastive phonemes in English (that is, they must be among the basic building blocks of the language) because two sequences of sounds that are otherwise identical have different meanings, and that difference in meaning must be linked to the difference between *p* and *b.* The kind of contrast demonstrated by *pat* and *bat* is called sequential contrast.

Sequential contrast is different from what is known as simultaneous contrast (that is, distinctions of one feature within a single, co-occurrent bundle of features). As we just saw, the contrast between the English sounds *p* and *b* (when these sounds are not in a sequence of sounds) is an example of simultaneous contrast. *P* and *b* each consist of co-occurrent features, and they differ only in one of those features, namely, voicing. Similarly, in the Stokoe view of signs as simultaneously produced parameters, there are many pairs of signs that are in contrast. For example, in the Stokoe system, the following pairs of signs are considered minimal pairs.

MOTHER	FATHER	contrast in location
SIT	CHAIR	contrast in movement
RED	SWEET	contrast in handshape

In all of the pairs, the signs differ in only one of the co-occurrent parts.

In the Stokoe system, contrast is seen as simultaneous contrast, and the issue of sequential contrast is not discussed. However, there are examples of sequential contrast in ASL, and because these examples exist, a system for describing ASL structure must be able to describe and account for any sign in the language. An example of sequential contrast in ASL can be seen in the pair of signs CHRISTIAN and CONGRESS. CONGRESS is produced with a sequence of locations on the upper chest; CHRISTIAN is produced almost exactly like CONGRESS, except that its final location is the lower torso. The contrast between the two signs lies in the difference in one feature, the final location. Similarly, in the one-handed version of the sign

CHILDREN, the palm orientation is down, while in the one-handed version of DIE, the palm is down and then up. The contrast between the two signs is in the sequence of orientation, down-down as opposed to down-up.

The Dictionary of American Sign Language (DASL) describes the location of the sign GIVE as Ø, the neutral location for signs without body contact. However, the contrast between the signs FIRST-PERSON-GIVE-TO-THIRD-PERSON and THIRD-PERSON-GIVE-TO-FIRST-PERSON is precisely in the location, and both of those signs show a sequence of locations.

It is very important to understand that many signs have sequences of handshapes, locations, orientations, or nonmanual signals but that the sequence is not contrastive. For example, some signs show a sequence of nonmanual signals, as with the sign ADMIT, which first has the lips pursed as the palm contacts the chest, and then the mouth opens as the hand moves away from the chest. A similar sequence occurs in one version of the sign FINALLY as the hands change orientation (see Figure 15). Without these nonmanual signals, the signs are not properly pro-

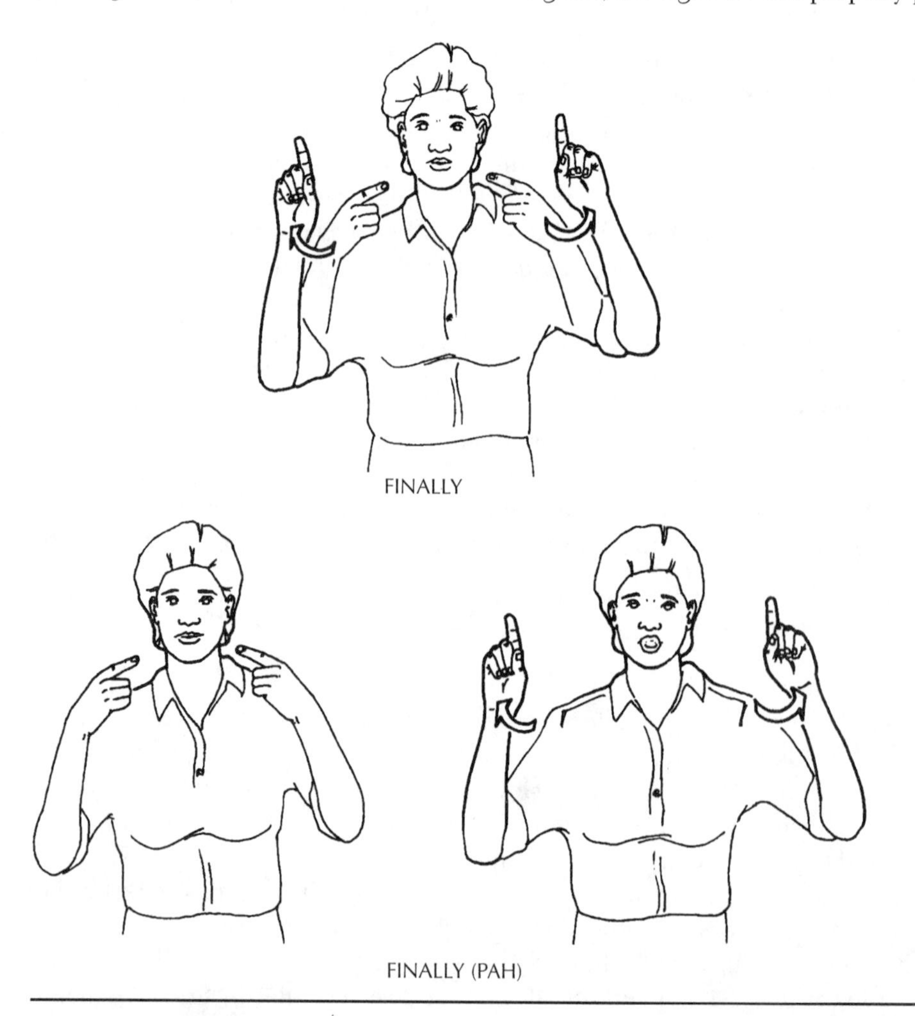

FIGURE 15. Two versions of FINALLY.

duced, and the sequence within the nonmanual signal cannot be reversed. It is not possible to begin with an open mouth and end with closed lips. It would seem then, that sequence in nonmanual signals is very important.

Many signs have a sequence of locations; that is, first one and then the other. For example, the sign DEAF begins just below the ear and ends on the chin. However, it can begin the other way around, on the chin, and end just below the ear. This is an example of variation in ASL, variation that occurs for stylistic or regional or grammatical reasons. What is important is that the variation lies in the sequence of locations. Since the sign means the same thing whether it begins at the ear or the chin, it is not an example of contrast, but the sequence of locations still is important in understanding the structure of ASL and how it can vary.

It is important to remember that sign languages show sequential contrast in the same way that spoken languages do, and it is very important for the system used to describe the sign language to represent that fact.

SUMMARY

The following list summarizes some of the problems with the Stokoe transcription system.

1. Detail in the description of ASL signs. For example,

	Location
HEAVEN	Ø
SIGN	Ø
CHILDREN	Ø
	Handshape
GIVE	O
NUMBER	O
NOTHING	O

2. The representation of sequence in ASL signs.
   a. MILLION BɑB̈$^{\dot{x}\perp\dot{x}}$ Movement repeated, sequence of movement.
   b. CONGRESS and CHRISTIAN both have a sequence of location, and the only difference between them is the final location. However, in the Stokoe system, this sequence of location is not shown. They are transcribed as follows:
   CONGRESS []C$^{x>x}$
   CHRISTIAN ::[]BB^{v}
   The same location is given for both, [], which means "trunk, body from shoulders to hips."
   c. DIE BɒBɑ$^{ɑ}_{ɒ}$
   The sign has two orientations in sequence (R:palm up→down;L:down→ up), and that is shown in the movement. However, signs like one-handed DIE and one-handed CHILDREN, which each have a sequence of orientations and seem to differ only in orientation, are not distinguished as such in the Stokoe system.
   d. DEAF ◡GΛ$^{x\top x}$
   The sign has two locations in sequence (chin→ cheek), and that is shown in the movement. This sign also can be made from cheek→ chin. The Stokoe system does not show this.

e. GIVE $\varnothing O_{\top} O_{\top\perp}^{\alpha}$
The specific location of the hand provides information about who is the subject and who is the object of the verb. The Stokoe system does not include this information.

f. ADMIT and FINALLY are among the many signs that include a nonmanual signal. The parts of the nonmanual signal must be produced in sequence. However, in the Stokoe system, no mention is made of the nonmanual signal, much less of the fact that the parts of the signal must occur in sequence.

UNIT 4

The Movement–Hold Model

GOAL
To explain the basic principles of the Movement–Hold Model

SUPPLEMENTAL READING
"American Sign Language: The Phonological Base," by Scott K. Liddell and Robert E. Johnson (1989); pp. 267–306

In unit 3, we examined ways in which the labelling system devised by Stokoe cannot adequately describe the structures of signs, specifically in the areas of level of detail and sequentiality. In this unit, we will very briefly describe a system developed by Scott K. Liddell and Robert E. Johnson. We will refer to this system as the Movement–Hold Model. Though details of the model are numerous and complex, its basic claims about sign language structure are important. The basic claims reflect a perspective about the structure of signs that significantly differs from Stokoe's perspective, and it is important to understand that difference in perspective.

The basic claim about the structure of signs in the Movement–Hold Model is that signs consist of hold segments and movement segments that are produced sequentially. Information about the handshape, location, orientation, and nonmanual signals is represented in bundles of articulatory features. These bundles of articulatory features are similar to the ones we described in unit 3 for the sounds of spoken languages. Holds are defined as periods of time during which all aspects of the articulation bundle are in a steady state; movements are defined as periods of time during which some aspect of the articulation is in transition. More than one parameter can change at once. A sign may only have a change of handshape or location, but it may have a change of both handshape and location, and these changes take place during the movement segment. For example, in the sign UNDERSTAND, only the handshape changes; in the sign FALSE, only the location changes; however, in the sign FASCINATING, both the handshape and the location change, while the sign is moving.

Let's look at some more examples. The sign WEEK is shown on this page in a simplified version of the Movement–Hold notation.

WEEK

	SEGMENTS			
RIGHT HAND	Hold (H)	Movement (M)	Hold (H)	
handshape	1		1	articulatory bundle
location	base of left hand		tip of left hand	
orientation	palm down		palm down	
nonmanual signal	—		—	
LEFT HAND				
handshape	B			articulatory bundle
location	front of torso			
orientation	palm			
nonmanual signal	—			

The sign WEEK begins with a hold (H), with the right hand (for right-handed signers) at the base of the left hand. It then moves (M) to the tip of the left hand and ends with a hold in that location. The change in the sign is in the location of the active hand, from base to tip of the passive hand.

The one-handed sign GUESS is written as follows:

GUESS

	SEGMENTS		
RIGHT HAND	H	M	H
handshape	C		S
location	right eye		left cheek
orientation	palm up		palm down
nonmanual signal	—		—

This sign begins with a hold at the level of the right eye and then moves left and ends in a hold near the left cheek. The sign begins with a C handshape and ends with an S handshape, and the palm orientation begins with the palm facing left and ends with the palm facing downward.

Not all signs have a hold-movement-hold (H M H) structure (see Table 1). While there are at least six possible sign structures, H M is not among them (see Figure 16). As you can see, not all combinations are acceptable in the structure of the language. Though the details of the complete Liddell and Johnson Movement–Hold system are beyond the scope of this course, it is important to understand three basic components of the system.

TABLE 1. Possible Sign Structures

STRUCTURE	SIGN
Movement (M)	ALWAYS, SOMETHING
Hold (H)	COLOR, STUDY[a]
M H	THINK, KNOW, MY
M H M H	CONGRESS,[b] FLOWER
M M M H	CHAIR, SCHOOL, PAPER

[a] The wiggling of the fingers in these signs is described as internal movement.

[b] Liddell and Johnson (1989) show the structure of CONGRESS as M H M M H (see p. 280).

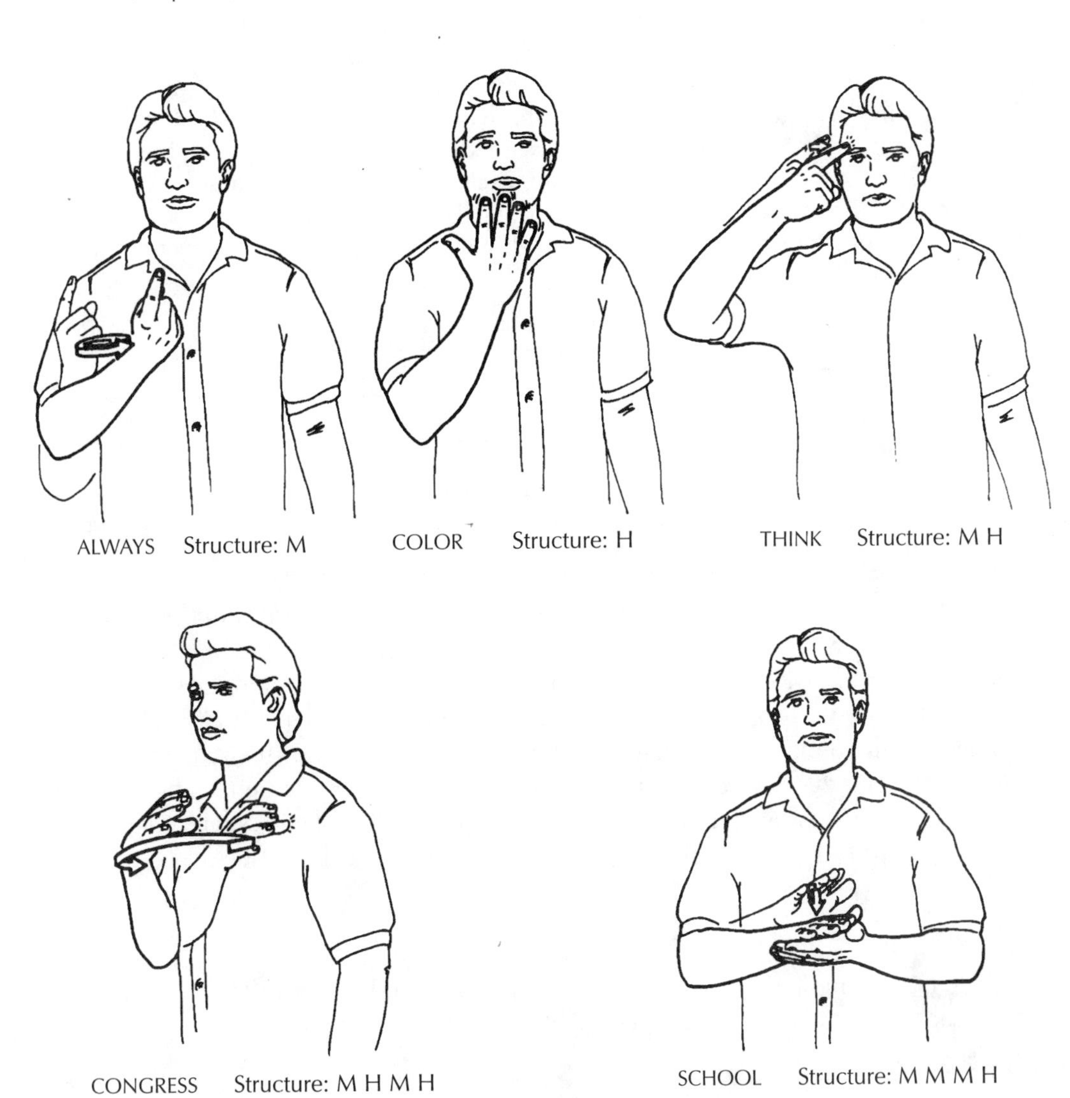

FIGURE 16. Examples of possible sign structures.

1. The Liddell and Johnson system makes the claim that the basic units of signs—movements and holds—are produced sequentially. The information about handshape, location, orientation, and nonmanual signals is represented in bundles of articulatory features found in each unit. This claim is very different from Stokoe's claim that the parameters of signs are produced simultaneously, but it parallels claims about the segmental structure of spoken languages. Liddell and Johnson claim sign languages and spoken languages are the same in their basic structure, adding support to arguments that sign languages are legitimate and viable languages. Sign languages are not unlike spoken languages, as Stokoe said. They are like them in the most basic way.
2. The Liddell and Johnson system solves the descriptive problems presented by the Stokoe system. Sequence is very important and contrastive in some signs, and this system can describe sequence very efficiently. The system also provides adequate detail for the description of signs, and it provides a way to clearly describe and explain the numerous processes that take place in sign language.
3. Linguists and others who analyze signs are able to identify the movements and holds in signs and explain where the information about handshape, location, orientation, and nonmanual signals is described. What may differ among linguists' analyses is the number of primes for each parameter—for example, Stokoe counted 19 handshape primes, while Liddell and Johnson counted more than 150. In the Movement–Hold model, a sign such as THINK, for example, would lead to the following representation:

THINK

	SEGMENTS	
	M	H
handshape	1	1
location	near forehead	forehead
orientation	palm down	palm down
nonmanual signal	—	—

Different segmental structure may reflect a difference in meaning. Another good example of this is the difference in segmental structure between SIT (M H) and CHAIR (M M M H). In the case of HELP, the difference in segmental structure may reflect a generational or regional difference—older signers may use the H M H variant, while younger signers may use the M H M M H one. The important concept to remember is that differences in meaning or regional and generational differences are differences in the actual way that the signs are put together. The Liddell and Johnson model provides a clear and precise way to describe these differences.

REFERENCE

Liddell, S. K., and Johnson, R. E. (1989). American Sign Language: The phonological base. *Sign Language Studies* 64:195–277.

Homework Assignment 4

1. Identify the segments in the following signs:

Example: DRY H M H

a. FALSE	**f.** SIT	**k.** HELP	**p.** BRING
b. ALWAYS	**g.** CHAIR	**l.** BROKE (no money)	**q.** WRITE
c. EAT	**h.** CAN'T	**m.** PREACH	**r.** KING
d. COLOR	**i.** INTERESTING	**n.** WEAK	**s.** WHERE
e. PAPER	**j.** WEEK	**o.** ARRIVE	**t.** BLACK

2. Transcribe the following five signs in the Liddell and Johnson model and in the Stokoe system and compare your transcriptions. If possible, consult the DASL directly for Stokoe's transcriptions of these signs.

a. UNDERSTAND

b. BLACK

c. DEAF

d. SIT

e. CHAIR

UNIT 5

Phonological Processes

GOAL
To understand some phonological processes in ASL

Now that we have talked about the parts of signs and how they are organized, we can talk about ways in which that order may vary. The parts of signs may occur in different orders, and the parts of signs may influence each other. These variations are due to phonological processes. In this unit, we will discuss four of them: movement epenthesis, hold deletion, metathesis, and assimilation.

MOVEMENT EPENTHESIS

Signs occur in sequence, which means that the segments that make up signs occur in sequence. Sometimes a movement segment is added between the last segment of one sign and the first segment of the next sign. This process of adding a movement segment is called *movement epenthesis.* It is illustrated in the sequence of signs FATHER STUDY (see Figure 17). The basic form of both signs is a hold with internal movement, as follows:

FATHER	STUDY (right hand)
H	H

When the two signs occur in sequence, a movement is inserted between the two holds, so that the sequence looks like this:

FATHER		STUDY
H	M	H

We will return to movement epenthesis when we discuss fingerspelling.

HOLD DELETION

Movement epenthesis is related to another phonological process called *hold deletion.* Hold deletion eliminates holds between movements when signs occur in se-

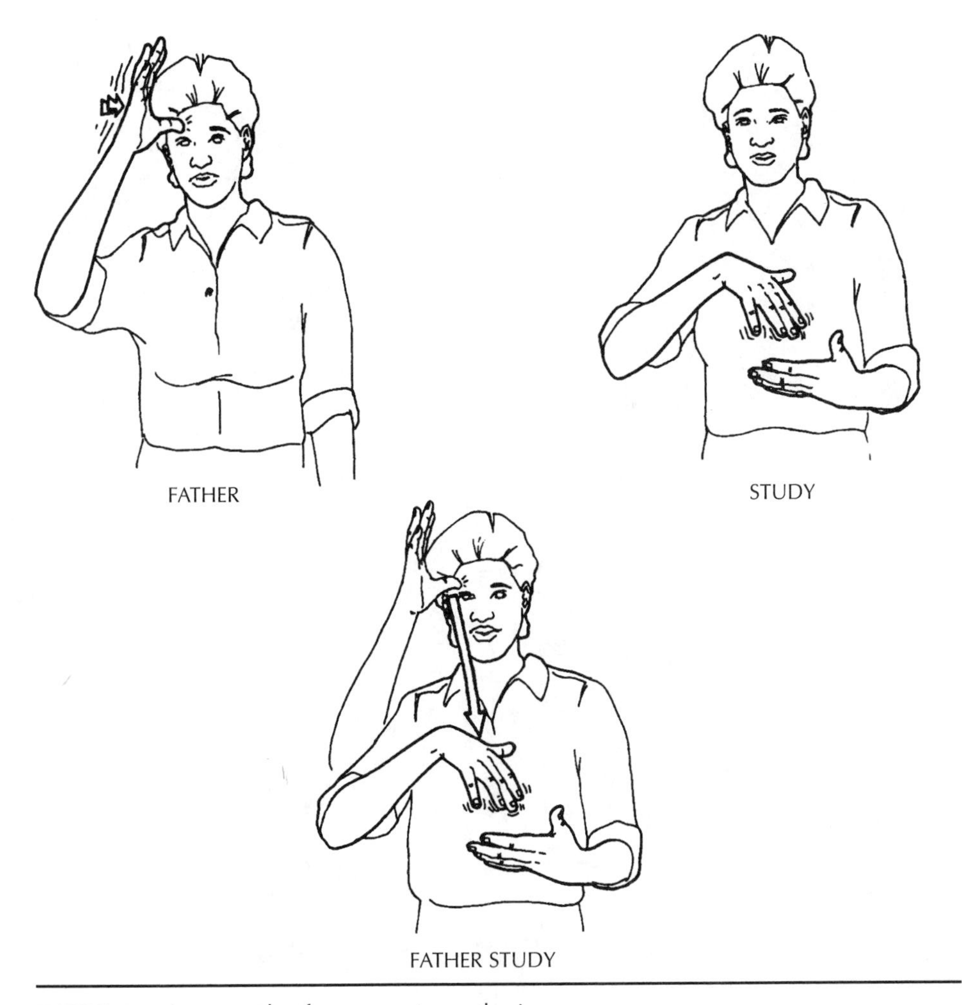

FIGURE 17. An example of movement epenthesis.

quence. For example, the sign GOOD is composed of a hold, a movement, and a hold. The sign IDEA is also composed of a hold, a movement, and a hold. When the two signs occur in sequence, a movement is inserted between the last segment of GOOD and the first segment of IDEA (another example of movement epenthesis). What also happens is that the last hold of GOOD and the first hold of IDEA are eliminated, so the structure is hold-movement-movement-movement-hold (see Figure 18). The whole process would look as follows:

Basic sign:		GOOD				IDEA	
	H	M	H		H	M	H
Movement Epenthesis:	H	M	H	M	H	M	H
Hold Deletion:	H	M		M		M	H

This is a fairly common process in ASL, and we will return to it when we talk about compounds.

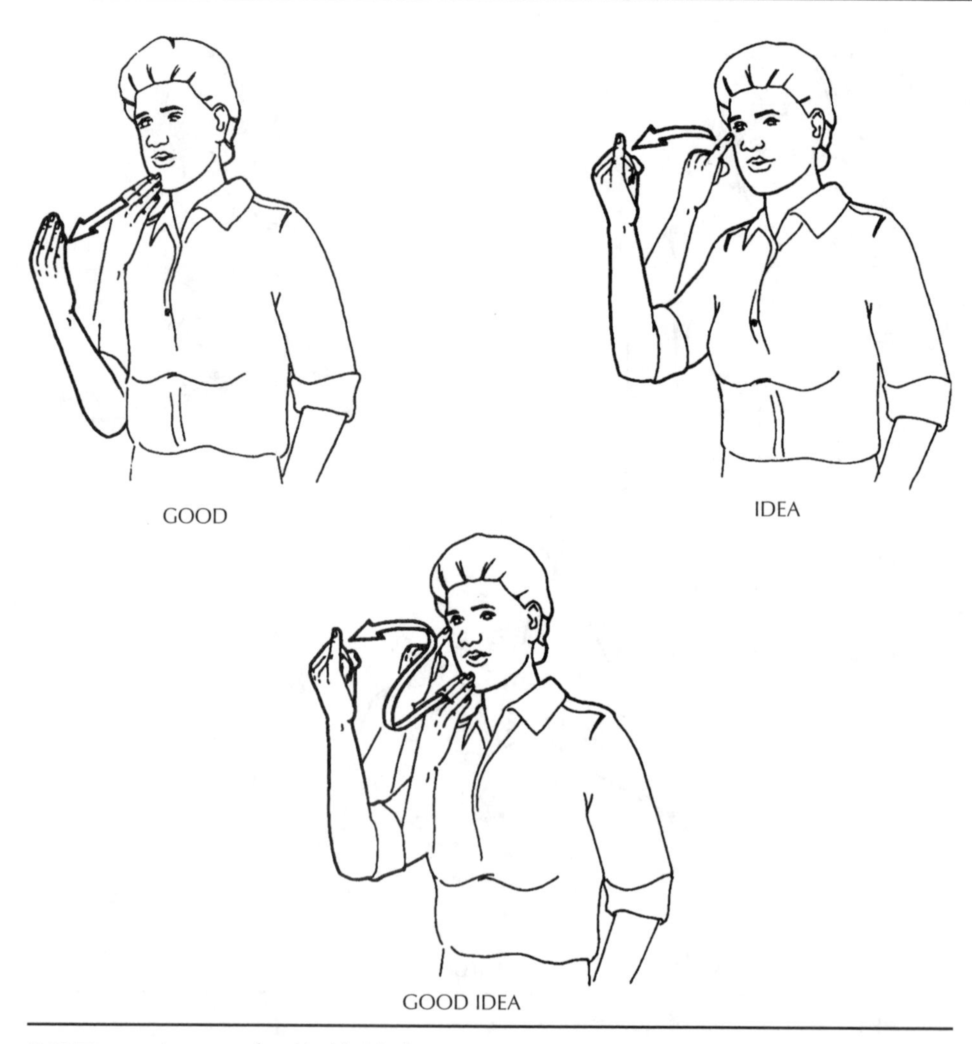

FIGURE 18. An example of hold deletion.

METATHESIS

Sometimes parts of the segments of a sign can change places. This process of changing place is called *metathesis*. To illustrate metathesis, look at the basic structure of the sign DEAF:

DEAF

	M	H	M	H
handshape	1	1	1	1
location	cheek	cheek	jaw	jaw
orientation	palm out	palm out	palm out	palm out

However, the location feature of the first and last segment might be reversed (see Figure 19). In that case, DEAF would look like this:

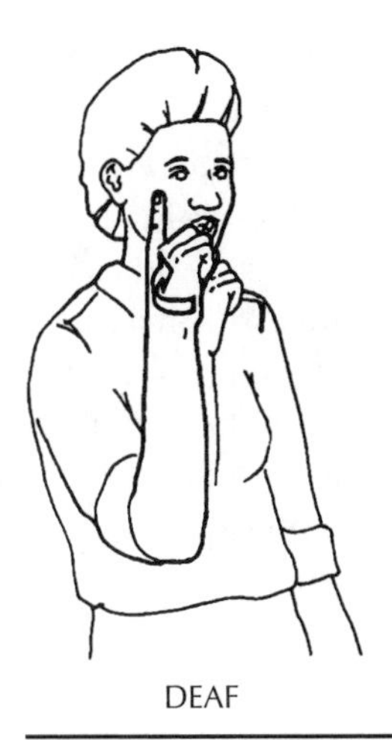
DEAF

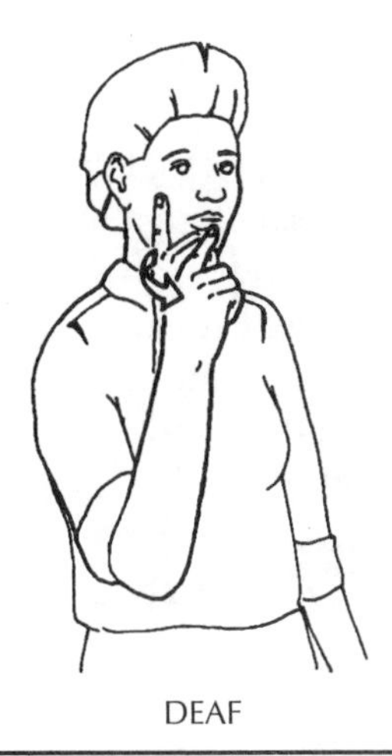
DEAF

FIGURE 19. An example of metathesis.

DEAF

	M	H	M	H
handshape	1	1	1	1
location	jaw	jaw	cheek	cheek
orientation	palm out	palm out	palm out	palm out

Many signs allow segments to change place, including CONGRESS, FLOWER, RESTAURANT, HONEYMOON, NAVY, TWINS, BACHELOR, PARENTS, HOME, and HEAD. Other signs do not allow the location feature of segments to change place, such as BODY, KING, CHRIST, INDIAN, BLOUSE, THANKSGIVING, CHILDREN, and THING. In unit 1 of part 6 we will talk about variation and what motivates signs like DEAF to exhibit variation.

ME INFORM

FIGURE 20. An example of assimilation.

ASSIMILATION

Assimilation means that a segment takes on the characteristics of another segment near it, usually the one just before it or after it. A good example of this is the handshape in the sign PRO.1 (1st person, "I"). The basic handshape is a 1, but when the sign occurs in a sequence, very often the handshape changes to match the handshape of another sign in the sequence. When signers produce the sequence PRO.1 INFORM, very often the handshape of PRO.1 changes from *1* to *O* because of the handshape of INFORM (see Figure 20). Likewise, when signers produce the sequence PRO.1 KNOW, very often the 1 handshape of PRO.1 becomes the Bent B handshape of KNOW. We will talk about assimilation more when we talk about compounds in part three.

UNIT 6

Summary

GOAL
To summarize the principles of ASL phonology

In this unit, we will summarize the material that has been covered on ASL phonology. The key points to remember are as follows:

1. Like the symbols of spoken languages, the symbols of sign languages have parts.
2. The study of the smallest contrastive parts of a language is called phonology.
3. Before Stokoe's analysis, signs were thought to be unanalyzable wholes.
4. Stokoe's model makes the claim that signs are composed of three simultaneously produced parameters—the location, the handshape, and the movement. Stokoe demonstrated simultaneous but not sequential contrast.
5. Liddell and Johnson's model makes the claim that signs are composed of sequentially produced movements and holds. The handshape, location, orientation, and nonmanual information is contained in bundles of articulatory features. Sequential contrast can be demonstrated.
6. The Movement–Hold Model allows for the level of detail needed for the adequate description of sign structure and of sign processes in ASL.
7. The Movement–Hold Model demonstrates that the fundamental structure of sign languages is parallel to the fundamental structure of spoken languages. Stokoe stated that the structure of sign language is fundamentally different from the structure of spoken languages. He supported this theory with his claim that the parameters are simultaneously produced.
8. There are phonological processes in ASL that may influence how the parts of signs are produced or the order in which the parts are produced.

PERSPECTIVES ON THE STRUCTURE OF SIGNS

1. Before Stokoe, signs were thought of as unanalyzable wholes.

   Stokoe (1960; 1965) described and analyzed signs. From his research, he concluded that signs have parts; signs have three parameters—handshape, movement, and location. (Orientation was added to the system later.) According to Stokoe, sign morphemes are different from the morphemes and words of spoken languages because they are seen as simultaneously, not sequentially produced.

Liddell and Johnson (1982 to the present) agreed with Stokoe that signs have parts, but they disagreed on the number of parts. Liddell and Johnson found that signs have five parameters—handshape, movement, location, orientation, and nonmanual signals.

2. Most signs can be segmented into movements and holds.

   Liddell and Johnson also found sign language phonology parallels spoken language phonology. Both spoken languages and sign languages divide the segments that make up the words or signs into two major types of units:

   a. Consonants and vowels in spoken languages.
   b. Holds and movements in sign languages.

PART THREE

MORPHOLOGY

UNIT 1

Phonology vs. Morphology: What's the Difference?

GOAL
To understand the difference between phonology and morphology

SUPPLEMENTAL READINGS
Files 40, 42, and 43 from *Language Files: Materials for an Introduction to Language,* by M. Crabtree and J. Powers (1991); pp. 307–317

In part two, we defined phonology as the study of the smallest *contrastive* parts of language. In American Sign Language, signs are made up of hold segments and movement segments. A hold segment has handshape, location, orientation, and nonmanual features, and likewise, a movement segment has handshape, location, orientation, and nonmanual features.

In comparing the signs LOUSY, AWKWARD, and PREACH with the signs THREE-MONTHS, THREE-DOLLARS, and NINE-WEEKS, we saw that the handshape in LOUSY, AWKWARD, and PREACH has no separate meaning. In those three signs, as in many others, the handshape, location, orientation and nonmanual information combine to produce one meaning. The separate parts can be identified, but they do not each have separate meaning. That is not the case, however, in THREE-MONTHS, THREE-DOLLARS, and NINE-WEEKS. In these three signs, the handshape does have a separate meaning—it indicates a specific quantity. To change the handshape in the sign THREE-DOLLARS immediately changes the meaning of the quantity of money being signed. To change the handshape in NINE-WEEKS or THREE-MONTHS changes the meaning of the number of weeks or months being talked about. (This process will be discussed more in unit 2, when we talk about numeral incorporation.)

Phonology is the study of the smallest contrastive parts of language. The parts of language that we study in phonology do not have meaning. So when we study phonology and we look at the sign THREE-MONTHS, we are simply interested in the fact that the sign has a handshape, a location, an orientation, and a movement. The fact that the handshape has the specific meaning of the quantity three is part of morphology.

MORPHOLOGY

Morphology is the study of the smallest *meaningful* units in language and of how those meaningful units are used to build new words or signs. Put another way, morphology is the study of word formation, of how a language uses smaller units to build larger units.

The smallest meaningful unit in a language is a *morpheme*. Some morphemes can occur by themselves, as independent units. These are called *free* morphemes. The English words *cat* and *sit* are examples of free morphemes; the ASL signs CAT and LOUSY are examples of free morphemes. Some morphemes cannot occur as independent units; they must occur with other morphemes. These are called *bound* morphemes. The English plural *-s* (*cats*) and third person *-s* (*sits*) are examples of bound morphemes; the 3 handshape in the ASL signs THREE-WEEKS and THREE-MONTHS are examples of bound morphemes. And as we will see, while a morpheme is often an identifiable form, a morpheme may also be a process.

Languages have many ways to build new words or signs. Using the patterns of words or signs that already exist, they can create totally new forms. They can also make compound words or signs by combining two forms that already exist. They can borrow words or signs from other languages, and ASL can create new signs based on the writing system of English. We will discuss examples of all these processes in ASL.

UNIT 2

Deriving Nouns from Verbs in ASL

GOAL

To be able to explain how nouns are derived from verbs in ASL

In unit 1, we said that morphology is the study of word formation, of how a language uses meaningful units to build new words or signs. One example of a morphological process is the way that a language uses verbs to derive nouns. That is, the verbs that are already in the language are used to create nouns. English has a group of verbs from which nouns have been made. In each of these cases, the difference between the verbs and nouns is found in the stress placed on different syllables (see Table 2).

From the examples in Table 2, two regular patterns emerge.

1. The verbs tend to be stressed on the second syllable (some verbs can receive stress on either syllable, such as *import* or *contrast*), and the nouns tend to be stressed on

TABLE 2. Nouns Derived from Verbs in English

VERBS	NOUNS
convíct	cónvict
segmént	ségment
subjéct	súbject
presént	présent
impáct	ímpact
impórt	ímport
incréase	íncrease
contrást	cóntrast
insúlt	ínsult
insért	ínsert
protést	prótest
convért	cónvert
projéct	próject
rebél	rébel
conflíct	cónflict

Note: The stress is indicated by the slash mark over the vowel.

the first syllable. Stress means that a particular sound in a word, usually a vowel, is more prominent; that is, it is said with more emphasis.
2. Because of the difference in stress between a noun and a verb, the vowels in the two words sound different. This means, for example, that the vowel sounds in the first syllable of the verb *convert* and in the noun *convert* sound different.

This is just one of the regular patterns in the relationship between verbs and nouns. Another example in English occurs when the suffix *-er* is added to verbs, which transforms the verbs into nouns. For example, adding *-er* to the English verbs *write, dance, walk,* and *think,* results in the nouns *writer, dancer, walker,* and *thinker.* Again, there is a regular pattern in the relationship between verbs and nouns. These patterns illustrate an earlier point—morphology is about the creation of new units, and one way to create new units is to take a form that already exists in the language and change it in some way.

These two examples from English morphology illustrate the difference between a morpheme that is a *form* and a morpheme that is a *process.* In the case of adding *-er* to a verb in order to form a noun (*walk/walker*), *-er* is a form that consists of two sounds; it is a form that is added on to other forms to create a new word. Since it cannot occur by itself, it is a bound morpheme. However, in the case of the verb *subjéct* and the noun *súbject,* we can't identify a specific form that is added to the verb to derive the noun; in other words, we can't see a morpheme. We can see that the stress on the verbs is consistently different from the stress on the nouns. On the verbs, it is generally on the second syllable, while on the nouns, it is on the first syllable (for example, contést/cóntest, progréss/prógress). The process of moving the stress to the first syllable results in the creation of a noun related to the verb. This concept of the morpheme as a process is important in understanding ASL morphology.

ASL also has verbs and nouns that show a regular pattern. Some examples of verbs and nouns that are related in ASL are listed in Table 3.

These noun-verb pairs were first analyzed by Ted Supalla and Elissa Newport, two researchers who published their findings in 1978. Supalla and Newport noticed that there are pairs of verbs and nouns in ASL that differ from each other only in the movement of the sign. For example, in the pair SIT and CHAIR, the handshape, location, and orientation of the two signs are the same, but the movement is different. It is the movement that creates the difference in meaning between the two signs. In the same way, the handshape, location, and orientation of FLY and AIRPLANE are the same, but the movement is different.

Supalla and Newport focused on movement and described the differences between verb movement and noun movement in great detail. By looking at pairs of verbs and nouns within the Liddell and Johnson framework for describing signs, we can say that related verbs and nouns may have the same handshape, location, and orientation, and that the noun simply repeats or reduplicates the segmental structure of the verb (see Figure 21). The segmental structure is the movements and holds of a sign. So, for example, the basic structure of the verb SIT is Movement-Hold, and the basic structure of the noun CHAIR is Movement-Hold-Movement-Movement-Hold. A diagram of the structure of the two signs is as follows:

SIT CHAIR

M H M H M M H

Notice the movement after the first hold in CHAIR. This is an example of movement epenthesis (see p. 42), which happens when nouns are derived from verbs in ASL. The basic structure of the verb is repeated, so when the last segment of the verb is a hold, a movement is added before the first segment of the verb is repeated. The result of reduplicating the verb structure is not simply M H M H; it is M H M M H. In production, the first H may be deleted, resulting in M M M H. Verbs have different segmental structure (the basic structure of SIT [M H] is different from the basic structure of OPEN-BOOK [H M H]), but in both cases, the basic structure of the verb is repeated, with movements added in order to form the noun. Look through the list of verbs and nouns below and describe the basic structure of the verbs; note how that basic structure is repeated to form the noun.

This process of repetition is called *reduplication*. Similar to the derivation of nouns from verbs in English, the morpheme in ASL is the process of reduplication. We do not add a form to the ASL morpheme SIT to derive the noun "chair"; we repeat the morpheme SIT.

The process of adding bound morphemes to other forms to create new units is called *affixation*. Plural *-s* (*cats*), third person *-s* (*follows*), and *-er* (*walker*) are all affixes in English; specifically, they are suffixes. English also has prefixes, such as *un-* in *untie* or *re-* in *reschedule*. There may be some examples of affixation in ASL, such

TABLE 3. Related Verbs and Nouns in ASL

VERBS	NOUNS
FLY	AIRPLANE
GO-BY-BOAT	BOAT
GO-BY-SKIS	SKIS
CALL	NAME
SELL	STORE
OPEN-BOOK	BOOK
SIT	CHAIR
PUT-GAS-IN	GAS
OPEN-DOOR	DOOR
CLOSE-WINDOW	WINDOW
PUT-ON-CLOTHES	CLOTHES
PUT-ON-HEARING-AID	HEARING-AID
PUT-ON-PERFUME	PERFUME
LICK-ICE-CREAM	ICE-CREAM
COMB-HAIR	COMB
USE-BROOM	BROOM
USE-SHOVEL	SHOVEL
PAINT	PAINT
IRON-CLOTHES	IRON
ICE-SKATE	ICE-SKATES
ROLLER-SKATE	ROLLER-SKATES
PRINT	NEWSPAPER

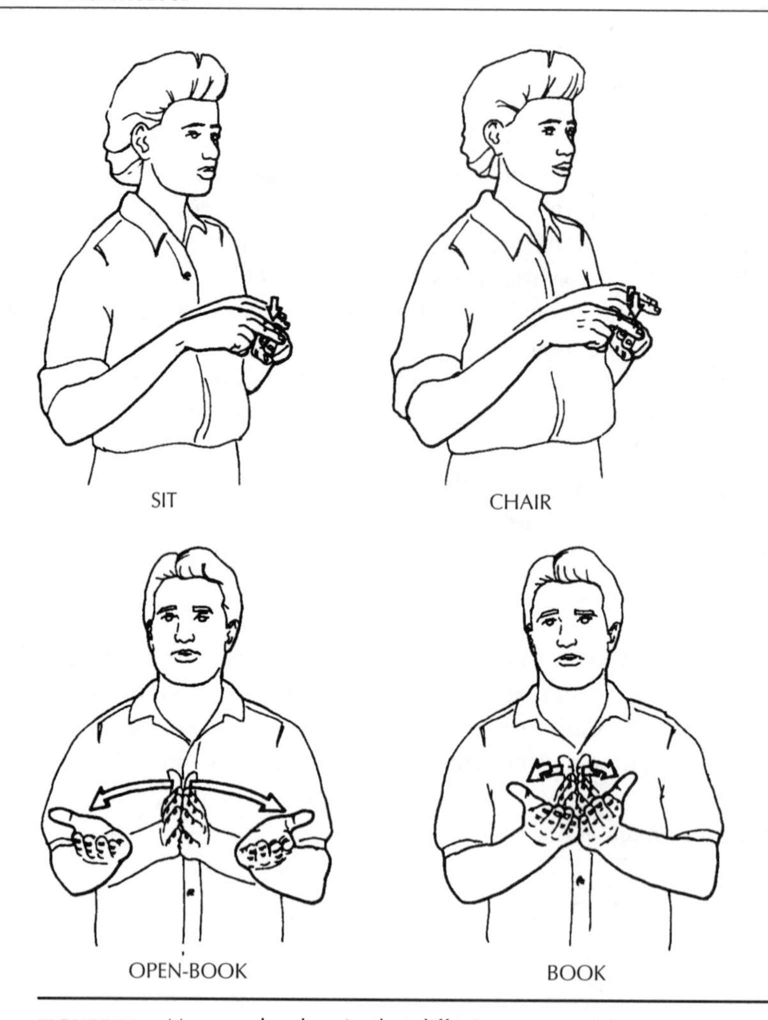

FIGURE 21. Noun and verb pairs that differ in movement.

as the agentive suffix in signs like TEACHER, LAWYER, and ACTOR, but the real origin of these signs is not clear. At this point, it seems that when ASL and English create new units from already existing units, they tend to do it in fundamentally different ways. English and many spoken languages frequently use affixation; ASL tends to repeat or change the segmental structure of the original form, while keeping parts of that form, including the handshape, the location, and the orientation. We will see other examples of this in later units.

REFERENCE

Supalla, T., and Newport, E. 1978. How many seats in a chair? The derivation of nouns and verbs in American Sign Language. In *Understanding language through sign language research*, ed. P. Siple, 91–132. New York: Academic Press.

Homework Assignment 5

1. The videotape (The Snowmobile story) has examples of nouns that have related verbs in ASL and examples of verbs that have related nouns in ASL. Find one example of each.

a. Noun on the videotape:

b. Related ASL verb (may not be on videotape):

c. Verb on the videotape:

d. Related ASL noun (may not be on videotape):

2. Find three more examples of noun-verb pairs not listed in the book.

a.

b.

c.

3. Which of the following sets are noun-verb pairs in ASL and which have related signs for the noun and the verb?

a. PUT-IN-JAIL	JAIL
b. PUT-ON-EARRING	EARRING
c. SHOOT-GUN	GUN
d. MAIL-LETTER	LETTER
e. DRIVE-CAR	CAR

UNIT 3

Compounds

GOAL
To be able to explain how compounds are formed in ASL

COMPOUNDS IN ASL

In unit 2, we saw that one way that ASL can create new signs is by deriving nouns from verbs. In this unit, we will look at another way that ASL can create new signs. Sometimes a language creates new words by taking two words (free morphemes) that it already has and putting them together. This process is called *compounding*. Both English and ASL have many compounds. We will first look at some examples from English.

In English, the word *green* is combined with the word *house* to make the word *greenhouse.* The word *black* is combined with the word *board* to make the word *blackboard.* Some other examples of English compounds are *hatrack, railroad, bookcase, blackberry, showroom,* and *homework.*

When nouns are derived from verbs in English or in ASL, a regular pattern can be described. A pattern can also be described for the formation of compounds. In English, when two words come together to form a compound, two fairly predictable changes take place.

1. The stress (that is, the emphasis) is usually on the first word of the compound, and the stress on the second word is usually reduced or lost. When the word *green* and the word *house* come together to form the compound *greenhouse,* the stress is on the word *green: gréenhouse.*
2. A new meaning is created when two words come together to form a compound. For example, greenhouse does not mean a house that is green, it has the specific meaning of a place where plants are grown. Blackboard does not mean a board that is black, it means a board that is used for instructional purposes, which may be black, green, or brown.

The research done by Supalla and Newport on nouns and verbs in ASL has already been mentioned. Another researcher, Scott Liddell, has done a great deal of research on compounds in ASL (see Table 4 for examples of ASL compounds). He noticed that when two signs come together to form a compound, predictable changes take place as the result of rule application, just as they do in English-compound formation. There are two kinds of rules that cause the changes—morphological and phonological.

Morphological rules are applied specifically to create new meaningful units (in this case, compounds). Three morphological rules are used to create compounds in ASL: (1) the first contact rule, (2) the single sequence rule, and (3) the weak hand anticipation rule.

1. Sometimes the hold segment of a sign includes contact on the body or the other hand (+c). In compounding, the first or only contact hold is kept. This means that if two signs come together to form a compound and the first sign has a contact hold in it, that hold will stay. A preceding movement may be deleted. If the first sign does not have a contact hold but the second sign does, that contact hold will stay. It is important to notice that while the hold may appear in the compound, the actual contact may not. For example, the sign GOOD has the structure

H	M	H
+ contact		+ contact

   The sign NIGHT has the structure:

M	H(+)
	+ contact

   The (+) following the H in NIGHT means that the sequence M H is repeated. When the sign GOOD and the sign NIGHT come together to form the compound GOOD⁀NIGHT, the first contact hold of GOOD is kept, and one movement-hold sequence of NIGHT is kept. The transition to the compound is as follows:

TABLE 4. ASL Compounds

ASL COMPOUND	ENGLISH TRANSLATION
GIRL⁀SAME	"sister"
BOY⁀SAME	"brother"
MOTHER⁀FATHER	"parents"
BLUE⁀SPOT	"bruise"
THINK⁀MARRY	"believe"
THINK⁀SAME-AS	"it's like"; "for example"
THINK⁀TOUCH	"be obsessed with"
TALK⁀NAME	"mention"
FACE⁀NEW	"stranger"
GOOD⁀ENOUGH	"just barely adequate"
JESUS⁀BOOK	"Bible"
LOOK⁀STRONG	"resemble"

Note: The symbol between the two glosses indicates that the sign is a compound.

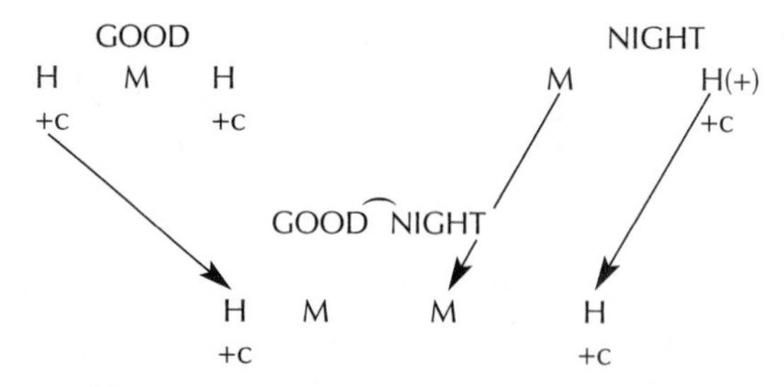

It happens that both GOOD and NIGHT have contact holds. But in the compound THINK⁀SAME, only THINK has a contact hold. The structure of THINK is

M H
+C

The structure of SAME is M H M H; it does not have contact holds. When THINK and SAME come together to form a compound, the contact hold in THINK is kept, and one movement hold sequence of SAME is dropped. The structure of THINK⁀SAME results from these changes.

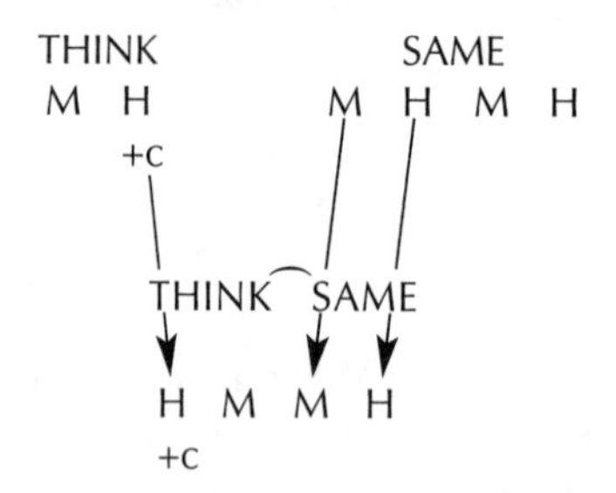

Notice that in the compounds GOOD⁀NIGHT and THINK⁀SAME, an M is added after the final H in GOOD and THINK. This is an epenthetic M, which we will discuss shortly.

2. When compounds are made in ASL, internal movement or the repetition of movement is eliminated. This is called the simple sequence rule. We saw in the sign NIGHT that the M H sequence is repeated. Other signs that show repetition include GIRL, WORK, and NAME. Signs that have internal movement include MOTHER and FATHER. The internal movement occurs while the hand is in the hold segment. In MOTHER and FATHER, the wiggling of the fingers is the internal movement. When these signs come together with other signs to form compounds, the repetition or internal movement is eliminated. For example, the following compounds don't show any repetition:

   GIRL⁀SAME "sister"

   TALK⁀NAME "mention"

   And in the sign for "parents," the fingers do not wiggle as they do in the individual signs MOTHER and FATHER.

3. When two signs are combined to form a compound, if often happens that the signer's weak hand anticipates the second sign in the compound. For example, in the compound SISTER (GIRL⁀SAME), you will notice that the weak hand appears in the space in front of the signer with the 1 handshape of the sign SAME *at the same time* that the active hand is producing the sign GIRL. This can also be seen in the compound BELIEVE (THINK⁀MARRY) in which the weak hand appears with the C handshape of the sign MARRY while the active hand produces the sign THINK.

Phonological rules may be applied whenever signs are produced in sequence and do not result in any changes in meaning. We see at least three different phonological rules occurring with compounding: (1) movement epenthesis, (2) hold deletion, and (3) assimilation.

1. We described movement epenthesis in the unit on phonological processes. It involves adding a movement segment between the last segment of one sign and the first segment of the next sign. An example of movement epenthesis in compounding can be seen in the compound THINK⁀SAME, where a movement segment is added between the final hold of THINK and the first movement of SAME. It should be noted that in the final production of a compound, the epenthetic movement may assimilate to a following movement. For example, in the sign SISTER, an epenthetic movement occurs between the final hold of the first sign, GIRL, and the initial movement of the second sign, SAME, producing the structure H M M H. However, the structure of the compound in actual production is H M H.
2. A second phonological rule that applies when two signs come together to form a compound is that noncontact holds between movements are eliminated. This is an example of the process of hold deletion that was discussed in part 2 unit 5. For example, the structure of the sign LOOK is M H. The structure of the sign STRONG is H M H. None of the holds in these two signs have contact with the body or with the other hand. When these two signs come together to form a compound, they look like this:

   LOOK STRONG
   M H M H M H

   An epenthetic M occurs between the two signs. The holds between the movements are eliminated and the result is

   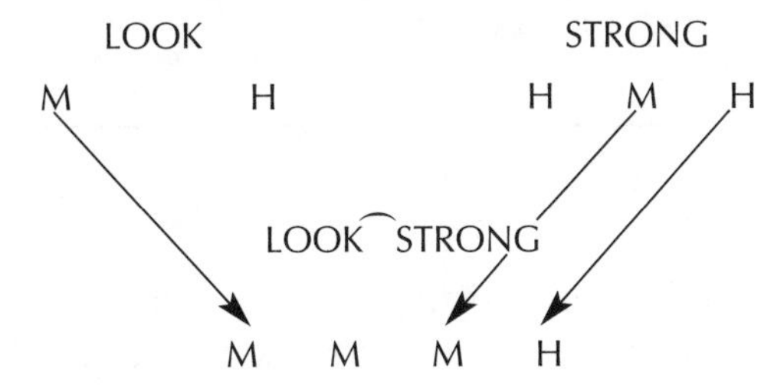

   Notice that this is the structure of the compound when it is first formed. Another version of the compound consists of H M H, with the index finger touching the nose on the first hold (see Figure 22).
3. As we said in the unit on phonological processes, assimilation means that a segment takes on the characteristics of another segment near it, usually the one just before it or after it. Assimilation occurs frequently in ASL compounds. In the compound BELIEVE, the handshape of the sign THINK may change to look more like the handshape of the sign MARRY; in RESEMBLE (LOOK⁀STRONG), the location of the sign STRONG may be closer to the location of the sign LOOK.

The result of compounding is that a new meaning is created. It may not be possible to predict the meaning of the new sign simply by looking at the two signs that form the compound. For example, the signs THINK and MARRY form the compound BELIEVE, but new signers cannot guess the meaning of the compound and many native signers are surprised to learn the origin of the compound. Likewise, the signs

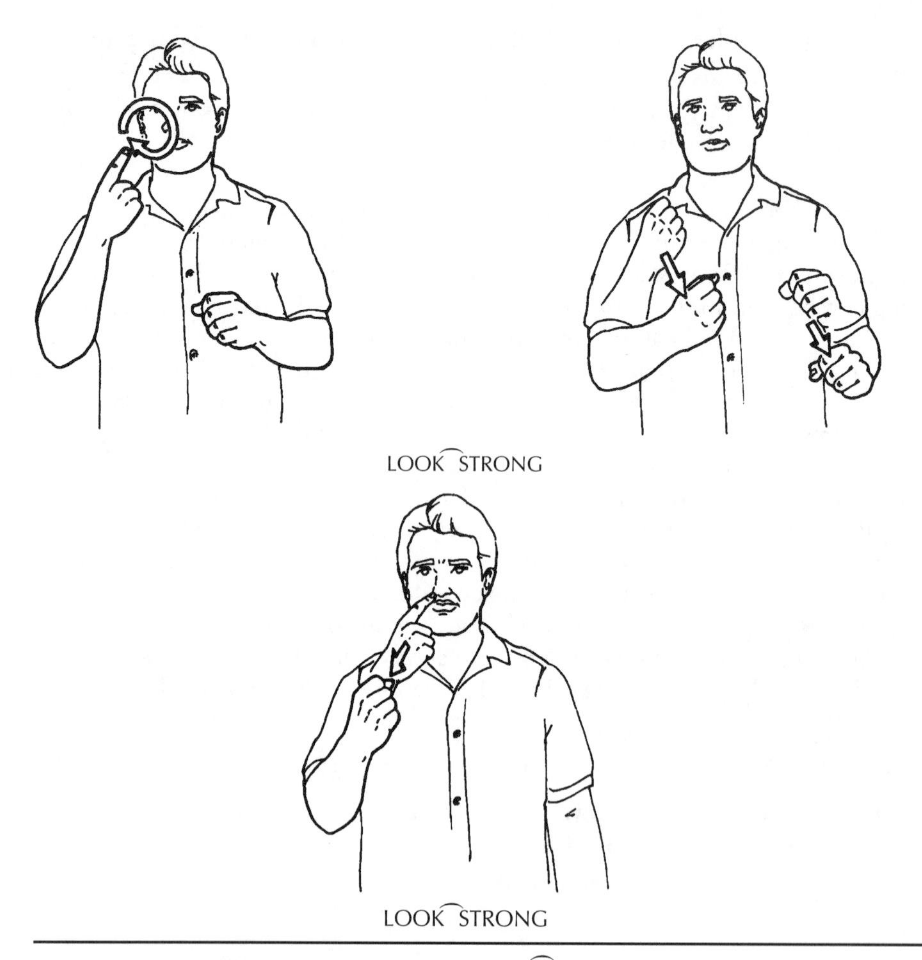

FIGURE 22. Two versions of the compound LOOK⁀STRONG.

LOOK and STRONG come together to form the sign RESEMBLE, but the meaning of the compound is not obvious simply from the joining of the two signs. Similarly in English, simply knowing the meaning of the words *green* and *house* that form the compound *greenhouse* will not be sufficient to figure out the meaning of the compound.

In summary, we see that, as in English, compound formation in ASL is a rule-governed process. ASL has a way of creating new signs by putting together signs that already exist in the language, and when two signs come together to form a compound, predictable and describable changes happen.

REFERENCES

Liddell, S. K. 1984. THINK and BELIEVE: Sequentiality in American Sign Language signs. *Language* 60: 372–399.

Liddell, S. K., and Johnson, R. E. Forthcoming. *Aspects of American Sign Language phonology.* New York: Academic Press.

Homework Assignment 6

1. For each of the English translations of ASL compounds listed below, write which two signs come together to form the compound and describe what changes happen when the two signs come together.

Example: "sister"			GIRL					SAME		
	M	H	M	M	H	M	H	M	M	H
Changes:		+c			+c		+c			+c
Morphological Rules:										
Single Sequence	M	H				M	H			
		+c					+c			
First Contact Hold		H				M	H			
		+c					+c			
Weak Hand Anticipation							yes			
Phonological Rules:										
Movement Epenthesis	H				M	M	H			
	+c						+c			

Assimilation (possibly handshape of GIRL, orientation of SAME, movement)

Result:	H	M	H
	+c		+c

a. "believe"
b. "wife"
c. "husband"
d. "home"
e. "Bible"
f. "resemble"
g. "mention"

2. List at least four other compounds in which the first sign is either THINK or MIND.
Example: THINK⁀TOUCH "be obsessed with"

3. There are three compound signs on the videotape. Find them and write down which two signs form each compound and its English translation.

UNIT 4

Lexicalized Fingerspelling and Loan Signs

GOAL
To be able to explain lexicalized fingerspelling and loan signs in ASL

FINGERSPELLING

ASL creates new signs in a third way—by representing the symbols of written English with ASL signs. This process is commonly referred to as fingerspelling (see Table 5). We will refer to these signs as fingerspelled signs. In the examples discussed in this unit, the symbol # placed before a gloss indicates that the sign is fingerspelled.

Robbin Battison, an ASL linguist, did the first research on fingerspelling in ASL. He noticed, among many things, that when a written English word is represented with ASL signs, different changes may take place. It is important to notice that what have traditionally been called the "letters" of fingerspelling are ASL signs, each with a segmental structure and a handshape, location, and orientation. It is true that the handshapes of the signs may resemble the written symbol and it is true that fingerspelling in ASL is the direct result of language contact with English. For example, the handshape of the sign C may look like the written English symbol C, but the sign is a sign and not a letter.

From a morphological perspective, these signs are free morphemes. A signer may produce each morpheme distinctly in what we will call full fingerspelling. This is represented with dashes, as in W-H-A-T (see Figure 23). In actual production, however, changes often take place when fingerspelling morphemes are produced in sequence. A number of separate morphemes may begin to act like one single morpheme, like a single sign. This what we refer to as lexicalized fingerspelling, and we use the symbol # to mark it, as in Figure 23. Eight of the changes that are part of the lexicalization process are described in the following section. These changes were first described by Battison (1978).

Some of the Signs May Be Deleted

In the fingerspelling of #YES, there is a sign Y and a sign S; there is no sign E. While there are signs in ASL with one handshape or two handshapes in sequence, there

TABLE 5. Fingerspelled Signs in ASL

#BANK	#DO
#BACK	#SO
#OFF	#OK
#ON	#KO
#IF	#JOB
#SALE	#YES
#EARLY	#NO
#BUT	#DOG
#BUS	#TOY
#CAR	#FIX
#HA	#WHAT

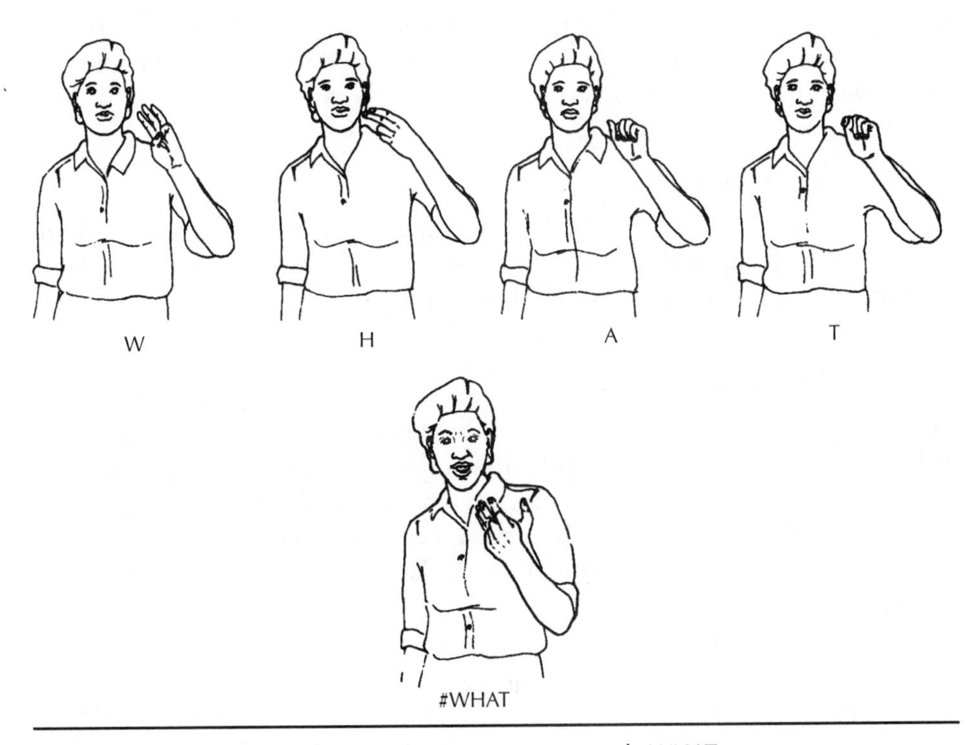

FIGURE 23. Fingerspelled versions of WHAT: W-H-A-T and #WHAT.

are no signs with more than two handshapes in sequence. However, many fingerspelled signs start out with four or more handshapes (for example, #BACK, #RARE, #SURE, #WHAT, and #EARLY). It seems that fingerspelled signs undergo pressure to conform to the rules of ASL structure. One of these rules seems to be "no more than two handshapes are allowed in a sign." This may explain why some signs in fingerspelled signs are deleted, as in #BACK.

Another rule seems to govern the acceptable sequence of handshapes in a sign. That is, it seems that some handshapes can only be followed by certain other handshapes. For example, the sequence of handshapes in the sign CHICKEN is from an Open L-like handshape to a closed Flat O-like handshape. This sequence occurs naturally in ASL. A very similar sequence occurs in the lexicalized fingerspelled sign #NO. The handshape sequence in #NO fits the pattern for handshape sequences in ASL. However, the sequence of handshapes in the lexicalized fingerspelled sign #JOB is unlike any ASL sign; it is not an acceptable sequence.

The Location May Change

Battison described the usual place for fingerspelling to take place as an area just below and in front of the signer's dominant shoulder. In fact, when names or English words are fingerspelled for the first time, they are often fingerspelled in this area. However, fingerspelling is not restricted to this area; the location can change. For example, if someone is obsessed with food, people can talk about the person in a teasing way by fingerspelling #FOOD on the forehead. In addition, we will see many examples in which the location of a fingerspelled sign includes grammatical information concerning the subject or object of a verb.

Handshapes May Change

In the fingerspelled sign #CAR, the C handshape has the thumb extended and involves principally the index and middle finger, and the R also has the thumb extended. The sign B in the fingerspelled sign #BACK has the fingers hooked.

Movement May Be Added

Within the Liddell and Johnson framework, a fingerspelled sign begins as individual signs that are symbols for English orthographic symbols. Each sign is basically a hold with a handshape, location, and orientation, and these holds are produced in sequence. When a series of holds are produced in sequence, movements are naturally added in the transition between holds. This is an example of the process of movement epenthesis.

The basic structure of the fingerspelled sign #BACK is as follows:

BACK

	H	H	H	H
handshape	B	A	C	K
location	sh	sh	sh	sh
orientation	palm out	palm out	palm out	palm out

However, when a signer produces the holds in sequence, movement is naturally added between the holds. The final structure of the fingerspelled sign could probably be described as H M H.

The addition of movement also may be accompanied by a change in location. For example, in the fingerspelling of #YES, the movement includes a dip in the wrist followed by a pulling back of the S sign; the fingerspelled sign #SALE includes a counterclockwise circular movement; the sign #SURE involves a movement forward with the R sign and a movement backward with the E sign.

The Orientation May Change

The palm orientation of a sign may change in a fingerspelled English word. For example, in the fingerspelling of #JOB, the final orientation of the B sign is opposite of its orientation if it were being signed alone; in the sign #HA, the orientation of the A sign goes from palm out to palm up.

There May Be Reduplication of the Movement

If one were to fingerspell the written word *ha*, there would be a sign H and a sign A. However, there is a fingerspelled sign #HA in which the index and middle finger are moved back and forth repeatedly. The repetition of the movement is called reduplication. Other examples include the signs #NO and #DO.

The Second Hand May Be Added

The fingerspelled sign #WHAT may be produced on both hands simultaneously as may the sign #BACK. Sometimes this is done for stylistic reasons, or to show emphasis. Other times it is because the left hand has different meaning from the right hand. This is discussed below.

Grammatical Information May Be Included

The location of the hands while fingerspelling can indicate the relationship between people or places. The location carries meaning and so is grammatical. For example, someone may be talking about a trip they took to a distant location. In the course of the conversation, they may have set up the location of that place in front of them to the right. When it comes time to talk about returning from that location, they may begin the fingerspelled sign #BACK in that location with the palm facing in, move the sign towards them, and complete it near their body. Similarly, a girlfriend and a boyfriend may have a history of breaking up and getting back together. Someone might describe this by fingerspelling #BACK simultaneously on the right hand and the left hand with the palms facing each other and the hands moving together, and by then signing #OFF with the hands moving away from each other. Another example is the fingerspelled sign #NO. It can be signed away from the signer, meaning "I say no to you or to a third person." However, it can also be signed with the palm facing the signer, with the meaning of "You (or someone) say no to me." Here the location and the orientation provide grammatical information about who is the subject and who is the object of the verb. We will discuss this more in the section on verb agreement.

LEXICALIZED FINGERSPELLING

Many people have noticed that the separate signs of fingerspelling tend to blend together when they are produced in fingerspelled signs. That is, they tend to "become like individual signs." In linguistics, the word *lexicalized* means "like a word," or "word-like," that is, like an independent unit. Examples of lexicalization in English include compounds such as *greenhouse*, *breakfast*, and *Christmas*, which are formed by uniting two separate lexical items that function as one word with a unique meaning. Acronyms such as NASA (National Air and Space Administration) and *scuba* (self-contained underwater breathing apparatus) are also examples of lexicalization in English. In these cases, a new word is formed by using the first letter of each word in the phrase.

Lexicalization describes the process of fingerspelling because the separate signs do seem to become like one, to be used like other ASL signs, and to follow the rules of ASL signs. For example, Battison noticed that in general, no sign uses more than two handshapes. This means that a fingerspelled sign like #IF or #OR can preserve both signs and still follow the rules of ASL. However, fingerspelled signs like #BACK or #EARLY present problems because they are formed from four and five signs. The result is that while all of the signs are not immediately lost, there is a tendency to reduce the number of signs as they become more like other ASL signs.

There is a difference between full, formal fingerspelling and lexicalized fingerspelling, but it is easy to see how quickly the process of lexicalization begins. Just think about how you would fingerspell someone's name if you were introducing them for the first time and then how the form of that fingerspelling would change if you used the name over and over again in a conversation. The changes that you observe are examples of lexicalization. The eight changes described earlier are also parts of the lexicalization process.

It is important to realize that lexicalization is a gradual process and that some fingerspelled signs may be more completely lexicalized than others. For example, #NO and #DO have undergone many changes and look like ASL signs, while signs like #BUSY and #EARLY are not as fully lexicalized. Similarly, the sign #MICH on the videotape, while it is a sign in terms of meaning and use (it is clearly used and understood as the name for the state of Michigan), is less lexicalized as it retains four handshapes in a sequence not found in natural ASL signs.

Three final observations about fingerspelled signs can be made.

1. Quite often, ASL has both a fingerspelled sign and a sign for the same concept. For example, CAR and #CAR, BED and #BED, BUSY and #BUSY.
2. People often produce combinations of fingerspelled signs and signs (such as LIFE#STYLE) or choose to fingerspell parts of sentences that could just as well be signed. Some very interesting research has been done on this by Arlene B. Kelly at Gallaudet University, but we don't yet have full explanations as to why this happens.
3. People often use both hands to fingerspell or they may sign with one hand and fingerspell with the other, either at the same time or alternately during a conversation. Again, research on this extremely interesting area is just beginning.

Researchers are also studying the two-handed fingerspelling used by British and Australian signers and the representation of writing systems used by deaf people who are in contact with written Chinese, written Arabic, written Hebrew, and written Russian. All of these languages have written symbol systems that are very different from written English. It seems that deaf people in contact with all of these written languages

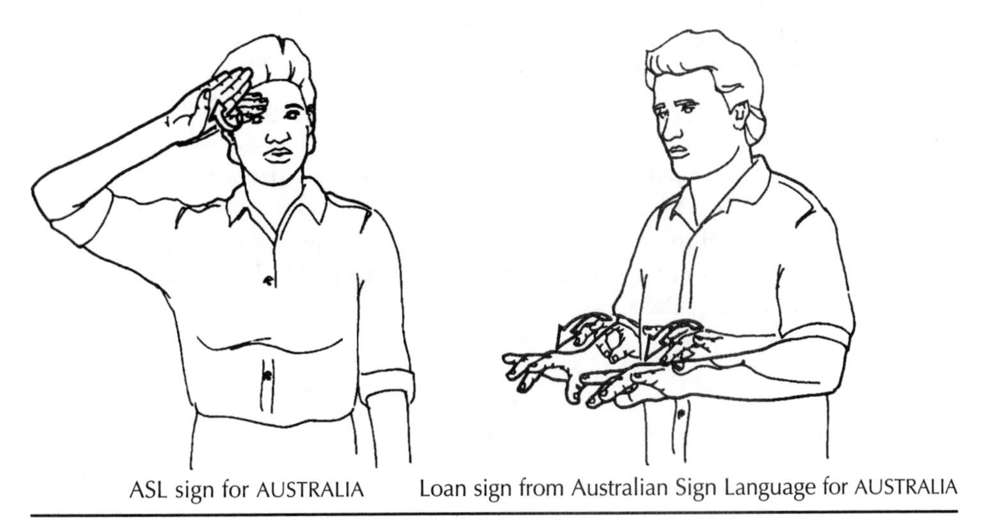

ASL sign for AUSTRALIA Loan sign from Australian Sign Language for AUSTRALIA

FIGURE 24. An example of a loan sign.

have manual ways of representing the written system, in the same way that American deaf people represent the alphabet with signs. For example, Jean Ann has found that deaf people who use Taiwan Sign Language produce signs that represent the characters of written Chinese. Like fingerspelling in ASL, the structure of these character signs is somewhat different from that of regular Taiwan Sign Language signs.

LOAN SIGNS

When two languages are in contact, one thing that happens is that the languages may borrow words from each other. English has borrowed words from Italian (pizza, spaghetti, ravioli), from Arabic (algebra, coffee), from French (quiche, bouquet), from American Indian languages (tobacco, squash), and from many other languages. ASL also borrows from other sign languages. The best examples are signs for the names of countries that are now being used instead of the American signs for those countries. Examples include JAPAN, ITALY, CHINA, and AUSTRALIA (Figure 24), and are the direct result of American deaf people coming in contact with deaf people from those countries. Another example is the sign CLUB, which was introduced at the Deaf Way conference in Washington, D.C., in 1989. The sign was adapted from a sign used widely in Europe meaning "deaf club," and it responded to the need for a sign that could be readily used and understood by 5,700 conference participants from around the world. Deaf people from different countries are interacting with each other more often than before as transportation has become more accessible and affordable. As a result of increased contact and interaction, they have begun to borrow signs from each other.

REFERENCES

Ann, J. 1998. Contact between a sign language and a written language: Character signs in Taiwan Sign Language. In *Pinky extension and eye gaze: Language use in Deaf communities,* ed. C. Lucas, 59–99. Sociolinguistics in Deaf Communities, vol. 4. Washington, DC: Gallaudet University Press.

Battison, R. 1978. *Lexical borrowing in American Sign Language.* Silver Spring, MD: Linstock Press.

Kelly, A. B. 1990. Fingerspelling use among the deaf senior citizens of Baltimore. Paper presented at NWAVE XIX, at University of Pennsylvania, Philadelphia.

———. 1995. Fingerspelling interaction: A set of deaf parents and their deaf daughter. In *Sociolinguistics in Deaf communities,* ed. C. Lucas, 62–73. Washington, DC: Gallaudet University Press.

Homework Assignment 7

1. The videotape has fourteen examples of fingerspelled signs. Find four and explain what changes have taken place in terms of the eight changes discussed in this unit: deletion/addition, location, handshape, movement, orientation, reduplication, second hand, and grammatical information.

2. Fingerspell your first name and describe the changes that take place when it is fingerspelled over and over, in terms of the eight changes.

UNIT 5

Numeral Incorporation

GOAL
To be able to explain numeral incorporation in ASL

So far in our discussion of ASL morphology, we have looked at how whole signs that already exist are used to derive new signs. We have seen how verbs are used to derive nouns, such as SIT and CHAIR; what changes we expect when two signs come together to form a compound, such as BELIEVE or SISTER; how English orthographic symbols are represented by ASL fingerspelling signs, such as #BACK or #JOB; and how signs from other sign languages are borrowed into ASL, such as ITALY or CHINA. It is important to notice that while the parts of signs may change or disappear as a result of the morphological processes described, the starting point for the processes are free morphemes.

In this unit, we will look at how bound morphemes (that is, meaningful units that cannot occur alone) can combine to create new meanings. Signs are composed of movements and holds, and the information about handshape, location, orientation, and nonmanual signals is contained in bundles of articulatory features that are a part of the movements and holds. For example, the sign WEEK would be represented as follows:

WEEK

DOMINANT HAND	H	M	H
handshape	1		1
location	base of hand		tip of fingers
orientation	palm down		palm down
nonmanual signal	—	—	

However, we know that the concept of *two weeks* or *three weeks* can be expressed in ASL by changing the handshape of this sign. By changing the handshape from a 1 to a 2 or a 3, the number of weeks referred to changes. The location, orientation, and nonmanual signal remain the same. This process in ASL is known as numeral

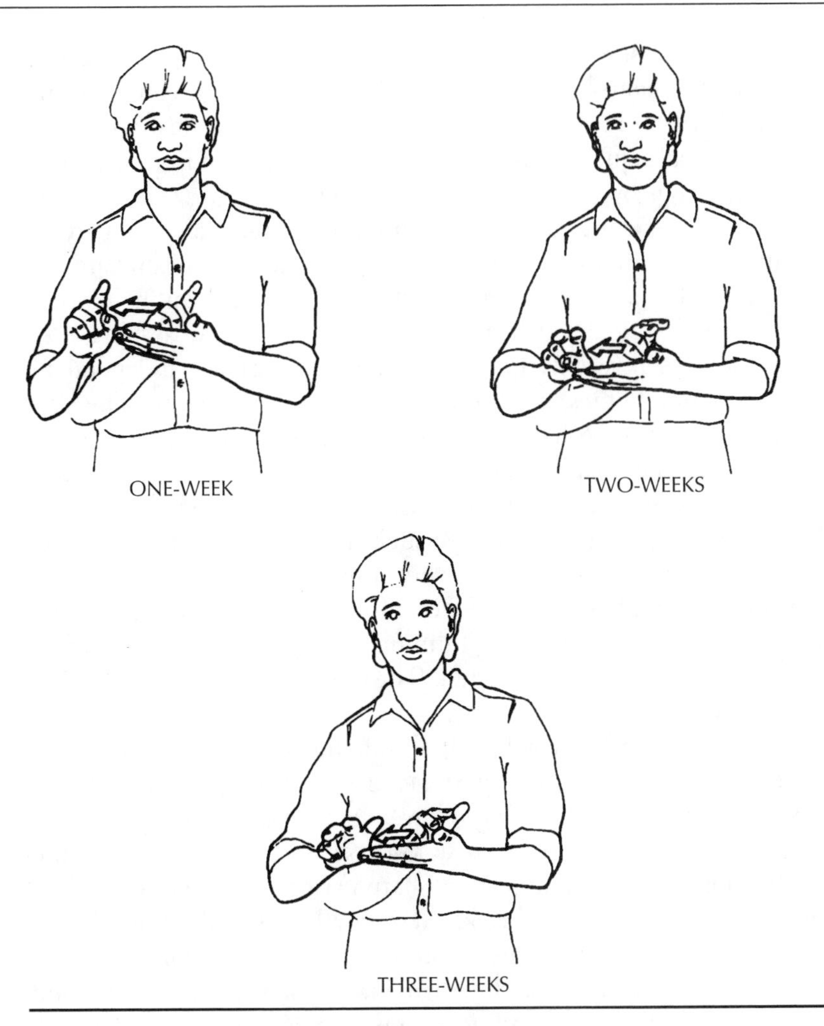

FIGURE 25. Numeral incorporation in ASL

incorporation (see Figure 25), and it has been described by Scott Liddell and Robert E. Johnson. We can say that the sign TWO-WEEKS has two meaningful parts (morphemes). One is the part that includes the segmental structure—the holds and the movement—and the location, orientation, and nonmanual signal. It means WEEK. The other meaningful part is the handshape, which has the meaning of a specific number. When the two parts are produced together, the meaning of the sign is "specific number of weeks." A diagram of the two morphemes would look like this:

NUMBER OF WEEKS

	H	M	H
handshape (varies)			
location	base of hand		tip of hand
orientation	palm down		palm down
nonmanual signal	—		—

The morphemes in this example are *bound* morphemes, that is, morphemes that must occur with other morphemes. For example, the handshape cannot occur by itself. It must occur within a segmental structure, with a location, an orientation, and possibly a nonmanual signal. Bound morphemes are different from *free* morphemes, which may occur by themselves. For example, the sign LOUSY in ASL (along with many other lexical signs) is a free morpheme. Its individual parts—handshape, location, orientation—do not have independent meaning and are not morphemes, but when they are all put together, the result is one meaningful unit, one morpheme. It is interesting to see the difference between the lexical sign LOUSY and the sign THREE-WEEKS. In LOUSY, the individual parts do not have independent meaning and are not morphemes, but the whole sign is a morpheme. The sign THREE-WEEKS has the same handshape as LOUSY, but in THREE-WEEKS, the handshape does have independent meaning and is a bound morpheme. In other words, the sign THREE-WEEKS is made up of two morphemes. What is interesting is that two signs with the same handshape can have such different linguistic structure.

The process of numeral incorporation is very common in ASL. Usually there is a limit to how high the numbers can go. For example, for most native signers, the handshape for WEEK can be changed from 1 through 9; for number 10 and higher the sign is signed separately from the sign WEEK. The same is true for MONTHS, DAYS, DOLLARS, and so forth.

Numeral incorporation in ASL can be found with the signs WEEK, MONTH, DAY, DOLLAR AMOUNT, PLACE IN A RACE, EXACT TIME, PERIOD OF TIME, and HEIGHT. It is important to notice that many of these signs have a characteristic movement, location, and orientation. For example, DOLLAR AMOUNT is generally signed in the area in front of the dominant shoulder, with a sharp twisting movement resulting in a change of orientation; EXACT TIME usually requires that the index finger of the dominant hand contact the passive wrist before moving outward from the wrist. What is important to understand is that the segmental structure (movements and holds) and the location, orientation, and nonmanual signal of each one does not change. All of those parts consist of one morpheme that communicates the main topic. The handshape does change to indicate the specific quantity being discussed.

Signs for age traditionally have been thought of as examples of numeral incorporation, especially for ages 1 through 9, in which the numeral handshape starts at the chin, with the palm out, and moves out. However, work by Scott Liddell has demonstrated that the sign OLD in these constructions functions more like a prefix and extends beyond ages 1 to 9 to include all ages (for example, OLD-22 and OLD-55). Thus, the handshape change that we see in ages 1 to 9, even though it resembles the numeral incorporation of WEEK or MONTH, is the result of phonological assimilation.

REFERENCES

Liddell, S. 1997. Numeral incorporating roots and non-incorporating prefixes in American Sign Language. *Sign Language Studies* 92: 201–226.

Liddell, S., Ramsey, C., Powell, F., and Corina, D. 1984. Numeral incorporation and numeral classifiers in American Sign Language. Department of Linguistics, Gallaudet University. Typescript.

Homework Assignment 8

1. Think about and briefly describe how you would sign the following signs.

Ex.: TIME: Touch passive wrist with active index finger, then move active hand back and forth in neutral space with handshape appropriate to time; 1–10, fine; seems to change for 11 and 12.

a. HEIGHT

b. FIRST, SECOND, THIRD PLACE

c. TV CHANNEL

d. PERIOD OF TIME (e.g., 6–9 p.m.)

e. DOLLAR AMOUNT (e.g., $1, $2)

f. NUMBERS ON A SHIRT

g. SPORTS SCORES (e.g., in racquetball, "I have 9 and you have 11")

2. The videotape shows three examples of signs involving numbers. Answer the following questions about these signs.

a. The three signs are:

b. What area do the signs refer to—for example, age, time, etc.

c. Are the signs examples of numeral incorporation?

UNIT 6

The Function of Space in ASL

GOAL
To understand the role of location in ASL morphology

SUPPLEMENTAL READING
"The Confluence of Space and Language in Signed Languages," by Karen Emmorey (1999); pp. 318–346

As we have said, morphology is the study of the smallest meaningful units of a language. We have seen how ASL signs have internal structure, how they are made up of separate parts. Those parts may have independent meaning, that is, they may be morphemes. In the preceding unit on numeral incorporation, we saw how handshape can be a morpheme in ASL. In this unit and in the next five units, we will focus on how location may have independent meaning in ASL signs. We will look at the function of space in ASL.

As we saw in the phonology units, location is a part of all ASL signs. Location may be on the body. For example, the location for the sign BORED is the nose, for FEEL it is the chest, and for RUSSIAN it is the waist. Location may also mean the signing space surrounding the signer, so that the location for the sign WHERE is in the space in front of the signer's dominant shoulder, while the location for SHOES or COFFEE is the space in front of the signer's torso. A very important point is that while all signs have a location on the body or in space, signers use location in many different ways. That is, location has many different functions in ASL signs.

Karen Emmorey (1999) has described some of the key functions of space in ASL and we will summarize her discussion here. The function of space may simply be *articulatory*. Remember that signs are composed of movement and hold segments and that segments include a bundle of articulatory features. Those features include handshape, location, orientation, and nonmanual signals. So the location of the sign (i.e., where the sign is made) may just be part of how the sign is made. Each sign is made in a particular location, and that location is part of the structure of the sign, but the location itself does not have independent meaning. Sometimes, changing the location of the sign changes its meaning, as in the signs SUMMER, UGLY, and DRY, and in this case, space is used to indicate *phonological contrasts.*

As we will see, while verbs in spoken languages are modified to show person and number by adding suffixes to a word stem, sign languages accomplish this partly with the use of space. We see this *morphological* use of space in verbs such as GIVE, for example. In the sentence FIRST-PERSON-GIVE-TO-SECOND-PERSON ("I give you"), the hand moves from the space associated with the first person (the signer) to the space associated with the second person. And in the sentence SECOND-PERSON-GIVE-TO-FIRST-PERSON ("You give me"), the hand moves in the opposite direction. We see the morphological use of space also in what are known as *aspectual markers.* For example, we can show that someone is giving continually or over and over again by the use of movement and space.

Space is also used for *referential* functions. That is, a location in space can be associated with a nominal. This may be accomplished by producing the sign for the nominal and then indexing (pointing to) a particular point in space. This point in space may continue to be referred to during the conversation by repeated indexing. Pronouns in ASL may also make use of indexing, such that a pronoun sign directed at a specific point in space can be understood to refer to the noun associated with it.

We see the *locative* function of space in classifier predicates and locative verbs. In this case, space provides information about the location of a person or object in a three-dimensional framework. For example, when a signer is talking about a car moving from one place to another, the sign would probably be made with a 3 handshape and would move from one part of the signing space to another.

Space can be used in ASL to indicate a signer's *frame of reference.* For example, within a *relative* frame of reference, a signer usually describes a scene from his or her perspective. Some signs have *intrinsic* features (for example, cars have identifiable fronts and backs), and we will see how classifier predicates represent these features. Signers also can make reference to *absolute* frames of reference, as when they use the signs for "east," "west," "north," and "south."

Finally, space in ASL can be related to *narrative perspective.* In the course of telling a story involving different characters, a signer may seem to take on the role of one of the characters. One of the ways the signer switches to a different role is through the use of space—the signer's body may shift to one side, the eye gaze may shift, and the position of the head may change.

As we can see, space has many functions in ASL. In the units that follow, we will take a closer look at some of these functions.

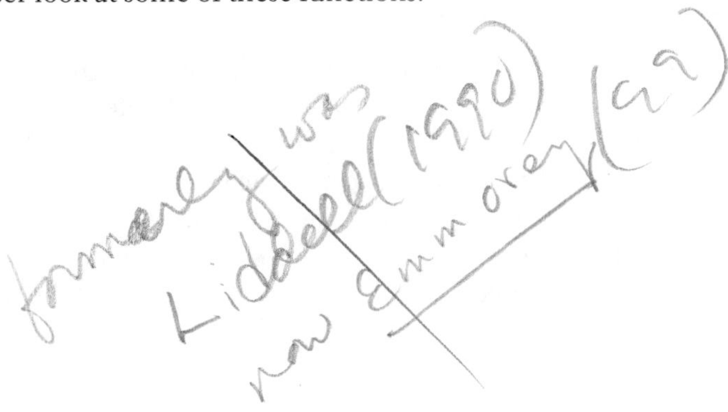

UNIT 7

Classifier Predicates and Locative Verbs

GOAL
To be able to explain classifier predicates in ASL

In our discussion of numeral incorporation, we introduced the concept of morphemes, and we saw how signs can be made up of different meaningful parts. In this section, we will talk about a class of verbs in ASL. These verbs are called *classifier predicates*, and we will see how they are made up of meaningful units. First, we must define the word *predicate*.

Languages have ways of referring to things or activities, and those ways are called nouns or noun phrases. Languages also have ways of saying something about those nouns or noun phrases, and those ways are called predicates. In the English sentence *The boy is home, the boy* is a noun phrase, and *is home* says something about the boy. In this sentence, *is home* is a predication about the boy; it can also be called a predicate. Predicates can have different forms, they are not limited to verbs. In fact, in the English sentence *The boy is home,* the predicate is a verb (is) with a noun (home). In the English sentence *The boy is sick,* the predicate is a verb (is) with an adjective (sick). We can look at the sentence like this:

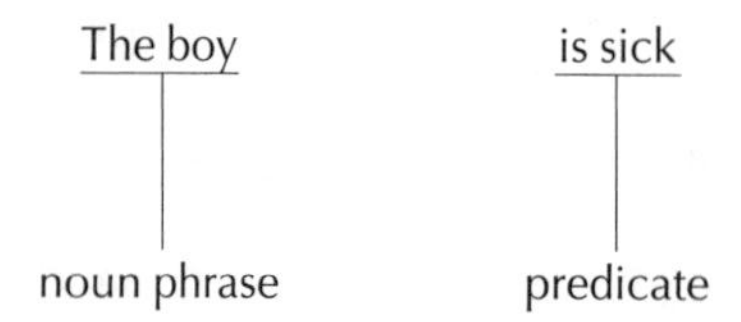

Many languages do not use the verb *to be*. In those languages, a predicate may consist of simply a verb, a noun, or an adjective. In ASL, for example, the sentence BOY EAT consists of a noun (BOY) and a predicate, the verb (EAT). The ASL sentence BOY HOME consists of a noun (BOY) and a predicate that is a noun, HOME. The ASL sentence BOY SICK consists of a noun and a predicate that is an adjective, SICK. These ASL sentences do not include the verb *is*, but the noun HOME and the adjective SICK function as predicates; they say something about the noun BOY. Verbs, nouns, and adjectives can be predicates in ASL.

CLASSIFIER PREDICATES

ASL has another class of predicates called classifier predicates. To understand these, we first have to understand what is meant by a classifier. We will start with an example. In ASL, when a signer describes how a car drove past, the sign CAR is used, followed by a sign with a 3 handshape, moving from right to left in front of the signer, with the palm facing in. A sign with the same handshape can be used to talk about the movement of a boat or a bicycle. The movement, orientation, and location can change to show how the car or boat or bicycle moved. This same handshape, used for all three signs, has the general meaning of VEHICLE. The 3 handshape is an example of a classifier: it is a symbol for a class of objects. The 3 handshape is the symbol for the class of objects VEHICLE. A classifier in ASL is a handshape that is combined with location, orientation, movement, and nonmanual signals to form a predicate. The English sentence *The car drove past* would be signed in ASL as CAR 3-CL (move from right to left of signer with palm facing in). The predicate is VEHICLE-DRIVE-BY, and the classifier is the handshape of the predicate. In the Liddell and Johnson system, the ASL predicate VEHICLE-DRIVE-BY looks like this:

VEHICLE-DRIVE-BY

	H	M	H
handshape	3		3
location	right		left
orientation	palm in		palm in
nonmanual signal	—		—

Note: The labels used in this book for classifier handshapes are different from the ones used by Liddell and Johnson in their system.

Another example of a classifier handshape is the Bent V handshape that symbolizes the class of animals sitting. To sign the ASL sentence CAT SIT, we first make the sign CAT and then the ASL predicate ANIMAL-SIT.

ANIMAL-SIT

	M	H
handshape	Bent V	Bent V
location	near shoulder	near shoulder
orientation	palm down	palm down

This same predicate can be used to say something about a bird or a dog or a squirrel. The classifier in this predicate is the handshape.

ASL has many classifier handshapes and many classifier predicates. Ted Supalla (1978) identified two basic parts in classifier predicates: the movement root and the handshape (Figures 26 and 27), which have been discussed further by Liddell and Johnson.

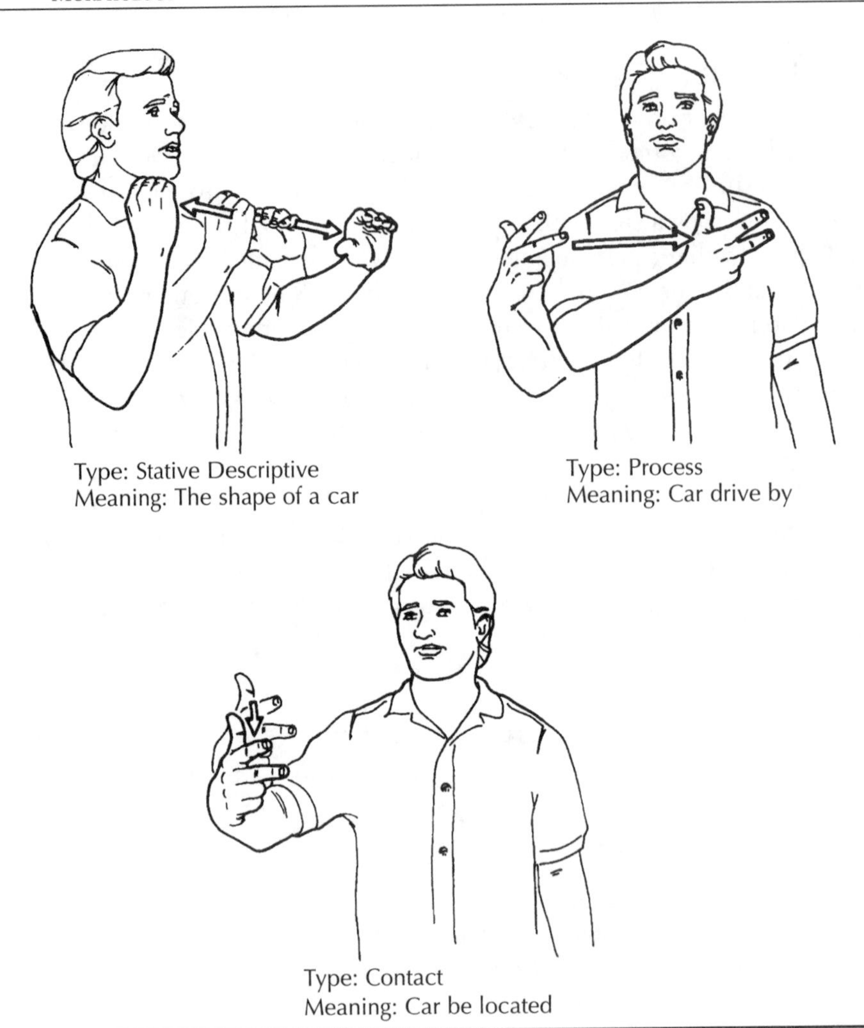

FIGURE 26. Movement roots of classifier predicates.

Movement Roots

1. Stative Descriptive: In this group of movement roots, the hand moves to describe an object, but the movement of the hand does not mean that the object itself is moving. An example of this is the predicate for FLAT-SURFACE, PILE-OF-COINS, or MOUND-OF-RICE.
2. Process: In this group, the hand moves, and the movement does mean that the object being described is moving or appears to be moving. The example we described earlier of CAR-DRIVE-BY is an example of a process root. Other examples include PERSON-WALK-BY or TREES-GO-BY.
3. Contact Root: In this group, the hand has a downward movement, but it does not mean that the object is moving, nor does it describe the shape of the object.

It has the meaning of BE-LOCATED-AT. Examples of the contact root include the earlier example of CAT SIT (that is, CAT BE-LOCATED-IN-THAT-PLACE), CAR-BE-

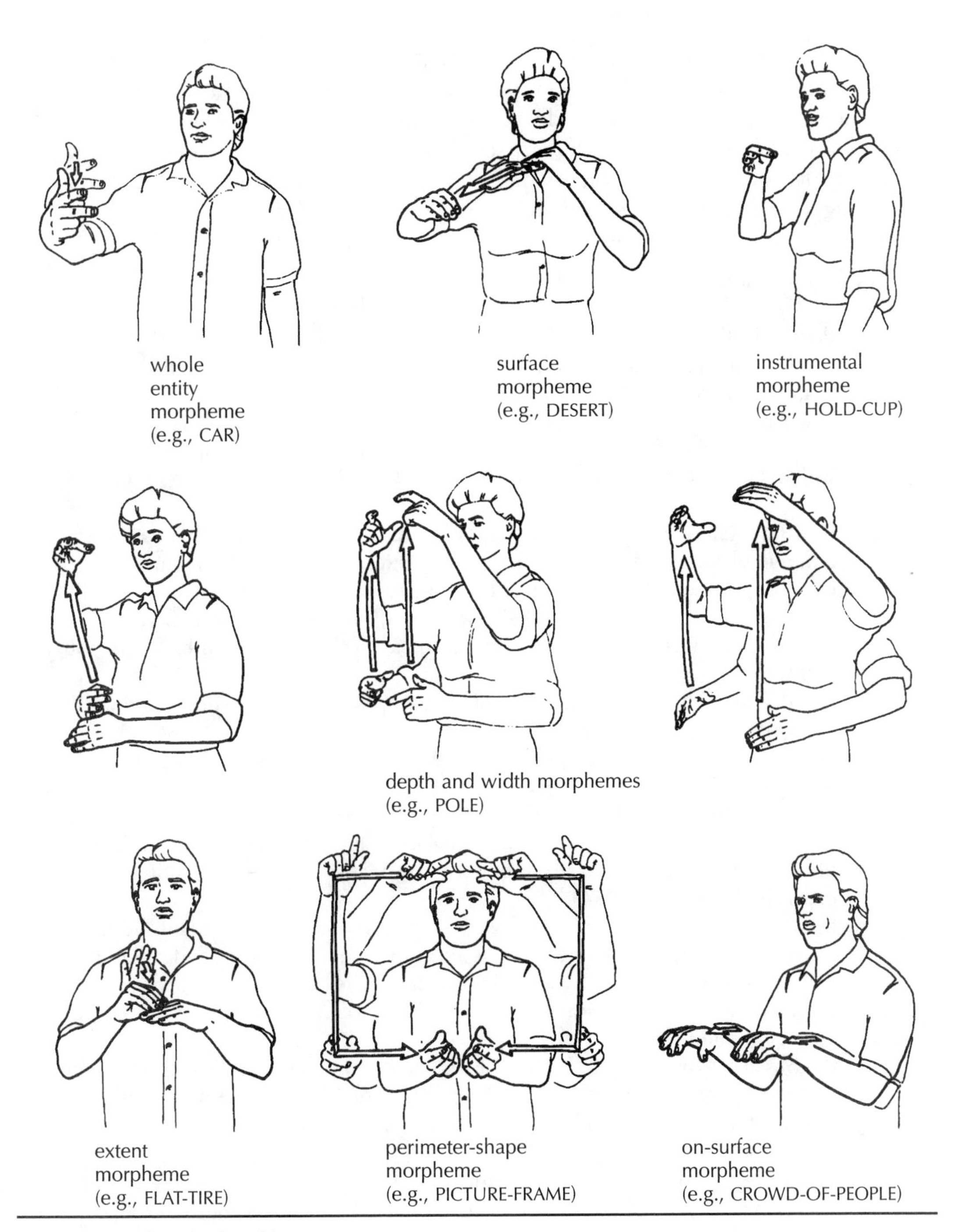

FIGURE 27. Classifier handshapes.

LOCATED, CUP-BE-LOCATED, or CITY-BE-LOCATED. Also in this group is the predicate produced with the pointing index finger, as in the sentence GIRL THERE. In that case, the sign would be produced with a downward movement towards a specific point in space. However, this sign can also occur in a sentence such as BALTIMORE THERE, D.C. HERE, in which the movement of the index finger might be straight out from the signer, as if indicating points on an imaginary map.

Classifier Handshapes

1. Whole Entity Morphemes: These are handshapes that refer to an object as a whole, such as a car, an animal, or a person standing. Other concepts that are represented by whole entity morphemes are airplanes, flying saucers, person lying down, person sitting, old person, many people standing in line, and piece of paper.
2. Surface Morphemes: These handshapes represent thin surfaces or wires, narrow surfaces, or wide surfaces. An example is a B handshape used to represent an expanse of desert.
3. Instrumental Morphemes: Handshapes in this category represent hands holding different objects or instruments as they act on objects. Examples include paper; cups of various kinds (for example, the handshape for holding a paper cup is different from the handshape for holding a tea cup); and instruments such as scissors, knives, tweezers, brushes, rakes, video cameras, syringes, baseball bats, and golf clubs.
4. Depth and Width Morphemes: These handshapes represent the depth and width of different things, such as tree trunks and pipes, and include the representation of layers, such as layer of thick make-up or layer of snow. These handshapes are also used for stripes of various widths.
5. Extent Morphemes: Handshapes in this group represent amounts or volumes, such as an amount of liquid in a glass, a stack of papers, or an increase or decrease of an amount. The handshape in DEFLATE-TIRE is in this class, representing the decrease in the volume of air.
6. Perimeter-Shape Morphemes: The handshapes in this group represent the external shape of an object. Shapes such as a rectangle, a round table, and a clump of mud or grass have specific classifier handshapes. The handshape used for describing a notecard or a playing card is in this group, as is the handshape for coins, poker chips, or buttons.
7. On-Surface Morphemes: Handshapes in this group represent large groups or crowds of people, animals, or objects. For example, handshapes are used to describe a crowd of people, a herd of cattle moving, an audience.

A classifier predicate consists of a movement root and a classifier handshape together. However, not all roots can go with all handshape types. For example, contact roots can be used with handshapes for whole entities, surface, and perimeter-shape morphemes, but not with instrumental, extent, or width and depth morphemes. Likewise, process roots can be used with instrumental, extent, surface, and whole entity morphemes, but not with width and depth or perimeter-shape morphemes. Furthermore, the same object may be represented with different handshapes. For example, a car may be described using a whole entity morpheme or a surface morpheme, depending on what is needed in a particular sentence. A piece of paper might be represented with a whole entity morpheme or with an instrumental morpheme, depending on whether the paper is lying on a table or being held in someone's hand.

Every classifier predicate has a location, and the location in classifier verbs typically represents a location in three-dimensional space. If the signer produces a classifier predicate with a 3 handshape and a contact movement root in a particular point in space, the meaning is that a vehicle is located at that point in three-dimensional space. In this case, the location of the classifier predicate also has the location fixing function that we discussed in unit 6. The exact point in space has meaning and refers to a point in real three-dimensional space. For example, suppose a signer is recounting that a vehicle is moving from one place to another. The signer must move the active hand from exactly one place to exactly another; to stop half-way would clearly mean that the vehicle stopped half-way, and the meaning of the half-way point is different from the meaning of the beginning and end points.

ASL has many classifier predicates, and it is one of the most important ways that ASL has to create new signs. Earlier descriptions of ASL structure have suggested that ASL shows pluralization with classifier predicates. However, pluralization is a process that applies to nouns, and classifier predicates are not nouns. They can represent the concept of "more than one" (think, for example, of how you would sign CARS-PARKED-IN-A-ROW or CROWD-OF-PEOPLE) but the concept of "more than one" is communicated with classifier predicates. For example, CARS-PARKED-IN-A-ROW could be signed several different ways: with repeated downward movement of the active hand (3 handshape) or with a "sweeping" movement of the active hand, with the passive hand (3 handshape) stationary in both cases. Both of these show "more than one," but with classifier predicates.

Classifier predicates are made by combining small meaningful units to create bigger units, the main units being the handshape and the movement. The location, orientation, and nonmanual signals are also important. In fact, the location information in a classifier predicate tells where an object is located. If an object moves, the location information tells the initial location and the final location. The nonmanual signals relay information also; just think how nonmanual signals are used for describing thin objects as opposed to fat or thick objects.

In some cases, the meaning of the small units in a classifier predicate cannot be easily separated out. All that is important, sometimes, is the meaning of the large unit. This is called *lexicalization*, the process whereby the meaning of the small units "gets lost" in the meaning of the large unit. ASL has many examples of signs that have become lexicalized. If one stops and looks carefully at the handshape, location, orientation, and movement of the sign, one can see how the sign was built, but the meaning of each part no longer plays a role. For example, the handshapes in the signs KEY, RING, PACK, or TRUST might be said to have been instrumental handshapes at the time that the sign was being built, but we hardly think of them as instrumental now. Likewise, the handshapes in TRAFFIC might have been surface morphemes meaning "surface pass by," and the handshape in COMMUTE might have been a whole entity morpheme meaning "object move between two places," but signers don't think of those meanings now. The handshape in the sign FALL might have been chosen as signers were building the sign because of its function as a whole entity morpheme representing human legs, but the sign can be used for HAIR-FALL-OUT, and the handshape does not refer to human legs.

The sign PEOPLE-WALK-TWO-BY-TWO is a *productive classifier predicate*. This means that each part of the sign has independent meaning. Each part can function as a morpheme. The handshape can be changed to mean THREE-BY-THREE or FOUR-BY-FOUR; people can walk TWO-BY-TWO in different locations; people can walk TWO-BY-TWO facing each other or facing the same way, that is, the orientation can have meaning; and the nonmanual signal can also have meaning. The signer selects each part and builds the sign from scratch each time it is used. But in the sign FUNERAL, while the sign may have started out as a classifier predicate (the handshape is clearly a whole entity morpheme for "standing person") the parts of the sign do not have independent meaning. They are not separate morphemes. The signer does not build the sign from scratch every time it is used. All of the parts work together to create one meaning. The parts cannot be changed and still have the same meaning of FUNERAL. FUNERAL is a good example of a *lexicalized classifier predicate* (see Figure 28).

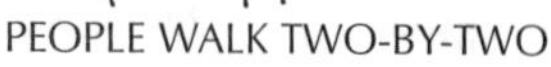

PEOPLE WALK TWO-BY-TWO

	M	M	M	H	
handshape	V	V	V	V	(but could be
location	depends⟶				1, 3. 4 . . .)
orientation	depends⟶				
nonmanual signal	depends⟶				

Productive Classifier Predicate: Each part has meaning and can be separated; the signer selects each part and *builds* the sign from scratch each time he or she uses it.

FUNERAL

	M	H	M	H	M	H
handshape		2		2		2
location	near right shoulder					
orientation	palm out⟶					
nonmanual signal	—					

Lexicalized Classifier Predicate: The parts of the sign may be the same as the parts of productive classifier predicates (for example, the handshape is clearly a whole entity morpheme for standing person), but the parts now *cannot* be separated out. They are no longer separate morphemes; they do not have independent meaning. They all function together to create one meaning. The signer does *not* build the sign from scratch every time. The sign is "ready to use."

FIGURE 28. Productive classifier predicates vs. Lexicalized classifier predicates.

Locative Verbs

Classifier predicates are composed of a movement root and a classifier handshape, and their location represents a location in three-dimensional space. There is another kind of verb in ASL—*locative verbs.* Locative verbs are like classifier verbs in that they use location to represent a location in three-dimensional space. A good example of a locative verb is THROW. When a signer signs the sentence JOHN THROW ROCK, the direction of the movement of the verb indicates the direction in which the object is thrown, and there is a lot of flexibility in the direction. For example, if the signer is talking about throwing something to someone standing on a balcony above him, the direction of the sign is upward; if the signer is talking about throwing something down to someone, the direction is downward; if the signer is talking about throwing something over his shoulder, the direction of the sign would show that, and so forth. Other examples of locative verb, are the fingerspelled sign #HURT, in which the sign functions as a verb that can be placed on the specific area of the body, and PUT.

Locative verbs are quite different from verbs like ENJOY, PUNISH, or UPSET, which are examples of plain verbs (Padden, 1988; see unit 9), signs in which the location feature is simply a part of how the sign is made. The function of the *location* in plain verbs is articulatory. In these signs, location does not have independent meaning.

Locative verbs share with classifier predicates the fact that location represents a place in three-dimensional space. One difference between locative verbs and classifier predicates is that the *handshape* in classifier predicates has independent meaning, but the handshape in locative verbs does not have independent meaning. That is, as we said in unit 7, a classifier handshape usually represents a class of objects (e.g., 3 handshape for vehicles), some aspect of the size or shape of an entity (e.g., F handshape for small round objects), or the hand holding an object (e.g., instrumental handshapes).

We cannot say that the handshapes in locative verbs such as PUT, #HURT, or THROW are classifiers. The best way to illustrate the difference is to compare the locative verb #HURT and the classifier predicate USE-SCALPEL (see Figure 29).

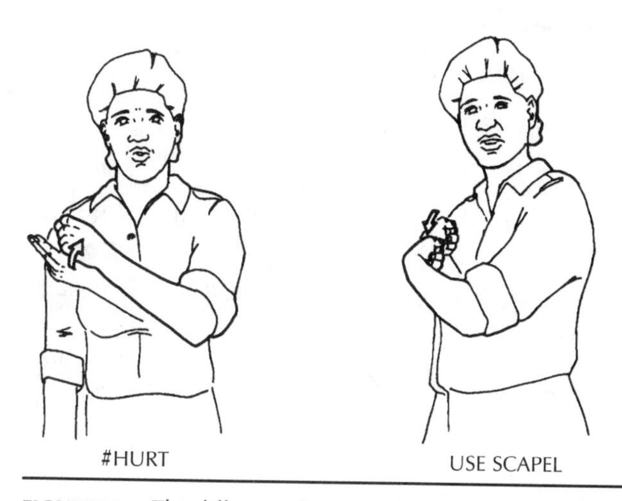

FIGURE 29. The difference between locative verbs and classifier predicates.

While we would say that the handshape in USE-SCALPEL is an instrumental classifier handshape, related to a hand holding a scalpel, the handshape of #HURT is not a classifier handshape, even though both signs can be used on specific body locations.

SUMMARY

The handshapes in classifier predicates may represent not only the whole entity, but also the surface, depth and width, extent, perimeter shape, and the instrument used for a particular action. Most of these handshapes are very iconic, and it may be from the large number of classifier verbs in ASL that people get the idea that ASL is "pictures in the air". After reading and discussing this section, you will understand that classifier predicates are morphological structures in ASL, and not "pictures in the air".

Some people say that ASL is made up of many gestures, and that these gestures account for as much as 60 percent of the language. This assumption may come from the fact that the structure of classifier predicates is highly iconic. However, what some people call gestures are really a part of ASL structure, a very important part.

Classifier predicates have two parts—movement roots and classifier handshapes. These can be divided into different types, as follows:

Movement Roots	*Classifier Handshapes*
stative descriptive	whole entity
process	surface
contact	instrumental
	depth and width
	extent
	perimeter shape
	on surface

We have also seen that locative verbs are like lexical signs and unlike classifier predicates in that their handshapes are not classifiers; and that locative verbs are like classifier predicates and unlike lexical signs in that their location has independent meaning.

REFERENCES

Liddell. S. K., and Johnson, R. E. 1987. An analysis of spatial locative predicates in American Sign Language. Paper presented at the Fourth International Symposium on Sign Language Research, July 15–19.

Padden, C. 1988. *Interaction of morphology and syntax in American Sign Language*. New York: Garland Publishing.

Supalla, T. 1978. Structure and acquisition of verbs of motion and location in American Sign Language. Ph.D. dissertation, University of California, San Diego.

Homework Assignment 9

1. In each sentence below, find the classifier predicates and name their movement roots and handshape morpheme types.

   Example: I parked the car in front of the house.

   CAR contact root, whole entity morpheme

   a. We were sitting there and this guy walked by.

   b. The book was in the middle of the table.

   c. There were five birds on the telephone line.

   d. One person was standing and the other was sitting.

   e. Baltimore is here and D.C. is there.

   f. From the window, I could see seven planes lined up.

   g. There were three poles in a row: a real skinny one, a medium-sized one, and a big fat one.

   h. From the space shuttle, the earth looks smooth.

   i. He got peanut butter out of the jar with a knife.

   j. Suddenly, the glass was empty.

2. There are many classifier predicates on the videotape. Find four and gloss them and describe their movement roots and classifier handshapes.

UNIT 8

Classifier Predicates and Signer Perspective

GOAL
To be able to explain classifier predicates and signer perspective in ASL

In an earlier unit, we discussed classifier predicates in ASL. These verbs are created by combining the small units of signs—handshape, location, orientation, and nonmanual signals—in the segmental structure (movements and holds). Some of these classifier predicates show *perceived motion;* that is, the hand (or hands) move to show a surface or an object that appears to be moving (see Figure 30). The information in this unit is based on our own research. We have found that the classifier predicate with a 3 handshape for vehicles can be signed with the base hand under it in a B handshape. This base hand can move repeatedly, making the meaning of the sign SURFACE-PASS-UNDER-VEHICLE, or that the car goes down the road. If the handshape of the base hand changes to a 3 handshape and moves in the direction opposite of the active hand the meaning becomes VEHICLE-PASS-VEHICLE. Another example is a 1 handshape used to represent a person and a 5 handshape moved next to the 1 handshape, meaning SURFACE-PASS-PERSON (for example, a person passing trees). Finally, an F handshape can be used to represent a coin while the base hand in a B handshape moves under it, meaning SURFACE-PASS-UNDER-COIN.

Perceived motion can also be indicated through orientation. Orientation used *productively* means that signers pay attention to it and use it to create different meanings. Examples include SURFACE-PASS-UNDER-VEHICLE-GOING-UPHILL and SURFACE-PASS-UNDER-VEHICLE-GOING-DOWNHILL (see Figure 31).

Signs in this class are not restricted to one kind of movement. We find that movement is highly productive and may have the meaning of speed or quantity of objects, depending on the situation. For example, to express the concept of passing objects and passing surfaces, greater speed is shown by faster signing of the segmental sequence, in this case movement hold. In the case of passing objects,

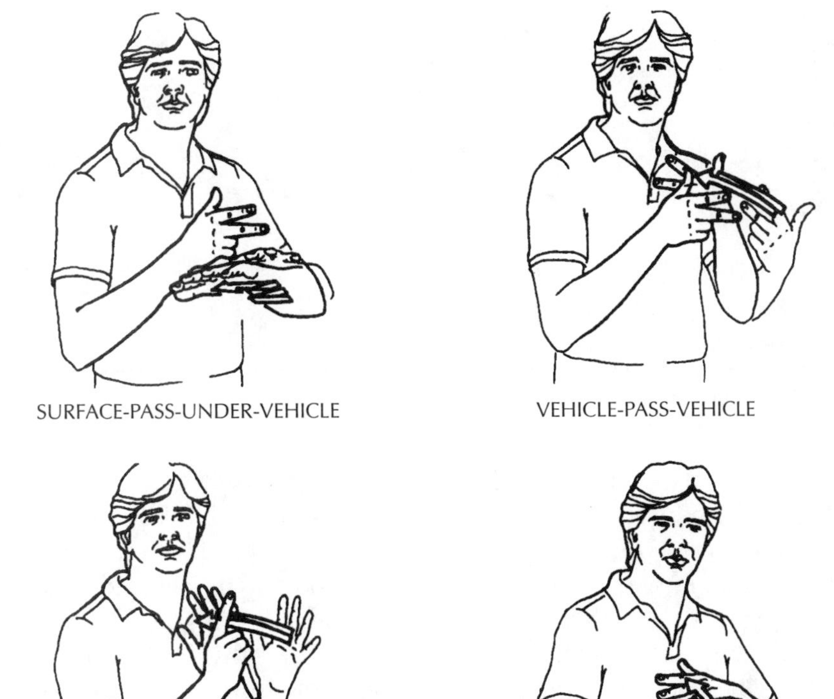

SURFACE-PASS-UNDER-VEHICLE

VEHICLE-PASS-VEHICLE

SURFACE-PASS-PERSON

SURFACE-PASS-UNDER-COIN

FIGURE 30. Examples of perceived motion.

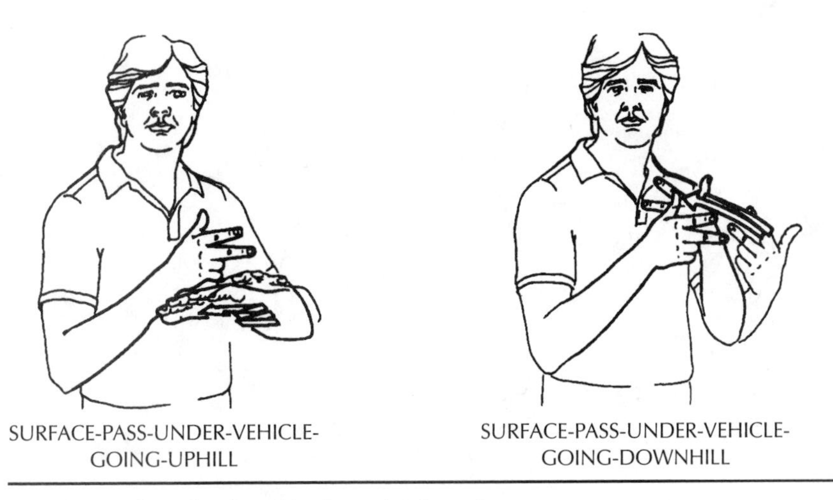

SURFACE-PASS-UNDER-VEHICLE-GOING-UPHILL

SURFACE-PASS-UNDER-VEHICLE-GOING-DOWNHILL

FIGURE 31. Perceived motion through orientation.

TWO VARIATIONS OF SURFACE-PASS-UNDER-VEHICLE-VERY-FAST

FIGURE 32. Examples of movement used to show great speed.

plurality can be shown by repetition of the sequence, so ONE-VEHICLE-PASS-VEHICLE-FAST (M H) contrasts with MANY-VEHICLES-PASS-VEHICLE (M H M H). Great speed may also be shown either by a structure that is a hold with internal movement, as in SURFACE-PASS-UNDER-VEHICLE-VERY-FAST or by an extended hold followed by a movement and a hold with internal movement (see Figure 32).

Location is also very important in classifier verbs, and the verbs are not limited to one location. One can sign SURFACE-PASS-VEHICLE-ON-SIDE, SURFACE-PASS-UNDER-VEHICLE, SURFACE-PASS-OVER-VEHICLE, and SURFACE-PASS-IN-FRONT-OF-VEHICLE. The surface in question may be the surface that the signer is moving on, the road her car is traveling on, or the ice that she is skating on. The difference between SURFACE-PASS-VEHICLE-ON-SIDE and SURFACE-PASS-SIGNER-ON-SIDE is a difference of location (see Figure 33). There is a clear difference between "object or surface pass other object" and "object or surface pass or appear to pass signer's body." Verbs showing objects or surfaces passing the signer's body show the same productivity in movement for objects or surfaces passing other objects. We can sign TREES-PASS-SIGNER, TELEPHONE-POLES-PASS-SIGNER, or ROOF-PASS-OVER-SIGNER.

FIGURE 33. A comparison of "object pass object" and "object pass signer."

So, for example, telephone poles can seem to go by fast or slow, depending on changes in the segmental structure.

The classifier handshape for many of these predicates is a whole entity handshape: tree, pole, car, and so forth. The movement root would be a process root because what is meant is actual motion by the signer. It is interesting to notice that in the two-handed predicates of this type, in which one hand represents the object that actually moves and the other represents the surface upon which it is moving, the process root is produced in the surface handshape and not in the whole entity handshape of the object moving. In fact, it does not seem acceptable or grammatical in these two-handed signs for the process root to be produced with the whole entity handshape.

Up to this point, we have talked about classifier predicates for objects or surfaces that move or appear to move. Location shows whether the signer's perspective is involved or not. But the interesting thing about these verbs is that they can show signer perspective, whether or not the object or surface is moving or appears to be moving. For example, it is possible to sign SURFACE-PASS-UNDER-VEHICLE at what we call a *general* level (at mid-torso). This is essentially a general description of a vehicle going along, with no specific reference to what the signer can see (see Figure 30).

SURFACE-PASS-UNDER-VEHICLE can also be signed at eye level. One might expect that at eye level, the sign indicates that the car itself is located at a higher level. But SURFACE-PASS-UNDER-VEHICLE at eye level means "I saw the car go by." This could happen if the signer were in a car behind the car being described and was explaining what the car in front looked like (see Figure 34).

We have also noticed that it is possible to produce a classifier predicate at eye level for an object or surface that is not moving or perceived to be moving. We can sign PERSON-BE-SEATED-IN-FRONT-OF-ME at eye level or PERSON-BE-SEATED, with no reference to signer perspective, at the general level. It is possible to sign CARS-BE-LOCATED-IN-PLACE at the general level, and CARS-BE-LOCATED-IN-FRONT-OF-ME at eye level. So the location information in a classifier predicate can have the meaning of "from signer perspective." The area meaning "from signer perspective"

FIGURE 34. SURFACE-PASS-UNDER-VEHICLE at eye level.

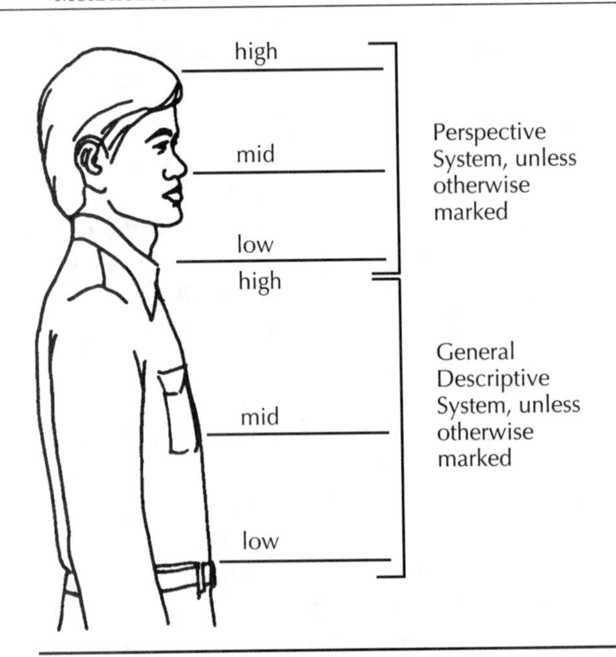

FIGURE 35. The perspective and general level systems of ASL.

seems to range between the upper chest and shoulders to the top of the head, but the level of a specific sign may depend on the relative location of the objects in the signer's perspective.

ASL appears to have two level systems (see Figure 35). The first system is used for representing the general location of objects and events. This system does not make reference to signer perspective. In the second system, specific reference is made to signer perspective, and this reference is specifically in the location part of the verb.

The second system has three basic levels, which are determined by the relative perspective of the signer. Examples of these levels are ROAD-PASS signed at the low level, VEHICLE-BE-LOCATED signed at the mid-level, and ROOF-PASS signed at the high level. It may be that (1) nonperspective verbs sometimes can be signed at a higher level and (2) perspective verbs sometimes may be signed at a lower level. When this happens, it is openly marked in the discourse. For example, TRAIN-PASS may be signed at waist level with the meaning of "from signer perspective," but the sentence before will establish that the signer is looking down from a hill. Therefore, if a verb happens at perspective level, it means "from signer perspective," unless it has been otherwise marked. And if a verb occurs at the general level, it does not include signer perspective unless otherwise marked.

REFERENCES

Lucas C., and Valli, C. 1990. Predicates of perceived motion in ASL. In *Theoretical issues in sign language research*, vol. 1: *Linguistics*, ed. S. D. Fischer and P. Siple, 153–166. Chicago: University of Chicago Press.

UNIT 9

Subject-Object Agreement

GOAL
To be able to explain subject-object agreement in ASL

We have seen that verbs in ASL can include information about how the action of the verb is performed. In this unit, we will look at how verbs in ASL can include information about the subject and object of a verb. When a verb includes this information, we say that the verb *agrees* with the subject or object, and the process is called subject-object agreement.

SUBJECT-OBJECT AGREEMENT IN ENGLISH

Some examples from English may help explain subject-object agreement. In the sentences *The boy sees the girl* and *The girl sees the boy*, we know who the subject is and who the object is partly by the *word order*, that is, by the position of the words in the sentence. *The boy* is the subject in the first sentence and it occurs before the verb, and *the girl* is the object. In the second sentence, *the girl* is the subject and it occurs before the verb, and *the boy* is the object. We also know that the subject is a third person because of the *s* on the verb sees. This is an example of subject agreement in English: the verb *includes* information about the subject. As we explained in unit 1, the third person *-s* is a bound morpheme.

In the sentence *I see the girl*, there is no special marking on the verb to indicate the subject. We know who the subject is from the word *I* and from the word order, but we cannot say that the verb *agrees* with the subject. English also uses some special words to indicate the subject or object, so that in the sentence *I saw the girl, I* is used for the subject, while in the sentence *The girl saw me, me* is used for the object. The sentences *Me saw the girl* or *The girl saw I* are not grammatical in English.

SUBJECT-OBJECT AGREEMENT IN ASL

English uses word order and some special pronouns, or a combination of the two, to indicate subject and object. There is not very much subject-object agreement in

English. That is, except for the third person -s, verbs don't generally include information about subject and object. ASL is very different from English in this way because many ASL verbs do include information about subject and object. This information is contained in the location part of the verb or in the orientation part, or sometimes in both the location and orientation parts. And since the location or the orientation are the parts of the sign that affect meaning, we can say that location and orientation are morphemes. Many verbs in ASL have a structure similar to what we saw with numeral incorporation: one morpheme consists of a kind of frame and has the basic meaning of the verb, and another morpheme consists of the location and/or orientation of the sign and indicates the subject and object of the verb. In this way, we can say that location and orientation are *morphemic*. We will look at seven different kinds of verbs in ASL. This information is based on research done by Liddell and Johnson.

Orientation

The *orientation* of some verbs includes information about the subject and object of the verb. In the verb HATE (the form of the verb with an 8 handshape), the palm faces the object and the back of the hand faces the subject. In the ASL translation of the English sentence *I hate him*, the back of the hand would face the signer and the palm would face the location in which the object had been established. The most important point is that there would be no *separate* signs for *I* or *him* because information about subject and object is included in the orientation part of the verb. If we label the signer A and the other person B, the sentence would look like this:

PRO.1HATEPRO.3

	H	M	H
handshape	8		Open 8
location	torso		torso
orientation: palm	B		B
back of hand	A		A
nonmanual signal	—		—

If we look at the sentence *He hates me*, the situation is reversed.

PRO.3HATEPRO.1

	H	M	H
handshape	8		Open 8
location	torso		torso
orientation: palm	A		A
back of hand	B		B
nonmanual signal	—		—

In both cases, the back of the hand faces the subject and the palm faces the object. TEASE is another example of a verb in which subject-object information may be included only in the orientation.

Location

Sometimes the subject-object information is included in the location, as in the verb HELP. The orientation does not change, but the location of the verb tells us who is the subject and who is the object. So, if we label the signer's location as A and the other person's location as B, the sentence *I help him* looks like this:

PRO.1HELPPRO.3

	H	M	H
handshape (with base hand)	A		A
location	A		B
orientation (base hand)	palm up		palm up
nonmanual signal	—		—

The sentence *He helps me* looks like this:

PRO.3HELPPRO.1

	H	M	H
handshape (with base hand)	A		A
location	B		A
orientation (base hand)	palm up		palm up
nonmanual signal	—		—

Once again, the location tells us who is the subject, and the *first* location includes this information.

Orientation and Location

There are ASL verbs in which both the orientation and the location include information about the subject and the object. For example, in the discussion of fingerspelling, we saw that ASL has a fingerspelled verb #SAY-NO-TO. In the sentence *I say no to him* we label the signer's orientation and location as A, and the other person's orientation and location as B. This is analyzed in the following chart. In this chart, the first location is the subject and the second location is the object, and as with HATE, the palm faces the object and the back of the hand faces the subject (see Figure 36). In the sentence *He says no to me*, the situation is reversed:

PRO.1SAY-NO-TOPRO.3

	M	H
handshape	V	Closed V
location	A	B
orientation: palm	B	B
back of hand	A	A
nonmanual signal	—	—

Note: These are not the handshapes used in the Liddell and Johnson system. We have chosen simplified descriptions for the sake of illustration.

SAY-NO-TO
"I say no to him."

FIGURE 36. Subject-object information in the location and orientation of the verb.

$_{\text{PRO.3}}\text{SAY-NO-TO}_{\text{PRO.1}}$

	M	H
handshape	V	Closed V
location	B	A
orientation: palm	A	A
back of hand	B	B
nonmanual signal	—	—

Other verbs in this category include GIVE and ASK and the two-handed signs BOTHER and FLATTER, in which the location and orientation of both hands show who is the subject and who is the object.

Object Information

All the verbs discussed so far have information about both the subject and the object included in their structure. In all these cases, the subject information occurs first. There are verbs, however, that show both subject and object, in which the object information occurs first, such as INVITE, HIRE, and COPY. So, if we label the signer's location as A and the other person's location as B, the sentence *I hire him* looks like this:

$_{\text{PRO.1}}\text{HIRE}_{\text{PRO.3}}$

	H	M	H
handshape	B		B
location	B		A
orientation	palm up		palm up
nonmanual signal	—		—

The verb starts at the object location and ends up at the subject location. And in the sentence *He hires me*, the same is true:

PRO.3HIREPRO.1

	H	M	H
handshape	B		B
location	A		B
orientation	palm up		palm up
nonmanual signal	—		—

Here again, the verb starts in the object location and ends up in the subject location.

Reciprocals

Other ASL verbs that include both subject and object information are called *reciprocals*. This means that there is information about two subjects and two objects simultaneously. An example of this is the verb UNDERSTAND-EACH-OTHER. In this verb, one hand is placed near the signer's forehead, with the palm facing out. The location of that hand indicates the subject, and the orientation indicates the object. The second hand is on the same level as the first hand, with the palm facing the signer. In the second hand, the location once again indicates the subject, that is, another person, and the orientation indicates the object, that is, the signer. So each hand shows both subject and object at the same time, with location and orientation. Other examples of this kind of verb are LOOK-AT-EACH-OTHER (Figure 37) and SEE-EACH-OTHER.

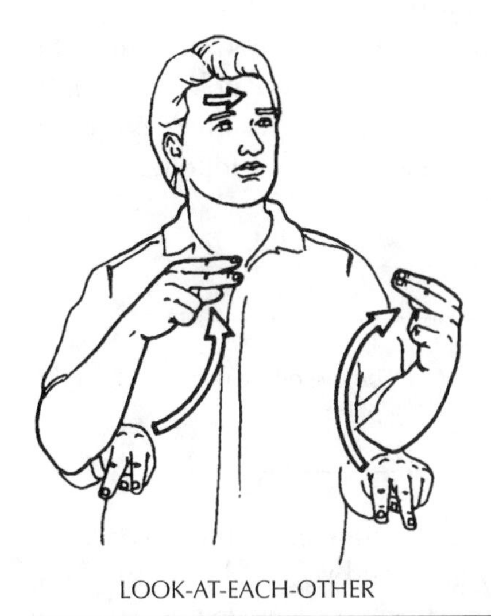

LOOK-AT-EACH-OTHER

FIGURE 37. A reciprocal verb.

Object-Only Verbs

Some verbs only include information about the object. An example is the verb TELL. The verb in the sentence *I tell him* looks like this:

PRO.1TELLPRO.3

	H	M	H
handshape	1		1
location	chin		away from chin
orientation	palm down		palm up
nonmanual signal	—		—

A separate sign is required for the sign PRO.1 because the information about the subject is not included in the location or the orientation. The same is true for the verb in the sentence *He tells me.*

PRO.3TELLPRO.1

	H	M	H
handshape	1		1
location	chin		sternum
orientation	palm down		palm down
nonmanual signal	—		—

A separate sign is required for HE because the information about the subject is not included in the verb.

Plain Verbs

There are verbs in ASL that do not include any information about the subject or the object. Some researchers call these verbs *plain* verbs (see Padden, 1988). All these verbs require separate signs for subjects and objects. One example is the verb PUNISH. The verb in the sentence *I punish you* is diagrammed as follows:

PUNISH

	H	M	H
handshape	1		1
location	near elbow		below elbow
orientation	palm side		palm left
nonmanual signal	—		—

No information is included in the verb about the subject or the object. The sentence requires the separate signing of the signs I and YOU. Other examples of verbs in this category include LOVE, LIKE, TASTE, THINK, UNDERSTAND, SHOCK, and KNOW.

SUMMARY

This is a basic introduction to subject-object agreement in ASL verbs. The most important points to remember are listed below.

1. Many verbs include information about subject and object in the verb and do not require or do not allow separate signs for subjects and objects.
2. There are different ways for information about subjects and objects to be included in a verb. Not all verbs include the information in the same way.

Finally, we have talked about how location is used in ASL, and we have pointed out that location in agreement verbs is different from location in classifier predicates or locatives. All three involve three-dimensional space. The location in an agreement verb identifies the subject or object of the verb, and the signer's hand does not have to move from precisely one point to precisely another to be correct. For example, in the ASL sentence PRO.1-GIVE-PRO.2 ("I give you") the location near the signer identifies the subject, while the location in front of the signer identifies the object. But there is no specific point to which the signer's hand must move in signing the verb. On the other hand, when a signer uses the classifier predicate 3-CL: MOVE, as in describing the movement of a car from one place to another, the signer's hand moves from one specific place to another, and if the hand stops halfway, the meaning is that the car stopped halfway to the second point. Similarly, when a signer uses a locative verb such as #HURT to indicate where there is pain, the specific location is important. The locations in classifier predicates and locatives do not identify subjects and objects, while the locations in agreement verbs do.

REFERENCES

Emmorey, K. 1999. The confluence of space and language in signed languages. In *Language and space*, ed. P. Bloom, M. A. Peterson, L. Nadel, and M. F. Garrett, pp. 171–205. Cambridge, MA: MIT Press.

Padden, C., 1988. *Interaction of morphology and syntax in American Sign Language.* New York: Garland Publishing.

Homework Assignment 10

1. Find two examples of verbs that include subject-object information on the videotape. Do they include both subject and object, or just object?

2. Find two examples of plain verbs (verbs that require separate signs for subject and object) on the videotape.

3. Carry some 3 × 5 cards or a small notepad with you for one day and write down all the verbs that you remember from your conversations. Divide them into plain verbs and verbs that include information about subject and object. (Write down at least two examples of each.)

UNIT 10

Pronouns and Determiners

GOAL
To understand pronouns and determiners in ASL

SUPPLEMENTAL READING
"A Class of Determiners in ASL," by June Zimmer and Cynthia Patschke (1990); pp. 347–353

PRONOUNS

A pronoun *represents* a person, place, or thing that has already been identified. Examples of pronouns in English are *he, she, it, them,* and *us.* Examples of English sentences with pronouns are *He came home early* and *She gave it to us.* When reading or hearing those sentences, we must know to what or to whom *he, she, it,* or *us* refers. If we do not know, we cannot understand the sentence. We understand the sentence because the referent (the noun that the pronoun represents) has been introduced earlier in the conversation or because we guess from the context. For example, if one sentence describes *the boy* and the next sentence uses the pronoun *he,* it is safe to assume that the pronoun *he* represents *the boy.* Or suppose three people are seated at a table. If one person looks at the person on her right and points to the person on her left and says *He told me something interesting,* the meaning of *he* comes from the context, and we can assume that *he* refers to the person on the left.

ASL also has pronouns. In this unit we will focus on subject and object pronouns. There are both similarities and differences between English and ASL pronouns (see Table 6). Consider the ASL sentence PRO.3 SILLY, which can be translated in English as "He is silly." In this ASL sentence, PRO.3 is a pronoun and is produced with the index finger pointing away from the signer. We use the gloss PRO.3-i (*i* = index finger) for this pronoun. While the sign is for a third person (as opposed to first person I or ME, glossed as PRO.1), it does not indicate whether the third person is masculine or feminine, in the way that the English words *he* and *she*

TABLE 6. A Comparison of Subject and Object Pronouns in English and ASL

PRONOUNS	ENGLISH	ASL
Subject Pronouns		
First person		
singular	I	PRO.1
plural	we	WE, TWO-OF-US, THREE-OF-US . . .
Second person		
singular	you	PRO.2 (singular)*
plural	you	PRO.2 (plural), TWO-OF-YOU, THREE-OF-YOU . . .*
Third person		
singular	he, she, it	PRO.3-index,* PRO.3-thumb
plural	they	THEY, TWO-OF-THEM, THREE-OF-THEM . . .*
Object Pronouns		
First person		
singular	me	PRO.1
plural	us	WE, TWO-OF-US, THREE-OF-US . . .
Second person		
singular	you	PRO.2*
plural	you	PRO.2 (plural), TWO-OF-YOU, THREE-OF-YOU . . .*
Third person		
singular	him, her, it	PRO.3-index, PRO.3-thumb
plural	them	THEM, TWO-OF-THEM, THREE-OF-THEM . . .*

*ASL may not have separate forms for second and third person pronouns.

do. The third person pronoun in ASL can also be produced with the thumb, and we gloss that pronoun as PRO.3-t (*t* = thumb).

Recent work by Liddell and Johnson suggests that there is no clear distinction between second and third person pronouns in ASL. In addition, the meaning of any given pronoun is determined by the context in which it is produced. For example, if the signer points away from her body, that same sign may refer to a second person or to a third person. Which one it refers to depends on the sentence in which it occurs. The asterisks in Table 6 indicate that ASL may not have separate forms for second and third person, even though we may gloss them as PRO.2 and PRO.3.

English also shows a distinction between subject and object pronouns—*he* (subject pronoun) and *him* (object pronoun), *we* and *us, she* and *her, they* and *them,* and so forth. ASL pronouns, like the pronouns in many other languages, do not show this distinction. Instead, subject and object are indicated in the sequence of signs. For example, ASL sentence PRO.1 PUNISH PRO.2 has two pronouns, one that points toward the signer and usually contacts the chest (glossed as PRO.1), and one that points away from the signer (glossed as PRO.2). The English translation of this sentence would be "I punish you."

ASL pronouns do show a number difference, so that the signs for PRO.2 referring to one person and PRO.2 referring to more than one person are different.

PRO.2 referring to one person is signed with one index finger pointing away from the signer. PRO.2 referring to more than one person might use a V handshape with the palm facing up, with movement back and forth between two points in front of the signer. Number differences are also indicated in third-person pronouns. For example, PRO.3 referring to one person might be a pointing index finger, while PRO.3 referring to more than one person might be a pointing index finger that moves in a sweeping motion from one place to another. PRO.3 referring to more than one person could also be signed using a number handshape, so that the pronoun could be glossed as TWO-OF-THEM or THREE-OF-THEM or even FOUR-OF-THEM.

Location serves an important function in pronoun signs. Many ASL pronouns consist of a pointing index finger, which leads us to two questions: (1) What is the function of the location of the sign itself? and (2) What is the function of the location to which the finger points? It seems that the function of the location of the sign itself is *articulatory*—that is, location is simply a part of the pronoun sign and it does not have independent morphological meaning. For example, PRO.3 can be produced either on the signer's right side or on the signer's left side to represent a third person. It doesn't seem to matter which side the signer chooses, but it is important to notice that once one side is chosen to refer to a specific third person, the same side must be used consistently during that conversation. One cannot point first to one side and then to the other to refer to the same person.

Pronouns represent a person, place, or thing that has already been introduced or is clear from the context. The location in space to which the finger points identifies the referent of the pronoun (the person, place, or thing being talked about). So, even though pronoun signs point at a location in space and are produced in a particular location near the signer's body, the function of location is very different from location in classifier predicates or locative verbs.

DETERMINERS

ASL has another kind of pointing sign—*determiners*. Determiners are words or signs that modify nouns. They indicate whether the noun referred to is a *specific* noun or any member of a particular class of nouns. Examples of determiners in English include *the*, *a*, and *an*. *The* indicates a specific noun, while *a* and *an* indicate any member of a particular class. For example, there is a difference in meaning between *the cat* and *a cat*. Other English determiners include *my*, *that*, and *every*.

ASL also has determiners. Determiners in ASL are pointing signs produced with the index finger. They always occur with a noun, and they may occur before, after, or simultaneously with the noun. Determiners in ASL are glossed as DET. Figure 38 is an example of a determiner occurring before a noun in the sentence PRO.1 ASK DET GIRL ("I ask the girl"). An example of a determiner after a noun is GIRL DET SILLY ("The girl is silly"), and an example of a determiner occurring simultaneously with a noun is MAN/DET SILLY ("The man is silly") (see Figure 39). We say that the

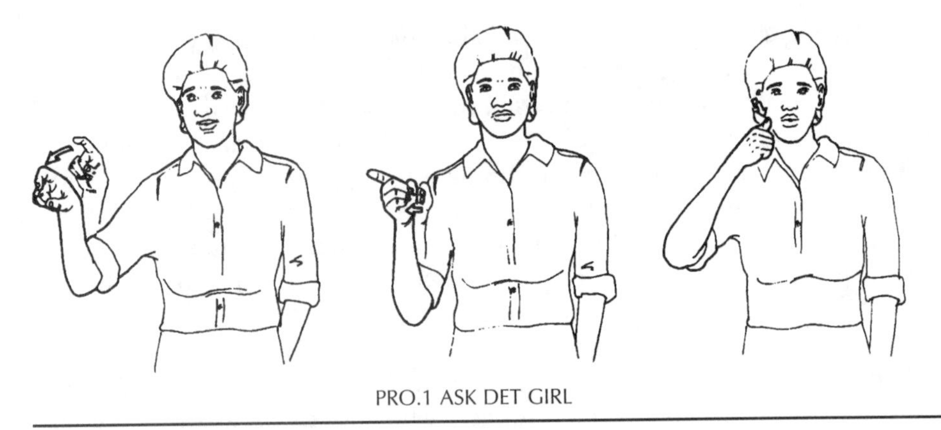

FIGURE 38. Determiner occurring before the noun.

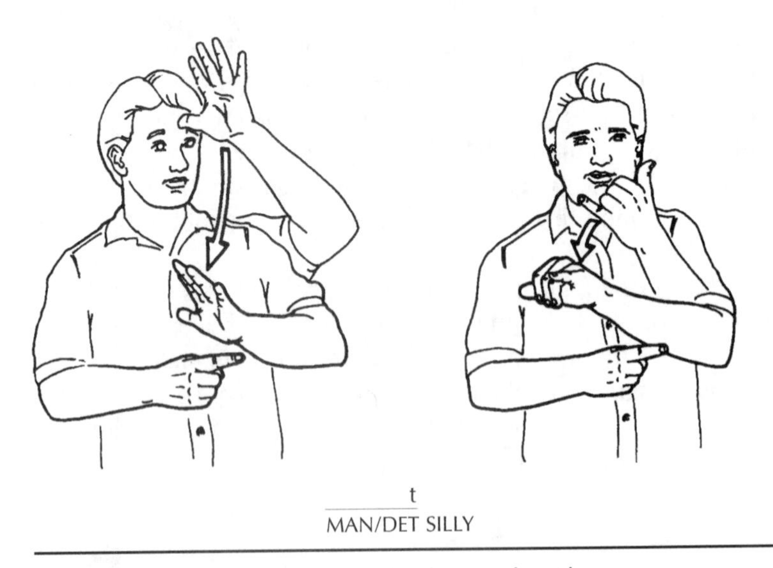

FIGURE 39. Determiner occurring simultaneously with noun.

noun and the determiner occur simultaneously because the determiner with the 1 handshape is produced with the passive hand at the same time that the dominant hand produces the sign MAN.

With regard to the function of location of the determiner, it seems that it is articulatory, that is, it is simply where the sign is produced. Researchers June Zimmer and Cynthia Patschke found that often the location of the determiner is the same or similar to the location of the noun that it accompanies. For example, in the sentence GIRL DET SILLY, the pointing sign that is the determiner occurs at the chin level of the sign GIRL, while in the sentence MAN DET SILLY, the determiner might occur at the chest level of MAN (see Figure 40). Furthermore, Zimmer and Patschke concluded that the actual direction in which the finger is pointing

FIGURE 40. Determiner produced at the same level as the noun it accompanies.

has no independent meaning and is not significant. So once again, we see a kind of sign whose location feature functions very differently from the location feature in other signs.

Homework Assignment 11

1. Look at the snowmobile story on the videotape and make a list of the pronouns that you see. You should find at least ten.

2. Collect and gloss four examples of ASL sentences with determiners that you see in everyday conversation. Provide an English translation of each.

UNIT 11

Temporal Aspect

GOAL
To understand the basic concept of temporal aspect in ASL

Aspect means information contained in a predicate that tells us how the action of the predicate is done. In ASL, aspect concerns forms that are verbs and adjectives both. Our discussion of aspect will be fairly short, because while this is a very productive area in ASL, not much research has been done on it. Most of our discussion is based on research done by Klima and Bellugi (1979).

Klima and Bellugi examined many different kinds of aspect markers in ASL, including markers that show that the activity of the verb is never-ending, frequent, drawn out, or intense. Many of the aspect markers they examined have to do with how the action of the verb is performed with reference to time. The linguistic term for this is *temporal aspect*, and we will discuss some examples of it.

One way to tell how the action of a predicate is done in ASL is through the segmental structure of the sign. For example, a basic form of the sign STUDY is a two-handed sign: the base hand is a hold with a B handshape with the palm facing up, and the active hand is a 5 handshape with the palm facing down. The fingers of the active hand wiggle. The sign would be described as a hold with internal movement. However, the sign STUDY can also be produced so that it means STUDY-CONTINUALLY. In this form, the handshape and orientation of the sign are the same as the basic form, and the location is basically the same. What is very different and what gives the meaning of CONTINUALLY is that the sign moves repeatedly in a circle. Within the Liddell and Johnson framework, the structure of this sign is an M. The movement of the circle looks like this:

The circular movement tells us how the action of the verb is performed with reference to time. The circular form of the verb STUDY is inflected for aspect. *Inflection* is the linguistic term for a morpheme that adds grammatical information to a word or a sign. In the discussion of noun-verb pairs in unit 1, we pointed out that there seems to be a fundamental difference between English morphology and ASL morphology. The difference is that English tends to "add things on" in the process of creating new units, while ASL tends to change the structure. A good example of this is temporal aspect in ASL (see Figure 41). As we explained in units 1 and 2, sometimes a morpheme is best identified as a process instead of an identifiable form. The result of this process is a new morpheme. When linguists study temporal aspect inflections in spoken languages, generally they describe morphemes that are added on to the beginning or the end of a verb. Those morphemes give information about how the action of the verb is performed.

In ASL, we cannot say that anything is added on to the verb STUDY to get the meaning of STUDY-CONTINUALLY. The handshape and the orientation stay the same, but the basic structure of the sign changes from a hold to a movement, and the lo-

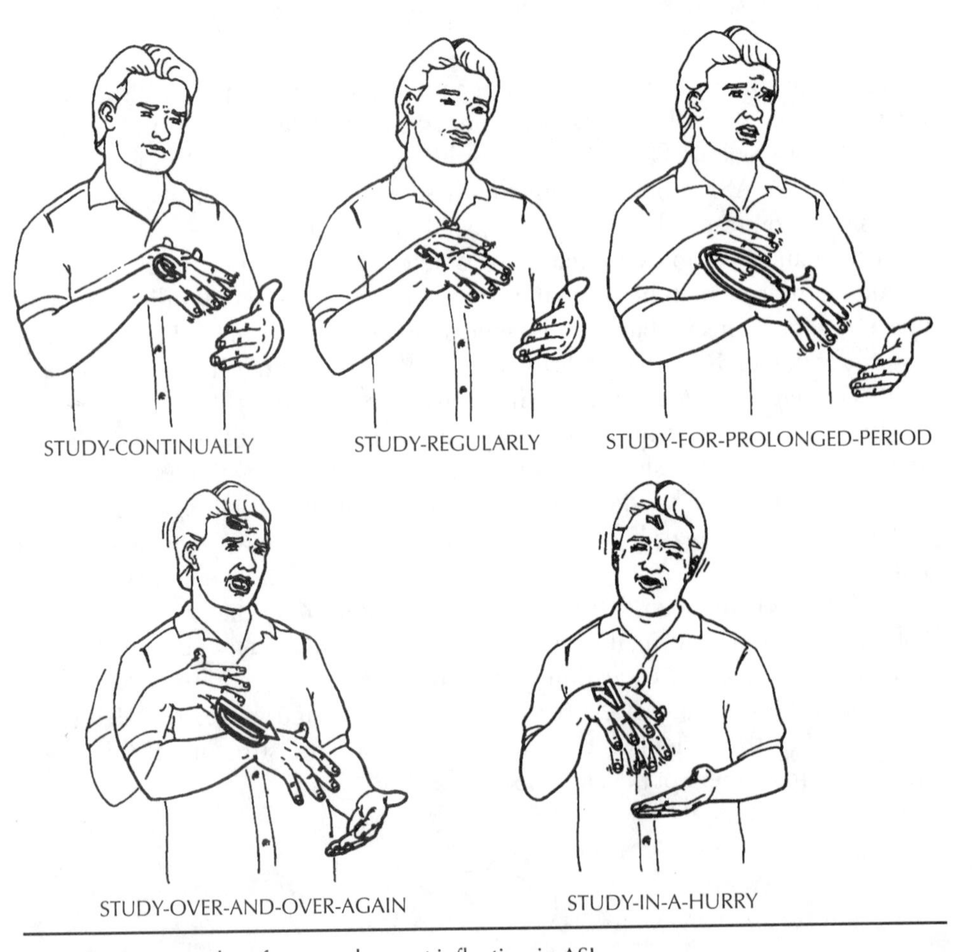

FIGURE 41. Examples of temporal aspect inflection in ASL.

cation changes as a result of the movement. Sometimes the change in structure is accomplished by the process of reduplication. (See p. 302–304 for Liddell and Johnson's discussion of reduplication and aspect.) Also, a very specific nonmanual signal adds to the meaning of continually. While linguists describe ASL verbs as being inflected—that is, having grammatical information added—the process of inflection seems to be very different from spoken language inflection. Many ASL verbs can have the aspect inflection meaning CONTINUALLY, including WRITE and SIT. Some adjective predicates that can have this inflection include WRONG and SILLY.

Another aspect inflection has the meaning of REGULARLY. This inflection is expressed by moving the sign in a straight line like this:

For example, the sign STUDY can have an M M H M M H structure in which the direction of the movement is a straight line. Signed this way, the meaning becomes STUDY-REGULARLY. Other predicates that can have this inflection are GO, PREACH, and SICK.

A third inflection has the structure of an M and has the meaning of FOR-A-PROLONGED-PERIOD-OF-TIME. It looks like this:

Verbs that can have this inflection include LOOK-AT, CRY, SIT, and STAND. SICK is an adjective predicate that can have this inflection.

A fourth aspect inflection has an M H M H structure and looks like this

It has the meaning of OVER-AND-OVER-AGAIN and can be used with verbs like STUDY and LOOK-AT.

During the fall of 1990, a Gallaudet University student, Randall Shank, did some research on a fifth temporal aspect inflection that is glossed as IN-A-HURRY. He found that when the signing space for a sign is reduced and the movement is done very quickly, the meaning of the sign is IN-A-HURRY. This inflection can be seen with verbs such as SEW, WRITE, EAT, and STUDY. We cannot define one single movement path for this inflection, as SEW-IN-A-HURRY has a circular movement, while EAT-IN-A-HURRY has a back and forth movement. But they have in common the increased speed of the movement and reduced signing space.

Another one of our students, Rosella Ottolini, observed that the meaning of I-A-HURRY can also be indicated with internal movement of the fingers. For example, the basic structure of the sign ANALYZE is Hold-Movement-Hold-Movement-Hold . . . , with the fingers repeatedly crooking and straightening during the movement. In ANALYZE-IN-A-HURRY, the hands move downward from one location to another with an H M H structure as the fingers rapidly straighten and crook. The latter is internal movement and looks like wiggling. This version of the sign is also usually accompanied by a particular facial expression, with the eyes squinted and the lips parted and tense.

Another temporal aspect marker observed by two other students, Martina Cosentino and Laura Clarke, conveys the meaning of "activity performed under pressure and then concluded." It includes a reference to time because it shows the performance of the activity and the end of the activity in two distinct parts. In the first part, the structure of the verb is produced as a hold (even if the basic form of the verb includes movement) and the lips are parted and tense, the eyes squinted. This part shows the on-going pressured activity. The second part shows the end of the activity, as the mouth drops open, the eyes relax, and the structure of the manual part of the sign is a short movement forward followed by a hold. Some verbs that show this marker include GIVE-BIRTH, DRIVE-CAR, RUN, STUDY, TYPE, STRUGGLE, READ, PUSH, and PULL.

While temporal aspect provides a good example of morphemes as process, it also shows how ASL sometimes uses what looks like the affixation used commonly in spoken languages. For example, signs that have a basic M H structure may add an initial hold to indicate a particular meaning. For instance, the basic structure of the sign ARRIVE is M H, but produced with an initial hold, it can have the meaning of ARRIVE-AT-LAST or ARRIVE-FOLLOWING-SOME-DELAY. This added initial hold is essentially an affix.

This is a very basic introduction to the topic of temporal aspect. We have not discussed all the temporal aspect inflections, but we have shown that ASL has a very structured way of indicating the way in which the action of a predicate is performed. Not all inflections can be used with all verbs. Clearly, a lot more research is needed in this area.

REFERENCES

Klima, E., and Bellugi, U. 1979. *The signs of language*. Cambridge, MA: Harvard University Press.

Homework Assignment 12

1. Using the descriptions of aspect in the text, find as many examples as you can from everyday conversations of verb and adjective predicates that can have aspect inflection.

   a. CONTINUALLY

   b. REGULARLY

   c. FOR-A-PROLONGED-PERIOD

   d. OVER-AND-OVER

   e. IN-A-HURRY

2. Can all of the verbs and adjectives take every inflection? Give two examples where a verb or adjective can take one inflection but not another.

UNIT 12

Derivational and Inflectional Morphology

GOAL
To understand the difference between derivational morphology and inflectional morphology

We have talked about morphology, the study of the smallest meaningful units in a language and of how those meaningful units are used to build new words or signs. Morphology is the study of word formation, of how a language uses smaller units to build larger units. As a language uses smaller units to build larger ones, two different processes are at work. Some of the larger units built from smaller units are the result of a *derivational* process, and some are the result of an *inflectional* process.

DERIVATIONAL MORPHOLOGY

Derivational morphology is the process of making new units for the language, in other words, deriving new units. An example of derivational morphology in English is the creation of nouns from verbs by the addition of the suffix *-er*. For example, when the suffix *-er* is added to the verbs *write, read,* and *sign,* the result is a noun with the meaning of "person who does the activity of the verb." The nouns *writer, reader,* and *signer* are derived from the verbs *write, read,* and *sign.* Another example from English is the derivation of verbs from adjectives by the addition of the suffix *-en*. For example, when *-en* is added to the adjectives *soft* and *hard,* the verbs *soften* and *harden* are derived.

The examples of derivational morphology that we have looked at in ASL include the derivation of nouns from verbs, as in the derivation of CHAIR from SIT, compounding, fingerspelled signs, numeral incorporation, classifier predicates, and perspective verbs. In all of these cases, small units of ASL are put together to create new large units. Nouns are derived from verbs, a series of fingerspelled signs become more like one sign, a handshape having the meaning of a specific number is incorporated into a segmental structure having the meaning of AGE or WEEK or MONTH, a movement root and a handshape are put together to make a classifier predicate, and the location of the classifier predicate provides specific information about the signer's perspective.

INFLECTIONAL MORPHOLOGY

Inflectional morphology is different from derivational morphology. While derivational morphology is about the creation of new units, inflectional morphology is the process of adding grammatical information to units that already exist. For example, when *-s* is added to nouns in English, the result is a meaning of plural—*cats, dogs, books.* The *-s* is known as an *inflection.* Another example is the *-s* that is added to verbs with the meaning of "third person," as in *walks, writes,* or *signs.* This *-s* is also an inflection. The inflections add grammatical information to a unit; they do not result in the creation of a new unit.

We have looked at two examples of inflectional morphology in ASL—aspect and subject-object agreement. In the case of aspect, the structure of a verb is changed to show a difference in the meaning of the verb. For example, the verb SIT is signed as M H, but if the sequence changes to a movement, the meaning becomes SIT-FOR-A-LONG-TIME. We would say that the verb SIT is *inflected.*

Verbs can include information about the subject and the object in the orientation or location parts of their structure. An ASL verb like GIVE is said to be *inflected* for both subject and object, while a verb like TELL is inflected only for object. The orientation and location parts of the structure provide grammatical information in the verbs. A new unit is not created; grammatical information is provided in already existing units.

Both derivational and inflectional processes in ASL may be fundamentally different from such processes in spoken languages. ASL does not tend to add on as spoken languages do. Instead, ASL tends to change the fundamental structure, as in the case of temporal aspect, or change one part of one segment, as in the case of subject-object agreement in verbs.

The same part of a language can be affected by both derivational and inflectional processes. For example, the ASL verb SIT can be used to derive the noun CHAIR, and it can be inflected to mean SIT-FOR-A-LONG-TIME. The ASL verb TALK can combine with the sign NAME to create the compound MENTION, which is a derivational process. The same ASL verb TALK can be inflected to mean TALK-FOR-A-LONG-TIME.

Some components of ASL become part of the language through a derivational process and then participate in inflectional processes. For example, the formation of the fingerspelled sign #NO is a derivational process. It is the creation of a new unit in ASL. That same fingerspelled sign can then be used as a verb, as in *He says no to me* or *I say no to him.* The information in the location and orientation part of the verb is inflectional, since it provides grammatical information about the subject and object of the verb.

Homework Assignment 13

1. The morphological processes that we have discussed in ASL include noun-verb pairs, compounds, subject-object agreement, aspect, fingerspelling, foreign loans, numeral incorporation, the formation of classifier predicates, the use of classifier predicates, the use of numeral incorporation, and use of fingerspelled signs as predicates. Assign each of the eleven processes listed here to derivational or inflectional morphology.

UNIT 13

Time in ASL

GOAL
To have a basic understanding of the role of time in ASL structure

One of the features that makes language unique as a communication system is that its users are not limited to talking about events in the here and now. Language allows its users to talk about things that are not immediately visible. We can talk about people or things or events in another room, another state, another country. Language also allows its users to talk about events that happened in the past or events that will happen in the future.

Certain parts of language structure allow us to show a difference among the present, the past, and the future. Sometimes we use independent lexical items. For example, in English we use the words *tomorrow, yesterday, soon,* or *two days ago* to indicate the time of an event. The word *will* is another independent lexical item in English that indicates a future event.

English also has special morphemes to indicate the time of what is being discussed. For example, the English sentence *He walks* has a different meaning from the English sentence *He walked.* In the first sentence, the letter *s* has the meaning of "third person present"; the letters *ed* in the second sentence are pronounced *t,* and this *t* has the meaning of "past." In these two sentences, the base form, *walk,* may be inflected with the morpheme *-s* if the meaning is "third person present" or with the morpheme *-t* if the meaning is "past." Forms like the *-s* and the *-t* are called *tense markers;* they show what tense is intended.

If we consider that spoken words are made up of consonant and vowel segments, we can see that inflecting a verb for third person present basically means adding the consonant *s* to the verb. The *s* is sometimes pronounced *z* or *iz,* depending on the last sound of the verb. Likewise, inflecting a verb for past tense essentially means adding the consonant *t* to the verb (the *t* is sometimes pronounced *d* or *id,* depending on the last sound of the verb).

Sometimes tense is shown by a whole different form altogether. For example, we recognize the English sentence *He sees* as having a present tense meaning; but most speakers of English would not accept *He seed* as the correct past tense form. The past form of the verb *see* is *saw*, so not all verbs add *-ed* to show the meaning of past. Forms in English like the third person present *-s* and the past tense *-ed* are called *bound morphemes:* they are meaningful units of language that cannot occur by themselves; they must be attached to another form. Bound morphemes are different from free morphemes that can stand by themselves. In the unit on numeral incorporation, we gave the example of the handshape as an example of a bound morpheme in ASL.

Tense in English is sometimes shown with independent lexical items and sometimes with special morphemes. Time is handled differently in ASL structure. In general, ASL does not use bound morphemes like third person present *-s* or past tense *-ed*. While we will see some bound morphemes in ASL time signs, ASL does not add segments to a sign to indicate tense.

EXPRESSING TENSE IN ASL

Traditionally, time in ASL has been described in terms of an imaginary time line that runs perpendicular to the signer's body. The area near the signer's torso has a general meaning of "present," the area farther away has a meaning of "future," and the area over the shoulder has a general meaning of "past."

In addition to the time line, many separate lexical items are used to specify the time of the event being described, including NOW, TODAY, YESTERDAY, TOMORROW, UP-UNTIL-NOW, NOT-YET, FROM-NOW-ON, RECENTLY, LATER, LONG TIME AGO, and FUTURE. Four of these signs—YESTERDAY, TOMORROW, NOT-YET, and RECENTLY—are independent lexical items whose meaning is only partly related to the imaginary time line. Their orientation, location, and movement do seem to be related to the time line—YESTERDAY moves backward and TOMORROW moves forward—but they are also full lexical items.

Two signs—UP-UNTIL-NOW and FROM-NOW-ON—clearly seem to depend, in part, on movement along an imaginary time line for their meaning. UP-UNTIL-NOW generally moves from the shoulders to a point in front of the signer, and FROM-NOW-ON generally moves from a point in front of the signer forward. The other signs—NOW, TODAY, LATER, LONG TIME AGO, and FUTURE—are like YESTERDAY, TOMORROW, NOT-YET, and RECENTLY in that they are independent lexical signs. It is true that they can all be produced further forward or back on the imaginary line, but it seems that the change in location adds emphasis to the meaning. For example, one can sign NOW in the area in front of the torso, with a general meaning of "in the present." But the sign can be produced at least two other ways, one much closer to the signer, with the wrists almost touching the torso, and one farther away, with the arms almost outstretched. In the first case, the movement might also be noticeably tense, while in the second case, the movement might be larger and sharper. Both signs also might have particular nonmanual features. The point is that while each one is at a different point on the so-called time line, the location of the sign has nothing to do with time. The location serves to emphasize the meaning of NOW.

As we said, the second example of NOW can be produced with the arms almost outstretched, relatively far away from the signer's body and far down the time line, but the location on the time line does not change the meaning to "now closer to the future." In fact, this sign means "not in the future *at all*." We can see the same thing with LATER. The basic sign might be produced fairly close to the signer's torso. Another form of the sign might be produced with the arm almost completely outstretched. A traditional description might say that this is farther along the time line, but we suggest that this different location may also be for emphasis. The location is only one part of this sign that gets a lot of its meaning from its segmental structure along with its handshape, orientation, and nonmanual signals.

Other independent lexical items for time include MORNING, AFTERNOON, NIGHT, NOON, and MIDNIGHT. ASL also has the signs YEAR, WEEK, MONTH, DAY, HOUR, MINUTE, and TIME, and these signs allow numeral incorporation. In other words, the handshape in these signs is a bound morpheme that has the meaning of the specific number being referred to—two weeks or three months or four years, while the other aspects of the sign function as one morpheme to mean WEEK or YEAR or MONTH. In addition, the basic signs YEAR and WEEK use location and orientation to indicate years or weeks in the past or in the future. For example, consider how you would sign THREE-WEEK-AGO or TWO-YEAR-PAST or FOUR-YEAR-FROM-NOW.

HABITUAL TIME

ASL structure also has a way of representing *habitual* time. For example, the way of signing EVERY WEEK or EVERY MONDAY or EVERY MONTH is different from the basic signs for these concepts. To sign the days of the week to mean "every Monday, Tuesday," etc., the basic structure is H M H, which moves from the height of the signer's dominant shoulder to the mid-torso, with the palm orientation toward the signer. The handshape is the one used for the specific day of the week. In the case of EVERY WEEK, the sign WEEK is produced in separate locations, each one lower than the preceding one. To sign EVERY night, the handshape and orientation of the basic sign are kept, while the segmental structure is H M H, and the sign moves from the signer's left to the signer's right.

In all the examples we've presented, the basic structure of the signs changed to achieve new meanings. The changes involve bound morphemes, similar to tense markers in spoken languages, but in ASL, bound morphemes are not added on to an existing sign. Rather, some parts of the basic sign are kept, and others are changed. In the case of EVERY MONDAY, the handshape and the orientation are the same as the basic sign MONDAY but the segmental structure (H M H) and the location are very different. ASL can also show the *duration* of time, as in the signs ALL-DAY-LONG and ALL-NIGHT-LONG.

WILL AND FINISH

ASL has two signs that can be glossed as WILL and FINISH and a fingerspelled sign #WILL. One might think that these signs have only the meaning of "in the future" and "in the past" and that they might be similar to their English counterparts, but it seems that they are also used for emphasis as well as for referring to the time of an event. For example, the English sentence "Tomorrow I will go to the store" can be produced in ASL as TOMORROW PRO.1 GO-STORE. The meaning of "future" comes from the separate lexical sign TOMORROW. The ASL sentence

nod
TOMORROW PRO.1 GO-STORE WILL PRO.1

would be translated as the emphatic English sentence "I will go to the store tomorrow!"

The sign FINISH, while often translated as "past" and used in some forms of signed English as the equivalent of English *-ed,* may also have the function of a *completive* marker. That is, it shows that the event being described is completely finished. For example, the sign FINISH would probably not appear in sentences that simply make reference to the past. The English sentence "Yesterday he walked down the street" would be rendered in ASL as YESTERDAY PRO.3 WALK and not as

nod
YESTERDAY PRO.3 WALK FINISH.

The second sentence would most aptly be translated as "Yesterday he did walk!" This sentence would be used to clear up doubt. It might also constitute the first half of a longer sentence meaning "Once he had finished his walk, he ate."

brow up
YESTERDAY PRO.3 WALK FINISH, EAT PRO.3

In either case, the sign FINISH does more than just indicate past tense; other elements in the sentence do that work.

This is a very brief introduction to time in ASL. The most important point to understand is that ASL has ways of representing time, and that they are different from the ways in which time is represented in English.

REFERENCES

Baker-Shenk, C., and Cokely, D. 1980. *American Sign Language: A teacher's resource text on grammar and culture.* Washington, DC: Gallaudet University Press.

PART FOUR

SYNTAX

UNIT 1

Definitions

GOAL
To understand the meaning of syntax

SUPPLEMENTAL READINGS
"Syntax: Sentences and Their Stucture," by Edward Finegan and Niko Besnier (1989); pp. 354–357

"The Study of Sentence Structure," by William O'Grady, Michael Dobrovolsky, and Mark Aronoff (1989); pp. 358–388

One of the features of language that makes it distinct from other communication systems is its productivity. The number of sentences that can be produced in a language is infinite, but each language has a finite set of rules for making sentences. Users of a language know these rules and use them to produce new sentences and to understand the sentences used by other people.

One of the interesting things about language is that a finite set of rules is used to produce an infinite set of sentences. Sometimes the users of a language cannot explain the rules of their language, but they know when a rule has been broken. They recognize grammatical and ungrammatical sentences. People sometimes make mistakes when they are using their language, and very often they correct themselves as they are using language. But just because they make mistakes does not mean that they don't know the rules. There is a difference between a user's *competence* in a language and a user's *performance* in a language, a difference between what a user knows about the language and how a user uses the language. One part of a user's competence is knowledge of the rules for making sentences, or the *syntax* of the language. Another word commonly used for syntax is *grammar*. It is important to recognize that theories about syntactic structure are continually developing and evolving. The theories now in existence include Noam Chomsky's minimalist approach (the latest step in a theory of syntax that began with transformational generative grammar and passed through government and binding), cognitive grammar (Langacker 1987), and functional grammar (Dik 1978). The discussion of ASL syntax in this book is based on the framework for ASL syntax presented by Liddell (1980).

Before we talk about sentence structure in ASL, we need to take a look at the work that specific signs do in sentences. That is, do the signs function as nouns, verbs, adjectives, or adverbs? These different categories of signs are called lexical categories.

Large groups of lexical signs in ASL have very similar properties. These shared characteristics allow us to organize lexical signs into lexical categories. Four major lexical categories to which members can be easily added are nouns (N), predicates (Pred), adjectives (Adj), and adverbs (Adv). There is also a group of minor lexical categories in which members are restricted to a fixed number of elements already in the language. The minor categories include determiners (Det), auxiliary verbs (Aux), prepositions (Prep), conjunctions (Conj), and pronouns (Pro).

Each lexical category has a unique set of morphological frames (the position of a sign with respect to the bound morphemes that can be attached to it with a sign) and syntactic frames (the position in which a sign occurs relative to other classes of signs in the same phrase). Both frames of a given sign can be used to determine the lexical category of that sign. The characteristics of the lexical categories in ASL are explained below. Even though there are some universal tendencies across languages in the area of lexical categories and the strategies we lay out here are valid tools in the investigation of other languages, it is important to note that what follows is a description of ASL lexical categories; the details are not the same in other languages.

MAJOR LEXICAL CATEGORIES

Nouns

Noun signs identify entities such as individuals (name signs like DAVID-on-temple, #ANN), places (CHICAGO, #SEARS, #DENNY'S), and concrete and abstract things (COMPUTER, TABLE, THEORY). While many English nouns form the plural by adding the bound morpheme *-s (door/doors)*, noun signs ASL tend to occur only in the syntactic frame. That is, unlike English nouns, it seems that there are no bound morphemes that attach to nouns in ASL to pluralize or to otherwise modify them. Instead, ASL nouns often use determiners (SOME, MANY, FEW) to indicate that a sign is plural. An example of a determiner (MANY and INDEX-arc) and noun that show plurality would be

<u>   t</u>
MANY #CAR INDEX-arc STILL NEW

In this example and others in this unit, the object of the sentence precedes the predicate. This is indicated by a *t* over the object. We will discuss this further in unit 4.

A small number of ASL nouns form the plural by reduplication. That is, the noun is repeated two or three times in an arc or linear movement path. Some examples of noun reduplication are BROTHER++, SISTER++, WORD++, TREE++, and PLANT++. Most nouns, however, cannot be reduplicated.

Nouns can combine with determiners and adjectives (signs that describe the noun). Some examples of the possible combinations are shown below.

t

Det + N INDEX-rt WOMAN NEAT

Det N Pred

In the following example, WOMAN/INDEX is produced simultaneously with both hands

t

N/Det WOMAN/INDEX-rt NEAT

N/Det Pred

t

Det + N + Det MANY #CAR INDEX-arc STILL NEW

Det N Det Adv Pred

Predicates

Predicates say something about the subject of a sentence, whether it is a noun or pronoun. In many languages, including ASL, adjectives and nouns function as predicates. English requires a verb as part of the predicate, while ASL does not. As we explained in the unit on classifier predicates, a predicate may consist of a verb, a noun, or an adjective. Here are some examples of predicate signs in ASL.

PRO.3 PLAY

PLAY is a verb, and it describes what the subject, PRO.3, is doing.

t

BOY INDEX-rt HOME

N Det Pred

HOME is a noun, but it can become a predicate when it says something about the noun, in this case BOY. It is often called a predicate noun or nominal predicate. In the sentence PRO.3 BOY, BOY is another example of a predicate noun.

t

INDEX-lf HOUSE YELLOW

Det N Pred

YELLOW is a predicate adjective since it describes something about the house—its color. Colors can be either adjectives or predicates, depending on where they appear in the sentence. An example of a color used as an adjective would be as follows:

t

YELLOW HOUSE OLD

Adj N Pred

t

SMALL DOG INDEX-lf SICK

Adj N Det Pred

SICK is a predicate. Even though its gloss looks like the English adjective *sick*, which can appear before or after the noun (as an adjective or predicate adjective), the ASL sign SICK seems to always function as a predicate. It seems that it cannot grammatically precede a noun in ASL, as it can in English—"the sick dog." Psychological, physiological, and emotional states like STUPID, FUNNY, HEALTHY, HAPPY, CONFUSED, and UPSET are all predicates in ASL. Therefore the sentence SICK DOG INDEX-rt SMALL is ungrammatical in ASL because SICK can only function as the predicate. It cannot be used as an adjective before the noun. However, physical characteristics like TALL, THIN, BIG, and UGLY tend to be either adjectives or predicates.

Members of the lexical category of ASL predicates indicate progressive tense by adding the progressive morpheme after the verb. This is different from English, which indicates progressive tense by adding the morpheme *-ing* (*sit/sitting*).

V + progressive morpheme SIT-with-tiny-circle-movements
READ-with-repeated-movements

Another class of predicates in ASL consists of classifier predicates. As we saw earlier, they consist of a movement root and a classifier handshape. Unlike ASL nouns, progressive tense and classifier predicate changes occur in the morphological frame, not the syntactic frame. Some examples of classifier predicates are described below.

classifier handshape + stative descriptive morpheme (2h)B-CL "pile of coins"

The active hand moves to describe the pile of coins while the passive hand acts as the surface.

classifier handshape + process morpheme 1-CL "person walks by"

The active hand moves to indicate the movement of the object being described.

classifier handshape + contact morpheme 3-CL "car is located"

The active hand moves downward a short distance when it is placed at a particular location. Its movement does not mean that it is a moving object; it represents the concept of being located.

One of the syntactic properties of predicates is that they can combine with auxiliary verbs (Aux) such as WILL, CAN, and FINISH (see the section on minor categories for more on Aux). This syntactic frame can be demonstrated as follows:

nodding
Aux + Pred WILL EAT PRO.1
Aux Pred CS (copy subject)

nodding
Pred + Aux EAT WILL PRO.1
Pred Aux CS

nodding
Aux + Pred + Aux WILL EAT WILL PRO.1
Aux Pred Aux CS

Another syntactic frame for predicates is that predicates can occur at the beginning or at the end of a command or request such as (PLEASE) LEAVE! FINISH! WATCH-PRO.1! and DON'T-MIND.

(PLEASE) + Pred   PLEASE STOP!

Pred + (PLEASE)   STOP PLEASE!

Adjectives

ASL adjectives (Adj) have the property of being placed before a noun. Both physical characteristics and colors often function as adjectives, but they can become predicates when they appear after nouns. In the morphological frame the movement can be produced in an emphatic way to show degrees of the adjective.

	t
Adj + stress movement	INDEX-rt VERY-TALL MAN, PRO.1 TELL-PRO.3-rt WILL
	DET Adj N N Pred Aux

This adjective property is reflected in a syntactical frame as follows:

	t
Adj + N + Det	TALL MAN INDEX-rt, PRO.1 TELL-PRO.3-rt FINISH
	Adj N Det N Pred Aux

Adverbs

Adverbs (Adv) usually modify adjectives and predicates by using particular nonmanual signals (NMS) and particular movements. However, it seems that in ASL, the features of a sign that carry adverbial meaning often are incorporated directly into the structure of the adjective sign or the predicate sign, as seen in the examples below. Figure 42 shows that the sign TALL is a two-handed sign in which the active hand moves from the base to the fingertips of the passive hand. The sign can be glossed VERY-TALL when the sign begins well below the passive hand, brushes it, and ends above the fingertips, along with a marked facial expression.

Adj + stress movement	VERY-TALL MAN
	Adj + Adv N
	t
Pred + stress movement	MAN INDEX-rt VERY-TALL
	N Det Pred + Adv
	t
Pred + temporal aspect	INDEX-lf CHILD SIT-FOR-LONG-TIME
	Det N Pred + Adv
	t
Pred + NMS	INDEX-rt MAN DRIVE-carelessly
	Det N Pred + Adv

FIGURE 42. An example of adverbial meaning incorporated into an adjective sign.

Adverbs can also indicate when an action or event took place—YESTERDAY, TWO-WEEKS-AGO, NEXT-TWO-DAYS, and STILL. They tend to occur at the beginning of a sentence. The following sentence provides an example of this syntactic frame:

```
                     ____________t
Adv + N + Pred       TOMORROW PRO.1 OFF
                          Adv     N   Pred
```

Other adverbs, such as NOT and *headshaking* also modify predicates. Headshaking is a morphological change, as the following sentence illustrates.

```
                         _____neg (headshaking)
Adv + Pred     #ANN HUNGRY
```

Adding the adverb NOT to the sentence is a syntactic change.

```
Adv + Pred      ANN NOT HUNGRY
                 N   Adv   Pred

Adv + Pred + Adv     #ANN NOT HUNGRY NOT INDEX-ann
                       N   Adv   Pred    Adv    CS
```

NOT can also function as a predicate, as is shown below:

```
__________rhet-q
ANN HUNGRY, NOT
```

MINOR LEXICAL CATEGORIES

The members of minor lexical categories have little meaning outside of their grammatical purpose and are used to relate phrases of various types to other phrases. These groups consist of determiners (Det), auxiliary verbs (Aux), prepositions (Prep), conjunctions (Conj), and pronouns (Pro).

Determiners

As we saw in the unit on pronouns and determiners, determiners (Det) occur with nouns. This class includes signs like INDEX (using index finger), MANY, SOME, ALL, MY, and YOUR. Some examples follow.

Det + N
t (over MY DAUGHTER)
MY DAUGHTER VERY-SICK
Det N Pred + Adv

N + Det
t (over GIRL INDEX-rt)
GIRL INDEX-rt L-CL "zoom off"
N Det Pred

N/Det
t (over MAN/INDEX-rt)
MAN/INDEX-rt SILLY
N/Det Pred

Det + N + Det
t (over SOME FOOD INDEX-rt-middle-lf)
SOME FOOD INDEX-rt-middle-lf #NG
Det N Det Pred

Det + Adj + N
t (over INDEX-lf YELLOW RED FLOWER)
INDEX-lf YELLOW RED FLOWER FALSE
Det Adj N Pred

Adj + N + Det
t (over YELLOW RED FLOWER INDEX-lf)
YELLOW RED FLOWER INDEX-lf FALSE
Adj N Det Pred

Auxiliary Verbs

Auxilliary verbs (Aux) like WILL, CAN, FINISH, MUST, and SHOULD tend to show up at the beginning or at the end of a sentence. Occasionally they are found both before and after the predicate. Auxiliary verbs accompany other verbs or predicates and are used to add tense and aspect information. Here are some examples in the syntactical frame:

Aux + Pred
nodding (over PRO.3 MUST EAT)
PRO.3 MUST EAT
N Aux Pred

Pred + Aux
nodding (over PRO.3 EAT MUST INDEX-PRO.3)
PRO.3 EAT MUST INDEX-PRO.3
N Pred Aux CS (copy subject)

Aux + Pred + Aux
nodding (over PRO.3 MUST EAT MUST INDEX-PRO.3)
PRO.3 MUST EAT MUST INDEX-PRO.3
N Aux Pred Aux CS

Morphemes can be added to auxiliary verbs by incorporating nonmanual signals. The concept of *may, might* is conveyed in this way.

Aux + NMS   brow up, lips drawn, slightly headshaking side to side
PRO.3 EAT

Prepositions

Prepositions (Prep) show relationships between nouns and predicates or pronouns. In ASL these relationships are typically expressed with classifier predicates, agreement verbs, and the index finger pointing to mean "at." ASL does not have many independent preposition signs like the English words *under, on, in, above, with,* and *to.* ASL does use signs like IN, ON, UNDER, and BEHIND; however, these signs function like predicates and not like prepositions in English. We could call them prepositional predicates. For example, the sign INSIDE produced on the chest with repeated movement to talk about inner feelings is such a predicate (see Figure 43).

t
OLD FEELING STILL INSIDE-my-chest
Adj N Adv Pred

Likewise, the sign BEHIND is the predicate in this sentence:

PRO.1 BEHIND
N Pred

This sentence has the meaning of "I've already planned for that," and in it, BEHIND functions as a predicate (see Figure 44). This function is syntactic in nature. Classifier predicates and agreement verbs also act as prepositions, and often the prepositional relationship is incorporated into the structure of the classifier predicate or agreement verb. This use is morphological and is shown in the examples below. The relationship is indicated by Pred + Prep.

t
Classifier predicate + from and to MY FRIEND 1-CL "walk from left side to right side"
Det N Pred + Prep

Classifier predicate + classifier predicate

t t
TABLE B-CL "be located" (left hand) BOOK B-CL "be located under the table" (right hand)
N Pred + Prep N Pred + Prep

FIGURE 43. An example of INSIDE used as a prepositional predicate.

FIGURE 44. An example of BEHIND functioning as a predicate.

Agreement verb + to

t
#JOHN, #ANN ann-GIVE-TO-john
N N Pred + Prep

It seems that there is only one sign that functions like an English preposition, and that is INDEX (using index finger), a concept similar to the English preposition *at*.

Prep + N PRO.3 LIVE INDEX-rt CHICAGO
N Pred Prep N

Conjunctions

Conjunctions (Conj) join words or phrases of the same category. In ASL, examples include BUT, UNDERSTAND, OR, and PLUS. Examples of conjunctions in the syntactical frame are as follows:

N + Conj + N PRO.3 BRING #TV, SHELF PLUS SOFA
N Pred N N Conj N

cond
Pred + Conj + Pred PLAY SAD #OR HAPPY, NO-MATTER
N Pred Conj Pred Pred

t
Adj + N + Copy + Adj + N RED CHAIR #OR RED TABLE, MUST CHOOSE ONE
Adj N Conj Adj N Aux Pred N

S + conj + S (S = sentence)

brow up
PRO.2 CAN GO STORE UNDERSTAND HELP MOTHER FIRST
Aux Pred N Conj Pred N Adv
S S

Pronouns

Pronouns include PRO.1 (first person), PRO.2 (second person), PRO.3 (third person), WE-TWO, THEY-THREE, and they are used as both subjects and objects. In a morphological frame, some numbers can be incorporated into pronouns.

Pro + number   WE-THREE LEAVE

Five seems to be the limit for incorporation into pronouns (6–9 are rarely used).

Also, pronouns can be incorporated into agreement verbs, another example of a morphological frame. (We discussed this in the unit on agreement verbs.)

agreement verb + PRO   PRO.2-GIVE-TO-PRO.1

Pronouns can also be expressed in a syntactical frame.

                                                q
PRO + plain verb + PRO   PRO.2 LOVE PRO.3

These are the main lexical categories that we will encounter as we look at the sentence structure of ASL. As we can see, ASL shares some features with spoken languages but is unique in other ways.

REFERENCES

Chomsky, N. 1965. *Aspects of the theory of syntax.* Cambridge, MA: MIT Press.

Dik, S. C. 1978. *Functional grammar.* Amsterdam: North-Holland.

Jannedy, S., Poletto, R., and Weldon, T., eds. 1994. *Language Files: Materials for an introduction to language and linguistics,* 6th ed. Columbus: Ohio State University Press.

Langacker, R. W. 1987. *Foundations of cognitive grammar.* Vol. 1 of *Theoretical Prerequisites.* Stanford, CA: Stanford University Press.

Liddell, S. K. 1990. *American Sign Language syntax.* The Hague: Mouton.

O'Grady, W., Dobrovolsky, M., and Aronoff, M. 1989. *Contemporary linguistics: An introduction.* New York: St. Martin's Press.

Homework Assignment 14

1. Gloss two sentences from the videotape and explain how you know they are sentences. What is it about the signs and the nonmanual features that tells you where one sentence begins and ends, for example?

2. Think of two ungrammatical (unacceptable) sentences in ASL and explain why they are ungrammatical.

3. Find one example of someone self-correcting while signing. How does the person indicate that he or she is correcting himself/herself? What is the mistake?

4. Using your gloss of the Snowmobile story, identify the lexical category of the signs in the first five sentences.

UNIT 2

Simple Sentences with Plain Verbs

GOAL
To understand how simple sentences with plain verbs work in ASL

INTRANSITIVE VERBS

Every language has certain basic structures for sentences. Sentences are made up of subjects and predicates. Some sentences include objects and others do not. The linguistic term for verbs or predicates that do not allow objects is *intransitive*. The basic word order for a sentence with an intransitive predicate in ASL is Subject-Verb. A sentence with this kind of predicate is BOY SILLY. In this case, the subject is a noun. The subject could also be a pronoun. The English sentence *He is silly* would be signed in ASL as PRO.3 SILLY. The pronoun in this case is represented by the index finger pointing in the direction of the space already established as referring to that person, often with eye gaze accompanying the pointing.

As we saw earlier, some ASL predicates do not contain information about the subject or object. These are called plain verbs. The basic word order for a simple sentence is Subject-Verb, but ASL has two other acceptable structures for simple sentences with plain verbs. One is Subject-Verb-Pronoun, where the pronoun copies the subject with the head nodding. We can write the structure as follows:

$$\text{S V } \overline{\text{Pro}}^{\,\text{nd}}$$

(*Note:* We use the abbreviation *nd* for nodding, in contrast to the word *nod* for a single downward movement of the head.)

An example of this structure is found in the following sentence:

$$\text{BOY SILLY } \overline{\text{PRO}}^{\,\text{nd}} \text{ (subject copy)}$$

The other possible structure is Verb-Pronoun, where the pronoun includes head nodding:

$$\text{V } \overline{\text{Pro}}^{\,\text{nd}}$$

The sample sentence then becomes SILLY PRO, or:

nd
SILLY PRO

This structure assumes that we have established that we are talking about a boy.

Every sentence in a language has a basic linguistic structure. As we mentioned earlier, there are a number of different theories about the structure of sentences. One theory, introduced by the linguist Noam Chomsky, proposed that a sentence has a basic form, deep structure, and that other forms of the sentence come from that basic form. In other words, additional sentences can be derived from the basic form of a sentence by a series of rules. Those rules are called *transformations*, and the resulting sentence that is produced is called the *surface structure*. Using this information, we can see that the sentence

nd
BOY SILLY PRO

is derived from the deep structure sentence BOY SILLY by a transformational rule. This rule allows a pronoun that refers to the subject to occur at the end of the sentence with head nodding. The derivation looks like this:

Deep Structure: BOY SILLY

nd
Subject Pronoun Copy Rule: BOY SILLY PRO

nd
Surface Structure: BOY SILLY PRO

The other possible structure for simple sentences with plain verbs is

nd nd
Verb Pro, as in SILLY PRO

In this case, the deep structure is still BOY SILLY, but two rules are used to derive the surface structure: the pronoun copy rule and the subject deletion rule. The derivation looks like this:

Deep Structure: BOY SILLY

nd
Subject Pronoun Copy Rule: BOY SILLY PRO

nd
Subject Deletion: _SILLY PRO

nd
Surface Structure: SILLY PRO

One combination that ASL does not allow is the verb followed by the noun subject, as in *V S. The asterisk in front of the sentence indicates that the sentence is not acceptable in ASL. Therefore, the sentence *SILLY BOY is ungrammatical in ASL.

TRANSITIVE VERBS

Many verbs in ASL do allow objects. The term for verbs that allow objects is *transitive.* The basic word order for a sentence with an object is Subject-Verb-Object, as in the sentence FATHER LOVE CHILD. However, as with intransitive verbs, different word orders are possible for sentences with transitive plain verbs. For example, during the course of conversation, FATHER LOVE CHILD can be changed to

nd
Subject Verb Object Subject copy
Pro Pro Pro

or

nd
FATHER LOVE CHILD FATHER
Pro Pro Pro

(In this and other examples, *Pro* under the noun means the third-person pronoun is used to refer to the noun.) The following structure is also possible:

nd
Verb Object Subject copy
Pro Pro

or

nd
LOVE CHILD FATHER
Pro Pro

Topicalization

While the basic word order for a sentence containing an object is Subject-Verb-Object, very often the object is the first element of the sentence. The placement of the object at the beginning of the sentence is called *topicalization* and is very common in ASL. The sentence FATHER LOVE CHILD can be changed so that the object occurs first. The sentence then becomes

t
CHILD, FATHER LOVE

The *t* over *child* indicates topicalization. It is marked by special nonmanual features, which we will discuss in unit 4.

As we saw before, this same sentence can occur with pronouns instead of nouns, and the object pronoun can be topicalized, as follows:

t
Object, Subject Love
Pro Pro

The same sentence can occur with the following word order:

t (Object) nd (Subject) t (CHILD) nd (FATHER)
Object, LOVE Subject or CHILD, LOVE FATHER
Pro Pro Pro Pro

The changes in word order of sentences with transitive verbs are the result of transformational rules.

SUMMARY

This unit is a basic introduction to the structure of simple sentences with plain verbs in ASL. The most important points are summarized in the chart and list below.

1. The basic word order in ASL sentences with intransitive verbs is Subject-Verb.
2. Other word orders are allowed, but if they are used, the fact that they are not Subject-Verb will be marked in some way. For example, if the subject is repeated as a pronoun, the repetition will be accompanied by nodding.
3. The basic word order in ASL sentences with transitive verbs is Subject-Verb-Object.
4. Other word orders are allowed, but if they are used, the fact that they are not Subject-Verb-Object is marked in some way. If the subject pronoun occurs after the verb or is repeated, the head nods. If the object is the first element in the sentence, so it occurs in front of the verb and the subject, the eyebrows are raised, the head is tilted, and there may be a slight pause before the rest of the sentence is signed.
5. The basic word order Subject-Verb-Object is not the most commonly used word order in ASL.

Sentences with Simple Plain Verbs

	SENTENCE	EXAMPLE
A. Intransitive Sentences:	S V	BOY SILLY
	S-Pro V	S-Pro SILLY
	nd (over final S-Pro) S-Pro V S-Pro	nd (over final S-Pro) S-Pro SILLY S-Pro
	nd (over S-Pro) V S-Pro	nd (over S-Pro) SILLY S-Pro
B. Transitive Sentences:	S V O	FATHER LOVE CHILD
	nd (over S-Pro-copy) S-Pro V O-Pro S-Pro-copy	nd (over S-Pro-copy) S-Pro LOVE O-Pro S-Pro-copy
	nd (over S-Pro-copy) V O-Pro S-Pro-copy	nd (over S-Pro-copy) LOVE O-Pro S-Pro-copy
	t (over O) O, S V	t (over CHILD) CHILD, FATHER LOVE
	t (over O-Pro) O-Pro, S-Pro V	t (over O-Pro) O-Pro, S-Pro LOVE
	t (over O-Pro) nd (over S-Pro) O-Pro, V S-Pro	t (over O-Pro) nd (over S-Pro) O-Pro, LOVE S-Pro

UNIT 3

Simple Sentences with Agreement Verbs

GOAL
To understand the basic structure of simple sentences with agreement verbs in ASL

Many verbs in ASL *do* include information about the subject and the object, and the structure of sentences with these verbs is different from the structure of sentences with plain verbs. We will discuss three possible structures.

1. Simple sentences with agreement verbs and no separate signs for the subject and the object. The gloss of the English sentence *I give you* is an example of this structure. The sentence could be signed as follows:

   $_{\text{PRO.1}}\text{GIVE}_{\text{PRO.2}}$

   and the structure of the sentence could be described as follows:

   $_{\text{Subj.}}\text{VERB}_{\text{Obj.}}$

   to indicate the fact that information about the subject and object is included in the verb.

2. Verbs that allow or require a separate sign for the subject. TELL is one of these verbs. The English sentence *He tells me* would be signed as follows:

   $_{\text{PRO.3}}\text{TELL}_{\text{PRO.1}}$

   HE would be represented with the index finger, while the information about the object (*me*) would be in the location part of the verb. It may also be that a separate sign for the subject is produced (perhaps for emphasis or to disambiguate the sentence) and included in the verb as well. The sentence *You give me* could be signed as follows:

   $\text{Pronoun}_{\text{PRO.2}}\text{VERB}_{\text{PRO.1}}$

   or

   $\text{YOU}_{\text{PRO.2}}\text{GIVE}_{\text{PRO.1}}$

3. Subject pronouns follow the verb, again, for emphasis or disambiguation. This structure would be as follows:

nd

VERB Subj.
Subj Obj Pro

An example of this would be the sentence *I give you.*

nd

PRO.1 GIVE PRO.2 PRO.1

Once again, the basic word order in all three sentence structures is Subject-Verb-Object (see chart below). Other word orders are used, and if they are, they are marked with head nods.

Simple Sentences with Agreement Verbs

$_{S}V_{O}$	PRO.1 GIVE PRO.2
S-Pro $_{S}V_{O}$	YOU PRO.2 GIVE PRO.1
$_{S}V_{O}$ S-Pro	PRO.1 GIVE PRO.2 PRO.1 (nd over PRO.1)

Homework Assignment 15

1. We described four possible structures for *intransitive* simple sentences with plain verbs in ASL. Write one example of each.

   a. Subject Verb

   b. Pronoun Verb

   nd (over "Pronoun")
   c. Pronoun Verb, Pronoun

   nd (over "Verb")
   d. Verb Pronoun

2. We described six possible structures for *transitive* simple sentences with plain verbs. Write one example of each.

   a. Subject Verb Object

   nd (over "Subj. Pro copy")
   b. Subj. Pro Verb Obj. Pro Subj. Pro copy

   nd (over "Subj. Pro")
   c. Verb Obj. Pro Subj. Pro

   t (over "Obj.")
   d. Obj., Subj. Verb

   t (over "Obj. Pro")
   e. Obj. Pro, Subj.

   t (over "Obj. Pro"); nd (over "Subj. Pro")
   f. Obj. Pro, Verb Subj. Pro

3. We described three structures for simple sentences with agreement verbs. List the three structures and give an example of each.

UNIT 4

Basic Sentence Types

GOAL
To understand the basic sentence types in ASL

In units 2 and 3, we looked at the basic rules for word order in ASL. In this unit, we will look at some basic sentence types in ASL, focusing specifically on the role that nonmanual signals play in ASL syntax. The five basic sentence types we will look at are questions, negations, commands, topicalization, and conditionals. ASL also has declarative sentences (that is, sentences that convey referential information). As a group, declarative sentences do not seem to be marked by one particular nonmanual signal as are other sentence types in ASL.

QUESTIONS

Yes-No Questions

Yes-no questions are questions that require a yes-no answer. An example of a yes-no question in English is *Is John home?* The word order for a yes-no question places the verb before the subject (as opposed to the order in a declarative sentence: *John is home*). When a speaker of English says this yes-no question, his or her voice usually rises at the end of the question. In English, then, yes-no questions have a definite form that is different from other kinds of sentences. The same is true of ASL. Yes-no questions in ASL do not have any particular word order, but they do have nonmanual signals that go with them. When someone asks a yes-no question, the eyebrows are raised, the eyes are widened, and the head and body may tilt forward; sometimes the shoulders are raised and sometimes the last sign is held (see Figure 45). The symbol that we use to represent the nonmanual signal that goes with a yes-no question is *q*. An example of a yes-no question is as follows:

```
________q
MAN HOME
```

This sentence would be translated into English as "Is the man home?"

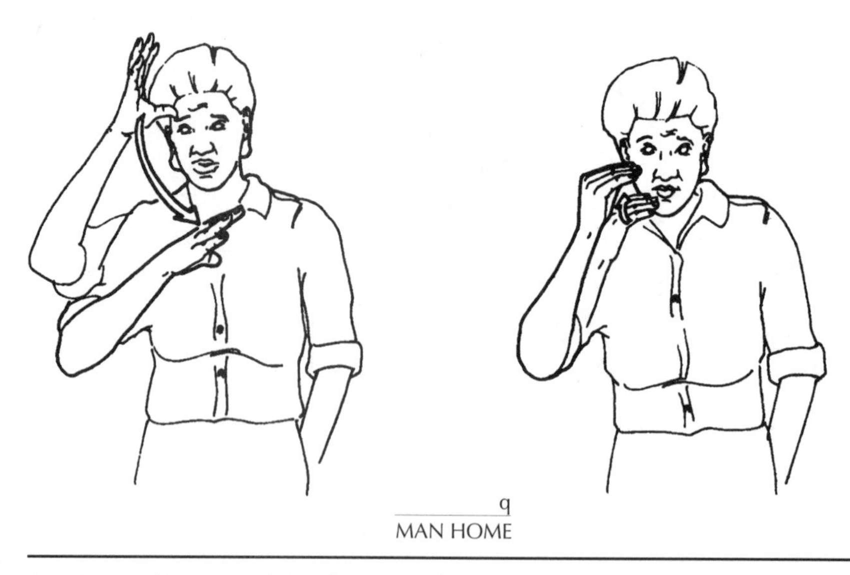

FIGURE 45. Nonmanual signals as part of a yes-no question.

Wh-questions

Wh-questions involve the use of words like *where, who, when, what,* and *why*. Examples of Wh-questions in English are *Where is John?* and *When is class finished?* Wh-questions in English have a special word order, with the verb usually preceding the subject. When a speaker asks a Wh-question, his or her voice usually goes down at the end of the question. Wh-questions in ASL also include the use of the signs WHERE, WHO, WHEN, WHAT, and WHY, and a very specific nonmanual signal. When someone asks a Wh-question, the eyebrows squint and the head tilts; also, the body may lean slightly forward and the shoulders may be raised (see Figure 46). The symbol used for a Wh-question is *wh,* and an example is as follows:

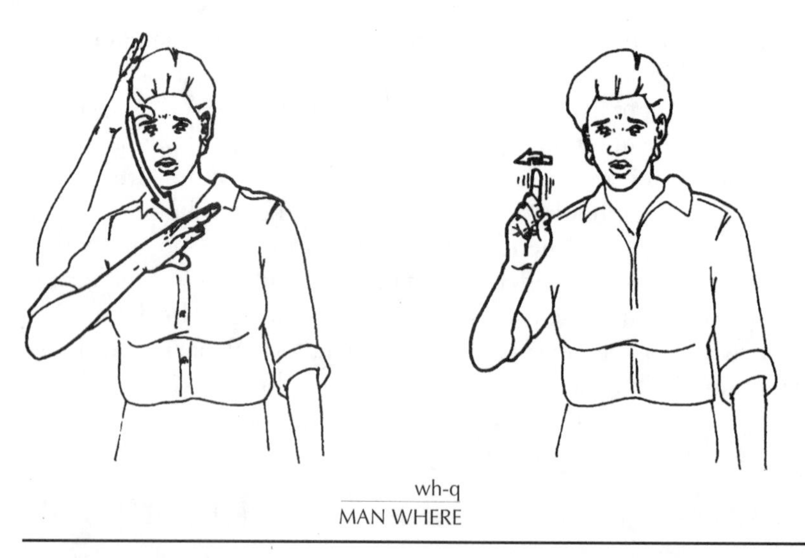

FIGURE 46. A Wh-question.

wh-q
MAN WHERE

This sentence would be translated into English as "Where is the man?"

Question Mark Wiggle

Sometimes questions in ASL include a sign that is glossed as QUESTION MARK WIGGLE (QM wg). These questions are often asked when the signer is surprised by the information he or she is being given, or when the signer wants to check what the other person is saying. QM wg is a sign with an X handshape with internal movement (wiggling). The nonmanual signal that accompanies sentences with this sign is the same as yes-no questions (eyebrows raised, eyes widened, head and body tilted forward) (see Figure 47). An example is as follows:

q
THINK TEST EASY QM wg

This sentence could be translated to English as "You really think that the test is easy?"

FIGURE 47. An example of question mark wiggle.

Rhetorical Questions

When people are speaking or signing, they often use forms that look like questions but that don't really behave like questions. They use forms that look like questions but they don't expect an answer from the person to whom they are speaking. These questions are called *rhetorical questions*, and their job is to provide the connections in what the speaker is saying. They are called rhetorical questions because while they look like questions, they do not do the work that real questions do. They are not seeking a yes or a no or the information that Wh-questions seek. An example of a rhetorical question in ASL is as follows:

              rhet
PRO.1 TIRED WHY STUDY ALL-NIGHT

The symbol that is used for rhetorical questions is *rhet*. An English translation of this sentence could be "I'm tired. Why? Because I studied all night." Other signs in ASL besides WHY that are used in rhetorical questions are REASON, WHEN, WHO, WHAT, WHERE, and FOR-FOR. The nonmanual signal used with rhetorical questions tells us that they do not have the same function as yes-no or Wh-questions. Most rhetorical questions use a Wh-word, and one might expect Wh-nonmanuals with them—squinted eyebrows and tilted head. But the nonmanuals used with rhetoricals include raised eyebrows and a slight shake or tilt of the head (see Figure 48). So even though the form may be a Wh-sign, the nonmanuals tell us that the function is not that of a Wh-question.

NEGATION

Sentences in ASL are not always *affirmative*. Signers often have occasion to use negative sentences, as do speakers of English. Some examples of negative sentences in English are *The man is not home* or *He cannot see me*. The process of changing an affirmative sentence to a negative is called *negation*. In ASL, negative sentences have specific nonmanual signals that include shaking the head from side to side, and possibly frowning or squinting. The symbol used for negation in ASL is *neg*, and an example is as follows:

          neg
MAN HOME

This could be translated to English as "The man is not home." It is interesting to note that the sign NOT is not required in negative sentences and may be used more for emphasis. The nonmanual signal is sufficient to produce a negative sentence.

COMMANDS

The sentences that people use to give commands are different from other kinds of sentences. In English, commands (or imperatives) often occur without a subject (the result of a transformational rule that deletes the subject *you*), as in *Sit down!* or *Come here!* In ASL the subject is also often deleted or occurs after the verb as a

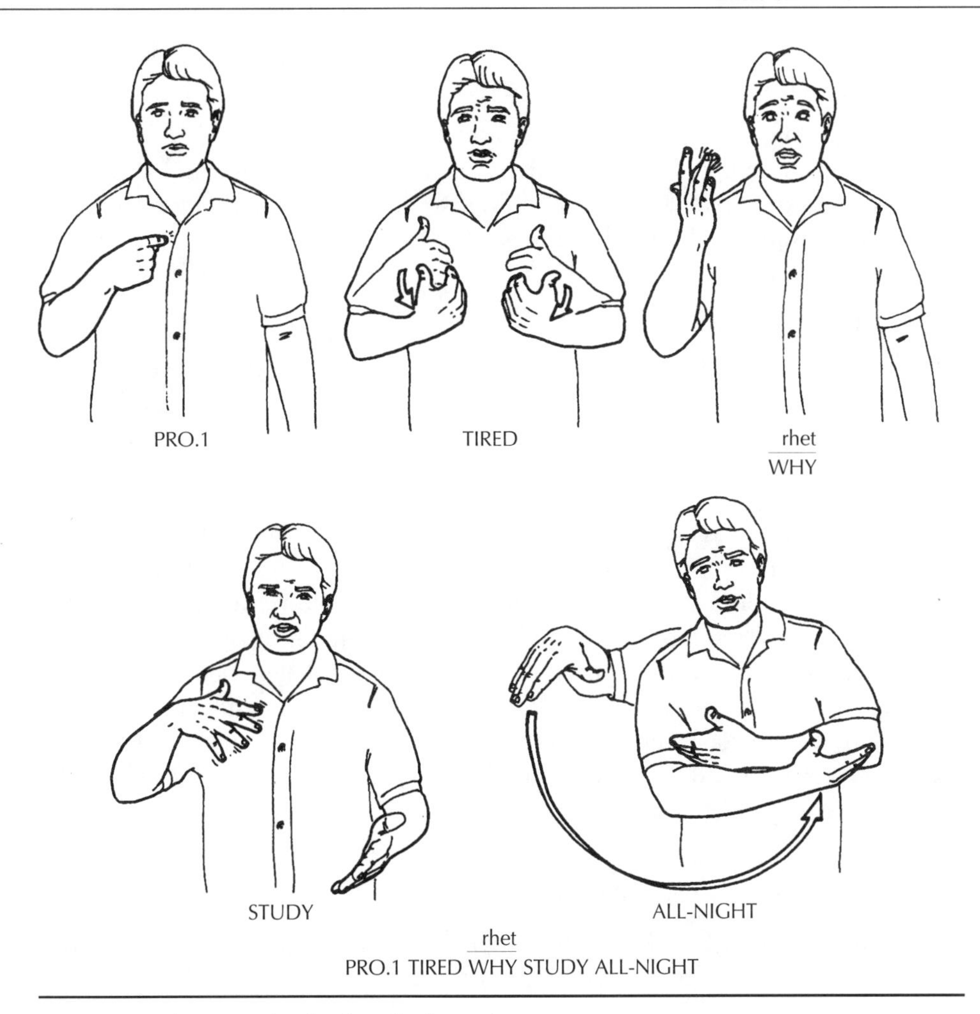

FIGURE 48. An example of a rhetorical question.

pronoun. ASL imperatives also have particular nonmanual signals, including making direct eye contact with the person being talked to, and possibly frowning. An example of an imperative in ASL is

SIT (with a line over it for the nonmanual signal)

The symbol * is used to indicate an imperative.

TOPICALIZATION

Topicalization occurs in ASL when the object of a sentence can be moved to the front of the sentence. The example we used in Unit 2 was as follows:

Deep Structure:	FATHER	LOVE	CHILD
	t		
Topicalization:	CHILD,	FATHER	LOVE

t
Surface Structure: CHILD, FATHER LOVE

The object that is moved to the front of the sentence and is topicalized is marked by particular nonmanual signals, which include raised eyebrows and a head tilt, and possibly a short pause. The symbol used for the nonmanuals of topicalization is *t*. Another example of topicalization is:

t
HOMEWORK, PRO.1 DETEST

This could be translated in English as "Homework, I detest it," or "As for homework, I detest it."

CONDITIONALS

Conditional sentences express a condition upon which the topics being discussed depend. An example of a conditional sentence in English is *If it rains tomorrow, the game will be cancelled.* In English, words such as *if* indicate a conditional. The ASL signs #IF and SUPPOSE also can be used to express conditionals. However, nonmanual signals play a very important role in conditional sentences. Conditional sentences can be constructed in ASL with nonmanual signals and without the use of signs to show the conditional. The nonmanual signals for conditionals include raised eyebrows, a head tilt, and possibly a short pause. The symbol used for conditionals is *cond*, and an example is as follows:

cond
TOMORROW RAIN, GAME CANCEL

It is important to note that the second part of the sentence is not conditional. It may be a negative or affirmative statement, a question, or a command.

THE IMPORTANCE OF NONMANUAL SIGNALS

Nonmanual signals, and not the signs, often determine the sentence type in ASL. The signs of a sentence can be identical, but it is the nonmanuals that make for the difference in sentence type. Consider, for example, the signs HOME YOU. These two signs can occur in four different sentence types. The signs themselves are the same; the nonmanuals are different.

nd
Declarative: HOME PRO.2 "You are home."

q
Yes-No Question: HOME PRO.2 "Are you going home?"

neg
Negation: HOME PRO.2 "You weren't home."

Command: *HOME PRO.2* "Go home."

In each of these examples, the nonmanual signal is vital in conveying the signer's intended message.

SUMMARY

We have seen here how important nonmanual signals are in syntax. In part 2 (Unit 1), we saw that many individual lexical signs require a nonmanual signal, such as FINALLY, NOT-YET, ADMIT, and so forth. This has to do with the phonological structure of individual signs. Nonmanual signals are also important in morphological structure because the signals can have independent meaning and may attach to a variety of signs. For example, the mouth configuration glossed as "mm" and having the meaning of "regularly" can be produced with many different verbs, for example, DRIVE, STUDY, READ, and WALK. A different mouth configuration glossed as "th" can be used with the same verbs (and many others) but with the meaning of "carelessly." Finally, nonmanual signals are important for ASL discourse, that is, the level of language use above the individual sentence. They may indicate the use of reported speech and they play a role in turn-taking and topic control. So we see that nonmanual signals are important in all areas of ASL structure: phonology, morphology, syntax, semantics, and discourse. The following chart summarizes the information on sentence types and nonmanual signals in ASL.

SENTENCE TYPE	NONMANUAL SIGNALS	EXAMPLE
1. Questions		
a. Yes-No Questions	Eyebrows raised, eyes widened, head and body may be tilted forward; shoulders may be raised; last sign may be held	q MAN HOME
b. Wh-Questions	Eyebrows squinted, head tilted; body may be forward; shoulders may be raised	wh MAN WHERE
c. Question Mark Wiggle	Same as yes-no questions	q THINK TEST EASY QM wg
d. Rhetorical Questions	Eyebrows raised, head may be tilted or may shake slightly	rhet PRO.1 TIRED WHY STUDY ALL-NIGHT
2. Negation	Head shakes side-to-side; may have frown or squint	neg MAN HOME
3. Commands	Direct eye contact with addressee, may frown	*SIT*
4. Topicalization	Eyebrows raised, head tilted, possibly a short pause	t HOMEWORK, PRO.1 DETEST
5. Conditionals	Eyebrows raised, head tilted; possibly a short pause and eye gaze shift	cond TOMORROW RAIN, GAME CANCEL

Homework Assignment 16

1. Look at the videotape and identify as many sentence types as you can. You should find examples of declaratives, topicalizations, yes-no questions, Wh questions, rhetorical questions, and negations. Gloss an example of each.

PART FIVE

SEMANTICS

UNIT 1

The Meaning of Individual Signs

GOAL
To gain a basic understanding of the semantics of signs

SUPPLEMENTAL READING
"The Study of Meaning," by William O'Grady, Michael Dobrovolsky, and Mark Aronoff (1989); pp. 374–388

Semantics is the study of the meaning of words and sentences. So far, we have looked at the basic units used to construct signs—movements and holds, handshapes, location, orientation, and nonmanual signals—that is, the phonological structure of ASL. We have seen how these parts can be used to construct new units, that is, the morphological component of the language, and we have seen how units are put together to form sentences. But for people who use language to communicate with each other, they not only need to share the phonology, morphology, and syntax of a language, but they also must share a system of meaning. The symbols and combinations of symbols must have shared value for the users of a language. Semantics is the study of the rule-governed ways in which languages structure meaning.

DETERMINING MEANING

How do we know what a sign means? When we see another signer use the sign CAT or HOUSE or THINK, how is it that we get the meaning intended by the signer from the combination of movements and holds, handshape, location, orientation, and nonmanual signals? Finding answers to these questions takes us back to the very first issue that we discussed, that is, the features that communication systems and languages have in common. You will recall that one feature that languages and other communications systems have in common is that they are shared by members of a community. The users of a language or variety of language determine what the meaning of a given combination of movements, holds, handshape, location, orientation, and nonmanual signals (that is, a specific sign) will mean.

Since meaning is determined by a specific community of users, the same combination of features, or the same sign, may have different meanings to different communities. For example, the combination of features that in ASL is glossed as

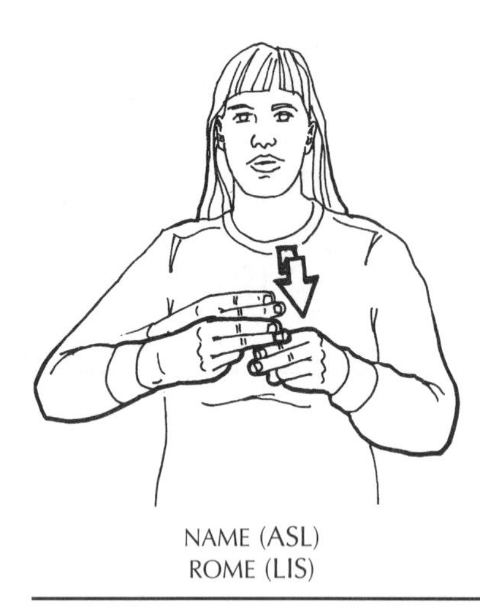

FIGURE 49. The same sign can have different meanings in different signing communities.

NAME is glossed as ROME (the name of the capital city) in Italian Sign Language (LIS) (see Figure 49). The same combination of sounds that in spoken Italian functions as a feminine plural definite article—*le*—in spoken Irish means "with."

Users of languages all over the world commonly look to written dictionaries as the definitive source for the meaning of words and signs, but it is important to remember that the people who write dictionaries derive their definitions of words or signs by carefully observing the way words and signs are used by real people. Dictionaries for sign languages are unique in that, while they may be organized to reflect the linguistic structure of the sign language, they seem to be almost necessarily bilingual. That is, in addition to providing an inventory of the signs in a sign language, sign language dictionaries almost always also provide written glosses for the signs in the majority language of the community in which the sign language is used. Stokoe's *Dictionary of American Sign Language* was an exception because it did not present the signs by an alphabetical list of their English glosses, but rather by the parameters of location, handshape, and movement. The potential problem with bilingual dictionaries is that the same sign may have different English glosses assigned to it or different signs may be assigned the same English gloss. Therefore, the meaning of the sign may not always be clear from the gloss assigned to it.

Types of Meaning

Researchers have identified three different kinds of meaning: *referential* meaning, *social* meaning, and *affective* meaning.

Referential Meaning. Referential meaning is the idea, thing, or state of affairs described by the sign or sentence. For example, the sign CAT refers to a four-legged mammal with a tail, whiskers, and so forth. The meaning of the sign CALIFORNIA is the western state that has the Pacific Ocean to the west, Mexico to the south, Oregon to the north, and so forth. That state is the referent of the sign.

Social Meaning. Signs and sentences also provide information about the social identity of the language user. For example, certain choices of signs may reveal where the person is from, whether the person is male or female, or whether the person is African American or Caucasian. This is the social meaning that can be conveyed by linguistic symbols.

Affective Meaning. Affective meaning provides information about the signer's feelings, attitudes, or opinions concerning a piece of information. Affective meaning can be conveyed by individual sign choice and by sentence structure. For example, a signer may be reporting a conversation that she had with another person in which the person talked about her work. One way to report the conversation would be to say "Alice explained to me about her fascinating research," while another way would be to say "Alice boasted to me about her boring old project again." Both sentences report the same basic information, that Alice talked about her work, but the signer's attitude toward what Alice said is completely different in each sentence. In the first sentence, the words *explained* and *fascinating* convey the meaning that the signer was really interested in what Alice had to say; in that second sentence, the words *boasted, boring old project,* and *again* clearly convey the message that the signer was not interested in what Alice had to say and had a negative opinion of her work. The difference in meaning between the two sentences is a difference in affective meaning.

Denotation and Connotation

The referential meaning of a sign or a sentence is often called its *denotation,* while the social and affective meaning is often called *connotation.* The difference between denotation and connotation can be illustrated with two signs in ASL that can be glossed as DEAF. The sign DEAF that is made with a 1 handshape that moves straight down from the ear to the chin denotes someone's audiological status and has a fairly neutral connotation. However, the form of the sign that is produced with a fairly slow arc movement and with a puffed cheek, while still denoting someone's audiological status, also conveys the message that the person is a full-fledged member of Deaf culture. This is a social connotation.

RELATIONSHIPS BETWEEN LEXICAL ITEMS

Users of a language know the phonological, morphological, and syntactic rules of their language, and they also know many individual words or signs. The collection of words or signs that they know is called the *lexicon,* and the individual words or signs in that collection are called *lexical items.* One area of semantics concerns the possible meaning relationships between lexical items in the lexicon. A number of different relationships can exist, including *hyponymy, part/whole relation-*

ships, *synonymy*, *antonymy*, *converseness*, and *metaphor*. We will briefly dicuss each relationship.

Hyponymy

Consider the signs BLUE, RED, YELLOW, GREEN, ORANGE, and PURPLE. You will quickly see that all of these signs are signs for colors. Now, ASL also has a sign COLOR. The referent for COLOR includes all of the signs in the set listed above, along with many other colors not listed. Each of the individual color signs has a meaning relationship with the sign COLOR: the sign COLOR is an inclusive term, and the meaning of each of the individual signs is included in the meaning of the sign COLOR. The signs for the individual colors are *hyponyms* (the prefix *hypo*-meaning "below"), and the sign COLOR is the *hypernym*. Another example is the hypernym SIGN LANGUAGE, which includes the hyponyms ASL, LSF (French Sign Language), LIS (Italian Sign Language), and LSQ (Quebec Sign Language).

Part/Whole Relationships

Another meaning relationship between signs is the one found between signs like HAND and ARM. This is not a hyponymic relationship because a hand is not a kind of arm. A hand is a part of an arm, and the referent of the sign HAND is included in the referent of the sign ARM. That is, an arm includes a hand. Another example might be the relationship between the signs PHONOLOGY and LINGUISTICS because phonology is a part of linguistics. The meaning of the sign LINGUISTICS includes the meaning of the sign PHONOLOGY.

Synonymy

We describe two signs as being synonymous if they "mean the same thing." When we say two words or signs "mean the same thing," we are generally talking about their referential meaning. For example, most users of English would agree that the words *sofa* and *couch* mean the same thing or that *soda* and *pop* refer to the same thing. But often words or signs that have the same referential meaning have different social or affective meaning. For example, the English words *think* and *cogitate* refer to the same mental activity, but *cogitate* tends to be used in fairly formal settings and not in more informal ones, unless the user is making a joke about the relative formality or informality of the situation. In ASL, DEAF signed with a 1 handshape from ear to chin has the same basic referential meaning of "audiological status" as DEAF signed with an A handshape at the ear then opening to a 5 handshape. However, the two signs have very different social and affective meanings. While the first is fairly neutral, the second generally has the meaning of "profoundly deaf," and its usage is sharply restricted—it is generally not considered socially appropriate for hearing non-native signers to use this sign. So while the two signs may look like synonyms and are at one level, they are not synonymous at another level.

Another interesting comparison involves the pairs of signs in ASL such as BED and #BED, CAR and #CAR, or BUSY and #BUSY. One member of each pair is a lexical sign, while the other is lexicalized fingerspelling. They appear to be synonymous, and yet their occurrence may be governed by discourse factors. Although this has not been researched as yet, it is possible that the fingerspelled sign is chosen for emphasis. Again, these pairs of signs seem to be synonymous at a referential level but not at a discourse level.

Antonymy

Antonymy describes the relationship between two signs that are opposite in meaning, and it is a binary relationship; it can only describe the relationship between two signs at a time. There are two basic kinds of antonymy—gradable and nongradable. The signs LARGE and SMALL are antonyms, but it is easy to see how the concept of "large" and "small" are relative. For example, in the domain of vegetables, a cucumber is larger than a pea but smaller than a pumpkin. Gradable antonyms can thus show degrees of the concept to which they refer. Something can be relatively larger or smaller, something can be relatively harder or easier, even though LARGE and SMALL and HARD and EASY are pairs of antonyms. The English words *alive* and *dead* and the ASL signs ALIVE and DEAD are considered to be nongradable antonyms, in that one is either alive or dead but not both. But it should be pointed out that users of both English and ASL sometimes use nongradable antonyms as if they were gradable, as in the English expressions "half-dead" or "barely alive" and their ASL equivalents.

This brings us to some interesting observations about antonyms in ASL. One concerns the way in which the language shows gradation. For example, in English, degrees of size (large or small) may be shown by suffixation, that is, by adding the suffix *-er* or *-est* as in *largest* or *smaller*, or with separate and formally unrelated lexical items—*tiny, enormous, midsize,* etc. In ASL, when the goal is to show degrees of meaning, the first question the signer may ask is "what exactly am I talking about?" Representing the size of an object, place, or person is usually accomplished with classifier predicates, and, as we know from the unit on classifier predicates, different handshapes and movement roots are used for different entities. For example, the classifier predicate used for representing the size of a car would vary depending on the actual size of the car being described. The handshape chosen to represent a limousine will be different from the handshape chosen to represent a small car, like a VW bug (see Figure 50). The handshape chosen to represent a thick book will be different from the one chosen to represent a thin book.

Specific classifier handshapes may be accompanied by specific nonmanual signals; pursed lips may accompany handshapes representing thin objects, while puffed cheeks may accompany handshapes representing larger objects. In addition, it is also possible to show gradation within a chosen classifier predicate. For example, the signer may choose a particular classifier handshape to represent a limousine, but the relative size of the limousine can be varied by changing the ending location of the sign. Normally, the sign begins with the hands touching or close together, and then they move apart from each other; how far they actually move apart indicates the relative size of the limousine (usually with an accompanying

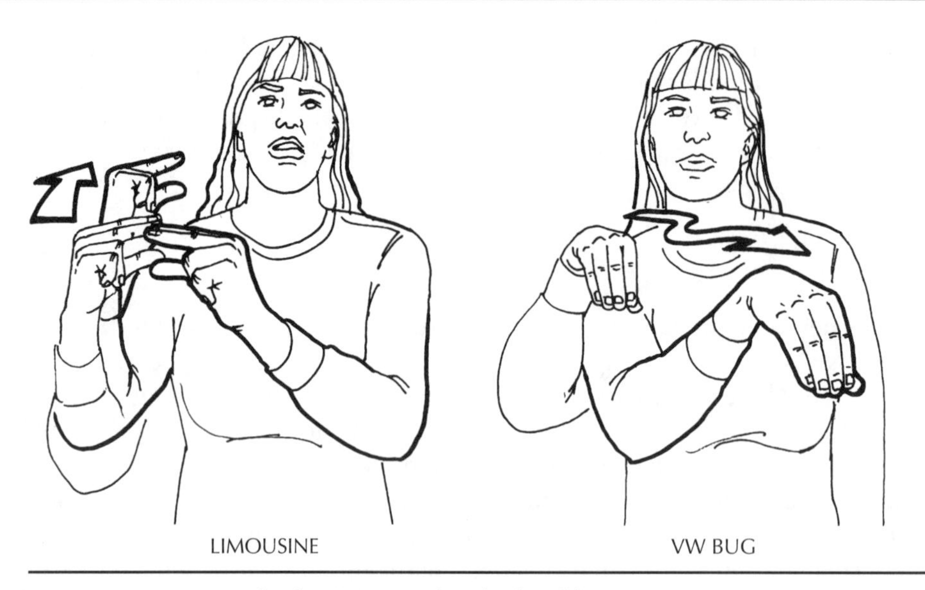

FIGURE 50. An example of variation in classifier handshapes.

nonmanual signal as well). This, then, shows gradation by changing some aspect of the sign structure, in this case, location and nonmanual signal.

This is also the case for lexical signs. For example, the ASL equivalent of "half-dead" might consist of producing the sign DEAD but producing the final hold in a location closer to the initial hold than where the final hold is produced in the citation form of the sign. Gradation, then, is not represented by adding a whole new sign, but rather by altering some feature of the already existing sign (see Figure 51).

In this regard, consider the ASL signs GOOD and BAD. In English, the words *good* and *bad* are antonyms, but their respective phonological forms are completely unrelated. The ASL signs GOOD and BAD are also antonyms, but unlike the English pairs, their phonological forms are clearly related—they share a hold-movement-hold structure, as well as handshape and location. The difference in meaning lies

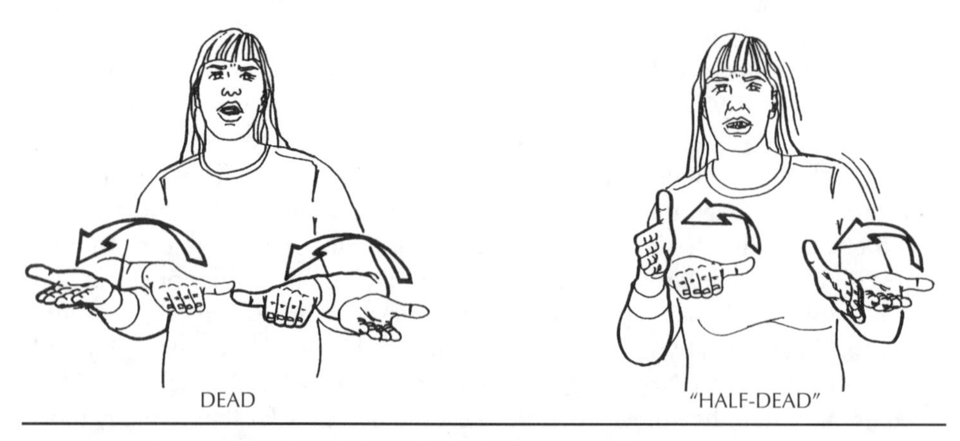

FIGURE 51. An example of gradation in lexical signs.

in the difference in the final palm orientation, up for GOOD and down for BAD. There are other pairs of signs like this in ASL, such as LIKE and DON'T-LIKE, WANT and DON'T-WANT, and KNOW and DON'T-KNOW, pairs that also represent opposition in meaning. It would appear that these antonyms are related by a morphological process because the change in the final palm orientation has the effect of changing the meaning of the sign. While it is not clear that this morphological process is productive, that is, that new pairs of antonyms are being created, there does seem to be a difference between these pairs of antonyms in ASL and pairs of antonyms in English.

Converseness

Another semantic relationship between signs or words is called *converseness*. It is similar to antonymy and is seen in pairs of signs like WIFE and HUSBAND. If A is the husband of B, then B is the wife of A; WIFE is said to be the *converse* of HUSBAND. Other examples in ASL are pairs of signs like TEACHER and STUDENT or AUNT and NIECE. As with antonymy, the English words *wife* and *husband* have no formal resemblance to each other. However, in ASL, it seems that many pairs of signs that exist in a converse relationship also resemble each other phonologically. For example, WIFE and HUSBAND are both compounds respectively resulting from the joining of WOMAN and MARRY and MAN and MARRY, and their form is very similar. Likewise TEACHER and STUDENT probably result from a process of affixation in ASL, whereby a form having its origin in a sign for PERSON is attached to verbs, in this case TEACH and STUDY. Likewise, AUNT and NIECE have the same structure and are produced in the same location with similar palm orientations; they differ only in handshape. So once again, it seems that in ASL, signs that have a semantic relationship may also share a phonological relationship.

Metaphor

The location feature of the ASL signs AUNT and NIECE brings us to another kind of meaning relationship between words and signs known as *metaphor*. A metaphor is generally defined as an extension of the use of a word or sign beyond its primary meaning to describe referents that are similar to the word or sign's primary referent. In English, for example, the word *head* (whose referent is "top part of an animal's body") is found in phrases such as *the head of the class* or *the head of the line*. In these phrases, the meaning of the word *head* has been extended to mean not only the top part of an animal but also the top part of other things.

In their book *Metaphors We Live By*, Lakoff and Johnson define three different kinds of metaphorical meaning: orientational, ontological, and structural. Orientational metaphors rely on spatial information to communicate the metaphor. For example, in many languages, the concept of *up* is related to positive meanings, while the concept of *down* is related to negative meanings. In English, this is seen in expressions such as *cheer up*, *lift one's spirits*, and *lighten up*, as opposed to *feeling down*, *what a downer*, and *being down and out*. Researchers such as Woll,

Wilbur, Boyes-Braem, Frishberg and Gough, and Wilcox have researched metaphor in ASL and have pointed out that ASL also makes use of orientational metaphors. We see this in signs such as DEPRESSED and TIRED, in which the movement of the sign is downward, as opposed to THRILLED and HAPPY, in which the movement is upward. Upward and downward movement in ASL signs can also carry a metaphor of presence or absence, as in the signs APPEAR and DISAPPEAR.

Sarah Taub (2000) has researched metaphor in sign languages and discovered that there is a strong link in sign languages between metaphor and iconicity. Metaphor is the use of one domain of experience, the concrete one, to describe or reason about the abstract domain, and the iconic system of classifier predicates in sign languages has movements, locations, and handshapes that can be used for the metaphorical description of abstract (nonphysical) situations. Taub explained that metaphor in sign languages involves *double mapping*—that is, there is a relationship between the concrete and the abstract, and a relationship between the concrete image chosen to represent the abstract and the forms (handshape, location, movement, palm orientation, nonmanual signals) of the language. The ASL metaphor ANALYSIS IS DIGGING shows this double mapping: DIGGING is a metaphor for the abstract concept of ANALYSIS, and this metaphor is represented in ASL by two oscillating Bent V handshapes moving downward in neutral space in a digging motion. This kind of double mapping for metaphor is widespread in sign languages.

Ontological metaphors treat abstract entities, states, and events as though they were objects. In English, for example, people talk about falling into or climbing out of a depression, as if the emotional state of depression were a tangible place. Likewise, they talk about working their way through a problem or being so busy that they feel like they are treading water or just barely keeping their heads above water. In all of these cases, abstract emotional states are represented as though they were actual locations or objects. ASL also has ontological metaphors. For example, a signer might express strong interest in a particular academic area by producing the sign that could be glossed as FALL-INTO, with a Bent V handshape moving sharply downwards (the base hand for this sign is a B handshape). The area of interest is thus portrayed as a location into which one can physically move. Likewise, during a discussion, a signer can indicate that a particular idea should be held until later in the discussion by producing a sign that consists of a C handshape closing to an S handshape. This sign strongly resembles the instrumental classifier handshape used to represent the holding of various real objects. In the case of its metaphorical use, the idea is being treated as an object that physically can be held.

Finally, structural metaphors treat one concept in terms of another more tangible concept. A common example from English is the expression "time is money," in which the abstract concept of time is treated as a tangible object that can be saved, wasted, spent, and so forth. Time is dealt with in a similar way in ASL, such that time that has run out may be represented with the same extent classifier handshape that is used to show a depletion of tangible substances like water or paper.

One kind of metaphor that occurs frequently in ASL has to do with handshapes. Frishberg and Gough make reference to "families of signs," that is, groups of signs that share the same handshape and that also share a portion of their meaning. For example, many signs produced with an Open 8 handshape have to do with emotions such as FEEL, EXCITE, DEPRESS, PITY, SENSITIVE, and SICK. Similarly, many signs having to do with negation and negative concepts are produced with an A handshape (e.g., NOT, DENY, REFUSE, BLAME, and SUFFER). Handshape would be considered metaphorical in these signs because while there is nothing inherently negative or emotional about the actual handshape, those handshapes have come to be associated with those meanings by users of the language. We cannot say that these handshapes are morphemes because they are not consistently associated with those meanings and handshape cannot be substituted in these signs to change the meaning of the sign in the way that it can in numeral incorporation, for example, where it is a morpheme. They are more like the examples of sound symbolism that we discussed for English, that is, groups of words like *lump*, *stump*, *hump*, and *bump*, that share the sounds *-ump*. We don't want to say that *-ump* is an English morpheme, but users of English would say that *-ump* symbolizes a meaning of heavy and thick.

This, then, is a brief introduction to some of the kinds of meaning relationships that may exist between signs. In the next unit, we will look at the semantics of sentences.

REFERENCES

Boyes-Braem, P. 1981. Distinctive features of the handshapes in ASL. Ph.D. diss., University of California, Berkeley.

Finegan, E., and Besnier, N. 1989. *Language: Its structure and use.* San Diego: Harcourt Brace Jovanovich.

Frishberg, N., and Gough, B. 1973. Morphology in ASL. Salk Institute for Biological Studies, La Jolla, Calif. Typescript.

Lakoff, G., and Johnson, M. 1980. *Metaphors we live by.* Chicago: University of Chicago Press.

Taub, S. 2000. *Language and the body: Iconicity and metaphor in American Sign Language.* Cambridge: Cambridge University Press.

Wilbur, R. 1990. Metaphors in ASL and English. In *SLR '87: Papers from the fourth international symposium on sign language research*, ed. W. H. Edmondson and F. Karlsson. Hamburg: Signum.

Wilcox, P. 1993. Metaphorical mapping in American Sign Language. Ph.D. diss., University of New Mexico.

Woll B. 1983. The Semantics of British Sign Language signs. In *Language in sign: An international perspective on sign language*, ed. J. Kyle and B. Woll. London: Croom Helm.

Homework Assignment 17

1. Find examples of ASL signs that illustrate the difference between *denotation* and *connotation.*

2. Find additional examples in ASL of the following meaning relationships:

   a. hyponymy

   b. part/whole relationships

   c. synonymy

   d. antonymy

   e. converseness

   f. metaphor

UNIT 2

The Meaning of Sentences

WORD ORDER AND SEMANTIC ROLES

We have seen some of the ways in which individual signs have meaning. We now turn our attention briefly to the ways in which sentences have meaning. First of all, we will see that it is not enough to simply say that the meaning of a sentence comes from just adding up the meanings of all the signs in the sentence. There is more to it than that. We can see this from the following two ASL sentences:

CAT CHASE DOG "The cat chases the dog."
DOG CHASE CAT "The dog chases the cat."

These two sentences have different meanings, and the difference in meaning comes from the *order* in which the signs appear. So, sign order or word order is an important factor in determining the meaning of a sentence. What is also important is the relative *semantic role* of each sign in a sentence. By *semantic role*, we mean how sentences show who did what to whom, with whom, or for whom. Examples of semantic roles are *agent*, *patient*, *experiencer*, *instrument*, and *cause*. For example, in the first sentence above, the cat is the agent, the "doer" of the action described by the verb, and the dog is the patient, the "receiver" of the cat's action. In the second sentence, the same signs have opposite semantic roles—the cat is now the patient, and the dog is now the agent, showing us how important knowing the semantic role of a sign is in understanding a sentence. In the sentence JOAN LIKE PIZZA, Joan is the *experiencer*. She is not really doing anything or receiving any action; she is experiencing some physical or psychological sensation. In the English sentence "The key opens the door," the semantic role of the word *key* is as *instrument*. The ASL version of that sentence might be as follows:

$\overline{\text{DOOR, KEY,}}^{\,t}$ CL: key-open-door

It is interesting to note that the semantic role of instrument is often realized in ASL with the classifier handshape of a classifier predicate, along with the sign for the instrument (see Figure 52).

FIGURE 52. An example of the semantic role *instrument.*

The final semantic role we will discuss is cause. In the English sentence "The tornado destroyed the trees," the semantic role of *tornado* is that of cause. The ASL version of this sentence (see Figure 53) might be as follows:

<u>   t</u>
TREES, TORNADO DESTROY

and, just as in the English sentence, the sign TORNADO would have the semantic role of cause.

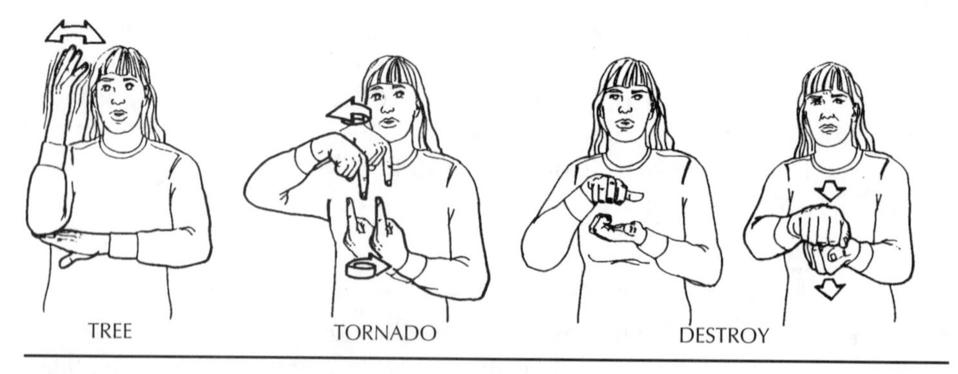

FIGURE 53. An example of the semantic role *cause.*

FUNCTION WORDS OR MORPHEMES

Another way in which we understand the meaning of sentences is through the *function words* or morphemes in a language. Function words or morphemes indicate *tense, aspect, reference*, and *deixis*.

In spoken languages, tense is often indicated by bound morphemes that attach to verbs, as in the English past tense marker *-ed*. Tense may also be indicated by separate lexical items such as *last night* or *next year*. As we saw in the chapter on time in ASL, tense in ASL is often indicated by separate signs in a sentence and possibly also by the position of the body and the location of the hands in the signing space. For example, a signer may lean slightly backward and to one side while talking about an event that happened earlier than another event being discussed. Other markers of tense may exist in ASL, but research in this area has just begun.

Aspect has to do with the manner in which the action of a verb is performed, as we saw in the unit on temporal aspect. While in spoken languages aspect may be indicated by bound morphemes or by separate lexical items, we saw that ASL aspect is often shown by altering the basic structure of the sign, as in the sign SIT-FOR-A-LONG-TIME as opposed to SIT, an M structure as opposed to an M H structure.

Reference provides information about the relationship between noun phrases and their referents. For example, the English sentences *A cat is on the porch* and *The cat is on the porch* mean different things, and the difference in meaning comes from the use of the deteminers *a* and *the*. The same holds true for ASL. The following sentences have different meanings:

MAN/DET SILLY "The man is silly."
MAN SILLY "A man is silly."

As we saw in the unit on pronouns and determiners, the determiner in ASL provides the meaning of "that specific man" as opposed to "any unspecified man" (see Figure 54).

FIGURE 54. An example of a determiner providing *reference*.

Deixis (which comes from the Greek verb *deiktikos* meaning "to point") marks the orientation or position of objects and events with respect to certain points of reference. For example, a teacher in a classroom asks the students "Do you have any questions about that?" while pointing to a problem on the blackboard. The pronoun *you* is considered an example of personal deixis (as are all personal pronouns) and refers to the students. The word *that* is an example of spatial deixis, and to understand it, the students must be able to see what it refers to (i.e., the problem on the board). A third kind of deixis, temporal deixis—the position or orientation of actions or events in time—is accomplished with separate lexical items or bound morphemes, such as the ones we discussed with relation to tense. Deixis is extremely complex for both spoken and signed languages, but it is easy to see that ASL has examples of all of the kinds of deixis mentioned (see Winston 1993 for examples). We see personal deixis in the personal pronoun system already discussed. When a signer mentions a place, a person, or an object during the course of a conversation and establishes it in space and then subsequently refers to that place, person, or object with an index finger or perhaps with eyegaze or both, that is an example of spatial deixis. And temporal deixis is done with separate lexical items and possibly body position and hand position, as we mentioned earlier.

CONTEXT

Even if we know the meaning of all the signs in a sentence and we can see what the semantic role of the signs is and can identify the function words or morphemes, sometimes that is still not enough to figure out the meaning of a sentence. Very often, the physical and social context in which the sentence is produced plays a central role in helping understand what the meaning is. It is important to know who is producing the sentence, what his or her relationship is to the person seeing or hearing the sentence, and where the sentence is being produced. For example, the English sentence "It's hot in here" may often be interpreted as a request for someone to open the window. There is nothing in the words themselves about a window or about opening a window. The sentence is simply a description of the condition of the room, but in many contexts it is seen as a request for action, and someone will get up and open a window. Given that there is nothing in the sentence itself that overtly mentions opening a window, that meaning must be coming from the situation or context in which the sentence is being produced. A similar sentence can be produced in ASL with similar results, so clearly context is important in understanding the meaning of ASL sentences as well.

The area of linguistics that investigates the role of context in understanding meaning is called *pragmatics*. In the Basic Concepts section of the text, we said that one thing that makes languages unique is that one sentence may have more than one meaning. What makes this possible is the role that the social and physical context plays in the meaning of the sentence. The example in that section is the ASL sentence

q
HOME YOU

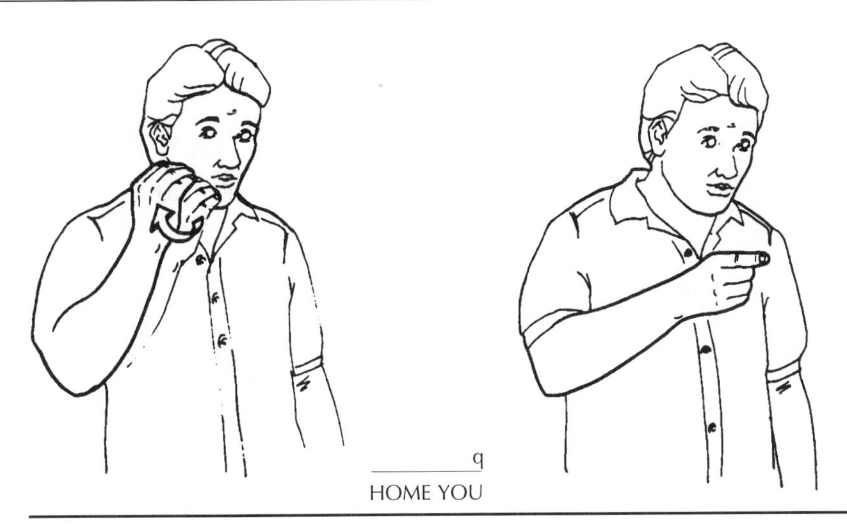

FIGURE 55. An example of the semantic role of *pragmatics*. The meaning of the sentence can vary depending on the context of the situation.

which may be simply a yes/no question with the function of requesting information (see Figure 55). However, it may also be a request for a ride home, even though there is no mention of a ride or of home, or it could also be a complaint by a boss to an employee who is leaving too early. Which meaning of the sentence is intended is in large part determined by the situation in which it is produced. We see, then, that what a sentence means is a lot more than just the sum of the signs or words produced.

REFERENCES

Finegan, E., and Besnier, N. 1989. *Language: Its structure and use.* San Diego: Harcourt Brace Jovanovich.

Jannedy, S., Poletto, R., and Weldon, T., eds. 1994. *Language files: Materials for an introduction to language and linguistics.* 6th ed. Columbus: Ohio State University Press.

Winston, E. A. 1993. Spatial mapping in comparative discourse frames in an American Sign Language lecture. Ph.D. diss., Georgetown University, Washington, DC.

Homework Assignment 18

1. Find an example of an ASL sentence in which word order changes the meaning of the sentence.

2. Find an example of an ASL sentence that can have different meanings depending on the context and explain what the different contexts are and what the different meanings of the sentence are.

PART SIX

LANGUAGE IN USE

UNIT 1

Variation and Historical Change

GOAL
To gain a basic understanding of sociolinguistic variation in ASL

SUPPLEMENTAL READINGS
Files 120 and 123 from *Language Files: Materials for an Introduction to Language,* by M. Crabtree and J. Powers (1991); pp. 389–393

"Analyzing Variation in Sign Languages: Theoretical and Methodological Issues," by Rob Hoopes, Mary Rose, Robert Bayley, Ceil Lucas, Alyssa Wulf, Karen Petronio, and Steven Collins (2000); pp. 394–415

"Sociolinguistic Aspects of the Black Deaf Community," by Anthony J. Aramburo (1989); pp. 416–428

When we study a language it is important not only to look at its structure (phonology, morphology, syntax, and semantics), but also how the language is used. Human beings use language every day in a variety of social settings and for a variety of reasons. Ralph Fasold (1984), a sociolinguist, pointed out that while we do use language to communicate information to each other, we also use language to define the social situation; in other words we use language to make our social and cultural identity clear, to show our group loyalties, to explain our relationships to other people, and to describe what kind of event we think we are involved in. Language, therefore, has different functions: it has communicative functions and it has social functions.

Dell Hymes, an anthropologist, introduced the concept of *communicative competence.* According to Hymes (1972), when someone knows a language, he or she knows how to use the forms of the language; knows the phonology, morphology, and syntax of the language; and knows how to use the language appropriately. This means the person knows how to enter or leave a conversation properly, what kind of language to use for a request or an apology, what kind of language is appropriate for different social situations, and so forth. When a user of a language is communicatively competent, he or she knows how to use language for both communicative and social functions.

Sociolinguistics is the study of the interrelationship of language and social structure. Sociolinguists study variation in language, contact between languages, language planning and policy, language attitudes, and the relationship between social interaction and language, including the structure of conversation. In this section, we will provide an introduction to three major areas of sociolinguistics—variation, discourse, and bilingualism and language contact.

VARIATION

Variation in language means that people have different ways of saying the same thing. The earliest studies of variation in language focused on *regional variation*. People in one geographic area may use a language differently from people in another geographic area, even though the language they are using has the same name. For example, in the United States, many regional differences are found in the vocabulary of spoken English. Some people use the word *sofa*, while others say *couch*, and still others say *davenport*; some people say *soda*, while others say *pop* or *coke* or *soft drink*; some people say *bag* while others say *sack* or *poke*; some people use the word *supper* while others use *dinner*, and so forth.

Regional differences can also be found in the phonological system of the language. Those differences may be referred to as *accents*. For example, someone from Boston may have a New England accent, while someone from Atlanta may have a southern accent. This simply means that certain sounds in the speaker's phonological system are consistently produced in a way that is different from the sounds in another speaker's phonological system. A speaker from Boston may say the *a* in the words *car* and *father* differently from a Chicagoan, and the Boston speaker may not produce the *r* in either word. There also may be some morphological and syntactical regional differences.

Variation is not limited to regional variation. Other kinds of variation include *social* variation, *ethnic* variation, *gender* variation, and *age* variation. For example, people from different socioeconomic groups within the same society may speak differently—differences have been described between working-class and middle-class speakers of American English. African American people may speak differently from white people, men may speak differently from women, and old people may speak differently from young people.

The same kind of variation exists in American Sign Language. We see variation at all levels of ASL structure: phonological variation, morphological variation, and lexical variation. Many examples of lexical variation have been documented. Ask a group of native ASL signers to show you their signs for PICNIC, BIRTHDAY, HALLOWEEN, EARLY, and SOON and you will see examples of regional variation (see Figure 56). Some of the variation exists because, in the past, deaf students attended the residential school in their region and did not have much contact with signers from other areas. Another reason for variation is that ASL was not formally taught or even recognized in the schools.

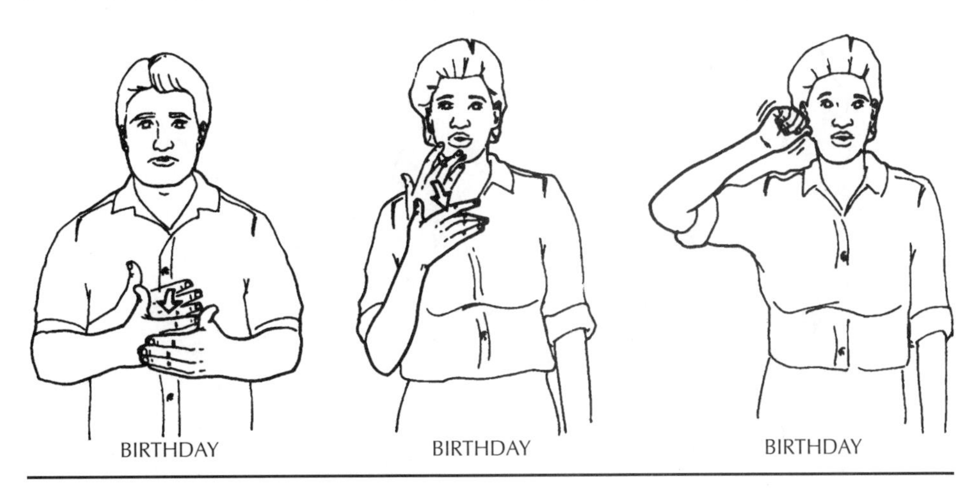

FIGURE 56. Regional variations of BIRTHDAY.

Despite the variations in ASL, it seems to be somewhat more standardized than other sign languages. LIS, for example, seems to have much more regional variation than ASL. This may be because when deaf education began in the United States, many teachers, both deaf and hearing, came to the American School for the Deaf in Hartford, Connecticut, from all over the country to learn Clerc's teaching method. They then returned to their schools. Many graduates of the school in Hartford established schools for the deaf in other parts of the country. As a result, both the teachers and the graduates took with them the ASL they had learned in Hartford. Not so in Italy, where there were few centralized schools and where only fairly recently the deaf communities in the different cities have begun to have contact. For a long time the many deaf communities were isolated from each other, each with its own sign language, and no attempt was made by school administrators to establish contact among students in schools for the deaf. The result is a lot of regional differences.

ASL also has ethnic variations. Anthony Aramburo has found that black signers and white signers use different signs for SCHOOL, BOSS, and FLIRT (see Figure 57). This variation is probably due to isolation and lack of contact between black and white deaf communities as a result of segregated education. Research on Ebonics in ASL is currently being done (Lewis 1997). Research has also been done on the sign language used by Navajo Indians of Arizona (Davis and Supalla, 1995) and on the Tactile ASL used by deaf-blind people (Collins and Petronio, 1998; Haas, Fleetwood, and Ernest, 1995). These studies have revealed some interesting variation patterns.

Signers also report gender variation, that is, differences between the way men and women sign, although this is an area that still needs to be researched. And there are also age differences, such that older signers may have ways of signing that differ from younger signers. Students often report forms of signs that they have seen used by older friends and relatives. This brings us to the issue of historical change.

FIGURE 57. Ethnic variations of SCHOOL.

As we said, variation means a different way of saying the same thing. Often, the same person will have different ways of saying the same thing and will make a choice depending on the situation. And often the different forms will stay in the language indefinitely. But many times, a change in an existing form will be introduced, or a whole new form will appear. The old form and the new form may coexist for a while, and then the old form may disappear. This process is called *historical change.*

Historical change in languages often takes place in the vocabulary and in the phonology, but some changes may happen in the morphology and syntax as well. An example from spoken languages is the evolution from Latin to the Romance languages (French, Italian, Spanish, Portuguese, and Romanian). The changes in Latin were the result of the passage of a great deal of time and social change. However, if we were able to visit what is now France in the year A.D. 800, we would see that older speakers in a given community on a given day in the marketplace spoke differently from speakers in the younger generation. For them at that moment in time, it would simply look like variation (i.e., "we have different ways of saying the same thing"). From our modern perspective, it looks like historical change. Gradual changes in all parts of the language took place over a very long period of time, such that modern French is completely different from the Latin that is its base.

Researchers such as Nancy Frishberg, James Woodward, Carol Erting, and Susan DeSantis have described historical change in ASL, and other researchers have described historical change in other sign languages. Many ASL signs bear a close resemblance to LSF signs because Clerc was a signer of LSF. We can see evidence of historical change from LSF to ASL. For example, signs such as CAT, COW, HORSE, and DEVIL that were produced with two hands in LSF are produced with one hand in ASL. Some signs that in LSF were produced on the elbow (HELP and GUIDE) are now produced on the passive hand in ASL.

Some changes have occurred as a result of assimilation, where the handshape of one hand has become like the handshape of the other. In an older form of the sign TOMATO, the dominant hand is a 1 handshape while the passive hand is an O handshape. Over time, the passive handshape has become a 1. We see this with other signs as well, such as LAST, BELIEVE, and HUSBAND. Sometimes the location feature of a sign changes with time, as in the sign WRONG, which in an older form was produced on the mouth and is now produced on the chin; or the sign FEEL, the location of which has moved from the left side of the chest to the middle. And while some signs have changed from being two-handed to one-handed, others such as DIE and JOURNEY have changed from being one-handed to two-handed. These are all examples of historical change in ASL.

One of the unique characteristics of language is that it changes over time, and the change is continual. We can see changes going on right now with the introduction of new terms for telephone, television, and computer technology. For example, the different signs that exist for COMPUTER reflect both regional differences and changes in technology. Similarly, the sign for changing the channels on a television, an iconic sign of a hand changing the channels on a television, is being replaced by a newer sign that is iconic of a remote control.

The older form of HOME was a compound consisting of the signs EAT and SLEEP. The handshape of SLEEP assimilated to the EAT handshape, and the location of EAT assimilated to the SLEEP location. The basic segmental structure is still M H M H. However, it is not uncommon now to see a form of the sign HOME that has the same handshape, but has the structure M M M H in *one* location. This sign looks like the handshape repeatedly tapping the same location on the lower cheek. As we said, language is always changing.

The most recent work on variation in ASL includes a five-year project done by the authors of this book with the participation of Robert Bayley, Mary Rose, Alyssa Wulf, Paul Dudis, Susan Schatz, and Laurie Sanheim (forthcoming). Beginning in 1994 we traveled to seven sites in the United States (Staunton, Va.; Frederick, Md.; Boston; New Orleans; Kansas City, Mo.; Fremont, Calif.; and Bellingham, Wash.) and videotaped 207 ASL users in everyday conversation. We are now analyzing the tapes to describe the phonological, morphosyntactic, and lexical variation that we observed. Phonological variation includes variation in signs made with a 1 handshape, variation in the sign DEAF (signed from ear to chin, from chin to ear, or as a single contact on the cheek), and variation in the location of signs such as THINK, KNOW, and SUPPOSE, which are produced on the forehead in citation form but can move down and be produced below the forehead.

In our analysis of phonological variation, we hypothesized that the variation observed in all three variables could be explained by phonological factors (that is, the characteristics of the location or handshape of the preceding or following signs). But when we analyzed almost 10,000 examples of the three variables (1,618 for DEAF, 2,862 for location signs, and 5,356 for 1 handshape signs), we found that while phonological variables do show some effect, the major factor in explaining the variation is the grammatical function of the sign. Specifically, DEAF can function as an adjective, noun, or predicate, and the noncitation forms (chin-to-ear or contact-cheek) are much more likely to be adjectives, while the citation form (ear-to-chin) is more likely to be a predicate. With location signs, verbs favor citation forms (at the forehead), while function words like prepositions favor the lower noncitation forms. First-person pronouns favor noncitation 1 handshapes (thumb open or all fingers open) second person is neutral, and third-person pronouns and content signs (nouns and verbs) favor citation forms (thumb and all fingers except index closed). We are also finding correlation with social factors. For example, with the sign DEAF, younger and older signers in general favor the chin-to-ear form, while middle-age signers favor the ear-to-chin form. Signers from Boston and Maryland strongly prefer the ear-to-chin form, while signers from the other areas are neutral or prefer the chin-to-ear form. And while older signers prefer the forehead level for the location signs, younger signers prefer the lower forms.

Morphosyntactic variation includes the dropping of the subject pronoun with verbs that usually require a subject, such as FEEL, KNOW, or LIKE. Our research focused on plain verbs, verbs that do not incorporate any information about the subject or object. Surprisingly, even though plain verbs do not contain subject information, they are more likely to occur without a signed pronoun than with one. Key factors in accounting for the variation are switch reference (whether the subject of the target verb is the same as the immediately preceding subject or different), the person and number of the pronoun (a first-person pronoun is more likely to be signed than other pronouns), and English influence (a pronoun is more likely to occur in a more English-like sentence). Older signers and women are more likely to produce pronoun subjects than leave them out.

Lexical variation involves asking signers what their sign for a list of concepts is, such as RABBIT, COMPUTER, AFRICA, and JAPAN. The signers in our study were asked to demonstrate 34 separate signs. We found a distinction between lexical innovation and phonological variation. For example, the new signs for AFRICA and JAPAN are lexical innovations and we see that these new signs have been adopted by all age groups in all seven regions. The old and new variants of signs like RABBIT (the old sign being produced at the forehead and the new one being made on the hands in neutral space) are used by all age groups, indicating that while there may be change in progress, it is not a completed change. If the change were completed, we would expect younger signers to use only the newer forms. This project shows that ASL, like other languages, has sociolinguistic variation, with both linguistic and social factors accounting for the variation.

REFERENCES

Collins, S., and Petronio, K. 1998. What happens in Tactile ASL? In *Pinky extension and eye gaze: Language use in Deaf communities*, ed. C. Lucas, 18–37. Sociolinguistics in Deaf Communities, vol. 4. Washington, DC: Gallaudet University Press.

Davis, J., and Supalla, S. 1995. A sociolinguistic description of sign language use in a Navajo family. In *Sociolinguistics in deaf communities*, ed. C. Lucas, 77–106. Washington, DC: Gallaudet University Press.

Fasold, R. 1984. *The sociolinguistics of society*. Oxford: Basil Blackwell.

Haas, C., E. Fleetwood, and M. Ernest. 1995. An analysis of ASL variation within deaf-blind interaction: Question forms, backchanneling, and turn-taking. In *Communication forum*, vol. 4, ed. L. Byers, J. Chaiken, and M. Mueller. Washington, DC: Gallaudet University School of Communication.

Hymes, D. 1972. On communicative competence. In *Sociolinguistics*, ed. J. Pride and J. Holmes, 269–293. Harmondsworth: Penguin.

Lewis, J. 1997. Ebonics in American Sign Language. Paper presented at Deaf Studies V, April, Gallaudet University.

Lucas, C., R. Bayley, and C. Valli, in collaboration with M. Rose, A. Wulf, P. Dudis, S. Schatz, and L. Sanheim. Forthcoming. *Sociolinguistic variation in American Sign Language*. Sociolinguistics in Deaf Communities, vol. 7. Washington, DC: Gallaudet University Press.

Homework Assignment 19

1. Find three examples of regional variation in ASL.

2. Find three examples of ethnic variation in ASL.

3. Find three examples of age variation in ASL.

4. There are at least two signs for TELEPHONE, an older form and a newer form. See if you can find some similar pairs of signs that reflect changes in technology.

5. Can you find any examples of differences between men's signing and women's signing? Look for signs that men use that women don't use or vice versa, or different ways that men and women produce the same sign.

UNIT 2

ASL Discourse

GOAL
To gain a basic understanding of ASL discourse

SUPPLEMENTAL READINGS
"Toward a Description of Register Variation in American Sign Language," by June Zimmer (1989); pp. 429–442

"Features of Discourse in an American Sign Language Lecture," by Cynthia B. Roy (1989); pp. 443–457

Throughout this textbook, we have seen that the different parts of ASL have internal structure. In the phonology section, we saw that signs have parts and that the parts are structured. In the morphology section, we looked at the smallest meaningful units of ASL and talked about how they are used to build new units in the language. In the section on syntax, we saw that ASL sentences are also structured; word order is not random, and nonmanual signals play a very important role in the construction of ASL sentences. So, we have seen that there is structure at each level of the language. But there is more to language than single isolated sentences. People talk to each other, they sign to each other, they write letters and novels and newspaper articles. These are all examples of the use of language, and the use of language involves using many sentences.

When people talk or sign or write, the language they use also has structure—words and sentences are not just thrown together in any order. In sociolinguistics, the term *discourse* is used to refer to any use of language that goes beyond the sentence. Discourse can refer to how language is organized in conversations, and it can also refer to how the sentences in a written text, such as a novel or a linguistics textbook, are organized. As we pointed out in Unit 1, language has social functions as well as communicative functions. Language is a kind of social behavior. The analysis of discourse has a lot to do with the social functions of language. In this unit, we will provide a brief introduction to discourse analysis and look at some examples of the structure of discourse in ASL.

As explained by the sociolinguist Hudson (1980), the study of discourse involves a number of different areas, four of which we will discuss here—the functions of language, language as skilled work, the norms and structure of language use, and language as a signal of social identity.

THE FUNCTIONS OF LANGUAGE

Language has social functions as well as communicative functions. We don't always use language just to communicate information. Often, language is used to establish or reinforce social relations or to control the behavior of other people. For example, imagine that you are walking down the street and you see an acquaintance—not someone you know well, not a friend, but someone you recognize—coming towards you. You don't really want to stop and chat, so you keep walking, but as you walk by, you make eye contact and either nod your head or sign a greeting. You may even sign the signs WHAT'S UP and FINE or nod your head as a greeting as you walk by, and the other person may sign the same signs or nod at the same time. The function of language in this situation is not only to exchange information but also to let the other person know that you see him and that you are not ignoring him.

To get a better understanding of the social functions of language, imagine how strange it would be to walk by an acquaintance and not sign anything! If someone you knew walked by you without a greeting, you might say that person was being rude or impolite. That leads us to ask what politeness means. In part, it means recognizing the existence of another person, and the way we accomplish that recognition is with language.

We use language for other social functions as well, such as apologizing, warning, threatening, commanding, and requesting. All of these functions go beyond the purely communicative function of telling someone something she does not already know. In fact, you may sometimes tell someone something she *does* already know, as a way of controlling behavior. For example, telling someone "It's cold in here," may have the function of requesting that the person close the window.

LANGUAGE AS SKILLED WORK

It is possible to be a good or a not-so-good user of a language. Some people are very skilled at getting what they want through the use of language, and others are not. And skilled language use tends to be respected in many cultures. In the American Deaf community, skilled storytellers and poets are recognized and respected, and the recognition and respect come precisely from their skill in the use of ASL.

It is not uncommon at social gatherings and parties for people to play ABC or number games in ASL, with respect shown for those who do it well.

THE NORMS AND STRUCTURE OF LANGUAGE USE

Discourse has internal structure and is governed by norms. By norms, we mean how many people can sign at once, how much one person should sign, what can be signed about, and so forth. It is easy to see the norms by looking at examples of when they are violated. For example, in a conversation, only one person signs at a time. If another person begins signing before the first has indicated that he is finished, the second person will be said to have interrupted. The first person may then indicate that he is not finished yet and that the other person should wait his turn. The fact that the second person's behavior is labeled an interruption shows that the norm is "one person signs at a time and when it is clear that she is finished, another person may begin."

Another norm governs what is appropriate behavior if you have to walk between two people who are signing to each other. In spoken language conversations, it is polite to say "excuse me" as you pass. That is, it is appropriate to use language to recognize the fact that you are temporarily in the way. However, in the deaf community, it is perfectly acceptable and polite to walk between two people having an ASL conversation without signing EXCUSE-ME. Not only is it polite, but to stop and sign EXCUSE-ME or to duck one's head or bend over as one walks by may even be unacceptable because it will almost always bring the conversation to a halt and cause an interruption. This is a norm that differs from the norms for spoken language conversations.

You probably know someone who has been described as being a nice person but who talks too much. The unspoken meaning is that the person always says more than is necessary or talks about things that he or she shouldn't. The norms here concern quantity and quality of discourse—how much and about what we should talk. Finally, norms dictate what topics can be discussed in which settings. Not all topics are considered appropriate for all settings. There seems to be a norm that says some topics are acceptable in public settings, and others are acceptable in private settings. Language users have ways of communicating to each other that the norm is not being followed, that what is being discussed should be discussed at another time. We also have ways of talking about private issues in public places (e.g., whispering), and we see examples of it in ASL, as well. Signers may use very reduced forms of signs or sign with one hand in a very reduced signing space. Unfortunately there is not much research on this aspect of ASL discourse as yet.

Internal Structure

Discourse has internal structure. This structure comes about in different ways. One way is *turn-taking*. Since everyone in a conversation does not sign at once, signers have different ways to get and keep a turn in conversation. For example, when a person is signing and then comes to the end of a thought, the person may pause. If another person in the conversation *self-selects*, that person will take the next turn. If the second person does not self-select, the first person may continue signing or the conversation may end. Another way to get a turn occurs when the first person asks the second person a question, thereby giving the next turn to the second person.

It is important to notice that turn-taking varies depending on the social setting. In a regular conversation, it is usual for conversational partners to self-select, unless one person asks a question of another person. In a classroom, however, it is generally the teacher's responsibility to select who gets the next turn; students generally don't self-select. In a courtroom, it is customary that an attorney asks questions of the witness on the stand and the witness answers; witnesses do not usually ask questions.

We also have ways of keeping a turn in conversation once we have gotten it. You will notice in sign conversations that often, if someone tries to interrupt a signer, the signer will lower or avert his eyes and perhaps hold up an index finger or an open hand to indicate that he is not done yet. In fact, as Baker (1977) and other researchers have found, eye gaze is very important in structuring conversations in ASL.

Discourse also may be structured by *topic*. That is, when a topic is introduced, it controls the flow of a conversation. We may stay on the topic, we may go from general to specific aspects of the topic, we may introduce issues related to the topic, and we may stray from the topic or introduce a new topic. Language has ways of showing how we are dealing with a topic. For example, speakers of English may say "On a related topic . . ." or "I don't mean to change the subject, but . . . ," both as ways of informing others that a change is taking place.

We see examples of structure by topic in ASL. Roy (1989, see p. 397) looked at the structure of a high school science lecture and saw that the teacher used the signs NOW and NOW-THAT to structure his talk. The talk was divided into very clear episodes, and the transitions between the episodes were marked with these signs. In this way, the students watching the lecture were easily able to follow the presentation of the topic and the subtopics. Roy also found that one feature of the lecture that made it very interesting for the students was *constructed dialogue*. Constructed dialogue is used in conversations to tell someone about a conversation that has already taken place—"He said . . . ," "Then I said . . . ," etc. During the constructed dialogue, the signer usually shifts her body and her eye gaze, so that it is perfectly clear when she is talking and when the other person is talking. Signers may even report a conversation between two other people and take the role of each by shifting the body and eye gaze.

Hudson suggested that discourse may also be structured by what he calls *encyclopedic knowledge*. That is, the knowledge about a topic that one person brings to a conversation may be very different from the knowledge that another person brings to the conversation. For example, if you are explaining ASL structure to someone who has no knowledge of it, you will go into much greater detail and have longer turns than if you are explaining it to someone who shares your knowledge. What we know and what we think the other person knows structures our conversations.

Register Variation

The structure of discourse may differ depending on the setting, that is, where and when a conversation takes place. This is known as *register variation*. Register, in this case, means "language appropriate for a certain occasion." This has traditionally been a very difficult area to describe in any language, but a fairly clear example can be seen by comparing the signs used in *informal* and *formal* settings. In informal settings, many two-handed signs may be signed with one hand (COFFEE, TEA, VOTE, PEOPLE, etc.; see Figure 58). In many pairs of signs that have the same meaning,

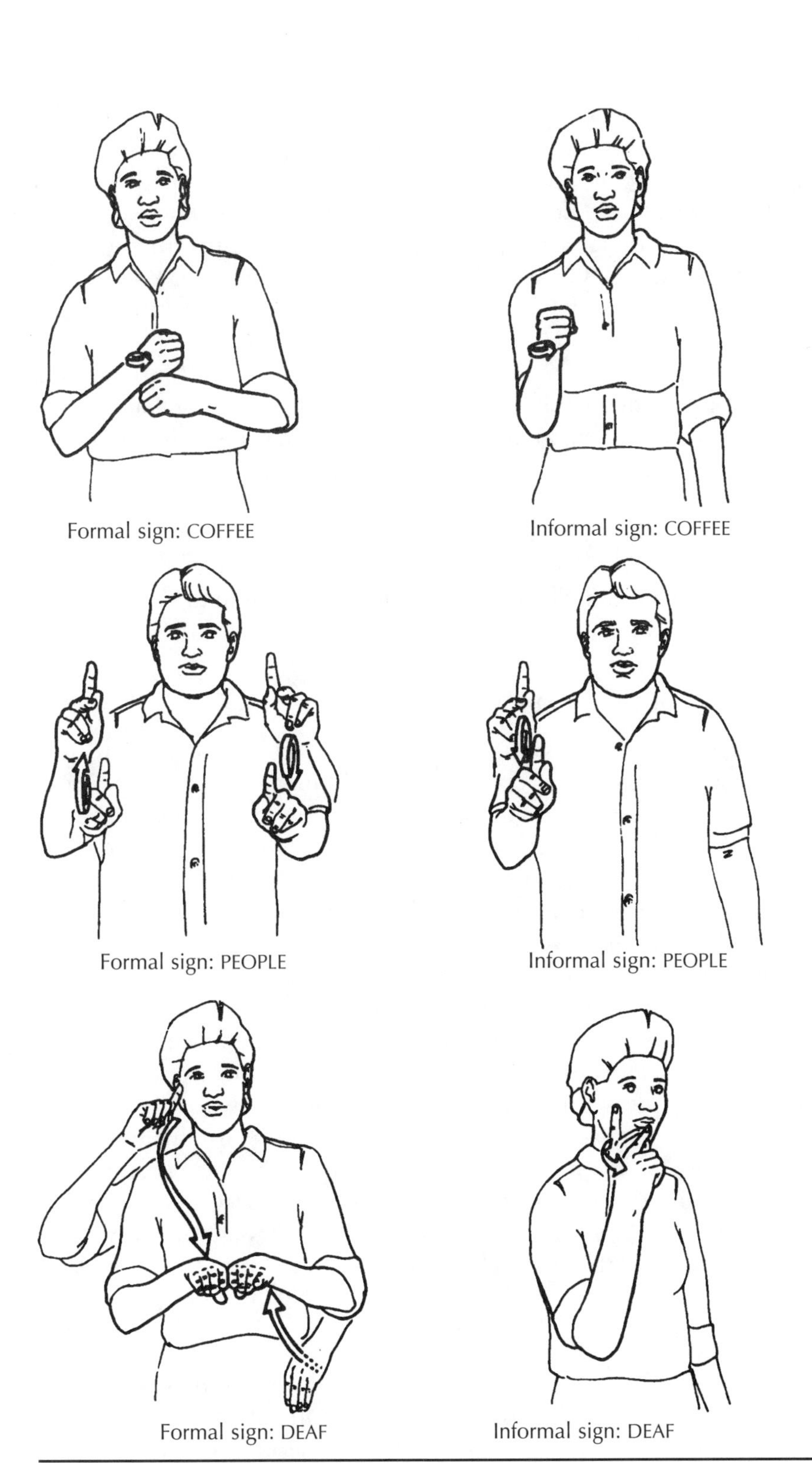

FIGURE 58. Examples of register variation.

one sign is used in formal settings, and the other sign is used in informal settings. The sign used in informal settings would be totally unacceptable in formal settings. For example, this is true of the two-handed form of DEAF, which is used in formal settings, and the form of DEAF produced at the ear location.

The location of signs may vary depending on the social setting. In formal settings, the sign KNOW may be made on the forehead, while it may be made on the cheek or in the space in front of the signer in informal settings, or it may be a wiggle of the nose.

Zimmer (1989, see p. 380) researched register variation in ASL. She compared one person's signing production in a formal lecture, in a television interview, and in an informal conversation, and found evidence of register variation in ASL. For example, she found that signs used in the informal setting did not occur in the formal setting, such as PEA-BRAIN, WHAT'S-UP, or KISS-FIST ("adore"). She found many rhetorical questions in the lecture, but none in the informal and television interview settings. She also found that the signing space in the lecture was much larger than in the other two settings. She found more topicalization in the informal setting than in the formal one.

LANGUAGE AS A SIGNAL OF SOCIAL IDENTITY

Finally, language may be used as a signal of social identity. A good example from English is the use of first names as opposed to a title with a last name. Do we call someone we have just met "Dr. Wilson" or "John"? And if we start out calling someone "Dr. Wilson," how do we know that it is acceptable to start calling that person by his first name? The use of a first name or of a title with a last name indicates the social identity of both the speaker and the person being spoken to. It shows what the social relationship between the two people is.

If you have studied Spanish, French, Italian, German, or other languages, you know that many languages have very complex ways of showing social relationships with pronouns. These languages have pronouns for formal situations and pronouns for informal situations. The pronouns used by a boss and an employee may be different from those used between friends. Not very much is known about how ASL or other sign languages signal social identity, but this is a very fruitful area for future research. Think about your own use of ASL: Do you use first names and names with titles in your conversations, as spoken languages do? How do you signal that you are a student and that you are talking to a boss or a professor? Do you sign differently with a good friend than with a teacher?

NEW AREAS OF RESEARCH

In recent years, the analysis of ASL discourse has focused on a variety of areas, including the use of nonmanual signals such as eye gaze and mouthing (Bahan and Supalla 1995; Bridges and Metzger 1996) and the use of space for reference (Emmorey, 1999 [see pp. 318–346]; Emmorey and Reilly, 1995; Winston, 1993, 1999; van Hoek, 1996). Studies also include the analysis of parent-child discourse

(Volterra and Erting 1994) and interpreted discourse (Roy 1993; Metzger 1995). Research about space and gesturing in ASL will provide important information about spoken language discourse as well.

REFERENCES

Bahan, B., and S. Supalla. 1995. Line segmentation and narrative structure: A study of eyegaze behavior in American Sign Language. In *Language, gesture, and space*, ed. K. Emmorey and J. Reilly. Hillsdale, NJ: Lawrence Erlbaum.

Baker, C. 1977. Regulators and turn-taking in American Sign Language discourse. In *On the other hand: New perspectives on American Sign Language*, ed. L. Friedman. New York: Academic Press.

Bridges, B., and M. Metzger. 1996. *DEAF TEND YOUR: Non-manual signals in American Sign Language*. Salem, OR: Sign Enhancers.

Emmorey, K. 1999. The confluence of space and language in signed languages. In *Language and space*, ed. P. Bloom, M. A. Peterson, L. Nadel, and M. F. Garrett, pp. 171–205. Cambridge, MA: MIT Press.

Emmorey, K., and J. Reilly. 1995. *Language, gesture, and space*. Hillsdale, NJ: Lawrence Erlbaum.

Hudson, R. A. 1980. *Sociolinguistics*. Cambridge: Cambridge University Press.

Metzger, M. 1995. The paradox of neutrality: A comparison of interpreters' goals with the realities of interactive discourse. Ph.D. diss., Georgetown University.

Roy, C. 1993. A sociolinguistic analysis of turn-taking in an interpreted event. *Multilingua*.

Winston, E. A. 1993. Spatial mapping in comparative discourse frames in an ASL lecture. Ph.D. diss., Georgetown University.

———., ed. 1999. *Storytelling and conversation: Discourse in Deaf communities*. Sociolinguistics in Deaf Communities, vol. 5. Washington, DC: Gallaudet University Press.

van Hoek, K. 1996. Conceptual locations for reference in American Sign Language. In *Spaces, worlds, and grammar*, ed. G. Fauconnier and E. Sweetser, 334–350. Chicago: University of Chicago Press.

Volterra, V., and C. Erting, eds. 1994. *From gesture to language in hearing and deaf children*. Washington, DC: Gallaudet University Press.

Homework Assignment 20

1. You are walking along and you see a group of your friends talking. You want to join the conversation. Think about and describe how you enter the group and how you get a turn to talk. What signs do you use? What about eye gaze? What is the correct way to enter a conversation and what is the "wrong" way?

2. What do you do in an ASL conversation when you want to change the topic? What signs do you use? Is there a particular way to change the subject?

3. Make a list of five signs that are signed differently in formal and informal situations, and describe how they differ. For example, KNOW may differ depending on the setting.

UNIT 3

Bilingualism and Language Contact

GOAL

To gain a basic understanding of bilingualism and language contact, especially as they relate to the deaf community

SUPPLEMENTAL READING

"Language Contact in the American Deaf Community," by Ceil Lucas and Clayton Valli (1989); pp. 458–480

Bilingualism and contact between languages is another important area of sociolinguistics. François Grosjean, who has done research on bilingualism, has stated that "bilingualism is present in practically every country of the world, in all classes of society, in all age groups; in fact, it has been estimated that half of the world's population is bilingual" (1982:vii). W. F. Mackey, another researcher, observed that "bilingualism, far from being exceptional, is a problem which affects the majority of the world's population" (1967:11). Obviously, bilingualism is an issue that is of interest to deaf people all over the world, for two reasons:

1. It is almost impossible for members of a deaf community not to have contact with the majority language of the country in which they live. In fact, most often they have been forced to learn that language in its spoken and written form while use of their natural sign has been forbidden. Deaf people almost always live in a situation of bilingualism and language contact.
2. Most of the research on bilingualism and language contact in the deaf community has focused on contact between the spoken language of the community at large and the natural sign language of the deaf community. However, the opportunity for language contact between natural sign languages has been increasing as the members of different deaf communities around the world begin to interact with each other. The results of this language contact are very interesting and deserve a lot of research attention.

THE REASONS FOR BILINGUALISM

Bilingual situations happen for many reasons. One main reason is that individuals or groups of people who speak one language move to an area where another language is spoken. This can happen as the result of military invasions or colonization. For example, English and French are spoken in many countries of the world as the result of colonization; the Romans invaded Britain many centuries ago and brought Latin with them; and Spain colonized South America beginning in the fifteenth century and brought Spanish.

People also move for social or economic reasons. In Europe, many "guest workers" have moved from Italy and Turkey to Germany and Sweden to find work, and have brought their native languages with them. Following the end of the war in Vietnam, many people from Southeast Asia came to the United States, bringing with them languages such as Cambodian, Hmong, and Vietnamese. Recently, many Soviet citizens have emigrated to Israel, bringing Russian with them. Some people move for reasons of trade and commerce. One of the earliest examples would be the Portuguese-speaking sailors who traveled to West Africa in the sixteenth century, coming in contact with different African languages.

Bilingual situations also come about through nationalism and political federalism. This has happened in many countries upon gaining independence from the European nations that colonized them. The newly independent nation chooses a national language to be used for education, government, newspapers, and so forth. A bilingual situation comes about because many people learn the national language but also want to keep their native language. Countries where this has happened include India and Nigeria.

Education and culture can also result in bilingualism. For example, the language of education in Europe during the Middle Ages was Latin, and educated people knew both their native language (e.g., French, Italian, or Spanish) as well as Latin. For many years before the revolution in Russia, the language of education and culture was French, and most educated people knew both Russian and French.

Urbanization and intermarriage can also result in bilingualism. When people from the country move to the city to find work, they may have to learn the language of the city. In Guatemala, for example, many people who live in the country speak one of twenty-two different Indian languages. If they move to a city or a big town to find work, they may have to learn Spanish, the official language of the country. Likewise, a speaker of one language may marry a speaker of another language, and they may learn each other's language.

In a deaf community, bilingualism comes about in different ways. In the American Deaf community, people who have Deaf parents learn ASL as their native language and English as a second language both from their parents and in school. However, for many years teachers and deaf students were not permitted to use ASL in classrooms. The language emphasis was either spoken English or some form of what we call sign-supported speech, that is, spoken English with signs added. Many deaf children have learned ASL from their peers in residential schools. Still other children have learned to sign from the interpreter provided to them in mainstream programs. Some deaf children do become bilingual in ASL and some form of English, but most deaf people do not become bilingual until they are adolescents or adults.

Maintained Bilingualism

When two languages happen to be used in the same location, they may both stay, or one of them may gradually disappear. The situation where they both stay is called *maintained bilingualism*. In one case, two separate monolingual communities can exist close together with some contact, as with French and English in the province of Quebec in Canada. In this situation, not everyone speaks both languages. Maintained bilingualism may also mean that everyone is bilingual and that the languages serve different purposes in the community. In Paraguay, for example, two languages are used—Spanish and Guaraní, an indigenous language. Almost everyone speaks both. They use Spanish for official purposes, such as school and government, and use Guaraní at home and among friends. The situation in the American Deaf community is generally one of maintained bilingualism. Most deaf people know some form of English and ASL.

Sometimes, bilingual situations result in a return to monolingualism. The second language may disappear, and the first may stay as it did following the Germanic invasions in Italy many centuries ago when the Germanic languages disappeared and Latin stayed. In other cases, the first language may disappear, and the second may stay. This has happened in the American West with many Native American languages that now have given way to English. One final situation may occur as a result of bilingualism: a new system may evolve through the processes of pidginization and creolization. The social conditions that usually accompany the emergence of pidgins and creoles are very special. Many people have suggested that there is a kind of pidgin in the American Deaf community, but we disagree with this perspective.

LANGUAGE CONTACT

A great deal of research has been done on what happens when two or more spoken languages are in contact with each other. We will focus on the contact between two sign languages and on the contact between a sign language and a spoken language.

Lexical Borrowing

When one language borrows a lexical item—a word or a sign—from another language and incorporates it into its system, this is called *lexical borrowing*. Examples of lexical borrowing in American English include the Italian words *pizza* and *spaghetti* and the French word *bouquet*. Generally, the form of the word or the sign changes as it becomes a part of the borrowing language's system. For example, the words *pizza* and *spaghetti* sound very different in American English than they do in Italian because they have become part of the American English system. Sign languages also borrow from each other. In recent years, for example, the ASL signs for many countries (AUSTRALIA, ITALY, JAPAN, and CHINA, etc.) have been replaced with the signs for those countries used by the native signers of the countries.

Code-Switching

Code-switching happens when a bilingual person is using one language and then switches to another language. The switch may be just one sign or it can be a part of a sentence, a whole sentence, or a whole paragraph. This might happen, for example, if a native signer of LIS switched for part of a sentence to ASL, and then switched back to LIS. Generally with code-switching, the forms do not change; they are not incorporated into the other language.

Foreigner Talk

Foreigner talk may occur when the user of one sign language (Signer A) is signing with the user of another sign language (Signer B). Suppose Signer B is trying to learn Signer A's sign language or does not know it well. Signer A may simplify her language so that Signer B will understand. She does not include signs from other languages; she just simplifies her own language for the foreigner.

Interference

Interference may happen when a bilingual person unconsciously uses parts of one language in another language. The signer may use a handshape or a movement that is not part of the language he is using, simply by accident.

Pidgins, Creoles, and Mixed Systems

Theoretically, contact between two sign languages can result in pidgins, creoles, and mixed systems. Researchers disagree as to what the words *pidgin* and *creole* mean, but there does seem to be some agreement that the conditions under which they occur are special. Usually a pidgin is the result of language contact between the adult users of mutually unintelligible languages. The language contact occurs for very specific purposes, like trade. These adult users are usually not trying to learn each other's language, but rather a third language that will help them improve their social and economic status. Often, they are removed from the situation in which they can continue to be exposed to their first language. They also may have restricted access to the language they are trying to learn and may end up learning it from each other. This was the sociolinguistic situation during the slave trade in West Africa and the West Indies, when many pidgins emerged.

The pidgins that emerge from these situations seem to share many linguistic features, including a greatly reduced morphology and syntax. Many linguists agree that when children are born in these situations and learn the pidgin as their native language, they begin to change it and make it more complex. The result is what linguists call a *creole*. Although such a situation has not yet been observed, it is possible to imagine a situation like this in the American Deaf community: Two signers of different sign languages are in contact and are trying to learn ASL, but basically only have access to ASL through each other; they are also removed from their native sign languages. The outcome of their interaction might look like what linguists have called pidgins. A final possibility is what linguists called a *mixed system,* a language resulting from language contact that combines elements of both languages.

LANGUAGE CONTACT BETWEEN SIGNED AND SPOKEN LANGUAGES

When language contact occurs between a sign language and spoken language, we make a further distinction between *unique phenomena* and *following spoken language criteria literally* (see Figure 59). Following spoken language criteria literally means following the rules of a language exactly. For example, when a signer code-switches from ASL to English, the signer *literally* stops signing ASL and begins speaking English, or vice versa. This can occur when a deaf person is signing ASL with a bilingual hearing person and then puts down her hand and speaks an English word, maybe for emphasis; or when a hearing bilingual is speaking English to another hearing bilingual and then stops speaking and uses an ASL sign.

Sign and spoken language may also borrow from each other, following the literal definition for borrowing. For example, the ASL signs BOY⌒FRIEND, GIRL⌒FRIEND, HOME⌒WORK, HOME⌒SICK, and BLACK⌒BOARD are all examples of English compounds that have been borrowed into ASL. Conversely, hearing bilinguals may take the mouth configuration from an ASL sign and turn it into an English word. For example, the mouth configuration that is part of the classifier predicate meaning "large pile of papers" or "thick book" can be glossed as "cha." We have heard this used by hearing students in a sentence such as "I have cha homework."

Unique phenomena are phenomena that seem to occur only as a result of the contact between a sign language and a spoken language. Fingerspelling, for example, is unique. As we pointed out earlier, fingerspelling is a representation with

Contact Between Two Sign Languages	*Contact Between a Sign Language and Spoken Language*	
Results in:	Results in:	
	Following spoken language criteria literally:	Unique phenomena:
Lexical borrowing	Code-switching	Fingerspelling
Code-switching	Lexical borrowing	Fingerspelling/Sign combination
Foreigner talk		Mouthing
Interference		Code-switching
Pidgins, creoles, and mixed systems		Contact signing (code-mixing)

FIGURE 59. Outcomes of language contact.

ASL forms of the orthographic system of English. Some researchers have said that fingerspelling is an example of borrowing, but borrowing is a relationship between two *phonologies*, be they signed or spoken. We have seen examples of borrowing between two sign languages. But fingerspelling is a relationship between the *phonology* of a sign language and the *orthography* of a spoken language, and the forms are always part of the sign language. Sometimes signers produce combinations of fingerspelling and signing, as in the sign LIFE#STYLE or the phrase #TAKE-CARE-OF.

Another unique phenomenon is *mouthing* of English words, distinct from the mouth configurations that are part of ASL signs. Davis (1989) discussed the difference between full English mouthing, where the word is essentially pronounced without voice, and reduced mouthing, where the word is not fully pronounced. Davis also described *lexicalized mouthing*, such as the mouth configurations in the signs FINISH or HAVE, which clearly derive from the English pronunciation of those words but have become part of the ASL signs.

A fourth unique phenomenon is the code-switching that may occur between ASL and one of the invented systems for coding English manually, such as SEE 1 or SEE 2. We describe this as a unique phenomenon and not as contact between two sign languages since these codes are not natural sign languages and are heavily influenced by the structure of spoken languages. We can imagine a situation, for example, in which a signer might switch from ASL to SEE 1 to represent a quote in English.

Contact signing is also a unique phenomenon. Contact signing results from the contact between English and ASL and has features of both. This is what has traditionally been called Pidgin Sign English (PSE) in the American Deaf community. We have done a lot of research on this kind of signing. We don't use the term *pidgin* because this kind of signing does not seem to have the linguistic features of what linguists call pidgins, and the social situations in which contact signing is used are not like the ones in which spoken language pidgins come about, as we explained earlier. We have seen contact signing being used not only by deaf people with hearing people, but also by deaf people with other deaf people. Its linguistic features include English word order, the use of prepositions, constructions with *that*, English expressions, and mouthing of English words, as well as ASL nonmanual signals, body and eye gaze shifting, and ASL use of space. It may also include the other unique phenomena we have mentioned (i.e., fingerspelling and combinations of fingerspelling and signs).

One important thing to keep in mind about contact signing is the wide variety of the language backgrounds of the people in contact situations. Everyone is unique, and so what happens in each contact situation will be unique. The contact signing produced by a hearing bilingual who is a native English speaker will be different from the contact signing produced by a deaf bilingual who is a native ASL signer. Their contact signing may share some of the same features, but it may not be identical in its structure. It is also possible for signers to switch during a conversation from ASL to contact signing or from contact signing to ASL. Again, we consider this to be unique, as contact signing itself is the result of contact between English and ASL.

REFERENCES

Davis, J. 1989. Distinguishing language contact phenomena in ASL interpretation. In *The sociolinguistics of the deaf community*, ed. C. Lucas, 85–102. San Diego: Academic Press.

Grosjean, F. 1982. *Life with two languages: An introduction to bilingualism.* Cambridge, MA: Harvard University Press.

Lucas, C., and Valli, C. 1992. *Language contact in the American deaf community.* San Diego: Academic Press.

Mackey, W. F. 1967. *Bilingualism as a world problem/Le bilinguisme: phenomène mondial.* Montreal: Harvest House.

UNIT 4

Language as Art

Goal
To gain a basic understanding of the different artistic forms in ASL

ASL is not used only for everyday communication. Artistic forms such as storytelling (which includes A-to-Z stories, numerical stories, and classifier stories), percussion signing, drama, comedy, and poetry have long existed in the Deaf community. The artistic forms of ASL have played an important role in the transmission of culture and history from generation to generation of Deaf people. The artistic forms of ASL are often quite distinct in their structure. For example, storytelling, a popular art form among Deaf people, demonstrates a complex structure that includes the extensive use of formulaic elements.

STORYTELLING

Storytelling is a fundamental part of Deaf culture. As with spoken language stories, ASL stories can be fables, personal experiences, anecdotes, or legends. Ben Bahan's "Bird of a Different Feather" (1992) is an excellent example of a fable. It tells the story of a singing bird who lives in the world of eagles and struggles to live up to their expectations. It very much applies to Deaf people's common experience of being raised with hearing people's expectations. "For a Decent Living" by Sam Supalla (1992) is a good example of a legend about a Deaf young man's dramatic fate. Like many other anecdotes and personal stories about funny experiences with house parents and teachers at residential schools, it also contains "paving the way" experiences (situations in which the Deaf hero of the story paves the way for other Deaf people through his pioneering experience).

A-to-Z Stories

A-to-Z stories (also called ABC stories) have been passed down through the generations dating back to the nineteenth century. In an A-to-Z story each sign represents one of the twenty-six handshapes in the manual alphabet, from A to Z. The stories cover a wide range of topics, including an operation, a haunted house, a romantic couple, a car race, and a basketball game. The transition from A to Z must be very smooth, as in a regular story. A-to-Z stories are not easy to translate into English since their meaning depends on the visual effect created by the alphabet handshapes. The following example illustrates a classic A-to-Z story about a car race:

Handshape	Equivalence
A	A driver gripping the steering wheel;
B	the back of the race car being raised, still not moving forward;
C	lights being flashed from top to bottom real fast;
D	the front of the race car being raised up as it is spinning;
E	the sound effect for the screeching tires, EEEEEEEEEE;
F	the audience's eyes following the race car that zooms off;

And the story continues until it ends with the Z handshape. Some very creative stories can also be told from Z to A!

Numerical Stories

Numerical stories are similar in form to A-to-Z stories. Each sign includes a handshape that represents a number from 1 to 15 or higher. A clever short, sharp, slap story, "Got it?!", starts with the sign for "hey you" made with a 1 handshape, followed by LOOK-AT-ME with the 2 handshape, TERRIBLY-LOUSY with the 3 handshape, and continues up to 11 where it ends with GOT-IT?! After several repetitions, the audience members finally understand what the narrator was trying to tell them about the hidden numbers and they nod, "Got it!" Stories can also be created with A-to-Z handshapes and numerical handshapes together.

Classifier Stories

The classifier story is a very rich, creative art form. The story is told exclusively with classifier predicates (see unit 7 in part 3). One of the many classic classifier predicate stories is about a golf ball. In this story the storyteller's head becomes a golf ball. It creates a point of view as it is put on a tee and watches a club approach several times before it is hit. After the ball is hit, it flies high over the trees, and then it descends and lands on the ground, bounces, rolls slowly, and finally stops. It is hit again, rolls toward the cup, and circles the rim of the cup before going down into the hole. Many funny visual images are created in this story.

PERCUSSION SIGNING

Percussion signing consists of using only one instrument, such as a bass drum, to beat rhythmic vibrations that Deaf people can feel while a performer signs with the beats. The beats are linked to the movements of the signs. Percussion signing started in the 1940s at Gallaudet University football games when it was performed for the song of the Gallaudet mascot. Now this art form is growing. It also can be done without an instrument, relying on the clapping of hands to create the rhythm for the performer. This kind of percussion signing was seen at the Deaf President Now events at Gallaudet University in 1988.

Drama

According to *A Journey into the Deaf-World* (Lane, Hoffmeister, and Bahan, 1996), ASL plays and skits probably emerged in the mid-nineteenth century in the residential schools. Dramatic performances have flourished in the twentieth century in Deaf clubs, Deaf colleges, Deaf theater groups, Deaf TV/film production groups, and Deaf celebration groups. Drama in ASL is characterized by large and rhythmic sign movements and clear visual facial information such as facial grammar (questions, adverbs, conjunctions, and so forth) and emotions.

In the early 1970s, the National Theatre of the Deaf debuted an original ASL play called *My Third Eye* about ASL and Deaf people, and it was a huge success. Regional Deaf theaters have sprung up around the U.S., including the Onyx Theater (New York City), The New York Deaf Theater, Cleveland Signstage Theater, Deaf Bailiwick Artists (Chicago), and Deaf West Theater (Los Angeles), as well as in college theaters at Gallaudet University and the National Technical Institute for the Deaf. There have also been efforts to create original productions in ASL. For example, *Tales from a Clubroom* by Bernard Bragg and Eugene Bergman, *Institution Blues* by Don Bangs, and *Broken Spokes* by Willy Conley have been produced in local and college theaters.

Some films have been created by Deaf people. A Deaf filmmaker named Ernest Marshall produced feature films between 1937 and 1963 in which all the actors used ASL. Another good example of Deaf film production is *Think Me Nothing* by Peter Wolf. It represents the strong core of the Deaf world. The big breakthrough for Deaf performers came in the 1980s when Marlee Matlin won an Oscar for her role in *Children of a Lesser God* (1986) and Juliana Fjeld received an Emmy award for her television production, *Love Is Never Silent* (1985). Since then, many Deaf actors and actresses have gone into the TV/film industry.

DEAF HUMOR

Deaf humor developed in the Deaf community partly as a way of coping with the oppression Deaf people face in the hearing world. ASL comedy amuses Deaf audiences. It includes funny stories, jokes, sketches, and other similar forms that make people laugh. One classic example of a funny story goes like this:

> A crowd goes crazy when a deaf giant comes into town. He spots one woman lying down frightened, comes toward her, and gently lifts her onto his huge palm. She lies motionless on his palm, still frightened. The giant says, "You are so beautiful! I want to marry . . . !" The audience laughs, knowing that the woman is smashed to death when the giant signs MARRY, as the active hand moves fast and hard toward the palm. Then the giant says, "Oh uh . . . oral is better, oh well."

This statement is very ironic and is intended to make Deaf people giggle uncomfortably since they know about the history of oral oppression.

Mary Beth Miller is a well-known comedienne. One of her more popular routines involves her "live" hands that fight each other in ASL. It is really masterful when she, the right hand, and the left hand are in turmoil. For example, the left hand protests that the right hand is being used most of the time and the left hand thinks this is not fair, so it won't cooperate with the right hand. This gives Mary Beth some trouble and she scolds the hands for their silly behavior. The skit goes on and on and it really makes the audience laugh very hard since they know the use of both hands is important in ASL.

Two ASL comedians, Charles McKinney and Al Barwiolek, formed a comedy team (CHALB) that had much success and performed in many places all over the world during the 1980s and 1990s. One of their most famous shows was called *Deaf Pa What?* It was about Deaf people's habits in the Deaf world. In one sketch they exaggerated Deaf people's "long good-bye": They put on coats and hats, indicating they are about ready to leave, but they continue chatting for another half hour. Then they realize they must go, but again they continue chatting for a half hour or more with coats and hats on. This is a big hit with all audiences in the Deaf community because it is so much a part of Deaf people's daily lives.

Poetry

ASL poetry emerged in the 1970s and is a fast developing art form. It is believed that from the 1840s (when residential schools flourished in the U.S.) to the 1960s (when William Stokoe recognized ASL as a language), there were some ASL poets, but they went unrecognized because of the oppression of ASL and the inability to document signs and sign performances. In the 1970s, videotape equipment became widely used, and, as a result, it became possible to record and preserve ASL and ASL poetry. Several ASL poets—Patrick Graybill, Ella Mae Lentz, and Clayton Valli—published their works on tape in the 1990s.

In *Deaf in America: Voices from a Culture* (1988), Carol Padden and Tom Humphries discuss rhythm of movement in two ASL poems, "Eye Music" by Ella Mae Lentz and "Windy Bright Morning" by Clayton Valli. They describe the rhythmic quality in both poems in an effort to point out how movement can express notions like harmony, dissonance, and resonance differently in poetry than in ASL prose.

Valli (1996) has also explored the features and functions in prose and poetry in ASL. At the phonological level, signs in prose are not specifically chosen for phonetic form. However, signs in poetry are chosen for specific phonetic form (physical image) to accomplish rhyme, rhythm, and meter; the signs also are more flexible in regard to changing of phonetic parameter(s). The morphological and lexical features are treated quite differently. Signers can create a new sign by compounding, inventing, borrowing, and other processes, but new signs must be approved by the community through use. Poets, on the other hand, can create new signs through invention. The new sign is created by the poet and does not require a history of use by the Deaf community. As for syntactic features, classifier predicates in prose tend to be used after identifying arguments of the verb. This is not so in ASL poetry, where classifier predicates often are used without explicitly identifying arguments. Gilbert Eastman, an ASL poet and performer, uses a lot of classifier predicates and physical images in his poem about the historic and dramatic Deaf President Now movement, "DPN Epic." This poem shows clearly that ASL poetry is very different from ASL prose.

Poetic Features. ASL poetry contains the same features found in spoken language poetry—rhyme, rhythm, and meter (Valli 1996). We can illustrate these features with two lines from Vivienne Simmons's poem, "White Rose." These lines look simple and smooth, but they are really quite complicated in terms of rhyme, rhythm, and meter.

CHATTING FLOWER-EVERYWHERE, HUMBLE-ROSE-OUT-THERE
COLORFUL FLOWER-EVERYWHERE, WHITE-ROSE-OUT-THERE

Several different kinds of rhyme are evident in these two lines. The transition from open handshape at the beginning (5 handshape or 4 handshape) to closed handshape at the end (Flat O) is repeated in each of these lines. This is called *handshape rhyme;* it also can be *end-rhyme* because of the closed handshapes at the ends of these lines. Another kind of rhyme, *movement path rhyme,* is present in the alternating circles and arcs in each of these lines. Location and nonmanual signals (NMS) are repeated also, producing *location rhyme* and *NMS rhyme.* The handedness in each line starts with two hands and ends with one hand. This is called *handedness rhyme.*

Rhythm in ASL poetry is created in a variety of ways: movement paths, assimilation, change of a sign, choice of a sign, handedness, alternating movement, movement duration, and movement size. The rhythm in our example is dominated by enlarged movement paths and use of handedness.

Meter is a count of something we can see. The essence of meter is the contrast between heavy and light syllables. We see this kind of meter in the example. They are *pentametric* (five feet in a line). The first signs in each line are *double-spondaic.* A spondaic foot shows equivalent stress in both of the syllables. The second signs in each line are *double-trochaic.* A trochaic foot consists of a stronger syllable followed by a weaker syllable. The last signs in each line are *iambic,* a weaker syllable followed by a stronger one. As you can see, the meter of ASL poetry depends heavily on visual movement (refer to the videotape that accompanies this text for a performance and an explanation in ASL of the example).

SUMMARY

One of the major aims of studying the artistic uses of ASL is to help learners discover the richness of the language, its multiple meanings, its enormous flexibility, and its complicated and very useful structures. Thus, this knowledge is the gateway to success in education and careers as well as to full participation in our bilingual/multicultural society.

REFERENCES

Bahan, B. 1992. "Bird of a Different Feather." In *ASL Literature Series.* Produced and directed by James R. DeBee. San Diego: DawnPictures. Videocassette and workbook.

Graybill, P. 1990. *Poetry in motion: Original works in ASL: Patrick Graybill.* Burtonsville, MD: Sign Media, Inc. Videocassette.

Lane, H., Hoffmeister, R., and Bahan, B. 1996. *A journey into the Deaf-World.* San Diego: DawnSign Press.

Lentz, E. M. 1995. *The treasure: Poems by Ella Mae Lentz.* Berkeley, CA: In Motion Press. Videocassette.

Supalla, S. 1992. "For a Decent Living." *ASL Literature Series.* Produced and directed by James R. DeBee. San Diego: DawnPictures. Videocassette and workbook.

Valli, C. 1993. Poetics of American Sign Language poetry. Ph.D. diss., Union Institute, Cincinnati, Ohio.

——. 1996. *ASL poetry: Selected works of Clayton Valli.* Produced by Joe Dannis, directed by Clayton Valli. San Diego: DawnPictures. Videocassette.

Homework Assignment 21

1. Think of a significant event that has taken place in your life, something that you may have told other people about before. Organize your thoughts into a story that you can present to your class. This is different from just telling someone about an event during a conversation—what you are preparing is more like a performance. As you rehearse your story, you may want to videotape yourself so you can see clearly what your story looks like and which parts you may want to change. Memorize your story and perform it for your class.

2. Analyze your story and describe how your presentation is different from just telling someone about the event during a conversation. Look at specific features such as the use of space, eye gaze, sign choice, speed and size of signing, handedness, possible repetition of signs and phrases, and so forth. What is the structure of your story? Does it have a clear beginning, middle, and end? How many parts does it have and what is the function of each part?

3. Can you identify any characteristics shared by all of the ASL art forms? What do they all seem to have in common?

PART SEVEN

SUPPLEMENTAL READINGS

Analyzing Signs

ROBBIN BATTISON

Sign language and speech are superficially unlike each other, since one involves a manually produced, visually received signal, while the other involves an orally produced, auditorily received signal. If we are to look for common features in the form of speech and sign behavior, then we must explore the organization of signs at a level general enough to permit some comparisons to spoken words. This necessitates a reexamination of the function of the phonological component of a grammar.

1.1 SUBLEXICAL STRUCTURE

The goals of a complete phonological description are to establish three interdependent aspects of linguistic form: (1) the sublexical analytical units which in combination with each other make up the morphemes of the language; for spoken languages these components would be segments (phonemes in the structuralist framework) described in terms of distinctive feature specifications (not to exclude tone, stress, etc.); (2) the allowable and nonallowable patterns of distribution of these units, whether stated at a deep underlying level by morpheme structure constraints, or at the surface level as the result of phonological rules and morphophonemic alternations; (3) the patterns of historical changes occurring over time; and (4) to link the above components, rules, and patterns of alternation with the physical or phonetic framework, and to seek motivation for these structures and constraints in the articulatory and perceptual processes which encode and decode the forms of the language.

What this adds up to is a set of rules and constraints that limit the possible forms which may be used in a given natural language to express meaning. For spoken languages, we may take the universe of forms to be the entire range of sounds produced by the human vocal apparatus, only a small set of which are potential human speech sounds. The phonology of a particular spoken language would further circumscribe this set, delimiting a finite set of sound elements combinable according to a set of rules and constraints to yield the allowable morphemes of the language, plus their alternative forms when used in strings (phrases or sentences).

For sign languages the task is analogous. Out of the entire range of gestures that it is possible to make with the human body (particularly torso, head and arms), the phonology of a sign language must specify the possible signs of a given sign language, and also specify their form when used in strings. In this sense a gesture is not necessarily a sign, but every sign is also a gesture.

I will continue to use the word "phonology" to refer to the analogous level of ab-

Source. Reprinted by permission of the publisher, from R. Battison, *Lexical Borrowing in American Sign Language* (1978):19–58. Silver Spring, MD: Linstok Press. The references for this reading can be found in the original volume.

stract structure in sign languages. Stokoe (1960) coined the term "cherology" to apply to much the same area. I choose to avoid this term for three reasons: (a) to avoid confusion between Stokoe's structural analysis and the present study, which is cast in a generative phonological framework; (b) to avoid using a new term where a familiar one seems both adequate and appropriate; (c) to highlight existing similarities between speech and signing.

The units of analysis posited by Stokoe still have a great deal of validity, however, and have been used by subsequent researchers in the field. He noted that signs in ASL required three different types of information about simultaneously occurring events to specify their information and to distinguish them from other signs. He refers to these as the *aspects* of a sign so as to avoid unnecessary confusion with a *sequence* of segments (Stokoe 1972):

a. The *location* of the sign in relation to the body, which Stokoe termed the *tabula* (or *tab*);
b. The *handshape(s)* or configuration(s) of the hand(s) involved in the sign, called the *designator* (or *dez*);
c. The movement executed by the hands, called the *signation* (or *sig*).

Besides the three aspects explicitly stated, Stokoe (1960) makes use of a fourth type of simultaneous formational information in his transcription system. This is the spatial *orientation* of the hands, in relation to each other and/or the rest of the body. Battison (1974), Frishberg (1974, 1975), Woodward (1973a), Woodward and Erting (1975), and others have since made orientation information more explicit in sign descriptions. Under this analysis, the lexical entry for each sign must be specified for each of these categories, and class relationships among signs can be stated in terms of shared specifications. Each of these categories of location, handshape, movement, and orientation thus may be viewed as comprising a sub-set of elements which make the equivalent of a phonological inventory. These units were termed *cheremes* by Stokoe (1960) and *primes* by Bellugi (1972). Naturally the interaction and interdependence of these hypothetical units are as important as the units themselves.

Stokoe (1960) and Stokoe et al. (1965) posited 19 distinct hand configurations, 12 distinct locations, and 24 distinct movements as the basic manual components of signs. In addition, Stokoe's (1960) analysis coded the passive hand of a two-handed sign as a location. In his structuralist analysis, independence of these units was based on their contrasting role in minimal pairs. All other variants of location, handshape, etc., were treated as "allochers" of these cheremes. At the more "phonetic" surface level there are many more possible distinctions, of course.

My own observations suggest that there are approximately 45 different handshapes and 25 different locations on the body or in space where signs are made. There are fewer different types of movements and orientations (perhaps on the order of one dozen each). Klima (1975) suggests that there are close to 40 significant handshapes, 12 locations, 16–18 orientations, and 12 simple movements. Newkirk (1975), in developing a transcription and orthography for ASL, noted more than 54 distinct handshapes, the remainder of his analysis not being comparable for enumeration.

The exact number of different primes depends upon more complete phonological and "phonetic" analyses than are now available, and depends upon the resolution of a number of descriptive problems. For one thing, there are many alternatives for coding the same type of information about the physical nature of signs: Direct linear movement between two locations could be coded entirely in terms of those locations; finer points about manual contact could be coded by orientation and locations, or they could be coded separately, as in Friedman and Battison (1973); fine movements of the fingers are sometimes (but not always) equivalent to recognizable changes of handshapes; orientation could be just a cross-classifier of handshapes rather than having a status equal to handshape, movement, and location aspects. For another thing, the state of the art has advanced to the point where information on the psychological reality of sign phonology is only just beginning to emerge (Bellugi et al. 1975, Lane et al. 1976, Poizner 1976).

The important point at present is not how many primes there are in each of the four categories, but that there is some justification in assuming that there are four separate categories, that each category is composed of a finite set of distinct elements, and that every simple sign comprises a prime specification for each of the four categories which are to be articulated simultaneously. These assumptions, which demand a refinement going beyond the scope of this study, are sufficient to facilitate the present descriptions and discussions.

Besides describing the physical formation of signs, these primes serve to distinguish signs from each other, often minimally. Not all of these primes contrast at an underlying level of representation, as we shall see later. Minimal pairs of signs can be found that differ in form only in one particular aspect. For the aspect of handshape, there are pairs of signs which are identical in all respects except for the particular handshape involved. An example is the pair of signs CAR[1] and WHICH (Figure 1). The only difference between them is that CAR uses the standard A or S handshape[2] (compact fist, thumb closed against side or knuckles), while WHICH uses the Å handshape (compact fist, thumb extended).

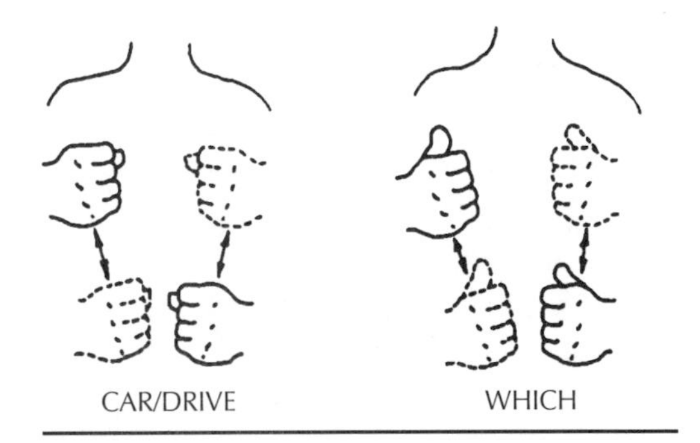

FIGURE 1.

In the case of location a minimal pair is CHINESE and SOUR (Figure 2). The two signs are identical except that CHINESE is made on the temple or high on the cheek and SOUR is made near the mouth.

A minimal pair for movement is found in NAME and SHORT (BRIEF) (Figure 3). NAME is made with simple contact (sometimes repeated) while SHORT (BRIEF) is made identically except for having a side-to-side brushing motion of the upper hand.

Finally, the pair NAME and SIT (CHAIR) differ minimally only by orientation. In the sign NAME, both *volar* (palm) surfaces are oriented more-or-less toward the body, and the fingers make contact on the edges. In SIT

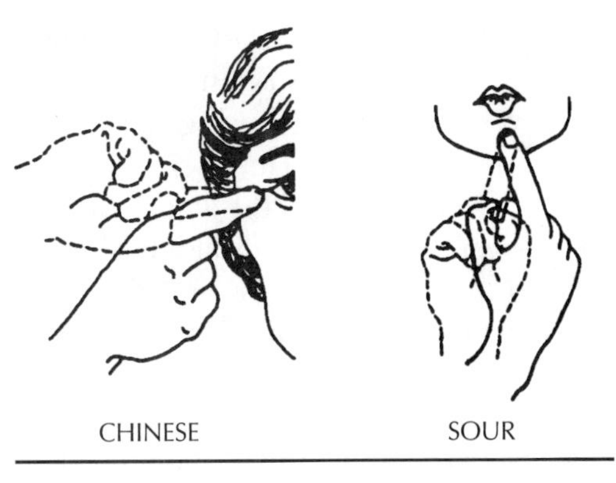

FIGURE 2.

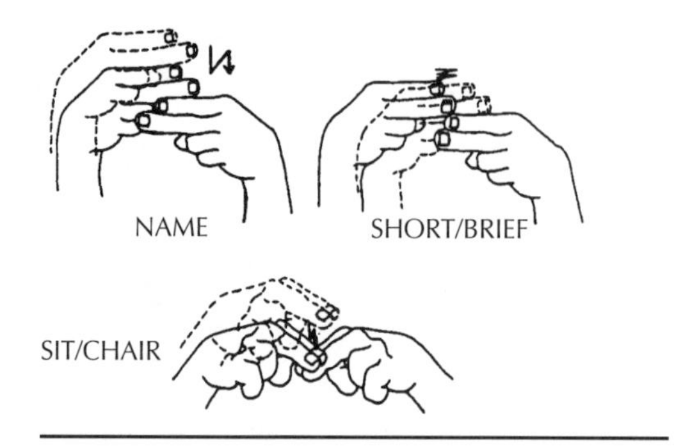

FIGURE 3.

(CHAIR), both volar surfaces point downward.

What we have seen so far is the beginning of a sublexical or phonological analysis of signs. The four categories of location, handshape, movement, and orientation comprise classes of units which may serve to distinguish signs from each other. Before moving on to other combinatorial aspects of these units, we should consider the form of the articulator, the human body.

1.2 THE BODY AS ARTICULATOR

It may be helpful to dissociate ourselves from our bodies temporarily and to consider our bodies as machines capable of generating manual visual signs. For our purposes here, there are actually two basic ways of viewing the body as a machine—one in terms of production of signs and the other in terms of perception of signs. In terms of perception, the body is a bilaterally symmetrical object with a very complicated moving organ (hand and arm) on each side. However, in terms of production of signs and the actual usage of the body, observations indicate that signers tend to use one hand and one side of the torso much more than the other.[3] It is a major thesis of this study that this opposition between potential visual symmetry and the actual manual asymmetry of the body creates a dynamic tension of great importance for the formational organization of signs, and we shall return to it often.

In the context of this study we shall need three pairs of terms to discuss the components and activities of the left and right sides of the body. The terms *left* and *right* themselves are superfluous, since they are arbitrary labels for sides unrelated to function, and because the opposition of *left* and *right* is nondistinctive for signs—it carries no meaning. A one-handed sign means the same thing regardless of whether it is performed by the left or right hand (except for cases where the sign refers to something to the left or to the right), and a two-handed sign does not change meaning regardless of whether the left and right hands reverse their formational roles.

The term *dominant* will be used to refer to the hand preferred for most motor tasks, and *nondominant* will refer to the other hand. For descriptions of signs involving two hands, we shall use the functional terms *active* and *passive*. A two-handed sign may either have two active (moving) hands, or it may have an active and a passive hand. The active hand has a much larger role and executes a more complex motor program than its passive partner, which can be absolutely stationary. Under certain circumstances the passive hand may be in motion due to transitions from the previous sign, or due to moving up into signing space from one of the rest positions. This motion is of course quite variable and quite irrelevant for the sign itself, except when considering transitions between adjacent signs and their potential metamorphosis into compounds.

Signers can be characterized as being either left-handed with respect to signing or right-handed with respect to signing. For most signers with right (left) hand dominance, their right (left) hand will assume the active role most of the time. This is the natural, or unmarked, state of affairs. In special circumstances there is switching of the hands (Battison 1974, Klima and Bellugi 1975, Frishberg 1976b).

A third pair of terms *ipsilateral* and *contralateral*, meaning same side and opposite side, respectively, are useful in discussing the orientation of signs with respect to where contact is made on the body. For signs which are not specified in terms of left or right, it is more germane to note which side of the body is touched in terms of *ipsilateral* (same side as that of the active hand) and *contralateral* (opposite side), rather than *right* and *left*. For example, in the American pledge of allegiance, the right hand contacts the contralateral breast; in a military salute, the right hand contacts the ipsilateral forehead or temple. Since we have already noted that left-right distinctions are superfluous to sign descriptions, the interaction between two articulators (body and hand), each having a left-right orientation, is easily described regardless of whether the left (right) hand touches the left (right) side of the body—ipsilateral contact—or whether the left (right) hand touches the right (left) side of the body—contralateral contact.

1.3 TYPOLOGY OF SIGNS

Given the preceding definitions, perspectives on the body as a sign-generating machine, and proposed elements of formation, it is now possible to return to the discussion of the formational qualities of signs in isolation. Our first task is to propose a tentative classification based on distinct types of motor acts.

For the purposes of this discussion, we shall posit six mutually exclusive, exhaustive, types of signs:

Type Ø: One-handed signs articulated in free space without contact (e.g. PREACH, Figure 4).

Type X: One-handed signs which contact the body in any place except the opposite hand (CHINESE, SOUR, Figure 2).

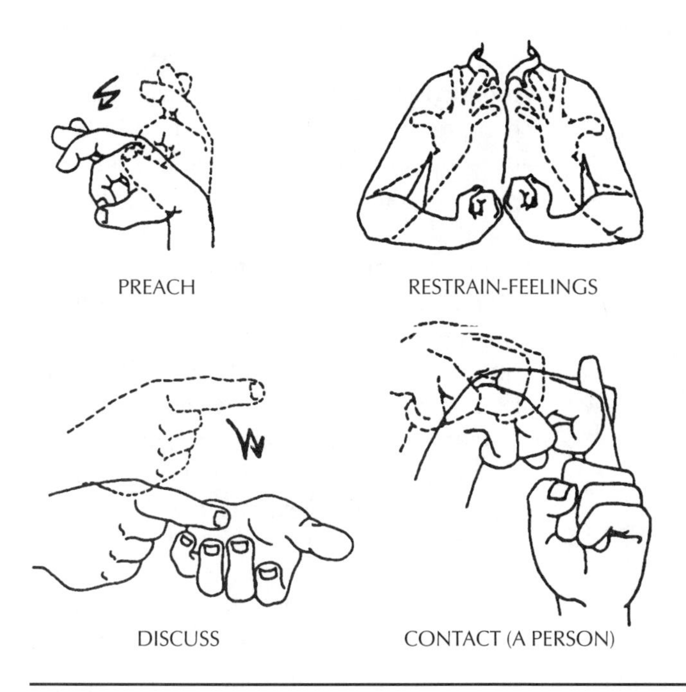

FIGURE 4.

Type 1: Two-handed signs in which both hands are active and perform identical motor acts; the hands may or may not contact each other, they may or may not contact the body, and they may be in either a synchronous or alternating pattern of movement (WHICH, CAR, Figure 1; RESTRAIN-FEELINGS, Figure 4).

Type 2: Two-handed signs in which one hand is active and one hand is passive, but both hands are specified for the same handshape (NAME, SHORT/BRIEF, SIT/CHAIR, Figure 3).

Type 3: Two-handed signs in which one hand is active and one hand is passive, and the two hands have different handshapes. Note that signs which were excluded specifically in Type X fit in Types 2 and 3—one hand contacts the other (DISCUSS, CONTACT (A PERSON), Figure 4).

We shall also need to posit a sixth type, *Type C,* to account for those compounds which combine two or more of the above types.

Computing the frequency of types illustrates the opposition between the principles of symmetry and asymmetry. If one includes both one- and two-handed signs, then a majority of them are asymmetrical; if one looks only at the two-handed signs, most of them are symmetrical:

> In a study of more than 2,000 signs of American Sign Language, we found that only 35% involve the use of both hands where both hands are active [type 1]. About 40% of the signs are made with one hand only [types Ø and X], and another 25% are made with one hand acting on the other hand which remains stationary as a base [types 2 and 3]. Thus, for almost two-thirds of these signs, one hand is used as the dominant hand. (Klima and Bellugi 1975:232)

This classification is not intended to be absolute and definitive, as there are other bases for classification, e.g., type of movement (Supalla 1976, Grosjean 1977) or type of contact. But this classification allows us to relate signs directly to the relative complexity of certain motor acts. As discussion warrants, this general schema will be amended and refined.

Types 1, 2, and 3, the two-handed signs, are of greatest interest, since (apart from type C), they are the more complex signs and lend themselves more easily to relative measures of complexity. We can demonstrate the relative complexity of types 1, 2, and 3 by reference to Figure 5, which represents an idealized procedure for identifying the handshape specifications of a two-handed sign. Note that this is only a linguistic-analytic model and not a psycho-linguistic model. It merely reflects the amount of information coded into a two-handed sign according to the analysis of handshape specifications presented.

In terms of this model, the chain of questions which leads to the specification of the handshapes of a two-handed sign is more complex for type 3 than for type 2, and more complex for type 2 than type 1, where complexity is indicated by the number of questions. This is summarized in Table 1.

According to this model, type 1 signs can involve a greater amount of redundancy in that fewer questions are required to arrive at the specification for the two handshapes involved. Conversely, the greater number of questions required to specify both handshapes of a type 3 sign reflects a greater amount of internal structure, more complexity and less redundancy. Type 2 signs lie between these two extremes.

1.4 MORPHEME STRUCTURE CONSTRAINTS ON TWO-HANDED SIGNS

The information presented thus far on two-handed signs can be described in terms

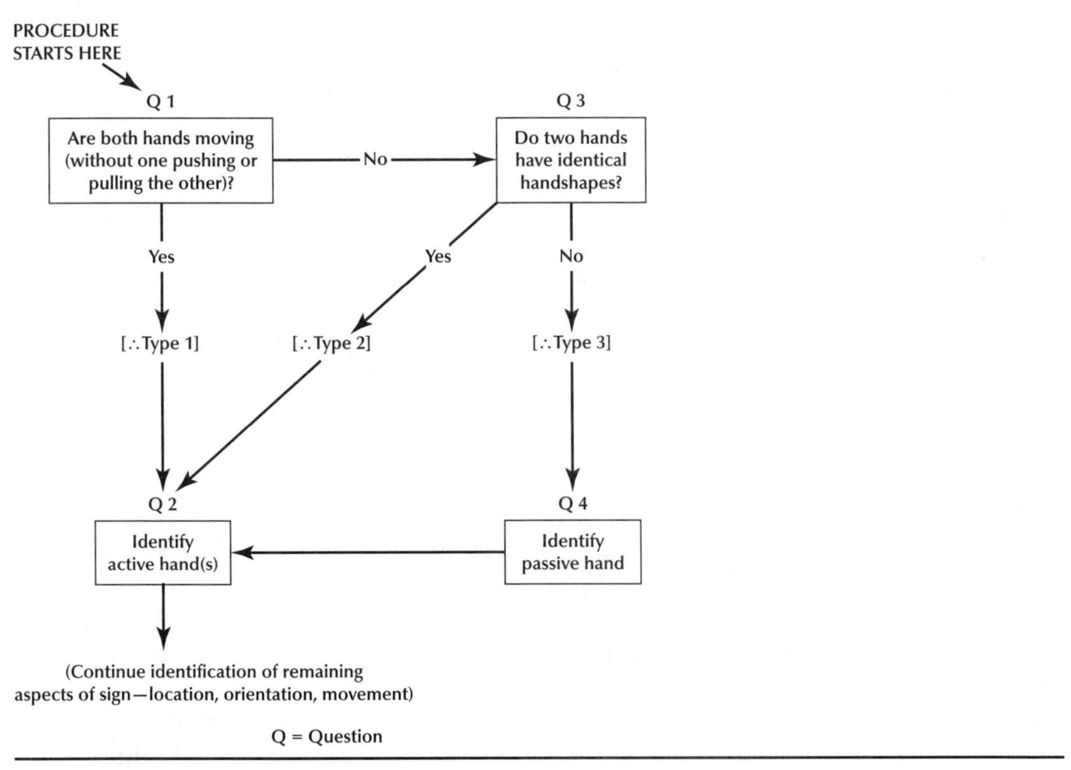

FIGURE 5. Idealized procedure for identifying the handshape specifications of a two-handed sign.

more compatible with linguistic descriptions, since they in fact reflect a hierarchy of constraints on the ways in which manual elements may combine to form sign morphemes. Simply by examining the descriptive definitions of types 1, 2, and 3, one can formulate two morpheme structure constraints stated over simultaneous primes which severely limit possible forms in a way which *excludes the more complex forms.* I call these two interlocking constraints the *Symmetry Condition* and the *Dominance Condition* (an earlier description can be found in Battison 1974). Both of these constraints can be stated in the familiar if-then form of morpheme structure conditions of spoken languages—*if* a certain structural configuration or element is present in the morpheme, *then* certain other things must be present (or absent) also.

The Symmetry Condition states that (a) if both hands of a sign move independently dur-

TABLE 1. Questions Required to Obtain Handshape Information on a Two-Handed Sign, Following Schema in Figure 5

	QUESTION (1)	QUESTION (2)	QUESTION (3)	QUESTION (4)
Type 1	XX	XX		
Type 2	XX	XX	XX	
Type 3	XX	XX	XX	XX

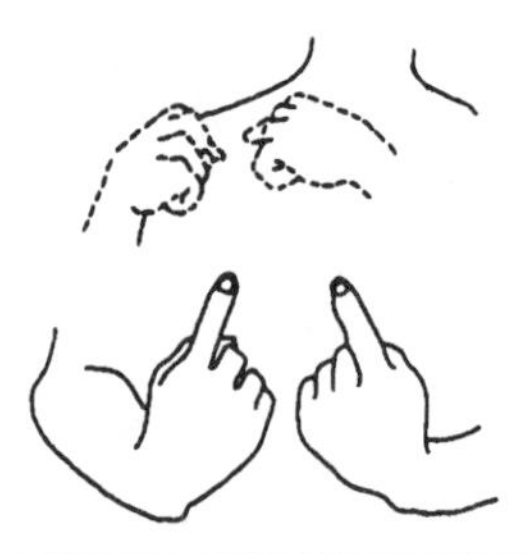

FIGURE 6. SINCE

ing its articulation, then (b) both hands must be specified for the same location, the same handshape, the same movement (whether performed simultaneously or in alternation), and the specifications for orientation must be either symmetrical or identical.

"Same location" in this case means either (a) the physically identical location—both hands are actually in the same area; or (b) the hands are in mirror-image locations on either side of the line of bilateral symmetry. An example of physically identical locations would be the sign SINCE (also glossed UP-TILL NOW) (Figure 6), in which both hands start from the same corner of the upper chest and flip outwards. An example of (b) would be the sign WHICH (Figure 1) in which each hand is equidistant from the line of bilateral symmetry.

"Symmetrical orientation" can be defined as any orientation in which identical parts (any parts) of the two hands have mirror image orientations with respect to the plane which separates them. "Identical orientation" means that both hands have the same orientation with respect to the body (e.g., fingers pointed out from the body and palms down), but it says nothing about the orientation of the hands with respect to each other. Both SINCE and WHICH have symmetrical (and identical) orientations—identical parts of the hands "face" each other across the line which separates them. The sign BE-

FIGURE 7. BE-PREPARED

PREPARED (Figure 7) illustrates identical orientation without symmetricality: Both hands have volar surfaces contralateral, metacarpals outward, but identical parts of the hand do not face each other across the line which separates the hands.

Rephrased very informally, the Symmetry Condition amounts to saying: "If a two-handed sign is going to bear the added complexity of having both hands move, then both hands must perform roughly the same motor acts." A large number of logically possible gestures in which two hands perform different motor activities are thus excluded from being potential sign morphemes.

The simple Dominance Condition, inversely related to the Symmetry Condition, states that (a) If the hands of a two-handed sign do not share the same specification for handshape (i.e., they are different), then (b) One hand must be passive while the active hand articulates the movement, *and* (c) The specification of the passive handshape is restricted to be one of a small set: A, S, B, 5, G, C, and O[4] (Figure 8).

Type 3 signs obey this constraint with very few exceptions. In effect, the Dominance Condition rules that if a two-handed sign is so complex as to involve two differ-

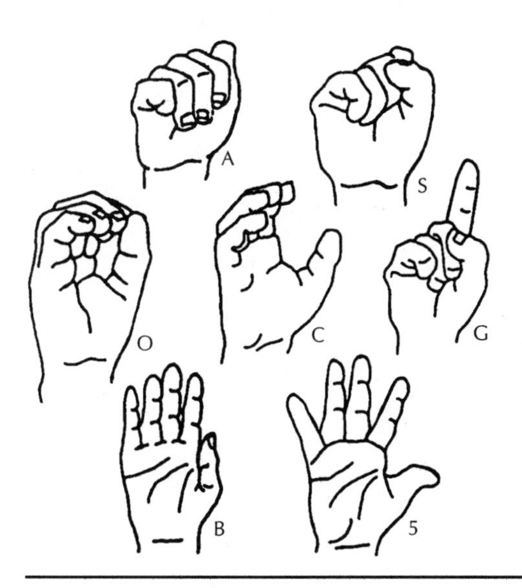

FIGURE 8.

ent handshapes, then the overall complexity of the sign must be reduced by (a) prohibiting movement of one hand (usually the nondominant) and (b) severely restricting the possible handshapes which may appear on this passive hand. The reduction from approximately 45 handshapes to a mere 7 greatly reduces the complexity of the sign and increases the redundancy, since a specification of one hand from among seven possibilities requires less information than a specification of one handshape among 45 possibilities. This constraint on complexity should tend to facilitate both the production and perception of such a complex sign. Looked at another way, the answer to question 4 of Table 1 does not carry as much information as the answer to question 2, since it chooses from among fewer possibilities.

Finally, it should be noted that the two-handed signs not delimited by either the Symmetry or the Dominance Condition constitute the in-between group, type 2, in which the handshapes are identical, but only one hand is active.

1.5 MARKED AND UNMARKED HANDSHAPES

The seven handshapes mentioned in reference to the Dominance Condition form an interesting group of critical importance. The first thing of note bears repeating: These particular seven handshapes may take the role of the passive hand in type 3 asymmetrical signs when dozens of others are proscribed. Secondly, a glance at Figure 8 suggests that these seven handshapes are maximally distinct, basic geometrical shapes. A and S are closed and maximally compact solids; B is a simple planar surface; 5 is the maximal extension and spreading of all projections; G is a single projection from a solid, the most linear; C is an arc; O is a full circle. They are thus the most basic possible handshapes, given these geometrical criteria, suggesting that they are maximally distinct in both articulatory and perceptual terms (with the exception of A and S, which are very distinct from the others, but very similar to each other).

There is also reason to believe that these seven are the most natural basic handshapes in a phonological sense also—i.e., that they are the unmarked elements in their set: (1) They have a high frequency of occurrence in a wide array of contexts (some of them exclusive contexts, as we have seen); (2) They are found in all other sign languages for which information is presently available to us; (3) They are among the first handshapes mastered by deaf children acquiring ASL from their parents (Boyes 1973, McIntire 1977); (4) In a visual perception experiment designed to test hypothetical feature analyses for 20 handshapes, Lane et al. (1976) found that the four hands least confused (i.e., most resistant to distortion by noise) were, in order, 5, B, C, and O, with A ranking 7th; (5) Children make production errors of handshape substitution which tend

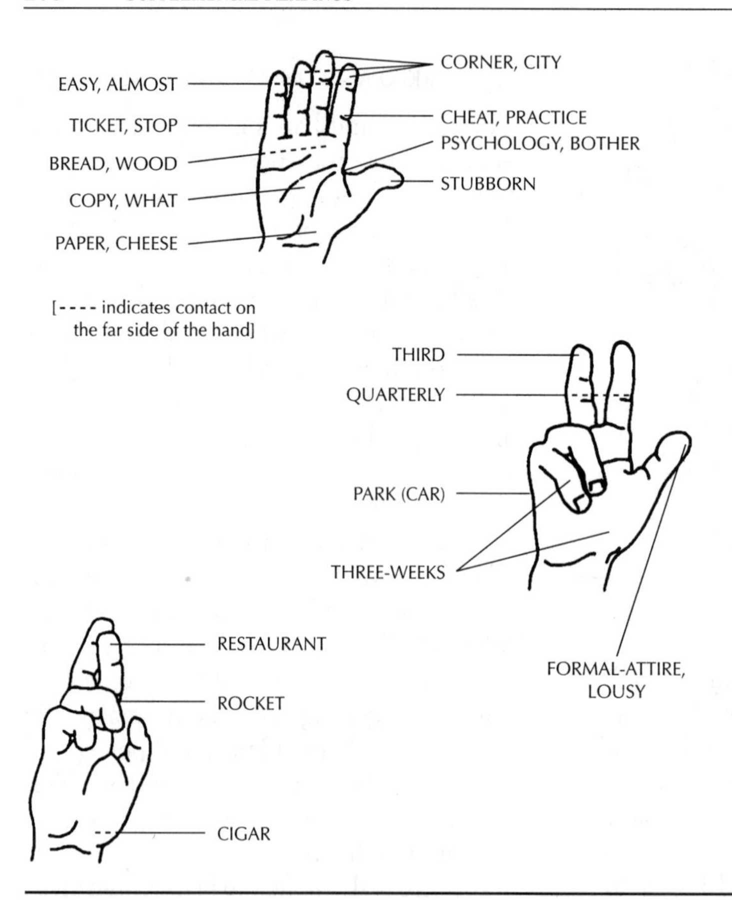

FIGURE 9. Comparison of potential points of contact of unmarked (B), intermediate (3), and marked (R) handshapes. (Glosses are examples of signs made by contacting these points.)

toward elements of this set (Boyes 1973); (6) This small set of unmarked handshapes functions less restrictively than other more marked handshapes—not only in terms of frequency as in (1) above, but in interaction with other elements of the sign: These seven handshapes have greater variety in how they may contact the body or the other hand in order to form signs; the more marked handshapes have greatly restricted points of contact (pointed out to me by Richard Lacy). Figure 9 compares the points of contact possible with an unmarked handshape (B), a handshape of intermediate status (3), and a highly marked handshape (R), which nearly always occurs in initialized[5] signs. These seven handshapes predominate in signs which require the active hand to change handshapes during the articulation of the sign. Of these 155 "dez-changing" or "double-handshape" signs, 136 (87.7%) have at least one unmarked handshape, and 98 (63.2%) change from one unmarked handshape to another (double-handshape signs are discussed in greater detail later in this chapter).

From the discussion thus far, it is evident that the complexity of handshapes individually and in simultaneous combinations are offset by quite stringent restrictions of distribution and co-occurrence. Unmarked handshapes have wider distribution and more freedom of co-occurrence than the more marked, more complex handshapes. The increased complexity of certain handshape combinations in two-handed signs also prompts certain restrictions to balance out the complexity: Where both hands are required to move in a sign, they must perform identical or nearly identical motor acts—they cannot move independently within a given sign (Symmetry Condition). For those signs which require two dissimilar handshapes, one of the hands must be passive, and must be one of the seven most basic, unmarked handshapes (Dominance Condition).

This dynamic tension between increased complexity of some aspects of a sign and decreased complexity in other areas is a theme which will recur frequently in this study. It suggests that there are some relative, and perhaps absolute, restrictions on the allowable complexity of ASL signs. This is well illustrated by the preceding data on handshapes. In the following sections we shall consider additional evidence from locations, and from the number of beats in the articulation of individual signs.

FIGURE 10. Fingerspelling (shaded) and signing areas.

1.6 MORPHEME STRUCTURE CONSTRAINTS ON LOCATION

The location aspect of signs is quite different from the handshape aspect, both in articulatory and perceptual terms. Handshapes are differentiated by the spatial configurations of the hand, involving the extension, contraction, contact, and divergence of the fingers. These relatively fine movements and configurations are acted out and displayed in an area of less than 50 square inches (the fully extended and open "5" hand of an average adult would not quite fill an area of 50 square inches). Fingerspelling, which relies almost totally on differentiation of handshapes, normally takes place in the region of the small circle in Figure 10 (shown for a right-handed person).

The manifestation and differentiation of the locational aspect of signs are necessarily grosser in many ways, since the extent of the space used is larger. Signs may be articulated freely in space, or they may involve contacting parts of the body. The general area in which signs are made is indicated by the large circle in Figure 10. Exaggerated signs, certain gestures, and pantomime may exceed these limits, but most signs would be made in this restricted area, which has been termed "signing space" by Bellugi (1972) and Frishberg and Gough (1973a).

The differentiations in location, whether on or off the body, are made within a much larger area than the differentiations for static handshapes. Obviously, there must be some compensation for this disparity in physical range. Three contributing factors act to balance out the motor-perceptual tasks on the relatively finely differentiated hand versus those on (or in front of) the more grossly differentiated body. The first of these is that the movements performed in this large signing space are performed by the brachial system, the movements of which probably cannot be as finely controlled or differentiated as those of the digital system. Thus locational targets within this large space should be further apart. The second factor involves the visual backdrop of the body itself. Locations in signing space are not differentiable by relative distance alone, but by their proximity or relations to the gross landmarks of the body—the head, chin, shoulders, waist, etc.

Third, the entire signing space is not used uniformly. Certain areas allow greater complexity of motor acts. This can be shown in two ways:

(1) Measuring vertically we could compare the discrete levels on the body where signs are made. For this purpose we need only consider signs made by contacting the head, neck, or trunk (the "height" of signs made by contacting the arm itself is difficult to establish, since the arm is a mobile organ). Figure 11 shows the different heights at which various signs may contact the body. Not all of these height differences are phonologically distinctive, and for many of them minimal pairs cannot be found—but this is not crucial to the argument. It is apparent that greater vertical location differentiation is possible as one moves from the waist to the head.

FIGURE 11. Vertical location distinctions.

(2) We could gauge the relative complexity of handshapes occurring in signs made at these various levels. One approach to this problem would be to trace the relationship between the unmarked handshapes (A, S, B, 5, G, C, and O) and the height of the location of the signs in which they occur.

Table 2 shows the number of unmarked and marked handshapes occurring in signs in either of two major areas: The head (including 15 signs made on the neck) and the trunk (from shoulders to waist). The signs were taken from DASL (Stokoe et al. 1965), and included signs which are normally made in close proximity without contact.

The percentage of marked handshapes in the head area is certainly higher than the percentage of marked handshapes occurring in the trunk area—33.1% as opposed to 24.1% ($\chi^2 = 4.10$; d.f. = 1; $p < .05$). While this is a significant difference, but not an overwhelming one, we should note additionally that 33 of the 34 signs made on the trunk with marked handshapes either involved contact on the upper or central trunk alone (e.g., RELIGION, EGOTISTIC, VOLUNTEER) or involve both upper and lower trunk contact (e.g., KING, LORD). Thus Table 2 does not reflect the fact that the lower portion of the trunk is almost "off limits" to marked handshapes. [We should note that, although DASL was compiled with the aid of many data corpora, it makes no claims to be complete. As more signs come to the attention of linguists and lexicographers, the counts in Table 2 will surely change, although the proportional results are assumed to be correct.]

Thus it does appear that the vertical location component of signs is systematically restricted in a manner consistent with the need to keep visual elements perceptually

TABLE 2. Number of Signs with Marked and Unmarked Handshapes Located in Two Major Areas

	UNMARKED HANDSHAPES	MARKED HANDSHAPES	TOTALS
Head and Neck Locations	311 (66.9%)	154 (33.1%)	465
Trunk Locations	107 (75.9%)	34 (24.1%)	141
Totals	418	188	606

Source: Enumeration of signs from Stokoe et al. (1965), Dictionary of ASL.
$\chi 2 = 4.10$, d.f. = 1, $p < .05$

distinct. Areas higher in the signing space permit more complex combinations of manual visual elements, both in terms of fineness of location distinctions and the complexity of individual handshapes.

An explanation for both these restrictions based on visual perception was proposed by Siple (1973), who suggested that in areas of high visual acuity, finer differentiation of handshapes and locations was to be expected. Signers in a conversation do not look at each other's hands, since the hands move radically and rapidly; instead we observe that they seem to fix their gaze on the lower part of the signer's face (regardless of whether the signer is accompanying the signs by mouthed or spoken words).

Thus Siple hypothesized that visual acuity should be highest in this area (the small circle in Figure 12), and should fall off rapidly as the distance from this central area increases. Siple also proposed that in the areas in the outer reaches of sign space, in areas of low visual acuity, not only should there be signs with simpler handshapes (i.e., more unmarked handshapes), but also more two-handed signs. Every two-handed sign that contacts the body is highly symmetrical (according to the criteria already discussed under the Symmetry Condition), and thus a greater proportion of two-handed signs insures a greater amount of articulatory and perceptual redundancy for the signs made in this area. Note also the finer differentiation of vertical locations in the combined head and neck area is also consistent with her explanation.

An alternative explanation to these findings is one based on visual "landmarks" rather than visual acuity. Coincidentally, the area delimited by Siple as corresponding to the highest visual acuity is also the area which has the greatest number of visually distinguishable (and readily nameable) body parts. On the visual backdrop of the facial surface we can readily distinguish the lips, chin, teeth, mouth, nose, nostril, cheek, jaw, dimple, moustache, temple, eye,

FIGURE 12. Central area of signing space.

eyebrow, etc., while the lower part of the signing space offers relatively fewer visible landmarks—shoulder, chest, side, waist. These distinguishable backdrop cues may facilitate the perception of the location of the sign.

The question of the relative merits of these two alternative explanations is best left to experimental determination; it is possible that the two systems interact and support one another. The issue of one- vs. two-handed signs in relation to sign locations will come up again in Chapter 2.

If we take a slightly different view of the body and consider the lateral, not the vertical, placement of signs, we find restrictions also. We can distinguish three types of contact laterally: *Ipsilateral,* in which the hand (whether left or right) touches the corresponding side of the body; *Contralateral,* in which the hand crosses the line of symmetry and contacts the opposite side of the body; *Central,* in which the hand contacts the midline of the body.

In general, we observe that no ipsilateral or central contact is restricted—most ipsilateral and midline areas (on the different levels specified previously in Figure 11) are utilized by some signs. Contralateral contact is somewhat more restricted. Compare the shaded areas on the bodies in Figures 13a and 13b.

The shaded areas indicate where a right hand is attested in making a bodily contact during the articulation of a sign (the corresponding areas for the left hand of a left-dominant signer would be depicted by holding the page to a mirror). If we consider *all* types of body-contact signs, then Figure 13a represents where these contacts may take place.

Figure 13b shows a reduced contact area where signs specified for only a single contact may be made. Note that the areas which are shaded in Figure 13a but unshaded in Figure 13b are just those where a specific type of sign is made—signs which require two contacts, one on each side of the body's midline.

FIGURE 13. (a) Body locations for all signs. (b) Body locations for single-contact signs.

In the forehead area, there are signs such as SUMMER and BLACK, both of which brush a forefinger from contralateral to ipsilateral. At midface there is FLOWER, which contacts first the ipsilateral, and then the contralateral side of the nose. At the chin are the examples FARM, BACHELOR, RESTAURANT, SLOPPY, DRY and BORING, which contact the contralateral side and then move to contact the ipsilateral side of the chin. At the marginal area of the waist we have the sign SAILOR, in which both hands (in the O configuration) contact first the side contralateral to the dominant hand, then the ipsilateral side.

Regarding the shaded areas which are not common to both bodies in Figure 13, a morpheme structure condition is suggested: If a sign is specified for contralateral contact for a place other than the opposite breast or arm, then it is also specified for ipsilateral contact; *contralateral contact does not occur on its own.* But this constraint actually has very few signs in its domain; most of them are listed above. This fact, coupled with the very restrictive nature of the constraint, suggests that ipsilateral locations are the more natural or unmarked, while contralateral locations are marked.

This seems in accordance with the intuitive notion that extra effort is required to move the manual articulator to a location on the opposite side of the body's midline. The exceptional nature of the opposite hand and arm as locations is likely due to the fact that they themselves are mobile and do assume a more central position when used as locations (e.g., as the passive hand in a type 2 or type 3 sign). The opposing hand, when used as a location where the moving hand articulates, is generally held in front of the central meridian of the body; it does not remain at the extreme edge of the body.

For locations of signs, we thus find that there are systematic restrictions on the use of certain locational elements, and some restrictions on combinations of these elements. This is true of both the vertical and lateral dimensions of location. We find some basis for these systematic restrictions in considering the dynamics of the moving articulator and principles of visual perception.

1.7 METRIC RESTRICTIONS

The last set of constraints to be proposed, before moving on to phonological processes in Chapter 2, involves specifying the temporal complexity of a sign by counting the number of manual articulations involved. Not surprisingly, there appears to be an upper limit, which shall be one of the principal concerns when we discuss the lexical restructuring of borrowed forms (loan signs) in Chapters 4 and 5.

In fact, *two* is the upper limit of complexity for the formation of signs. A simple sign can be specified for no more than two different locations (a sign may require moving from one location to another), and no more than two different handshapes (a sign may require that the handshape changes during the sign). It is not clear whether such an absolute metric restriction applies to either orientations or movements. Note that these restrictions are claimed for simple signs only, not compound signs. However, it is interesting to note that many, if not most, compounds are themselves composed of no more than two simple signs.

1.71 Locations

We have already discussed some restrictions on signs with double locations; now we can look at the range and variety of the occurrence of these signs. No sign is specified for more than two locations, which themselves must be located in the same major area. Figure 14 demarcates four major areas on the body where signs make contact. Any sign which makes two separate contacts with the body confines those contacts to the same major area. The only exceptions to this are

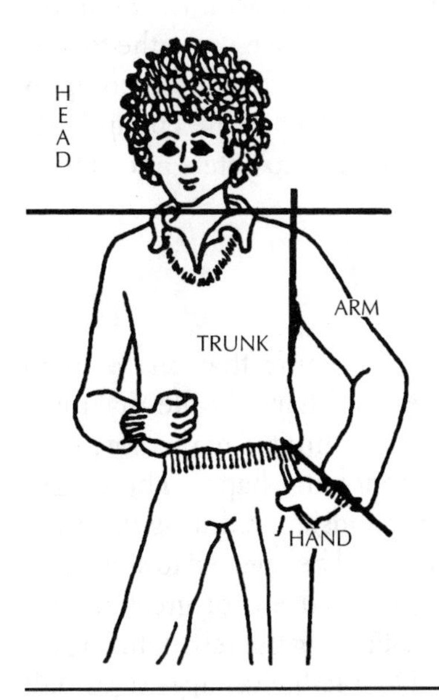

FIGURE 14. Four major areas.

compound signs or signs derived from compound signs.

Examples of signs made in two separate locations are (a) *Head area*—FLOWER (both sides of the nose), INDIAN (nose to crown or temple), BACHELOR (chin, contralateral to ipsilateral); (b) *Trunk area*—KING (contralateral breast to ipsilateral waist), SAILOR (both hips), OUR (breast, ipsilateral to contralateral); (c) *Arm area*—BRIDGE (wrist to elbow), IMPROVE (wrist to forearm), POWER (shoulder to forearm); (d) *Hand area*—TOAST (i.e., toasted bread; volar and dorsal surface), FLATTER (volar and dorsal surface of extended index finger), THEN (thumb tip to index tip).

In contrast to this restriction on simple signs, compound signs (or signs derived from compounds) may move from a location in one major area to a location in another major area: SISTER, derived from GIRL + SAME, contacts the cheek and then the opposite hand; REMEMBER, derived from THINK + SEAL, may contact the forehead before contacting the opposite hand; DAUGHTER, derived from GIRL + BABY, contacts the cheek and then the forearm. An examination of phonological processes in the following chapter will show that these complex compounds crossing major area boundaries are unstable, and tend to delete one of their locations.

1.72 Handshapes

Some signs may require that one or both hands change handshapes while making a sign; these signs are limited to no more than two such different handshapes. These signs which change handshapes during the articulation of a sign will be referred to as *double-handshape* signs, and are of great importance to understanding the restructurings of Chapter 4. Double-handshape signs fall into two broad types—those which also involve moving from one location to another, and those which remain in one relatively confined area. Both of these types include signs made in space and signs made on the body. Examples of each of these follow.

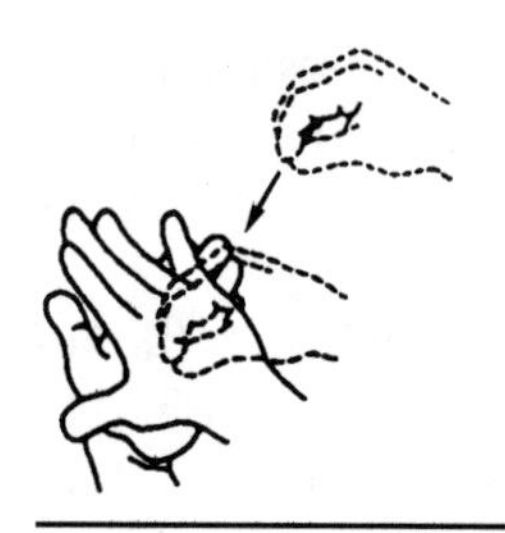

FIGURE 15. NOTE-DOWN

NOTE-DOWN (Figure 15) is made on the opposite palm, and involves changing the active hand from an O to a 5, without any additional movement. (This sign means "to make a note of something important," not "taking notes in a class.") Other double-handshape signs made in one location on the body include ACCEPT (5 becomes O, contacting the trunk), ORANGE (C closes to S, in front of the mouth or chin), CHEWING-GUM (V becomes $\ddot{V}$ [Bent V], fingertips contacting cheek).

Double-handshape signs which move on the body include RESTRAIN-FEELINGS (Figure 16) (5 becomes S, moving down the trunk), SPLIT/DISAPPEAR (L becomes bO [baby O], moving along the extended index of the opposite hand), FAR-OUT (5 becomes S, with the same location and movement as SPLIT).

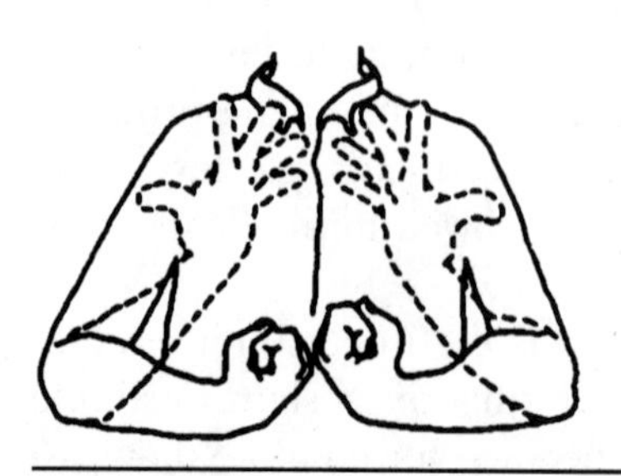

FIGURE 16. RESTRAIN-FEELINGS

Double-handshape signs made in space, off the body, may also be either static or moving, although locational points are not as easy to supply, since there are no convenient reference points in space without reference to the body. Static double-handshape signs made in space include MILK (hand held about shoulder height, C becomes S, repeatedly), and one of the signs for BEAT/OVERCOME (S becomes H). Other signs which might fit this class include 81 of the signs for the numbers between ELEVEN and NINETY-EIGHT. However, these are all transparently analyzable as compounds.

Finally, signs which move in space and also change handshapes: SIGN-ASL (verb; Figure 17) (each hand alternatively moves forward, changing from S to 5, repeatedly); WELFARE/SUBSCRIBE (hand moves from head height to shoulder height, changing from L to bO (baby O)); BE-PREPARED (Figure 18) (ulnar surface of one S-hand contacts thumb surface of the other S-hand, hands thrust forward and change to 5-hands, once); BAWL-OUT (same as BE-PREPARED, but rapidly reduplicated).

Double-handshape signs, in spite of their apparent complexity, appear to be a stable part of the language if we judge on the basis of their prominence—there are 155 double-handshape signs listed in *DASL*. They exhibit a number of interesting characteristics which bear on the present discus-

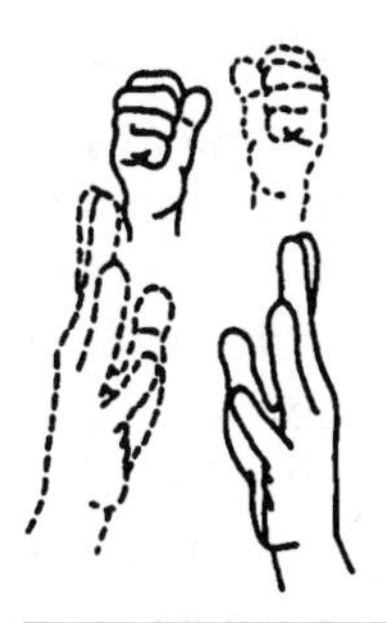

FIGURE 17. SIGN-ASL (repeated)

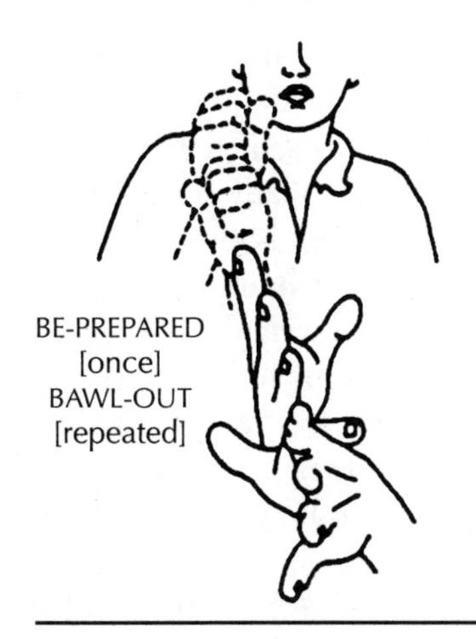

FIGURE 18.

sion and on the later discussion of loan signs. There are four major points to be made about the *type* of handshapes which occur in double-handshape signs:

(1) As already pointed out, the handshapes which predominate in these signs are the unmarked seven—A, S, 5, B, G, C, and O. Of the 155 signs which change handshapes, 136, or 87.7%, involve at least one member of this select set; in 98 of the signs, or 63.2%, both handshapes are unmarked.

(2) The dimension of change which is most often involved in these handshape changes is that of relative *openness* and *closedness* of the handshapes. Thus straight, extended fingers may bend or fully contract into the palm (B→˙B̈˙, V→˙V̈˙, 5→S); extended fingers which are bent or curved may straighten out (˙B̈˙→B, ˙V̈˙→V, O→5, X→G) or they may close (C→S); fingers which are contracted into a compact fist may extend fully (A→5, S→5). 153 signs, or 98.7%, vary in this way along the closed/open dimension. (The two exceptions are HAIRCUT and BOTH, in which V→U; the fingers converge but do not close or bend.)

(3) It follows from the above that most of these handshapes involve *maximal* changes

along the closed/open dimension. If we consider the two handshapes A and S to be the maximally compact, closed handshapes, and B and 5 as the maximally open handshapes, then these two end-points enjoy a prominent role in double-handshape signs. 125 signs, or 80.6%, involve at least one element from the set A, S, B, and 5 (83 as the initial handshape, 73 as the final handshape, and 31 signs which involve a maximal change from A/S to B/5, or vice-versa).

(4) The handshape changes on the dimension of open/closed are generally relevant to all involved fingers. Thus, if two fingers are extended, both will be bent; if five fingers are extended, all of them will be bent over or closed completely, etc. In measuring this tendency, we find that 136 signs, or 87.7% of the double-handshape signs, change the closed/open dimension of all involved fingers, instead of merely some of them. So while there are signs where C →S (closing all fingers), we do not find C →V̈ (leaving two bent extended fingers); we find O opening all its fingers to 5 and closing all its fingers to S, but we do not find signs where an O opens two of its fingers to an L, nor do we find signs where O closes three of its fingers to bO (baby O).

Double-handshape signs exhibit restricting tendencies on handshapes which exclude many logically possible, but overly complex gestures. Complexity of these signs is held to a minimum by favoring the involvement of unmarked handshapes which make simple transitions to other unmarked handshapes along a single dimension of *open* vs. *closed* hand.

1.73 Iterations

Besides measuring the number of locations and number of handshapes included in a sign, we can also measure the number of unit *executions* or beats that are required to articulate a sign. Execution here means the production of the basic specified units of the sign—its location, handshapes, orientation, and movements all in one bundle (some of these locations or handshapes may be doubled or complex, as we have just seen). Thus a single execution or beat is one complete cycle of a sign, with no part of it being repeated.

Some signs require internal repetition; the individual lexical item may consist of a reduplicated gesture. Sometimes this serves to mark an inflection on a sign which commonly consists of one execution. Some noun plurals are formed this way, for example, and some verb inflections are marked by special types of repetition (Fischer 1973). But what concerns us here are the parameters of monomorphemic lexical description and differentiation. In this regard, it turns out that some signs simply require two beats, some for seemingly arbitrary reasons, and some because they are derived from signs which once had two different locations, but currently have a reiterated gesture made in one location (Frishberg 1975, 1976).

Examples of signs that require two metrical beats include MANY (which itself is a double-handshape sign in which S→5, so the sign consists of a chain of handshapes; S→5→S→5), SCHOOL, KNOCK (on a door), GO-BACK-AND-FORTH (or COMMUTE), BAWL-OUT (Figure 18), DISCUSS (Figure 4), PAIN, PREACH (Figure 4), and NAME (Figure 3).

There are also some signs which always have only a single beat, the movements of these often being sharp. Reduplication in these forms is either not attested, or only found when the sign is inflected in some other manner. These include the signs: BE-PREPARED (Figure 18), TRICK ("to trick someone;" volar side of active A hand hits dorsal side of upright passive G, once); ILLEGAL (volar knuckles of active L strikes and rebounds from volar surface of passive B, once); LOSE ("to lose a game;" volar folded knuckles of active V contacts volar surface of passive B, once); CONVINCE (ulnar edge of B strikes edge of upright G, once); KNACK/CAN-DO (tips of thumb and index of F contact chin, once; see DASL pp. 155–156).

Further, we should note two things. First, while there are signs which are limited to one beat in unmarked contexts, the signs which require at least two beats have no absolute limit on the actual number of iterations. The number two is a required minimum; such a sign may be produced with three iterations, or four iterations, etc. There are no lexical distinctions based on the difference between two and four iterations, or two and five iterations, etc.; the difference is between signs with one beat and those with iterations.

1.8 SUMMARY

We have seen that for the submorphemic level of American Sign Language, the formational level, one can establish goals of description and explanation which are consonant with those of generative phonology. In particular, the phonological component of a language must determine the permissible and inadmissible forms of a language. Starting with a brief description of the manual visual elements of ASL, the primes which fall into the four aspects of location (tab), handshape (dez), movement (sig), and orientation, we have seen that ASL restricts the formation of admissible signs:

(1) The units themselves have a hierarchy of complexity which is measurable. Certain handshapes (A, S, B, 5, C, G, and O) are unmarked handshapes. Certain locations of the body are favored over others for the complexity of signs they enter into: Ipsilateral and central locations are unmarked in this regard, and contralateral locations are marked; locations in proximity to the head area allow finer differentiation of handshapes and locations than in the trunk area, and this is in accordance with strategies for visual perception available to the sign perceiver.

(2) Other constraints regulate the combinational properties of these elements as they form morphemes. The Symmetry Condition requires symmetry if both hands of a sign are moving, in order to limit the complexity of the sign; likewise, the Dominance Condition restricts the movements and possible handshapes of the passive hand in signs which have two different handshapes, one on either hand. Bilateral symmetry is thus unmarked, and asymmetry is marked.

(3) For double-handshape signs (signs which change handshapes during the sign), signs which have two locations, and signs which have a double execution (or reduplication), we also find restrictions. We have posited an upper limit on the underlying form of a sign, which states that it may not require more than two handshapes, two locations, or two separate executions of the basic gestural motor act. Double-handshape signs themselves are restricted in the types of handshapes which they may involve.

There remains another very important question: Do these proposed constraints systematically disallow certain manual formations in ASL, or do they merely represent accidental gaps in the lexicon which could be filled but are not? A tentative answer will be proposed after more evidence is presented in Chapter 2.

In conclusion, these are the basic points:

a. It is possible to describe and measure formational complexity of signs.
b. There are severe restrictions on the for-

mation of signs which exclude the more complex combinations of manual-visual components.

c. Therefore not all possible manual-visual gestures are permissible signs in ASL.

d. The restrictions on possible occurring signs of ASL are motivated by the dynamics inherent in manual articulation and visual perception: The restrictions are linguistic limitations on information coding, partly brought about by a need for systematic redundancy in the signals.

In informal terms, Chapter 1 has pointed out "what signs look like, and why." In Chapter 2 we shall see how these principles and structures take a more active role in determining the shape and substance of American Sign Language—in other words, how signs behave, both in terms of passage of time, and in terms of juxtaposition to other signs.

NOTES

1. Sign glosses are given in small capital letters. The gloss is simply a common translation of the sign into an English word, and the semantic, syntactic, and morphological properties of the word and the corresponding sign do not necessarily coincide. For example, the English word "attend" has two different ASL translations, one sign meaning "pay attention," and the other meaning "to go to an event." Conversely, the single ASL sign SINCE can also be translated into English as "lately," "up till now," "has been," etc. As such, *the capitalized gloss is merely a convenient label or name of a sign.* As much as possible, the same capitalized gloss (name) will always be applied to the same sign. Additional notes on other transcription conventions will be found in Chapter 4.
2. The capital letters and numerals used in descriptions of signs are names (or symbols) of handshapes, and should not be confused with letters of any alphabet (although in some cases that is the motivation for the symbol). The symbols in this study are based on Stokoe's (1960) transcriptional system. The reader who is unfamiliar with the handshapes involved in fingerspelling and in American Sign Language should consult Appendix A; Stokoe's symbols for handshapes appear in Appendix B.
3. This concurs with Kimura's findings (1973a, b) that the dominant hand makes more free movements while accompanying speaking activity. From these studies and many more, including cases of aphasia in deaf signers, she makes a strong case for left hemispheric control (in right handers) of the motor activities underlying verbal and gestural activity, including sign language (Kimura 1974, Kimura, Battison, and Lubert 1976).
4. For the purpose of simplifying the discussion here, this "select set of seven handshapes" includes phonetically distinct variants which do not always contrast at any underlying level of representation. A permissible variant of A on the passive hand (and certain other contexts) is S, which differs only in that the thumb is more compact—placed over the knuckles rather than at the side of the index finger—the A is generally found in signs requiring volar contact and the S hand with ulnar contact. B (with thumb held at side of index finger—not folded into palm as with fingerspelled B) and 5 also co-vary or freely vary in many contexts. See Friedman (1976) for a more detailed description of the distributional patterns of handshapes.
5. "Initialized" signs (or "initial dez" signs, or "initial handshape" signs) are those whose handshapes correspond (via fingerspelling) to the first letter of the English word which commonly translates the sign. Thus the sign WAY may use a W handshape, although it is standardly made with a B handshape. More commonly, many signs use one of the handshapes that do not correspond to a letter of the fingerspelled alphabet (e.g. AIRPLANE, HATE, and THIRD); recall that there are more than 26 different handshapes. Other signs coincidentally use handshapes which correspond to fingerspelled letters, but they may have no connection to an English gloss (e. g. SCHOOL with B handshapes, TELEPHONE with a Y handshape, SIGN(ATURE) with a B and an H hand). For some handshapes (e.g. D, E, R, T, and W), nearly all the signs which employ them are initialized signs. In this sense they can be said to occur in a restricted context, since they are not freely productive handshapes. For example, signs commonly made with an R handshape include RESTAURANT, ROCKET, ROOM, RAT, RATHSKELLAR, RED, REGISTER, RESEARCH, RULE, REASON, RESPOND, and REHEARSE.

File 4—Introduction: *What Do You Know When You Know a Language?*

M. Crabtree and J. Powers

As a speaker of English, you know a great deal about your language—but suppose someone were to ask you to put all that knowledge down into a textbook to be used to teach English to others. You would soon find out that although you know perfectly well how to speak English, you are not consciously aware of most of that knowledge. Linguists are interested in this "hidden" knowledge, which they call *linguistic competence.* In this course we will be examining (among other things) the elements of linguistic competence—that is, what you know when you know a language.

But if linguistic competence isn't available to conscious thought, how can we find out what this competence is like? We can observe speakers' *linguistic performance,* and draw conclusions about the knowledge that underlies it. You can think of linguistic competence as being a person's potential to speak a language, and his or her linguistic performance as the realization of that potential. Compare it with riding a bicycle. You can have the ability to ride a bike even when you're not using that ability, and even though you probably aren't fully aware of all the complex motor tasks and feats of balance and timing that are involved. When you get on a bike and go, that's bicycling performance.

Now suppose you're riding along, and you hit a bump and fall off. That doesn't mean you're not a competent cyclist, even though your performance was impaired. Maybe you just weren't paying attention to where you were going, or a squirrel ran in front of your tire, or it was dark and you couldn't see well. Linguistic performance is quite similar; speech usually contains lots of mistakes and hesitations, but that doesn't mean that the competence underlying that speech is flawed. Since competence can't be observed directly, linguists use linguistic performance as a basis for drawing conclusions about what competence must be like. However, they try to abstract away from performance factors (the inevitable speech errors, incomplete utterances, and so on) in their study of linguistic competence.

So what are some of the things you know about your language? Here is a brief survey.

PHONETICS

Part of your linguistic competence has to do with your knowledge of the sounds of your language. You know how to produce them though you may have never had to really think about the mechanics of doing so. Imagine, for instance, that you are trying to describe to someone else how the first sound in the word *the* is pronounced (*the*, by the way, contains only two sounds). Or suppose you had to explain the differences between

Source. Reprinted by permission of the publisher, from M. Crabtree and J. Powers, compilers, *Language Files: Materials for an Introduction to Language* (1991): 9–12. Columbus: Ohio State University Press.

the vowels in the words *bat*, *beat*, and *boot*. You have probably been producing these sounds for years without having to think twice about them. When you attempt to learn another language, you become acutely aware that other languages have sounds that English does not have—for example, French *r*, French or Spanish *p*, the German *ü* and *ö* vowels, the *ch* of German (which has more than a single pronunciation), or the clicks of some languages of Africa such as Xhosa and Zulu.

PHONOLOGY

Not only can you produce and perceive the sounds of your language, you know how these sounds work together as a system. For instance, you know what sequences of sounds are possible in different positions. In words like *ptomaine* or *Ptolemy* English speakers usually omit the *p*, because *pt* is not a combination that can occur at the beginning of English words. There is nothing inherently difficult about this cluster, however; it occurs non-initially in many English words such as *apt*, *captive*, and *lapped*, and some languages (including Greek) do allow *pt* clusters to occur word-initially.

An even more dramatic demonstration of your inherent knowledge of possible sound sequences appears when you consider *Jumbles* and *Scrambles* from the newspapers. (These are actually concerned with unscrambling letters, not sounds, but the same principles apply.) For example, *gisnt* has five letters. There are 5! ($5 \times 4 \times 3 \times 2 \times 1 = 120$) possible arrangements of these letters. When you do a *Jumble*, however, you rarely consider many of the possibilities: you've probably already grouped *n* and *g* as *ng*, put the one vowel somewhere in the middle, and put *s* and *t* together in *st*. You don't even think of beginning words with *ng*, *gt* or *gs* or ending them with *gnt* or *tn*, or even *gn* (this does occur, but it's rare and pronounced as *n*). Your inherent knowledge of what is a possible sequence of sounds in the English language enables you to eliminate these possibilities.

Your knowledge of phonology also allows you to make substitutions for unfamiliar sounds. Consider the sounds discussed earlier that are foreign to an English speaker. When we try to pronounce words containing such sounds, we usually replace them with sounds from our own language. For instance, English speakers often pronounce the German name *Bach* with a final *k* sound, and replace the *ü* in German *grun* "green" with the same vowel as in English *moon*. Or English speakers may ignore differences that are important in other languages but not in English, such as the tones in Thai and the Chinese languages.

MORPHOLOGY

For the most part, speech consists of a continuous stream of sound with few pauses between words. Speakers, however, have little trouble breaking utterances down into the words that make them up. Thus an English speaker can easily analyze (a) as containing the sequence of words in (b), and a Welsh speaker can just as easily break (c) down into (d) [which means the same thing as (b)].

(a) Ihavetogohomeearlytoday.
(b) I have to go home early today.
(c) Rhaidimifyndadre'ngynnarheddiw.
(d) Rhaid i mi fynd adre'n gynnar heddiw.

You also know how to break individual words down into smaller parts that have a meaning or some other function, and you know how to create words by combining these smaller parts. For instance, how many parts are there to the words *desk*, *oranges*, and *unbelievability*? Can you produce an example of a word you've never heard or read before? You can certainly understand newly composed words—for example, *uncoffeelike.* As a speaker of some language, you know which such combinations are possible and which ones aren't. Compare *baker* with the nonword **erbake,* or nicely with **bookly* (the "*" is used to mark that something is ungrammatical—in this case, that it is not a possible word). What is wrong with these starred words?

SYNTAX

You can recognize well-formed—that is, grammatical—sentences:

(a) *You up pick at o'clock will eight.
(b) *I will picks you up at eight o'clock.
(c) I will pick you up at eight o'clock.
(d) At eight o'clock, I will pick you up.

(a) and (b) are ungrammatical; (a) is just nonsense and (b) violates the standard English rules of subject-verb agreement; (c) and (d) are grammatical, and they are also syntactically related to each other. Why is (d) grammatical but (e) not?

(e) *You up at, I will pick eight o'clock.

There is an important difference between the grammaticality of a sentence (whether it is structurally well-formed) and semantic acceptability (whether it makes sense). Below, (f) is structurally well-formed [compare it with the structurally parallel sentence in (g)], but semantically odd.

(f) Colorless green ideas sleep furiously.
(g) Contented little cats purr loudly.

SEMANTICS

Part of your linguistic competence has to do with your ability to determine the meaning of sentences. Your competence also allows you to determine when a sentence has more than one meaning. Consider the following ambiguous sentences; what are the different meanings each one can have?

(a) I like chocolate cakes and pies.
(b) I'll meet you at the bank.
(c) Visiting relatives can be dreadful.
(d) I saw her duck.

You also know when different sentences mean the same thing.

(e) John is an unmarried male.
(f) John is a bachelor.

(g) The car bumped the truck.
(h) The truck was bumped by the car.

Above, (e) and (f) are synonymous sentences, as are (g) and (h). In addition, (g) and (h) are syntactically related (one is the passive of the other).

PRAGMATICS

Your understanding of the meaning of sentences and larger utterances also involves an understanding of how the context of those utterances influences their meaning. For instance, suppose you're a student in a classroom; there's a lot of noise out in the hall, and the instructor says to you "Can you close the door?" Taken quite literally, this is an inquiry about your door-closing abilities, but you would probably not even think of taking the question in that way. Instead, you would understand it as a request that you close the door.

As a speaker of a language, you subscribe to unspoken conventions that enable you to use and interpret language correctly, though you may have never consciously become aware of these "rules." You also know how to use language to do things—to perform what are called *speech acts.* In the example above, your instructor performed the act of requesting you to close the door. Think about the many different ways you could use language to perform the act of, for example, finding out from someone what time it is, requesting information from someone, or giving someone a warning.

STYLES OF SPEECH

You also understand the contexts or situations in which different styles of language may be used. Suppose, for instance, you are explaining what it is you plan to do after college (a question most students are relentlessly subjected to). In what ways would your answer be different if you were talking to your roommate, to your parents, or to a prospective employer at a job interview? Speech styles can vary in pronunciation, vocabulary, and syntax, among other things. (Who are you more likely to use a sentence like this one with? *With whom is there a greater likelihood that one will employ a sentence of this genre?)*

You are also probably quite aware that not all speakers of your language talk in exactly the same way. Everyone speaks a dialect, and dialects can vary in subtle or striking ways. You can often draw conclusions about where a speaker is from, and you may make assumptions about their ethnic background or socioeconomic class based on the way they talk. Justified or not, most people have opinions about their own speech and that of others; though they may not realize it, these opinions are strongly influenced by nonlinguistic factors.

File 5—Introduction: *Prescriptive vs. Descriptive Rules of Grammar*

M. Crabtree and J. Powers

To most people, the word "grammar" means the sort of thing they learned in English classes, when they were taught about subjects and predicates and parts of speech, and told not to dangle participles or strand prepositions. To a linguist, however, "grammar" means something rather different; it is the set of elements and rules that make up a language. Actually, linguistics recognize three distinct things called "grammar."

The first kind of grammar was discussed in File 4. It is those aspects of a speaker's knowledge of language that allow him or her to produce grammatical utterances—that is, a speaker's *linguistic competence.* This kind of grammar is made up of knowledge of phonetics, phonology, morphology, syntax, and semantics. Everyone who speaks a language has a grammar of that language in his or her head, but details of this grammar will vary among dialect groups and even among speakers of the same dialect. Note that this grammar determines the structural wellformedness of utterances, not their appropriateness. You can imagine producing perfectly grammatical sentences that are pragmatically unacceptable or stylistically odd—for example, answering a question with a wholly irrelevant statement or using lots of slang on a graduate school application. Knowledge of pragmatics and language variation is not usually considered to be part of grammar proper, though it is an important part of your knowledge about language.

Linguists concern themselves with discovering what speakers know about a language, and describing that knowledge objectively. They devise rules of *descriptive grammar.* For instance, a linguist describing English might formulate rules (i.e., descriptive generalizations) such as these:

1. Adjectives precede the nouns they modify.
2. To form the plural of a noun, add *-s*.
3. The vowel sound in the word suit is produced with rounded lips.

Descriptive grammar, then, is created by linguists as a model of speakers' linguistic competence.

When most people think of "grammatical rules," they think of what linguists call rules of *prescriptive grammar.* Prescriptive rules tell you how to speak or write, according to someone's idea of what is "good" or "bad." Of course, there is nothing inherently good or bad about any use of language; prescriptive rules serve only to mold your spoken and written English to some standard norm. Here are a few examples of prescriptive rules; you can probably think of others.

4. *Never end a sentence with a preposition.*
   NO: Where do you come from?
   YES: From where do you come?

Source. Reprinted by permission of the publisher, from M. Crabtree and J. Powers, compilers, *Language Files: Materials for an Introduction to Language* (1991): 13–15. Columbus: Ohio State University Press.

5. *Never split an infinitive.*
   NO: . . . to boldly go where no one has gone before
   YES: . . . to go boldly where no one has gone before
6. *Never use double negatives.*
   NO: I don't have nothing.
   YES: I don't have anything. I have nothing.

Notice that the prescriptive rules make a value judgment about the correctness of an utterance and try to force a usage that aligns with one formal norm. Descriptive rules, on the other hand, accept the patterns a speaker actually uses and try to account for them. Descriptive rules allow for different varieties of a language; they don't ignore a construction simply because some prescriptive grammarian doesn't like it.

So, if prescriptive rules are not based on actual use, how did they arise? Many of these rules were literally created by someone. During the seventeenth and eighteenth centuries, scholars became preoccupied with the art, ideas, and language of ancient Greece and Rome. The Classical Period was regarded as a golden age and Latin as the perfect language. The notion that Latin was somehow better or purer than contemporary languages was strengthened by the fact that Latin was strictly a written language and had long ceased to undergo the changes natural to spoken language. John Dryden's preoccupation with Latin led him to write: "I am often put to a stand in considering whether what I write be the idiom of the tongue . . . and have no other way to clear my doubts but by translating my English into Latin." For many writers of the seventeenth and eighteenth centuries the rules of Latin became, whenever remotely feasible, the rules of English. The rules above are all results of this phenomenon.

Speakers of English have been ending sentences with prepositions freely since the beginning of the Middle English period (about 1100). There are even some instances of this construction in Old English. Speakers who attempt to avoid this often sound stilted and stuffy. The fact that ending sentences with prepositions is perfectly natural in English did not stop John Dryden from forbidding it because he found it to be non-Latin. His rule has been with us ever since.

Since the early Middle English period, English has had a two-word infinitive composed of "to" plus an uninflected verb (e.g., "to win"). English speakers have always been able to split this two-word infinitive by inserting words (usually adverbs) between the "to" and the verb (e.g., "to quickly hide"). There have been periods in English literary history when splitting infinitives was very fashionable. However, 18th century grammarians noticed that Latin infinitives were never split. Of course, it was impossible to split a Latin infinitive because it was a single word (e.g., *describere*, "to write down"). But that fact did not prevent the early grammarians from formulating another prescriptive rule of English grammar.

The double negative rule has a different source. In Old and Middle English, double and triple negatives were common, and even quadruple negatives existed. The following sentence from Old English illustrates this; it contains two negative words, and was entirely grammatical.

7. ne bið ðær nænig ealo gebrowen mid Estum
   not is there not-any ale brewed among Estonians
   "No ale is brewed among the Estonians."

By Shakespeare's time, however, the double negative was rarely used by educated speakers, although it was still common in many dialects. In 1762, Bishop Robert Lowth attempted to argue against the double negative by invoking rules of logic: ". . . two negatives in English destroy one another or are equivalent to an affirmative." Of course, language and formal logic are different systems, and there are many languages (e.g., Russian) in which multiple negation is required for grammaticality. Certainly no one misunderstands the English-speaking child or adult who says "I don't want none." But Lowth ignored the fact that it is usage, not logic, that must determine the descriptive rules of a grammar.

It is somewhat surprising that rules which do not reflect actual language use should survive. There are several reasons, however, for the continued existence of prescriptive rules. First, they provide a standard form of a language that is accepted by most speakers of that language; adherence to prescriptive rules allows a speaker to be understood by the greatest possible number of individuals. This is especially important for a language such as German, which has dialects so different from one another that their speakers cannot always understand each other. Second, a set of standard rules is necessary for students learning English (or any other language) as a second language. Imagine the chaos if there were no guidelines for learning English (or Spanish, or German, or Russian, etc.). Thus they serve a very useful purpose for language teachers and learners as well. Finally, and most importantly, there are *social* reasons for their existence. Nonstandard dialects are still frowned upon by many groups and can inhibit one's progress in society. The existence of prescriptive rules allows a speaker of a nonstandard dialect to learn the rules of the standard dialect and employ them in appropriate social circumstances. Therefore, prescriptive rules are used as an aid in social mobility. This does *not* mean, however, that these judgments about dialects are *linguistically* valid. The idea that one dialect of a language is intrinsically better than another is simply false; from a linguistic point of view all dialects are equally good and equally valid. To look down on nonstandard dialects is to exercise a form of social and linguistic prejudice.

EXERCISES

1. Which of the following are prescriptive statements, and which are descriptive?

   a. *It's me* is ungrammatical; *It's I* is the correct way to say this.

   b. *Between you and me* is correct; *between you and I* is ungrammatical.

   c. People who say *ain't* may suffer some negative social consequences because many speakers of English associate *ain't* with the dialects of the working classes.

   d. In casual styles of speaking, English speakers frequently end sentences with prepositions; ending sentences with prepositions is avoided in formal styles.

File 6—Introduction: *Arbitrariness in Language*

M. Crabtree and J. Powers

It is generally recognized that the words of a language and the pieces that make up these words (all of which are discussed in some detail in later files) represent a connection between a group of sounds, which give the word or word-piece its form, and a meaning. For example, the word for the inner core of a peach is represented in English by the sounds we spell as *p*, *i* and *t*, occurring in that order to give the form *pit*. The combination of a form and a meaning connected in this way gives what may be called a *linguistic sign*.

An important fact about linguistic signs is that, in the typical instance in a language, the connection between form and meaning is *arbitrary*. The term "arbitrary" here refers to the fact that the meaning is not in any way predictable from the form, nor is the form dictated by the meaning. The opposite of *arbitrariness* in this sense is *nonarbitrariness*, and the most extreme examples of nonarbitrary form-meaning connections are said to be iconic. Iconic forms are directly representational of their meanings (for example, a "No Smoking" sign that has a large red X through a cigarette). Moreover, the connection in such cases is not a matter of logic or reason, nor is it derivable from laws of nature.

Thus, the fact that the inner core of a peach may be called a *stone* or even a *seed* as well as a *pit* points to arbitrariness in the above example, for if the connection between the form and the meaning here were nonarbitrary (because the form determined the meaning, or vice versa), there should only be one possible form to express this meaning. Also, there is nothing intrinsic in the combination of the sounds represented by *p*, *i* and *t* that suggests the meaning "inner core of a peach," for the same sounds combined in a different order have an entirely different meaning in the word spelled *tip*.

Arbitrariness in language is shown by other considerations. For instance, it is usually the case cross-linguistically that words with the same meaning have different forms in different languages and that similar forms express different meanings. Thus, what is *water* in English is *eau* in French, *Wasser* in German, *shui* in Mandarin Chinese, and so on. And the same form (pronounced like the English name *Lee*) means "bed" in French (spelled *lit*), marks a question in Russian, and means "meadow" or "side sheltered from the wind" in English (spelled *lea* and *lee* respectively), as well as being an English proper name. If there were an inherent, nonarbitrary connection between form and meaning in all languages, with the meaning being determined by the form, then such cross linguistic differences should not occur.

Similarly, the pronunciation of particular words can change over time (see File 92

Source. Reprinted by permission of the publisher, from M. Crabtree and J. Powers, compilers, *Language Files: Materials for an Introduction to Language* (1991): 17–21. Columbus: Ohio State University Press.

Crosslinguistic Examples of Onomatopoeia

SOUND	ENGLISH	GERMAN	FRENCH	SPANISH	HEBREW	ARABIC	MANDARIN	JAPANESE
1. Dog barking	[bawwaw]	[vawvaw]	[wahwah]	[wawwaw]	[hawhaw]	[ʕawə] (baby talk)	[wãwwãw]	[wãwa]
2. Rooster crowing	[kakəduədldu]	[kikəRiki]	[kokoRiko]	[kikr̃iki] or [kokoroko]	[kikuRiku]	[kikiki:s]	[kuku]	[kokekokko]
3. Cat meowing	[miaw]	[miaw]	[miaw]	[miaw]	[miaw]	[mawmaw]	[meaw] (baby talk)	[niaw]
4. Cow lowing	[mu:]	[mu]	[mø:]	[mu]	[mu]	[ʕu:]	[mo]	[mo:mo:]
5. Sheep bleating	[ba:]	[mɛ:]	[be:]	[bɛ:]	[mɛ:mɛ:]	[ma:ʔ]	[mɛ:mɛ]	[mɛ:mɛ:]
6. Bird chirping	[twit-twit]	[pip]	[kwikwi]	[pippip]	[tswits tswits]	[zægzæg]	[čiči]	[čiči]
7. Bomb exploding	[bum]	[bum]	[bRum] or [vRum]	[bum]	[bum]	[bɔm]	[bɔ̃ŋ]	[bãŋ]
8. Sound of laughing	[haha]	[haha]	[haha]	[xaxa]	[haha]	[qahqah]	[haha]	[haha]
9. Sound of sneezing	[aču]	[hači]	[ačum]	[aču] or [ači]	[apči]	[ʕats]	[hačũ:]	[hakšɔ̃ŋ]
10. Sound of something juicy hitting a hard surface	[splæt]	[pač]	[flæk]	—	[flox]	[ʔax]	[pyaʔ]	[gušaʔ]
11. Sound of a clock	[tɪ̆ktak]	[tɪ̆ktɪ̆k]	[tɪ̆ktak]	[tɪ̆ktak]	[tɪ̆ktak]	[tɪ̆ktɪ̆k]	[tiktɔk]	[ciktakɯ̣]

*Buffalo cow

on sound change). For instance, from a variety of evidence, including their spelling, we know that words such as *wrong*, *knight*, and *gnaw* must have had an initial *w*, *k*, and *g* respectively at some point in the history of English, and have thus undergone a change in their pronunciation, i.e., in their form. If we hold to the view that the form-meaning connection is determined and nonarbitrary, and if we further suppose that the original pronunciations of these words reflected this inherent and nonarbitrary relationship between form and meaning, then how can we maintain this inherent connection when the pronunciation changes without any accompanying changes in meaning? The relationship between the form and meaning of a word, therefore, has to be arbitrary in order to allow for inevitable changes it may undergo.

It is clear, therefore, that arbitrariness is the norm in language, at least as far as the basic relationship between the form of a word and its meaning is concerned. At the same time, though, it turns out that there are many nonarbitrary aspects to language. Again, to focus just on vocabulary and the form-meaning connection (though nonarbitrariness can be found in other domains of language), notice that a small portion of the vocabulary of all languages consists of items whose forms are largely determined by their meanings. Most notable and obvious are the so-called *onomatopoetic* (or *onomatopoeic*) words, i.e., words that are imitative of natural sounds or have meanings that are associated with such sounds of nature.

Examples of onomatopoetic words in English include noise-words such as *bow-wow* for the noise a dog makes, *moo* for a cow's noise, *splat* for the sound of a rotten tomato hitting a wall, *swish* or *swoosh* for the sound of a basketball dropping cleanly through the hoop, *cockadoodle-doo* for the noise a rooster makes, and so on. Further examples include derivatives of noise-words, such as *cuckoo*, a bird name derived from the noise the bird makes, *babble*, a verb for the making of inarticulate noises derived from the perception of what such noises sound like, *burble*, a verb for the making of a rushing noise by running water derived from the sound itself, and so on. In all of these words, the match-up between the form of the word and the meaning of the word is very close: the meaning is very strongly suggested by the sound of the word itself.

Even in such onomatopoetic words, however, an argument for arbitrariness is to be found. While the form is largely determined by the meaning, the form is not an exact copy of the natural noise; roosters, for instance, do not actually say *cockadoodle-doo*—English speakers have just arbitrarily conventionalized this noise in that form. Moreover, when different languages imitate the same sound, they have to make use of their own linguistic resources. Different languages admit different sound combinations, so even the same natural sound may end up with a different form in different languages, though each of the forms is somewhat imitative. For example, a rooster says *cockadoodle-doo* in English but *kukuku* in Mandarin Chinese, even though (presumably) roosters sound the same in China as in America. If there were an inherent and determined connection between the meaning and the form of even onomatopoetic words, we would expect the same meaning to be represented by the same sounds in different languages. Thus, the strongest evidence for nonarbitrariness, namely the existence of onomatopoetic words, is not quite so strong after all; in fact, comparison of such words in different languages can be used to argue *for* a degree of arbitrariness in linguistic signs. To make this point more clearly, we give below eleven natural sounds that are represented by onomatopoetic words in eight languages. The similarity among them is expected, due both to the nature of the words and to possibility of borrowing between geographically neighboring languages; still, the variation is also great.

In what may perhaps be considered a special subcase of onomatopoeia, it is often found that certain sounds occur in words not by virtue of being directly imitative of some sound but rather by simply being evocative of a particular meaning; that is, these words more abstractly suggest some physical characteristics by the way they sound. This phenomenon is known as *sound symbolism*. For instance, in many languages, words for "small" and small objects or words which have smallness as part of their meaning often contain a vowel which is pronounced with the tongue high in the front part of the mouth (see File 22), which we will represent by the symbol [i]. This occurs in English *teeny* "extra-small," *petite* and *wee* "small," and dialectal *leetle* for "little," in Greek *mikros* "small," in Spanish diminutive nouns (i.e., those with the meaning "little X") such as *perrito* "little dog" where *-ito* is a suffix indicating "little," and so on. Such universal sound symbolism—with [i] suggesting "smallness"—seems to be motivated by several factors: first, the high, front vowel [i] uses a very small space in the front of the mouth, and second, [i] is a high-pitched vowel and thus more like the high-pitched sounds given off by small objects. Thus the use of [i] in "small" words gives a situation where an aspect of the form—the occurrence of [i]—is determined by an aspect of the meaning—"smallness"—and where the form to a certain extent has an inherent connection with the meaning, even though not directly imitative in any way. We may thus characterize the appearance of [i] in such words as somewhat iconic—the "small" vowel [i] is an *icon* for the meaning "small(ness)."

In addition to such universal sound symbolism, there are also cases of language particular sound symbolism, in which some sound or sequence of sounds can come to be associated in a suggestive way with some abstract and vague but often sensory-based meaning. For example, in English, words beginning with *fl-*, such as *fly, flee, flow, flimsy, flicker,* and *fluid,* are often suggestive of lightness and quickness. Also, there are many words in English that begin with *gl-* and refer to brightness (such as *gleam, glisten, glow, glint, glitter,* and *glimmer*), as well as a group of words signifying a violent or sudden action that all end in *-ash* (such as *bash, mash, crash,* and *flash*). In all such groups, an identifiable aspect of the form relates in a nonarbitrary way to the meaning.

Even in such cases, however, arbitrary aspects are again identifiable. Thus there are words which have the appropriate sequences of sounds but do not fit into the group semantically, such as *glove* and *glue* with respect to the *gl-* group, or *sash* and *cash* with respect to the *-ash* group. There are also words with appropriate meanings that do not fit in formally, such as *shine* or *hit;* note too that the English word *small* does not contain the "small" vowel [i], but instead a relatively "open" or "large" vowel (think about what a dentist or doctor might tell you to say in order to get your mouth open wide, and compare that to the vowel of *small*). Also, from a cross-linguistic perspective, it turns out that other languages do not (necessarily) have the same clustering of words with similar meanings and a similar form. For example, the Greek words for "fly," "flee," "flow" and "fluid" are *petó, févo, troéxo,* and *iró,* respectively, showing that the *fl-* sound symbol is an English-particular fact and so cannot be a matter of a necessary and inherent connection between form and meaning.

All in all, these examples show that nonarbitrariness and iconicity have at best a somewhat marginal place in language. At the same time, though, it cannot be denied that they do play a role in language and moreover that speakers are aware of their potential effects. Poets often manipulate onomatopoeia and sound symbolism in order to achieve the right phonic impression in their poetry; for example, Alfred Tennyson in his poem *The Princess* utilized nasal consonants to mimic the noise made by the bees he refers to:

> The **m**oa**n** of doves i**n** i**mm**e**m**orial el**m**s
> A**n**d **m**ur**m**uring of i**nn**u**m**erable bees
> (V11.206–7)

Similarly, the successful creation of new words often plays on sound symbolic effects; for instance, the recently coined word *glitzy* meaning (roughly) "flashily and gaudily extravagant" fits in well with the group of English words discussed above with initial *gl-*. It seems, therefore, that even though arbitrariness is the norm in language and is an important distinguishing characteristic separating human language from other forms of communication (see File 10), an awareness of nonarbitrary aspects of language is part of the linguistic competence of all native speakers and thus is worthy of study by linguists.

EXERCISES

1. In what ways do compound words such as *blackboard* or *outfox* show a degree of nonarbitrariness in their form-meaning connection? Will this be true for all compound words? (Hint: think about the color of objects we call *blackboards.*)
2. In Chinese, expressions for moving from one city to another by way of yet another city must take the form "from X pass-through Y to Z," and cannot be expressed as "from X to Z pass-through Y;" this is il-

lustrated in the examples below ("*" indicates that a sentence is unacceptable).

a. *ta cong San Francisco jinguo*
he from pass-through
Chicago dao New York
to
"He went from San Francisco through Chicago to New York"

b. **ta cong San Francisco dao New York*
he from to
jinguo Chicago
pass-through

How would you characterize the form-meaning relationship exhibited by these Chinese expressions?

3. Onomatopoetic words often show a resistance to change in their pronunciation over time; for example, in earlier stages of English the word *cuckoo* had roughly the same pronunciation as now, and failed to undergo a regular change in the pronunciation of vowels that would have made it sound roughly like *cowcow;* similarly, the word *babble* has had *b* sounds in it for over 2,000 years and did not undergo the sound shift that is characteristic of all the Germanic languages (see File 102) by which original *b* came to be pronounced as *p*. Can you suggest a reason for this resistance to change on the part of these (and similar) words?

4. One piece of evidence for sound symbolism is the often quite consistent responses that speakers of a language give to the judgment of the relative meanings of pairs of nonsense words, where the only clue to work from is the sound (i.e., the form) of the words. For example, speakers of English typically judge the nonsense word *feeg* to refer to something smaller than the nonsense word *foag*. Try the following experiment out on a friend and then compare your friend's responses with your own and compare your results with those of others in your class:

Pronounce the words below according to regular English spelling, and decide for each pair of words which member of the pair could refer to something *heavy* and which to something *light* (you might want to ask if given a pair x and y, it is possible to say that "an x is a heavier y" or vice-versa).

a. lat–loat
b. foon–feen
c. mobe–meeb
d. toos–tace
e. fleen–feen
f. seeg–sleeg
g. poas–poat
h. toos–tood

Signs Have Parts: A Simple Idea

ROBBIN BATTISON

It was December of 1971 and I was flying from San Diego to Europe to attend some meetings and see some friends. I had been working with American Sign Language for about a year, and one of the books that I kept going through again and again was the Dictionary of American Sign Language. *I decided to meet the principal author of that book as long as I was stopping in at Washington, D.C. Who knew when I would have a chance like that again? I called up Bill Stokoe and he invited me to lunch. At lunch, we chatted; he was friendly and full of ideas and wanted to know about mine.*

He later surprised me when he wrote to offer me a job that summer (the Watergate summer of 1972) in the Linguistics Research Lab. Of course I accepted; the salary he offered was twice what I would have asked for. I made several false starts that first summer and actually wrote up very little of my research or my ideas; but the following year Bill asked me to come out again. After the second summer in the Lab, I did not return to graduate school in San Diego. After all, I had finished my course work, and at Gallaudet College I could write my dissertation while surrounded by hundreds of skilled signers, the people who could help me discover new things about this very peculiar language that I had chosen to study. I had some ideas but very little direction at this point. Bill gave me the support I needed to develop my ideas and to shape my work into something coherent. It took years . . .

Robbin Battison first became interested in Sign Language in 1970, while studying linguistics at the University of California, San Diego, and working in Ursula Bellugi's laboratory at the neighboring Salk Institute for Biological Studies. He spent the years 1973–1976 at the Linguistics Research Lab, Gallaudet College, and received his Ph.D. in Linguistics from UCSD in 1977. His dissertation, Lexical Borrowing in American Sign Language, *was published in 1978. From 1976 to 1979, Robbin conducted research and taught American Sign Language in the Psychology Department of Northeastern University in Boston. Since 1979, he has pursued his interest in bureaucratic language and language comprehension as Manager of the Document Design Center at the American Institutes for Research in Washington, D.C. He edits a newsletter,* *Fine Print, *and other publications which discuss the language and design of public documents.*

INTRODUCTION

The thing that interested me most about Bill Stokoe was that he had hold of an exciting idea, one that clearly was going to lead somewhere. He said that Sign Language was a language like any other language and that it could be analyzed as a language. This simple idea contradicted many popular beliefs: for who could see similarities between the movements of hands and body and the audible sounds produced by speaking? What possible basis of comparison was there? And, as the argument went, even if they did have some casual similarity, we would still know that signed languages were fundamentally different from spoken languages: after all, signs are

Source. Reprinted by permission of the publisher, from C. Baker and R. Battison, eds., *Sign Language and the Deaf Community* (1980): 35–51. Silver Spring, MD: National Association of the Deaf.

like pictures drawn in the air with hands, aren't they, while words are quite abstract?

This is actually the crucial part of the argument, and the basic idea that Bill developed. Bill believed that the basic way to think of a sign was *not* as a picture, but as a complex and abstract symbol that could be analyzed into parts. This heretical idea contradicted what most experts had always said about signed languages, but eventually it took hold, because it opened new doors of understanding. Analyzing signs into parts allowed us to develop new theories about how signed languages work, where they came from, where they are going, and what is the best way to teach them. This simple idea also later influenced the way in which Sign Language is used in classrooms, and how it is used by interpreters. In this chapter I would like to give a short history of how this simple idea developed, the scientific inquiries that it inspired, and the social action and professional policies that derive from it. The story is not yet at an end.

SIGNS AS PICTURES

There are perhaps several reasons for the tradition of thinking of signs as pictures: they are visual; they involve space and size and shape; and they sometimes seem to represent things wholly and directly, just like a picture or a drawing. I would not argue against any of those very common observations. Signs are like pictures in many ways. But to stop there is to miss an important point. Saying that signs are like pictures is like saying that speech is like music. Spoken languages certainly have their musical aspects, but there are so many things about words and connected speech that are not like music—especially how they transmit meanings. There is more to signs than meets the eye; even if a sign does seem like a picture, that may not be the most important aspect of a sign to investigate.

There are several kinds of evidence which demonstrate that the pictorial or graphic nature of signs is not the most important aspect of Sign Language. First, several different kinds of experiments show that people who don't know Sign Language have a hard time guessing what very common signs mean, even in a multiple-choice test. Second, if we compare signs from different countries, we find that not everyone uses the same kind of gesture to represent the same meaning; in other words, different signed languages may represent the same thing with different kinds of gestures. Third, if we look very carefully at written and filmed records of older signs, we find that very often these signs have changed to become *less* graphic or picture-like, and have become more like a standardized gesture that must be pronounced in a particular way to be "just right." For example, the sign STUDENT (based on the sign LEARN) originally was made so that it seemed to create the image of taking something from a book and absorbing it into the mind; however, the modern sign looks very much like taking something and tossing it away! Fourth, sometimes even if you know what a sign means, you may find it hard or impossible to decide just exactly what pictorial image connects the meaning with the gesture. Some signs are just less pictorial than others.

For all these reasons and others (which are reviewed more carefully by Klima and Bellugi in their 1979 book) it is evident that we cannot learn very much or explain very much about Sign Language by depending on the weak idea that they are graphic pictures written in the air with the hands. There has to be something more.

WRITING ABOUT SIGNS

Bill Stokoe had a lot of faith in his ideas; that is, he always was a stubborn man, unwilling to change his opinions just because very few people agreed with him. Faith and stubbornness are sometimes just two ways of looking at the same thing.

At first his ideas didn't make sense to anyone. Many respected experts (including some of the authors in this volume) dismissed his ideas as worthless; he was wasting his time. But knowledge comes step by step, and Bill Stokoe had a plan for studying Sign Language. First, he would need to describe the language in an elemental sense: he must write a dictionary. But before he could do that, he would need to write signs down on paper, in order to "capture" them accurately and describe how they are made. So first he would have to invent an adequate writing system—and that's where the idea began to take real shape.

In order to develop a transcription (writing) system for signs, Bill was forced to take a good hard look at how signs are made: what parts of the body move or don't move, how the fingers bend or extend, how the hands contact the body, where they touch, the speed and repetition of movements, and so on. If he could just think of a written symbol for each of the *important* elements in making signs, then he could write them down, collect signs, and begin even further analyses that could provide important information about these very strange communication systems.

Very early on, he proposed that every sign had at least three independent parts:

location— where on the body or in space is the sign being made? On the cheek, the chest, in front of the body, etc.?

handshape—how are the fingers extended and bent in this particular sign? Is the hand a fist, or does it have some fingers extended, etc.?

movement— how does the hand (or hands) move? In a circle, up-and-down, forward, etc.?

From his experience and training with other languages, Stokoe then made an assumption that turned out to be true. He assumed that within each of these three categories, there were probably a limited number of different ways of making these sign parts. For example, there might be ten different handshapes, or there might be one hundred; the important thing was that he could probably develop a list of all the possibilities, and then develop symbols for each one of them—the list was not going to be infinitely long. The same would be true of different locations and movements. The possibilities were not endless. There was probably a system to it, waiting to be discovered.

In the end, he came up with a system that worked: he had 19 different basic symbols for handshapes, 12 different basic symbols for locations, and 24 different basic symbols for types of movements. In much the same way that the symbols 0123456789 allow us to express any number, Stokoe now had a system that would allow him to express any sign on paper. He published a list of symbols and some of his early thoughts about how to use them in a thin volume in 1960 called *Sign Language Structure*. Table 1 shows the chart he published.

Regardless of how well this system captured the important parts of signs, it was an advance for the time, and it gave us some new tools to work with in probing Sign Language further. There were also practical applications. Using a transcription system, for example, a dramatist could use the transcription system to record exactly the signs needed for a play, a poem, or some other dramatic presentation; a Sign Language teacher could begin to organize lesson material according to which signs are similar, or which signs are different. The most important thing that Stokoe went on to create, however, was the first true dictionary of Sign Language. With Carl Croneberg and

TABLE 1. Stokoe's Transcription Symbols

Tab symbols

1.	Ø	zero, the neutral place where the hands move, in contrast with all places below
2.	⌓	face or whole head
3.	⌒	forehead or brow, upper face
4.	△	mid-face, the eye and nose region
5.	∪	chin, lower face
6.	3	cheek, temple, ear, side-face
7.	Π	neck
8.	[]	trunk, body from shoulders to hips
9.	\	upper arm
10.	√	elbow, forearm
11.	ɑ	wrist, arm in supinated position (on its back)
12.	D	wrist, arm in pronated position (face down)

Dez symbols, some also used as tab

13.	A	compact hand, fist; may be like 'a', 's', or 't' of manual alphabet
14.	B	flat hand
15.	5	spread hand; fingers and thumb spread like '5' of manual numeration
16.	C	curved hand; may be like 'c' or more open
17.	E	contracted hand; like 'e' or more claw-like
18.	F	"three-ring" hand; from spread hand, thumb and index finger touch or cross
19.	G	index hand; like 'g' or sometimes like 'd'; index finger points from fist
20.	H	index and second finger, side by side, extended
21.	I	"pinkie" hand; little finger extended from compact hand
22.	K	like G except that thumb touches middle phalanx of second finger; like 'k' and 'p' of manual alphabet
23.	L	angle hand; thumb, index finger in right angle, other fingers usually bent into palm
24.	3	"cock" hand; thumb and first two fingers spread, like '3' of manual numeration
25.	O	tapered hand; fingers curved and squeezed together over thumb; may be like 'o' of manual alphabet
26.	R	"warding off" hand; second finger crossed over index finger, like 'r' of manual alphabet
27.	V	"victory" hand; index and second fingers extended and spread apart
28.	W	three-finger hand; thumb and little finger touch, others extended spread
29.	X	hook hand; index finger bent in hook from fist, thumb tip may touch fingertip
30.	Y	"horns" hand; thumb and little finger spread out extended from fist; or index finger and little finger extended, parallel
31.	8	(allocheric variant of Y); second finger bent in from spread hand, thumb may touch fingertip

Sig symbols

No.	Symbol	Description	Group
32.	^	upward movement	vertical action
33.	v	downward movement	vertical action
34.	N	up-and-down movement	vertical action
35.	>	rightward movement	sideways action
36.	<	leftward movement	sideways action
37.	z	side to side movement	sideways action
38.	⊤	movement toward signer	horizontal action
39.	⊥	movement away from signer	horizontal action
40.	I	to-and-fro movement	horizontal action
41.	ɑ	supinating rotation (palm up)	rotary action
42.	D	pronating rotation (palm down)	rotary action
43.	ω	twisting movement	rotary action
44.	ŋ	nodding or bending action	
45.	□	opening action (final dez configuration shown in brackets)	
46.	#	closing action (final dez configuration shown in brackets)	
47.	ℛ	wiggling action of fingers	
48.	⊚	circular action	
49.	)(	convergent action, approach	interaction
50.	×	contactual action, touch	interaction
51.	⌶	linking action, grasp	interaction
52.	†	crossing action	interaction
53.	⊙	entering action	interaction
54.	÷	divergent action, separate	interaction
55.	″	interchanging action	

KEY
Tab = location
Dez = handshape
Sig = movement

Dorothy Casterline, he collected, organized, and described more than 2000 different signs from the language he had begun to call American Sign Language. The dictionary was published in 1965.

We must remember the social and intellectual climate of fifteen years ago: many people were still denying that there was such a thing as a signed *language.* Certainly there was nothing that deserved the elegant title of American Sign Language (displayed in capital letters like that). And whatever kind of language it was, it was certainly nothing like the very large, complicated, and elegant spoken languages that were known in the world. As a matter of fact, some people belittled the language by referring to the dictionary and saying, "Only 2000 signs? This clearly indicates the impoverished, simple nature of Sign Language." What these people forgot is that our scientific knowledge of spoken languages has been developed and refined over several thousand years. By contrast, the scientific study of signed languages has only been progressing for twenty years, if we date it from Stokoe's first publication in 1960. We were only scratching the surface, so far.

Why was the dictionary so important? Surely there were other books that listed signs that deaf people use? But none were like this. A dictionary gives several different kinds of information about the words (or signs) of a language. For each *lexical entry* (separate word or sign), it gives: a coded physical description, telling us how to physically reproduce (pronounce) the word or sign; the meaning of that word or sign, including special nuances; the grammatical functions and properties of that word or sign, telling us how we might use it in a sentence and what variations we might expect depending upon its grammatical form; something of the history of that word or sign, especially a history that relates to other words or items in the language. *The Dictionary of American Sign Language* gave us all that. Previous books had given us only scattered and incomplete (and sometimes misleading) information about signs and Sign Language. Without a writing or transcription system, signs cannot be faithfully reproduced, unless especially clever photos or illustrations are used (and they usually were not).

The Dictionary of American Sign Language was remarkable for another reason: the signs were arranged according to a principle of the language. Just as spoken language dictionaries arrange their words alphabetically (according to the order of the first letter, then the second letter of the word, and so on), Stokoe arranged his sign dictionary according to the parts of the signs that he used for transcription. Thus, this idea that signs are complex objects with parts not only led to a writing system, but also led to a principle of *organizing* all the signs that could be related to each other, depending upon which parts they shared. This is like the way we think of different words as being related if they share the same sounds, particularly at the beginnings of words. This arrangement also shows a lot of *respect* for the language.

Considering the obvious usefulness of Bill's analysis, the reader might expect that he received a lot of support for his work from members of the Deaf community and from professionals in the field of deafness. But this was certainly not the case. Why didn't his ideas catch on more rapidly? Why was there such resistance and even hostility to his ideas about analyzing, transcribing, and describing signs?

There are two interesting reasons for this lack of support that are not usually considered. The first reason concerns the prevailing attitudes among educators of deaf people and deaf people themselves. At that time, you must remember, Sign Language was only accepted if it could be justified as a contribution to the educational system. Any new idea about Sign Language was discussed as a tool for classroom use. As several stories have it, students and faculty at Gallaudet and at some residential schools mistakenly assumed that they were going to be forced to learn this new transcription system for signs, and that all their books would be written in these complex symbols. Of course, nothing was further from the truth: the transcription system was intended as a scientific tool. But there were enough rumors and feelings going around to prevent anyone from really seeing the transcription system as Bill had intended it.

The second reason was a strategic error on Bill's part. Bill gave new technical names to the things he was describing. Perhaps he didn't realize that he was creating resistance to learning when he gave complex names to simple and familiar things. He referred to *dez*, *tab*, and *sig* when he could have simply said *handshape*, *location*, and *movement*. Some people were probably put off by these strange words and had some difficulty learning what they meant and keeping them separate; I certainly did, and I worked hard at it.

PARTS OF SIGNS

Comparing, grouping, and classifying signs according to what parts they have in common and what parts they don't is not simply a convenience for organizing dictionaries. Like words, signs must be broken up into parts in order to perceive what they mean. This is especially true of the kinds of complex signs that Ursula Bellugi describes in the next chapter, but it is also true of very simple signs.

Just as we know that the two English words "skim" and "skin" are different words with different meanings, we know that they are *minimally different*. That is, the only difference between these two words is the final sound unit: "m" or "n." Of course we can find thousands of these *minimal pairs* (pairs of words that differ in only one *minimal* way). From them we can determine what types of sound units play an important role in distinguishing meanings in a spoken language. We can do the same with a signed language.

We can find minimal pairs of signs that differ in only one aspect of their production. For the aspect of handshape, there are pairs of signs that are identical except for their handshape. An example is the pair of signs CAR and WHICH (Figure 1). The only difference between them is that CAR has a fist with the thumb closed against the knuckles, while WHICH has a fist with the thumb extended. In the case of location, a minimal pair of CHINESE and SOUR (Figure 2). The

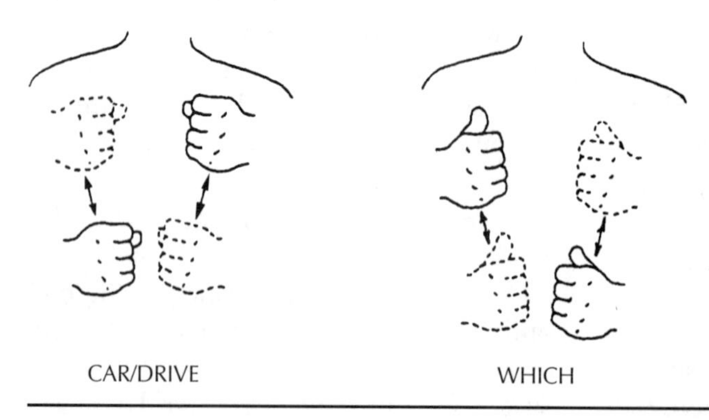

FIGURE 1.

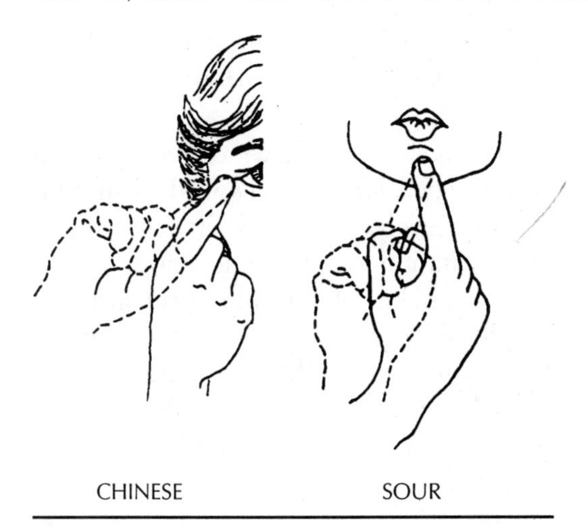

FIGURE 2.

two signs are identical except that CHINESE is made on the temple or high on the cheek and SOUR is made near the mouth.

A minimal pair for movement is found in NAME and SHORT (Figure 3). NAME is made with simple contact (sometimes repeated), while SHORT is made identically except for its brushing motion of the upper hand. Figure 3 also shows that the *orientation* of the hands might also be a distinctive aspect of signs. The pair of signs NAME and CHAIR differ only by their orientation: in NAME, both palm surfaces point towards the body, but in CHAIR the palm surfaces point downward. These and many other examples of minimal pairs show that there are critical

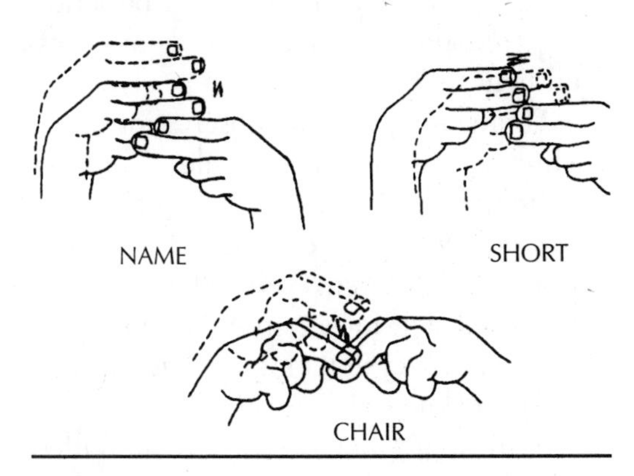

FIGURE 3.

parts of a sign that allow us to distinguish it from other signs.

There is also reason to think that this is not just a convenient way to speculate about words and signs. This kind of division into parts seems to reflect the way deaf native signers think in signs. Several memory experiments with both spoken and signed languages have shown that the errors people make when trying to recall lists of vocabulary items are frequently related to the other member of a minimal pair. In a spoken experiment, for example, someone who heard "vote" might later recall it as "note;" in a signed experiment, someone might see the sign TREE (with the hand completely open and fingers extended and spread, the entire upright forearm shakes on its axis) but later recall it as the sign NOON (same gesture, without the shaking). The same principles of analysis into parts seem to guide the structure and use of signed languages and spoken languages.

There are several other different types of constructive arguments that are based on an analysis of signs into component parts like the one that Stokoe proposed. If we are trying to argue that signs are not simply random gestures that our bodies just happen to be able to perform, and if we also want to argue that a sign does not have to be a "picture" and does not have to "graphically" represent an idea or an object, then we might look for some other factors or forces that determine how signers use their hands and their bodies to make signs.

From work with spoken languages, it is well known that the individual sounds in a language and the way those sounds can come together to make words in a language are always only a small portion of what humans are able to articulate. Not every possible vocal sound is used in a spoken language. Of the sound units that a language uses, not every possible combination of these units is used to form syllables or words—many are unlikely or impossible combinations, such as "frtps." This is because sounds and their combinations are governed and limited by psychological and physiological laws relating to the speech organs, and by the way that the ear takes in and processes information.

It is easy to show that the same kinds of principles determine how the different elements of signs—handshapes, locations, and movements—can come together (or *co-occur*) to form complete signs. Of course, some things are quite impossible to do with the hands because of physical limitations. But what about things that are *possible*, but *too complex and unnatural* for the kind of rapid signing that is common in conversation? Are there such things? Linguistic research has shown that there are.

The example I will offer here is from some work I did while studying how signs limit the ways that different parts can occur together. (At that time, I was looking for something parallel to what we call *morpheme structure constraints* in spoken languages.) In ASL, as in all signed languages that we know about, many signs are made with both hands. Logically then, the handshapes could either be the same (for example, two fists), or they could be different (for example, a fist on the left hand and a "V" shape on the right hand). As it turns out for the signs that I studied, there are a number of rules and predictions that you can make on the basis of the handshapes used in signs made with both hands. For example, if the two handshapes are different:

- only one hand will move during the sign—usually the "dominant" hand.
- the hand that does not move will not be just any one of dozens of handshapes—it will be one of the simplest, or most natural, handshapes (the closed fist, the open palm, the open hand with fingers spread, the fist with index finger extended, the "O" hand, or the "C" hand).

This kind of limitation, which is observed in other signed languages as well as in ASL leads to several further observations. First, the limitation is systematic and excludes large numbers of possible hand arrangements; there are only a very few existing signs which break the two "rules" above. Second, there seems to be a physiological reason for the way these "rules" operate: complex and moving things are most often on the dominant hand; simple and static things will most often be on the nondominant hand (the one that is usually not as skilled in doing things). Other reasons may include perceptual factors, such as how many different things the eye and the brain can take in and keep track of when a person watches signs. There is quite a bit of evidence that perceptual limitations play a role in "shaping" possible signs.

There is no need here to continue listing and describing the many different kinds of constraints that people have hypothesized for the structure of signed languages. For the purposes of this paper, the important theoretical point is that these constraints are like those that explain how spoken languages operate: the forms of a language are constrained by physiological and perceptual factors on the production and perception of spoken words and gestural signs.

There are practical observations that are linked to this small set of rules. Consider the problem that faces many professionals who work with signs, especially teachers of young deaf children. Very often teachers will want a sign for a particular word or a concept, but they don't know what that sign is, or even know if it exists. Occasionally, they will appropriately ask several skilled signers to determine what they should sign.

Much more often, they will either fingerspell the word or invent their own sign.

Now, what about all these signs that get invented? Many schools have continuing discussions in committees whose main purpose seems to be to invent signs. But are these invented signs appropriate? Do they fit the natural rules of how signs can be constructed out of parts? The answer is that many of the invented signs, particularly the signs that have been invented to transliterate English words, are unnaturally complex. Many of the signs that have been invented for children, including the names of animals and toys, violate some of the rules that natural signs obey. The results of this situation have been observed by many people in many different places: both children and adults have difficulty learning how to make the signs; both children and adults tend to change the signs, to pronounce them in a little more natural way; and experienced signers often view some of these signs as being unnatural ("they don't fit in"), and in some cases peculiar, silly, or even crude. The lesson is quite clear: we should study how deaf people use signs in a conversational context, and we should pay attention to the detail of how the signs are made. Only then, and only cautiously, should anyone attempt to invent a sign on their own—and only as a last resort.

EXTENDING THE IDEA THAT SIGNS HAVE PARTS

The first summer working in the Linguistics Research Lab was one of exploration and discovery for me. Contrary to what I expected, Bill did not order me to carry out a specific research plan; he didn't order me to transcribe videotapes, and he didn't have me compiling information from dusty books on a hot summer day. He allowed me to think about what I wanted to do, and to take it from there. I kept thinking about breaking signs down into parts and comparing them; I knew that this would be the way to discover all sorts of things about signing, and that this would provide a basis for comparing signs with words. That summer, Lynn Friedman (another summer research assistant) and I began to talk about another level of structure. We knew that it was interesting and useful to think of signs broken down into handshapes, locations, and movements . . . but what was beyond that? What was a handshape? What was a movement, really? These things could also be analyzed into finer parts, and perhaps that division would be useful too. We felt that if we could isolate the different levels of structure of a sign, we might compare them to the different levels of structure of a word. We felt that a word corresponded to a sign pretty well, and the three aspects that Stokoe had discovered might correspond roughly to individual sounds in a spoken word. But we also knew that even individual sounds were composed of finer parts called *distinctive features*, and perhaps we would also find a corresponding level of structure in signs.

Distinctive features in spoken language can refer to many things, but for our purposes here I might say that they refer to different *acts* that the vocal organs (mouth, lips, tongue, etc.) perform in order to make the sounds of language. For example, the feature of *lip rounding* is a distinctive feature of many sounds in many languages. We felt that we might discover a similarity, so we began by breaking down handshapes into features that we called *bent* (if the fingers were *bent*), *crossed* (if some of the fingers crossed each other), *spread* (if the fingers were not touching each other), etc. We eventually came up with a preliminary analysis of features for handshapes, locations, and movements, and we later pursued this track of investigation more thoroughly in our ways.

By now you may be asking yourself, "Why bother breaking down signs into finer and finer details?" The answer is that we were creating a tool for understanding how Sign Language works. Since all of us were continually trying to think of new ways to get valid and meaningful information about signs, it made sense to at least experiment with the very lowest, very finest level of description: how different parts of the body had to arrange themselves and move in order to compose a sign. It was also good practice for learning how to describe signs adequately, and eventually might help us sort out what were the important, as opposed to the unimportant, parts of signs.

The second set of reasons had to do with the general strategy among sign researchers at the time. We were always looking for familiar things that would help alert us to how signs really worked. Since spoken languages had been studied for many centuries, there was a set of traditions (sometimes misleading) and set of theories (sometimes conflicting) about how human beings managed to move their mouths and tongues and make sounds, and how they could listen to those sounds and somehow form the impression that the other person had given them information. There is something magical about it, after all. But for spoken languages, we had at least made a dent in the problem. There are large dictionaries of spoken languages and many scholars who study those languages. Even elementary school children learn something about grammar and composition in their classrooms. More importantly, there is a vocabulary of technical terms for discussing spoken languages. The natural thing to do, although cautiously, was to try to find things in signed languages that looked like, or seemed to act like, familiar things in spoken languages. In this way, we were trying to answer the question: "In what ways are signed languages like spoken languages?" If we kept finding similarities despite their different production mechanisms (the hands and body versus the voice) and despite their different perceptual mechanisms (the eyes versus the ears), then we would feel sure that we were somehow getting closer to discovering ways for producing and perceiving language that all humans share, regardless of whether a given human can hear or not. Any time that a researcher did find a similarity, it might lead that researcher onto a very productive path. This was true of the distinctive feature analysis. As it turns out, allowing us to think about distinctive features of signs allowed us to make a connection to three different kinds of psychological studies that had been done with spoken languages. These offered researchers three new bases for comparing signs and words as people actually used them.

The first kind of study concerned psychological processes like perception and memory. Experiments had showed that the "inner language" of the mind may operate in terms of something like distinctive features. This led to a whole series of investigations by various researchers on the memory and perception of signs.

The second type of study concerned the effects of brain damage on language production and perception. Some of the descriptive work on hearing people who have suffered brain damage used an analysis of distinctive features; this work could now be extended to studies of deaf people (usually elderly) with brain damage.

A third type of study was even more exciting than the other two. People who study "slips of the tongue" (everyday speech errors) have found that these errors help us understand how the brain controls the parts of the body that express speech and language.

One of the only ways to describe some of the errors is in terms of distinctive features. This suggested a new avenue of investigation for sign researchers, who then began to study "slips of the hand," or sign errors.

The point of these little anecdotes is not to inform you about distinctive features. The point is to show the logical progression of ideas leading to further ideas and action.

I think it is very easy to show, for example, that the original idea that signs have parts influences the ways in which we think about the grammar of a signed language. Just to take one point, many writers have said (even into the 1970's) that a signed language has no distinction between nouns, verbs, and adjectives, as spoken languages do. The truth is quite the opposite, as Ursula Bellugi explains in the following chapter; we just weren't paying attention to the right parts of the sign. Normally, a spoken language will add some additional sounds to a word (a suffix or prefix) to indicate whether it functions as a noun or a verb in the sentence. For example, "claw" can be either a noun or a verb, but "claw*ed*," "claw*ing*," and "*de*-claw" can only be verbs. Anyone who looked for signs that "added on" bits of signs in this way was disappointed, because there weren't any. But as Ted Supalla later noticed, there are systematic differences between nouns and verbs in American Sign Language: they are expressed as different types of movement. Bellugi describes this in greater detail in her chapter. I only raise the point now to show how one observation can build on, and make use of, another. Once movements had been separated (in a sense) from other parts of signs, it became easier to notice different roles that individual movements might play.

Another way that we can use the information about the structure of individual signs is when we try to decide if two different "pronunciations" of a sign make two different signs, or if they are just alternate pronunciations of the same sign. This becomes an issue when we consider what an "idiom" is in American Sign Language. Without discussing it in any great detail, we can show that things that are often called sign "idioms" are often just ordinary signs that are difficult to translate into English (see similar comments in Hansen's paper on Danish Sign Language), or are signs that are confused with other signs. For example, some people claim that the sign SUCCEED has an idiomatic or special meaning, "finally" or "at last." But these two signs are made differently: SUCCEED has two distinctive movements, while the sign that I call AT-LAST has only one sharp movement. If two signs are made differently, and have different meanings, this is good evidence that they are separate signs. So AT-LAST is not an idiom, even though it might historically derive from the sign we call SUCCEED. One of the ways ASL expands its vocabulary is through such changes in movement. Again, we see one more reason for paying attention to the fine details of how signs are formed.

This is just one example of how the term "idiom" has been often misused when it is applied to Sign Language; the effect is often to obscure how the language really works, and to make it seem as if the language is unstructured and simple. Of course, nothing could be further from the truth.

CONCLUSION

In this essay I have described some of the research findings that have come out of the last twenty years of thinking about the structure of signed languages. This description has pointed out a few general principles and a few practical results that have sprung from a very simple idea: signs have parts. The discussion has also shown that when we investigate signed languages, we find many parallels to the structure of spoken languages. I think that this will become a very significant factor in how we hearing people think about deaf people, and in how deaf people think about themselves. It is becoming harder and harder these days to maintain that Sign Languages are very "simple" and "primitive." On the contrary, they are very rich and complex systems. Future investigations in which signing and speaking are compared will tell us more about the wonderful capacity the mind has to deal in abstract symbols.

In closing, let me say that simple ideas are usually the most valuable ones. The work that Bill Stokoe began more than twenty years ago, and which he continues today, has produced ideas that have generated interest among scholars everywhere. They have led to a re-examination of policies and attitudes towards deaf people; they have contributed to the emergence of deaf people as a cultural group; and they have let all of us, deaf and hearing, come a little bit closer to each other.

REFERENCES AND SELECTED BIBLIOGRAPHY

Battison, R., *Lexical Borrowing in American Sign Language.* Silver Spring, MD: Linstok Press, 1978.

Battison, R. & Cogen, C., The Implications of Teaching American Sign Language as a Second Language. Paper presented at the 2nd Annual National Symposium on Sign Language Research and Teaching. Coronado, CA, October, 1978.

Klima, E. & Bellugi, U., *The Signs of Language.* Cambridge, MA: Harvard Press, 1979.

Stokoe, W., Sign Language Structure: An Outline of the Visual Communication Systems of the American Deaf. *Studies in Linguistics: Occasional Papers* 8, 1960. Revised 1978, Silver Spring, MD: Linstok Press.

Stokoe, W., Casterline, D., & Croneberg, C., *A Dictionary of American Sign Language on Linguistic Principles.* Washington, DC: Gallaudet College Press, 1965. 2nd Edition, Silver Spring, MD: Linstok Press, 1976.

Introduction to
A Dictionary of American Sign Language

William C. Stokoe, Dorothy C. Casterline, and Carl G. Croneberg

1. THE ELEMENTS OF AMERICAN SIGN LANGUAGE

A first look into a dictionary may be more perplexing than enlightening to one unfamiliar with the language, but even those readers who know American Sign Language best will find this dictionary strange at first because the language has never before been written. It is written here and can be written because of what we know of its structure. Each sign of this language has three things which distinguish it from all other signs in the language. Let us call these things *aspects* since they are ways of looking at something that can happen all at once. The three aspects of a sign are (1) the place where it is made, (2) the distinctive configuration of the hand or hands making it, and (3) the action of the hand or hands. In the early stages of the structural analysis of this language it was decided to call the place the *tabula* or *tab*, to call the active hand the *designator* or *dez*, and the action it made the *signation* or *sig*. These three terms, *tab*, *dez* and *sig* are used throughout the dictionary as brief and convenient labels for the three aspects of signs. The reader who becomes completely familiar with them and the aspects of signs they refer to will find his thinking and reading about signs and his study of unfamiliar signs in the dictionary entries made much easier.

What happens when a person makes a sign may be described in many different ways, from a kind of telegraphic mention of some essentials to a leisurely description of every detail of the activity. To supplement written descriptions of signs line drawings and photographs have long been used, but these can show only a static moment in the process of signing. To indicate sig motion dotted lines, arrows drawn on the film, double exposures, and sequences of views have been used—none really successfully. Full representation of signs in motion pictures is unsatisfactory too, for it is expensive, cumbersome, and essentially artificial. Although it is usual to deal with languages, especially in dictionaries, a word at a time, a language is really a whole of which words are somewhat artificial parts. Users of sign language find it harder to get what a person is signing in a carefully made motion picture than what a live signer is signing. When a film is cut to separate individual signs, that difficulty is increased. One sign blends or merges with another as a signer proceeds. Students of other languages are aware of the same difficulty. We write: "I want to see what he is doing to them," but we say and hear something more like: "aywannaseewoteesdointoem."

1.1 Writing American Sign Language

With the understanding that all separation of real human communication into word-size units is a little artificial, we can proceed

Source. Reprinted by permission of the publisher, from W. C. Stokoe, D. C. Casterline, and C. G. Croneberg, *A Dictionary of American Sign Language* (rev.). (1976): vii–xxxi. Silver Spring, MD: Linstok Press.

to a representation of the separate signs of the American sign language by symbols for the three elemental aspects of a sign. If we use "T," "D," and "s" as cover symbols for any possible tab, dez, and sig, we can write a sign thus: TD^{s}. This formula or convention for writing a sign indicates that at or in some place (T), visibly distinguished from all other sign language places, a hand configuration (D), distinctly different from all others used in sign language, performs an action (s), visibly unlike all other such actions.

Not all signs are made in just this way, because the sig may be a combination of movements. Some signs will be written like this: TD$^{\substack{s \\ s}}$. Here two sig actions are combined; that is they are done at the same time. Thus "down" and "touch" ($\substack{\vee \\ \times}$) written one above the other will indicate that the dez moves down while in contact with the tab. In other words it grazes, brushes, or scrapes down across the tab. Or two straight-line sigs, 'right' and 'down' ($\substack{> \\ \vee}$), done together combine to make a motion downward and to the signer's right.

Another kind of formula shows the sig symbols side by side: TD^{ss}. This way of writing a sign indicates that one sig action is done first and a second follows.

A third kind of formula shows two dez symbols: TDD^{s}. This way of writing a sign indicates that both the signer's hands serve as a double dez. A double-dez sign like this may have a single sig symbol as shown or have a compound ($\substack{s \\ s}$) or a double (^{ss}) sig. Indeed, some double-dez signs and some with single dez may have three sig symbols ($\substack{s \\ s}{}^{s}$) or (^{sss}) and some even four ($\substack{s\,s \\ s\,s}$).

All that is needed now to read a sign written in the dictionary is a knowledge of what specific symbols may be used to replace these general cover symbols in the formulation, and a knowledge of what visible aspects of sign activity are represented by the specific symbols. The fifty-five symbols shown in the following table (and on the endpapers for handy reference) may seem more burden-some to learn than the English alphabet of twenty-six symbols. But the writing of signs is both simpler and more consistent than English spelling. Our conventions of spelling in English allow o-u-g-h to have five separate pronunciations, for instance, and one vowel sound may be spelled with *e, ee, ei, ie, ea, ae, ay, i, y, oe,* and otherwise. The fifty-five symbols used to write American sign language stand for just fifty-five things visibly unlike all the rest. Moreover, grouping within the fifty-five helps to learn the symbols and what they stand for.

The first twelve symbols stand only for tab aspects. The next nineteen stand for hand configurations used as dez and some of these are also used as tab. Most of this group of nineteen will be immediately recognized by the reader who knows and uses the American manual alphabet, but appearances are misleading.

The dez and tab hand configurations of American sign language are similar to but not identical with the configurations of finger spelling. In finger spelling the configurations and the direction in which the hand and fingers point must be kept within very close limits, but in American sign language the configuration symbolized "A" for instance may look more like the "s" or the "t" of the manual alphabet than the "a," or it may look like nothing used in finger spelling at all—depending on what sign is being made, on who is making it, or on where he learned the language. Again, the sign language configuration symbolized "H" may look at times like the manual alphabet "h" or "u" or "n," depending on the direction the fingers point as the dez moves in making the sig.

The last twenty-four of the symbols in the table below stand for sig aspects only and divide into subgroups. First there are four subgroups of three symbols each, showing a similar relationship within the subgroup. Vertical motion, for instance, might be considered one sig and given one symbol; but some signs are identical in every respect except that the sig of one is upward motion, of another downward motion, and of a third up-and-down motion. The same three-way distinction, of sideways motion, of to-and-fro motion, and of rotational motion of the forearm gives three more of these subgroups of three members. The last seven of the twenty-four symbols for sig motion also form a subgroup as they all indicate interaction between the tab and dez of a sign or between the two hands of a double-dez sign.

1.2 Table of Symbols Used for Writing the Signs of the American Sign Language

Tab symbols

1. Ø zero, the neutral place where the hands move, in contrast with all places below
2. ○ face or whole head
3. ⌒ forehead or brow, upper face
4. △ mid-face, the eye and nose region
5. ∪ chin, lower face
6. 3 cheek, temple, ear, side-face
7. Π neck
8. [] trunk, body from shoulders to hips
9. \ upper arm
10. √ elbow, forearm
11. a wrist, arm in supinated position (on its back)
12. D wrist, arm in pronated position (face down)

Dez symbols, some also used as tab

13. A compact hand, fist; may be like 'a', 's', or 't' of manual alphabet
14. B flat hand
15. 5 spread hand; fingers and thumb spread like '5' of manual numeration
16. C curved hand; may be like 'c' or more open
17. E contracted hand; like 'e' or more claw-like
18. F "three-ring" hand; from spread hand, thumb and index finger touch or cross
19. G index hand; like 'g' or sometimes like 'd'; index finger points from fist
20. H index and second finger, side by side, extended
21. I "pinkie" hand; little finger extended from compact hand
22. K like G except that thumb touches middle phalanx of second finger; like 'k' and 'p' of manual alphabet
23. L angle hand; thumb, index finger in right angle, other fingers usually bent into palm
24. 3 "cock" hand; thumb and first two fingers spread, like '3' of manual numeration
25. O tapered hand; fingers curved and squeezed together over thumb; may be like 'o' of manual alphabet
26. R "warding off" hand; second finger crossed over index finger, like 'r' of manual alphabet
27. V "victory" hand; index and second fingers extended and spread apart
28. W three-finger hand; thumb and little finger touch, others extended spread
29. X hook hand; index finger bent in hook from fist, thumb tip may touch fingertip
30. Y "horns" hand; thumb and little finger spread out extended from fist; or index finger and little finger extended, parallel
31. ȣ (allocheric variant of Y); second finger bent in from spread hand, thumb may touch fingertip

Sig symbols

32.	^	upward movement	vertical action
33.	v	downward movement	
34.	N	up-and-down movement	
35.	>	rightward movement	sideways action
36.	<	leftward movement	
37.	z	side to side movement	
38.	⊤	movement toward signer	horizontal action
39.	⊥	movement away from signer	
40.	I	to-and-fro movement	
41.	a	supinating rotation (palm up)	rotary action
42.	D	pronating rotation (palm down)	
43.	ω	twisting movement	
44.	ŋ	nodding or bending action	
45.	□	opening action (final dez configuration shown in brackets)	
46.	#	closing action (final dez configuration shown in brackets)	
47.	ℓ	wiggling action of fingers	

48. ⊚ circular action
49.)(convergent action, approach
50. × contactual action, touch
51. ⌶ linking action, grasp
52. † crossing action
53. ⊙ entering action
54. ÷ divergent action, separate
55. " interchanging action

(49–54: interaction)

1.3 Conventions of Writing American Sign Language

When the tab, dez, and sig of a sign have been identified as three or more of the fifty-five aspects in the table above, that sign has been uniquely described and the appropriate symbols should suffice to show it in written formulation in this order: TD^S. However, a few additional symbols and some conventions of using the symbols to write signs have been adopted to make the notation more explicit.

First, many signs begin with the tab and dez or the two hands of the double dez in a particular relationship. This may be looked at as a stage in the process of sig action, but in writing signs it is easier to show it as part of the tab-dez picture. Thus when one hand rests on or is held above the other, the symbol for the lower hand will be shown with a line above it, as in A̅A⊚× "coffee." A line below the symbol indicates that the hand represented is uppermost as in A̲Ȧ× "assistant" (the dot over the dez is explained below). A vertical line between the symbols indicates that the hands are side by side, close together or touching, as in ØA|A× "with." A subscript symbol (ǫ) between indicates that one hand is held, with or without contact, behind the other, as in ØAǫA⊥ "follow." A cross, the same symbol used for "crossing" sig, between configuration symbols indicates that as the sign begins the forearms, wrists, hands, or fingers are crossed as in ØB†B÷ᴅ "divide." The symbol for "linking" sig used in this way indicates initially clasped hands or fingers as in ØF*F⊚ "cooperate," and the symbol for entrant sig indicates one configuration within the other, as in 5⊙Gɑ "begin."

Second, sig symbols written as subscripts to tab or dez symbols will show the way the hand or hands are held. Hence, the sign translated "school" is written BɑBᴅ×· to show that the tab is supinated, turned palm up, and the dez is pronated, turned palm down. A different sign, translated "money," is written BɑBɑ×·; in it both hands are palm up. The dot after the sig symbol is explained below.

Third, some special features of a configuration may need noting. Thus a dot above a tab or dez symbol shows that the thumb or other finger not usually prominent is extended or used in the sig action, as in ∪Ȧ⊥ "not." Again, if the configuration is displayed or used with the fingers bent it will be shown with a triple mark (‴) above, as in BɑC‴ᴅ⊥ "rough." When the forearm is prominent, the "forearm" tab symbol is placed before the configuration symbol, as in Ø√Gɑ⊚ "always."

Three other marks are used to show sig action more explicitly than may be done with sig symbols alone. A dot above the sig symbol indicates a short, sharp, tense or checked movement, as in △V‴ẋ "strict." A dot used to the right of a sig symbol indicates a repetition of the whole sig, as in BɑBᴅ×· "school." Two dots indicate two or more repetitions, as in B|B‴×·· "often." A curve (~) after the sig symbol indicates that the sig action of the hands in a double-dez sign is done first by one then by the other, as in ØFFɴ~ "if."

When the sig includes the actions "open" or "close," the dez configuration changes, and, to show what the hand becomes, the new dez symbol may be shown in brackets, as in ∩B#<>[A] "forget."

Some signs occur in pairs, or rarely triplets, for a single concept. These compounds, analogous to compound words or word-phrases of English are shown with a symbol (::) between to indicate the compounding.

The foregoing explanation of the system with the table of symbols should adequately introduce written signs to a user of American sign language. However, for the reader who does not already know the language, the following photographic illustrations may be more enlightening.

1.4 Illustrations of Tab and Dez Notation

No attempt has been made here to illustrate sig aspects. Only carefully made motion picture studies or observation of actual signing can give an adequate idea of the nature of sig action and the wide variation a sig action may show and still be accepted as the same.

Note that right and left may be reversed. Although the photographs show the right hand as dez and the left, when used, as tab, any sign may be made with dez left- and tab right-handed. Signers who are left-handed often use left hand as dez; and in a long utterance, as in interpreting for a non-

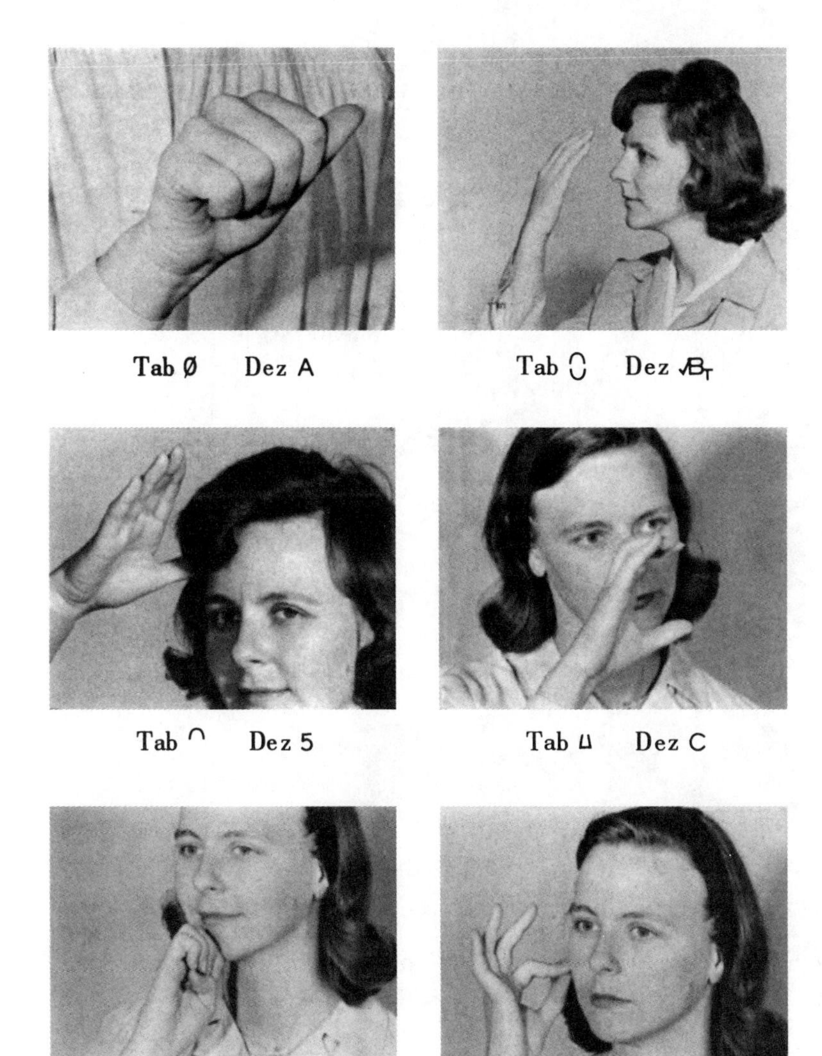

Tab Ø Dez A

Tab ⌒ Dez √B$_T$

Tab ∩ Dez 5

Tab ⊔ Dez C

Tab ∪ Dez E

Tab 3 Dez F

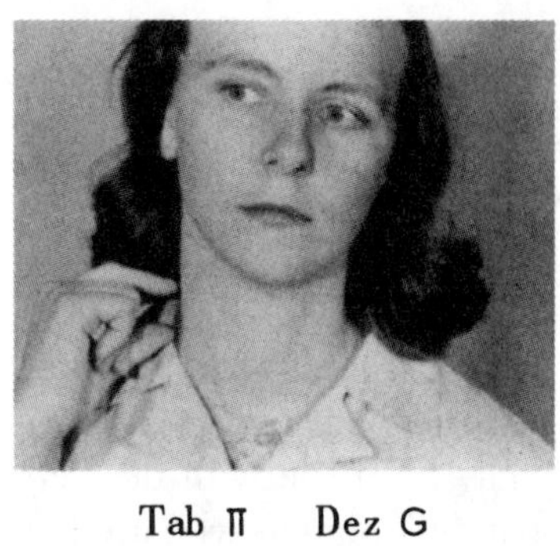

Tab Π Dez G

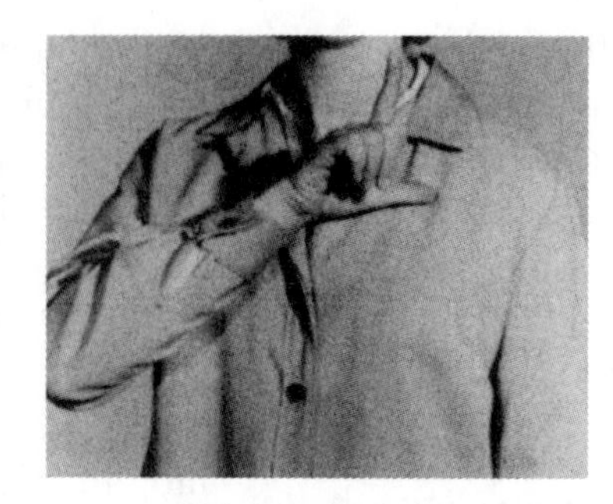

Tab [] Dez L

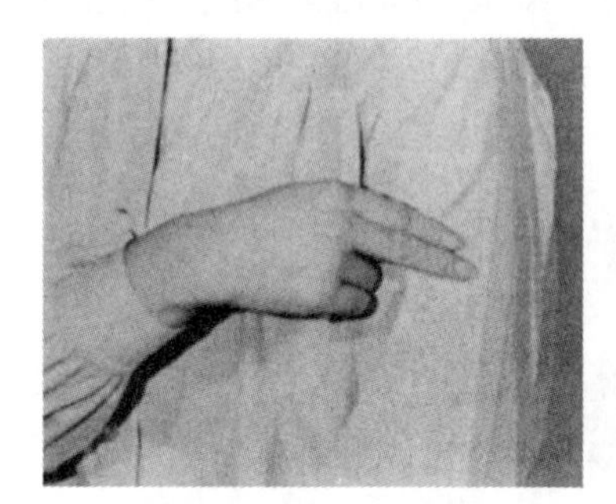

Tab \ Dez H

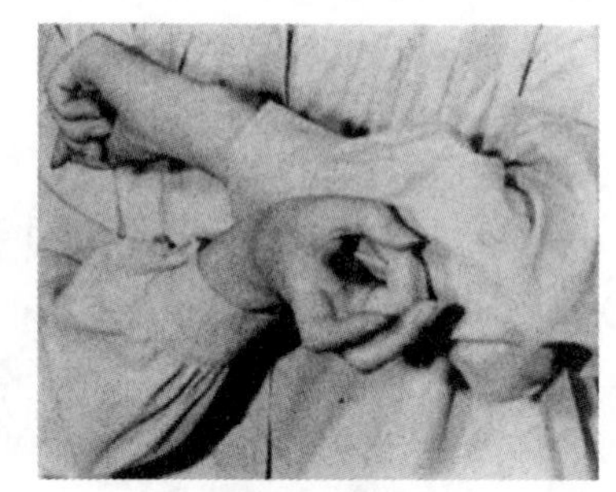

Tab ✓ Dez V̈

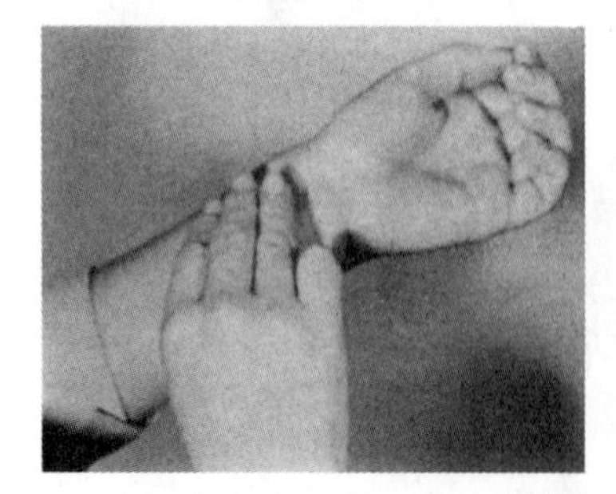

Tab ɑ Dez W_{D}

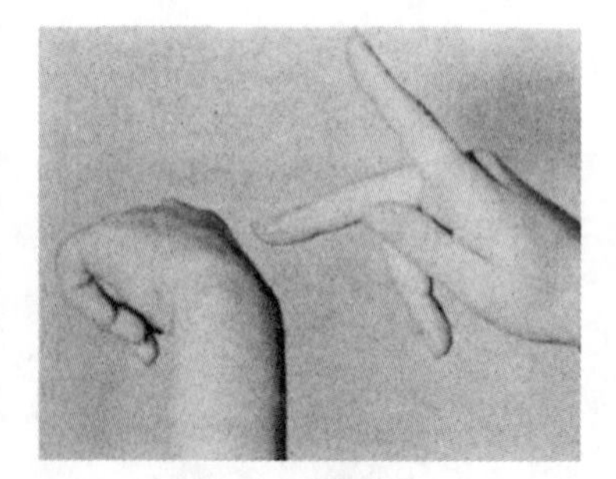

Tab D Dez K_{v}

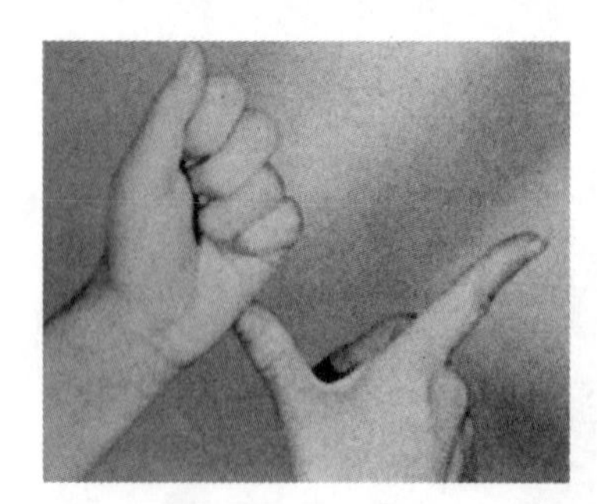

Tab A̲ Dez L

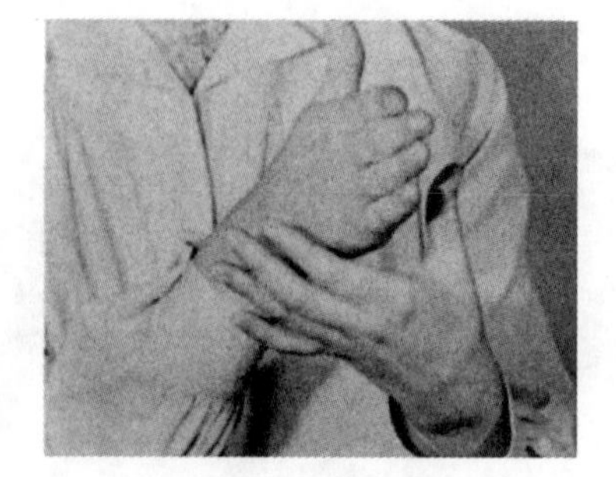

Tab B_{a} Dez B

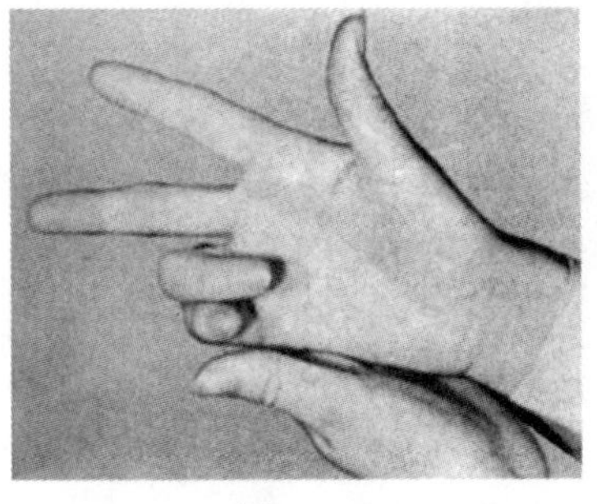

Tab $\bar{B}_a$ Dez 3

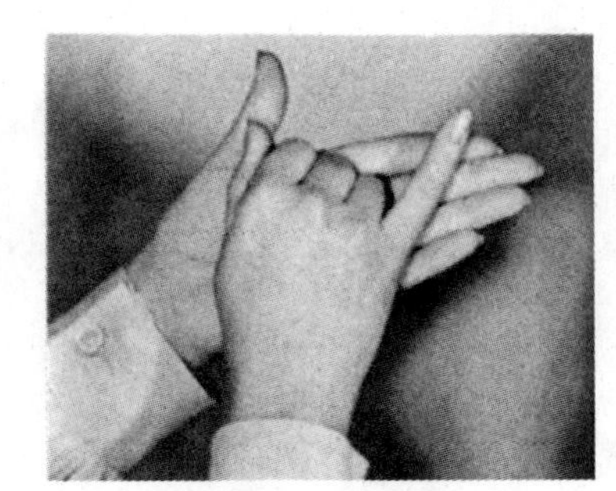

Tab $\bar{B}_a$ Dez Y_D

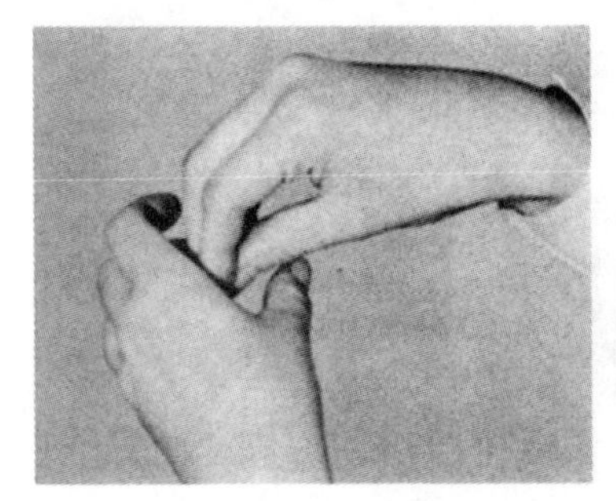

Tab C Dez $O_\vee$

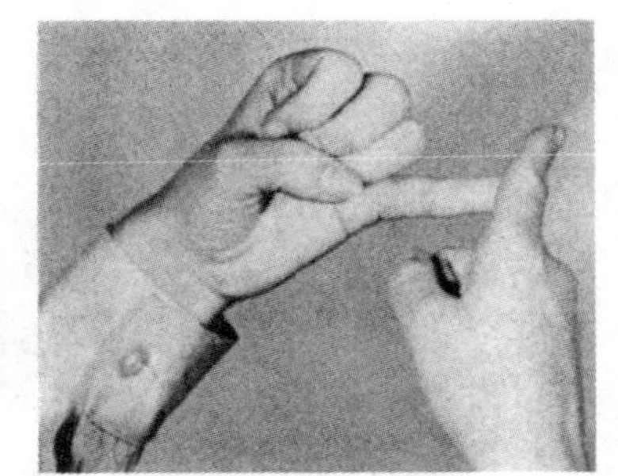

Tab I Dez G

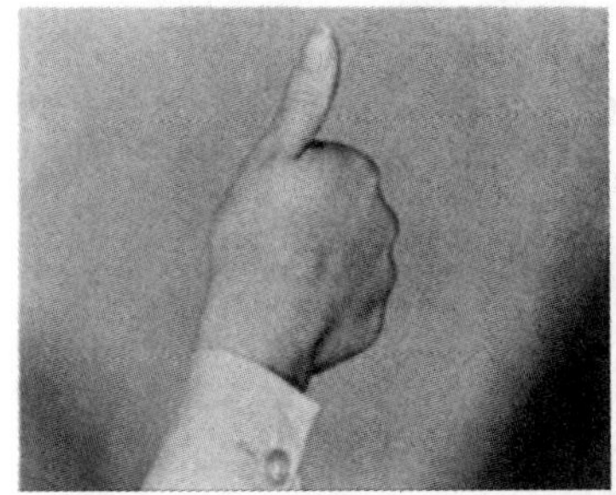

Tab Ø Dez $\dot{A}$

Tab Ø Dez √B

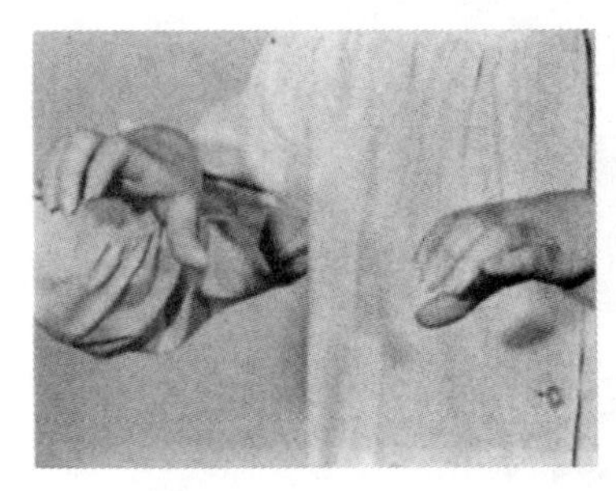

Tab Ø Dez $C_D C_D$

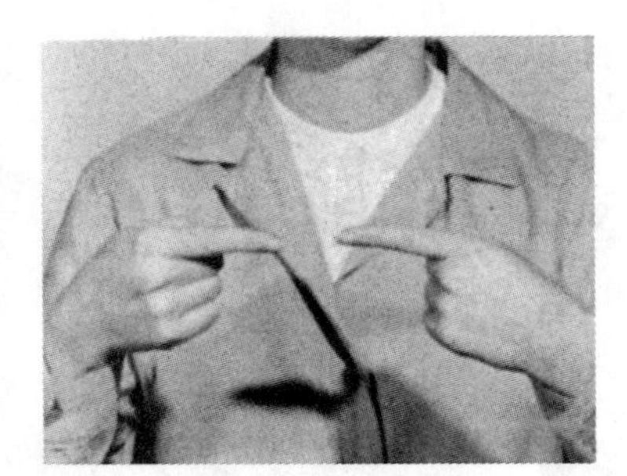

Tab Ø Dez $G_> G_<$

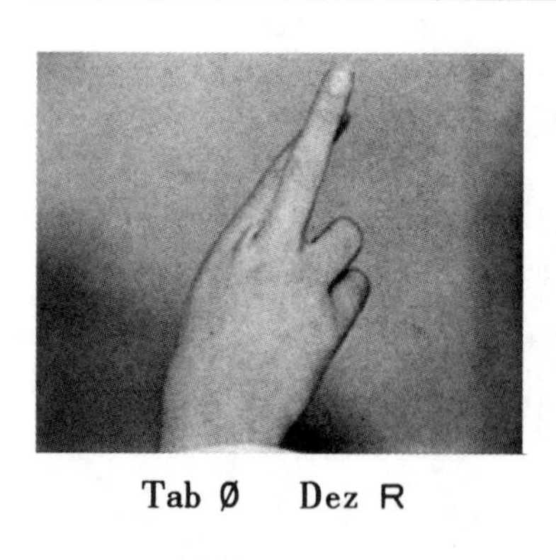

Tab Ø Dez R

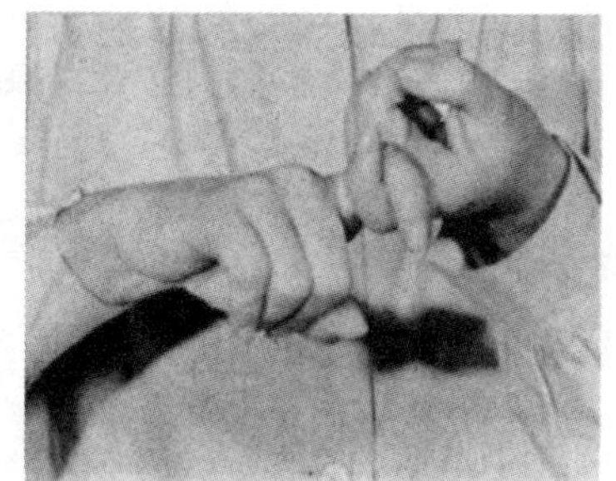

Tab Ø Dez X^{II}X

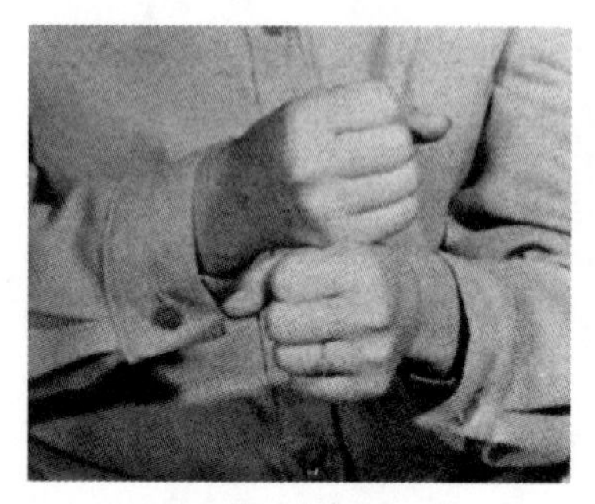

Tab $\overline{\text{A}}$ Dez A

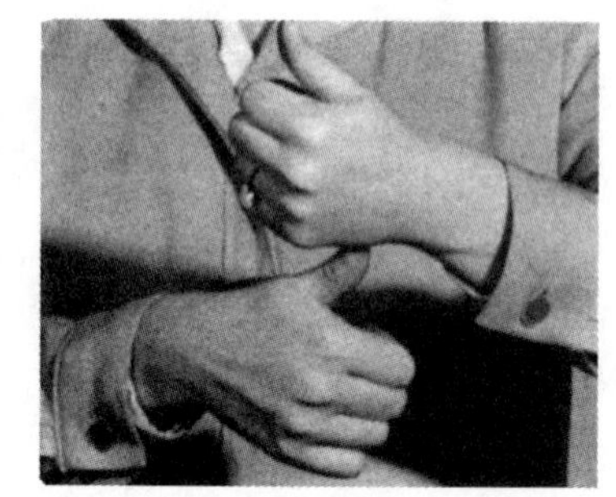

Tab $\underline{\text{A}}$ Dez Ȧ

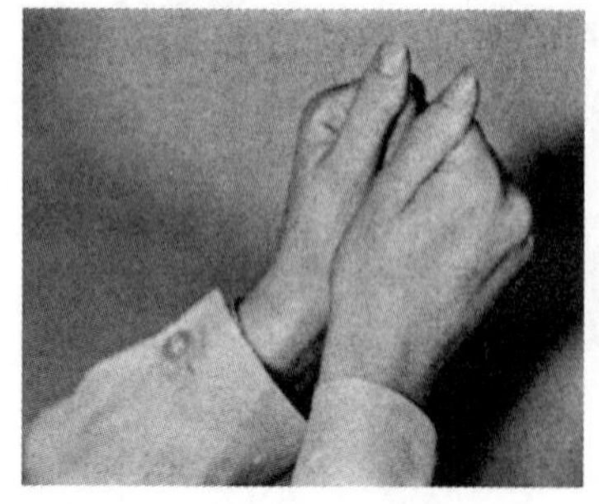

Tab Ø Dez A^{I}A

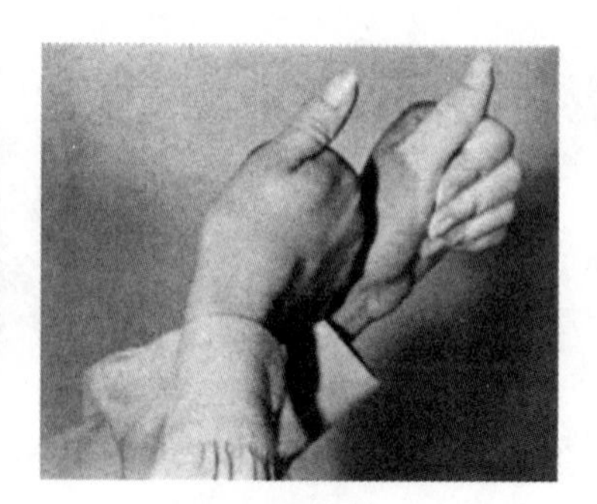

Tab Ø Dez A$_{\text{♀}}$ A

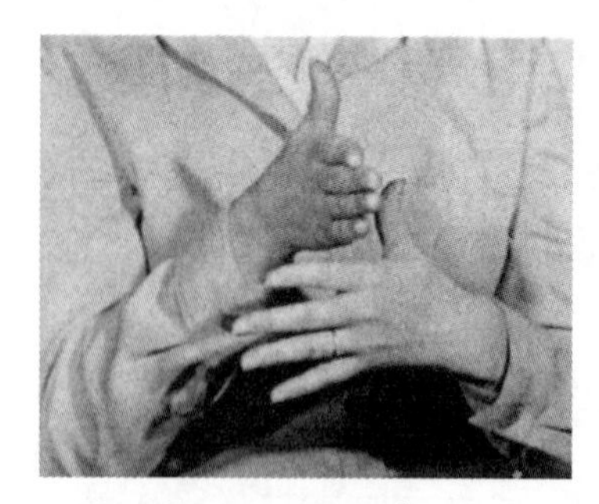

Tab Ø Dez B†B

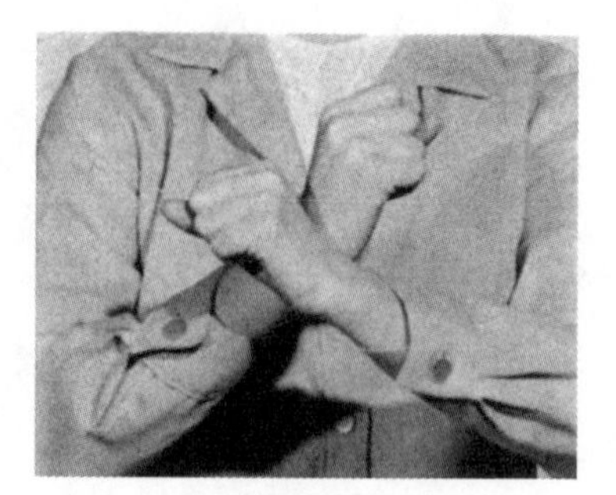

Tab Ø Dez √A†√A

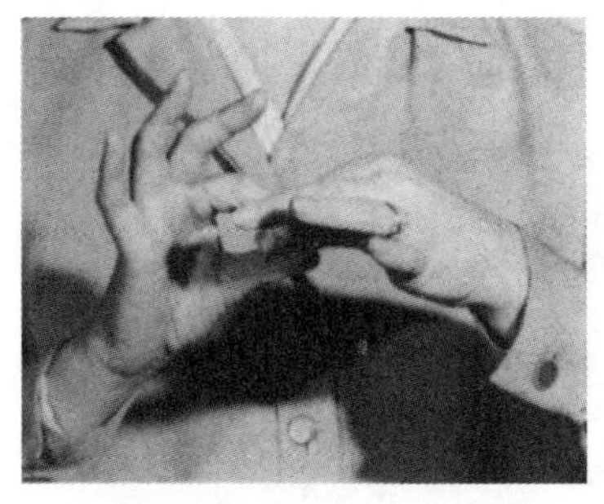

Tab Ø Dez F^{x}F

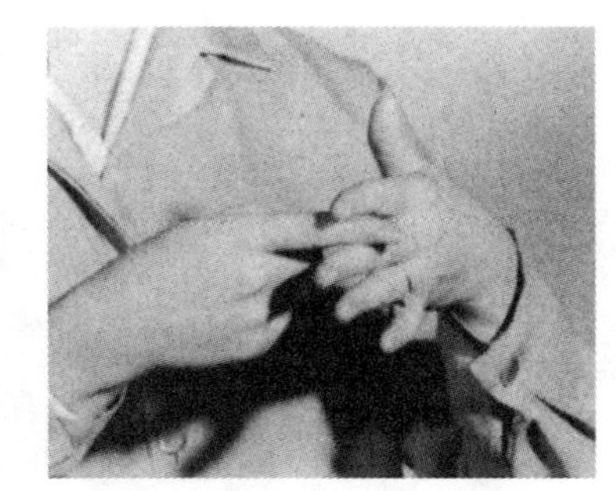

Tab $5^{\odot}$ Dez G

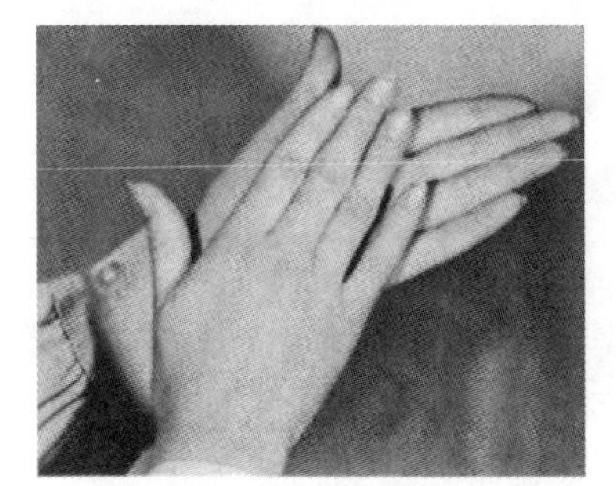

Tab B_{a} Dez $B_{ɒ}$

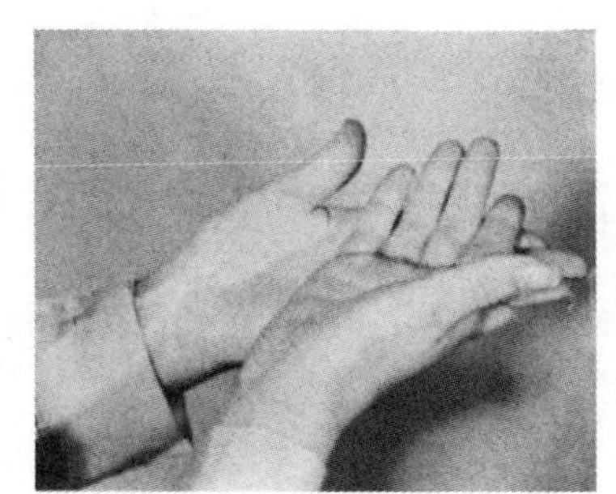

Tab B_{a} Dez B_{a}

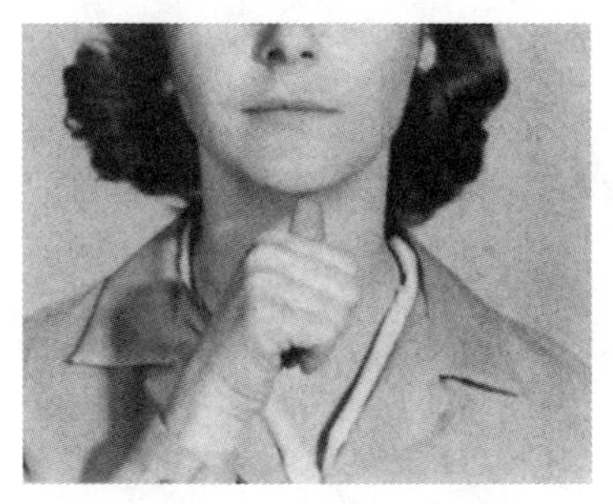

Tab ∪ Dez Ȧ

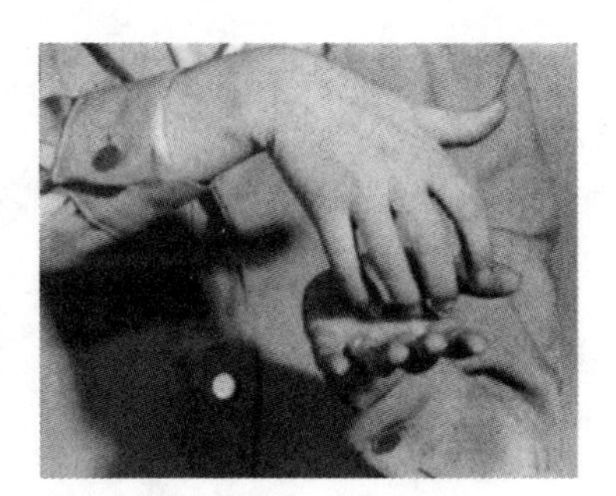

Tab B_{a} Dez $\overset{\therefore}{C}_{ɒ}$

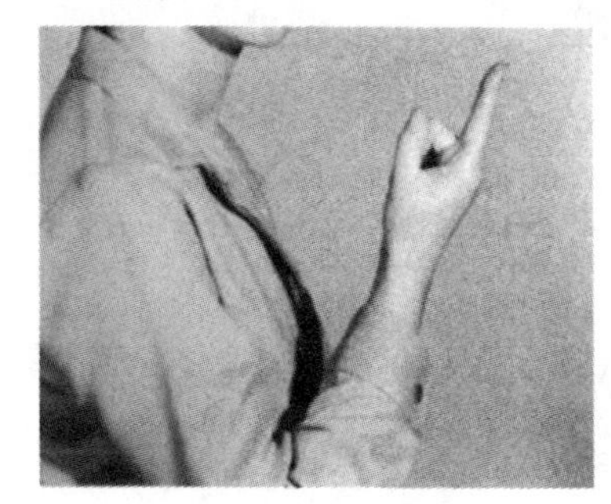

Tab Ø Dez √G_{a}

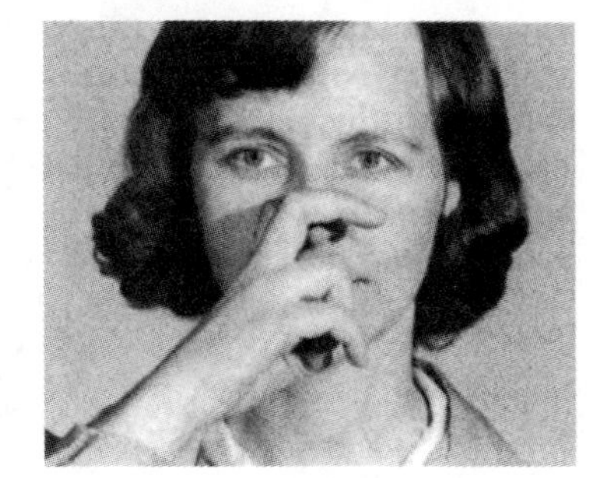

Tab ⊔ Dez $\overset{\therefore}{V}$

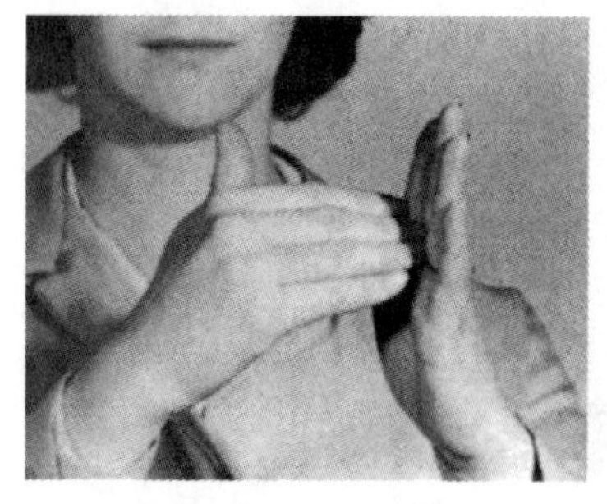

Tab B' Dez $\dddot{B}$

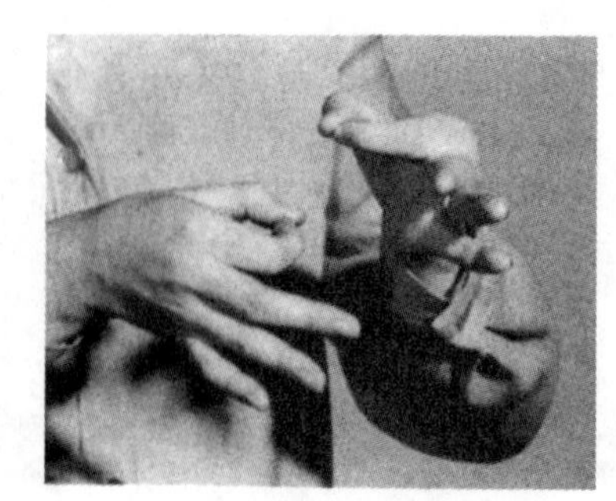

Tab Ø Dez FF

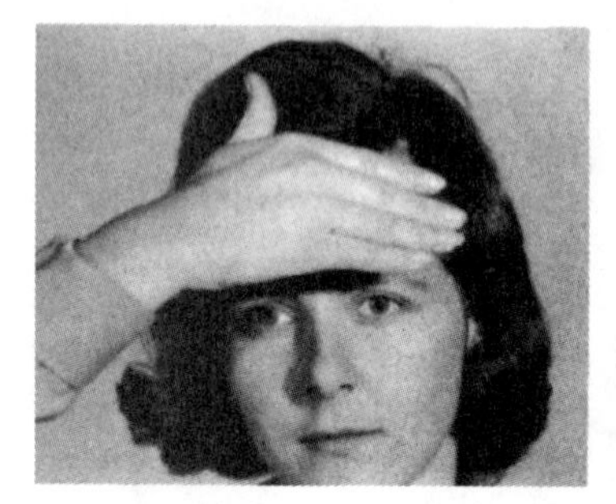

Tab ∩ Dez $B_{<}$

Tab ∩ Dez $A_{<}$

signing speaker, even a right-handed signer may change to the use of left hand as dez. Most of the illustrations show the dez and tab as it would be seen by one to whom the sign is addressed. To show some configurations clearly, however, the camera has looked over the signer's shoulder, picturing the dez nearly as the signer himself would see it.

1.5 Table of the American Manual Alphabet

Although finger spelling, a one-for-one representation of alphabetical symbols, and sign language are totally different modes of communication, many of the hand configurations are shared or similar. Furthermore there are signs that use as dez the alphabetical configuration of the initial letter of the English gloss. For these reasons a table showing the configurations of the manual alphabet is reproduced on this page.

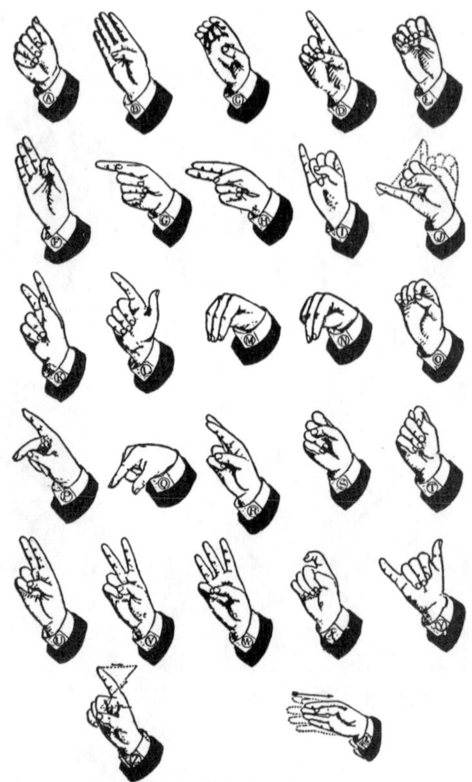

American Manual Alphabet

2. THE DICTIONARY ENTRIES

An entry in the dictionary will give information on some or all of these points:

1 the sign in symbols
2 variants of the sign
3 the nature of the sign
4 notes on how the sign is made
5 special usage indications
6 syntactic value: ^{N}, ^{V}, ^{x}
7 glosses, English equivalents
8 notes on usage, related signs, examples
9 cross-reference.

2.1 The Sign in Symbols

Signs in the dictionary are listed in the order of the symbols used to write them. This is the order shown in 1.2, Table of Symbols, and also in the endpapers. Thus signs with the same tab are arranged according to the order of their dez symbols, and signs with the same tab and dez are arranged according to the order of their sig symbols.

2.2 Variants of the Sign

Following the main listing at a little distance are shown variants of the sign which are either slightly different ways of making the sign or different ways that the same sign may be written.

2.3 Nature of the Sign

After the variants or after the sign itself if none are shown, a parenthesis may occur. The first item within parentheses is an indication of the nature of the sign, when this can be given with assurance. Most signs, like the words in any language, are associated with a meaning simply because users of the language use them so. However, American Sign Language uses visible human activity instead of sounds, hence there may often be a relationship of some kind between a sign and its referent. Onomatopoeia, the imitation in language sounds of the sound referred to (*buzz, quack, hum, etc.*) has a parallel in sign language, but the ways that signs relate to their referents may be distinguished:

Pantomimic signs, like all signs of American sign language, have tab, dez, and sig; but together these make an action which represents itself. Thus "knock" ØA$_{\perp}^{\perp\cdot}$ is a sign but is also exactly what a person does when knocking on a door. Again "cold" ØAA$^{\times\cdot}$ may be accepted as a likely reaction of anyone feeling cold. Real pantomime has no more place in signing than chanting has in speaking but the label will be shown wherever there is a reasonable supposition that the sign has a pantomimic origin.

Imitative signs are similar to pantomimic except that they single out some feature or object of the whole meaning to imitate more or less closely. Thus "car" and "drive" ØAA$^{N\sim}$ imitate the hands gripping an imaginary wheel but still represent the rest of the car or the whole activity of driving it. Again in "pipe" ∪Y$^{\times\cdot}$ the dez hand itself indicates the object but there is no attempt in signing "pipe" to pantomime the whole activity of smoking. In the sign "dance" BɑVv^{z} the sig indicates, does not pantomime, the action while the dez indicates the legs of the dancer. Here the sig is as much smaller than the real action of dancing as the dez hand is smaller than the body; but in "amazed" Ø$\underline{\ddot{V}}$ɒ$\ddot{V}$ɑ$^{+}$ the hands and fingers imitate the jaws and teeth dropping open in amazement so that the sign is larger, not smaller, than the imitated action.

Metonymic signs are occasionally marked as a special class of imitative signs which pick a relatively unexpected feature or object of the whole meaning to represent or imitate.

Indicative signs are not always so labeled in the dictionary, for the action of pointing toward the referent makes further indication redundant. It should be noted, however, that there are different degrees of indicative signs. The signs for "I" and "me" are made close to the referent; the latter usually makes actual contact with the signer's body. But the sign for "you" indicating several persons simply sweeps an arc that more or less precisely indicates the width of the group. Still further from direct and tactile indication are the signs for third person which do not require the referent or referents to be present or visible.

Name signs form a special class, not only because they are unique appellations for individual persons but also because they use a set of tab, dez, and sig aspects somewhat different from those of other signs. See Appendix B.

Initial-dez signs are coinages to translate a particular English word and have as dez the manual alphabet configuration for the first letter of that word. Although this is an open class and still used in coinage of new signs, it is by no means an innovation. The American sign language signs for colors, the days of the week, for *wine,* and others are direct translations from cognate French signs and use different initials of course when the English spelling differs. Many of the earliest French initial-dez signs can be attributed with certainty to the Abbe de l'Epée who describes his inventions of *signes methodiques* to augment the *signes naturelles* in use by Parisian deaf-mutes in the eighteenth century.

2.4 Notes on How the Sign Is Made

For the reader who knows American Sign Language the symbolic notation will suffice to indicate a sign and may even, with its subscripts and modifications, be a redundant symbolization. However, for those who use the dictionary as an aid to learning the sign language, the symbols alone may not be enough to allow exact reproduction of a sign. Therefore, within the parentheses in the entry are notes on the special features of tab, dez and sig, if these need further explanation. These notes for the sake of concision are expressed in terminology taken from structural linguistics. Explanation of the terms will be found in Section 3 below.

2.5 Special Usage Indications

Most signs are used and may be used in any situation where sign language may be used, and these signs need no special marking. There are, however, signs which are seen invariably or usually in *formal, religious, platform* (public or academic lecture), *dramatic, colloquial,* or *humorous* contexts. These will be so labeled within the parentheses. Other signs are known to be locally rather than nationally used and will be labeled *local, dialectal,* or *regional* with further specification where possible. Within the categories above there are also subdivisions. Since several denominations conduct religious work with the deaf and have their own traditions of translating liturgical and scriptural language into signs, the special usage label may be *Roman Catholic, Lutheran,* and the like, instead of the general *religious.* There is no attempt to list exhaustively all the signs peculiar to denominational linguistic communities. Some sign language manuals approach this task. See "Bibliography," Appendix E.

2.6 Syntactic Value

Although the description of the grammatical and syntactical structure of a language cannot be adequately given piecemeal in dictionary entries, each entry does indicate by the use of labels "N," "V," and "X" whether the sign is of the sort which may be used alone or as the center of a phrase of nominal, verbal, or adjectival-adverbial function. A full discussion of these matters will be found in Appendix A, "American Sign Language Syntax." At times the similarity of an idea expressed in English and in American sign language may lead one to suppose more structural parallels than really exist. Moreover, the practice of glossing signs with English words may mislead one to suppose that the sign and word are grammatical as well as semantic counterparts. However, both suppositions are fallacious; and even though a noun, for instance, is used to gloss a sign, it is more accurate to understand from the label "N" that "this sign has nominal uses" than to classify it mentally as a noun and so engraft the whole "parts of speech" concatenation on a language which has a different system of syntax.

2.7 Glosses, English Equivalents

A dictionary of American Sign Language could conceivably contain no words of English at all, just as a dictionary of English might have no words of any other language within its pages. However, two considerations have kept this dictionary from being made on such strict lines. First, it is hoped that it will have some usefulness as a bilingual dictionary and yet avoid the most serious errors such hyphenated works fall into. Its users may be especially interested in the problem of translating from English into ASL or the reverse. They will therefore give careful consideration to these remarks and to the appendices in which the grammar and syntax of sign language are described. Second, American Sign Language is in a different case from those languages like French, Spanish, and Italian that coexist with English in American communities. The deaf user of ASL, no matter how pure his sign language usage among his deaf fellows, is also a part of the general American culture and no further justification should be needed for the commingling of sign language and English in these pages.

Therefore, following the syntactic label in each entry will be given one or more English words which will, at least sometimes, adequately translate the sign. However, the reader is warned, here generally and in the entries specifically, that there may be uses of the signs that the word will not translate and uses of the word for which the sign would be inappropriate.

2.8 Notes on Usage, Related Signs, Examples

Because single word glosses for a sign are so often inadequate and approximate, there follows in many entries a note on the kind of context in which the sign will be used, the environment in which the gloss will serve, and the uses of the gloss which the sign will not fit. These are followed often with examples in sign phrases or sentences and the translations of the latter. In these notes considerable reference will be made to other signs, synonyms, or signs of similar structure.

2.9 Cross-Reference

Finally, many entries conclude with a reference to one or more other signs in the dictionary. These references are intended to help the user of the dictionary find several entries, which taken together, will cover a certain semantic ensemble; will show signs related in their aspects but distinct in meaning; or will lead to a longer entry, an article in which a number of related signs are discussed and differentiated.

There is another kind of cross-reference as a feature of the dictionary. At the back will be found an alphabetical list of the words used as glosses. These are followed by numbers that refer to the page on which the sign so glossed may be found.

3. SIGN LANGUAGE STRUCTURE[1] AND VARIATION

In linguistics a first consideration is the *phonology* of any language under study, what sounds it uses as its elemental units and how they are selected and used. Language sounds, *phones*, are rigorously classified into *phonemes*, classes of language sounds whose members are called *allophones* (the suffix *-eme* for "same," and the prefix *allo-* for other). All the sounds—which will be different if measured phonetically—that constitute one phoneme are allophones of that phoneme and are treated by the speakers of the language as alike. Thus the vowel of *hat*, *had*, and *has* is a phoneme, even though its allophone in *hat* is very short and its allophone in *has* is two or three times as long. An even more striking illustration of this sameness with a difference is furnished by the English of Chinese speakers whose own language has sounds like English "l" and "r" as allophones of the same phoneme. To them "flied lice" is no different from *fried rice*.

For the scientific description of a language, especially that actual production of language a linguist observes, a set of distinct symbols for each of the phonemes of the language is necessary and sufficient. However, a strictly phonemic writing system would not be practical. If a speaker sometimes says /blows/ and sometimes says /blowz/ for the same garment (*blouse*) the writing will have to have two ways to spell the same thing. And if speakers from different regions or social strata differ in "pronunciation," a phonemic writing system will be full of different spellings; for instance: *brush, bresh, bersh; just, jist, jest, jerst; idea, idear, idee, ijea*. A more practical system of writing, and one that much more accurately accounts for the social phenomena of languages, is *morphophonic*.

A *morphophone* is a unit of language out of which the minimum meaning bearing units, *morphemes*, are made. A morphophone is *actualized* as one or another phoneme. Thus the "u" in *just* represents a morphophone of English which some speakers actualize as the phoneme /e/, some as /i/, some as /u/ and some as /ə/. Allowing for individual and dialect differences in actualization, morphophones serve to represent the language of those whose speech is different yet mutually intelligible, just as phonemic symbols represent classes of allophones that have phonetic differences.

3.1 Cheremes and Allochers

The nature of sign language structure is not very different from that of spoken language structure, once account is taken of the vocal-visual difference. Sign language uses, not sounds, but visible distinct elemental units. Looked at simply as different things to see, the activity of signing can show infinite variety. However, sign language, like other language, puts these many things into classes. Analogous with the *phoneme* is the sign language *chereme* (CARE-eem, the first syllable from a Homeric Greek word meaning "handy"). It is a class of visual units that may differ in visible ways but that are just the same in their use in American Sign Language. These units, *allochers*, may look so different to one unaccustomed to the language that he misses the essential fact that they are the same. For example, the dez chereme symbolized in this dictionary as "Y" may look like the hand configuration for "y" in the manual alphabet—that is one allocher. It may have the three middle fingers only loosely curled—that is another allocher of "Y." It may have the three middle fingers at right angles with the palm—still another. It may have the forefinger and little finger parallel and extended, the thumb either bent or extended—two more allochers. All these allochers are represented by the cheremic symbol "Y." Some of them are in free variation; others are selected automatically (are in complementary distribution) according to the tab and sig used with them in signs. Thus "mistake" which ends with the middle of the dez against the chin uses the tightly curled fingers, but "why," which begins (for some signers) with the middle fingers of the dez lightly brushing down the forehead, selects the open allocher of "Y."

There is a chereme somewhat like "Y." But this, like other cheremic contrasts, produces a different sign, while the allocheric differences merely mean "a different way of making that sign." It is symbolized "8." It too has allochers: open with the hand rigid, the middle finger at right angles to the rest; tense, the middle fingernail caught by the ball of the thumb; and lax, the tips of middle finger and thumb lightly touching. The problem in writing sign language, and in recording it in a dictionary is to take account of such differences but at the same time not to treat as different those things that users of the language react to as same.

3.2 Morphophonics

The concept of the morphophone and morphophonic notation, which allows for interchange, alternation, and replacement of phonemes, was first publicly enunciated (by Henry Lee Smith, Jr., at the January 1965 meeting of the Washington Linguistics Club) after much of this dictionary had been completed. The symbols used herein for the elemental units, cheremes, of signs cover allocheric differences at least. The user of the dictionary, aware of the morphophonic concept, may find it very helpful to think of the notation, however, as "morphocheric," that is, a sign printed with "Y" for dez may sometimes be seen with an allocher of "8," or even of "B." This kind of variation is easier to find and describe than to account for in a writing system serving all users of a language. Just as the southern American English speaker's identical pronunciation of *pin* and *pen* does not negate the many primary contrasts between /i/ and /e/, so the actual occurrence of American Sign Language in one signer's performance does not negate the primary contrasts the editors have observed and recorded. In short, *pin* and *pen* are spelled differently in English and yet may be said as different or as same in actual use. So too the signs listed in this dictionary as using different cheremes may have different or the same cheremes in actual use. This caution, to be aware of sameness and difference simultaneously and at different levels, is needed in any study of language, more especially in one so different in nature from other languages but so similar in submorphemic structure.

3.3 Variation and Flexibility

The reason for introducing such technicalities of linguistic theory into a dictionary of sign language is eminently practical. Almost all that has been put into print about American Sign Language gives, intentionally or not, the impression that a sign must be made precisely so, will always be seen made that way, and admits of no variation. Nothing could be further from the truth. Individual, local, regional, and other differences operate at all levels in all languages. One person's "idee" is another's "idear" even though they both write *idea*. Just so, one person's "Y" will look like another's "I." Once the student of American Sign Language grasps the nature of the "allo-" and "-eme" distinctions, he will be in a much better attitude for learning and understanding than if he expects all sign language activity to look like what some person or book lays down as *the* sign.

NOTES

1. For a more detailed treatment see Stokoe, "Sign Language Structure: An Outline of the Visual Communication System of the American Deaf," *Studies in Linguistics, Occasional Papers:* 8. Buffalo, N.Y., 1960.

File 20—Phonetics: *The Sounds of Speech*

M. Crabtree and J. Powers

Although languages can in principle use modes of communication other than sound (for instance, visual signals) to convey meaning, it is nevertheless true that most human languages are spoken. This may not be an accident: some theorists have claimed that using the vocal apparatus for language freed human hands to engage in other activities and so had survival value in the evolution of the race. Note that people all over the world adopted spoken language, but sign language is only used in special circumstances. *Phonetics* is the study of speech sounds, which are known more technically as *phones*.

A whole chain of activities is involved in communicating meaning by sound. First of all, a speaker encodes meaning into sounds which he or she produces using the tongue, lips, and other articulatory organs. These sounds are transmitted through the air to reach the hearer. Then the hearer perceives them through auditory processes, finally translating them back into meaning. There are therefore three aspects to the study of speech sounds: *articulatory phonetics*, the study of the production of speech sounds; *acoustic phonetics*, the study of the transmission and the physical properties of speech sounds (such as intensity, frequency and duration); and *auditory phonetics*, the study of the perception of speech sounds.

The study of articulatory phonetics has had the longest history among the three subbranches of phonetics; it was already fairly developed by the 19th century. In the popular musical *My Fair Lady*, based on Bernard Shaw's play *Pygmalion*, the eccentric professor Higgins was actually modeled after the phonetician Henry Sweet. Acoustic phonetics, however, has mostly developed only in the last few decades. Acoustic phonetics has had to rely heavily on the use of sophisticated instruments that perform analyses of sound vibration. A particularly important instrument, the spectrograph, was invented only in the 1940s. Among the three branches of phonetics, auditory phonetics is the least understood, due to gaps that remain in our understanding of human neurology and perception.

Articulatory phonetics involves the study of how phones are produced by speakers, and the description and classification of those sounds according to their properties. Each of these aspects of articulatory phonetics will be considered in the files that follow, and the basic concepts of acoustic phonetics will be introduced. We will also be learning and using a system of phonetic symbols that linguists have developed for representing speech sounds. In a phonetic transcription one sound is represented by one symbol, and each symbol represents a single sound.

Source. Reprinted by permission of the publisher, from M. Crabtree and J. Powers, compilers, *Language Files: Materials for an Introduction to Language* (1991): 45–47. Columbus: Ohio State University Press.

Compare this system with English orthography (i.e., spelling), which is full of inconsistencies—for example:

- sometimes the same sound is spelled using different letters, as in *sea*, *see*, *scene*, *receive*, *thief*, *amoeba*, *machine*, and *Aesop*.
- sometimes the same letters can stand for different sounds, as in *sign*, *pleasure*, and *resign*, or *charter* and *character*, or *father*, *all*, *about*, *apple*, *any*, and *age*.
- sometimes a single sound is spelled by a combination of letters, as in *lock*, *that*, *book*, *boast*, *shop*, *apple*, or *special*.
- sometimes a single letter represents more than one sound, as in *exit* or *use*.
- sometimes letters stand for no sound at all, as in *know*, *doubt*, *though*, *island*, *rhubarb*, or *moose*.

Phonetic transcription, however, is consistent and unambiguous because there is always a one-to-one correspondence between sounds and symbols. This is even true across languages, so that the symbols you will be learning can be used to transcribe the sounds of any language. Phonetic symbols are written within square brackets, [ ], to distinguish them from letters or words written in ordinary orthography. It is important to remember that these symbols are not the same as letters, and that they represent the sounds of language, not letters of a writing system.

PHONETIC SYMBOLS FOR THE CONSONANTS OF ENGLISH

SYMBOL	SAMPLE WORDS
[p]	pit, tip, spit, hiccough, appear
[b]	ball, globe, amble, brick, bubble
[t]	tag, pat, stick, pterodactyl, stuffed
[d]	dip, card, drop, loved, batted
[k]	kit, scoot, character, critique, exceed
[g]	guard, bag, longer, designate, Pittsburgh
[ʔ]	uh-oh, hatrack, Batman
[f]	foot, laugh, philosophy, coffee, carafe
[v]	vest, dove, gravel, anvil, average
[θ]	through, wrath, thistle, ether, teeth
[ð]	the, their, mother, either, teeth
[s]	soap, psychology, packs, descent, peace
[z]	zip, roads, kisses, Xerox, design
[š]	shy, mission, nation, glacial, sure
[ž]	measure, vision, azure, casualty, decision
[h]	who, hat, rehash, hole, whole
[č]	choke, match, feature, righteous, constituent
[ǰ]	judge, George, Jell-O, region, residual
[m]	moose, lamb, smack, amnesty, ample
[n]	nap, design, snow, know, mnemonic
[ŋ]	sing, think, finger, singer, ankle
[l]	leaf, feel, Lloyd, mild, applaud
[r]	reef, fear, Harris, prune, carp
[w]	with, swim, mowing, queen, twilight
[y]	you, beautiful, feud, use, yell
[w̥]	which, where, what, whale, why (*for those dialects in which* witch *and* which *do not sound the same)*

SYLLABIC CONSONANTS

[m̩]	possum, chasm, Adam, bottomless
[n̩]	button, chicken, lesson, kittenish
[l̩]	little, single, simple, stabilize
[r̩]	ladder, singer, burp, percent

PHONETIC SYMBOLS FOR THE VOWELS OF ENGLISH

SYMBOLS	EXAMPLES
[i]	beat, we, believe, people, money
[ɪ]	bit, consist, injury, malignant, business

[ə]	b*u*t, t*ou*gh, *a*mong, *o*ven, sof*a*
[o]	b*oa*t, be*au*, gr*ow*, th*ou*gh, *o*ver
[ɔ]	b*ou*ght, c*au*ght, wr*on*g, sta*l*k, c*o*re
[a]	p*o*t, f*a*ther, s*e*rgeant, h*o*nor, h*os*pital

DIPHTHONGS

SYMBOLS	**EXAMPLES**
[ay]	b*i*te Ste*i*n *ai*sle ch*oi*r *is*land
[aw]	b*ou*t, br*ow*n, d*ou*bt, fl*ow*er, l*ou*d
[oy]	b*oy*, d*oi*ly, rej*oi*ce, perestr*oi*ka, ann*oy*

File 30—Phonology: *The Value of Sounds: Phonemes*

M. Crabtree and J. Powers

DISTINCTIVE AND NONDISTINCTIVE SOUNDS

Suppose we drew up a list of all the phones in some language (though as discussed in File 27, this is not actually possible: there is a potentially infinite number of speech sounds in a language, since no sound is ever pronounced quite the same way twice). Such a list still would not give us information about a very important aspect of the sound structure of a language, namely the values that these sounds have to its native speakers. In every language, certain sounds are considered to be the "same" sound, even though they may be phonetically distinct. For example, native speakers of English consider the [l] in *lay* to be the same sound as that in *play*, even though the former is voiced and the later voiceless, as discussed in File 27. And if you ask a native speaker of English how many different sounds are represented by the underlined letters in the words *pin*, *bin*, and *spin*, he or she will probably say "two," grouping the aspirated [pʰ] of *pin* and unaspirated [p] of *spin* together. Though [pʰ] and [p] are phonetically different sounds, native English speakers overlook this difference.

A native speaker of Hindi, however, could not ignore this difference. To a speaker of Hindi, [pʰ] is as different from [p] as [pʰ] is from [b] to our ears. The difference between aspirated and unaspirated stops must be noticed by Hindi speakers because their language contains many words that are phonetically identical, except that one word will have an aspirated stop where the other has an unaspirated stop. The data below illustrate this.

[kʰəl]	"wicked person"
[kəl]	"yesterday"
[kapi]	"copy"
[kapʰi]	"ample"
[pʰəl]	"fruit"
[pəl]	"moment"
[bəl]	"strength"

A native speaker of English can overlook the difference between aspirated and unaspirated stops because aspiration will never make a difference in the meanings of English words. If we hear someone say [mæp] and mæpʰ] we may recognize them as different pronunciations of the same word *map*, but not as different words. Because of the different ways in which [p], [pʰ] and [b] lead to meaning distinctions in English and Hindi, these sounds have different values in the phonological systems of the two languages.

In general, speakers will attend to phonetic differences between two (or more) sounds only when the choice between the sounds can change the meaning of a word—that is, can cause a distinction in

Source. Reprinted by permission of the publisher, from M. Crabtree and J. Powers, compilers, *Language Files: Materials for an Introduction to Language* (1991): 89–93. Columbus: Ohio State University Press.

meaning. Such sounds are said to be *distinctive* with respect to one another. One way to determine whether two sounds in a language are distinctive is to identify a *minimal pair*, which is a pair of words that differ only by a single sound in the same position, and which have different meanings, but which are otherwise identical. For example, the English words [tʰæp] and [tʰap] form a minimal pair in which [æ] and [a] contrast. This pair of words demonstrates that the sounds [æ] and [a] are distinctive relative to one another in English. [pʰəl] and [bəl] constitute a minimal pair in Hindi, contrasting [pʰ] and [b]; [pʰəl] and [pəl] also form a minimal pair in Hindi. But notice that there are no English minimal pairs involving [pʰ] and [p]. These two sounds are never distinctive with respect to one another in English.

Consider another example in which two languages make different distinctions using the same set of sounds. In English it is possible to find minimal pairs in which [l] and [r] are contrasted; for example, *leaf* [lif], *reef* [rif]; *lack* [læk], *rack* [ræk]. However, [l] and [r] are never distinctive in Korean. Consider the data below ([ɨ] represents a high central lax unrounded vowel).

[param] "wind"
[irɨm] "name"
[pal] "foot"
[mal] "horse"

As these examples illustrate, minimal pairs can never be found for [r] and [l] in Korean because these two sounds do not appear in the same positions in words: [r] appears only between two vowels, while [l] does not appear in this position. And this observation about the distribution of [r] and [l] is not merely a property of these isolated examples, but is true of all Korean words containing these sounds. Observations of this sort play an important role in determining which sounds are considered to be the "same" by a native speaker.

PHONEMES AND ALLOPHONES

So far, we have seen that there is phonological information (namely, information about which sounds are distinctive relative to which others) that cannot be extracted from a list of the sounds of a language. This information, however, is part of the "internal grammar" or linguistic competence that speakers have. Linguists attempt to characterize this information about the sound system of a language by grouping the sounds in the language's phonetic inventory into classes. Each class contains all of the sounds that a native speaker considers to be the "same" sound. For example, [p] and [pʰ] in English would be members of the same class. But [p] and [b] are members of different classes because they are distinctive. A class of speech sounds which are identified by a native speaker as the same sound is called a *phoneme*. The members of these classes, which are actual phonetic segments produced by a speaker, are called *allophones*—thus an allophone is a phone that has been classified as belonging to some class, or phoneme. In the above example, [p] and [pʰ] are allophones of the same phoneme in English, which we can label /p/. However, in Hindi, these sounds are allophones of different phonemes. Note that symbols representing phonemes are written between slash brackets; this distinguishes them from symbols representing phones.

By giving a description like this, linguists attempt to show that the phonological system of a language has two levels. The more concrete level involves the physical reality of phonetic segments. Phonemes are something more abstract. Note that when linguists group sounds into phonemic classes, it is necessary to appeal to psychological notions like meaning. This is no accident, because phonemes are psychological units of linguistic structure.

To emphasize this point, linguists sometimes describe phonemes as the form in which we store sounds in our memory. It makes sense to remember words in terms of phonemes because it is much more efficient not to store information about phonetic details. As we will see, the details about the phonetic form of a word can be predicted from its phonemic form. For example, when we attempt to memorize a word like *path*, we notice that it begins with /p/, not /s/ or /j/. But we need not learn as a particular fact about this word that the *p* must be aspirated; this is done automatically whenever the word is pronounced.

The first sound in a word like *path* is pronounced when the brain sends signals to the articulatory organs to produce a phonetic realization of the phoneme /p/—or, in everyday terms, to make the *p*-sound. [pʰ], an allophone of the phoneme /p/, is the product of these instructions. Since phonemes are psychological concepts, they are not directly observable in a stream of speech. Only allophones of phonemes are.

The phoneme is a unit of linguistic structure which is just as significant to the native speaker as the word or the sentence. Native speakers reveal their knowledge of phonemes in a number of ways. When an English speaker makes a slip of the tongue and says [či ken] for *key chain*, reversing [č] and [k], he or she has demonstrated that [č] functions mentally as a single unit, just as [k] does. Recall from File 21 that this is not the only way to conceptualize [č]: it is phonetically complex, consisting of [t] followed immediately by [š]. (Thus *key chain* can be transcribed as either [ki čen] or as [ki tšen].) Yet since [č] represents the pronunciation of a single phoneme /č/ in English, no native speaker would make an error which would involve splitting up its phonetic components: you will never hear [ti kšen] as a slip of the tongue.

Knowledge of phonemes is also revealed in spelling systems. For example, English does not have separate letters for [pʰ] and [p]; they are both spelled with the letter *p*. Examples like this show that the English spelling system ignores the differences in pronunciation that don't result in meaning distinctions. For the most part, the English spelling system attempts to provide symbols for phonemes, not phonetic segments. In general, alphabetic writing systems tend to be phonemic rather than phonetic, although they achieve this goal with varying degrees of success.

DISTRIBUTION OF SPEECH SOUNDS

To find out which sounds are thought of by a native speaker as the same sound and which sounds are distinctive relative to one another, it is important to look at where these sounds occur in a language. In other words, linguists try to discover what the phonemes of a language are by examining the *distribution* of that language's phones. The distribution of a phone is the set of phonetic environments in which it occurs. For example, we saw in file 27 that nasalized vowels in English appear in the environment of a nasal consonant. More precisely, a linguist would describe the distribution of English [ĩ], [õ], and so on by stating that they occur immediately preceding a nasal consonant.

We can also describe the distribution of one phone relative to that of another. Two speech sounds in a language will either be in *overlapping distribution* or *complementary distribution* with respect to one another.

We will consider each of these distribution patterns in turn.

Two sounds are in *overlapping distribution* when the sets of phonetic environments in which they can occur are partially or completely identical. For example, consider a small selection of English words in which the sounds [b] and [d] appear. (Recall that "*" indicates that a word is unacceptable. *[dlit] is not a possible English word.)

bait	[bet]	*date*	[det]
lobe	[lob]	*load*	[lod]
knobs	[nabz]	*nods*	[nadz]
bleat	[blit]		*[dlit]

You can see that the set of environments of [b] is partially similar to that of [d]: both sounds occur word-initially before a vowel, and they both occur between [a] and [z]. (Of course, their actual distributions are much wider than this, but we are using a very limited set of data.) The distribution of these two sounds is not identical, however, because [b] can occur word-initially before /l/ but [d] cannot. Nevertheless, their sets of possible phonetic environments overlap, and so we say that [b] and [d] are in overlapping distribution in English.

Some (but not all—see the paragraph below) sounds that are in overlapping distribution are *contrastive* with respect to one another, which is another way of saying that they are distinctive sounds. Consider the [b] and [d] words above. *Bait* and *date* form a minimal pair, as do *lobe* and *load*, and *knobs* and *nods*. The choice between [b] and [d] in the environments [_et], [lo_], and [na_z] makes a difference in the meanings of these words. Because the difference between [b] and [d] can result in a contrast in meaning (*bait* vs. *date* and so on), we say that [b] and [d] are in *contrastive distribution*. As you know, two distinctive (or contrastive) phones are classified as being allophones of separate phonemes. Thus [b] is an allophone of the phoneme /b/, and [d] is an allophone of the phoneme /d/.

Other phones that are in overlapping distribution are in *free variation*. As an example, consider the following words containing [p] and [p°] (recall from File 27 that [p°] represents an unreleased voiceless bilabial stop).

leap	[lip]	*leap*	[lip°]
soap	[sop]	*soap*	[sop°]
troop	[trup]	*troop*	[trup°]
happy	[hæpi]		*[hæp°i]

It should be clear that these sounds are also in overlapping distribution, because they share some of the same environments: they both can appear at the ends of words. Unlike the [b] vs. [d] examples, however, there are no minimal pairs in these data. Although there are pairs of words containing the same sounds but one, these words do not contrast in meaning. Thus the choice between [p] and [p°] in *leap*, *soap*, and *troop* does not make a difference in meaning; rather, these sounds are interchangeable in word final position. To a native speaker, sounds like [p] and [p°] which are in free variation are perceived as being the "same" sound, and so we conclude that they are allophones of the same phoneme.

Complementary distribution is just the opposite of overlapping distribution. To understand this better, think about what the term *complementary* means: two complementary parts of something make up the whole. For example, the set of people in your class at any given moment can be divided into the set of people who are wearing glasses and the set of people who are not. These two sets of people complement each other. They are mutually exclusive—i.e., nonoverlapping—but together they make up the whole class. Therefore they are complementary sets.

Now let's consider a linguistic example. The sounds [p] and [pʰ] occur in English words such as the following.

spat	[spæt]	*pat*	[pʰæt]
spool	[spul]	*pool*	[pʰul]
speak	[spik]	*peek*	[pʰik]

As you can see, [p] and [pʰ] are not in overlapping distribution: they do not occur in the same phonetic environment. In fact, they are in complementary distribution. [p] occurs after [s] but not word-initially. [pʰ] occurs word-initially but not after [s]. There are no minimal pairs involving a [p]-[pʰ] contrast; since these sounds appear in different phonetic environments there can be no pair of words composed of identical strings of sounds except for [p] in one and [pʰ] in the other. Phones that are in complementary distribution are allophones of a single phoneme. In this case, [p] and [pʰ] are both allophones of the phoneme we can represent as /p/. The appearance of one allophone or the other is *predictable* when those allophones are in complementary distribution. Here we can predict that [pʰ] (but never [p]) will appear in word-initial position in words other than those listed above, and that [p] (but never [pʰ]) will follow [s] in other words.

To summarize, a phone's distribution is the collection of phonetic environments in which the phone may appear; when linguists describe a phone's distribution they describe this collection. Relative to each other, two (or more) phones will be in overlapping or complementary distribution. If they are in overlapping distribution, they are either in contrastive distribution or in free variation. Phones in contrastive distribution may appear in minimal pairs, and are allophones of different phonemes. Phones in free variation may appear in the same phonetic environments but never cause a contrast in meaning; they are allophones of the same phoneme. In either kind of overlapping distribution, given a particular phonetic environment (such as [be_] or [li_]) one cannot predict which of the phones will occur. If the two (or more) phones are in complementary distribution, their appearance in particular phonetic environments (such as [s_æt] or [_æt]) is predictable, they can never appear in minimal pairs, and they are allophones of the same phonemes.

American Sign Language: The Phonological Base

Scott K. Liddell and Robert E. Johnson

ABSTRACT

This paper has the ambitious goal of outlining the phonological structures and processes we have analyzed in American Sign Language (ASL). In order to do this we have divided the paper into five parts. In section 1 we detail the types of sequential phenomena found in the production of individual signs, allowing us to argue that ASL signs are composed of sequences of phonological segments, just as are words in spoken languages. Section 2 provides the details of a segmental phonetic transcription system. Using the descriptions made available by the transcription system, Section 3 briefly discusses both paradigmatic and syntagmatic contrast in ASL signs. Section 4 deals with the various types of phonological processes at work in the language, processes remarkable in their similarity to phonological processes found in spoken languages. We conclude the paper with an overview of the major types of phonological effects of ASL's rich system of morphological processes.

We realize that the majority of readers will come to this paper with neither sign language proficiency nor a knowledge of sign language structure. As a result, many will encounter reference to ASL signs without knowing their form. Although we have been unable to illustrate all the examples, we hope we have provided sufficient illustrations to make the paper more accessible.

1. SEQUENTIAL PHENOMENA IN SIGN FORMATION

1.1 Background

The fact that all spoken languages combine meaningless elements to form meaningful symbols is regarded as one of the defining features of human language. Stokoe (1960) demonstrated that ASL signs may also be viewed as compositional rather than holistic and thereby provided the first structural evidence that ASL should be regarded as a language rather than merely a gesture system. His pioneering work has had a profound effect on all subsequent research into ASL structure.

He proposed that a sign consists of three parts which combine simultaneously: the tab (location of the sign), the dez (handshape), and the sig (the movement). Influenced by the American structuralists, Stokoe referred to these three aspects of a sign as "cheremes." He regarded cheremes as meaningless elements which combined to form all the signs in the language, in a manner analogous to that of spoken language phonemes.

The Stokoe model has been adopted almost universally by sign language researchers. The most recent treatments of the model hold signs to be temporally unitary phenomena, composed of some number of simultaneously occurring gestural

Source. Reprinted by permission of the publisher, from William C. Stokoe, ed., Fall 1989, *Sign Language Studies*, 64(195–277).

primes. According to this view of sign structure, the entire set of gestures comprising a sign is seen to be analogous to the set of articulatory primes that comprise a single segment in spoken language (Studdert-Kennedy and Lane 1980; Klima and Bellugi 1979:85–194).

Differences among signs are described by the substitution of primes within the simultaneous bundle. Thus, the difference between the signs MOTHER (an Open "5" hand touches the chin twice with the thumb) and FATHER (an Open "5" hand touches the forehead twice with the thumb) is described as a difference in location in the bundles of otherwise identical primes. Analogously, the difference between [p] and [t] is commonly described as a difference in the place of articulation primes in bundles of otherwise identical primes. Because of this view, sign languages have been seen to be unusual in that meaning is attached to such simultaneous bundles rather than to sequences of such bundles as it is in spoken languages.

In this model of sign structure (as in the model of spoken language segment structure), however, the claim that signs are simultaneous bundles of primes is not a claim that there are no sequential events within signs. It is a claim that within signs sequential organization is phonologically unimportant. Thus, while Stokoe and more recent workers recognize sequence within signs, they typically hold it to be phonologically insignificant (Stokoe 1960, Battison 1978). This is similar to the recognition that the onset-closure sequence present in the stops [p] and [t] is phonologically insignificant.

Liddell (1984a) argues that an adequate description of many phenomena in ASL requires the recognition of sequences of primes, and demonstrates that such sequences are capable of signaling contrast among signs. Below we will describe several descriptively important sequences of primes, and then return to the issue of contrast.

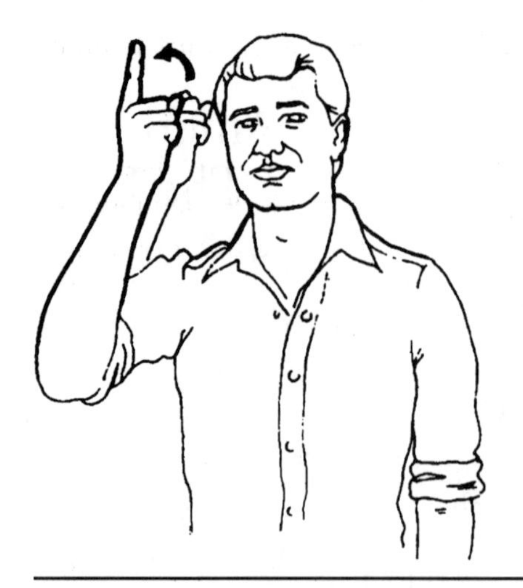

FIGURE 1. UNDERSTAND

1.2 Handshapes

A significant number of signs in the ASL lexicon are produced with changes in handshape. For example, UNDERSTAND begins with an S handshape but ends with a 1 handshape.

This handshape change is described by Stokoe et al. (1965) as a unitary movement they call an "opening movement" wherein a handshape changes from a "Closed" handshape to an "Open" handshape. Table 1 presents a sampling of signs which all begin

TABLE 1. Signs with Initial S Handshape Changing to Second Shape

SIGN	INITIAL HANDSHAPE	FINAL HANDSHAPE
UNDERSTAND	S	1
THROW	S	H
TWELVE	S	V
SO-WHAT	S	O
FINGERSPELL-TO	S	4
GAMBLE	S	5

with an S handshape, but end with different handshapes.

Many other sequences of two handshapes occur in ASL signs. A smaller number of signs are produced with a sequence of three handshapes. In SHOCKED the handshape sequence is S-C-S. In THINK-SAME-THOUGHT the sequence is S-1-S. In GOVERNMENT the sequence is 1-Bent 1-1.

1.3 Locations

It is quite common for the hand to move from one location to another location during the production of a single sign. Such relocations occur frequently in simple signs and are especially common in compound signs, almost all of which move from one location to another.

The sign PARENTS is such a compound sign, derived from the signs MOTHER and FATHER. It begins at the chin (the location of MOTHER) and then moves to the forehead (the location for FATHER). Table 2 lists several examples of signs in which the location of the hand changes.

Compounds are marked with a "(C)." Because Stokoe's sign schema permits a sign to have only one location, his notations treat relocations in simple signs as complexes of movements. Thus, for example, NAVY might be said to be located at the left side of the waist and then to move to the right and make contact. The actual location at the right side of the waist would not be specified. Compounds are treated as linked notations of two complete signs, each of which has its own location.

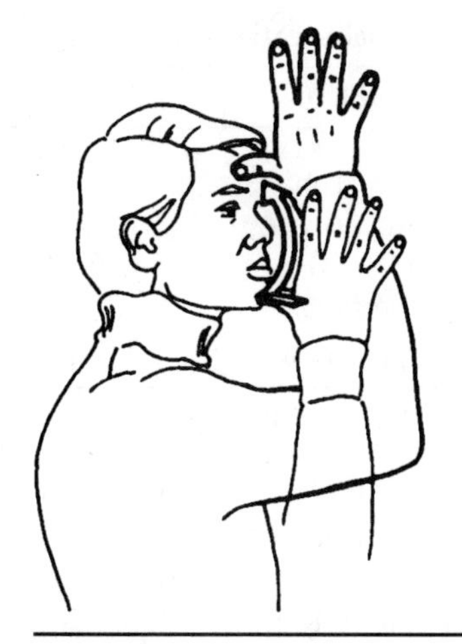

FIGURE 2. PARENTS

Numerous verbs in ASL are marked for subject and object agreement and typically move from one location to another. Table 3 shows the locations involved with two verbs

TABLE 2. Initial and Final Locations of Some Common Signs

	SIGN	INITIAL LOCATION	FINAL LOCATION
	SANTA-CLAUS	chin	chest
	GOOD	chin	base hand
	NAVY	left side of waist	right side of waist
	KING	left side of chest	right side of waist
	INDIAN	nose	side of forehead
	AHEM	chin	chest
(C)	PARENTS	chin	forehead
(C)	SON	forehead	forearm
(C)	PALE	chest	face
(C)	BROTHER	forehead	base hand
(C)	PROMISE	chin	base hand

TABLE 3. Initial and Final Locations for Two Agreement Verbs

VERB	SUBJ.	OBJ.	INITIAL LOC.	FINAL LOC.
TELL	—	1st person	chin	chest
TELL	—	3rd person(a)	chin	place(a)
GIVE	1st person	3rd person(b)	chest	place(b)
GIVE	3rd person(a)	3rd person(b)	place(a)	place(b)
GIVE	3rd person(b)	1st person	place(b)	chest

marked for agreement. TELL always begins in contact with the chin, and then moves to a location which reflects agreement with its object. GIVE agrees with both its subject and object. Its initial and final locations are determined by the subject and object agreement morphemes which are inserted into the verb stem. Subject and object marking is not capable of being represented in Stokoe's notation system. We will discuss this in more detail in section 1.6.

1.4 Movements

Stokoe's original observations demonstrated that some signs require movements to be carried out in sequence. He describes CHICAGO as being made with a rightward movement followed by a downward movement; WHEN with a circular movement followed by a contacting movement; YEAR with a circular movement followed by a contacting movement; and ALSO with a contact movement followed by a rightward movement, then another contacting movement.

Supalla and Newport (1978) demonstrate that very finely detailed differences in movement could distinguish some nouns from related verbs. Whereas Stokoe et al. (1965) reports the existence of a single sign meaning both "sit" and "chair," Supalla and Newport claim that SIT and CHAIR are separate signs. They find that for more than 100 such noun-verb pairs, the pattern of movement of the noun differs in predictable ways from that of the verb. They distinguish these formational differences in terms of three "manners of movement." They describe the movement of the sign SIT as a single, unidirectional movement with a "hold manner" and that of CHAIR as a repeated, unidirectional movement with "restrained manner."

FIGURE 3a. WHEN

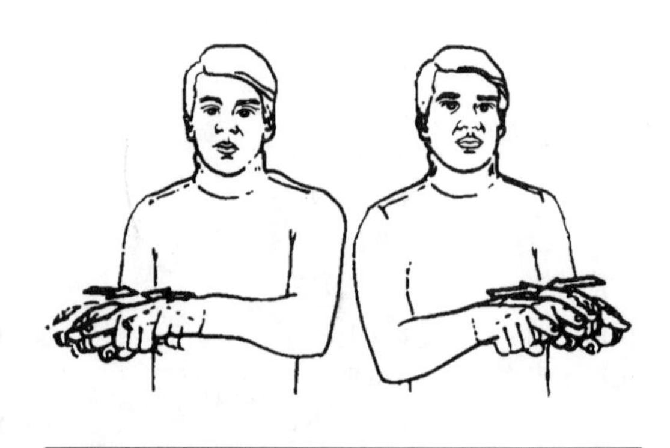

FIGURE 3b. ALSO

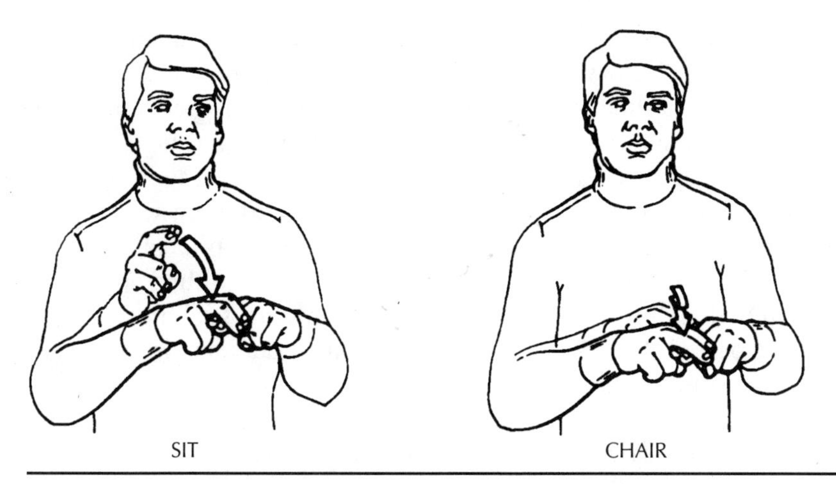

FIGURE 4. The movement differences between SIT and CHAIR.

Their manners of movement demonstrate a significant type of sequentiality in the formation of signs. The sign SIT begins with a motion toward the base hand and ends with the two hands in contact, but not moving. A sign ending with the hands immobile is said to have "hold manner" at the end of the sign. In their view such motionless periods are as important in providing contrast as are the periods of movement. They note (1978:96) that one of the possible implications of their findings is that signs may have sequential internal segments rather than a simultaneous bundle of features.[1]

1.5 Local Movements

Local movements are small repeated movements of the fingers and wrist which accompany the major movements of the hand. For example, LONG-AGO is produced with a "5" hand configuration which moves backward to a hold at a point just over the shoulder. During the backward movement itself the fingers wiggle, but the final hold is produced without finger wiggling.

Thus LONG-AGO contains the sequence: local movement, no local movement. In other signs, such as JUMP-FOR-JOY the wiggling is restricted to the middle of the sign where the active hand does not contact the base hand. This produces the sequence: no local movement, local movement, no local movement.

1.6 Nonmanual Signals

Many nonmanual signals involve no sequentiality. For example, the combination of raised eyebrows and backward head tilt which accompanies topics (Liddell, 1977) is

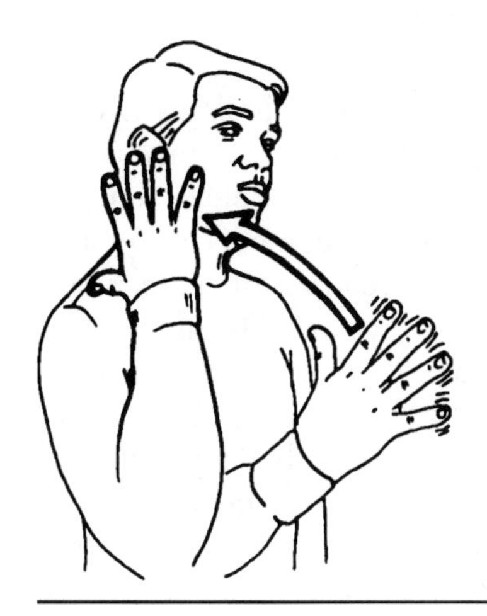

FIGURE 5. LONG-AGO

purely configurational, with no internal changes. Some nonmanual signals, however, are produced by sequencing nonmanual activities. Some such nonmanual signals occur as part of lexical items and others occur as part of morphological processes. A lexical item which requires a sequence of nonmanual activities is GIVE-IN. During the initial part of its production the lips are closed but during the final part of its production the lips are open. ALL-GONE, on the other hand, begins with the lips apart and the tongue slightly protruding and ends with the lips closed.

Sequences of nonmanual activities are also important as part of morphological processes. Liddell (1984b) describes a sequence of nonmanual activities required as part of the inflection for unrealized-inceptive aspect. When this inflection is applied to a verb, specific, predictable changes occur in both the manual and nonmanual portions of the sign. The sequence of nonmanual behaviors associated with this inflection require the signer to inhale through the mouth while rotating the trunk, and then to hold the resulting configuration during the final portion of the sign.

1.7 Contrast in ASL

We have illustrated several types of sequentiality in ASL signing, including sequences of handshapes, locations, nonmanual signals, local movements, and movements and holds. The simultaneous model of sign structure is not able to represent these sequential details in an effective way. This alone argues for a descriptive device which is able to represent important aspects of ASL sequence.

Specifically, given that signs have sequential structure, that sequence can be shown to correspond to phonological segments responsible for sequential contrast of the sort found in spoken languages. The identification of physical sequence in the linguistic signal provides the evidence needed to argue that signs are composed of sequenced, abstract, linguistic segments. Support for the existence of such linguistic segments comes, in part, from a demonstration that ASL, like spoken languages, contains pairs of signs distinguished only by differences in sign-internal sequence.

It has become traditional in treatments of ASL structure to illustrate "minimal pairs" of signs as a demonstration of phonological contrast. However, because the simultaneous model of sign structure dictates that signs are composed of a single, simultaneous bundle of gestural features, such pairs of signs are able to demonstrate only simultaneous contrast of the sort found within segments in spoken languages. Thus, staying for the moment with the notion that signs are simultaneous, most "minimal pairs" of signs identified in the literature on ASL exhibit contrasts analogous to the differences between [p], [t], and [b]. They are distinctions of one feature within a single, co-occurrent bundle of features.

By contrast, in spoken language analysis, the notion of "minimal pair" has typically been used to demonstrate sequential contrast. Thus, a minimal pair is usually considered to be two words, contrastive in meaning, which are identical in all segments except one, in which they differ by only one feature. The kinds of ASL sequential details we have identified above provide this kind of evidence for sequential contrast.

THANK-YOU and BULLSHIT are minimal pairs in this sense. Both begin with identical holds produced at the chin and move to holds produced at a location about six inches out and slightly below the chin. In both signs, the orientation of the hand remains constant, with the palm toward the face and the wrist toward the ground. Thus, from the perspective of movement, location, and ori-

TABLE 4. Sequential Contrast Between Minimal Pairs THANK-YOU and BULLSHIT.

	THANK-YOU		
	first part	*middle part*	*last part*
movement	hold	move out	hold
location	chin	transitional	out from chin
orientation	palm to chin	transitional	palm to chin
hand configuration	B	transitional	B
	BULLSHIT		
movement	hold	move out	hold
location	chin	transitional	out from chin
orientation	palm to chin	transitional	palm to chin
hand configuration	B	transitional	S

entation the signs have identical sequences. They differ only in hand configuration sequence. Specifically, during the production of the sign THANK-YOU, the hand configuration begins and ends as a "B." In the sign BULLSHIT, however, it begins as a "B" and ends as an "S." In Table 4 the parts of THANK-YOU and BULLSHIT are aligned.

Although true minimal pairs such as these are not abundant in ASL, there are similar pairs that demonstrate sequential contrast in each of the major descriptive parameters of signs. Together they demonstrate that segments function to signal contrast in ASL in much the same manner as in spoken languages, and suggest that the description of segments is central to an adequate phonological analysis of ASL signs. In addition, the value of a segmental description in the analysis of the phonological and morphological processes of ASL will become more apparent as we proceed.

2. A PHONETIC TRANSCRIPTION SYSTEM FOR ASL

At first glance, it may seem inappropriate to use "phonology," "phonetics," and other seemingly vocally-based terms in referring to details of sign language and its organization. As we mentioned earlier, Stokoe's work explicitly avoids this difficulty by positing terminology such as "chereme" and "cherology," which are specific to sign language. Battison (1974) demonstrates that sign language descriptions contain a sublexical level of analysis that appears in certain ways to be organizationally and functionally equivalent to the level of phonology in spoken languages. He argues convincingly that standard phonological terminology refers appropriately to those levels. A part of what we will be demonstrating in this paper is that an analysis of the patterns of organization of sign language signals yields levels of analysis quite similar to those known to exist in spoken language phonologies.

It is a matter of historical accident that, during the period of development of modern linguistic terminology, all languages known to linguists were spoken languages. Even so, for the most part, phonological terminology refers to the patterns of organization of linguistic signals, rather than to the signals themselves. Thus, the vocal reference of the *phone-* stem in words such as *phoneme* is largely unnecessary. We use phonological terminology in referring to the organization of sign languages, with the understanding that the terminology here, as in studies of other languages, refers to general principles of organization probably found in all languages rather than to the specific vocal gestures of spoken languages.

2.1 Goals of Transcription

A transcription system for a language or set of languages should meet the dual goals of at once providing for the accurate representation of the detail of the "facts" of a language and assuring that those representations are useful in characterizing the organization of the facts.

We have attempted to devise a system that provides a linkage between the abstract and concrete aspects of phonological systems without committing overwhelmingly to either. Clearly, an adequate system of transcription must have elements of both. On the concrete end, a transcription must account for all the linguistically interesting details of the production of the signal. For our purposes, such phonetic transcription will be roughly equivalent in its concreteness to the "systematic phonetic representations" of standard generative phonology (Chomsky and Halle 1968). While such representations must account for a great deal of detail, they exclude (a) linguistically nondistinctive differences such as the difference between apical and laminal [s] in English; (b) sequential detail within phonologically functional units, e.g., elimination of onset and closure information from the description of English stop consonants; (c) detail stemming from universal physiological conditions; (d) detail stemming from individual physiological conditions, e.g., absolute voice pitch; and (e) traditionally nonlinguistic detail such as rate, loudness, and affect marking features.

On the abstract end, an adequate notation system must provide descriptive devices that permit a plausible linkage between the detailed surface representation and the underlying forms of the individual lexical items that are present in it. Thus, a single set of descriptive devices should at once be capable of characterizing each of the following: (a) the phonological shape (underlying form) of lexical items; (b) the phonological aspects of the morphology; (c) phonological processes; and (d) the surface forms of signs in running signed productions (at the level of concreteness specified above). To the extent that a system of notation succeeds in achieving this balance, it provides phonetic motivation for phonological features and phonetic plausibility for the abstract structures and processes of the phonological component.

That the system be usable is a second, more pragmatic goal which has influenced the current form of our notation system. Thus, while sign notations will ultimately be reducible to matrices of binary phonological features, most of the notations presented here contain taxonomic entries that represent bundles of such features. The use of such taxonomic entries is primarily a matter of clerical and typographical convenience, reducing the number of symbols required to transcribe a sign.

2.2 Overview of Sign Structure

2.2.1 Describing Segments. The segment is the central element in our view of the structure of signs. Thus, the representation of segments is the essential task of our notation system. In our system, each segment is represented individually and signs (and discourse strings) are represented as strings of segments.[2]

Segments in sign languages are composed of two major components. One describes the *posture* of the hand; the other describes its *activity*. A description of the posture of the hand is concerned with where it is, how it is oriented, how its own movable parts are configured, and so on. The features that describe these details are collectively called *articulatory features*. We refer to the combination of articulatory features needed to specify a given posture of the hand as an "articulatory bundle."

The articulatory bundle contains four major clusters of features. The first represents the *hand configuration*, i.e., the state of the fingers and thumb. The second cluster represents *point of contact*, which specifies the primary location with respect to which the hand is located, the part of the hand that points to or contacts that location, and the spatial relationship between that hand part and that location. The third cluster represents *facing*, which is composed of sets of features specifying a second location, and features indicating the part of the hand which faces that location. The fourth cluster of features in the articulatory bundle, *orientation*, contains features specifying a plane toward which a part of the hand faces. Orientation features distinguish THING (a sequence of movements made with the palm up) from CHILDREN (like THING but with the palm down). The four clusters, all taken together, describe the posture of the hand at a particular point in the production of a sign. They do not describe the activity of the hand.

The features that specify the activity of the hand during the production of the segment are grouped into a separate segmental feature bundle. They describe whether or not the hand is moving, and, if so, in what manner. The elemental work of this class of features is to distinguish movements from holds. *Movements* are defined as periods of time during which some aspect of the articulation is in transition. *Holds* are defined as periods of time during which all aspects of the articulation bundle are in a steady state.

While the descriptive work of the segmental features is to detail the movement of the articulators, they function within signed strings to divide the flow of gestures into segments. By definition, then, the features that distinguish movements from holds also define the segmental structure of larger units such as signs, which we represent as strings of juxtaposed segments. This is not unlike the manner in which the major class features of generative phonology function. In spoken language phonology, major class features specify phonetic details of segments such as spontaneous voicing, interruption of the airstream, and syllabicity. These same feature values distinguish consonants from vowels and therefore also function to specify the manner in which the flow of speech is divided.

The remaining features in the segmental bundle specify the finer detail of segments such as contour of movement, simultaneous local movement of the fingers, and precise timing information such as length. We will discuss these features in detail below.

We have presented the articulatory bundles and segmental bundles separately, and in fact they function independently from each other in the specification of entire segments. The articulatory features combine to describe postural states. By definition, movement segments are those during which there is a change in state in some complex of articulatory features, and hold segments are those during which no such change occurs. Because they involve a steady state, a single matrix of features will be sufficient to describe holds. This matrix will contain both the segmental bundle of features including the specification of fine detail of the segment and the articulatory bundle of features describing the postural state present during the production of the hold segment.

Movement segments, however, present another problem. During a movement the hand changes from one posture to another. Thus, because our articulatory features represent states, our system requires the specification of an initial and final bundle of articulatory features to indicate the changes during the production of the segment. Movement segments contain one bundle of segmental features containing the specification of the segment type and the fine details of the movement and two bundles of articulatory features, the first of which specifies the postural state at the inception of the movement and the second of which specifies the postural state of the hand at the conclusion of the movement. Hold segments contain one articulatory bundle; movement segments contain two articulatory bundles.

Both hold and movement segments may be represented by matrices of features, but following the discussion above the matrices will be different. The hold segment would correspond to be a straightforward and traditional feature matrix as in Figure 6, while the movement segment will have one set of segmental specifications and two sets of articulatory specifications, as in Figure 7.

An apparent alternative solution to the use of two kinds of matrices might be to use

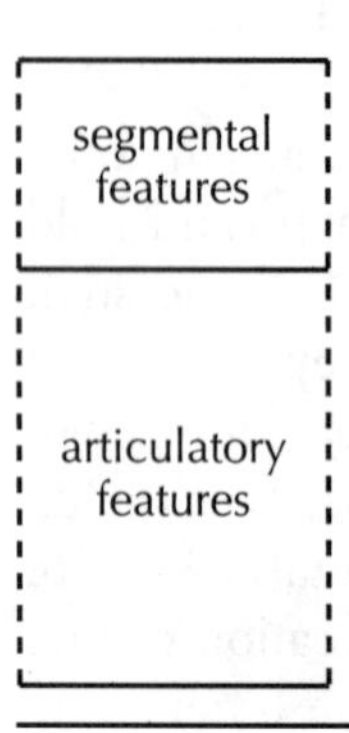

FIGURE 6. A hold matrix.

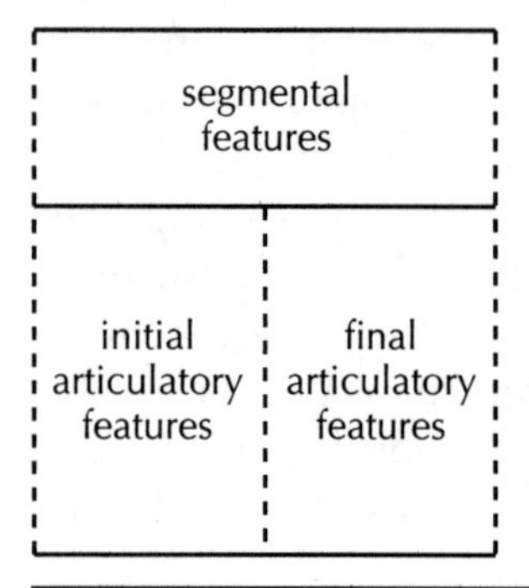

FIGURE 7. A movement matrix.

only hold matrices, let them define segmental structure, and have movement take place as a result of transitions from one state to the next. As we present more detailed descriptions of signs it will become apparent that independent movement features are necessary. This is because the fine details of movement production are features of the movement itself, not of either of the individual articulatory bundles. For example, when the hand moves on a path from one location to another, that path may take any of three contours. It may move in a straight line, on an arc, or on an indirect path with a sharp change of direction in the middle. These differences in path are contrastive and therefore must be recorded. They are not a feature of the initial articulatory posture nor of the final articulatory posture nor of both at once. They are a feature of the period of time during which the hand is changing from the initial posture to the final posture. Thus, they are details of the movement itself and must be specified independently of the articulatory information. Considerations presented below will confirm this claim of independence of the segmental and articulatory bundles of features.

2.2.2 Non-Manual Behaviors. The segmental structure of signs also bears on the representation of the non-manual behaviors that have linguistic function in ASL. At times, non-manual behaviors clearly have functions that are independent of the segment. Examples of such non-manual behaviors are those that have syntactic function and those that have clear morphological status. Others appear to be tied to specific segments within specific signs (Liddell 1984a). In both cases, although possibly independent in function, the behaviors are timed to the production of segments, and need to be specified in the transcription system. The exact nature of this specification will be taken up later.

2.2.3 Describing Sequences of Segments. In the view of sign structure presented here, individual signs and larger constructions are all composed of sequences of segments. Thus, a sign or a piece of discourse may be represented as a sequence of hold and movement matrices, each composed of the appropriate number of segmental and articulatory bundles. The sign GOOD, for example, is composed of three segments: a hold, a movement, and a hold (see Figure 26b). The first hold occurs with the finger pads of a flat hand in contact with the chin. For convenience, we will call this complex of articulatory information "posture a." From this hold, the hand moves outward and downward to a final hold, which occurs in space about a foot in front of the sternum with the same flat hand configuration oriented so that the palm of the hand is facing (roughly) upward and the tips of the fingers are pointing outward at about a forty-five degree angle. We can call this complex of articulatory information "posture b." In our matrix format we can represent this sign as in Figure 8.

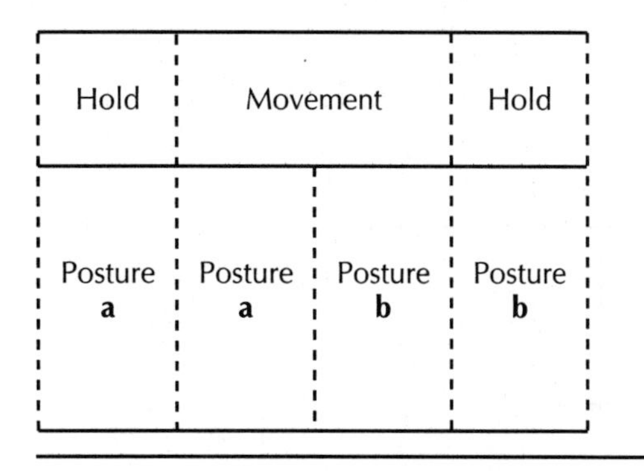

FIGURE 8. Representation of feature matrix for sign GOOD.

Notice that in the representation of GOOD the initial articulatory specification of the movement segment is the same as the articulatory specification of the first hold segment. Similarly, the final articulatory specification of the movement segment is the same as the articulatory specification of the second hold segment. An initial posture of any segment in a string is identical to the final posture of the preceding segment. This is true by definition because a given line of transcription represents a sequence of behaviors of a single articulator, which can only start a gesture from the posture in which it terminated the preceding gesture. From this perspective it is unnecessary to record every articulatory bundle of information because (within signs) two articulatory bundles that share a common segmental boundary must be identical.

This observation stands as additional evidence for the independence of the articulatory features from the segmental features. It also recommends the use of an autosegmental representation which permits the attachment of single clusters of features of one sort to single clusters of features of another sort (Goldsmith 1976, McCarthy 1979), as in Figure 9.

Autosegmental representations of the sort presented in Figure 9, in addition to enhancing clerical economy, provide additional support for the earlier suggestion that the articulatory bundle of features is autonomous in function from the segmental

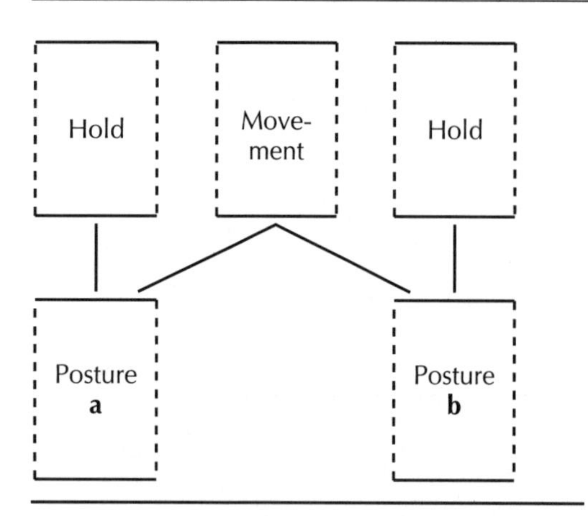

FIGURE 9. Representation of autosegmental attachment of feature bundles of the sign GOOD.

bundle of features. It is also quite likely that certain of the clusters of features within the articulatory bundle itself enjoy a similar kind of autonomy, particularly at the lower levels of the phonology where the independent postural and movement components must be finely timed to one another. Similarly, there may be more autonomous tiers of feature clusters at the level of the phonology that controls the production of fast speech, in which muscular activities and postures are reinterpreted and produced as perceptually and productively similar (though linguistically different) muscular behaviors. Autosegmental analyses of these phenomena may prove to be worthwhile. For our purposes, however, it is sufficient to use only the articulatory and segmental tiers, together with a tier for non-manual behaviors.

A number of the combinations of segments that may occur in ASL signs are presented in Figure 10.

2.2.4 Describing Signs Requiring Two Hands. As we indicated above, many signs make use of both hands as articulators. From a phonetic perspective, each hand is independent of the other. Moreover, the hands may carry different phonetic information at a given moment. For example, one may be moving while the other is not. One may be in one location or orientation or hand configuration while the other hand is specified differently for one or more of these details. As one might expect, there appear to be fairly strong conditions on the nature and extent of the simultaneous articulation of two segments (Battison 1974, 1978), so the two hands are not completely independent phonologically. While a notation system may ultimately be able to eliminate certain aspects of the information that is predictable from such constraints on simultaneous articulations, it is useful at early stages of analysis to be able to represent each hand in its full phonetic configuration.

From the perspective of the segmental notation system described above, there is no difference between the productions of one hand and those of the other. Given this and their phonetic independence, each hand must be represented as a separate string of segmental notations, and the segments of one hand must be attached (for timing purposes) to the co-occurrent segments of the other hand.

The first difficulty encountered in the representation of the behaviors of both hands is that right and left are not absolute in signing. First, left-handed and right-handed signers sign mirror images of the same sign sequence with no change in meaning. A notation system should describe both the left-handed, left-dominant and the right-handed, right-dominant versions identically. Secondly, certain constructions treat spatial locations on the right and the left as absolute. A notation system must be able to distinguish right from left under these conditions. Third, certain constructions allow a signer to meaningfully alternate between right-dominant and left-dominant signing. The notation system must be able to describe this sort of alternation.

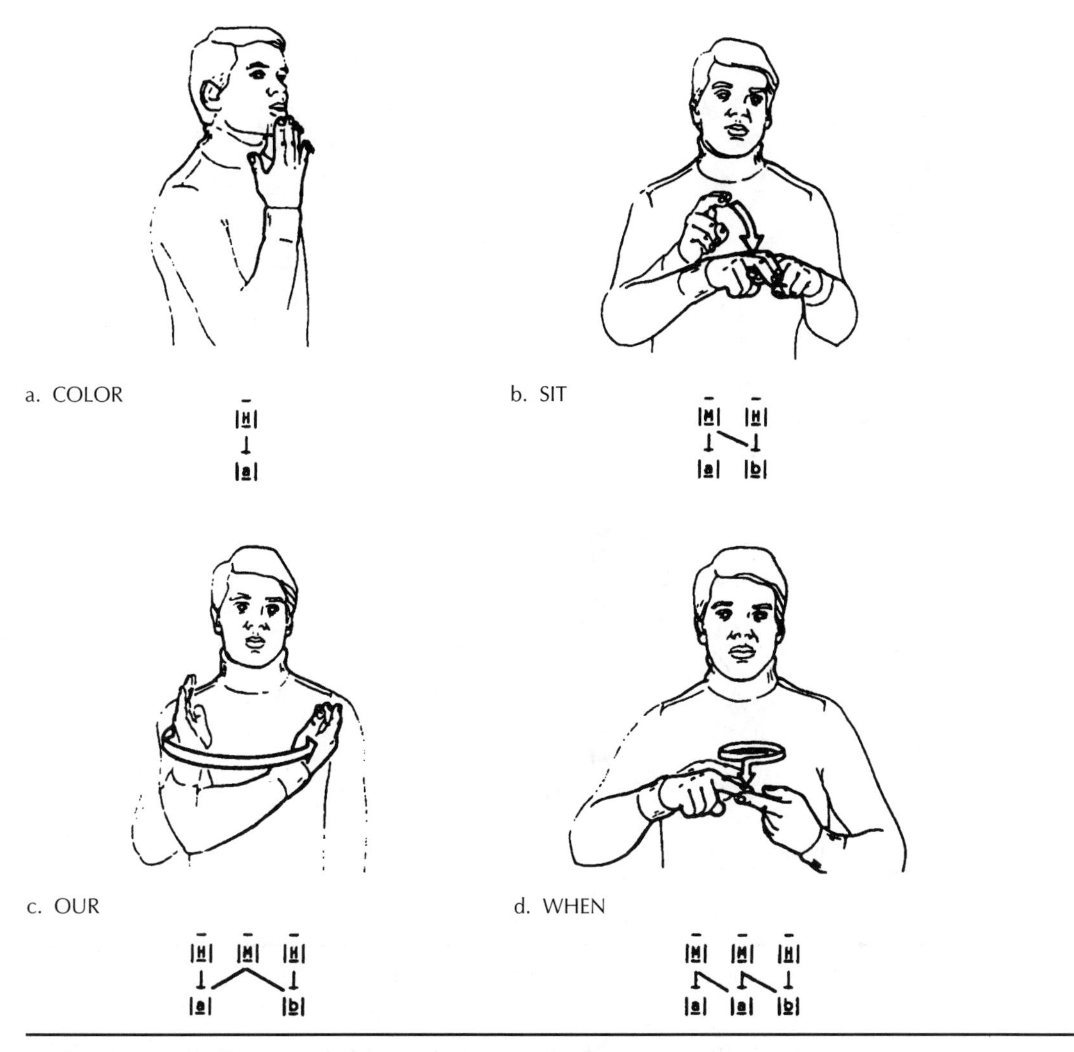

FIGURE 10. Signs illustrating common segment combinations.

Padden and Perlmutter (1984) introduce the terms "strong" and "weak" to describe the active hand and the hand it acts upon. Adopting those terms for our notation system will permit signs to be specified in a single way although signed in mirror image by right- and left-handed signers. We have chosen to use two vertically stacked strings of segments for two-handed signing. The top line represents the strong hand and the bottom line represents the weak hand. In such cases, the strong hand is understood to be the dominant hand of the signer. Particular transcriptions of running sign will need to be marked for the dominance of the signer. When a signer shifts from expected-dominance signing to opposite-dominance signing the strong label will be shifted to the bottom line and the weak to the top line. In those instances when each hand is actually operating independently, the top line will be right for right-dominant signers or left for left-dominant signers.

It appears that the strong hand segments function as the central organizing elements for the timing of strings of co-occurrent

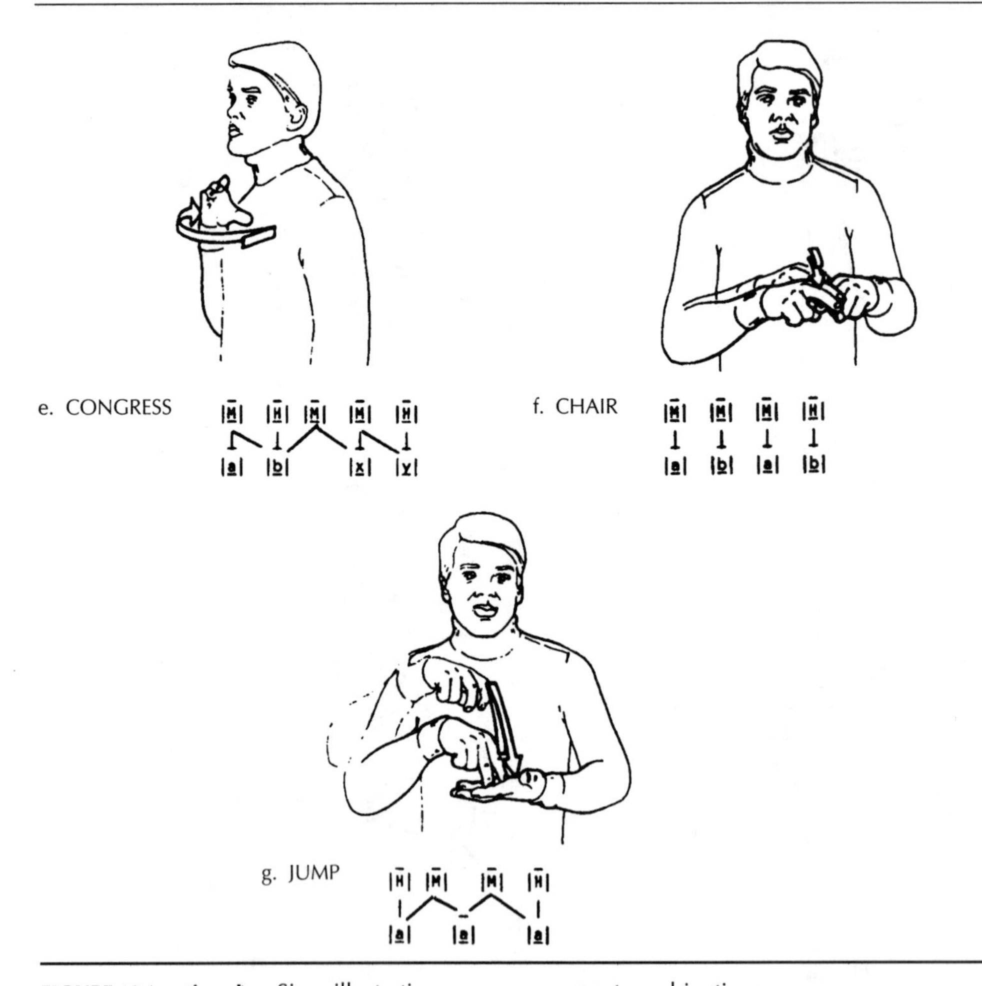

FIGURE 10 (continued). Signs illustrating common segment combinations.

segments. Therefore, the segments of the weak hand must be attached to those of the strong hand. Several combinations of strong and weak hands within signs and our conventions for attaching them are presented in Figures 11–13.

2.3 Detailed Description of Segmental Bundles

Segmental feature bundles specify the detail of movements and holds. Each such cluster defines one segment in the string of gestures in the transcription of a running signed production. Ultimately, the segmental bundle will contain numerous binary features. At present it contains five slots for the entry of taxonomic symbols representing clusters of features. The five types of entries within the segmental bundle are laid out as shown in Figure 14.

2.3.1 Major Classes of Segments. There are two major classes of segments in ASL: holds and movements. As described above, a movement (M) segment is characterized by a change in one or more of its articulatory features and hold (H) segments are not. Notice that not all movement segments involve movement from one location to another. The change in articulatory specification may occur in the hand configuration

FIGURE 11. FIRED, a two-handed sign in which the strong hand moves with respect to the weak hand.

FIGURE 12. LARGE, a two-handed sign in which two hands move independently, simultaneously, and symmetrically.

(UNDERSTAND), the orientation (START), or other clusters of the specification. Such non-path movements do not appear to have a phonological status different from that of path movements (those in which there is a change in the point of contact specification) and so need not be distinguished by a special feature.

2.3.2 Contours of Movement. Those movement segments that move on a path between two locations may do so on one of several contours. *Straight* [str] movements traverse a direct, straight path between two points (GOOD). There are two types of indirect contour paths: *round* [rnd] and *seven* [7]. The seven contour describes an indirect path that is sharply angled (CHICAGO). The round contour describes an indirect path that is smooth. Arcs (OUR) and circles (FACE) both describe *round* paths but are distinguished by the fact that an arc begins at one

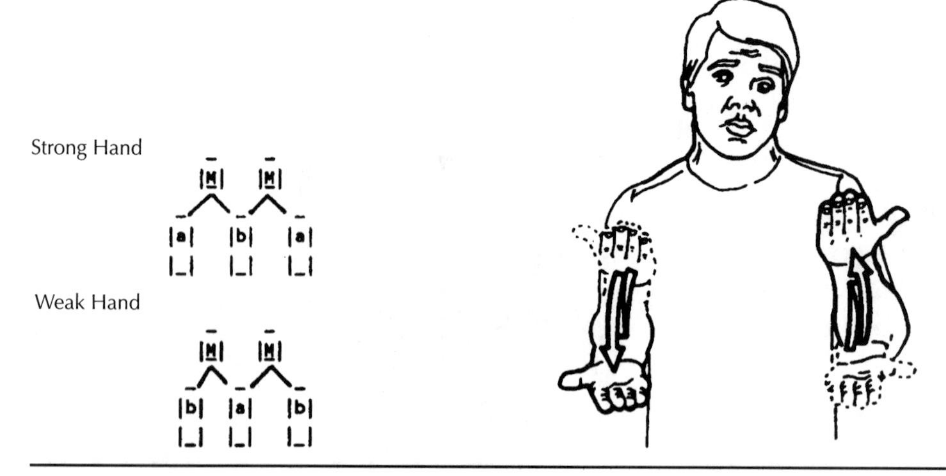

FIGURE 13. MAYBE, a two-handed sign in which the strong and weak hands perform independent movements but in temporal alternation.

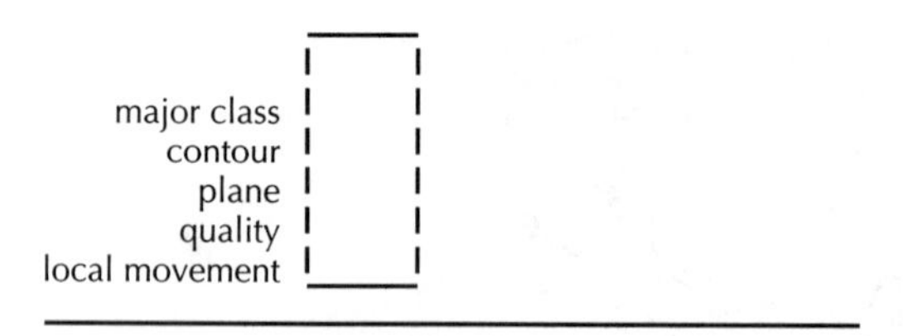

FIGURE 14. Organization of segmental features.

location and ends at another whereas a circle begins at a point, traverses a round path, and ends at its beginning point.

2.3.3 Contour Planes. When a path movement is not straight, it is necessary to specify an additional piece of information, which functions to orient the path. The entries indicate the plane upon which the hand travels as it moves between points. We currently record five planes. The *horizontal plane* [HP] is the plane parallel to the floor (OUR). The *vertical plane* [VP] is that plane parallel to the front of the torso (RAINBOW). The *surface plane* [SP] is the plane parallel to the surface at a location on the body or hand (FACE). The *midline plane* [MP] is a plane that intersects the surface plane along the midsaggital line of the body (BLOUSE, SIGN), or the plane through the long midline of the bones of the arm or the hand (BASKET). We currently use the designation *oblique plane* [OP] to represent the plane that is horizontal from side to side but angled up and away from the body.

2.3.4 Quality Features. Quality features describe fine details of a segment. Among these are the temporal qualities *prolonged* [long], *shortened* [short], and *accelerating* [acc], and the nontemporal qualities *tense* [tns], *reduced path* [sm], and *enlarged path* [lg]. The quality feature *contacting* [contact] indicates that the hand makes contact with the other hand or a body location during the course of the movement. It describes brushing movements, in which the hand travels between points on two sides of a location, making brief contact with that location as it passes. It is also useful in describing the movement in which the hand moves to a location, makes brief contact, and rebounds to a point near that location.

2.3.5 Local Movements. The major classes of segments (H and M) reflect activity of the hand taken as a whole. It is common for signs simultaneously to exhibit movement at the finger, wrist or elbow joints. Such movements are overlaid on the actual segmental activity, occurring together sometimes with H segments and sometimes with M segments. Thus, they are secondary, though linguistically significant activities. Each of the local movements is characterized by rapid, uncountable repetition. All may occur in H segments. At least wiggling, twisting, nodding, and hooking may occur in M segments.[3]

Wiggling [wg] represents repeated, sequentially alternating retraction at the first joint of all fingers extended at the first joint (COLOR). *Hooking* [hk] involves repeated, simultaneous retraction at the second and third joints of all fingers that are extended at the first joint and retracted at the second and third joints ("hooked" hand configurations) (WORM). *Flattening* [fl] is repeated, simultaneous retraction at the first joint of all fingers that are extended at the second and third joints and retracted at the first joint ("flat" hand configurations) (STICKY).[4] *Twisting* [tw] describes repeated, alternating rotations of the wrist (WHERE). *Nodding* [nod] is a repeated retraction and extension of the wrist joint (YES).[5] *Releasing* [rel] involves rapid, repeated opening of fingers that have thumb restraint (SHIRK-RESPONSIBILITY). *Rubbing* [rub] is repeated, back and forth rubbing of the thumb and the finger pads (DIRT). *Circling* is a repeated, uncountable local circling about a central point simultaneously with either an H or M. It requires the specification of a plane.

2.4 Detailed Description of Articulatory Bundles

Each articulatory bundle is composed of eight entries, each representing a complex of features. The entries cluster into four possibly autonomous groupings, described above as hand configuration (HC), point of

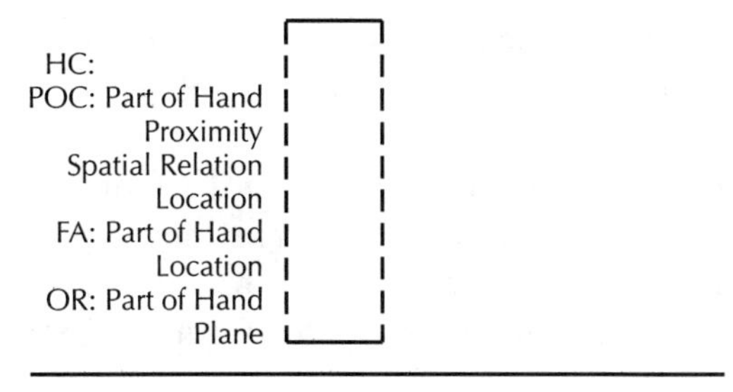

FIGURE 15. Organization of articulatory bundle.

contact (POC), facing (FA), and orientation (OR). They are organized as shown in Figure 15.

2.4.1 Hand Configuration. We have found more than 150 HCs in ASL lexical signs. Many more occur in the surface forms of running sign. A system of thirteen mostly binary features will distinguish all HCs we know to exist in sign languages. The taxonomic symbols we use as HC entries in our notations are capable of describing all the HCs of ASL and many more. They translate to features in a very straightforward way.

The HC entry is organized according to the following schema (see Figure 16).

While most HC use only the hand, others use the entire hand and forearm as a unit (ALL-DAY). Following Stokoe (1960), the symbol indicates the presence of such forearm involvement in the HC. If / is absent, the HC is assumed to use only the hand itself.

The HC description we have developed differs from most other approaches in that it notes finger configuration and thumb configuration separately. The portion of the HC

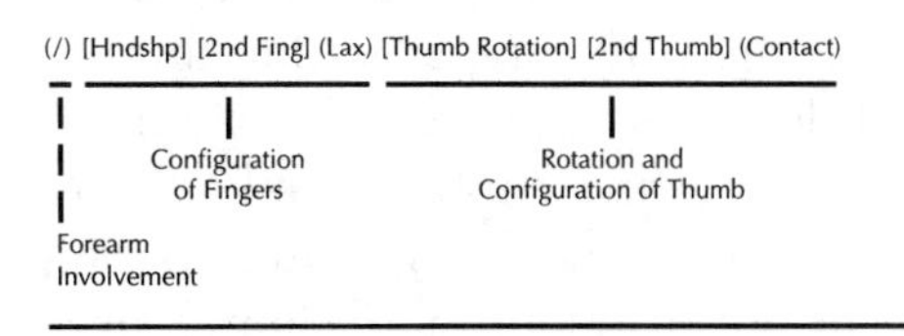

FIGURE 16. Organization of handshape features.

notation concerned with finger configuration contains slots for three symbols. The first is *handshape*, which indicates the state of extension and retraction of the four fingers. The symbols presented in Table 5 represent those combinations of open and closed fingers we know to occur in ASL signing.

TABLE 5. Symbols for Taxonomic Description of Major Finger Combination

SYMBOL	CONFIGURATION
A	Four fingers closed (pads contact palm)
S	Four fingers closed (tips contact palm)
1	All but index closed
!	All but middle closed
I	All but pinky closed
Y	All but pinky closed; pinky spread
=	All but pinky and index closed; unspread
>	All but pinky and index closed; pinky and index spread
H	All but index and middle closed; unspread
V	All but index and middle closed; spread
K	Ring and pinky closed; index open; middle partly open
D	Index open; all others partly open
R	Ring and pinky closed; index and middle crossed
r	Ring and pinky closed; middle open; index partly open and crossed under middle
W	All but pinky open and unspread
6	All but pinky open and spread
7	All but ring open and spread
8	All but middle open and spread
F	All but index open and unspread
9	All but index open and spread
B	All four fingers open and unspread
4	All four fingers open and spread
T	All fingers closed; thumb under index
N	All fingers closed; thumb under middle
M	All fingers closed; thumb under ring

Each of the four fingers is independently capable of being in one of four basic configurations: *open* (proximal joint (PJ) and distal joint (DJ) extended); *closed* (PJ and DJ flexed); *hooked* (PJ *extended*, DJ flexed); *flattened* (PJ flexed, DJ extended). The taxonomic symbols presented here function primarily to indicate which fingers are open and which are closed. The slot labeled [*2nd Fing*] in the schema contains diacritics for the hooking and flattening of those fingers ordinarily extended in a given handshape. Hooked is indicated by [″]; flattened is indicated by [^]. Thus, the symbol 1″ indicates that the index is extended at the proximal joint and flexed at the distal joints and the symbol B^ indicates that all four fingers are flexed at the proximal joints and extended at the distal joints.

The diacritic for *lax* [~] indicates an additional modification to the finger configuration. It relaxes (slightly reverses) the prominent muscle action at both the proximal and distal joints. If the joint is extended lax will flex it slightly, although not enough to be fully flexed. Similarly, if the joint is flexed, lax will extend it slightly, although not enough to be perceived as fully extended. Thus, the effect of laxing is that the finger remains as specified but not rigidly so. Lax tends to affect all four fingers but has no effect on the configuration of the thumb.

All details of thumb configuration are specified in the final cluster of symbols. The primary value for the thumb is thumb rotation. The proximal joint of the thumb (near the wrist) is capable of rotating about ninety degrees on its axis. When the thumb is relaxed and roughly adjacent to the plane created by the palm of the hand, it is in its *unopposed* [u] rotation. When the thumb is unopposed, its friction pad faces across the palm, and is capable of contacting the radial side of the middle joint of any (flattened) finger or the radial side of the palm. Typically, if the thumb is touching the palm, it is in unopposed position.

The thumb may also be rotated so that its friction pad faces the palmar surface. This is its *opposed* [o] rotation, in which the tip of the thumb may easily contact the tip of any of the fingers. The opposed thumb typically cannot touch the palm of the hand except at the base of the little finger. It often contacts the fingers at the tip, pad, or nail, and if the fingers are closed may contact the back of the penultimate finger bones.

Both opposed and unopposed thumbs must also be specified for one of four values of secondary extension and flexion, indicated in the [*2nd Thumb*] slot. The proximal joint of the thumb is near the wrist and along with the two more distal joints operates to define the same four values of extension and flexion available to the fingers. Because the thumb features are descriptive rather than taxonomic, however, open and closed must be indicated. An *open* thumb is one in which the proximal and distal joints are both extended. Thus the symbol Bu will indicate a handshape with all fingers extended and unspread and a thumb that is on the plane created by the palm and extended at about ninety degrees outward from the radial side of the hand. The symbol Bo will designate the same finger configuration with the thumb extended at a ninety degree angle from the palmar surface. Leaving the PJ extended and flexing the DJ provides the *hooked* ["] thumb configuration. In *flat* [^] thumb configurations the PJ is flexed and the DJ is extended. In the [^] configuration the degree of flexion of the middle joint is typically adjusted to bring the thumb pad into contact with either a finger pad (for [o^] thumbs) or the middle joint of the first finger flexed at the PJ (for [u^] thumbs). When the [u^] thumb is not in contact with a finger it is in pad contact with the radial side of the palm. The *closed* [-] configuration flexes both the PJ and the DJ. The symbol Bu- indicates the B fingers with the thumb flexed and in contact with the palm. Ho- indicates a hand configuration in which the index and middle fingers are extended and the thumb is closed over the ring and little fingers.

In many hand configurations the thumb contacts one or more of the fingers. The specifications for this are the final entry in the hand configuration schema. There are four kinds of contact: *tip* contact [c]; thumb *pad* contact [p], in which the thumb pad contacts either the finger pad or the radial side of the finger; *finger restrained* contact [f], in which the thumb pad contacts the finger nail; and *thumb restraint* [t], in which the finger pad contacts the thumb nail. These symbols combine to describe every hand configuration we know to exist in ASL. A selection of them is presented in tabular form in Appendix A.

2.4.2 Point of Contact. The Point of Contact (POC) cluster contains slots for four symbols. These are: *location*, analogous in function to place of articulation in that it identifies a place on the passive articulator; *handpart*, the part of the hand that is located there; *proximity*, how near the handpart is to the location; and the *spatial relationship* between the handpart and the location.

Three different kinds of location specification may be entered in the location slot. Some signs are made with reference to a location on the body, some are made in the signing space surrounding the front of the head and torso, and some are made at a specific place on the weak hand.

Body Locations are those places where lexically distinctive signs may be made on the head, neck, torso, upper legs, or arms (exclusive of the hands). We have found that the accurate description of ASL requires

TABLE 6. The Twenty Major Body Locations

BH	back of head	CN	chin
TH	top of head	NK	neck
FH	forehead	SH	shoulder
SF	side of forehead	ST	sternum
NS	nose	CH	chest
CK	cheek	TR	trunk
ER	ear	UA	upper arm
MO	mouth	FA	forearm
LP	lip	AB	abdomen
JW	jaw	LG	leg

many more phonetically distinctive body locations than proposed in earlier treatments of sign notation. The entries describing body location are composed according to the following schema:

(%) (i) location (t or b)

The slot labeled location is filled by one of the twenty major body locations shown in Table 6.

Diacritic symbols may be added to each of the major body location descriptions in order to specify other locations near them. The diacritic [%] indicates that the location specified is on the side of the body contralateral to the signing hand. If this slot is empty the location is assumed to be ipsilateral.

Most of the major locations specified above are surrounded by a set of corresponding locations that may be described by adding two diacritics to the basic location symbol. The first is *ipsilateral* [i], indicating that the hand is at a location slightly toward the outside of the body from the major location. The second indicates a location in the *top* [t] portion or *bottom* [b] portion of the major location. Combining these entries provides the locations represented in Figures 17, 18, and 19. Appendix B presents examples of lexical signs made at each of the locations we know to be distinctive in ASL.

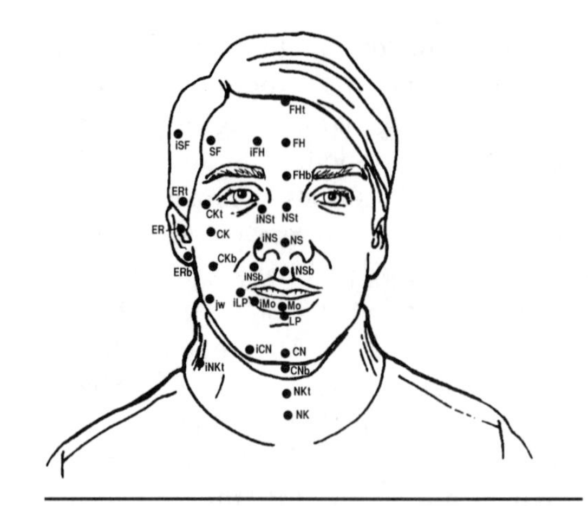

FIGURE 17. Articulatory locations on the head and neck.

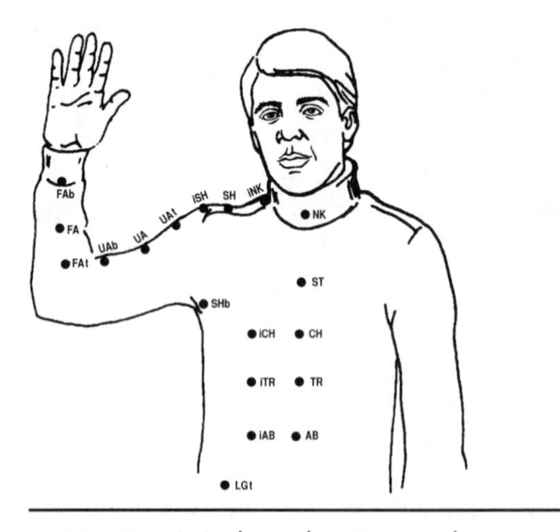

FIGURE 18. Articulatory locations on the torso.

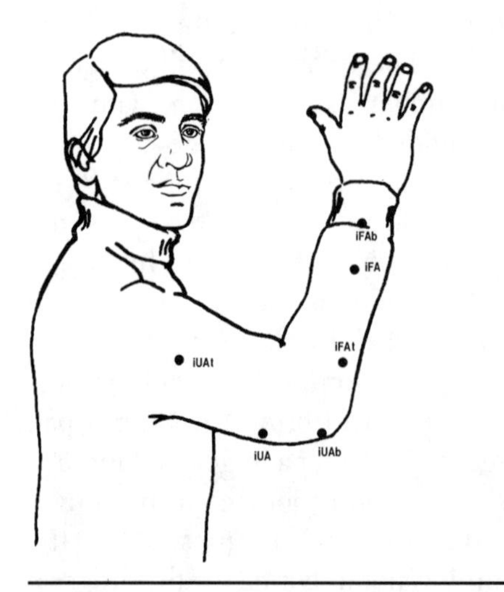

FIGURE 19. Articulatory locations on the arms.

Signs may also be produced at locations in the signing space surrounding the front of the body and head. Such *spatial locations* are described by a combination of a diacritic indicating a distance forward from the body on a perpendicular line, a symbol indicating the extent of ipsilateral offset from the midline, and the symbol for a major central body location:

Proximity—Ipsilateral Offset—Central Location

We currently distinguish four degrees of forward distance for spatial locations: *proximal* [p], indicating a location within a few inches of the body location; *medial* [m], a position roughly an elbow's length from the body location; *distal* [d], a comfortable arm's length from the body; and *extended* [e], a full arm's length from the body location.

The side-to-side dimension appears to require two degrees of ipsilateral offset. The first of these is roughly in line with the breast and the second is roughly in line with the outside edge of the shoulder. In order to avoid confusion with the set of finer distinctions among ipsilateral offset for the body locations, we refer to the degrees of ipsilateral offset for spatial signs with the numbers [0] (no offset), [1], and [2], respectively.

The last symbol indicates the height of the spatial location. It is chosen from among the major body location symbols that refer to points along the midline of the body (TH, FH, NS, MO, CN, NK, ST, CH, TR, AB). Thus, each spatial location is represented by a complex of three symbols. For example, the symbol m-0-TR describes a location about an elbow's length directly in front of the solarplexis. The symbol m-1-TR indicates a location at the same height and distance forward, but on the breastline. Similarly, the symbol d-2-FH describes a location about an arm's length forward and a shoulder's width to the ipsilateral side of the center of the forehead. Appendix C presents selected signs produced at different spatial locations.

Most signs appear to locate on points like those described above. However, one important class of signs makes use of locations created by vectors radiating from midline locations. We have found use for seven such vectors. These vectors ([L3] [L2] [L1] [0] [R1] [R2] [R3]) and the locations they create around their intersection with the lines representing degrees of distance from the body are presented in Figure 20. One such semicircular system of locations may exist at each contrastive height along the

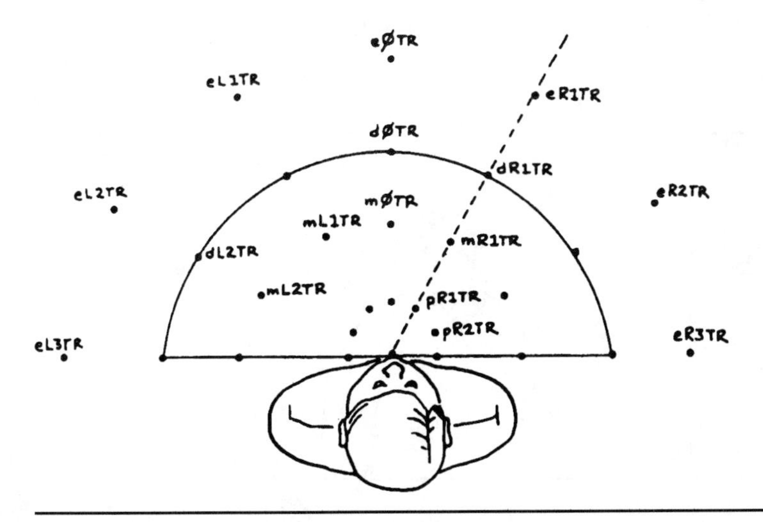

FIGURE 20. Spatial vectors used by agreement verbs.

midline. The vector specification substitutes in the spatial location schema for the ipsilateral offset number.

Thus, m-R1-TR specifies a location at TR height, about an elbow's length out from the center line on an approximately thirty degree right vector. Although the addition of a second set of location specifications may appear to be excessive, the behavior of predicates inflected for subject and object agreement and the behavior of locative predicates require it. We will return to this issue in more detail below.

For many signs, the location of the strong hand is a point on the weak hand (FIRED). The schema describing *weak hand locations* is composed of two symbols: one indicating a major part of the hand (hand, fingers, forearm, thumb, etc.), and the other indicating a zone in that major hand part (inside, back, radial edge, etc.). The specifications for locations on the weak hand and examples we have found in ASL appear in Appendix D.

The *handpart* slot of the POC complex will contain a handpart specification constructed in the same way as those described above. Whereas the handpart specifications exemplified in Appendix D specify weak hand locations, the handpart slot proper indicates which part of the strong hand makes reference to or contacts the location of the POC. An inventory of strong hand handparts we know to occur in ASL is presented in Appendix E. Combining handpart and location in POC, we would find that the first segment of the sign GOOD, for example, contacts the LP location with the fingerpads of the strong hand. The POC of this segment will contain PDFI in the handpart slot and LP in the location slot. In the final segment of the sign STOP, the handpart is UL and the location is PA.

The *proximity* slot of the POC cluster specifies whether the handpart is in *contact* [c] with the location or, if not in contact, then its distance from the location. It appears that three distance specifications (proximal [p], medial [m], and distal [d]) are sufficient.

The spatial relationship slot of the POC cluster describes the direction at which the handpart is offset from the location. In brushing signs the hand moves between points on two sides of a location, making brief contact as it passes the location. For example, in the sign FALSE the handpart is the RAFI of a 1o- (index extended) hand configuration. The location is NS, the tip of the nose. The hand begins at a point proximal and to the ipsilateral side of the nose and moves to point proximal and to the contralateral side of the nose, briefly contacting it as it passes (Figure 21).

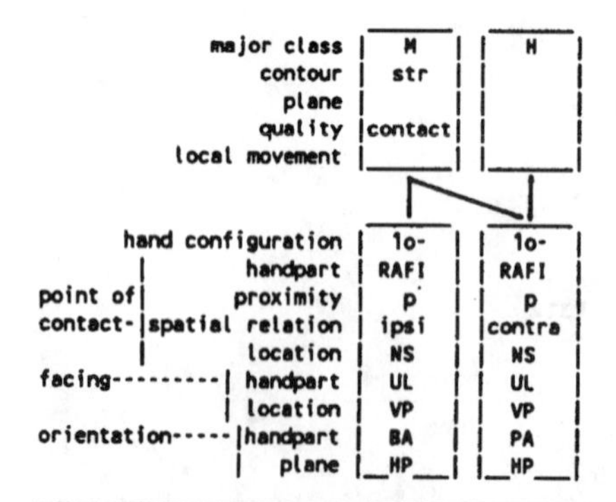

FIGURE 21. FALSE

We use two sets of spatial relationship symbols. One set refers to locations on the body or in space and the other set refers to locations on the weak hand. Those for body and spatial locations are the absolute directions over, under, behind (toward body from spatial location), ahead, contra, and ipsi. Because the weak hand can move, the spatial relations specified with respect to weak hand locations are relative to parts of the hand. The set includes: tipward [toti], baseward [toba], toward ulnar side [toul], toward radial side [tora], palmward [topa], and backward [tobk]. An articulatory bundle specified c in the proximity slot may be left unspecified in the spatial relation slot.

2.4.3 *Describing Hand Orientation.*

The POC entries in the notation simply place a part of the hand at a location. At any location it is possible for the hand to assume countless orientations. The orientation of the hand is important in ASL signs, for both lexical contrast and morphological functioning. It appears that signs make use of two dimensions functioning together to orient the hand. The first of these is *facing,* which "points" a part of the hand at a location. The second is *orientation* proper which usually indicates which part of the hand is pointing toward the ground. The facing cluster is composed of two entries: one for a handpart and one for a location. The orientation cluster is also composed of two entries: one for a handpart (other than that used in facing) and one for a plane (usually HP). The sign STARE exemplifies the interaction of facing and orientation. In citation form it is produced as a hold with the hand located near and in front of the shoulder, with a V^o-hand configuration. If the third person object is associated with the vector R1, the tips of the fingers point directly forward toward R1 and the base of the hand points toward the ground. If the object is associated with the vector L2, the hand re-

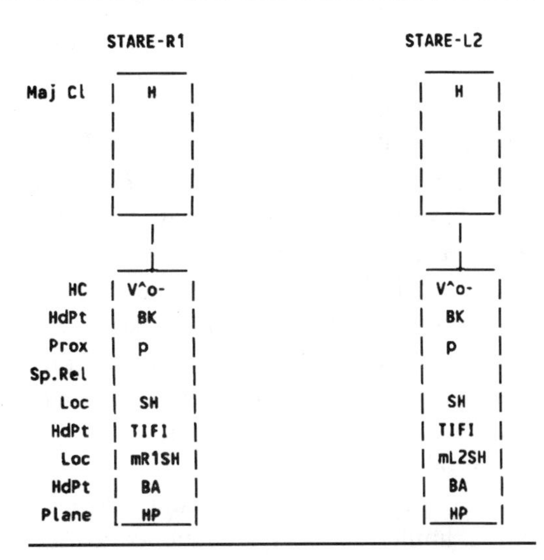

FIGURE 22. STARE: Two different third person objects

mains in front of the shoulder, and the base continues to point to the ground, but the tips point to the object agreement location, in this case mL2SH.[6] Numerous object agreement inflections may be achieved by altering the facing complex of STARE, independently from POC and orientation.

3. MORPHEME STRUCTURE CONSTRAINTS

Upon recording a corpus of connected signs using the system described above, it becomes clear that certain phonetic details of the segmental strings are predictable. For example, some details of phonetic representations recur as consistent patterns in the lexicon. These may be stated as *morpheme structure constraints* (MSC) on the combinations of features and segments permissible in novel lexical forms.

Battison (1974, 1978) identifies several MSCs in ASL, based on the notations present in Stokoe et al. (1965). As a result, they are stated largely in terms of a simultaneous model of sign structure. Nonetheless, he identifies both simultaneous and sequential conditions on the structure of ASL signs. For example, he observes that the hand configuration R may contact locations in only a relatively limited number of ways (1978:38). This observation can be restated explicitly as a segmental MSC: If the hand configuration of a segment is specified as Ro-, then the hand part specification in POC will be one of the following: TIFI (DONUT), PDFI (RESTAURANT), BAFI (CIGAR), BA (ROCKET).[7] Segmental MSCs such as this will constrain the inventory of segments that may be utilized in forming novel morphemes.

Similarly, Battison noted that in signs in which the hand configuration changes, only a limited number of sequences occur. One such sequential MSC states that if two segments of a sign contain different hand configuration specifications and the final hand configuration is 1o-, then the first hand configuration will be 1″o-f (UNDERSTAND). Similar sequential constraints appear to pertain to the following final/initial pairs of hand configurations: Ho- / Ho″-f (BEAT), Vo- / Vo″-f (TWELVE). Such constraints describe the preferential structure of lexical items but do not operate as phonological processes across word boundaries. For example, in the clause EXTREMELY-FOND-OF ## NAME "I am extremely fond of that name," the Ho-hand configuration of the final sign NAME does not predict a H″o-f hand configuration for the preceding sign. EXTREMELY-FOND-OF retains its So-hand configuration, resulting in the sequence So-Ho-. The sequence H″o-f Ho- would be ungrammatical for this clause. Many other constraints such as these appear to exist in the lexicon, and will ultimately describe the extensive harmonic sequencing observable in ASL signs.

Battison also identifies another, more unusual sort of MSC, which specifies co-occurrence relationships between the two hands (1974). Spoken languages have little need for specifying the possibilities of co-occurrence among the independent articulators, although constraints on the feature [round] and constraints describing coarticulated implosives are probably similar in function. In ASL it is possible to have fully specified strong and weak hands performing identical activities (LARGE) or mirror image activities (MAYBE), or completely different activities (FIRED). Moreover, there are minimal contrasts among one-handed and two-handed signs (LIKE; INTERESTING), so the weak hand is not completely predictable, and must be specified. Battison's Dominance Condition specifies rather rigid limitations on differences between the hands. He points out that if the two hands have different hand configurations then the hand configuration of the weak hand must be chosen from a very limited set of easily discriminable hand configurations, while the hand configuration of the strong hand is much less constrained. The refinement of MSCs of this type promises to be a rich area of research in the segmental phonology of ASL.

4. PHONOLOGICAL PROCESSES

The phonological strings contain still another sort of predictable detail, traceable to *phonological processes*, producing alternations among surface forms. These processes are typically described by a complex of phonological rules, each of which may alter some detail of the representation of a form or add nonlexical phonological information to a string. The combined action of these processes ultimately derives the surface representation of the string.

4.1 Movement Epenthesis

Phonological processes proper influence the phonetic shape of phonological strings. Many of the phonological processes known to occur in spoken languages appear also in ASL. The most easily described is a process which inserts a movement between concatenated seg-

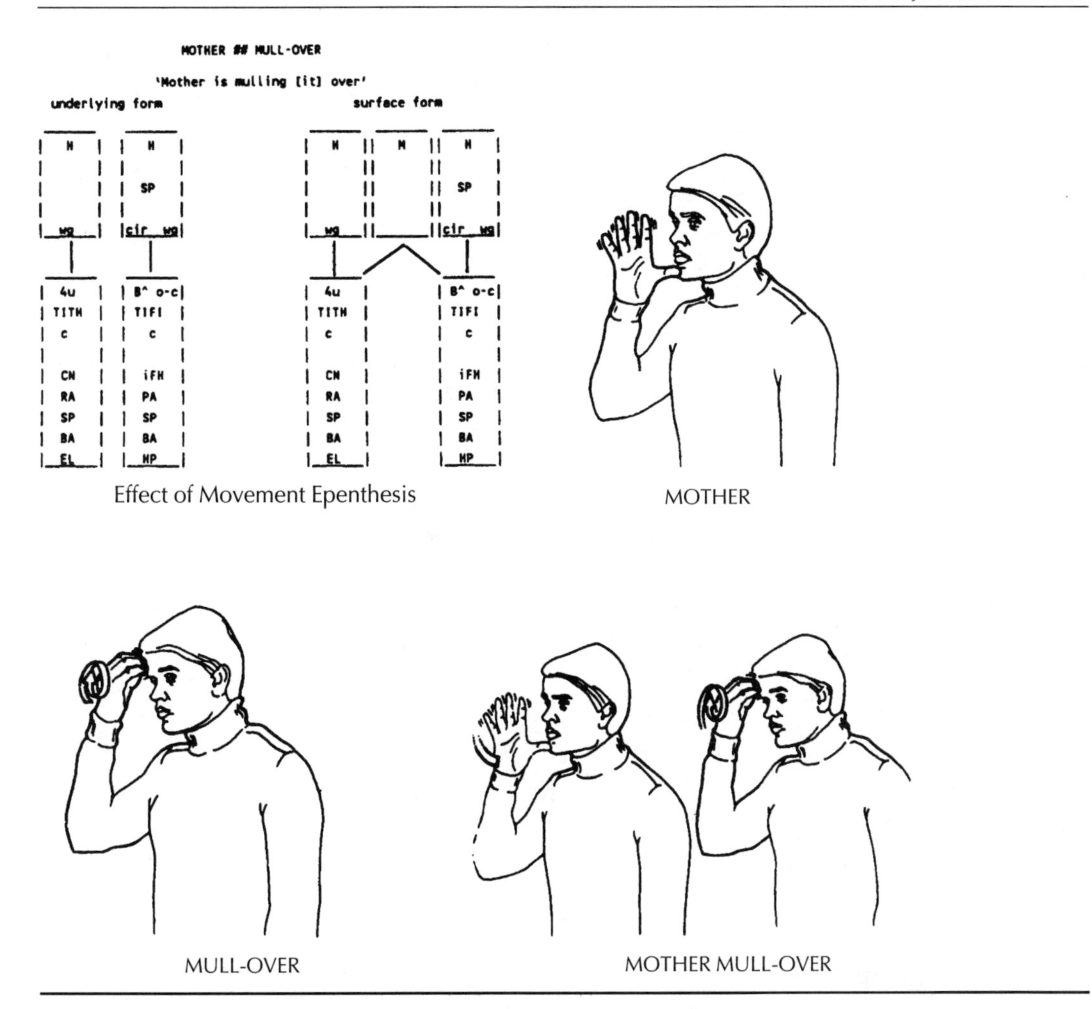

FIGURE 23. The effect of M Epenthesis in the string MOTHER MULL-OVER.

ments, the second of which begins with an initial articulatory bundle different from the final articulatory bundle of the preceding segment. For the most part, this process applies at the boundary between signs and enjoys the relatively straightforward function of moving the hand from the articulatory posture that ends one sign to the articulatory posture that begins the next. In the case of MOTHER MULL-OVER the Movement Epenthesis Rule inserts an M segment between the last segment of MOTHER and the first segment of MULL-OVER.

Although it may seem to be unnecessary to propose a rule describing a process so predictable, pervasive, and physiologically motivated, the M segment introduced into strings by the M Epenthesis Rule functions as a critical part of the environment that feeds another phonological process.

4.2 Hold Deletion

That process is Hold Deletion, which, with certain exceptions, eliminates hold segments occurring between movement segments. The surface form of the phrase GOOD ## IDEA "good idea" demonstrates the application of the H Deletion Rule.

Because the sign GOOD ends with a segment articulated in a different way from the

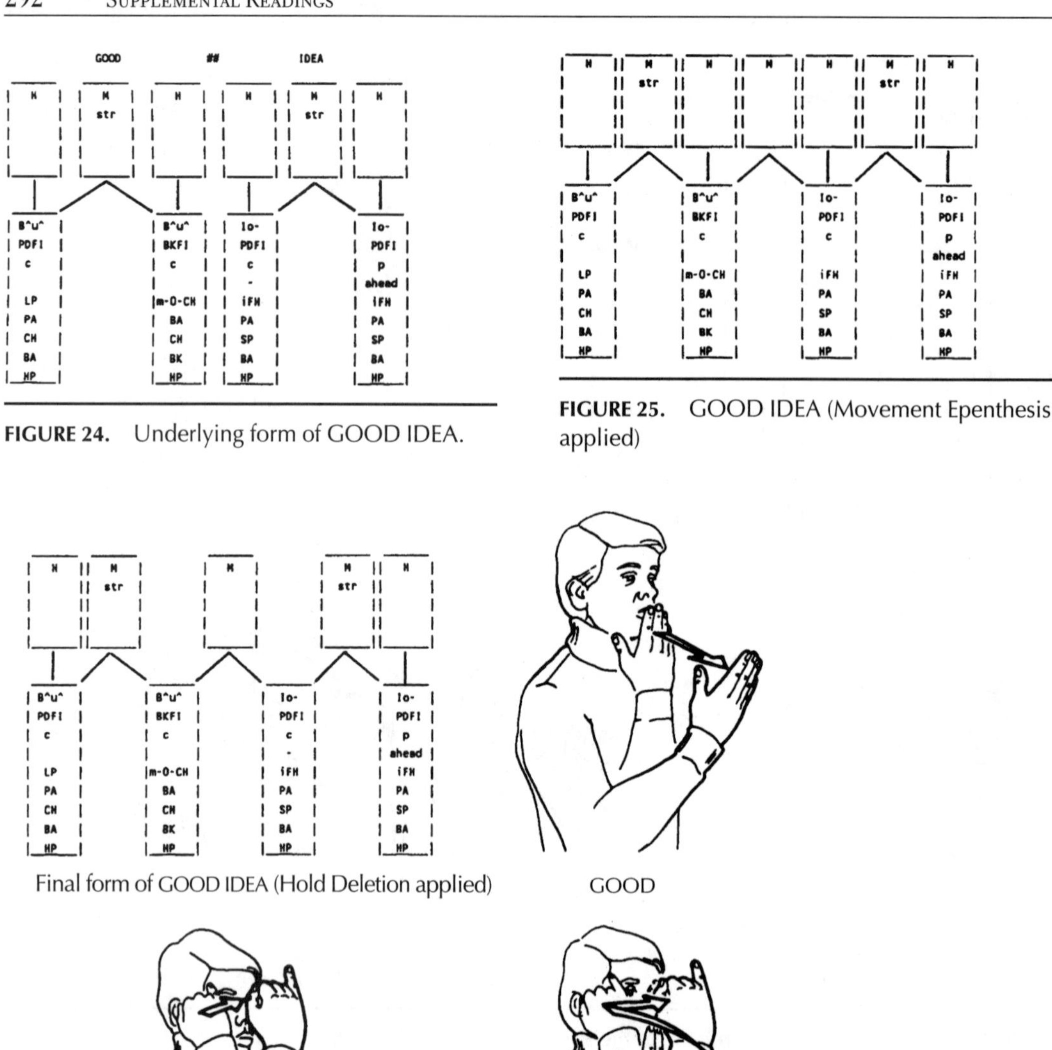

FIGURE 24. Underlying form of GOOD IDEA.

FIGURE 25. GOOD IDEA (Movement Epenthesis applied)

Final form of GOOD IDEA (Hold Deletion applied)

GOOD

IDEA

GOOD IDEA

FIGURE 26. The effect of M Epenthesis in the string GOOD IDEA.

initial segment of IDEA, the M Epenthesis Rule will insert a segmental bundle, specified as M, between the two signs. This has the effect of moving the hand from the area immediately in front of the chest to a location in contact with the side of the forehead and simultaneously changing the other articulatory specifications from those describing an open hand oriented with its back to the HP to those of a hand with only the little finger extended and oriented with the tip of the little finger upward.

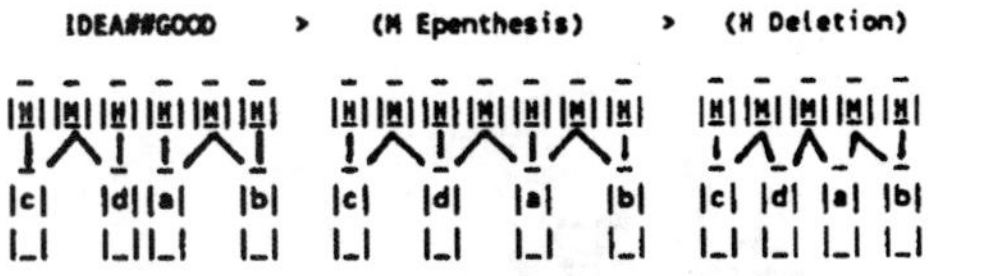

IDEA##GOOD > (M Epenthesis) > (H Deletion)

FIGURE 27. M Epenthesis and H Deletion.

Whereas the isolated signs GOOD and IDEA end and begin with substantial holds, when juxtaposed in this phrase the final H of GOOD and the initial H of IDEA are deleted. The critical environment for the application of this rule seems to be the M segments that surround each H segment.[8]

The surface form of the clause IDEA # # GOOD "The idea is good" is also affected by the H Deletion rule, which again causes only the inter-M holds to be deleted [Figure 27].

Certain conditions prohibit application of the H Deletion Rule. Holds that are lengthened, either by the presence of local movement or by morphological processes such as the one which produces a lengthened H at the beginning of emphatic forms, tend not to delete. Moreover, it appears that the application of H Deletion is variable by context. Although the extent and exact nature of the variation is not yet clear, it appears that H segments that do not contact the body or the other hand are generally deleted in inter-M contexts (as long as they are not lengthened), whereas those that do contact another body part are variably deleted. The following combinations result (+ indicates body contact) [Figure 28].

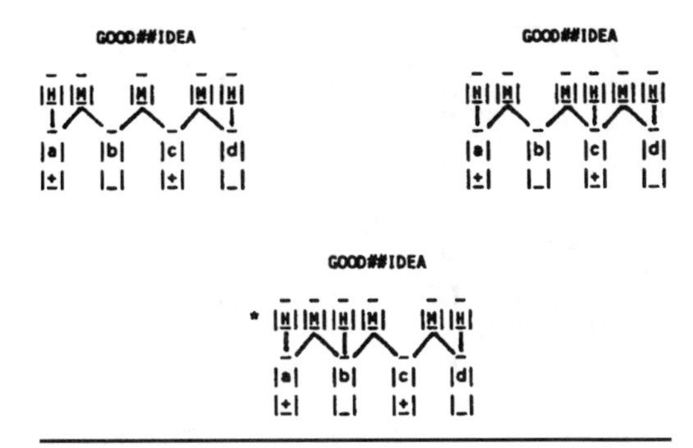

FIGURE 28. Possible and disallowed application of H Deletion.

4.3 Metathesis

A number of signs exchange an initial sequence of segments with a sequence of final segments in certain contexts that appear to be purely phonological. The sign DEAF is typical of such metathesizing signs.

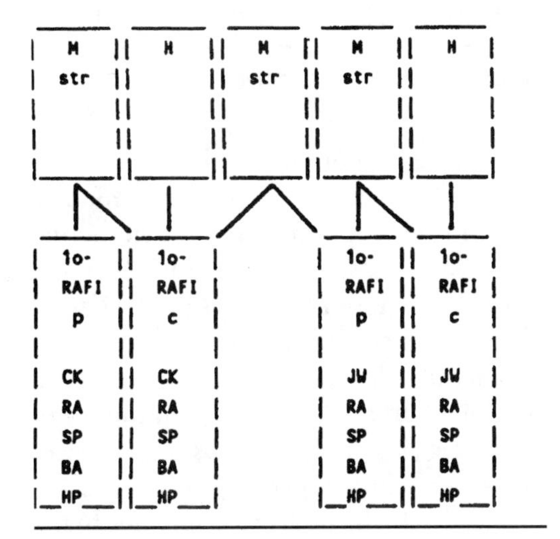

FIGURE 29a. DEAF

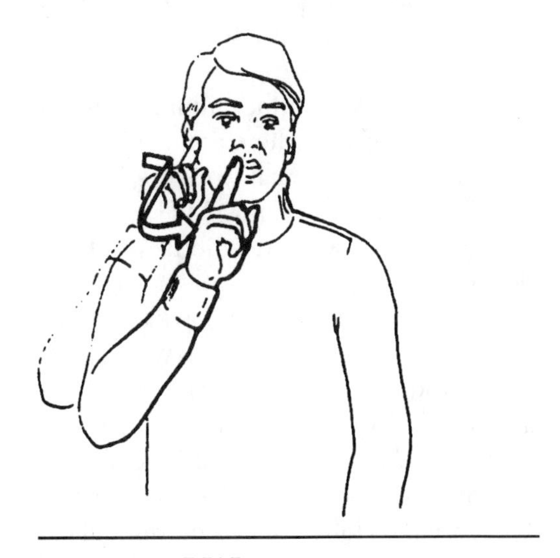

FIGURE 29b. DEAF

In this form of the sign the index finger first moves to contact the cheek and

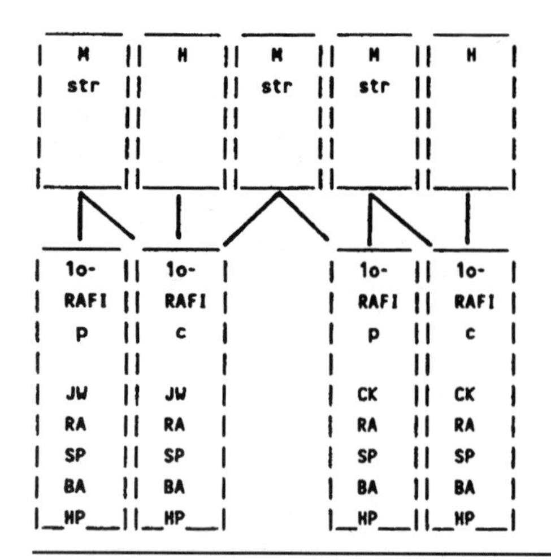

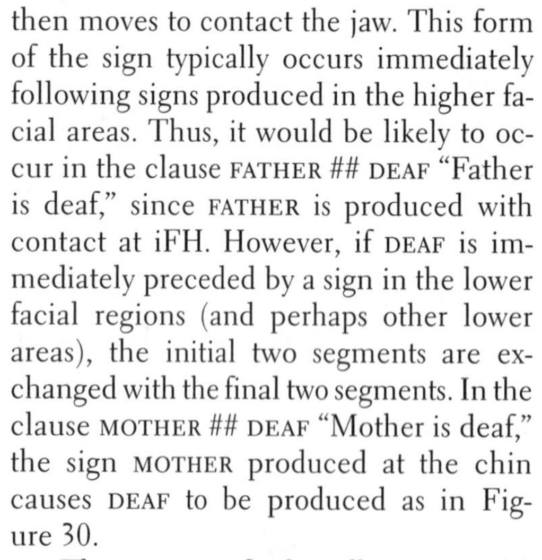

FIGURE 30a. DEAF (after metathesis).

FIGURE 30b. DEAF (after metathesis).

then moves to contact the jaw. This form of the sign typically occurs immediately following signs produced in the higher facial areas. Thus, it would be likely to occur in the clause FATHER ## DEAF "Father is deaf," since FATHER is produced with contact at iFH. However, if DEAF is immediately preceded by a sign in the lower facial regions (and perhaps other lower areas), the initial two segments are exchanged with the final two segments. In the clause MOTHER ## DEAF "Mother is deaf," the sign MOTHER produced at the chin causes DEAF to be produced as in Figure 30.

The sign WE further illuminates the metathesis process. There are two forms of WE; one has a segmental structure like that of DEAF, the other has an H M H sequence, with an arc M. WE_1 metathesizes but WE_2 does not (Figure 31).[9]

The signs CONGRESS, FLOWER, RESTAURANT, DEAF, HONEYMOON, NAVY, TWINS, BACHELOR, PARENTS, HOME, and HEAD have all been observed to undergo metathesis. All these signs have the same basic segmental structure as DEAF, i.e., a movement to a hold at one location followed by a movement to a hold at another location. Because no sign with another segmental structure has been observed to metathesize, application of the phonological rule appears to require this underlying segmental structure. However not all signs with this underlying segmental structure may metathesize. BODY, KING, CHRIST, INDIAN, BLOUSE, THANKSGIVING, CHILDREN, and THING all have the appropriate segmental structure but may not metathesize. Most of these share the characteristic that their two contacts are in markedly different locations on the body. The last two do not make contact with the body. These tentatively appear to be additional phonological constraints on the application of the rule.

These observations carry two important implications for the general theory of the structure of signs we are proposing here. The first is that we have some justification for treating signs with this segmental structure as having two lexical parts. Specifically, we propose that the underlying form of such signs contains two unconnected M H sequences, which are subject to metathesis and which (whether or not metathesis has applied) are connected by the M Epenthesis Rule, as represented in Figure 32.[10] Signs such as WE_2 have a unitary lexical form

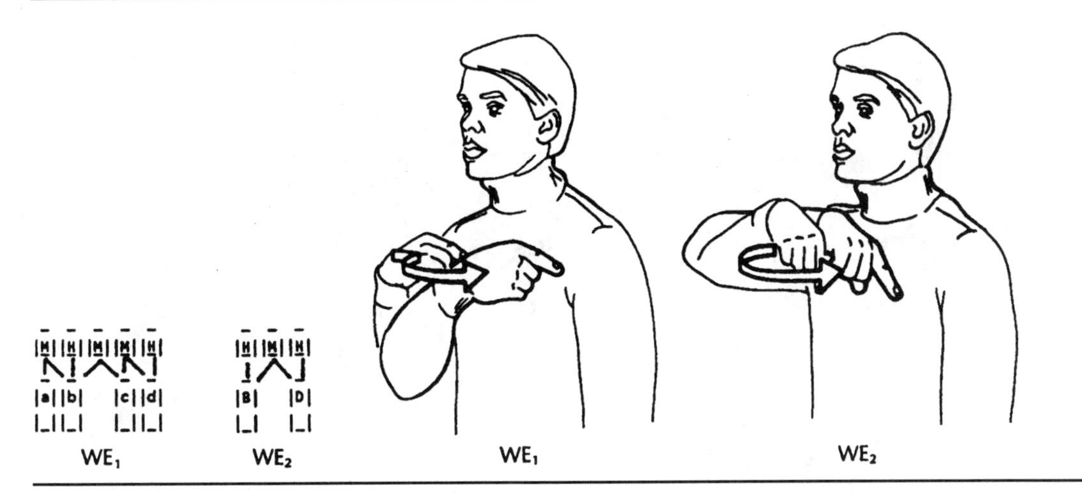

FIGURE 31. Alternate forms of WE.

H M H, which may not be permuted by metathesis and in which the segmental information in the M must be specified as an arc.

The second important implication of these observations suggests that a complete feature analysis of locations will provide insights into the nature of phonological processes. First it is probable that some feature or set of features unites the sets of locations between which metathesis may occur and distinguishes those which are saliently distant enough to prohibit metathesis. Moreover, the conditioning of the Metathesis Rule by prior signs will depend on a feature analysis that recognizes that certain locations are more to the left or right or below or above certain other locations. Only features that carry this sort of information may condition the appropriate application of the Metathesis Rule. Such featural information will account for the fact that signs made on the stomach, the chest, or the chin may all provide the condition that selects initial occurrence of the lowermost sequence of DEAF.

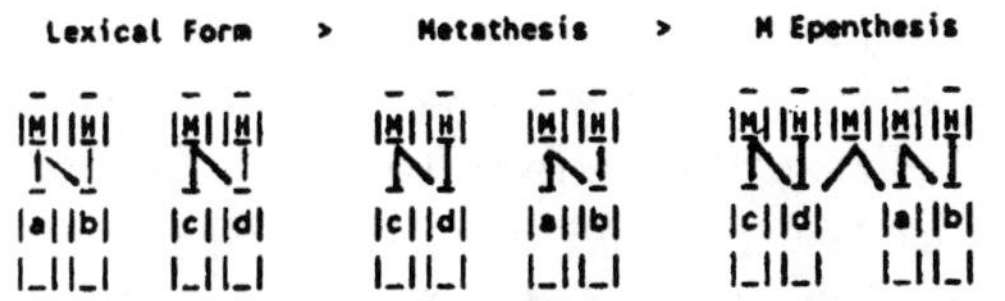

Lexical Form > Metathesis > M Epenthesis

FIGURE 32. Relationship between metathesis and epenthesis.

4.4 Gemination

Although such occurrences are rather rare in ASL, it sometimes happens that the terminal segment of one sign is identical to the initial segment of the following sign. In the sentence,

> SPAGHETTI$_{3A}$, MOTHER REPULSED-BY$_{3A}$
> "Mother really hates spaghetti"

the final segment of MOTHER (the form of MOTHER without local movement) and the initial segment of REPULSED-BY are identical holds. The result is a single long hold. An epenthetic movement away from the chin or a hold of normal length is ungrammatical.

4.5 Assimilation

There are numerous instances of assimilation in ASL. For example, the hand configuration of the sign ME typically assimilates to that of a contiguous predicate in the same

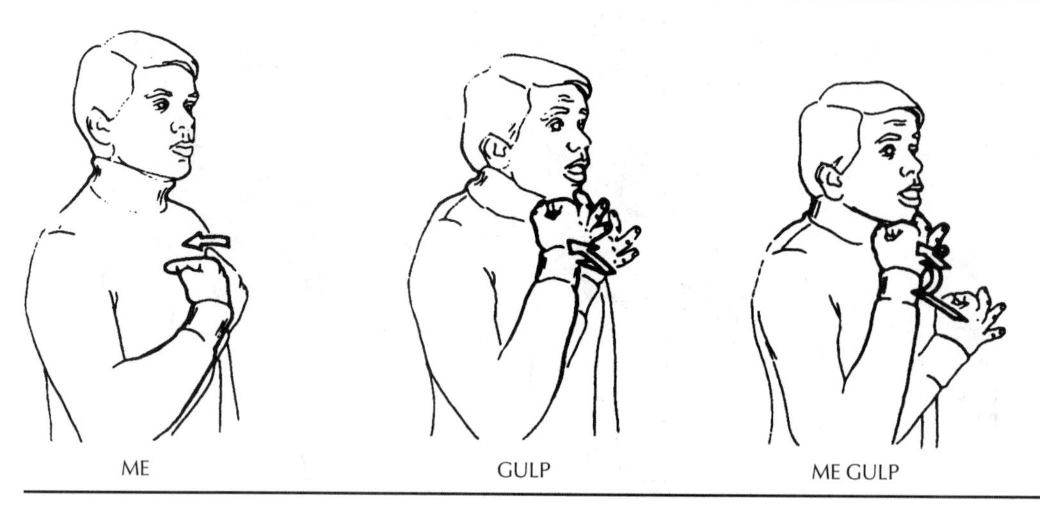

FIGURE 33. Phonological assimilation of handshape features in the string ME GULP.

clause. Thus, whereas the underlying form of ME contains a 1o- hand configuration, in the string

> MOTHER$_{3A}$STARE-AT$_{1}$. ME GULP.
>
> "Mother was staring at me and I was nervous about what was to come"

ME assumes the 9o-c hand configuration of GULP. The extent to which signs other than ME assimilate to the hand configuration of another sign, although not yet thoroughly investigated, appears to be considerably more limited.

Assimilation of the hand configuration of the weak hand to that of the strong hand in two-handed signs is quite common. For most signers it appears to be variable, probably controlled by formality and fast-signing constraints. Thus, it is common that in signs in which the strong and weak hand configurations are different in formal signing, the weak hand configuration will be fully assimilated to the strong hand configuration in casual or fast signing.

We have observed numerous other examples of assimilation in ASL. Among these are the assimilation of orientation and facing features of the weak hand to those of the strong hand; assimilation of features specifying location in POC of an initial segment of one sign to the location features of the final segment of the preceding sign; assimilation of location features of the final segment of a sign to the location of the initial segment of a following sign; two-handed signs becoming one-handed as a result of assimilation to a one-handed sign in the same string; one-handed signs assimilating to two-handed signs. These processes await more detailed description.

4.6 Reduction

Frishberg (1975) notes a number of historical trends in ASL which she identifies as "displacement." Each of these involves the diachronic relocation of certain signs to areas either less central to the face (and thereby less likely to obscure important facial signals) or to areas more central to the lower head and upper body regions of the signing space (and thereby more readily perceptible).

Although such forms appear to be lexicalized at their new locations, the phonological processes that originally must have moved them are still active in contemporary ASL. The rules which account for them appear to be variably selected by casual signing, and, like vowel reduction rules in spoken languages, have the effect of neutralizing contrasts of location. Thus, many signs that are produced with contact at the SFH location in formal signing may be produced in casual signing at the CK location. Similarly, signs produced at the CK location (including those moved from the SFH location) may be produced at the JW location. These same signs also appear at times without contact in the area immediately in front of the iNK location. The first segment of the sign KNOW-THAT is produced formally at the SFH location but may occur in casual signing at any of the other locations described above.

In a somewhat similar manner, signs produced at a location proximal to, but not in contact with FH or NS in citation form (KNOW-NOTHING, DOUBT) and signs produced with contact at the mouth (GLASS) may be produced at the CH location. Signs that do have underlying contact at the FH or NS locations are not subject to the effects of this rule (FATHER, BLIND). Similar rules exist to reduce peripheral locations on the torso to more centralized locations.

It appears also that there are rules that reduce the distance between the locations of two-location signs in casual signing. The M M M H sequence of the type isolated by the metathesis rule (CONGRESS, HOME) is commonly reduced by such a rule, and it appears that many other segment sequences also undergo a similar reduction process (GOOD, GIVE, etc.). Similarly, the size of the first (round) movement in M M H sequences such as YEAR, WHEN, POLITICS, and QUESTION is often reduced in casual signing.

4.7 Perseveration and Anticipation

Typically, signed strings contain both one-handed and two-handed signs. When a one-handed sign follows a two-handed sign, although the weak hand is not required, in casual and fast signing it commonly either perseverates features of the former sign or anticipates features of the following sign, or both, rather than returning to a resting position. Although these processes and other very late phonological processes such as reduction have the relatively trivial phonological function of speeding and smoothing the phonetic string, they apply very broadly. Thus, because they apply to most forms produced in comfortable signing, these processes commonly have a substantial impact on the underlying form of lexicalized compounds and other lexical entries that result from the lexicalization of productively produced forms.

5. MORPHOLOGICAL PROCESSES

Another sort of predictable detail originates in the morphology, where *morphological processes* create words. Across languages, words are formed by attaching lexical forms to one another and by moving, reproducing, deleting from, adding to, and altering the phonological information carried by lexical forms. Although both morphological processes and phonological processes may add, delete, alter, or move phonological details, they differ in that phonological processes do not account for meaning changes whereas morphological processes do.

Below we will describe a small selection of ASL morphological processes that illustrate the diverse phonological effects which result from their application. We have divided these processes into two broad categories. In the first, meaningful feature bundles (morphemes) are inserted into one or more segments of a root with incomplete articulatory feature bundles. This insertion results in a phonologically fully specified stem. In the second major category, the morphological processes operate on a completely formed stem either by removing some of its phonological features and inserting them in a segmental frame, by modifying them through reduplication, or, rarely, by attaching an affix.

5.1 Processes that Insert Features in Roots

For many ASL signs, we posit lexical forms of roots with empty spaces (or "cells") in their underlying feature specifications. A number of ASL morphological processes "fill out" such incompletely specified roots with morphemes which consist of the small bits of phonological information used to fill the empty cells in the root. The three signs in Figure 34 are representative of a large class of such signs, built from roots specified for all their features except hand configuration.

These three signs are identical except for their hand configuration. FIRST-PLACE is produced with a 1o- hand configuration, SECOND-PLACE has a Vo- hand configuration, and THIRD-PLACE has a Vu hand configuration. Signs meaning FOURTH-PLACE through NINTH-PLACE can be formed by using other hand configurations. In numerous other signs the same hand configurations convey equivalent meanings of numerosity.

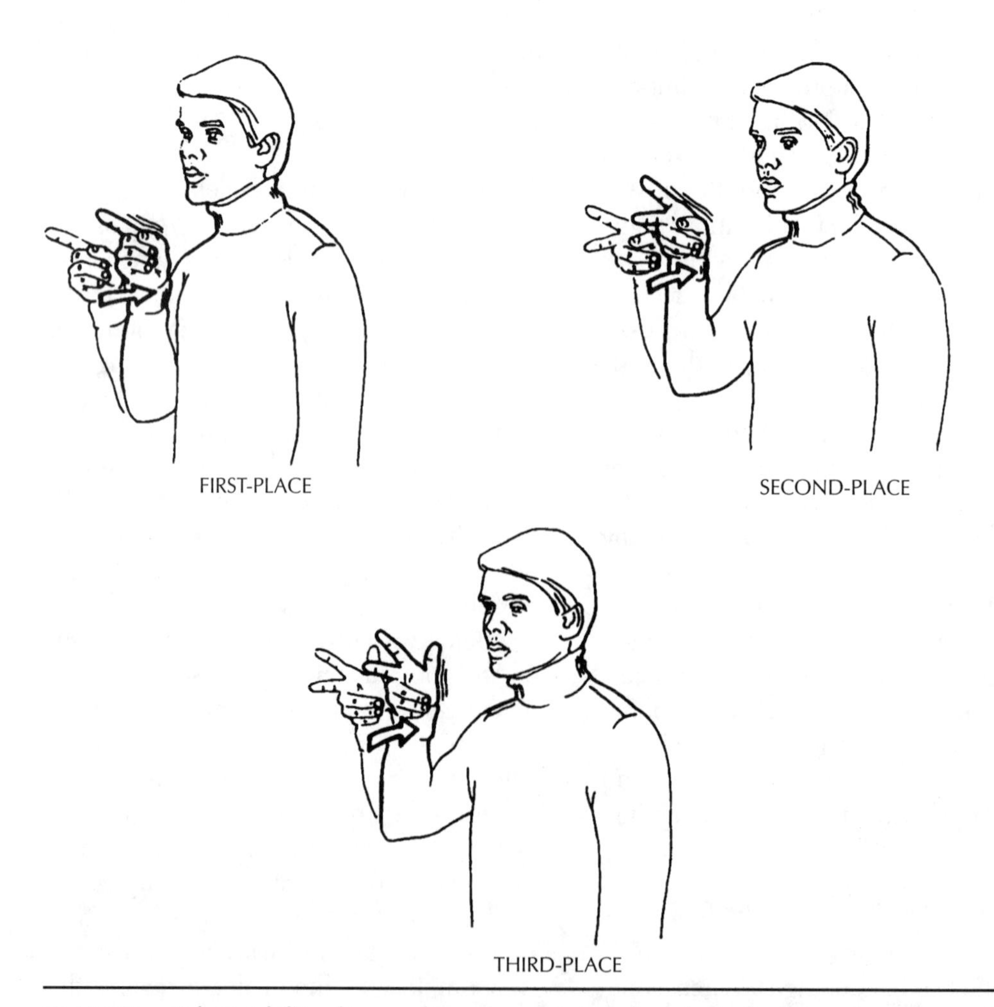

FIGURE 34. Substitutability of numeral morphemes into a phonologically incomplete root morpheme.

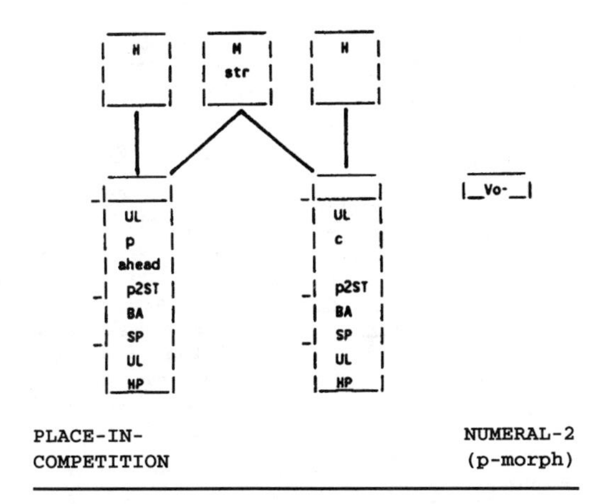

FIGURE 35. The two bound morphemes required for "first place," "second place," etc.

We contend that these signs (and others with numeral hand configurations) contain at least two morphemes: the root morpheme, a numeral classifier which means "place in a competition," and the numeral morpheme. The two morphemes in SECOND-PLACE and their phonological relationship to one another are sketched in Figure 35. The root, PLACE-IN-COMPETITION, is composed of three segments and two incompletely specified articulatory feature bundles. A numeral morpheme is required to complete the phonological representation of the stem SECOND-PLACE.

We refer to roots such as PLACE-IN-COMPETITION as "Incomplete S-morphs," since their phonological representation is segmental, but incomplete (Johnson and Liddell 1984). The numeral morpheme is referred to as a "P-morph" since it only provides paradigmatic contrast (i.e., it contains no segmental information). It can be inserted into a root consisting of one or more segments and its features simply spread according to autosegmental principles. We have identified more than thirty different incomplete S-morphs which, like PLACE-IN-COMPETITION, require the insertion of a numeral morpheme.[11]

A second major category of incomplete S-morph contains verb roots with unspecified location information. The completed form of the verb stem of such signs contains location (vector) specifications received through the insertion of subject and/or object agreement morphemes. Two such verbs, ASK and TELL, are illustrated in Figure 36.

The initial location for TELL is the chin. Its final location, however, is determined by the insertion of an object agreement morpheme. In Figure 37, TELL agrees in location with the 3rd person object already indexed on the signer's left.[12] ASK is structured so as to allow both object agreement and subject agreement morphemes to be inserted.

The subject agreement morpheme pictured on the left in Figure 38 is determined by the person and location of the subject

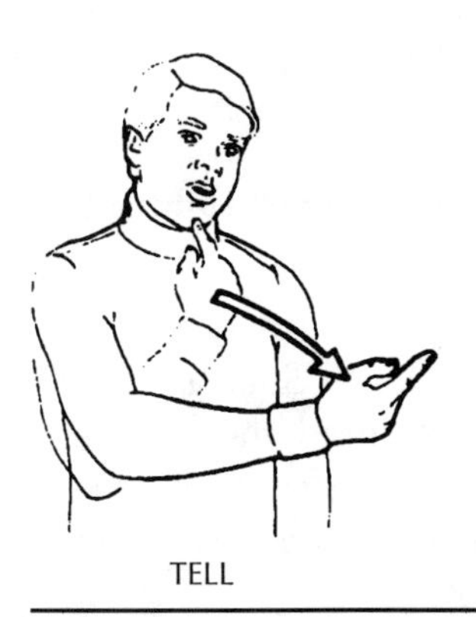

FIGURE 36. An object agreement verb (TELL) and a subject-object agreement verb (ASK).

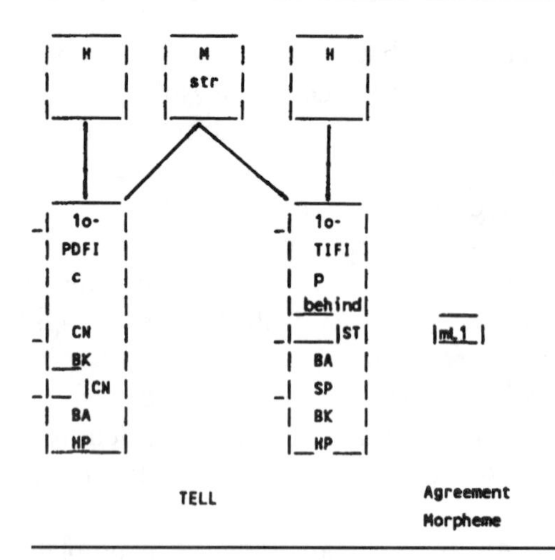

FIGURE 37. The shape of TELL with an object agreement morpheme.

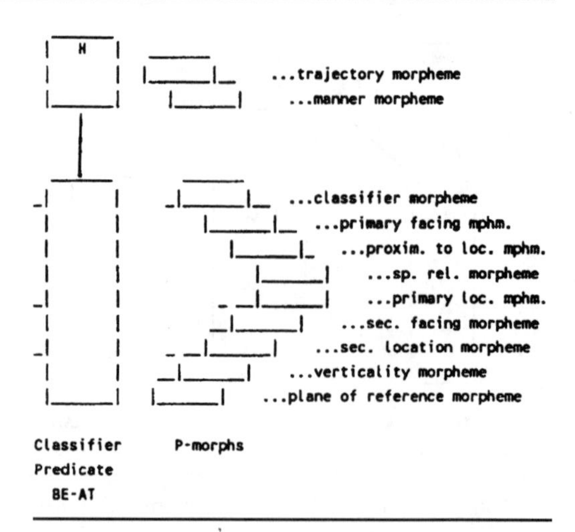

FIGURE 39. The composition of a classifier predicate.

nominal, and is inserted into specific places in the two feature bundles. The object agreement morpheme is determined by the person and location of the object and is similarly inserted into both articulatory bundles. Thus, the completed verb stem 3a-ASK-3b is composed of three morphemes: one root and two agreement morphemes.

In the examples of feature insertion discussed so far, the root contains only a small number of empty cells. Many other signs are built from roots that are specified only for segment type, and contain empty cells for

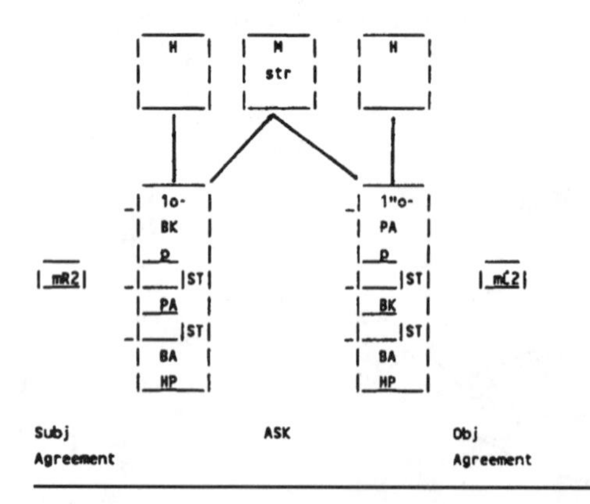

FIGURE 38. The shape of ASK with subject and object agreement morphemes.

all other segment features and all articulatory features. This class of signs has been referred to as "classifier predicates" by Liddell (1977), and "verbs of motion and location" by Supalla (1978), who first proposed the idea of movement roots in the analysis of these signs. Morphological processes insert a number of morphemes in appropriate cells to derive a polysynthetic predicate stem.

The type of information which can be inserted into such movement roots has been investigated in depth by Supalla (1978). We will not provide additional analysis here, but simply observe that this category of predicate is highly productive in ASL and is responsible for a significant number of the signs observed in ASL discourse.

5.2 Processes that Operate on Fully Specified Stems

The processes we describe below all operate on fully specified stems. Such stems can either come directly from the lexicon as completely specified s-morphs, or become fully specified through processes like those described above.

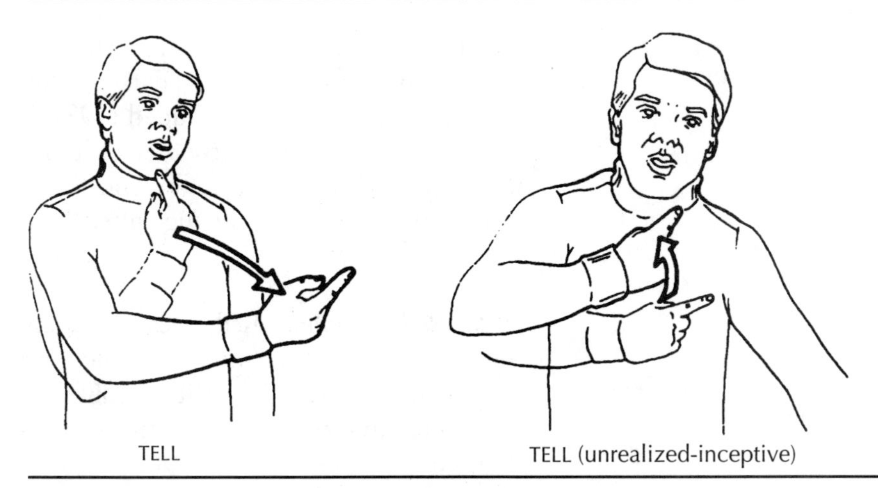

FIGURE 40. TELL and its unrealized-inceptive form.

5.2.1 Frames. Many ASL inflections have an unusual characteristic. Regardless of the syllable structure of the uninflected stem (the input to the process), the syllable structure of the inflected form (the output) is completely uniform. For example, Liddell (1984b) describes the verb inflection for unrealized-inceptive aspect. The input to the inflection could be a verb with a single segment, two segments, or even three segments. The inflected verbs, however, uniformly have the shape M H.

In this analysis the inflected verb is not strictly a modification of the verb stem, but rather results from feeding a small piece of articulatory information from the verb stem into a segmental structure referred to as an "inflectional frame." Figure 41 shows the shape of the uninflected verb stem TELL, and its form when inflected for the unrealized-inceptive (U-I) aspect.

For verb stems in the same verb class as TELL, the initial feature bundle of the stem is identical to the final feature bundle of the U-I form of the verb. Further, all of their U-I forms have the form M H, and all have the same location features in the initial feature bundle. The inflectional frame is the phonological structure provided by the inflection itself. This frame is not prefixed or suffixed onto the stem, but rather, serves as the phonological framework used to construct the inflected sign. The frame has a partially specified initial feature bundle, but no final bundle of features. For verbs like TELL, which begin in contact with the body, the initial bundle of articulatory features is removed from the stem and inserted into final position in the frame. The remainder of the phonological information from the verb stem does not appear in the inflected form.[13] The resulting sign begins at the location specified by the inflectional frame and moves to what

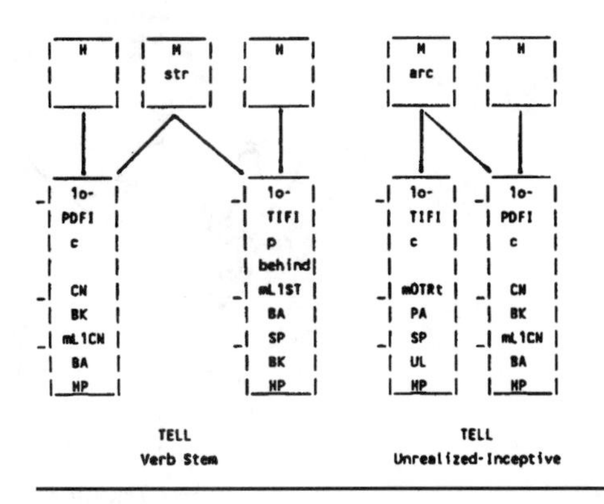

FIGURE 41. The stem TELL and its unrealized-inceptive form.

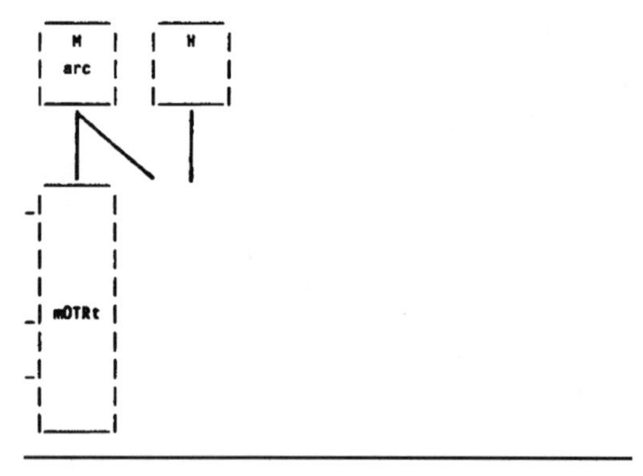

FIGURE 42. Unrealized-Inceptive Frame.

was the original location specified in the stem.

Many details have been left out of our description of this inflection. In fact, three such frames (i.e., three allomorphs) are needed to account for the U-I data. A fuller account can be found in Liddell (1984b). There are a number of other ASL inflections which will naturally lend themselves to an analysis utilizing inflectional frames.

5.2.2 Reduplication. Reduplication is common in ASL. Habitual aspect and iterative aspect are each marked in ASL by a different type of reduplication rule.[14] Figure 43 illustrates the form of the verb LOOK along with its habitual and iterative forms.

For purposes of our discussion, we will use the verb stem ASK, described earlier, and its habitual and iterative forms. The shape of

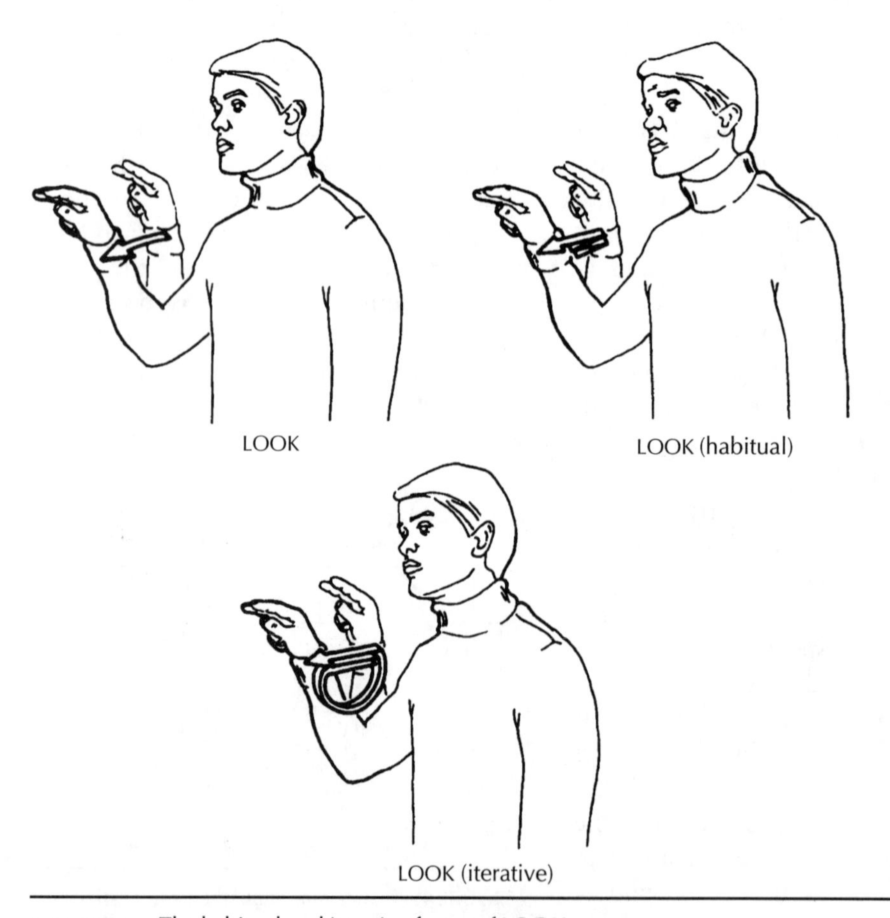

FIGURE 43. The habitual and iterative forms of LOOK.

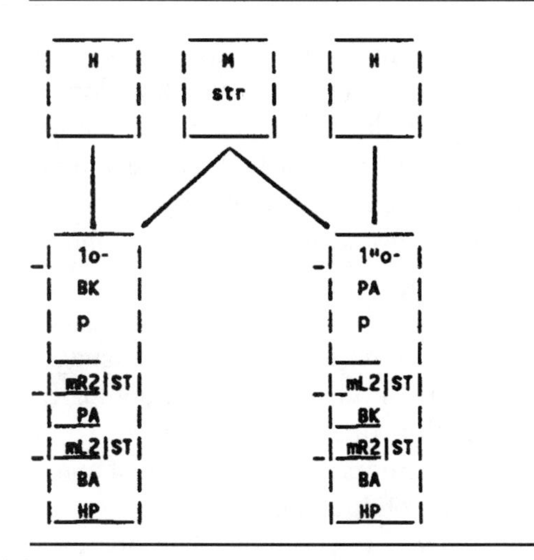

FIGURE 44. ASK

the movement of these forms is the same as that seen in Figure 44. The verb stem ASK is an incomplete S-morph. It has phonological cells which are filled with subject and object agreement morphemes.

After the subject and object agreement morphemes are inserted, the phonological structure of the stem is complete. Habitual aspect is then marked for the verb ASK through the application of a reduplication rule like the following:

Habitual Aspect Rule:
(for H M H signs)

1 2 3 → 1 2 3 1 2 3 1 2 3 1 2 3
srt srt srt srt

The rule produces four copies of the verb stem and shortens each of the movements (srt).[15] The application of this rule creates the environment for the M Epenthesis Rule described under phonological processes above.

The circled Ms are inserted between the final H of one repetition and the initial H of the next by the M Epenthesis Rule. Because none of those Hs are attached to articulatory bundles specified for body contact, the H Deletion Rule applies. It deletes every

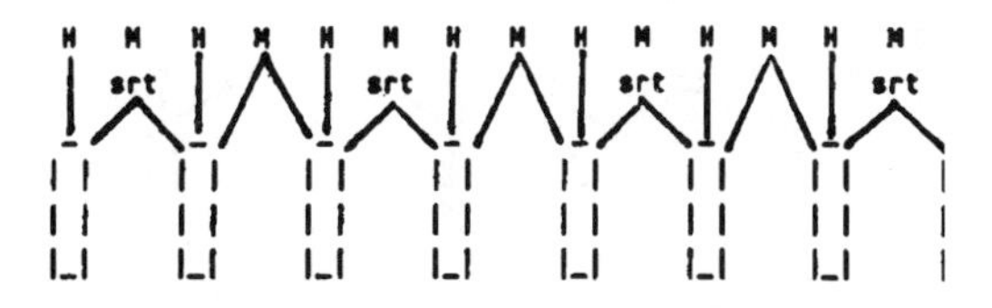

FIGURE 45. Habitual form after application of M Epenthesis.

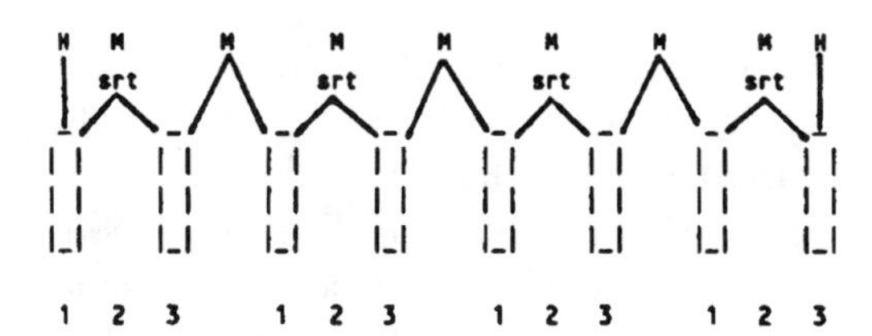

FIGURE 46. Surface form of ASK (habitual aspect.)

H except for the first and the last, producing the structure in Figure 45.

The epenthetic Ms and the feature bundles attach as shown in Figure 46. This produces what, for ASL, is a relatively long word consisting of nine segments.

A different and slightly more complicated reduplication rule could have applied, producing the iterative aspect.

Iterative rule:

1 2 3 → 1 2 3 M 1 2 3 M 1 2 3
Long arc Long arc Long

The application of this rule to ASK will produce the following structure (see Figure 47).

In this case the M Epenthesis Rule will not apply because the reduplication rule itself has already inserted a particular type of M

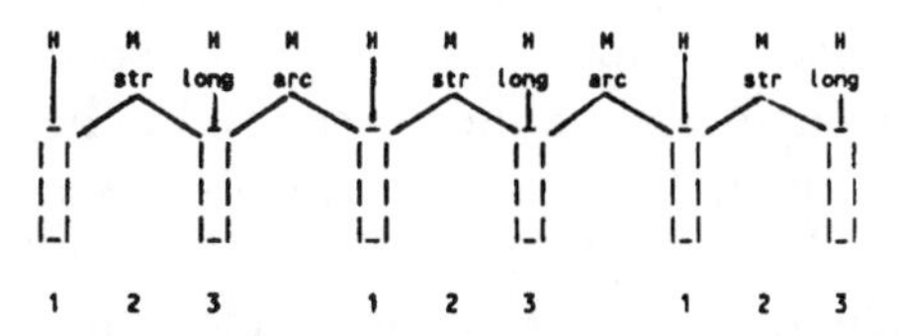

FIGURE 47. Result of application of iterative rule to ASK.

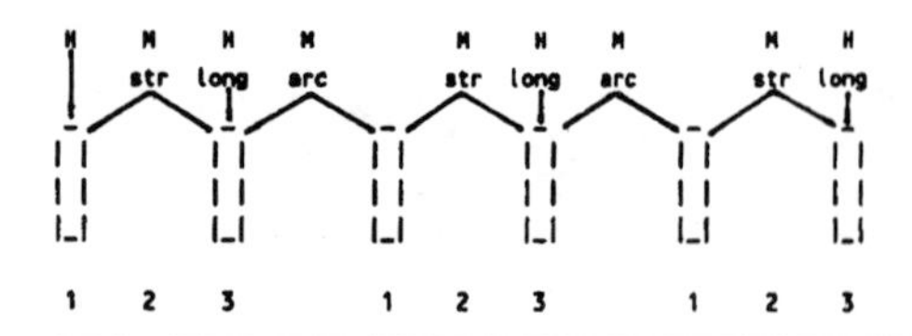

FIGURE 48. ASK (Iterative form) after H deletion is applied.

(with the feature "arc") between each repetition of the stem. The rule has also marked some of the Hs with the feature [long], which prohibits application of the H Deletion Rule. The H Deletion Rule may apply to unlengthened Hs, however. Its application produces the structure in Figure 48.

The application of the Iterative Rule has also produced a rather long ASL sign, though its structure is significantly different from that produced by the Habitual Aspect Rule.

We will now summarize the morphological and phonological processes which have interacted to form these two forms of ASK. Each began as a phonologically incomplete stem. The stem was made complete through a morphological rule which inserts agreement morphemes into the stem. The completed stem then underwent one of the reduplication rules, which produced an aspectual inflection. The application of either of the reduplicative rules creates the environment for the application of one or more phonological rules. The phonological rules then apply to produce the correct surface form.

It has been common practice in the past to refer to signs which have undergone reduplication process as being marked by the phonological feature [+ redup] (Fischer and Gough, 1978; Supalla and Newport, 1978; Klima and Bellugi, 1979; Padden and Perlmutter, 1984). It should be clear from the two reduplication rules we have examined that such an approach is not adequate. The two reduplicated forms do not differ from their stems by the single phonological feature [+/- redup]. They have undergone a reduplicative process which copies phonological segments, adds phonological features, and triggers the application of phonological rules.

5.2.3 Affixation. Across spoken languages, one of the most common phonological means for marking the application of a morphological process is the affixation of one or more segments to a stem. This also occurs in ASL, but it is uncommon. The one clear case is a nominalizing suffix having the structure M H. When suffixed to the verb TEACH, it produces a word meaning "teacher," and, when suffixed to the noun LAW, it produces "lawyer." This is the only ASL morpheme we know of which clearly has the status of an affix. Most ASL morphological activity involves filling in cells in phonologically incomplete segments, or operations on phonologically complete stems, which either modify them through the use of frames, or through some type of reduplicative process.

6. CONCLUSION

Early in this paper we suggested that, although the terminology of modern phonology would appear to eliminate signed languages from phonological analysis, the concepts that underlie the terminology are sufficiently broad to permit its application to the levels of organization of sign language. Our discussion of the phonetic, phonological, and morphological structures of ASL has been aimed at demonstrating the often surprising degree to which both the levels of organization and the processes and structures of ASL parallel those found in spoken languages. Thus, it should now be possible to refer to the phonetic structure, the morpheme structure conditions, or the phonological processes of sign languages and be confident that what is being described is analogous to similar phenomena in spoken languages. This potential for comparison permits an expansion of our knowledge about language universals, and should encourage the description of some of the dozens of independent sign languages of the world.

More importantly, the unique lexical structures and morphological processes we have identified and described add to our knowledge of the variety of forms of human language.

REFERENCES

Battison, R. 1974. Phonological deletion in American Sign Language. *Sign Language Studies* 5:1–19.

——. 1978. *Lexical Borrowing in American Sign Language.* Silver Spring, MD: Linstok Press.

Chomsky, N. & M. Halle. 1968. *The Sound Pattern of English.* New York, NY: Harper and Row.

Fischer, S. & B. Gough. 1978. Verbs in American Sign Language. *Sign Language Studies* 18:17–48.

Frishberg, N. 1975. Arbitrariness and iconicity: Historical change in American Sign Language. *Lg.* 51:676–710.

Goldsmith, J. 1976. Autosegmental phonology. MIT dissertation.

Johnson, R. & S. Liddell. 1984. Structural diversity in the American Sign Language lexicon. In *Papers from the Parassession on Lexical Semantics,* Testen, Mishra, & Drogo, (eds.). Chicago, IL: Chicago Linguistic Society. 173–186.

Klima, E. & U. Bellugi. 1979. *The Signs of Language.* Cambridge, MA: Harvard University Press.

Liddell, S. 1977. An investigation into the syntactic structure of American Sign Language. UCSD dissertation.

——. 1984a. THINK and BELIEVE: Sequentiality in American Sign Language signs. *Lg.* 60:372–399.

——. 1984b. Unrealized inceptive aspect in American Sign Language: Feature insertion in syllabic frames. In *Papers from the Twentieth Regional Meeting of the Chicago Linguistic Society,* Drogo, Mishra, & Testen, (eds.). Chicago, IL: Chicago Linguistic Society. 257–270.

Liddell, S, C. Ramsey, F. Powell, & D. Corina. 1984. Numeral incorporation and numeral classifiers in American Sign Language. Gallaudet University, ms.

McCarthy, J. 1979. Formal problems in Semitic phonology and morphology. MIT dissertation.

Padden, C. & D. Perlmutter. 1984. American Sign Language and the architecture of grammatical theory, ms.

Stokoe, W., Jr. 1960. *Sign Language structure: An outline of the visual communication Systems of the American Deaf* (Studies in linguistics: occasional papers 8) Buffalo, NY: University of Buffalo. [Rev. ed., Silver Spring, MD: Linstok Press, 1978].

——, D. Casterline, & C. Croneberg. 1965. *A Dictionary of American Sign Language on Linguistic Principles.* Washington, DC: Gallaudet College Press. [Rev. ed., Silver Spring, MD: Linstok Press, 1976.]

Studdert-Kennedy, M. & H. Lane. 1980. Clues from the differences between signed and spoken language. In *Signed and Spoken Language: Biological constraints on linguistic form,* Bellugi & Studdert-Kennedy, (eds.). Weinheim: Verlag Chemie. 29–39.

Supalla, T. 1978. Morphology of verbs of motion and location in American Sign Language. In *Papers from the Second National Symposium on Sign Language Research and Teaching.* Caccamise & Hicks, (eds.). Silver Spring, MD: NAD. 27–45.

—— & E. Newport. 1978. How many seats in a chair? The derivation of nouns and verbs in American Sign Language. In *Understanding Language Through Sign Language Research,* Siple, (ed.). New York: Academic Press. 91–132.

AUTHOR NOTE

Many individuals have commented on earlier versions of the work presented here and we have benefited from their insights. In particular, we would like to thank Ursula Bellugi, Edward Klima, Ceil Lucas, Carol Padden, David Perlmutter, William Stokoe, the participants at the 1984 Clear Lake Conference on Sign Language Linguistics, and our students over the past three years. In addition, we would like to thank the Gallaudet Research Institute for supporting the production of the illustrations used in this paper. We consider the authorship of this paper to be equal. This is an unrevised version of the original unpublished manuscript of the same title cited as Liddell and Johnson (1984), in many recent papers on ASL phonology. It is published here to provide access to that paper as a stage in the development of ASL phonological theory.

NOTES

1. It might be possible to argue that in many cases, the hold at the end of a sign is simply the physiological result of making contact with the body. It is not difficult to demonstrate that this is not so. The sign KNOW moves toward the forehead, makes contact, then stops briefly in contact with the fore-

head. It can be described as ending with hold manner. Liddell (1984a) reports the occurrence of a noncontacting form of the sign in which the hand approaches but does not touch the forehead and in which the sign still ends with hold manner.

2. In actuality, discourse strings must be represented as several simultaneous strings: one for each hand, since each produces segments, and one for each linguistically independent complex of torso, head, and facial behaviors. For the moment we are focusing on segments and strings of segments produced by a single hand.
3. Earlier work treated these as features of hand configuration (Liddell, 1984a). There is evidence for their independence from hand configuration, however, in the fact that certain of the local movements function as the sole manual markers of inflectional morphemes attached to signs which have plain (i.e., nonmoving) hand configurations in their uninflected forms.
4. It may be that a single feature such as "contracting" unifies both hooking and flattening.
5. For certain hand configurations and under certain discourse conditions it is possible to achieve twisting and nodding with the elbow joint rather than the wrist joint. For example, the sign WHERE is typically performed by twisting the wrist but by changing the hand configuration to one with a straight, rigid wrist the twisting can be transferred to the elbow. Similarly, YES which normally nods at the wrist may nod at the elbow in its emphatic form.
6. This sign also inflects for subject agreement. In fact, the example shown in Fig. 22 is the appropriate one for a first person subject, but we will not deal with this issue here.
7. Recently introduced signs for representing English words whose spellings begin with r use three other hand parts in POC: PA (RELAX), UL (RIGHT), RAFI (REALLY), but the use of such introduced signs is highly constrained.
8. A treatment whereby lexical forms of such signs contain terminal M segments and H segments are inserted finally would also have to propose that the initial H segments were also inserted by phonological process. This is not an appealing solution, however, since there exist signs with initial M segments that are not preceded by H segments, even in isolation (WHEN). We know of no principled way to predict which signs would add an H and which would not. Moreover, a number of signs consist of only a hold in isolation but are deleted between Ms. The underlying M solution would clearly not work for such signs since they have no M. The alternative proposal would amount to a claim that they have no segmental structure in their underlying forms which appears to introduce unnecessary complication to a theory of lexical structure of ASL.
9. The feature bundles in these two signs share many features. That is, feature bundle "b" is closely related to feature bundle "B." Likewise, feature bundle "d" is very similar to feature bundle "D."
10. Hold Deletion may optionally apply to the first hold of this string, yielding an M M M H surface form. In addition, although the derivation is presented in ordered form, M Epenthesis and Metathesis appear to be unordered with respect to each other.
11. Many of these are analyzed in detail in Liddell, Ramsey, Powell, and Corina (1984).
12. In ASL discourse any nominal may be assigned a grammatical association with a spatial location or vector. The process of assigning this association has been called "indexing" and the location or vector associated with the nominal has been called its "index." While ASL pronouns may make reference to a nominal by pointing at its index, verbs such as TELL and ASK agree with their subject and object nominals through the insertion of agreement morphemes. The agreement morphemes are morphs, the phonological form of which is a specification determined by the location of the index of a nominal.
13. We hesitate to talk about "deletion" here since this constructive process may take place within the lexicon. If so, then the process merely copies (reads, selects) specific information from the lexical entry of the stem and there is nothing to delete.
14. The data on these aspects are from Klima and Bellugi (1979), who first described them.
15. The actual number of repetitions can vary. For example, it could easily be produced with three rather than four repetitions.

File 40—Morphology: *The Minimal Units of Meaning: Morphemes*

M. Crabtree and J. Powers

A continuous stream of speech can be broken up by the listener (or linguist) into smaller, meaningful parts. A conversation, for example, can be divided into the sentences of the conversation, which can be divided up further into the words that make up each of the sentences. It is obvious to most people that a sentence has a meaning, and that each of the words in it has a meaning as well. Can we go further and divide words into smaller units which still have meanings? Many people think not; their immediate intuition is that words are the basic meaningful elements of a language. This is, however, not the case. Many words can be broken down into still smaller units. Think, for example, of words such as *unlucky*, *unhappy*, and *unsatisfied*. The *un-* in each of these words has the same meaning, loosely, that of "not," but *un* is not a word by itself. Thus, we have identified units—smaller than the word—which have meanings. These are called *morphemes*. Now consider the words *look*, *looks*, and *looked*. What about the *s* in *looks* and the *ed* in *looked?* These segments can be separated from the meaningful unit *look*, and although they do not really have an identifiable meaning themselves, each does have a particular function. The *s* is required for agreement with certain subjects (*she looks*, but not **she look*), and the *ed* signifies that the action of the verb *look* has already taken place. Segments such as these are also considered morphemes. Thus, a *morpheme* is the smallest linguistic unit which has a meaning or grammatical function.

Some words, of course, are not composed of other morphemes. *Car*, *spider*, and *race*, for example, are words, but they are also morphemes since they cannot be broken down into smaller meaningful parts. Morphemes which are also words are called *free morphemes* since they can stand alone. *Bound morphemes*, on the other hand, never exist as words themselves, but are always attached to some other morpheme. Some examples of bound morphemes in English are *un*, *ed*, and *s*.

When we identify the number and types of morphemes a given word consists of, we are looking at what is referred to as the *structure* of the word. Morphology is the study of how words are structured and how they are put together from smaller parts. Morphologists not only identify the different classes of morphemes but also study the patterns that occur in the combination of morphemes in a given language. For example, consider the words *rewrite*, *retake*, and *relive*. Notice that *re* is a bound morpheme which attaches only to verbs, and, furthermore, attaches to the beginning of the verb, not the end. Every speaker of English knows you can't say *write-re* or *take-re* (where *re-* is connected to the end of the free morpheme), nor can

Source. Reprinted by permission of the publisher, from M. Crabtree and J. Powers, compilers, *Language Files: Materials for an Introduction to Language* (1991): 127–130. Columbus: Ohio State University Press.

you say *rechoice* or *repretty* (where *re-* is connected to a morpheme which is not a verb). In other words, part of a speaker's linguistic competence is knowing, in addition to the meaning of the morphemes of a language, the ways in which the morphemes are allowed to combine with other morphemes.

Morphemes can be classified as either bound or free, as we have seen. There are three additional ways of characterizing morphemes. The first is to label *bound* morphemes according to whether they attach to the beginning or end of a word. You are most likely familiar with these terms. A *prefix* attaches to the beginning and a *suffix* attaches to the end of a word. The general term for prefixes and suffixes is *affix*, so bound morphemes are also referred to as *affixes*. The second way of characterizing morphemes is to classify *bound* morphemes according to their function in the complex words of which they are a part. When some morphemes attach to words, they create, or *derive*, new words, either by changing the meaning of the word or by changing its part of speech. For example, *un-* in *unhappy* creates a new word with the opposite meaning of *happy*. Notice that both *unhappy* and *happy* are adjectives. The suffix *ness* in *quickness*, however, changes the part of speech of quick, an adjective, into a noun, *quickness*. Morphemes that change the meaning or part of speech of a word they attach to are called *derivational* morphemes. Other morphemes do not alter words in this way, but only refine and give extra grammatical information about the word's already existing meaning. For example, *cat* and *cats* are both nouns which basically have the same meaning (i.e., they refer to the same sort of thing), but *cats*, with the plural morpheme *-s*, contains only the additional information that there are more than one of these things referred to. The morphemes which serve a purely grammatical function, never creating a new word but only a different *form* of the same word, are called *inflectional* morphemes.

In every word we find that there is at least one free morpheme. In a morphologically complex word, i.e., one composed of a free morpheme and any number of bound affixes, the free morpheme is referred to as the *stem*, *root*, or *base*. However, if there is more than one affix in a word, we cannot say that all of the affixes attach to the stem. Consider the word *happenings*, for example. When *-ing* is added to *happen*, we note that a new word is derived; it is morphologically complex, but it is a word. The plural morpheme *-s* is added onto the word happening, not the suffix *-ing*.

In English the derivational morphemes are either prefixes or suffixes, but, by chance, the inflectional morphemes are all suffixes. Of course, this is not the same in other languages. There are only eight inflectional morphemes in English. They are listed below along with an example of the type of stem each can attach to.

The difference between inflectional and derivational morphemes is sometimes difficult to see at first. Some characteristics of each are listed here and on the next page to help make the distinction clearer.

DERIVATIONAL MORPHEMES

1. Change the part of speech or the meaning of a word, e.g., *-ment* added to a verb forms a noun (*judg-ment*) *re-activate* means "activate again."
2. Syntax does not require the presence of derivational morphemes. They typically indicate semantic relations *within* a word, but no syntactic relations outside the word (compare this with #2 below) e.g., *un-kind* relates *-un* "not" to *kind*, but has no particular syntactic connections outside the word—note that the same word can be used in *he is unkind* and *they are unkind*.
3. Are usually not very productive—derivational morphemes generally are selective

about what they'll combine with e.g., the suffix *-hood* occurs with just a few nouns such as *brother, neighbor,* and *knight,* but not with most others, e.g., *friend, daughter,* or *candle.*

4. Typically occur before inflectional suffixes, e.g., *govern-ment-s: -ment,* a derivational suffix, precedes *-s,* an inflectional suffix.
5. May be prefixes or suffixes (in English), e.g., *pre-arrange, arrange-ment.*

INFLECTIONAL MORPHEMES

1. Do not change meaning or part of speech, e.g., *big, bigg-er, bigg-est* are all adjectives.
2. Are required by the syntax. They typically indicate syntactic or semantic relations *between* different words in a sentence, e.g., *Nim love-s bananas: -s* marks the 3rd person singular present form of the verb, relating it to the 3rd singular subject *Nim.*
3. Are very productive. They typically occur with all members of some large class of morphemes, e.g., the plural morpheme /-s/ occurs with almost all nouns.
4. Occur at the margin of a word, after any derivational morphemes, e.g., *ration-al-iz-ation-s: -s* is inflectional, and appears at the very end of the word.
5. Are suffixes only (in English).

There is one final distinction between types of morphemes which is useful to make. Some morphemes have semantic content. That is, they either have some kind of independent, identifiable meaning or indicate a change in meaning when added to a word. Others serve only to provide information about grammatical function by relating certain words in a sentence to each other (see 2 under inflectional morphemes, above). The former are called *content* morphemes, and the latter are called *function* morphemes. This might appear at first to be the same as the inflectional and derivational distinction. They do overlap, but not completely. All derivational morphemes are content morphemes, and all inflectional morphemes are function morphemes, as you might have surmised. However, some words can be merely function morphemes. Examples in English of such free morphemes that are also function morphemes are prepositions, articles, pronouns, and conjunctions.

In this file, we have been using conventional spelling to represent morphemes. But it is important to realize that morphemes are pairings of *sounds* with meanings, not spellings with meanings, and representing morphemes phonetically reveals some interesting facts. We find that just as different free morphemes can have the same phonetic representations, as in *ear* (for hearing) and *ear* (of corn), the same is true of bound morphemes. For example, the plural, possessive, and third person singular suffixes can all sound identical in English (e.g., *cats* [kæts], *Frank's* [fræŋks], and *walks* [waks]). These three suffixes are completely different morphemes, they just happen to be homophonous, or sound alike, in English. Similarly, there are two morphemes in English that sound like [in]. One means "not" as in *inoperable* or *intolerable,* and the other means "in" as in *intake* or *inside.*

One of the more interesting things revealed by transcribing morphemes phonetically is the interaction of phonological and morphological processes. For example, some morphemes have more than one phonetic representation depending on which sounds precede or follow them, but since each of the pronunciations serves the same function or has the same meaning, it is considered to be the same morpheme. In other words, the same morpheme can be pronounced differently depending upon the sounds that follow or precede it. Of course, these different pronunciations will be patterned. For example, the phonetic representation of the plural morpheme is either [s] as in *cats,* [z] as in *dogs*, or [əz] as in *churches*. Each of these three pronunciations is said to be an *allomorph* of the *same* morpheme because [s], [z], and [əz] all have the same function (making some word plural) and because they are similar phonetically. Note that this same phonological process which causes the plural morpheme /s/ to be pronounced as [s] after voiceless sounds, [z] after voiced sounds, and [əz] after sibilants also applies to the possessive morpheme /s/ and the 3rd person singular morpheme /s/. Consider the morpheme /in/ which means "not" in the words *inoperable, incongruent,* and *impossible.* What are the allomorphs of this morpheme?

We now call your attention to a few pitfalls of identifying morphemes. First, don't confuse morphemes with syllables. A few examples will show that the number of morphemes and syllables in a word are independent of each other. Consider the word *coats.* It is a one-syllable word composed of two morphemes. *Coat* happens to be one morpheme and consists of a single syllable, but *-s* is not even a syllable, although it is a morpheme. Note that *syllable* is a three-syllable word composed only of one morpheme.

Secondly, note that a given morpheme has a particular sound or sound sequence associated with it, but not every instance of that sound sequence in the language represents that morpheme. For example, take the plural morpheme /s/. When you hear the word [karts] in isolation, you can't determine if the [s] is an instance of this plural morpheme (*the carts are back in the store*), or an instance of the possessive morpheme (*the cart's wheels turn funny*) or of the 3rd person singular morpheme (*He carts those books around everyday*). That sound sequence may not even be a morpheme at all. The [s] in [sun], for example, is not a morpheme. Likewise, the [in] of *inexcusable* is the morpheme which means "not," but the [in] of *print* is not a morpheme.

Third, remember to analyze the phonetic representations of morphemes and not their spellings. A morpheme can have one or more allomorphs, and these allomorphs might be represented by the same or different spellings. The *-er* in *writer* is the same morpheme as the *-or* in *editor,* and the *-ar* in *liar,* since all three mean "one who," but they do not represent separate allomorphs since their pronunciations are identical, namely, [r]. On the other hand, the -s in *Mark's, John's* and *Charles's* are the same morpheme, but represent three different allomorphs, since each is pronounced differently.

Finally, we include below a summary list of criteria which might help you to identify the different types of morphemes.

Given a morpheme,

1. Can it stand alone as a word?
   YES → it's a *free* morpheme (e.g., *bubble, orange*)
   NO → it's a *bound* morpheme (e. g., *-er* in beater, -s in *oranges*)
2. Does it have the principal meaning of the word it's in?
   YES → it's the *stem* (e.g., *happy* in *un-happiness*)
   NO → it's *an affix* (e.g., *-or* in *contributor* or, *pre-* in *preview*)
3. Does it create a new word by changing the meaning and/or part of speech?
   YES → it's a *derivational* affix (e.g., *re-* in *rewind, -ist* in *artist*)
   NO → it's an *inflectional* affix (e.g., *-est* in *smartest*)
4. Does it have a meaning, or cause a change in meaning when added to a word?
   YES → it's a *content* morpheme (e.g., *-un* in *untrue*
   NO → it's a *function* morpheme (e.g., *the, to, or, -s* in *books*)

File 42—Morphology: *The Hierarchical Structure of Words*

M. Crabtree and J. Powers

When we examine words composed of only two morphemes, we implicitly know two facts about the ways in which affixes join with their stems. First, the stems with which a given affix may combine normally belong to the same part of speech. For example, the suffix *-able* attaches freely to verbs, but not to adjectives or nouns; thus, we can add this suffix to the verbs *adjust, break, compare,* and *debate,* but not to the adjectives *asleep, lovely, happy,* and *strong,* nor the nouns *anger, morning, student,* or *success.* Second, the words formed by the addition of a given affix to some word or morpheme also normally belong to the same part of speech. For example, the expressions resulting from the addition of *-able* to a verb are always adjectives; thus *adjustable, breakable, comparable,* and *debatable* are all adjectives

These two facts have an important consequence for determining the way in which words with more than one affix must be formed. What it means is that words are formed in steps, with one affix attaching to a complete word, which can be a free morpheme or a morphologically complex word. Words with more than one affix are not formed in one single step with the affixes and stem just strung together. For example, consider the word *unusable,* which is composed of a prefix *un-* a stem *use,* and a suffix *-able.* One possible way this morphologically complex word might be formed is all at once, as in: *un* + *use* + *able,* where the prefix and the suffix attach at the same time to the verb stem *use.* However, this cannot be the case knowing what we know about how affixes attach only to certain parts of speech and create words of certain parts of speech. The prefix *un-,* meaning "not," attaches only to adjectives and creates new words which are also adjectives. (Compare with *unkind, unwise,* and *unhappy.*) The suffix *-able,* on the other hand, attaches to verbs and forms words which are adjectives. (Compare with *stoppable, doable,* and *washable.*) Therefore, *un-* cannot attach to *use,* since use is a verb and not an adjective. However, if *-able* attaches *first* to the stem *use,* then it creates an adjective, *usable,* and the prefix *-un* is allowed to combine with it. Thus, the formation of the word *unusable* is a two-step process whereby *use* and *-able* attach first, then *un-* attaches to the word *usable.*

Recall that what we are analyzing is the internal *structure* of words. Words, since they are formed by steps, have a special type of structure characterized as *hierarchical.* This hierarchical structure can be schematically represented by means of a "tree" which indicates the steps involved in the formation of the word, i.e., which morphemes joined together first and so on. The tree for *unusable* is:

Source. Reprinted by permission of the publisher, from M. Crabtree and J. Powers, compilers, *Language Files: Materials for an Introduction to Language* (1991): 133–135. Columbus: Ohio State University Press.

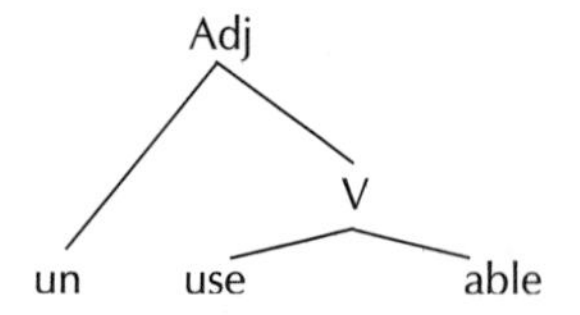

Now consider the word *reusable*. Both the prefix *re-* and the suffix *-able* attach to verbs, but we have already shown that one must attach first. Which is it? Notice that *reusable* cannot be regarded as the result of adding the prefix *re-* to the word *usable* since *re-* attaches only to verbs (compare with *redo*, *relive*, and *refuel*) and *usable* is an adjective. However, *-able* can attach to the verb *reuse* since *-able* attaches to verbs. Thus, our understanding of how the affixes *re-* and *-able* combine with other morphemes allows us to conclude that the verb *reuse*, but not the adjective *usable*, is a step in the formation of the adjective *reusable*.

Interestingly, some words are ambiguous in that they have more than one meaning. When we examine their internal structure, we find an explanation for this: their structure may be analyzed in more than one way. Consider, for example, the word *unlockable*. This could mean either "not able to be locked" or "able to be unlocked." If we made a list to determine the parts of speech the affix *un-* attaches to, we would discover that there are not one but two prefixes which sound like *un-*. The first combines with adjectives to form new adjectives, and means "not." (Compare with *unaware*, *unintelligent*, or *unwise*.) The second prefix *un-* combines with verbs to form new verbs, and means "do the reverse of." (Compare with *untie*, *undo*, or *undress*.)

Remember from Files 40 and 41 that even though these prefixes sound alike, they are entirely different morphemes. Because of these two different sorts of *un-* in English, *unlockable* may be analyzed in two different ways. First, the suffix *-able* may join with the verb *lock* to form the adjective *lockable*. *un-* may then join with this adjective to form the new adjective *unlockable*, with the meaning "not able to be locked." This way of forming *unlockable* is schematized in the following tree:

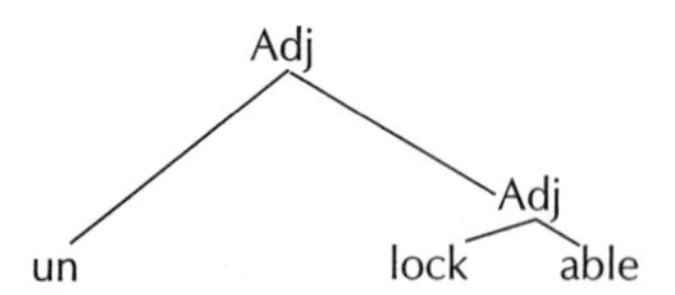

The second way of forming *unlockable* is as follows. The prefix *un-* joins with the verb *lock* to form the verb *unlock*. The suffix *-able* then joins with this verb to form the adjective *unlockable* with the meaning of "able to be unlocked." This manner of forming *unlockable* is represented by the following tree:

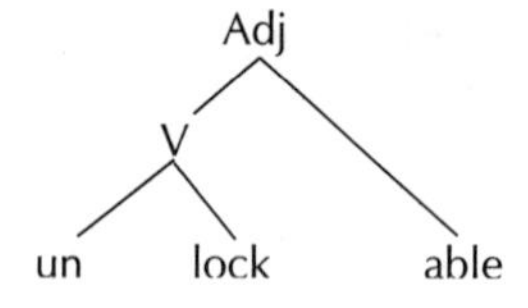

SOME SUGGESTIONS

There are a few prefixes which do not attach exclusively to one part of speech. For example, consider the prefix *pre-*. *Pre-* attaches to verbs and does not change the part of speech as the following examples show:

preexist
predecide
predetermine
predefine
premeditate

However, there are examples of words with the prefix *pre-* which do not follow the same pattern as those cited above:

preseason
predawn
prewar
pregame

In these words *pre-* attaches to a noun and forms an adjective (*the preseason game, the prewar propaganda, the pregame warmup*). However, the "meaning" of the prefix is the same as in *preexist, predecide*, etc. (although its function is different). In addition, there are sets such as:

prefrontal
predental
preinvasive
prehistoric

In these words, *pre-* is attaching to an adjective, forming adjectives, and has the same "meaning" as in *preexist, predecide*, etc. So this is a bit problematic. We don't want to throw out the idea that a given affix attaches only to one part of speech, since the overwhelming majority of affixes adhere to this pattern. Apparently, some morphemes become so productive that their combinatorial possibilities can be extended. Such must be the case with *pre-*. Note, however, that its combinations are nevertheless rule-governed. When *pre-* attaches to verbs, it forms only verbs. When it attaches to nouns, it forms only adjectives, and when it attaches to adjectives, it forms only adjectives. So, it is advisable to consider many examples when attempting to determine the rules by which a given affix combines.

EXERCISES

1. Draw a tree diagram for the word prejudgment.
2. Draw tree diagrams for each of the following words:

   a. reconstruction
   b. unaffordable
   c. un-American
   d. manliness
   e. impersonal
   f. irreplaceability
   g. oversimplification
   h. unhappiness
   i. impotency
   j. international
   k. misunderstandable
   l. dehumidifier
   m. unrespectable
   n. nonrefundable
   o. mismanagement
   p. underspecification
   q. restatement
   r. inflammability
   s. unmistakable
   t. insincerity
   u. dysfunctional
   v. inconclusive
   w. premeditatively
   x. overgeneralization
   y. reformer
   z. infertility
   aa. dishonesty

3. We said that polar opposite ("not") unattaches only to adjectives, but two exceptions to this rule are Uncola and Uncar. Why are these exceptions? Why would advertisers have made them up in the first place when the words fail to follow the rule?

File 43—Morphology: *Word Formation Processes*

M. CRABTREE AND J. POWERS

In the previous files of this section, we have been looking at how words are put together out of smaller parts. We have seen that English makes use of derivational morphemes to create more words than would exist with only free morphemes, and, of course, English is not the only language that enlarges its vocabulary in this way. When linguists observe a language which uses the combining of bound and free morphemes to form additional words, they note that the occurring combinations are systematic, i.e., rule-governed, as we have certainly seen is the case in English. To illustrate, recall that the prefix *un-*, meaning "not" attaches only to adjectives, the prefix *re-* attaches only to verbs, and the suffix *-ful* attaches only to nouns. Because these combinations are rule-governed, we can say that a *process* is at work, namely a *word formation process,* since new words are being formed. What we will consider in this file are the ways in which languages create new words from bound and free morphemes. There are other ways in which new words come into use in a language, but they will be discussed in Files 95 and 96 in Historical Linguistics.

Before describing some of the word formation processes found in the world's languages, we must first address the question: in what sense is it meant that new words are being "formed?" Do we mean that every time a speaker uses a morphologically complex word that the brain reconstructs it? Some linguists would maintain that this is the case. They would claim that in a speaker's mental dictionary, called the *lexicon,* each morpheme is listed individually, along with other information such as what it means, its part of speech (if a free morpheme), and possibly a rule naming what it can combine with, if it is a bound morpheme. Thus, each time a word was used, it could be reformed from the separate entries in the lexicon. However there is evidence which indicates this is not actually the case; even morphologically complex words apparently have a separate entry in the adult lexicon. There are other reasons, though, to consider *derivation* a process of word formation. A linguist analyzing a language uses the term *formation* to mean that the lexicon of a language includes many items which are systematically related to one another. Speakers of a given language, however, are also often aware of these relationships. We see evidence of this when new words actually are formed based on patterns that exist in the lexicon. For example, a speaker of English may never have heard words such as *unsmelly, smellless,* or *smellful* before, but he or she would certainly understand what they mean. The word *stick-to-it-ive-ness* causes some prescriptiv-

Source. Reprinted by permission of the publisher, from M. Crabtree and J. Powers, compilers, *Language Files: Materials for an Introduction to Language* (1991): 137–141. Columbus: Ohio State University Press.

ists to wail; why create this new word when a perfectly good word, *perseverance,* already exists? This word illustrates that speakers of a language have no problem accessing the patterns in their lexicons and applying them for new creations. Thus, the term *formation* is applicable. Rules which speakers actually apply to form words that are not currently in use in a language are termed *productive.* English has examples of nonproductive morphemes as well; for example, the suffix *-tion* is not used by speakers to form new nouns, whereas the suffix *-ness* is.

AFFIXATION

Words formed by the combination of bound affixes and free morphemes are the result of the process of *affixation.* Although English uses only prefixes and suffixes, many other languages use *infixes* as well. Infixes are inserted within the root morpheme. Note that English really has no infixes. At first glance at a word like *doubtfully* some students think that *-ful* is an infix because it occurs in the middle of a word. Recall from File 42, however, that *doubtfully* has a hierarchical structure which indicates that the *-ly* suffix is not attaching to the affix *-ful,* but rather is attaching to a complete word, *doubtful.* Thus *-ful* attaches to the word *doubt* as a suffix and does not break up the morpheme *doubt.* Tagalog, one of the major languages of the Philippines, uses infixes quite extensively. For example, the infix *-um* is used to form the infinitive form of verbs:

[sulat]	"write"	[sumulat]	"to write"
[bili]	"buy"	[bumili]	"to buy"
[kuha]	"take, get"	[kumuha]	"to take, to get"

COMPOUNDING

Compounding is a process which forms new words not from bound affixes but from two or more independent words. The words that are the parts of the compound can be free morphemes, words derived by affixation, or even words formed by compounding themselves. Examples in English of these three types include:

girlfriend	air conditioner	lifeguard chair
blackbird	looking glass	aircraft carrier
textbook	watch maker	life insurance salesman

Notice that in English compound words are not represented consistently in the orthography. Sometimes they are written together, sometimes they are written with a dash, and sometimes they are written separately. We know, however, that compounding forms *words* and not just syntactic phrases, regardless of how the compound is spelled, because the stress patterns are different for compounds. Think about how you would say the words *red neck* in each of the two following sentences:

1. The wool sweater gave the man a red neck.
2. The redneck in the bar got drunk and started yelling.

Compounds which have words in the same order as phrases have primary stress on the first word only, while individual words in phrases have independent primary stress. Some other examples are listed below. (Primary stress is indicated by ´.)

Compounds	*Phrases*
bláckbird	bláck bírd
mákeup	máke úp

Other compounds can have phrasal stress patterns, but only if they *can't* possibly be phrases. These same compounds might also have stress on the first word only, like other compounds. For example:

eásy-góing	eásy-going
mán-máde	mán-made
hómemáde	hómemade

German is one of the many languages which also uses compounding to form new words. Some examples of the numerous compounds in German are:

Muttersprache	"native language" < "mother tongue"
Schreibtisch	"desk" < "writing table"
stehenbleiben	"stand (still)" < "stay remain"
wunderkind	"child prodigy" < "miracle child"
Geschwindigkeitsbegrenzung	"speed limit" < "speed limit"

REDUPLICATION

Reduplication is a process of forming new words either by doubling an entire free morpheme (*total reduplication*) or part of it (*partial reduplication*). English makes use of reduplication very sporadically. Some English examples are *higglety-pigglety*, *hoity-toity*, and *hocus-pocus*. However, note that these partial reduplications are not a single morpheme. Other languages do, however, make use of reduplication more extensively. Indonesian uses total reduplication to form the plurals of nouns:

[rumah]	"houses"	[rumahrumah]	"house"
[ibu]	"mother"	[ibuibu]	"mothers"
[lalat]	"fly"	[lalatlalat]	"flies"

Tagalog uses partial reduplication to indicate the future tense:

[bili]	"buy"	[bibili]	"will buy"
[kain]	"eat"	[kakain]	"will eat"
[pasok]	"enter"	[papasok]	"will enter"

In conjunction with the prefix *-maŋ* (which often changes the initial consonant of a following morpheme to a nasal with the same place of articulation as the original initial consonant), Tagalog uses reduplication to derive words for occupations:

[mamimili]	"a buyer"	</maŋ + bi + bili/ (cf. [bili] "buy")
[manunulat]	"a writer"	</maŋ + su + sulat/ (cf. [sulat] "write")
[maŋʔiʔisda]	"a fisherman"	</maŋ + ʔi + ʔisda/ (cf. [ʔisda] "fish")

MORPHEME-INTERNAL CHANGES

Besides adding an affix to a morpheme or copying all or part of the morpheme to make new words or make morphological distinctions, it is also possible to make morpheme-internal modifications. There are a few examples of this in English.

1. Although the usual pattern of plural formation is to add an inflectional morpheme, some English plurals make an internal modification:

man	men
woman	women
goose	geese
foot	feet

2. The usual pattern of past and past participle formation is to add an affix, but some verbs also show an internal change:

ring	rang	rung
sing	sang	sung
swim	swam	swum

   Some verbs show both an internal change and the addition of an affix to one form:

break	broke	broken
bite	bit	bitten

3. Some word class changes are also indicated only via internal changes

strife	strive
teeth	teethe
breath	breathe
life	live (V)
life	live (Adj)

SUPPLETION

Languages that employ morphological processes to form words will usually have a regular, productive way of doing so according to one or more of the processes discussed above. They might also have some smaller classes of words that are irregular because they mark the same morphological distinction by another of these processes. Sometimes, however, the same distinction can be represented by two different words which don't have any systematic difference in form—they are exceptions to all of the processes. This completely irregular situation is called *suppletion* and usually only occurs in a few words of a language.

In English, for example, the regular past tense is formed by the ending realized by the allomorphs [t], [d] or [əd]. Most English verbs, and any newly made-up words such as *scroosh* or *blat*, will have this past tense form:

[wak]	"walk"	[wakt]	"walked"
[skruš]	"scroosh"	[skrušt]	"scrooshed"
[blæt]	"blat"	[blætəd]	"blatted"

There are also some smaller classes of very common words that form the past tense by an internal vowel change:

[siŋ]	"sing"	[sæŋ]	"sang"
[reŋ]	"run"	[ræŋ]	"ran"

But a small number of individual verbs have *suppletive* past tenses:

[æm]	"am"	[wez]	"was"
[go]	"go"	[wɛnt]	"went"

Note there is no systematic similarity between the past and present tense forms of these verbs.

Classical Arabic provides another example of suppletion (as could most languages). The normal plural form for nouns ending in [at] in Arabic involves the lengthening of the vowel of this ending (a morpheme internal change):

[dira:sat]	"(a) study"	[dira:sa:t]	"studies"
[harakat]	"movement"	[haraka:t]	"movements"

There are also some irregular plurals of nouns ending in [at] that involve other internal changes:

[ǰumlat]	"sentence"	[ǰumal]	"sentences"
[fikrat]	"strength"	[fikar]	"thoughts"

However, the plurals of other forms are clearly cases of suppletion, for example:

[marʔa+t]	"woman"	[nisa:ʔ]	"women"

EXERCISES

1. Imagine for a moment that *-ful* is an infix in English. How would it attach to a morpheme like doubt? What would the entire word look like? (Note, there are four possibilities.)
2. Think up other examples of suppletion in English. (Hint: start with some common adjectives.)

The Confluence of Space and Language in Signed Languages

Karen Emmorey

Expressed by hands and face rather than by voice, and perceived by eye rather than by ear, signed languages have evolved in a completely different biological medium from spoken languages. Used primarily by deaf people throughout the world, they have arisen as autonomous languages not derived from spoken language and are passed down from one generation of deaf people to the next (Klima and Bellugi 1979; Wilbur 1987). Deaf children with deaf parents acquire sign language in much the same way that hearing children acquire spoken language (Newport and Meier 1985; Meier 1991). Sign languages are rich and complex linguistic systems that manifest the universal properties found in all human languages (Lillo-Martin 1991).

In this chapter, I will explore a unique aspect of sign languages: the linguistic use of physical space. Because they directly use space to linguistically express spatial locations, object orientation, and point of view, sign languages can provide important insight into the relation between linguistic and spatial representations. Four major topics will be examined: how space functions as part of a linguistic system (American Sign Language) at various grammatical levels; the relative efficiency of signed and spoken languages for overt spatial description tasks; the impact of a visually based linguistic system on performance with nonlinguistic tasks; and finally, aspects of the neurolinguistics of sign language.

5.1 MULTIFUNCTIONALITY OF SPACE IN SIGNED LANGUAGES

In this section, I describe several linguistic functions of space in American Sign Language (ASL). The list is not exhaustive (for example, I do not discuss the use of space to create discourse frames; see Winston 1995), but the discussion should illustrate how spatial contrasts permeate the linguistic structure of sign language. Although the discussion is limited to ASL, other signed languages are likely to share most of the spatial properties discussed here.

5.1.1 Phonological Contrasts

Spatial distinctions function at the sublexical level in signed languages to indicate phonological contrasts. Sign phonology does not involve sound patterning or vocally based features, but linguists have recently broadened the term *phonology* to mean the "patterning of the formational units of the expression system of a natural language" (Coulter and Anderson 1993, 5). Location is one of the formational units of sign language phonology, claimed to be somewhat analogous to consonants in spoken language (see Sandler 1989). For example, the

Source. Reprinted by permission of the publisher, from P. Bloom, M. S. Peterson, L. Nadel, and M F. Garrett, eds., *Language and Space*, (1999): 171–209. Cambridge, Mass.: MIT Press.

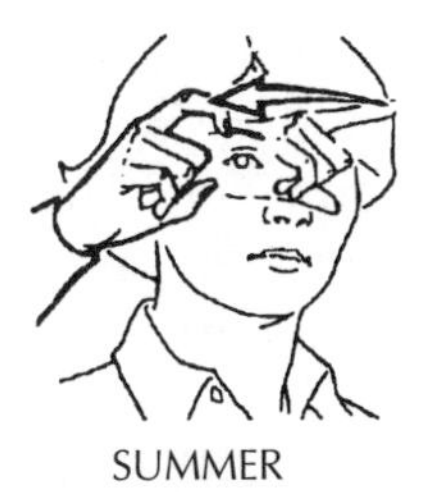

FIGURE 5.1. Example of a phonological contrast in ASL. These signs differ only in the location of their articulation.

ASL signs SUMMER, UGLY, and DRY[1] differ only in where they are articulated on the body, as shown in Figure 1.

At the purely phonological level, the location of a sign is articulatory and does not carry any specific meaning. Where a sign is articulated is stored in the lexicon as part of its phonological representation.[2] Sign languages differ with respect to the phonotactic constraints they place on possible sign locations or combinations of locations. For example, in ASL no one-handed signs are articulated by contacting the contralateral side of the face (Battison 1978). For all signed languages, whether a sign is made with the right or left hand is not distinctive (left-handers and right-handers produce the same signs—what is distinctive is a contrast between a dominant and nondominant hand). Furthermore, I have found no phonological contrasts in ASL that involve left-right in signing space. That is, there are no phonological minimal pairs that are distinguished solely on the basis of whether the signs are articulated on the right or left side of signing space. Such left-right distinctions appear to be reserved for the referential and topographic functions of space within the discourse structure, syntax, and morphology of ASL (see below). For a recent and comprehensive review of the nature of phonological structure in sign language, see Corina and Sandler (1993).

5.1.2 Morphological Inflection

In many spoken languages, morphologically complex words are formed by adding prefixes or suffixes to a word stem. In ASL and other signed languages, complex forms are most often created by nesting a sign stem within dynamic movement contours and planes in space. Figure 2 illustrates the base form GIVE along with several inflected forms. ASL has many verbal inflections that convey temporal information about the action denoted by the verb, for example, whether the action was habitual, iterative,

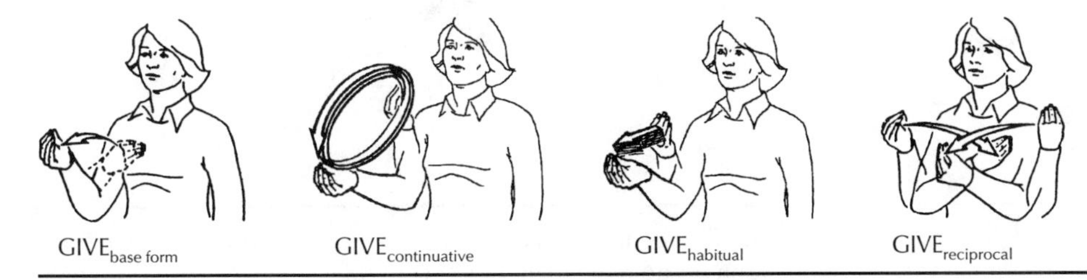

FIGURE 5.2. Examples of nonconcatenative morphology in ASL.

or continual. Generally, these distinctions are marked by different movement patterns overlaid onto a sign stem. This type of morphological encoding contrasts with the primarily linear affixation found in spoken languages. For spoken languages, simultaneous affixation processes such as templatic morphology (e.g., in the Semitic languages), infixation, or reduplication are relatively rare. Signed languages, by contrast, prefer nonconcatenative processes such as reduplication; and prefixation and suffixation are rare. Sign languages' preference for simultaneously producing affixes and stems may have its origin in the visual-manual modality.

For example, the articulators for speech (the tongue, lips, jaw) can move quite rapidly, producing easily perceived distinctions on the order of every 50–200 milliseconds. In contrast, the major articulators for sign (the hands) move relatively slowly such that the duration of an isolated sign is about 1,000 milliseconds; the duration of an average spoken word is more like 500 milliseconds. If language processing in real time has equal timing constraints for spoken and signed languages, then there is strong pressure for signed languages to express more distinctions simultaneously. The articulatory pressures seem to work in concert with the differing capacities of the visual and auditory systems for expressing simultaneous versus sequential information. That is, the visual system is well suited for simultaneously perceiving a large amount of information, whereas the auditory system seems particularly adept at perceiving fast temporal distinctions. Thus both sign and speech have exploited the advantages of their respective modalities.

5.1.3 Coreference and Anaphora

Another hypothesized universal use of space within sign languages is for referential functions. In ASL and other sign languages, nominals can be associated with locations in signing space. This association can be established by "indexing" or pointing to a location in space after producing a lexical sign, as shown in Figure 3. Another device for establishing the nominal-locus association is to articulate the nominal sign(s) at a particular location or by eye gaze toward that location. In Figure 3, the nominal DOG is associated with a spatial locus on the signer's left and CAT is associated with a locus on the signer's right. The verb BITE moves between these locations identifying the subject and object of the sentence "[The dog] bites [the cat]." BITE belongs to a subset of ASL verbs

FIGURE 5.3. Example of the sentential use of space in ASL. Nominals (*cat, dog*) are first associated with spatial loci through indexation. The direction of the movement of the verb (BITE) indicates the grammatical role of subject and object.

termed *agreeing* verbs, whose movement and/or orientation signal grammatical role.[3] ASL pronouns also make use of established associations between nominals and spatial loci. A pronominal sign directed toward a specific locus refers back to the nominal associated with that locus. Further description of coreference and anaphora in ASL can be found in Lillo-Martin (1991) and Padden (1988).

Recently, there has been some controversy within sign linguistics concerning whether space itself performs a syntactic function in ASL. Liddell (1993, 1994, 1995) has argued that spatial loci are not morphemic. He proposes that space in sentences illustrated in Figure 3 is being used deictically rather than anaphorically. That is, the signer deictically points to a locus in the same way he would point to a physically present person. In contrast, other researchers have argued that these spatial loci are agreement morphemes or clitics that are attached to pronouns and verbs (e.g., Janis 1995; Padden 1990). As evidence for his position, Liddell (1993, 1995) argues that just as there is an unlimited number of spatial positions in which a physically present referent could be located, there also appears to be an unlimited number of potential locations within signing space (both vertically and horizontally) toward which a verb or pronominal form can be directed (see also Lillo-Martin and Klima 1990). If this is the case, then location specifications are not listable or categorizable and therefore cannot be agreement morphemes or clitics. The syntactic role of subject or object is assigned, not by the spatial loci, but either by word order or by the orientation or the temporal end points of the verb itself.[4] According to this view, the particular location at which a verb begins or ends serves to identify the *referent* of the subject and object roles. The space itself, Liddell has argued, is not part of a syntactic representation; rather, space is used nonmorphemically and deictically (much as deictic gesture is used when accompanying speech). This hypothesis is quite radical, and many of the details have not been worked out. For example, even if space itself does not perform a syntactic function, it does perform both a referential and a locative function within the language (see Emmorey, Corina, and Bellugi 1995). The association of a nominal with a particular location in space needs to be part of the linguistic representation at some level in order to express coreference relations between a proform and its antecedent. If this association is not part of the linguistic representation, then there must be an extremely intimate mixing of linguistic structure and nonlinguistic representations of space.

5.1.4 Locative Expressions

The spatial positions associated with referents can also convey locative information about the referent. For example, the phrase DOG INDEX, shown in Figure 3 could be interpreted as "the dog is there on my left," but such an interpretation is not required by the grammar. Under the nonlocative reading, INDEX simply establishes a reference relation between DOG and a spatial locus that happens to be on the signer's left. To ensure a locative reading, signers may add a specific facial expression (e.g., spread tight lips with eye gaze to the locus), produced simultaneously with the INDEX sign. Furthermore, ASL has a set of classifier forms for conveying specific locative information, which can be embedded in locative and motion predicates; for these predicates, signing space is most often interpreted as corresponding to a physical location in real (or imagined) space. The use of space to directly represent spatial relations stands in marked contrast to spoken languages, in which spatial information must be recovered from an acoustic signal that does not map onto the information content in a one-to-one correspondence. In locative expressions in ASL, the identity of each object is provided by a lexical sign (e.g., TABLE, T-V, CHAIR); the location of the objects, their orientation, and their spatial relation vis-a-vis one another are indicated by where the appropriate accompanying classifier sign is articulated in the space in front of the signer. The Flat B handshape is the classifier handshape for rectangular, flat-topped, surface-prominent objects like tables or sheets of paper. The C handshape is the classifier handshape for bulky boxlike objects like televisions or microwaves. The Bent V is the classifier handshape for squat, "legged" objects like chairs, small animals, and seated people.

Flat B handshape:

C handshape:

Bent V handshape:

These handshapes occur in verbs that express the spatial relation of one object to another and the manner and direction of motion (for moving objects/people). Figure 4 illustrates an ASL description of the room that is sketched at the far left. An English translation of the ASL description would be "I enter the room; there is a table to my left, a TV on the far side, and a chair to my right." Where English uses separate words to express such spatial relations, ASL uses the actual visual layout displayed by the array of classifier signs to express the spatial relations of the objects.

Landau and Jackendoff (1993) have recently argued that languages universally encode very little information about object shape in their locative closed-class vocabulary (e.g., prepositions) compared to the amount of spatial detail they encode in object names (see also Landau, Chapter 8, this volume). As one can surmise from our discussion and from Figure 4, ASL appears to have a rich representation of shape in its locative expressions. Like the locational predicates in Tzeltal (Brown 1991; Levinson 1992a), ASL verbs of location incorporate detailed information about the shape of objects. It is unclear whether these languages are counterexamples to Landau and Jackendoff's claims for two reasons. First, both Tzeltal and ASL express locative information through verbal predicates that form an open-class category, unlike prepositions (although the morphemes that make up these verbal predicates belong to a closed class). The distinction may hinge on whether these forms are considered grammaticized closed-class elements or not (see also Talmy 1988). Second, in ASL the *degree* of shape detail is less in classifier forms than in object names. For example, the Flat B handshape classifier is used for both TABLE and for PAPER—the count nouns encode more detailed shape information about these objects than the classifier form.

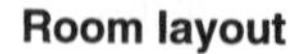

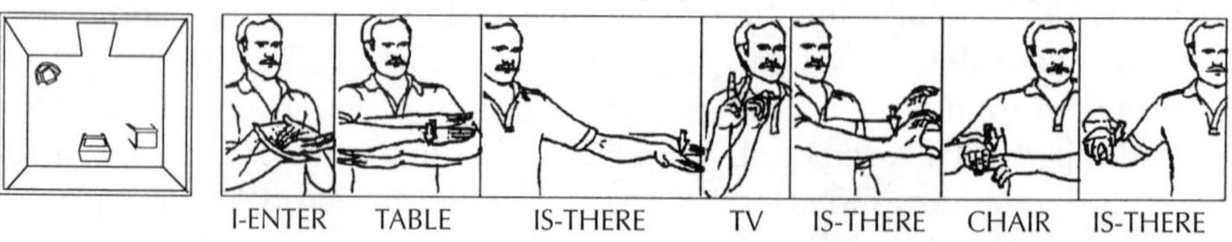

FIGURE 4. Example of an ASL spatial description using classifier constructions.

Thus, although the contrast is much less striking in ASL than in English, it still appears to hold.

Talmy (1983) has proposed several universal features that are associated with the figure object (i.e., the located object) and with the reference object or ground. For example, the figure tends to be smaller and more movable than the ground object. This asymmetry can be seen in the following sentences (from Talmy 1983):[5]

(1) a. The bike is near the house.
b. ?The house is near the bike.

In English, the figure occurs first, and the ground is specified by the object of the preposition. When a large unmovable entity such as a house is expressed as the figure, the sentence is semantically odd. This same asymmetry between figure and ground objects occurs in ASL, except that the syntactic order of the figure and ground is reversed compared to English, as shown in (2a) and (2b) (the subscripts indicate locations in space). In these examples, the classifier in the first phrase is held in space (indicated by the extended line) during the articulation of the second phrase (produced with one hand). In this way, the classifier handshape representing the figure can be located with respect to the classifier handshape representing the ground object, as illustrated in Figure 5 (the signer's left hand shows the classifier form for HOUSE; her right hand shows the classifier form for BIKE). The final classifier configuration is the same for either (2a) or (2b)—what differs is phrasal order.

(2)
a. HOUSE OBJECT-CLASSIFIER$_a$ ______________
BIKE VEHICLE-CLASSIFIER$_{near\ a}$

b. ?BIKE VEHICLE-CLASSIFIER$_a$ ______________
HOUSE OBJECT-CLASSIFIER$_{near\ a}$

Recently, I asked eight native signers[6] to describe a series of fifty-six pictures depicting simple relations between two objects (e.g., a dog under a chair, a car behind a tree). The signers almost invariably expressed the ground first, and then located the figure with respect to the ground object. This ordering may be an effect of the visual-spatial modality of sign language. For example, to present a scene visually through drawing, the ground tends to be produced first, and then the figure is located within that ground. Thus, when drawing a picture of a cup on a table, one generally would draw the table first and then the cup; rather than draw the cup in midair and then draw the table beneath it.[7] More crosslinguistic work will help determine whether the visual-spatial modality conditions all signed languages to prefer to initially express the ground and then the figure in locative constructions.

FIGURE 5.5. Final classifier configuration of either (2a) or (2b).

Talmy (1983) also argues that prepositions (for languages like English) ascribe particular geometries to figure and ground objects. He presents evidence that all languages characterize the figure's geometry much more simply than the ground. The figure is often conceived of as a simple point, whereas the ground object can have more complex geometric specifications. For example, Talmy argues that the English

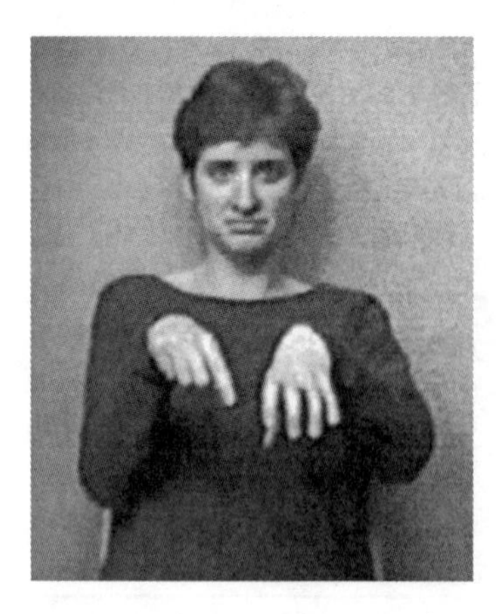

FIGURE 5.6. Final classifier construction for (3a). Final classifier construction for (3b).

prepositions *across, between, along, and among* all pick out different ground geometries. At first glance, it appears that there is no such asymmetry in ASL. For example, the classifier construction in (2a) for the ground (the house) does not appear to be more geometrically complex than the figure (the bike) with respect to specifications for shape (indicated by classifier handshape) or for spatial geometry. The locative expression in (2a) does not appear to have a linguistic element that differentially encodes figure and ground geometries in the way that prepositions do in spoken languages. Nonetheless, the grammar of ASL reflects that fact that signers conceive of the figure as a point with respect to a more complex ground. As shown in (3a) and (3b) and illustrated in Figure 6, expression of the figure can be reduced to a point, but expression of the ground cannot:

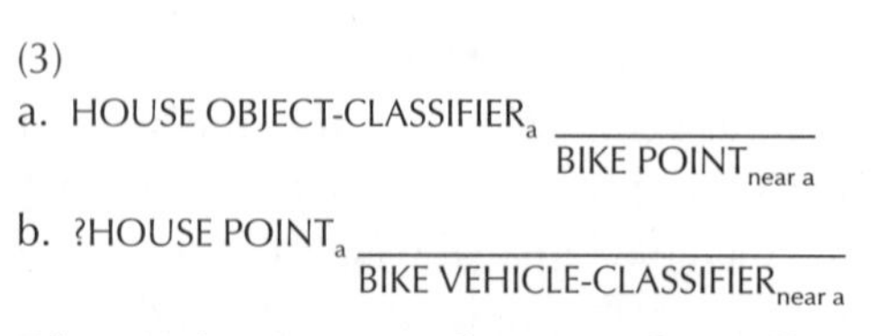

(3)

a. HOUSE OBJECT-CLASSIFIER$_{a}$ __________
BIKE POINT$_{near\ a}$

b. ?HOUSE POINT$_{a}$ ________________
BIKE VEHICLE-CLASSIFIER$_{near\ a}$

Thus Talmy's generalization about figure-ground complexity appears to hold even for languages that can use spatial geometry itself to encode spatial relations.

5.1.5 Frames of Reference

ASL can express spatial relations using an intrinsic, relative, or absolute frame of reference (see Levinson, Chapter 4, this volume, for discussion of the linguistic and spatial properties of these reference frames).[8] Within a relative frame of reference, scenes are most often described from the perspective of the person who is signing. In this case, the origin of the coordinate system is the viewpoint of the signer. For example, eight ASL signers were asked to describe the picture shown in Figure 7. All but one indicated that the bowl was on their left with the banana on their right (one signer provided a description of the scene without using signing space in a topographic way, producing the neutral phrase ON S-I-D-E instead). To indicate that the banana was on their right, signers produced the classifier form for bowl on the left side of signing space, and then a classifier form for banana was simultaneously articulated on the right.

Descriptions from the addressee's viewpoints[9] turn out to be more likely in the front-back dimension than in the left-right dimension (the signer's perspective is still the most likely for both dimensions). In describing the picture shown in Figure 8, five

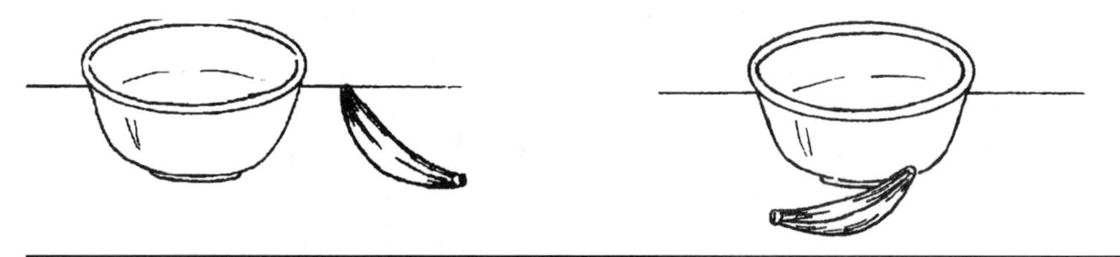

FIGURE 5.7. Illustration of one of the pictures that signers were asked to describe.

of eight signers preferred their own viewpoint and produced the classifier for banana near the chest with the classifier for bowl articulated away from the chest behind the classifier for banana, as shown in Figure 8a. This spatial configuration of classifier signs maps directly onto the view presented in Figure 8 (remember that you as the reader are facing both the signer and the picture). In contrast, three signers described the picture from the addressee's viewpoint, producing the classifier for bowl near the chest and the classifier for banana in line with the bowl but further out in signing space, as shown in Figure 8b. This configuration would be the spatial arrangement seen by an addressee standing opposite the signer (as you the reader are doing when viewing these figures). There were no overt linguistic cues that indicated which point of view the signer was adopting. However, signers were very consistent in what point of view they adopted. For example, when the signers were shown the reverse of Figure 8, in which the banana is behind the bowl, all signers reversed their descriptions according to the viewpoint they had selected previously. Note that the lack of an overt marker of point of view, the potential ambiguity, and the consistency within an adopted point of view also occur in English and other spoken languages (see Levelt 1984).

Bananas and bowls do not have intrinsic front/back features, and thus signers could not use an intrinsic frame of reference to describe these pictures. In contrast, cars do have these intrinsic properties, and the classifier form for vehicles encodes intrinsic features: the front of the car is represented roughly by the tips of the index and middle fingers, which are extended. Figures 9 and 10 illustrate ASL constructions using the vehicle classifier, along with the corresponding pictures of a car in different locations with respect to a tree. Again the majority of signers expressed their own view of the pic-

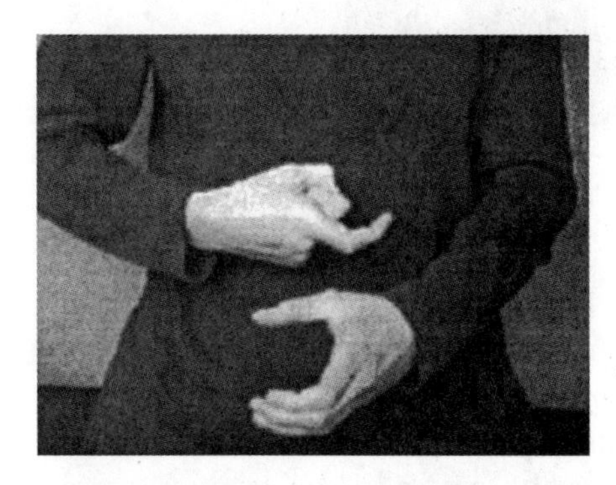

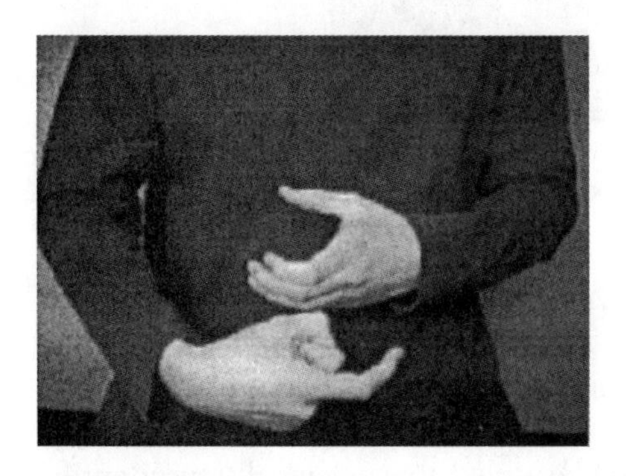

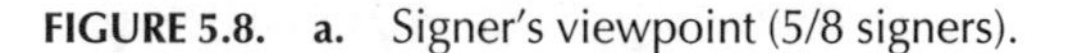

FIGURE 5.8. **a.** Signer's viewpoint (5/8 signers). **b.** Addressee's viewpoint (3/8 signers).

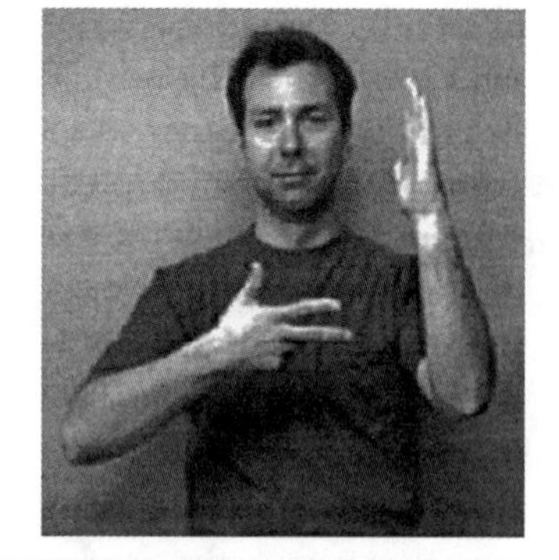

FIGURE 5.9. **a.** Signer's viewpoint (6/7 signers). **b.** Addressee's viewpoint (1/7).

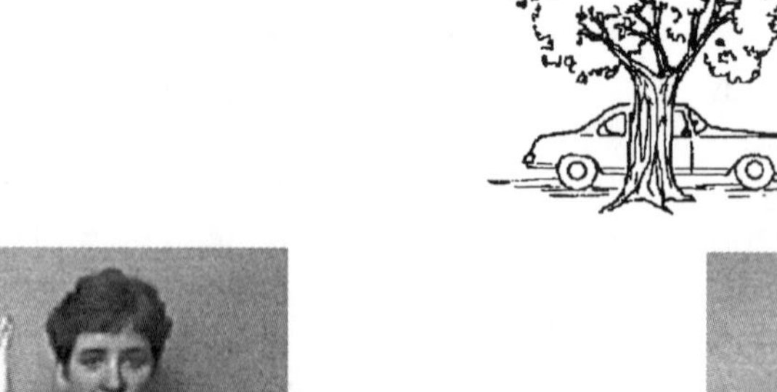

FIGURE 5.10. **a.** Signer's viewpoint (5/7 signers). **b.** Addressee's viewpoint (2/7 signers).

ture. In Figures 9 and 10, the pictured female signer adopts her own perspective (describing the picture as she sees it), while the male signer adopts the addressee's viewpoint. As noted above, lexical signs identifying the referents of the classifier signs are given first. Also as noted, the ground object (the tree) is expressed first and generally held in space while the lexical sign for car is articulated and the vehicle classifier is placed with respect to the classifier for tree. The illustrations in Figures 9 and 10 represent the final classifier construction in the description. As you can see, signers orient the vehicle classifier to indicate the direction the car is facing. Note that the orientation of the car is consistent with the point of view adopted—the vehicle classifier is always oriented toward the tree.[10] The majority of signers described Figure 9 by placing the vehicle classifier to their left in signing space. Only one signer placed the car on his right and the tree on his left. Again all signers were very consistent in which point of view they adopted, although one signer switched from her own viewpoint in describing Figure 9 to the addressee's viewpoint for Figure 10. There were no switches in viewpoint within either the left-right or front-back dimension. Signers were also consistent within the intrinsic frame of reference, almost always changing the orientation of the vehicle classifier appropriately (e.g., toward the left/right or away from/facing the signer).[11]

One question of interest is whether signers can escape the relative point of view that is imposed "automatically" by the fact that signers (and addressees) view their own articulators in space and these articulators express locative relations using this space. The answer appears to be that a relative framework is not necessarily entailed in locative expressions in ASL. That is, the expressions shown in Figure 9a and 9b could be interpreted as the rough equivalent of "the tree is in front of the car" without reference to the signer's (or addressee's) viewpoint. The car could actually be in any left-right or front-back relation with respect to the signer—what is critical to the intrinsic expression is that the vehicle classifier is oriented toward (facing) the tree. Thus the intrinsic frame of reference is not dependent upon the relative frame; in ASL these two frames of reference can be expressed simultaneously. That is, linguistic expression within an intrinsic frame occurs via the intrinsic properties of certain classifier forms, and a relative frame can be imposed simultaneously on signing space if a viewpoint is adopted by the signer. Figures 9 and 10 illustrate such simultaneous expression of reference frames. The linguistic and nonlinguistic factors that influence choice of viewpoint within a relative reference frame have not been determined, although it is likely that several different linguistic and nonlinguistic factors are involved. And just as in English (Levelt 1982a, 1984), frame of reference ambiguities can abound in ASL; further research will determine how addressee and signer viewpoints are established, altered, and disambiguated during discourse. Preliminary evidence suggests that, like English speakers (Schober 1993), "solo" ASL signers (such as those in this study) are less explicit about spatial perspective than signers with conversation partners.

Finally, ASL signers can use an absolute reference frame by referring to the cardinal points east, west, north, and south. The signs for these directions are articulated as follows: WEST: W handshape, palm in, hand moves toward left[12]; EAST: E handshape, palm out, hand moves toward right; NORTH: N handshape, hand moves up; SOUTH: S handshape, hand moves down.

N handshape: 

E handshape: 

S handshape: 

W handshape: 

These signs are articulated in this manner, regardless of where the person is standing, that is, regardless of true west or north. This situation contrasts sharply with how speakers gesture in cultures that employ absolute systems of reference such as certain Aboriginal cultures in Australia (see Levinson

1992b and Chapter 4, this volume). In these cultures, directional gestures are articulated toward cardinal points and vary depending upon where the speaker is oriented.

Although the direction of the citation forms of ASL cardinal signs is fixed, the movement of these signs can be changed to label directions within a "map" created in signing space. For example, the following directions were elicited from two signers describing the layout of a town shown on a map (from Taylor and Tversky 1992):

(4) YOU DRIVE — STRAIGHT (right hand traces a path outward from the signer) — EAST (E handshape traces the same path, palm to left)

"You drive straight eastward."

(5) UNDERSTAND MOUNTAIN R-D — PATH (right hand traces path toward left, near signer) — NORTH (N handshape traces same path, palm in near signer)

"Understand that Mountain Road goes north in this direction."

The signer who uttered (5) then shifted the map, such that north was centered outward from the signer, and the sign NORTH[13] then traced a path similar to the one in (4), that is, centered and outward from the signer. It appears that ASL direction signs are either fixed with respect to the body in their citation form or they are used relative to the space mapped out in front of the signer. As in English, it is the direction words themselves that pick out an absolute framework within which the discourse must be interpreted.

5.1.6 Narrative Perspective

In a narrative, a spatial frame of reference can be associated with a particular character (see discussions of viewpoint in Franklin, Tversky, and Coon 1992; and Tversky, Chapter 12, this volume). The frame of reference is relative, and the origin of the coordinate system is the viewpoint of that character in the story. The linguistic mechanisms used to express point of view in signed languages appear to be more explicit than in spoken languages. Both signers and speakers use linguistic devices to indicate whether utterances should be understood as expressing the point of view of the signer/speaker or of another person. Within narrative, "point of view" can mean either a visual perspective or the nonspatial perspective of a character, namely, that character's thoughts, words, or feelings. Spoken languages have several different devices for expressing either type of perspective: pronominal deixis (e.g., use of *I* vs. *you*), demonstratives (*here, there*), syntactic structure (active vs. passive), and literary styles (e.g., "free indirect" discourse). Signed languages use these mechanisms as well, but in addition, point of view (in either sense) can be marked overtly (and often continuously) by a "referential shift." Referential shift is expressed by a slight shift in body position and/or changes in eye gaze, head position, or facial expression (for discussions of this complex phenomenon, see Loew 1983; Engberg-Pedersen 1993; Padden 1986; Lillo-Martin 1995; Poulin and Miller 1995).

The following is an example of a referential shift that would require overt marking of a spatial viewpoint. Suppose a signer were telling a story in which a boy and a girl were facing each other, and to the left of the boy was a tall tree. If the signer wanted to indicate that the boy looked up at the tree, he or she could signal a referential shift, indicating that the following sentence(s) should be understood from the perspective of the boy. To do this, the signer would produce the sign LOOK-AT upward and to the left. If the signer then wanted to shift to the perspective of the girl, he or she would produce the sign LOOK-AT and direct it upward and to the *right.* Signers often express not only a character's attitudinal perspective, but also that character's spatial viewpoint through signs marked for location and/or deixis. Slobin and Hoiting (1994, p. 14) have noted that "directional deixis plays a key role in signed languages, in that a path verb moves not only with respect to source and goal, but also with respect to sender and receiver, as well as with respect to points that may be established in signing space to indicate the locations and viewpoints of protagonists set up in the discourse." That spoken languages express deixis and path through separate elements (either through two verbs or through a satellite expression and a verb) reflects, they suggest, an inherent limitation of spoken languages. That is, spoken language must linearize deictic and path information, rather than express this information simultaneously, as is easily done in signed languages. Deixis is easily expressed in signed languages because words are articulated in the space surrounding the signer, such that "toward" and "away from" can be encoded simply by the direction of motion with respect to the signer or a referential locus in space. I would further hypothesize that this simultaneous expression of deictic and other locative information within the verbs of signed languages may lead to habitual expression of spatial viewpoint within discourse.

In sum, signed languages use space in several different linguistic domains, including phonological contrast, coreference, and locatives. The visual-gestural modality of signed languages appears to influence the nature of grammatical encoding by compelling signed languages to prefer nonconcatenative morphological processes (see also Emmorey 1995; Supalla 1991; Gee and Goodhart 1988). Signed languages offer important insight into how different frames of reference are specified linguistically. A unique aspect of the visual-gestural modality may be that intrinsic and relative reference frames can be simultaneously adopted. In addition, shifts in reference are often accompanied by shifts in visual perspective that must be overtly marked on deictic and locative verbs. Although spoken languages also have mechanisms to express deictic and locative relations, what is unique about signed languages is that such relations are directly encoded in space.

5.2 SOME RAMIFICATIONS OF THE DIRECT REPRESENTATION OF SPACE

In the studies reported below, I explore some possible ramifications of the spatial encoding of locative and spatial contrasts for producing spatial descriptions and solving spatial problems. Specifically, I investigate (1) how ASL signers use space to express spatial commands and directions, (2) to what extent signers use lexicalized locatives in spatial directions, (3) whether the use of sign language provides an advantage for certain spatial tasks, and (4) how differences in linguistic encoding between English and ASL affect the nature of spatial commands and directions.

5.2.1 Solving Spatial Puzzles with Spatialized Language

To investigate these questions, ten hearing English speakers and ten deaf ASL native signers were compared using a task in which they had to solve three spatial puzzles by instructing an experimenter,[14] where to place blocks of different colors, shapes, and sizes onto a puzzle grid (see Figure 11). To solve the problem, all blocks must fit within the puzzle outline. The data from English speakers were collected by Mark St. John (1992), and a similar but not identical protocol was used with ASL signers. English

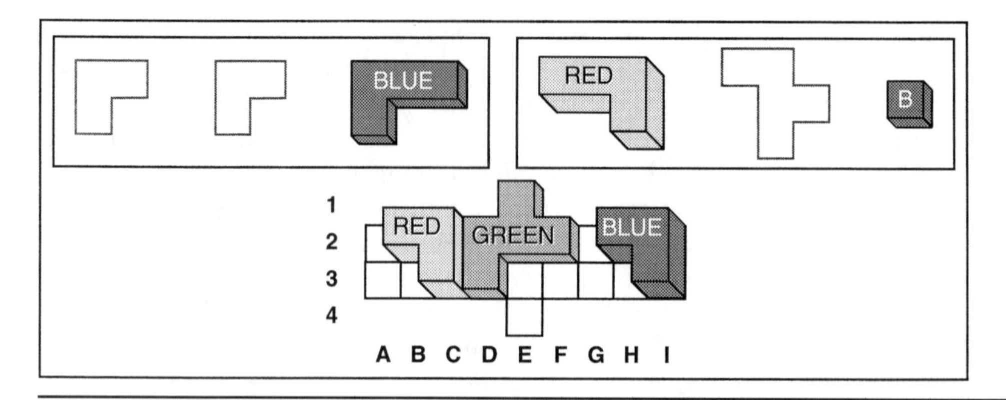

FIGURE 5.11. Solving a spatial puzzle: Subjects describe how to place blocks on a puzzle grid.

speakers were instructed to sit on their hands and were not permitted to point to the puzzle or to the pieces. Of course, ASL signers could use their hands, but they were also not permitted to point to the pieces or puzzle. For both signers and speakers, the subject and experimenter sat side by side, such that each had the same visual perspective on the puzzle board.

To explore how speakers and signers use spatial language—encoded in either space or sound—we examined different types of English and ASL instructions. We hypothesized that ASL signers may be able to use signing space as a rough Cartesian coordinate system, and therefore would rely less on the coordinates labeled on the puzzle board. This prediction was confirmed: 67% of the English speakers' commands referred to the puzzle grid, whereas only 28% of the commands given by ASL signers referred to the puzzle coordinates. This difference in grid reference was statistically reliable [$F(1,18) = 9.65; p < .01$]. The following are sample commands containing references to the puzzle grid given by English speakers:

(6) Take the blue L piece and put it on H1 H2 G2.

(7) Place the red block in 3G H 2G.

(8) Green piece on El, E2, D2, C2, and D3.

Instead of referring to grid coordinates, ASL signers used space in various ways to indicate the positions on the puzzle board—for example, by tracing a distinctive part of the board in space or by holding the nondominant hand in space, representing a part of the puzzle board (often an edge).

We also compared how signers and speakers identified the puzzle pieces to be placed for a given command (see Figure 12a). There were no significant differences in how either ASL or English was used to label a particular block. We had hypothesized that signers might make more references to shape because shape is often encoded in classifier handshapes (see discussion above). However, the numerical difference seen in Figure 12a was not statistically significant. Language did not appear to influence how subjects labeled the puzzle pieces within this task.

There were significant differences, however, in the types of commands used by ASL signers and English speakers (see Figure 12b). Puzzle commands could be exhaustively divided into three categories: (1) commands referring to a *position* on the puzzle board, (2) commands expressing a *relation* between two pieces, and (3) the *orientation* of a single piece. These categories were able to account for all of the com-

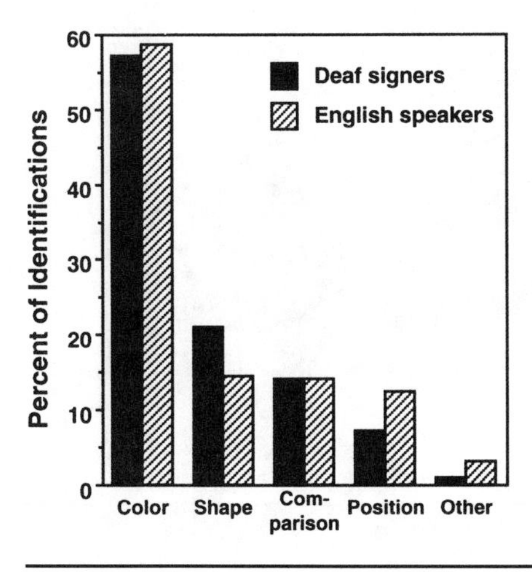

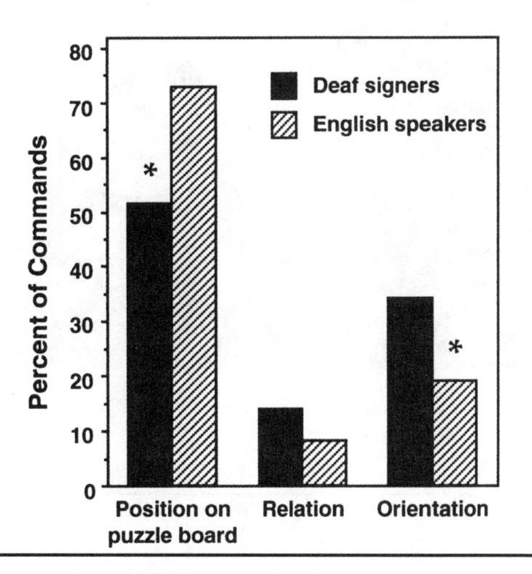

FIGURE 5.12. **a.** Type of puzzle piece identification. **b.** Type of command reference.

mands given by the twenty subjects. The only difference was that in ASL, two command types could be expressed simultaneously. For example, signers could simultaneously describe the orientation of a piece (through the orientation of a classifier handshape) and that piece's relation to another block through two-handed classifier constructions (see Figure 15, as well as the constructions illustrated in Figures 5, 9, and 10).

English speakers produced significantly more commands referring to a position on the puzzle board compared to ASL signers [$F(1,18) = 4.47$; $p < .05$]. English speakers' reliance on commands involving coordinate specifications (see examples [6]–[8]) appears to account for this difference in command type. It is interesting to note that even when ASL signers referred to grid coordinates, they often specified these coordinates within a vertical spatial plane, signing the letter coordinates moving crosswise and the number coordinates moving downward. Thus the true horizontal plane of the board laying on the tabletop was "reoriented" into a vertical plane within signing space, as if the puzzle board were set upright. The linguistic and pragmatic constraints on using a vertical versus horizontal plane to represent spatial layouts are yet to be determined, but clearly use of a vertical plane does not necessarily indicate a true vertical relation between objects. Subjects did not differ significantly in the percentage of commands that referred to the relation of one piece to another. Examples of English relation commands are given in (9)–(1 1):

(9) Put the other blue L next to the green one.

(10) Put it to the left of the green piece.

(11) Switch the red and the blue blocks.

ASL signers also produced these types of commands, but generally space, rather than prepositional phrases, conveyed the relation between pieces. For example, the nondominant hand can represent one block, and the dominant hand either points to a spatial locus to the left or right (somewhat like the construction illustrated in Figure 6a) or the dominant hand represents another block and is positioned with respect to the nondominant hand (see Figure 15).

Finally, ASL signers produced significantly more commands that referred to the orientation of a puzzle piece [$F(1, 18) = 5.24$; $p < .05$]. Examples from English

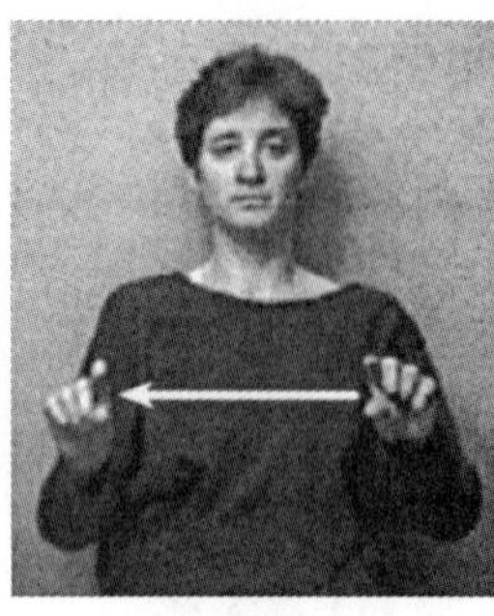

GREEN CL:G ________
CL:G-*orientation*
"Orient the green block in this way." See green block in figure 5.11; note signer's perspective.

FIGURE 5.13.

of commands referring to orientation are given in (12)–(14):

(12) Turn the red one counterclockwise.

(13) Rotate it 90 degrees.

(14) Flip it back the other way.

For English speakers, a change in orientation was often inferred from where the piece had to fit on the board, given other non-orientation-specific commands. In contrast, ASL signers often overtly specified orientation. For example, Figure 13 illustrates an ASL command that indicates a change in orientation by tracing a block's ultimate orientation in signing space (the vertical plane was often used to trace shape and orientation). Figure 14 illustrates a command in which orientation change is specified by a change in the orientation of the classifier handshape itself. Figure 15 illustrates the simultaneous production of a command indicating the orientation of an L-shaped piece and its relation to another piece. Signers also used the sign ROTATE quite often and indicated the direction of rotation by movement of the wrist (clockwise vs. counterclockwise).

ASL also has a set of lexicalized locative signs that are used much less frequently than classifier constructions in spatial descriptions. The lexicalized locatives that were produced by signers in this study included IN, ON, AGAINST, NEAR, and BETWEEN.

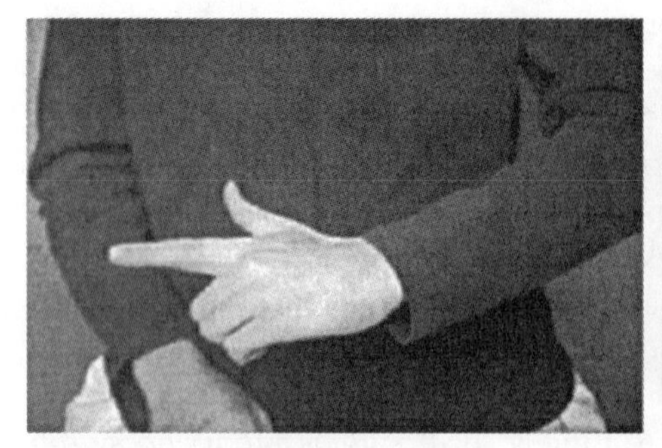

BLUE L CL:L-*orientation*
"Move the blue L so it is oriented with the long end outward."

FIGURE 5.14.

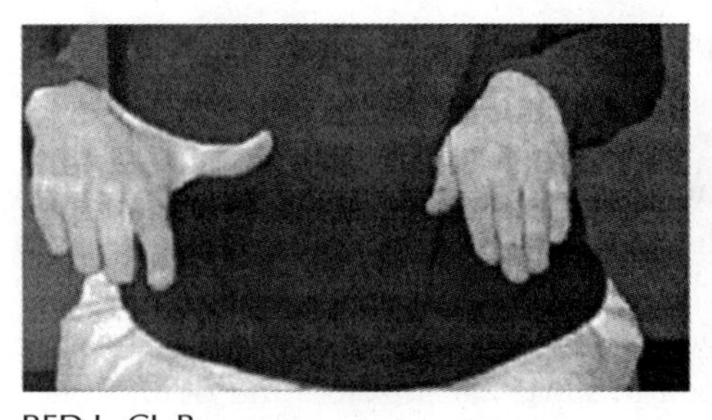
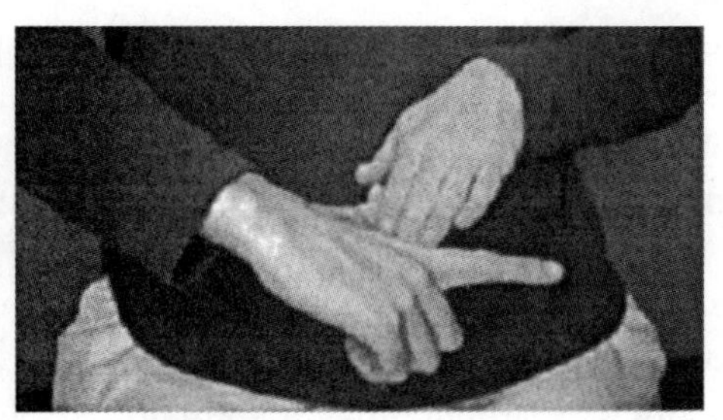

RED L CL:B ______________
CL:L-*orientation*
"Move the blue L so it is oriented with the long end outward."

FIGURE 5.15.

Only about 20% of ASL commands involved lexical locatives, and these were almost always produced in conjunction with commands involving classifier constructions. The grammatical structure of these forms is not well understood—are they adpositions (see McIntire 1980) or verbs (see Shepard-Kegl 1985)—and their semantics has not been well studied either (see McIntire 1980 for some discussion of IN, UNDER, and OUT). The linguistic data from our study provided some interesting insight into the semantics of IN and ON (these signs are shown in Figure 16).

English speakers used the prepositions *in* and *on* interchangeably to specify grid coordinates, for example, "in G2 H2" or "on G2 H2" (see sample commands 6 and 7 above). ASL signers used the lexical locative ON in this context, but never IN:

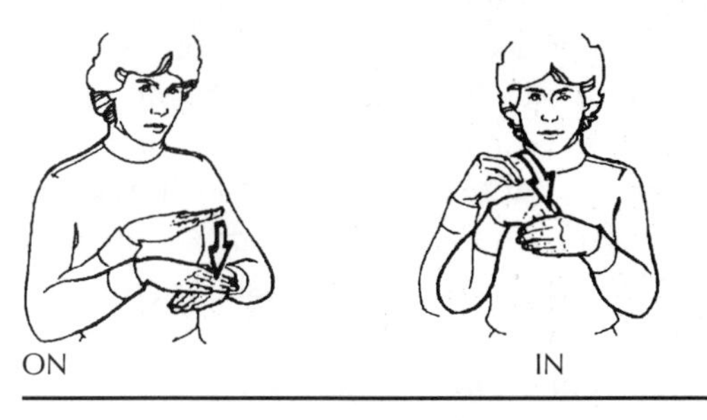

FIGURE 5.16. ASL lexicalized locative signs. Illustration by Frank Allen Paul in Newell (1983).

(15) PUT RED 1 ON G2 H2 I2 I3

(16) PUT BLUE [CL:G—*shape*][15] ON 3E 4F 3F 3G
shape traced in
vertical plane

(17) *PUT RED 1 IN G2 H2

The use of the preposition *in* for describing grid positions on the puzzle board falls under Herskovitz's (1986) category "spatial entity in area," namely, "the reference object must be one of several areas arising from a dividing surface" (p. 153). This particular semantic structure does not appear to be available for the ASL sign IN. Signers did use IN when aspects of the puzzle could be construed as container-like (falling under Herskovitz's "spatial entity in a container"). For example, signers would direct pieces to be placed IN CORNER;[16] in this case, two lines meet to form a type of container (see Herskovitz 1986, 149). IN was also used when a block (most often the small blue square) was placed in a "hole" created by other blocks on the board or when a part of a block was inserted into the part of the puzzle grid that stuck out (see Figure 11). In both cases, the reference object forms a type of container into which a block could be placed. The use of the ASL lexical locative IN appears to be more restricted than English *in*, applying only when there is a clear containment relation.

One might conjecture that the iconicity of the sign IN renders its semantics transparent—one hand represents a container, and the other locates an object within it. However, iconicity can be misleading. For example, the iconic properties of ON might lead one to expect that its use depends upon a support relation, with the nondominant hand representing the support object. The data from our experiment, however, are not compatible with this hypothesis. ASL signers used ON when placing one block next to and contacting another block (e.g., the red piece ON the green in Figure 11):

(18) RED MOVE [CL:G—*orientation*] ON GREEN
new orientation traced in horizontal plane

"Move the red one so that it is oriented lengthwise next to the green."

(19) RED [(CL:G–shape] THAT-ONE ROTATE
shape traced in upper horizontal plane; clockwise to lower left

[CL:L—*orientation*] ON GREEN
[CL:B–*reference obj.*]
L classifier (right hand) oriented and positioned with respect to B classifier (left hand) as in Figure 5.15

"Rotate that red L-shaped block clockwise so that it is oriented lengthwise at the top of the green."

English speakers never produced commands relating one block to another using only the preposition *on*. Given the nature of the puzzle, subjects never said "put the red block on the green one." The support requirements described by Herskovitz for *on* in English do not appear to apply to the lexical locative glossed as ON in ASL. This difference in semantic structure highlights the difficulties of transcribing one language using glosses of another (see also discussion in Shepard-Kegl 1985). English *on* is not equivalent in semantics or syntax to ASL ON (see Bowerman, Chapter 10, this volume, for further discussion of language variation and topological concepts).

Finally, the ability to linguistically represent objects and their orientations in space did not provide signers with an advantage on this complex spatial task. Signers and speakers did not differ in the number of moves required to solve the puzzles nor in the number of commands within a move. In addition, ASL signers and English speakers did not differ significantly in the time they took to solve the puzzles, and both groups appeared to use similar strategies in solving the puzzle. For example, subjects tended to place the most constraining piece first (the green block shown in Figure 11).

In summary, English speakers and ASL signers differed in the nature of the spatial commands that they used for positioning objects. Signers used both vertical and horizontal planes of space itself as a rough Cartesian coordinate system. Changes in object orientation were expressed directly through changes in the spatial position of classifiers and by tracing shape and orientation in signing space. In contrast, English speakers were less likely to overtly express changes in orientation and relied heavily on direct reference to labels for coordinate positions. The heart of this different use of spatial language appears to lie in the properties of the aural-vocal and visual-manual linguistic modalities. For example, in ASL, the hands can directly express orientation by their own orientation in space—such direct representation within the linguistic signal is not available to English speakers. Finally, ASL and English differ in the semantics they assign to lexicalized locatives for the topological concepts *in* and *on*, and the semantic structure of the ASL locatives cannot be extracted from the iconic properties of the forms. In the following study, we further explore the effect modality may exert on the nature of spatial language for both spoken and signed language.

5.2.2 Room Description Study

Eight ASL signers and eight English speakers were asked to describe the layout of objects in a room to another person ("the manipulator") who had to place the objects (pieces of furniture) in a dollhouse.[17] In order to elicit very specific instructions and to eliminate (or vastly reduce) interchanges, feedback, and interruptions, "the describer" (the person giving the instructions) could not see the manipulator, but the manipulator could see the describer through a one-way mirror (see Figure 17). The manipulator could not ask questions but could request that the describer pause or produce a summary. Subjects described six rooms with canonical placements of furniture ("normal rooms") and six rooms in which the furniture had been strewn about haphazardly without regard to function ("haphazard rooms"). The linguistic data and analysis arising from this study are discussed elsewhere (Emmorey, Clothier, and McCullough). However, certain results emerged from the study that illuminate some ramifications of the direct representation of space for signed languages.

Signers were significantly faster than speakers in describing the rooms [$F(1,14)$ 5.00; $p < .05$; see Figure 18a]. Mean description time for ASL signers was 2 min, 4 sec; English speakers required an average of 2 min, 48 sec to describe the same rooms. In one way, the speed of the signers' descriptions is quite striking because, on average, ASL signs take twice as long as English words to articulate (Klima and Bellugi 1979; Emmorey and Corina 1990). However, as we have seen thus far in our discussion of spatial language in ASL, there are several modality-specific factors that would lead to efficient spatial descriptions and lessen the need for discourse linearization (Levelt 1982a,b), at least to some degree. For example, the two hands can represent two objects simultaneously through classifier handshapes, and the orientation of the hands can also simultaneously represent the objects' orientation. The position of the hands in space represents the position of the objects with respect to each other. The simultaneous expression of two objects, their position, and their orientation stands in contrast to the linear strings of prepositions and adjunct phrases that must be combined to express the same information in English.

The difference in description time was not due to a speed-accuracy trade-off. Signers and speakers produced equally accurate descriptions, as measured by the percent of furniture placed correctly by the manipulators in each group (see Figure 18b). There

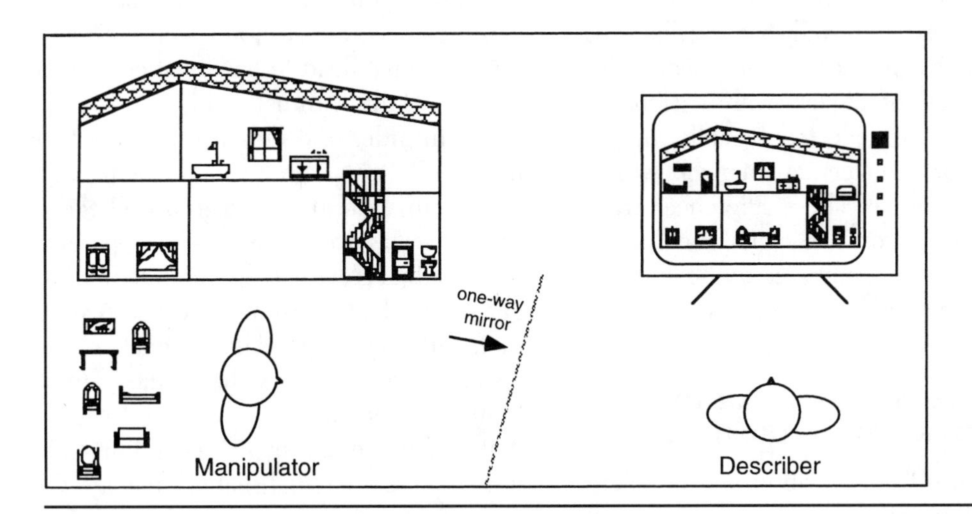

FIGURE 5.17. Experimental set-up for room descriptions.

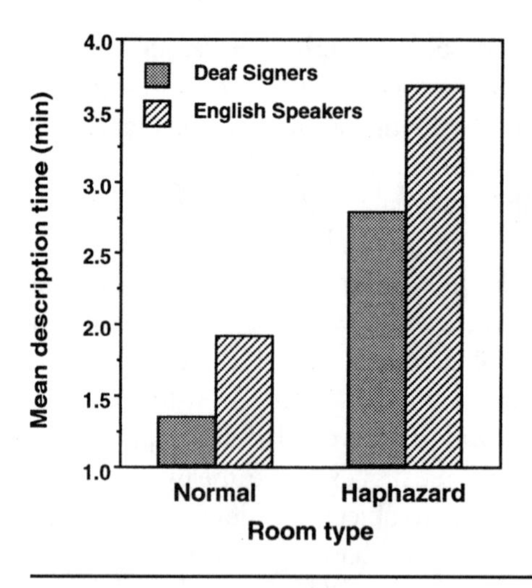

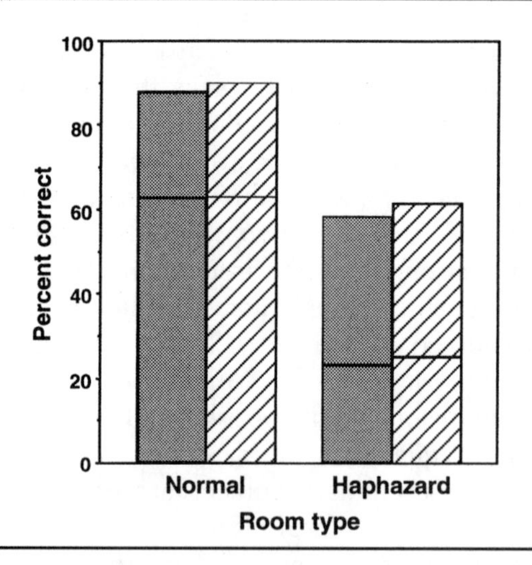

FIGURE 5.18. **a.** Dollhouse room description. **b.** Accuracy of manipulators.

was no significant difference in percent correct, regardless of whether a lenient scoring measure was used (object misplaced by more than 3 cm or misoriented by 45 degrees; represented by height of the bars in Figure 18b) or a strict scoring measure was used (object misplaced by 1 cm or misoriented by 15 degrees; shown by the line in each bar in Figure 18b).

To summarize, this second study suggests that the spatialization of American Sign Language allows for relatively rapid and efficient expression of spatial relations and locations. In the previous study, we saw that ASL signers and English speakers focused on different aspects of objects within a spatial arrangement, as reflected by differing instructions for the placement of blocks within a coordinate plane. These differences arise, at least in part, from the spatial medium of signed languages, compared to the auditory transmission of spoken languages.

5.3 INTERPLAY BETWEEN SPATIALIZED LANGUAGE AND SPATIAL COGNITION

We now turn to the relation between general nonlinguistic spatial cognition and processing a visual-spatial linguistic signal. Does knowing a signed language have any impact on nonlinguistic spatial processing? In a recent investigation, Emmorey, Kosslyn, and Bellugi (1993) examined the relation between processing ASL and the use of visual mental imagery. Specifically, we examined the ability of deaf and hearing subjects to mentally rotate images, to generate mental images, and to maintain images in memory (this last skill will not be discussed here). We hypothesized that these imagery abilities are integral to the production and comprehension of ASL and that their constant use may lead to an enhancement of imagery skills within a non-linguistic domain. In order to distinguish the effects of using ASL from the effects of being deaf from birth, we also tested a group of hearing subjects who were born to deaf parents. These subjects learned ASL as their first language and have continued to use ASL in their daily lives. If these hearing native signers have visual-spatial skills similar to those found for deaf signers, this would suggest that differences in spatial cognition arise from the use of a visual-spatial language. On the other hand, if these signers have visual-spatial skills similar to those found in hearing subjects, this would suggest that differences in spatial cognition may be due to auditory deprivation from birth.

We hypothesized that mental rotation may play a crucial role in sign language processing because of the changes in spatial perspective that can occur during referential shifts in narrative (see above) and the shifts in visual perspective that occur between signer and addressee. As discussed earlier, during sign comprehension the perceiver (i.e., the addressee) often must mentally reverse the spatial arrays created by the signer such that, for example, a spatial locus established on the right of the person signing (and thus on the left of the addressee) is understood as on the right in the scene being described by the signer (see Figures 9a and 10a). Because scenes are most often described from the signer's perspective and not the addressee's, this transformation process may occur frequently. The problem is not unlike that facing understanders of spoken languages who have to keep in mind the directions "left" and "right" with regard to the speaker. The crucial difference for ASL is that these directions are encoded spatially by the signer. The spatial loci used by the signer to depict a scene (e.g., describing the position of objects and people) must therefore be understood as the reverse of what the addressee actually *observes* during discourse (assuming a face to face interaction). Furthermore, in order to understand and process sign, the addressee must perceive the reverse of what they themselves would produce. Anecdotally, hearing subjects have great difficulty with this aspect of learning ASL; they do not easily transform a signer's articulations into the reversal that must be used to produce the signs. Given these linguistic processing requirements, we hypothesized that signers would be better than hearing subjects at mentally rotating imaged objects and making mirror image judgments. To test this hypothesis, we used a task similar to the one devised by Shepard and Metzler (1971) in which subjects were shown two forms created by juxtaposing cubes to form angular shapes. Subjects were asked to decide whether the two shapes were the same or mirror images, regardless of orientation (see Figure 19).

Our results support the hypothesis that use of ASL can enhance mental rotation skills (see the top illustration in Figure 19); both deaf and hearing signers had faster reaction times compared to nonsigners at all degrees of rotation. Note that the slopes for the angle of rotation did not differ between signing and nonsigning groups, and this indicates that signers do not actually rotate images faster than nonsigning subjects. Emmorey, Kosslyn, and Bellugi (1993) originally suggested that ASL signers may be faster in detecting mirror reversals, particularly because they were faster even when no rotation was required (i.e., at zero degrees). However, recent research by Ilan and Miller (1994)[18] indicates that different processes may be involved when mirror-same judgments are made at zero degrees within a mental rotation experiment, compared to when mental rotation is not required on any of the trials. In addition, preliminary results from Emmorey and Bettger indicate that when native ASL signers and hearing nonsigners are asked to make mirror-same judgments in a comparison task that does not involve mental rotation, these groups do not differ in accuracy or reaction time. The faster response times exhibited by signers on the mental rotation task may reflect faster times to initiate mental rotation or faster times to generate a mental image (as suggested by the next experiment). Finally, the finding that hearing native signers performed like deaf signers indicates that enhancement on this mental rotation task is

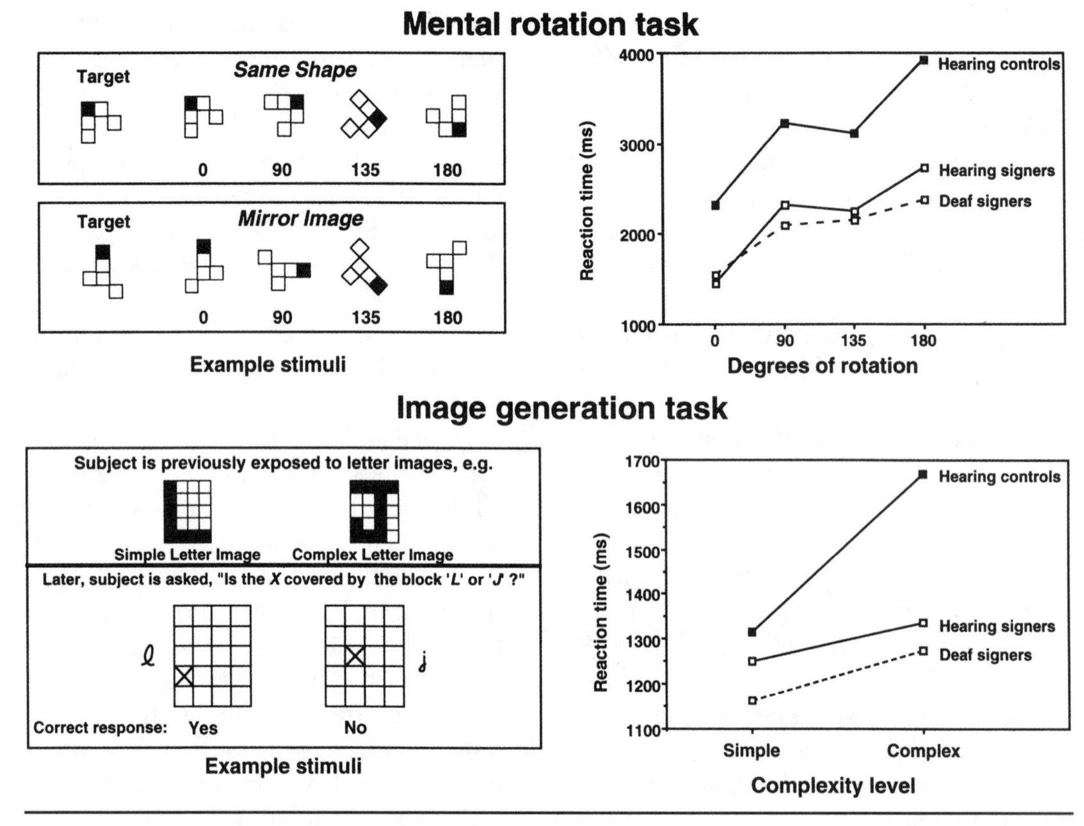

FIGURE 5.19. Illustration of the mental rotation and image generation tasks used by Emmorey et al. (1993).

not a consequence of auditory deprivation. Rather, it appears to be due to experience with a visual language whose production and interpretation may involve mental rotation (see also Talbot and Haude 1993).

Another visual imagery skill we investigated was the ability to generate mental images, that is, the ability to create an image (i.e., a short-term visual memory representation) on the basis of information stored in long-term memory (see Kosslyn et al. 1985). In ASL, image generation may be an important process underlying aspects of referential shift. Liddell (1990) argues that under referential shift, signers may imagine referents as physically present, and these visualized referents are relevant to the expression of verb agreement morphology. Liddell gives the following example involving the verb ASK which is lexically specified to be directed at chin height (see Figure 20):

> To direct the verb ASK toward an imagined referent, the signer must conceive of the location of the imaginary referent's head. For example, if the signer and addressee were to imagine that Wilt Chamberlain was standing beside them ready to give them advice on playing basketball, the sign ASK would be directed upward toward the imaged height of Wilt Chamberlain's head (Figure [20a]). It would be incorrect to sign the verb at the height of the signer's chin (Figure [20b]). This is exactly the way agreement works when a referent is present. Naturally, if the referent is imagined as laying down, standing on a chair,

a. addressee-ASK-imagined tall referent

b. * addressee-ASK-imagined tall referent

FIGURE 5.20. Agreement verbs and referents imagined as present. Illustration from Liddell (1990).

> etc., the height and direction of the agreement verb reflects this. Since the signer must conceptualize the location of body parts of the referent imagined to be present, there is a sense in which an invisible body is present. The signer must conceptualize such a body in order to properly direct agreement verbs. (Liddell 1990, 184)

If deaf subjects are in fact generating visual images prior to or during sign production, then the speed of forming these images would be important, and we might expect signers to develop enhanced abilities to generate images. The image generation task we used is illustrated at the bottom of Figure 19. Subjects first memorized uppercase block letters and then were shown a series of grids (or sets of brackets) that contained an X mark. A lowercase letter preceded each grid, and subjects were asked to decide as quickly as possible whether the corresponding uppercase block letter would cover the X if it were in the grid. The crucial aspect of the experiment was that the probe mark appeared in the grid only 500 ms after the lowercase cue letter was presented. This was not enough time for the subjects to complete forming the letter image; thus response times reflect in part the time to generate the image. Kosslyn and colleagues have used this task to show that visual mental images are constructed serially from parts (e.g., Kosslyn et al. 1988; Roth and Kosslyn 1988). Subjects tend to generate letter images segment by segment in the same order that the letter is drawn. Therefore, when the probe X is covered by a segment that is generated early (e.g., on the first stroke of the letter *F*), subjects have faster reaction times, compared to when the probe is located under a late-imaged segment. Crucially, this difference in response time based on probe location is not found when image generation is not involved, that is, when both the probe X and letter (shaded gray) are physically present.

Our results indicated that both deaf and hearing signers formed images of complex letters significantly faster than nonsigners (see Figure 19). This finding suggests that experience with ASL can affect the ability to mentally generate visual images. Results from a perceptual baseline task indicated that this enhancement was due to a difference in image generation ability, rather than to differences in scanning or inspection—signers and nonsigners did not differ in their ability to evaluate probe marks when the shape was physically present. The signing and nonsigning subjects were equally accurate, which suggests that although signers create complex images faster than nonsigners, both groups generate equally good images. Furthermore, deaf and hearing subjects appeared to image letters in the same way: both groups of subjects required more time and made more errors for probes located on late-imaged segments, and these effects were of comparable magnitude in the two groups. This result indicates that neither group of subjects generated images of letters as complete wholes, and both groups imaged segments in the same order. Again, the finding that hearing signers performed similarly to deaf signers suggests that their enhanced image generation ability is due to experience with ASL, rather than to auditory deprivation.

This research establishes a relation between visual-spatial imagery within linguistic and nonlinguistic domains. Image generation and mental rotation appear to be deeply embedded in using ASL, and these are not processes that must obviously be involved in both visual imagery and ASL perception. Note that these experiments have focused on ASL processing; whether there is a more direct relation in sign language between linguistic *representations* (e.g., conceptual structure, see Jackendoff, Chapter 1, this volume) and spatial representations is a topic for future research.

5.4 NEURAL CORRELATES FOR SIGNED AND SPOKEN LANGUAGES

Finally, sign language exhibits properties for which each of the cerebral hemispheres of hearing people shows different predominant functioning. In general, the left hemisphere has been shown to subserve linguistic functions, whereas the right hemisphere is dominant for visual-spatial functions. Given that ASL expresses linguistic functions by manipulating spatial contrasts, what is the brain organization for sign language? Is sign language controlled by the right hemisphere along with many other visual-spatial functions or does the left hemisphere subserve sign language as it does spoken language? Or is sign language represented equally in both hemispheres of the brain? Howard Poizner, Ursula Bellugi, and Edward Klima have shown that the brain honors the distinction between language and nonlanguage visual-spatial functions (Poizner, Klima, and Bellugi 1987; Bellugi, Poizner, and Klima 1989). Despite the visual-spatial modality of signed languages, linguistic processing occurs primarily within the left hemisphere of deaf signers, whereas the right hemisphere is specialized for nonlinguistic visual-spatial processing in these signers. Poizner, Bellugi, and Klima have shown that damage to the left hemisphere of the brain leads to sign aphasias similar to classic aphasias observed in speaking patients. For example, adult signers with left-hemisphere damage may produce "agrammatic" signing, characterized by a lack of morphological and syntactic markings and often accompanied by halting, effortful signing. An agrammatic signer will produce single-sign utterances that lack the grammatically required inflectional movements and use of space (see discussion above). In contrast, right-hemisphere damage produces impairments of many visual-spatial abilities, but does not produce sign language aphasias. When given tests of sign language comprehension and production (e.g., from the Salk Sign Aphasia Exam; Poizner, Klima, and Bellugi 1987), signers with right-hemisphere damage perform normally, but these same signers show marked impairment on nonlinguistic tests of visual-spatial functions. For example, when given a set of colored blocks and asked to assemble them to match a model (the WAIS blocks test), right-hemisphere-damaged signers have great difficulty and are unable to capture the overall configuration of the block design. Similar impairments on this task are found with hearing, speaking subjects with right-hemisphere damage.

Poizner, Klima, and Bellugi (1987) also reported that some signing patients with right-hemisphere damage show a selective impairment in their ability to use space to express spatial relations in ASL, for example when describing the layout of furniture in their room or apartment. Their descriptions are not ungrammatical, but they are incorrect when compared to the actual layout of objects. One hypothesis for this dysfunction following right-hemisphere damage is that, unlike spoken language, ASL requires that the cognitive representation of spatial relations be recovered from and instantiated within a spatialized linguistic encoding (i.e., cognitive spatial relations map to space, not to sound). Evidence supporting this hypothesis comes from a bilingual hearing patient with right-hemisphere damage studied by David Corina and colleagues (Corina et al. 1990; Emmorey, Corina, and Bellugi 1995; Emmorey, Hickok, and Corina 1993). The data from this case suggest that there may be more right-hemisphere involvement when processing spatial information encoded within a linguistic description for signed compared to spoken languages.

The case involves female patient D.N.,[19] a young hearing signer (age 39), bilingual in ASL and English, who was exposed to ASL early in childhood. She underwent surgical evacuation of a right parietal-occipital hematoma and an arteriovenous malformation. Examination of a magnetic resonance imaging (MRI) scan done six months after the surgery revealed a predominantly mesial superior occipital-parietal lesion. The superior parietal lobule was involved, while the inferior parietal lobule was spared, although some of the deep white matter coming from this structure may also be involved. The comparison test between English and ASL spatial commands (see below and Figure 21)

English instruction:
"The pencil is on the paper."
D.N.'s correct response to English instruction

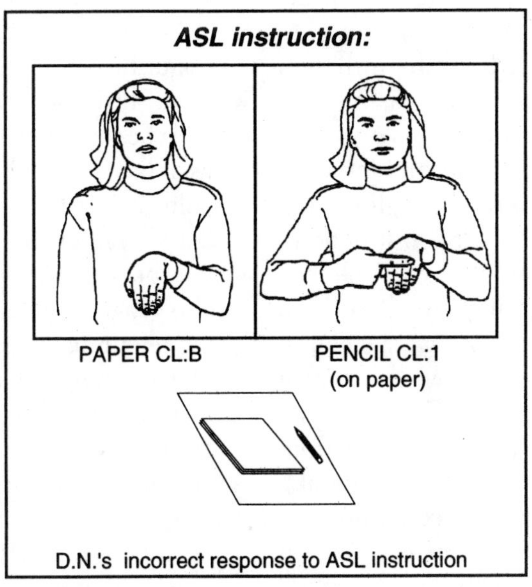

FIGURE 5.21. Illustration of an RHD patient's differential performance in comprehending English versus ASL spatial commands (the lexical signs PAPER and PENCIL are not shown).

was conducted by Corina approximately one year after D.N.'s surgery.

D.N. was not aphasic for either English or ASL. Her performance on the Salk Sign Diagnostic Aphasia Exam was excellent, and she showed no linguistic deficits for English. Nevertheless, she exhibited a striking dissociation between her ability to comprehend and produce spatial descriptions in English compared to ASL. Although her English description had no evident spatial distortions, she was impaired in her ability to describe the spatial layout of her room using ASL. Her ASL description showed a marked disorganization of the elements in the room. Her attempts to place one set of objects in relation to others were particularly impaired, and she incorrectly specified the orientation and location of items of furniture (see also Emmorey, Corina, and Bellugi 1995).

Corina (1989) developed a specific set of tasks to investigate D.N.'s comprehension of locative relations in English and ASL. One of these tasks required D.N. to set up real objects in accordance with spatial descriptions given in either English or in ASL. An example of a simple English instruction would be "The pen is on the paper." The English and ASL instructions along with D.N.'s responses are illustrated in Figure 21. D.N. correctly interprets the English command, but fails with the ASL instructions. This particular example was elicited through informal testing by Corina in which the same instructions were given in both English and ASL. D.N. was later given 36 different spatial commands (18 in English and 18 in ASL) which involved from two to four objects (e.g., cup, pen, book). The instructions were matched for number of spatial relations that were encoded in each language. When D.N. was given instructions in English to locate objects with respect to one another, she performed relatively well—83% correct. Her score was worse than her normal age-matched bilingual control (100% correct), but better than other right-hemisphere-damaged subjects who were given the English test (69% correct). However, when presented with similar information in ASL—in which spatial relations are presented topographically in sign space—D.N. made many more spatial errors, scoring only 39% correct. This result is particularly striking, given the iconicity of the ASL descriptions (see Figure 21).

We hypothesize that the dissociation between D.N.'s comprehension of English and ASL spatial commands arises because of the highly specific spatial realization of ASL classifier constructions. That is, spatial relations must be recovered from a visual-spatial signal in which much more information is encoded about the relative position and orientation of objects, compared to English. Furthermore, the requirement of reading off spatial relations directly from the orientation and position of classifier signs in space may make additional demands on spatial cognitive processes within the right hemisphere. D.N.'s comprehension impairment is not linguistic per se, but stems from the fact that linguistic information about spatial relations must be recovered from a representation that itself is spatialized; D.N. does not have difficulty understanding ASL spatial contrasts that do not encode information about location or orientation. Thus the case of D.N. also bears on our earlier discussion concerning referential versus topographic functions of space in ASL. D.N. exhibits a dissociation between the use of signing space as a linguistic device for marking sentence-level referential distinctions and the use of signing space as a topographic mapping device (see Emmorey et al. 1995 for a complete discussion of this dissociation and for additional evidence from language-processing experiments with normal ASL signers).

In conclusion, signed languages offer a unique window into the relation between language and space. All current evidence indicates that signed languages are constrained by the same principles that shape spoken languages. Thus far, there is no evidence that signed languages grammaticize different aspects of the spatial world compared to spoken languages (see Supalla 1982). What is different and unusual about signed languages is their visual-spatial form—the fact that space and movement can be used to linguistically represent space and movement in the world. This chapter has explored the ramifications of this spatialized encoding for the nature of linguistic structure, for language processing, for spatial cognition in general, and for the neural substrate of sign language. Future research might include investigations of the following: (1) the semantic and grammatical structure of locative constructions in different sign languages (how do sign languages vary in the way they utilize physical space to represent topological and other spatial concepts?); (2) when and how signing children acquire locative vocabulary (what is the developmental relation between spatial cognition and sign language acquisition? See Mandler, Chapter 9, this volume, and Bowerman, Chapter 10, this volume, for discussion of spatial cognition and spoken language acquisition); (3) spatial attention in sign language perception and nonlinguistic visual-spatial perception (do signers show differences in spatial attention that could be attributed to experience with sign language?); (4) how signers build spatial mental models (does signing space operate like a diagram? See Johnson-Laird, Chapter 11, this volume); and (5) the neural substrate and psychological mechanisms that underlie the mapping between a linguistic signal (both signed and spoken) and an amodal spatial representation. These are only some of the areas in which the study of sign language could enhance our understanding of the relation between language and space.

ACKNOWLEDGMENTS

This work was supported by National Institutes of Health grants ROI DC 00201, ROI DC 00146, and R37 HD 13249. I thank David Corina, Greg Hickok, and Ed Klima for many insightful discussions about the issues presented here. Merrill Garrett and Mary Peterson provided valuable comments on an earlier draft of this chapter. I also thank Bonita Ewan and Steve McCullough, who were my primary language consultants and who were the sign language models for the figures. Mark Williams helped create many of the figures in this chapter. Finally, I am particularly grateful to the Gallaudet University students who participated in these studies.

NOTES

1. Words in small capital letters represent English glosses for ASL signs. The gloss represents the meaning of the unmarked, unmodulated root form of a sign. A subscripted word following a sign gloss indicates that the sign is made with some regular change in form associated with a systematic change in meaning, and thus indicates grammatical morphology in ASL (e.g., $\text{GIVE}_{\text{habitual}}$). Multiword glosses connected by hyphens are used when more than one English word is required to translate a single sign (e.g., LOOK-AT). Subscripts are used to indicate spatial loci; nouns, pronouns, and agreeing verbs are marked with a subscript to indicate the loci at which they are signed (e.g. INDEX_{a}, BITE_{b}). Classifier forms are abbreviated CL, followed by the handshape of the classifier and a description of the meaning in italics (CL:G—*shape*). Descriptions of how a classifier sign is articulated may be given underneath the gloss. English translations are provided in quotes.
2. Some signs such as personal pronouns may not be specified in the lexicon for location (see Lillo-Martin and Klima 1990; Liddell 1994).
3. Other terms that have been used for these verbs are *indicating* (Liddell 1995) and *inflecting* (Padden 1988).

4. Whether subject is associated with the beginning or end of the verb's movement depends upon the class of verb (cf. "backwards" verbs, Padden 1988; Brentari 1988).
5. Following traditional linguistic typography, a question mark (?) indicates that a sentence is considered marginal; a star (*) indicates that the sentence is unacceptable.
6. In this study, native signers were deaf individuals who were exposed to ASL from birth.
7. The example of drawing was suggested to me by Dan Slobin, who has made similar arguments about scene setting and the effect of modality on signed languages (Slobin and Hoiting 1994).
8. Sign linguists often use "frame of reference" in a nonspatial sense, referring to anaphoric reference in a discourse (see especially Engberg-Pedersen 1993).
9. The addressee is assumed to be facing the signer. Signers described these pictures to a video camera rather than to an actual addressee. In understanding this discussion of point of view in ASL, it might be useful for you the reader to imagine that you and the signer viewed the display from the same vantage point, and now the signer is facing you (the addressee) to describe it.
10. It should be noted that occasionally a signer may ignore the orientation features of the vehicle classifier, say, pointing the vehicle classifier toward the tree classifier, when in actual fact the car is facing away from the tree. This may occur when it is difficult to produce the correct orientation, say, pointing the vehicle classifier to the right with the right hand, palm out (try it).
11. There were only six examples (out of thirty-five) in which a signer ignored the orientation of the car because it was awkward to articulate. Also, signers did not always alternate which hand produced the classifier for TREE, as might be implied by Figures 9 and 10.
12. Except for the sign LEFT, WEST is perhaps the only sign that is specified as moving toward the signer's left rather than toward the "nondominant side." For both left- and right-handers, the sign WEST moves toward the left, and the sign EAST moves toward the right. The direction of movement is fixed with respect to the signer's left and right, unlike other signs. For example, right- and left-handers would articulate the signs illustrated in Figure 1, which also move across the body, with opposite directions of motion (left to right vs. right to left, respectively). However, there is some change in articulation for left-handers, perhaps due to phonological constraints. For EAST and WEST the orientation of the palm is reversed: outward for WEST and inward for EAST. This change in palm orientation also occurs when a right-handed signer articulates EAST or WEST with the left hand (switches in hand dominance are phonologically and discourse governed).
13. When the signs NORTH and SOUTH are used to label paths within a spatial map, they often retain some of their upward and downward movement.
14. This study was conducted in collaboration with Shannon Casey; the experimenter was either a native speaker of English (for the English subjects) or a deaf ASL signer (for the deaf subjects).
15. This is not an orientation command but a shape description, namely, a classifier construction in which the shape of the blue puzzle piece is traced in the vertical plane (see Figure 13 for an example).
16. CORNER is a frozen classifier construction produced with nominal movement (Supalla and Newport 1978). The sign can be articulated at various positions in space to indicate where the corner is located (e.g., top left or bottom right).
17. This study was conducted with Marci Clothier and Stephen McCullough.
18. I thank Mary Peterson for bringing this work to my attention.
19. Poizner and Kegl (1992) also discuss this patient, but use the pseudonym initials A.S.

REFERENCES

Battison, R. (1978). *Lexical borrowing in American Sign Language.* Silver Spring, MD: Linstok Press.

Bellugi, U., Poizner, H., and Klima, E. S. (1989). Language, modality, and the brain. *Trends in Neurosciences,* 10, 380–388.

Brentari, D. (1988). Backwards verbs in ASL: Agreement re-opened. In *Papers from the Parasession on Agreement in Grammatical Theory,* vol. 24, no. 2, 16–27. Chicago: Chicago Linguistic Society.

Brown, P. (1991). Spatial conceptualization in Tzeltal. Working paper no. 6, Cognitive Anthropology Research Group, Max Planck Institute for Psycholinguistics, Nijmegen.

Corina, D. (1989). Topographic relations test battery for ASL. Unpublished manuscript, Salk Institute for Biological Studies, La Jolla, CA.

Corina, D., Bellugi, U., Kritchevsky, M., O'Grady-Batch, L., and Norman, F. (1990). Spatial relations in signed versus spoken language: Clues to right parietal functions. Paper presented at the Academy of Aphasia, Baltimore.

Corina, D., and Sandler, W. (1993). On the nature of phonological structure in sign language. *Phonology, 10,* 165–207.

Coulter, G. R., and Anderson, S R. (1993). Introduction to G. R. Coulter (Ed.), *Phonetics and phonology: Current issues in ASL phonology.* San Diego, CA: Academic Press.

Emmorey, K., and Corina, D. (1990). Lexical recognition in sign language: Effects of phonetic structure and morphology. *Perceptual and Motor Skills, 71,* 1227–1252.

Emmorey, K., Corina, D., and Bellugi, U. (1995). Differential processing of topographic and referential functions of space. In K. Emmorey and J. Reilly (Eds.), *Language, gesture, and space,* 43–62. Hillsdale, NJ: Erlbaum.

Emmorey, K., Hickok, G., and Corina, D. (1993). Dissociation between topographic and syntactic functions of space in ASL. Paper presented at the Academy of Aphasia Meeting, Tucson, AZ, October.

Emmorey, K., Kosslyn, S. M., and Bellugi, U. (1993). Visual imagery and visual-spatial language: Enhanced imagery abilities in deaf and hearing ASL signers. *Cognition, 46,* 139–181.

Engberg-Pedersen, E. (1993). *Space in Danish Sign Language: The semantics and morphosyntax of the use of space in a visual language.* International Studies on Sign Language Research and Communication of the Deaf, vol. 19. Hamburg: Signum.

Franklin, N., Tversky, B., and Coon, V. (1992). Switching points of view in spatial mental models. *Memory and Cognition, 20*(5), 507–518.

Gee, J., and Goodhart, W. (1988). American Sign Language and the human biological capacity for language. In M. Strong (Ed.), *Language learning and deafness,* 49–74. New York: Cambridge University Press.

Herskovits, A. (1986). *Language and spatial cognition: An interdisciplinary study of the prepositions in English.* Cambridge: Cambridge University Press.

Ilan, A. B., and Miller, J. (1994). A violation of pure insertion: Mental rotation and choice reaction time. *Journal of Experimental Psychology: Human Perception and Performance.* 20(3), 520–536.

Janis, W. (1995). A crosslinguistic perspective on ASL verb agreement. In K. Emmorey and J. Reilly (Eds.), *Language, gesture, and space,* 195–224. Hillsdale, NJ: Erlbaum.

Klima, E. S., and Bellugi, U. (1979). *The signs of language.* Cambridge, MA: Harvard University Press.

Kosslyn, S. M., Brunn, J. L., Cave, K. R., and Wallach, R. W. (1985). Individual differences in mental imagery ability: A computational analysis. *Cognition, 18,* 195–243.

Kosslyn, S., Cave, K., Provost, D., and Von Gierke, S. (1988). Sequential processes in image generation. *Cognitive Psychology, 20,* 319–343.

Landau, B., and Jackendoff, R. (1993). "What" and "where" in spatial language and spatial cognition. *Behavioral and Brain Sciences, 16,* 217–238.

Levelt, W. (1982a). Cognitive styles in the use of spatial direction terms. In R. Jarvella and W. Klein (Eds.), *Speech, place, and action,* 251–268. New York: Wiley.

Levelt, W. (1982b). Linearization in describing spatial networks. In S. Peters and E. Saarinen (Eds.), *Processes, beliefs, and questions,* 199–220. Dordrecht: Reidel.

Levelt, W. (1984). Some perceptual limitations on talking about space. In A. J. van Doorn, W. A. van de Grind, and J. J. Koenderink (Eds.), *Limits in perception,* 323–358. Utrecht: VNU Science Press.

Levinson, S. (1992a). Vision, shape, and linguistic description: Tzeltal body-part terminology and object descriptions. Working paper no. 12, Cognitive Anthropology Research Group, Max Planck Institute for Psycholinguistics, Nijmegen.

Levinson, S. (1992b). Language and cognition: The cognitive consequences of spatial description in Guugu Yimithirr. Working paper no. 13, Cognitive Anthropology Research Group, Max Planck Institute for Psycholinguistics, Nijmegen.

Liddell, S. (1990). Four functions of a locus: Reexamining the structure of space in ASL. In C. Lucas (Ed.), *Sign language research: Theoretical issues,* 176–198. Washington, DC: Gallaudet University Press.

Liddell, S. (1993). Conceptual and linguistic issues in spatial mapping: Comparing spoken and signed languages. Paper presented at the Phonology and Morphology of Sign Language Workshop, Amsterdam, August.

Liddell, S. (1994). Tokens and surrogates. In I. Ahlgren, B. Bergman, and M. Brennan (Eds.), *Perspectives on sign language structure.* Durham, UK: ISLA.

Liddell, S. (1995). Real, surrogate, and token space: Grammatical consequences in ASL. In K. Emmorey and J. Reilly (Eds.), *Language, gesture, and space,* 19–42. Hillsdale, NJ: Erlbaum.

Lillo-Martin, D. (1991). *Universal grammar and American sign language: Setting the null argument parameters.* Dordrecht: Kluwer.

Lillo-Martin, D. (1995). The point of view predicate in American Sign Language. In K. Emmorey and J. Reilly (Eds.), *Language, gesture, and space,* 155–170. Hillsdale, NJ: Erlbaum.

Lillo-Martin, D., and Klima, E. (1990). Pointing out differences: ASL pronouns in syntactic theory. In S.-D. Fischer and P. Siple (Eds.), *Theoretical issues in sign language research,* vol. 1, 191–210. Chicago: University of Chicago Press.

Loew, R. (1983). Roles and reference in American Sign Language: A developmental perspective. Ph.D. diss., University of Minnesota.

McIntire, M. (1980). Locatives in American Sign Language. Ph.D. diss., University of California, Los Angeles.

Meier, R. (1991). Language acquisition by deaf children. *American Scientist,* 79, 60–70.
Newell, W. (Ed.) (1983). *Basic sign communication.* Silver Spring, MD: National Association of the Deaf.
Newport, E., and Meier, R. (1985). The acquisition of American Sign Language. In D. I. Slobin (Ed.), *The Crosslinguistic study of language acquisition.* Vol. 1, *The data,* 881–938. Hillsdale, NJ: Erlbaum.
Padden, C. (1986). Verbs and role-shifting in ASL. In C. Padden (Eds.), *Proceedings of the Fourth National Symposium on Sign Language Research and Teaching,* 44–57. Silver Spring, MD: National Association of the Deaf.
Padden, C. (1988). *Interaction of morphology and syntax in ASL.* Garland Outstanding Dissertations in Linguistics, ser. 4. New York: Garland. 1983 Ph.D. diss., University of California, San Diego.
Padden, C. (1990). The relation between space and grammar in ASL verb morphology. In C. Lucas (Ed.), *Sign language research: Theoretical issues,* 118–132. Washington, DC: Gallaudet University Press.
Poizner, H., and Kegl, J. (1992). Neural basis of language and motor behavior: Perspectives from American Sign Language. *Aphasiology,* 6(3), 219–256.
Poizner, H., Klima, E. S., and Bellugi, U. (1987). *What the hands reveal about the brain.* Cambridge, MA: MIT Press.
Poulin, C., and Miller, C. (1994). On narrative discourse and point of view in Quebec Sign Language. In K. Emmorey and J. Reilly (Eds.), *Language, gesture, and space,* 117–132. Hillsdale, NJ: Erlbaum.
Roth, J., and Kosslyn, S. M. (1988). Construction of the third dimension in mental imagery. *Cognitive Psychology,* 20, 344–361.
Sandler, W. (1989). *Phonological representation of the sign: Linearity and nonlinearity in American Sign Language.* Dordrecht: Foris.
Schober, M. (1993). Spatial perspective taking in conversation. *Cognition,* 47, 1–24.
Shepard, R., and Metzler, J. (1971). Mental rotation of three-dimensional objects. *Science, 171,* 701–703.
Shepard-Kegl, J. (1985). Locative relations in American Sign Language word formation, syntax, and discourse. Ph.D. diss., Massachusetts Institute of Technology.
Slobin, D., and Hoiting, N. (1994). Reference to movement in spoken and signed languages: Typological considerations. *Proceedings of the Nineteenth Annual Meeting of the Berkeley Linguistic Society,* 1–19. Berkeley, CA: Berkeley Linguistics Society.
St. John, M.–F. (1992). Learning language in the service of a task. In *Proceedings of the Fourteenth Annual Conference of the Cognitive Science Society.* Hillsdale, NJ: Erlbaum.
Supalla, S. (1991). Manually coded English: The modality question in signed language development. In P. Siple and S. D. Fischer (Eds.), *Theoretical issues in sign language research,* vol. 2, 85–109. Chicago: University of Chicago Press.
Supalla, T. (1982). Structure and acquisition of verbs of motion and location in American Sign Language. Ph.D. diss., University of California, San Diego.
Supalla, T., and Newport, E. (1978). How many seats in a chair? The derivation of nouns and verbs in American Sign Language. In P. Siple (Ed.), *Understanding language through sign language research,* 91–132. New York: Academic Press.
Talbot, K. F., and Haude, R. H. (1993). The relationship between sign language skill and spatial visualization ability: Mental rotation of three-dimensional objects. *Perceptual and Motor Skills,* 77(3), 1387–1391.
Talmy, L. (1983). How language structures space. In H. Pick and L. Acredolo (Eds.), *Spatial orientation: Theory, research, and application.* New York: Plenum Press.
Talmy, L. (1988). The relation of grammar to cognition. In B. Rudzka-Ostyn (Ed.), *Topics in cognitive linguistics,* 165–207. Amsterdam: Benjamins.
Taylor, H., and Tversky, B. (1992). Spatial mental models derived from survey and route descriptions. *Journal of Memory and Language, 31,* 261–292.
Wilbur, R. (1987). *American Sign Language: Linguistic and applied dimensions.* Boston: Little, Brown.
Winston, E. (1995). Spatial mapping in comparative discourse frames. In K. Emmorey and J. Reilly (Eds.), *Language, gesture, and space,* 87–114. Hillsdale, NJ: Erlbaum.

A Class of Determiners in ASL

June Zimmer and Cynthia Patschke

This paper examines a particular class of pointing signs in ASL. It will be shown that this class of signs is distinct from other pointing signs in several ways. The analysis provided here gives support to the idea that these signs act as determiners.

Sign language researchers who discuss pointing signs in ASL have arrived at diverse conclusions as to their syntactic, semantic, and pragmatic functions. Lacy (1973) finds that signers establish referents in particular locations in signing space and use pointing signs that act as pronouns to reference these locations. O'Malley (1975) distinguishes two types of pronouns: deictic, which refer to objects that are physically present; and anaphoric, which refer to objects that are not actually present.

Mandel (1977) and Wilbur (1979) propose that the pronoun is the point in space rather than the pointing gesture, and that the pointing gesture merely indicates which referent is meant. However, most researchers (Coulter 1977; Liddell 1980; Pettito 1983; Padden 1983) agree that these signs do function as pronouns. Liddell (1980) has shown that they appear in the syntactic positions reserved for subjects and objects, thus acting in the same way as personal pronouns in spoken languages like English.

Freidman (1975) speaks of these signs in terms of "proforms," which are used to achieve all pronominal, most locative, and some temporal references. Edge and Herrman (1977) and Hoffmeister (1977) also use the term "proforms." Edge and Herrman state that proforms can reference people, objects, time, and locations. Like Mandel (1977) and Wilbur (1979), they claim that the pointing sign merely functions as an indicator rather than a lexical item. In their view, the proforms consist of locations in space or of "markers," which can take the form of the signer's body or hand "which are understood or explicity labeled to take on the identity of referents" (1977, 142). Hoffmeister (1978), on the other hand, calls the pointing sign itself the proform and says that it functions as a personal pronoun, a demonstrative pronoun, or a prolocative.

Several researchers (Liddell 1980; Padden 1983; Aramburo 1986) have studied pointing signs used as locatives. Ingram (1978) notes that the pointing of the finger is one of the many possible markers for ASL topics. Hoffmeister (1977, 1978) and Wilbur (1979) briefly mention that pointing signs also function as determiners.

From this discussion it is obvious that descriptions of the forms and uses of pointing gestures are diverse and ambiguous. One might assume from the literature that one sign performs many different functions, and that this sign is made by pointing to a particular location in neutral space. However, a close examination indicates that

Source. Reprinted by permission of the publisher, from C. Lucas, ed., *Sign Language Research: Theoretical Issues*, (1990): 201–210. Washington, DC: Gallaudet University Press.

pointing signs constitute several different lexical items.

This paper focuses on a class of pointing signs that are phonologically and syntactically distinguished from other pointing signs. The analysis and discussion support the notion that this class of signs act as determiners.

METHODOLOGY

The data for this project come from two main sources. The first set comes from videotape recordings of ten deaf native signers of ASL. The tapes were transcribed using a system of written English glosses, and drawings were made to document the various forms pointing signs could take.

The second set of data comes from work with several deaf informants. The time spent with the informants was mainly used to elicit particular types of data, to ask specific questions, and to check hypotheses. These data were collected in the form of notes in which ASL signs were recorded using English glosses.

In the analysis of these written transcripts and notes, each occurrence of a pointing sign was described according to its phonological form, placement in a clause or phrase, signs preceding or following it, and apparent meaning and function.

PHONOLOGICAL ANALYSIS

Although the pointing signs mentioned in the literature are composed of a variety of movements, locations, and orientations, the category of signs examined in this paper is quite restricted in form. The vast majority of these signs point slightly upward (see Figure 1). These signs, made with the nondominant hand, are often simultaneous with a sign on the dominant hand. In this case, they are sometimes lowered (see Figure 2).

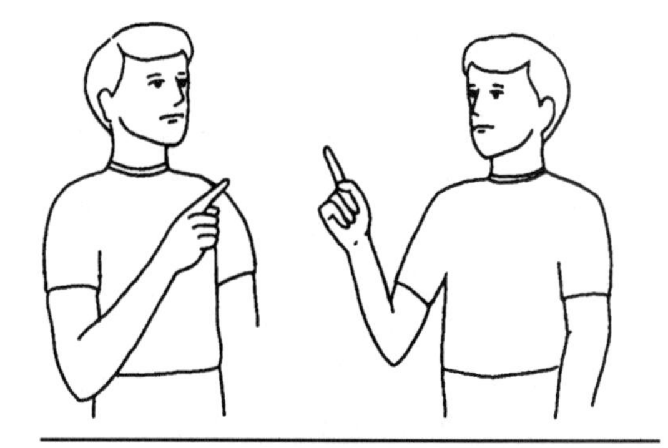

FIGURE 1. Pointing signs on dominant hand.

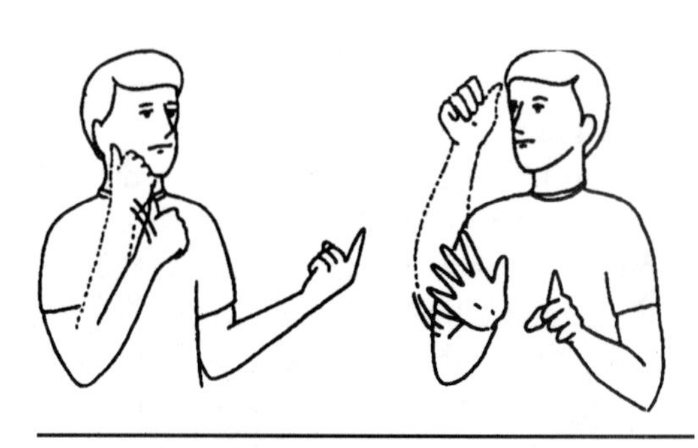

FIGURE 2. Pointing signs on nondominant hand simultaneously produced with sign on dominant hand.

Eye gaze is variable, sometimes remaining on the addressee, sometimes following the direction of the point.

These signs are phonologically distinct from other pointing signs with arcing or jabbing movements. Aramburo (1986) describes varying forms of locative pointing signs, all of which involve an arcing movement. Other pointing signs in our data have a jabbing movement, which is often repeated. Neither of these classes of pointing signs will be discussed here. This paper focuses on signs that move slightly or not at all, never arc or jab, and most often point slightly upward.

SYNTACTIC ANALYSIS

A large corpus of signs with this particular phonological form were analyzed according to their syntactic function. It soon became apparent that these signs could be divided into two syntactic categories: pronouns and determiners.[1]

The use of pointing signs as pronouns has been well documented, but will be briefly reviewed here. Pronominalization in ASL has been said to involve the indexing of a particular area in signing space. A pointing sign acting as a pronoun is distinguished by its function and by its placement within a clause. In ASL, the first-person-singular pronoun is signed with the tip of the index finger moving to make contact with the chest (transcribed as PRO.1). Describing the syntactic function of this pronoun helps to identify other pronouns in ASL, and to help discriminate them from other uses of pointing signs. Examples 1 and 2 are examples of first-person-singular pronouns.

(1) PRO.1 CL:PICK-UP-PIECES
"I picked up the pieces."

(2) NEVER SEE BOY BREAK-INTO-TEARS FOR PRO.1
"I'd never seen a boy burst out crying over me."

The pronouns all stand alone. In accordance with the definition of pronouns, they are "noun phrases of the simplest possible structure, which, as a rule, allow neither premodification nor postmodification" (Aarts and Aarts 1982, 49). ASL pronouns function in a similar way to English pronouns, except that there is no gender marking or case marking.

Pointing signs acting as pronouns are shown in sentences 3 and 4. (Henceforth [p.s.] will be used to indicate a pointing sign.)

(3) [p.s.] COOK THAT GREEN CL:SMALL-CYLINDER
"He cooked celery."

(4) PRO.1 LIKE [p.s.]
"I liked him."

In accordance with the definition of third-person pronouns, these signs can be replaced by the noun phrase for the person, place, or thing to which they refer. The pointing sign constitutes the whole noun phrase. This is illustrated in the phrase structure trees of sentences 3 and 4 (see Figure 3).

Many of the pointing signs in this corpus do not act as pronouns. A pronoun, as mentioned above, must stand alone in a nounphrase. However, pointing signs sometimes occur with nouns rather than replacing them, as in sentences 5 and 6.

(5) [p.s.] GIRL ALL-DAY WORK
"The girl worked all day long."

(6) OTHER MAN [p.s.] STEAL
"The other man had stolen it."

The data collected for this study are consistent with the notion put forward by Hoffmeister (1977) and Wilbur (1979) that

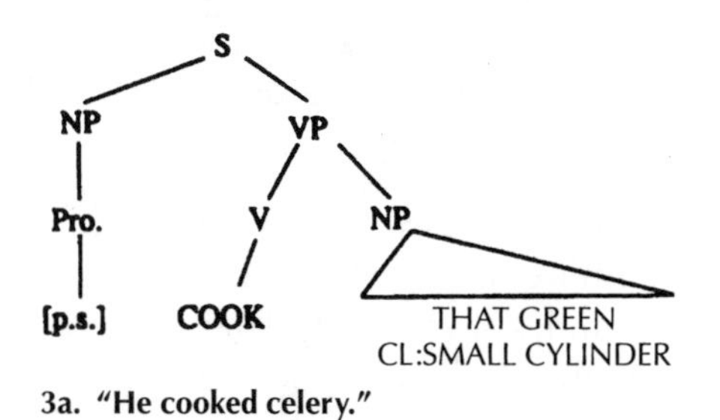

3a. "He cooked celery."

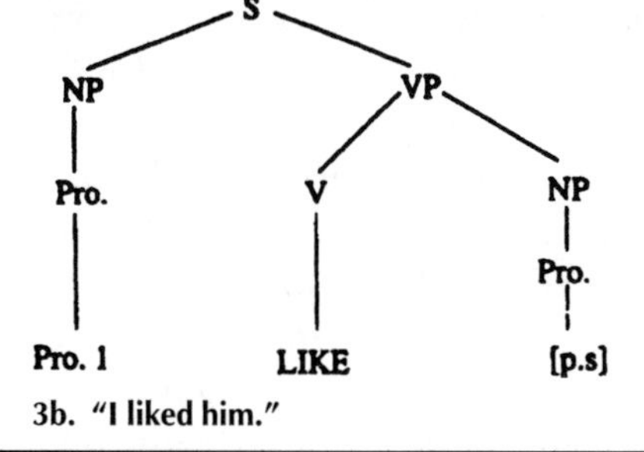

3b. "I liked him."

FIGURE 3. Phrase structure trees for "He cooked celery" and "I liked him."

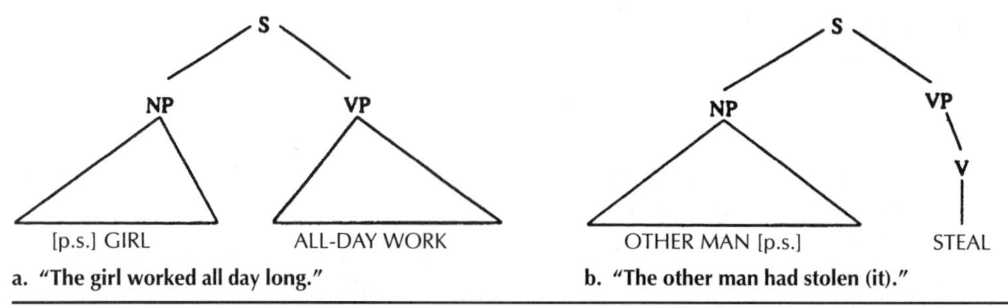

FIGURE 4. Tree diagrams indicating pointing signs.

pointing signs may act as determiners. The tree diagrams of sentences 5 and 6 indicate that the pointing sign, together with the noun, constitutes the noun phrase (see Figure 4).

POINTING SIGNS AS DETERMINERS

Since the pointing signs discussed above occur with nouns in noun phrases, they serve to modify nouns. They don't contain a great deal of semantic content nor do they describe nouns. Thus they do not function as adjectives. When asked why these signs were being used, the informants stated that they "specify" the noun. These observations indicate that these signs function as some type of determiner.

In English, determiners are usually considered to include the articles "a" and "the," the demonstrative pronouns ("this," "that," "these," and "those"), possessive pronouns, and quantifiers like "any," "other," "some," "none," etc. (Stockwell, Schachter, and Partee 1973; Huddleston 1984; Givon 1984). They help "determine" which object is being referred to. Determiners can be either definite or indefinite. The factors that dictate whether a definite or an indefinite determiner will be used have not been fully described. However, it is generally agreed that a definite determiner is used when the interlocutor can be expected to be able to locate a referent (for example, "the girl," "that book," "my mother") because such a determiner is anaphoric (makes reference to prior discourse) or deictic (makes reference to an entity that is present). An indefinite determiner will be used when the particular referent cannot be identified (for example, "a girl," "some books," "anyone's mother"). A noun phrase in English can contain up to three determiners as in "all her many friends" (Huddleston 1984).

The data examined for this study support Wilbur's (1979) claim that pointing determiners may occur before, after, or simultaneously with a noun, as in sentences 7 through 10: (Pointing determiners will be labeled "DET" throughout the rest of the paper.)

(7) Before the noun
SEE DET GIRL
"He saw a girl."

(8) After the noun
OTHER SISTER DET COME
"The other sister came over."

(9) Simultaneously with the noun
SAME MAN/DET CL:ONE PERSON-MOVES-TOWARD-ANOTHER
"The same man was walking towards her."

As in English, ASL permits more than one determiner to occur in a noun phrase. Many examples of a pointing determiner occurring with other signs that act as determiners, such as OTHER and THAT, were found in these data, as in sentence 10:[2]

(10) OTHER MAN DET THAT^DET ENTER
"The other man, that one, came in."

Wilbur (1979) hypothesizes that the definite/indefinite distinction in ASL may be made by the contrast between the existence of a surface determiner (in which case a noun phrase is definite) or the lack of a surface determiner (in which case it is indefinite). The data in this study, however, are not consistent with this hypothesis. One clear case in which one would expect to see an indefinite determiner is that in which a character in a story who is unknown to the interlocutor is being mentioned for the first time. But, we found many instances in which a noun being mentioned for the first time does occur with a determiner. In sentence 11, one of the signers is telling a story about an experience he and a friend had at the beach. A clumsy man walks by and spills a can of soda on his friend. In this utterance, the man is being mentioned for the first time.

(11) DET FAT-KLUTZ MAN CL:WALK-CLUMSILY
"A fat klutzy guy was walking clumsily toward us."

We found several instances in which a newly mentioned noun occurs without a determiner, but by far the most usual case was that in which a determiner is present.

Determiners with Specific and Concrete Nouns

We found no instances of pointing signs being used with generic nouns. The informants in this study indicated that pointing determiners are used to describe only specific entities. Sentences 12 and 13 provide examples of a permissible utterance and an ungrammatical utterance:

(12) MY CAR DET BETTER THAN POSS.3 CAR DET
"My car is better than his car."

(13) *TOYOTA DET BETTER THAN HONDA DET
"The Toyotas are better than the Hondas."

In addition, we found no instances of pointing determiners being used with abstract nouns. The informants also judged as ungrammatical the use of pointing signs simultaneously with signs such as CONCEPT and THEORY.

These data seem to indicate, therefore, that pointing determiners in ASL are used only with concrete nouns that refer to specific entities. It is also possible that pointing determiners are used only with count nouns, although this needs to be investigated further. As yet, we have identified no process marking the definite/indefinite distinction. Our original hypothesis was that this distinction is marked by whether the determiner occurs before or after the noun, but a thorough investigation proved this hypothesis to be unfounded.

Arbitrary Direction of the Point

One particularly interesting discovery is that the direction of the point is most often insignificant. It has been generally accepted that signers set up entities at different locations in space. In a story with several different characters, the claim has been that each character is identified with one particular location in the signing space. In this view, the location remains constant until the signer indicates that the character has moved to a new location (Padden 1983). This view also claims that a pointing gesture in the direction of a location associated with a character is used when referring back to this character.

The characters in the stories we examined, however, are typically not set up in this way. In most cases, the determiners used with many different characters point to the same location. In fact, the data indicate that signers tend to have a preferred location that they use consistently for their determiners. When we asked one of the informants to tell the story of "Cinderella," the determiners used with nouns to indicate each of the characters were most often identical in form—that is, handshape, orientation, and (most notably) location were the same. These observations show that the locations to which these signs point do not distinguish characters from one another. Furthermore, even determiners occurring with nouns indicating places (for example, HOME and B-A-L-L) show no distinction in location. Also the determiners used with one character are not consistently directed toward one location. Occasionally the determiners used with GIRL (indicating Cinderella), were directed toward a different location, with no apparent semantic or pragmatic reason for doing so. It appears, then, that the direction in which a determiner points is arbitrary. One particularly clear example of this occurs in sentence 14. This utterance occurred in a story in which one of the characters was a woman sitting in the back seat of a car. The story teller, referring to the woman in the back seat signed the utterance (LOC here refers to a pointing sign functioning as a locative).

(14) DET (to the left) WOMAN LOC (to the back)
"The woman in the back . . ."

The determiner in this case points toward the left, whereas the locative points toward the back.

Determiners with Plural Nouns

We also found determiners of the same form used with plural nouns, as in sentence 15.

(15) FLIRT MANY GIRL DET SERVE KING
"He was flirting with the king's serving girls."

In sentence 15 the determiner follows the noun GIRL, which is pluralized by the addition of the sign MANY. However, the form of the determiner is the same as that used with a singular noun. Plural pronouns, on the other hand, use an arcing movement as in sentence 16.

(16) PRO.1 ASK PRO.3 (arcing movement).
"I asked them."

Determiners with Personal Names and Possessives

We found that pointing signs can occur with personal names, indicating another difference between English determiners and ASL determiners. We observed occurrences of ASL determiners being used with proper nouns in both the videotaped narratives and in the work with informants. Sentence 17 is one example of a determiner used with a personal name:

(17) BILL DET TAKE-ADVANTAGE ANN
"Bill took advantage of Ann."

ASL determiners also appear with possessives, as in sentence 18:

(18) MY CAR DET BETTER THAN POSS.3 CAR DET
"My car is better than his car."

SUMMARY

In this study, pointing signs that act as determiners have been phonologically and syntactically distinguished from other pointing signs. Evidence has been provided that indicates that such pointing signs occur with nouns in a noun phrase and are used to mark specific entities in a discourse. This analysis shows how ASL determiners are similar to and different from English determiners. Unlike English determiners, ASL determiners can occur with proper nouns and possessives, and apparently cannot occur with generic or abstract nouns. It is particularly interesting that the direction in which a determiner points is generally insignificant.

This is a preliminary study of how pointing determiners behave in one visual/gestural language, ASL. Areas for future research include the exploration of the definite/indefinite distinction, the interaction of pointing determiners with other determiners like THAT and OTHER, and the possibility that some pointing signs (possibly those with a jabbing movement) act as demonstratives. Finally, it would be of interest to examine whether pointing signs are ever used to "set up" entities in space for later reference, and if so, whether these signs act as determiners or have some other syntactic function.

NOTES

The authors wish to thank Scott Liddell for his guidance and encouragement.

1. The fact that pronouns and determiners have the same phonological form is not unique to ASL. As noted by Sera de Vriendt (personal communication), this phenomenon is also found in other languages. In French, for example, the masculine "le" and feminine "la" are used as both pronouns and determiners.
2. The form THAT^DET, although not addressed in this paper, is worthy of special note. It may be that it is one lexical item since it appears that the two parts cannot be interrupted by additional details or by a pause. Its function warrants further investigation. One possibility is that it acts as some type of discourse marker.

REFERENCES

Aarts, F. and J. Aarts. (1982). *English syntactic structures: Functions and categories in sentence analysis.* Oxford: Pergamon Press, Ltd.

Aramburo, A. (1986). *Locative features of deictics in American Sign Language.* Gallaudet University. Unpublished manuscript.

Coulter, G. (1977). Continuous representation in American Sign Language. In *Proceedings of the national symposium on sign language research and teaching,* edited by W. Stokoe, 247–57. Silver Spring, MD: National Association of the Deaf.

Edge, V. and Herrman, L. (1977). Verbs and the determination of subject. In *On the other hand: New perspectives in American sign language research,* edited by L. Friedman, 137–79. New York: Academic Press.

Friedman, L. (1975). Space, time, and person reference in American Sign Language. *Language* 51:940–61.

Givon, T. (1984). *Syntax: A functional-typological introduction,* vol. 1. Philadelphia: John Benjamins Publishing Co.

Hoffmeister, R. (1977). The influential point. In *Proceedings of the national symposium on sign language research and teaching,* edited by W. Stokoe, 177–91. Silver Spring, MD: National Association of the Deaf.

———. (1978). *The development of demonstrative pronouns, locatives, and personal pronouns in the acquisition of ASL by deaf children of deaf parents.* Ph.D. diss., University of Minnesota.

Huddleston, R. (1984). *Introduction to the grammar of English.* Cambridge: Cambridge University Press.

Ingram, R. (1978). Theme, rheme, topic and comment in the syntax of American Sign Language. *Sign Language Studies* 20: 193–218.

Lacy, R. (1973). Directional verb marking in the American Sign Language. Paper presented at the Summer Linguistic Institute, Linguistic Society of America, 3–5 August, University of Michigan, Ann Arbor.

———. (1974). Putting some of syntax back into semantics. Paper presented at the Linguistic Society of America Annual Meeting, December, New York.

Liddell, S. (1980). *American Sign Language syntax.* The Hague: Mouton.

Mandel, M. (1977). Iconic devices in American Sign Language. In *On the other hand: new perspectives on American Sign Language research,* edited by L. Friedman, 57–107. New York: Academic.

O'Malley, P. (1975). *The grammatical function of indexic reference in American Sign Language.* Research, Development and Demonstration Center in Education of the Handicapped, University of Minnesota, Minneapolis. Unpublished manuscript.

Padden, C. (1983). *Interaction of morphology and syntax in American Sign Language.* Ph.D. diss., University of California, San Diego.

Petitto, L. (1983). *From gestures to symbol: the relationship between form and meaning in the acquisition of personal pronouns in American Sign Language.* Ed.D. diss., Harvard University.

Stockwell, R., Schachter, P., and Partee, B. H. (1973). *The major syntactic structures of English.* New York: Holt, Rinehart, and Winston.

Wilbur, R. (1979). *American Sign Language and sign systems.* Baltimore, MD: University Park.

Syntax: Sentences and Their Structure

E. FINEGAN AND N. BESNIER

INTRODUCTION

This chapter explores how morphemes and words are organized within sentences. It examines the parts of a sentence, the relationships among them, and the relationships among various kinds of sentences such as statements and questions. The structure of a sentence, as well as its study, is called *syntax*.

The first observation to be made in studying sentence structure is that all languages have ways of referring to entities—to people, places, things, ideas, events, and so on. *Referring expressions* are nouns or noun phrases. There are simple ones like the proper nouns *Lauren*, *Paris*, and *Labor Day*, the common nouns *books* and *justice*, and the personal pronouns *you* and *it*. There are also more complicated expressions like these noun phrases: *a magical book, the ghost, his mother, the star of the film, a judge he had known forty years earlier,* and *the strict-constructionist way that Wapner settled another dispute over the ownership of a dog.*

The second observation to be made about syntax is that all languages have ways of saying something about the entities they make reference to. In other words, all languages can make *predications* about the things referred to by the referring expressions. All languages have ways of making statements, both affirmative and negative. They can also ask questions, issue directives, and so on.

Let's illustrate with affirmative statements. In the following sentences, reference is made to an entity and then a predication is made about it.

Referring Expression	Predication
Judge Wapner	uses an answering machine.
She	has a daughter.
The ghost	reappeared last night.

In the first example, reference is made to "Judge Wapner"; something is then predicated of him—namely, that he "uses an answering machine." Likewise for the second and third examples.

Sentences often consist of more elaborate referring expressions and more elaborate predications than these. The two sentences below illustrate more elaborate predications. In the first example, reference is made "to the dog" and then a predication about the dog is made. In the second example, reference is made to "the bride" and then a predication is made about her. In these examples, the predication is underlined.

The dog <u>bit the man who had agreed to care for it.</u>

The bride <u>swore that her father had promised to foot the bill.</u>

The processes that a language uses to refer to things and make predications about

Source. Reprinted by permission of the publisher, from E. Finegan and N. Besnier, *Language: Its Structure and Use,* (1989): 125–130. San Diego: Harcourt Brace Jovanovich.

them are part of its syntax. Syntax governs the way a language makes statements, asks questions, gives directives, and so on. In other words, the study of syntax treats the structure of sentences and their structural relationships to one another. To repeat: A typical sentence consists of two parts, one a referring expression and the other a predication about the entity referred to. In syntactic terms, referring expressions are noun phrases, and predicates are verb phrases. All languages, however much they differ from one another in the other categories or parts of speech, have nouns (and noun phrases) and verbs (and verb phrases).

SENTENCE TYPES

In many traditional grammars three major sentences types are distinguished. A *simple sentence* consists of a single clause that stands alone as its own sentence. In a *coordinate sentence* (called "compound" in traditional grammars), two or more clauses are joined by a conjunction in a coordinate relationship. A *complex sentence* combines two (or more) clauses in such a way that one clause functions as a grammatical part of the other one.

Simple Sentences

Simple sentences are those that contain one clause; a *clause* contains a single verb (or predicate). The following are examples of simple sentences:

(a) Dan washed the dishes.
(b) Karim assembled the new grill.
(c) Joe cooked the hot dogs.
(d) A runner from Ohio won the marathon last year.
(e) Denise will buy a new raincoat this fall.
(f) Her uncle had put the gifts in the car.
(g) The psychiatrist should have believed in banshees.

Each of these sentences contains only one verb, but you can see that a verb itself can consist of a single word (as in *washed, assembled, cooked,* and *won*) or of more than one word (as in *will buy, had put,* and *should have believed*). The clauses just cited are called sentences because they stand independently as sentences; if they were incorporated into other sentences, they would be called clauses. In English and many other languages, the central element in a clause is the verb; each clause—and therefore each simple sentence—contains just one verb.

Coordinate Sentences

Two clauses can be joined to make a coordinate sentence, as in these examples:

(a) Karim assembled the new grill, and Joe cooked the hot dogs.
(b) Denise bought a new coat, but she didn't wear it often.

A coordinate sentence consists of two clauses joined by a word such as *and,* but, or *or,* which are called *coordinating conjunctions,* or simply *conjunctions.* Conjunctions can be used to join sentences (as we have just seen), but they can also join other constructions; for example, nouns in *trick or treat* and *dungeons and dragons:* verbs in *trip and fall* and *break and enter;* adjectives in *slow and painful* and *tried and true.* To repeat a point made in the preceding section, when clauses are combined to form a single sentence we generally reserve the word *sentence* for the larger structure and refer to the structures that make it up as *clauses.*

The clauses in a coordinate sentence hold equal status as parts of the sentence: neither is part of the other one, and each could stand by itself as an independent sentence. Figure 1 represents the structure of a coordinate sentence and illustrates the equivalent status of the clauses (called *coordinate clauses*). We use the label S for both

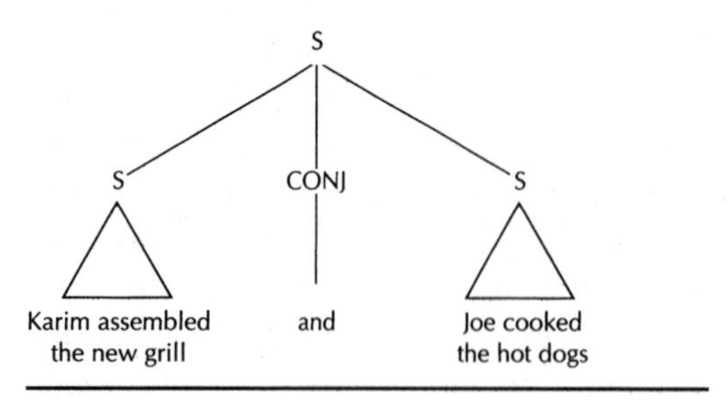

FIGURE 1.

the whole sentence and for each coordinate clause in it: CONJ stands for conjunction.

Complex Sentences

Embedded Clauses. One clause can be incorporated into another clause. The clause *Dan washed the dishes* can be incorporated into another clause to produce the sentence *Sue said Dan washed the dishes*. In each of the following examples, the underlined portion is a clause that is incorporated (or *embedded*) into another clause.

(a) Sue said Dan washed the dishes.
(b) That the runner from Ohio won the marathon surprised us.
(c) She is wondering whether Denise will buy a new raincoat.
(d) She didn't suspect a party until her uncle put the gifts in the car.
(e) It was clear that the patient should have received a refund.

In sentence (a), the clause *Dan washed the dishes* is embedded into the clausal structure *Sue said* __________. The clause *Dan washed the dishes* functions as the direct object of the verb *said*. It is thus functionally equivalent (though not semantically equivalent) to the word *something* in the sentence *Sue said something*; both are direct objects. In (b), the clause *That the runner from Ohio won the marathon* is embedded into the clausal structure ______ *surprised us*. In this case, the embedded clause functions as the subject of the verb *surprised*. The embedded clause in (b) (*That the runner from Ohio won the marathon*) is grammatically equivalent to *It* in *It surprised us* or to *The news* in *The news surprised us*. In (c) the clause *whether Denise will buy a new raincoat* is embedded into the clause *She is wondering* _____; it serves as a complement to the verb *is wondering*.

Subordinators. In most of the examples just given, the embedded clause is introduced by a word that would not occur there if the clause were standing as an independent sentence: words like *that* in (b) and (e), *whether* in (c) and *until* in (d). When a clause is embedded into another clause, it is often introduced by such a *subordinator*. Subordinators serve to mark the beginning of an embedded clause and to help identify its function in the sentence. Not all embedded clauses must be introduced by a subordinator, although in English they usually can be. Compare these sentence pairs:

(a) Sue said that Dan washed the dishes.
(b) Sue said Dan washed the dishes.

(c) That she won surprised us.
(d) *She won surprised us.

Notice that (a) and (b) are well formed with or without the subordinator. But of the pair (c) and (d), only (c) is well formed. (The asterisk preceding (d) indicates a structure that is not well formed.)

The Form of Embedded Clauses. When a clause is embedded within certain other clauses, its form may differ from the form it would have if it stood independently as a simple sentence. In these pairs, compare sentence (a) with (b) and (c) with (d):

(a) Sue said Dan washed the dishes.
(b) Sue wanted Dan to wash the dishes.

(c) That the runner from Ohio won the marathon surprised us.

(d) For the runner from Ohio to win the marathon surprised us.

The clause *Dan to wash the dishes* is not a well-formed English sentence; yet when it is embedded into the clausal structure *Sue wanted* ______, it is perfectly well formed. As a matter of fact, any other form would be unacceptable, as illustrated:

(a) *Sue wanted Dan washed the dishes.

(b) *Sue wanted that Dan will wash the dishes.

(c) *Sue wanted Dan washes the dishes.

The form of an embedded clause can depend on the particular verb of the clause in which it is embedded. Compare the sentences in each of these pairs:

(a) Sue wanted Dan to wash the dishes.

(b) *Sue wanted Dan washed the dishes.

(c) Sue said Dan washed the dishes.

(d) *Sue said Dan to wash the dishes.

These sentences suggest that the verb *want* requires a clause form with *to*, as in *wanted Dan to wash the dishes*; whereas the verb *say* does not permit an embedded clause to take the form *Dan to wash the dishes* but does permit the independent sentence form *Dan washed the dishes*.

Unlike coordinate sentences, which contain clauses of equal status, *complex* sentences contain clauses of unequal status. In the complex sentences we have been examining, one clause is subordinate to another clause and functions as a grammatical part of that clause. We call the subordinate clause an *embedded clause* and the clause into which it is embedded a *matrix clause*. Every subordinate clause is by definition embedded in a matrix clause, in which it serves in a grammatical function such as subject, direct object, or adverbial. For example, in the next sentences, in which brackets set off the embedded clauses, each embedded clause functions as a grammatical unit in its matrix clause. Each embedded clause has the same grammatical function in its matrix clause as the underlined word has in the sentence directly below it:

(a) Sally said [she saw a ghost].

(b) Sally said it. (it is the direct object of the verb *said*)

(c) [That Jack feared witches] upset his wife.

(d) It upset his wife. (It is the subject of the sentence)

(e) Joe cooked the hot dogs [after Karim assembled the grill].

(f) Joe cooked the hot dogs then. (then is an adverbial modifier)

In (a), the embedded clause *she saw a ghost* functions as the direct object of the verb *said*, just as the word *it* does in (b). In (c), the embedded clause *That Jack feared witches* functions as the subject of the verb *upset*, just as *it* does in sentence (d). In (e), *after Karim assembled the grill* functions as an adverbial modifying the verb phrase *cooked the hot dogs*, just as *then* does in (f).

Syntax: The Study of Sentence Structure

W. O'Grady, M. Dobrovolsky, and M. Aronoff

Noun-substantives, the names of things declare,
And adjectives, what kind of things these are . . .
A structure: and the toil of grammar's past.
Israel Tonge (c. 1680)

One of the underlying themes of this book is that language is a highly structured system of communication. Utterances are not formed by randomly combining linguistic elements. Rather, as you saw in Chapter 3, words consist of phonological units called syllables, which in turn are made up of segments and features. This chapter focuses on *syntax*, the system of rules and categories that allows words to be combined to form sentences.

The data that linguists use to study syntax consist primarily of judgments about the grammaticality of individual sentences. Roughly speaking, a sentence is considered *grammatical* if speakers judge it to be a possible sentence of their language. Example 1a is not a possible sentence in English, although the same words can be combined in a different way to form the grammatical structure in 1b.

1. a) *house painted student a the
   b) A student painted the house.

Often, it is not obvious why a particular sentence has to be ungrammatical. Consider in this respect the following examples.

2. a) Mike will leave tomorrow at 3:00 P.M.
   b) Will Mike leave tomorrow at 3:00 P.M.?

3. a) Mike leaves tomorrow at 3:00 P.M.
   b) *Leaves Mike tomorrow at 3:00 P.M.

While 2a and 3a mean essentially the same thing, only one of them has a question structure formed by reversing the order of the first two words. There is nothing logically wrong with sentence 3b. Such structures are found in many human languages and, until a few centuries ago, were pefectly acceptable in English. For some reason, however, the rules that form sentences in Modern English do not allow this pattern.

In the following pages, we will use information about grammaticality to illustrate the workings of the syntactic component of the grammar. We will begin by considering the role of word classes in sentence formation. Next, we will examine the various types of rules that form sentences by arranging words into patterns appropriate to English. Finally, we will consider some basic syntactic phenomena in languages other than English.

5.1 SYNTACTIC CATEGORIES

The first step in syntactic analysis is the identification of the categories to which the words of a language belong. If words could not be assigned to a small group of categories, it would be very hard to learn or use a language. Each of the ten thousand or so lexical items in the average person's every-

Source. Reprinted by permission of the publisher, from W. O'Grady, M. Dobrovolsky, and M. Aronoff, *Contemporary Linguistics*, (1989): 126–147. New York: St. Martin's Press.

day spoken vocabulary would have its own set of properties that would have to be memorized—a rather daunting task.

Lexical Categories

Fortunately, such a feat of memory is unnecessary since large groups of words have very similar properties. These shared characteristics allow us to organize words into a relatively small number of *lexical categories* or classes (see Table 1). Four *major lexical categories* are typically recognized, namely *noun (N)*, *verb (V)*, *adjective (Adj)*, and *adverb (Adv)*. Membership in these categories is open in the sense that new words are always being added. There is also a group of *minor* or closed categories in which membership is open in the sense that new words are always being added. There is also a group of *minor* or closed categories in which membership is restricted to a fixed set of elements already in the language. Minor lexical categories include *determiner (Det)*, *auxiliary verb (Aux)*, *preposition (P)*, *pronoun (Pro)*, and *conjunction (C)*. How are lexical categories defined? As noted previously, the words in each lexical category share certain properties. Some of these properties pertain to meaning. Nouns, for instance, typically name entities such as individuals (*Shawn*, *Marie*) and concrete and abstract things (*book*, *desk*, *policy*). Verbs, on the other hand, designate actions (*run*, *jump*), sensations (*feel*, *hurt*), and states (*be*, *remain*).

The meanings associated with nouns and verbs can be modified in various ways. The typical function of an adjective, for instance, is to designate a property or attribute that is applicable to the individuals and things named by nouns. Thus, adjectives such as *tall*, *old*, and *red* name properties that can be attributed to individuals and things. When we say *That building is tall*, we are attributing the property "tall" to the building named by the noun.

Just as adjectives bear a special relationship to nouns, so adverbs typically name properties and attributes that can be applied to the actions, states, and sensations designated by verbs. In the following sentences, for example, the adverb *quickly* indicates the manner of Janet's leaving and the adverb *early* specifies its time.

4. a) Janet left quickly.
   b) Janet left early.

TABLE 5.1 Lexical Categories

Major lexical categories		Examples
Noun	(N)	Pierre, butterfly, wheat, policy
Verb	(V)	arrive, discuss, melt, feel, remain
Adjective	(Adj)	good, tall, silent, old, expensive
Adverb	(Adv)	yesterday, silently, slowly, quietly, quickly
Minor lexical categories		**Examples**
Determiner	(Det)	the, a, this, these
Auxiliary verb	(Aux)	will, can, may, must, be, have
Preposition	(P)	to, in, on, near, at, by
Pronoun	(Pro)	he, she, him, his, her
Conjunction	(C)	and, or, but

a.

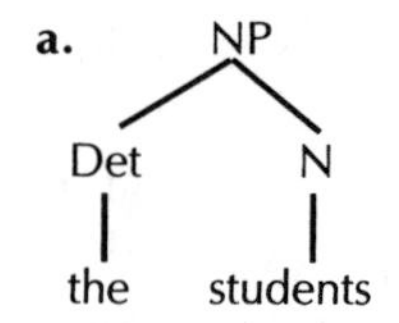

$[_{NP}$ $[_{Det}$ the] $[_{N}$ students]]

b.

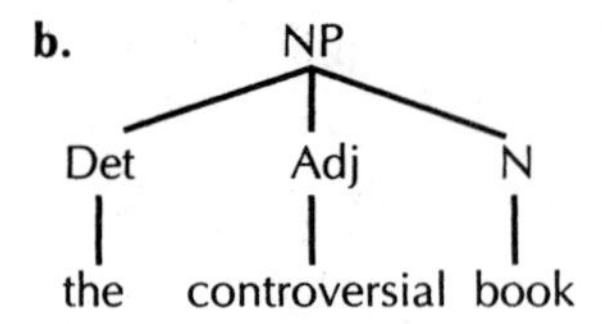

$[_{NP}$ $[_{Det}$ the] $[_{Adj}$ controversial] $[_{N}$ book]]

FIGURE 5.1.

The members of each lexical category also share certain combinatorial properties. This means that they can combine with certain other types of words to form larger units.

Noun Phrases. The words that we have grouped together as nouns can all combine with determiners and adjectives to form larger phrases such as the following:

5. a) the books
   b) the controversial books

In 5, the adjective *controversial* modifies the noun *books* while the determiner *the* indicates that the speaker has in mind a definite set of books. Such a group of words, called a *noun phrase* or *NP*, can be represented by either a tree structure or a set of labeled brackets. In Figure 5.1, each word is marked by the appropriate lexical category label and is shown to be part of a larger phrasal unit (NP). Evidence that NPs are syntactic units comes from the fact they can often be replaced by a single word such as the pronoun *they* or *it*. This is illustrated in 6, where *they* replaces *the students* and *it* replaces *the controversial book*. (This is called a *substitution test.*)

6. The students read *the controversial book,* and then *they* returned *it* to the library. (*they* = *the students, it* = *the controversial book*)

Even though the sequence of words *the controversial book* is longer and contains more information than the single word *it*, both are NPs and both can occur in the same places in sentences. In fact, a pronoun can replace any NP, no matter how long or complex it may be. In 7, for example, *it* can replace the considerably longer NP:

7. *The controversial book that the teacher almost forgot to remind the students to return to the library* was banned by the committee.

From the syntactic point of view, a pronoun like *it* or *she* counts as a full NP, even though it would be listed in the dictionary as a pronoun only one word long (see Figure 5.2).

Note that the pronoun substitutes for the entire NP and not simply for the N, as shown in 8.

8. a) The students read *it.*
   b) *The students read the controversial *it.*

Prepositional Phrases. The class of words making up the minor lexical category of preposition includes such items as *near, in, on, before,* and *after.* In terms of meaning, these words typically designate relations in space (such as *in*), time (such as *before,*) or

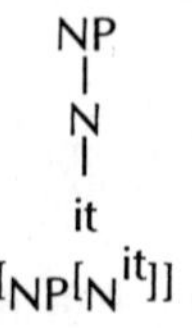

FIGURE 5.2.

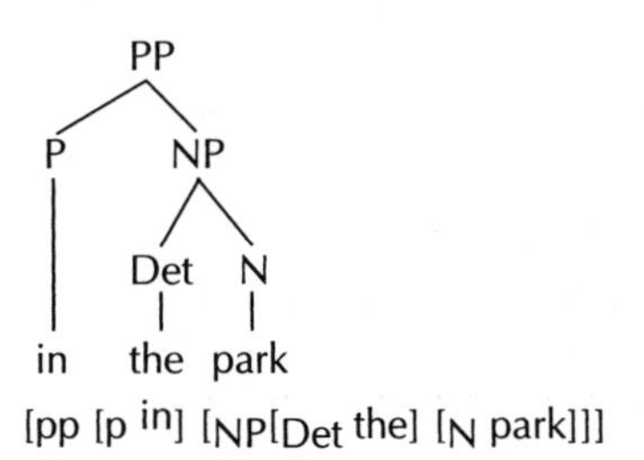

FIGURE 5.3.

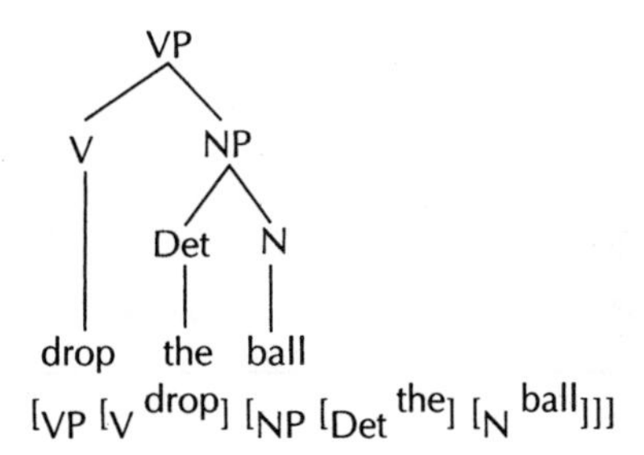

FIGURE 5.4.

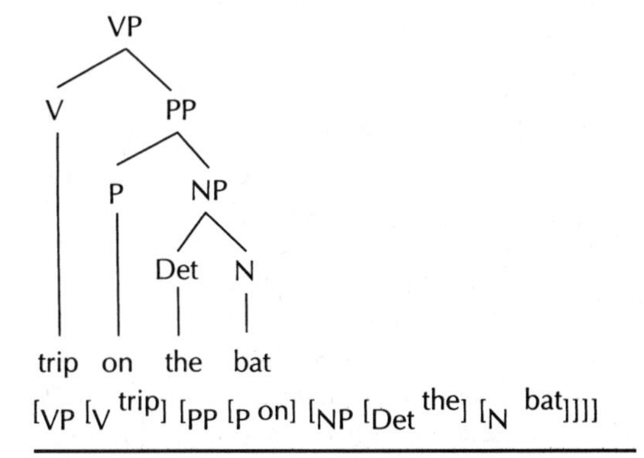

FIGURE 5.5.

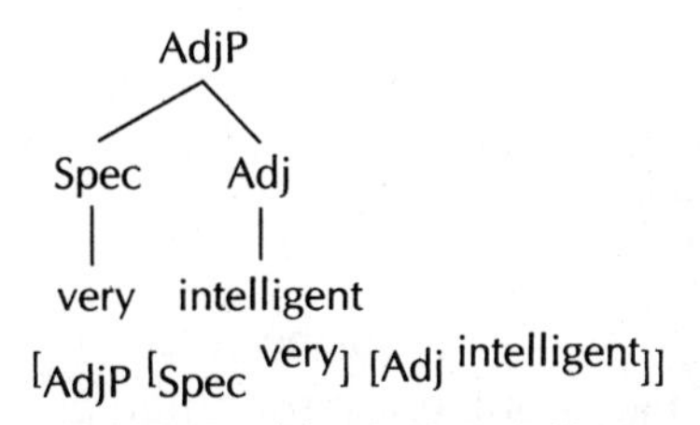

FIGURE 5.6.

direction (such as *to* or *from*). A preposition combines with an NP to form a *prepositional phrase* or *PP* (see Figure 5.3).

The substitution test confirms that *in the park* is a unit since it can be replaced by a single word in sentences such as 9.

9. The team practiced *in the park,* and Lisa trained *there* too.
   (*there = in the park*)

A second indication that *in the park* forms a phrase is that it can be moved as a single unit to different positions within the sentence. (This is called a *movement test.*) In 10 for instance, *in the park* occurs at the beginning of the sentence.

10. *In the park,* the team practiced for the championship game.

Verb Phrases. The lexical category consisting of verbs has yet another set of combinatorial properties. As Figures 5.4 and 5.5 show, elements in this class can combine with NPs and/or PPs (among other categories) to form a *verb phrase* or *VP.* We know that *drop the ball* and *trip on the bat* form syntactic units because they can be replaced by the single word *did.*

11. a) The catcher *dropped the ball,* and the pitcher *did* too.
       (*did = dropped the ball*)
    b) The player *tripped on the bat* and the coach *did* too.
       (*did = tripped on the bat*)

Other Phrases Two other types of phrasal categories are commonly found in language. An adjective can combine with a *degree specifier (Spec)* such as *very, quite,* or *really* to form an *adjectival phrase* or AdjP, as in Figure 5.6. AdjPs can be replaced by the word *so* in structures such as 12.

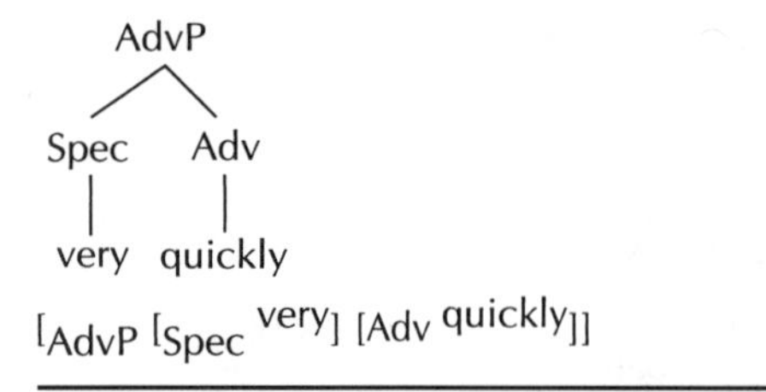

FIGURE 5.7.

12. Linda is *very intelligent,* and Mark appears *so* too.
(*so = very intelligent*)

Adverbial Phrases. (*AdvPs*) consist of an adverb and an optional specifier as in Figure 5.7. AdvPs expressing times can usually be replaced by the word *then.*

13. Jeremy arrived *very early,* and Cheryl arrived *then* too.
(*then = very early*)

Other types of AdvPs cannot be easily replaced by a single word, but substitution by larger units is possible.

14. Doug types *very quickly,* and Caroline types *that way* too.
(*that way = very quickly*)

A small number of time expressions such as *yesterday, today,* and *now* are problematic for syntactic analysis. In terms of the meaning they express, such elements appear to be adverbs in that they provide information about the time of actions. In terms of form, however, these elements do not combine with specifiers such as *very.* For the purposes of this book, we will consider these expressions to make up an exceptional class of adverbs.

Intermediate Structures. The substitution test that we used to justify the claim that NPs are syntactic units can also be used to show that there is a syntactic unit larger than an N but smaller than an NP. This new category is N′ (pronounced N-bar). It is sometimes also written as $\bar{N}$. An item that substitutes for N′ is the word *one.*

15. a) This book is longer than that *one.*
(*one = book*)
b) This book about Australia is longer than that *one* about New Guinea.
(*one = book*)
c) This book about Australia is longer than that one.
(*one = book,* or *book about Australia.*)

Here we see that word *one* can substitute for something the size of an N or something larger than an N but smaller than an NP. If we postulate N′ as a category intermediate between N and NP, we can think of these examples as involving the same kind of substitution. Another set of examples illustrating this is shown below.

16. a) This book is heavier than that *one.*
(*one = book*)
b) This book on the shelf is heavier than that one on the table.
(*one = book*)
c) This book on the table is better than that one.
(*one = book,* or *book on the table*)

In general, we can think of the NP as initially branching in two directions, to *Det* and N′. N′ can go directly to N, or it can branch to N′ and something else, such as PP. At each level, *one* may substitute for N′. This is diagrammed in Figure 5.8.

The substitutability of *one* in other cases involving adjectives shows that an AdjP can be a subconstituent of N′ (see Figure 5.9). That is, *one* may substitute for an AdjP + N sequence, as in 17a. In fact, there is even more structure in this example, since *one* may also replace only *book,* as in 17b.

17. a) This controversial book is longer than that *one.*
(*one = controversial book*)
b) This controversial book is longer than this innocuous *one.*
(*one = book*)

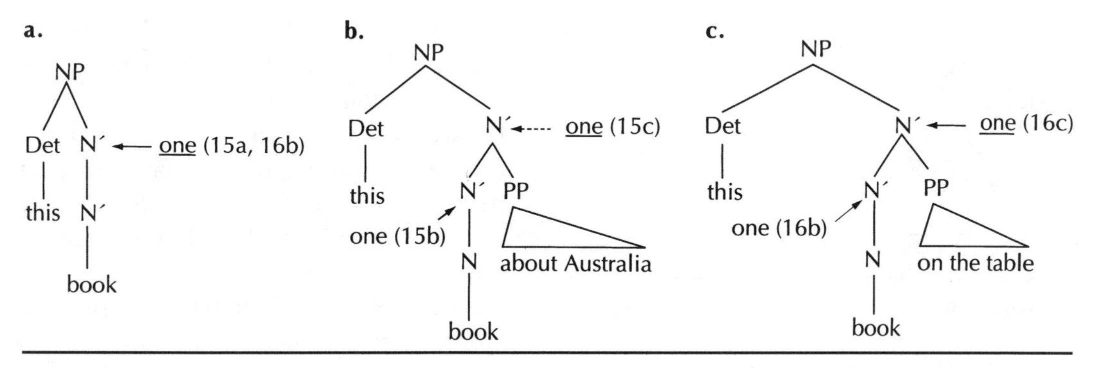

FIGURE 5.8.

(Because this section is optional, the NPs diagrammed in the following sections do not reflect the N′ innovation discussed here.)

Heads. As we have seen, each phrasal category is built around a lexical category—NP around N, VP around V, AdjP around Adj, and so on. The lexical category around which a phrasal category is built is called the *head* of that phrase. The head of a phrase has two distinctive properties. First, it is the one component of a phrase that is invariably present. Thus, it is not possible to have a VP without a verb, although it is possible to have such a phrase without an NP or a PP.

18. a) No NP: They [$_{VP}$ left early].
    b) No PP: They [$_{VP}$ left the room].
    c) No NP or PP: They [VP left].
    d) No verb: *They [$_{VP}$ the room]

Second, the type of meaning associated with the head is also associated with the phrase.

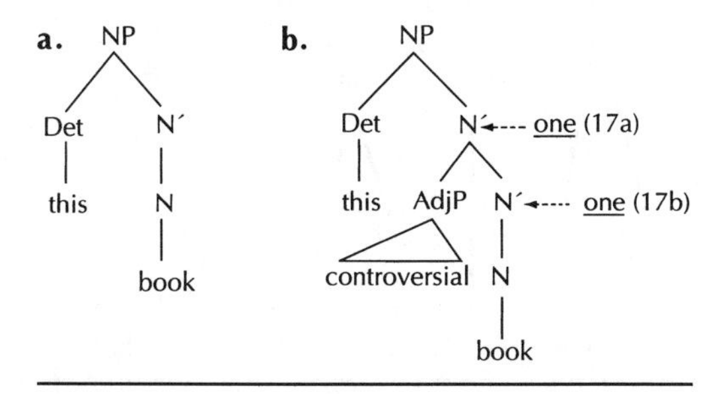

FIGURE 5.9.

Thus, just as the noun *girls* designates a group of individuals, so does the NP *the young girls.* Similarly, just as the verb *run* names an action, so does the VP *run to the store.*

This head–phrase relation can be expressed by using the variable X to stand for N, V, Adj, or P. Every XP contains an X as its head, and many of the properties of the X, as illustrated above in the previous paragraph, are shared by the XP. This way of looking at phrases leads us to expect that an XP will always have an X as its head. It should therefore come as a great surprise if we were to find a VP with something other than a V as its head—an N for instance.

19. a) [VP[Vrun] to the store]
    b) [VP[N noun] to the store]

A system of phrase structure called X′ (X-bar) theory, incorporating the notion of head discussed here as well as intermediate-sized categories like the N′ discussed earlier, has been elaborated and applied in much recent work in syntactic theory.

Recursion

One very important property of any natural language is that it contains an indefinite number of possible sentences; given any grammatical sentence of the language, it is always possible to form a sentence that is longer. This property is called *recursion,* and

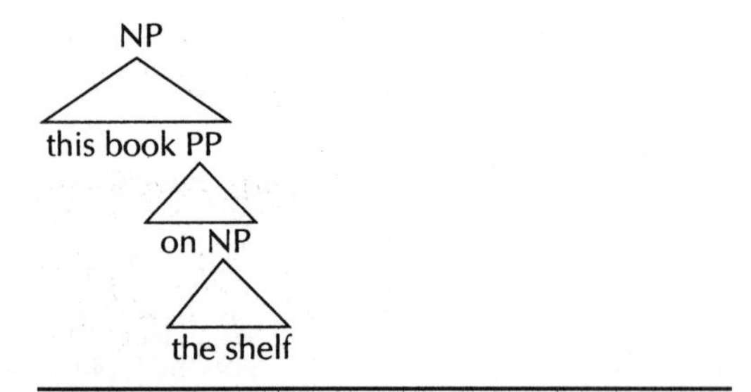

FIGURE 5.10.

it can be illustrated with notions introduced in this section. Take, for example, the NP in 16b, *this book on the shelf.* Note that this NP contains a PP (*on the shelf*) as a subconstituent, and note further that this PP contains an NP (*the shelf*) as a subconstituent.

Now imagine that this NP itself contained a PP, *this book on the shelf in the corner.* Here we have a longer sentence, formed by the introduction of a PP into the NP, a reapplication of the procedure used to form the NP in Figure 5.10. The following general pattern is emerging: an NP may contain a PP which in turn contains an NP, which may contain a PP, and so on (see Figure 5.11).

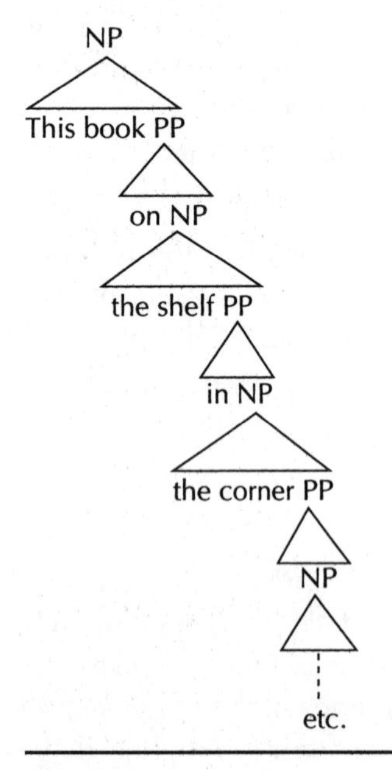

FIGURE 5.11.

Were it not for the fact that the NP need not contain a PP, the sentence would never end.

Recursion is exhibited in other parts of the syntax of a language. We have seen that AdjPs, for example, may contain the specifier *very*, as in the AdjP *very* quiet. We may also have an AdjP that contains two occurrences of very (*very, very quiet*), or three (*very, very, very quiet*), or in fact any number. Nor is there a numerical limit on the number of AdjPs that can occur inside NP, as in *the small, white poodle,* or *the very, very large, very black, quite silly, rather undignified bulldog.*

Sentence Structure

A *sentence* (S) consists of an NP and a VP, each of which can itself consist of other categories. This is illustrated in Figure 5.12. (For clarity of exposition, tree structures rather than labeled bracketing will be used to represent full sentences in many cases.) Tree structures such as Figure 5.12 express a fundamental insight of syntactic analysis. That insight is that sentences do not simply consist of strings of lexical categories. Rather, within any sentence, words are grouped together to form phrases, and so on. As we have seen, the presence of each phrasal unit can be verified with the help of substitution and movement tests.

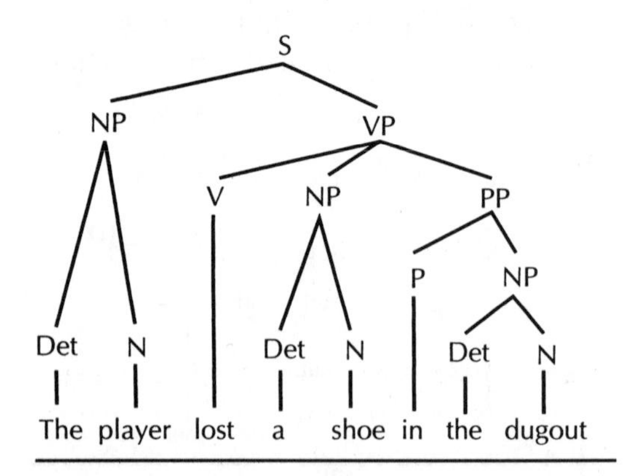

FIGURE 5.12.

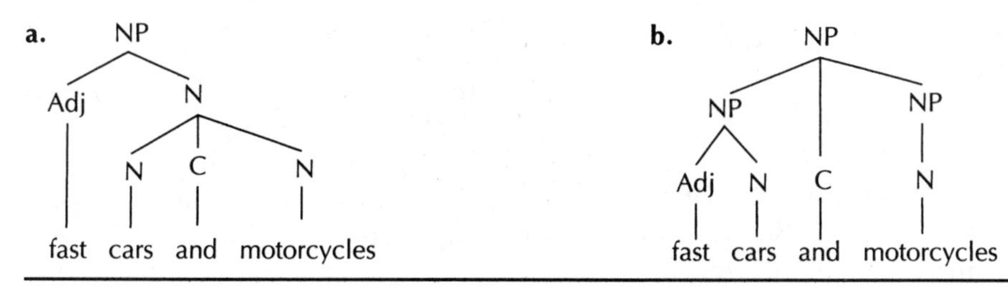

FIGURE 5.13.

Some Syntactic Relations. Tree structures can be used to define various important syntactic notions. The points where category labels appear in Figure 5.12 are called *nodes*. One node is said to *dominate* another if there is a path in the tree from the first node down to the second. Thus, the S node in Figure 5.12 dominates all other nodes, while the NP node dominates only Det and N. Two or more categories that have the same node immediately above them are called *sisters*. In Figure 5.12, for example, each determiner and the noun to its right are sisters as are the verb and the NP and PP to its right. In contrast, the noun *player* and the verb *lost* are not sisters since they do not occur immediately beneath the same node.

Dominance and sisterhood allow us to define the following important distinction between two structural positions in the sentence.

20. *Subject:* the NP immediately dominated by S (it is the sister of VP)
    Direct object: the NP immediately dominated by VP (it is the sister of V)

When applied to Figure 5.12, these definitions identify *the player* as subject and *a shoe* as direct object. Frequent reference to subjects and direct objects is made in the remainder of this chapter.

Structural Ambiguity The grouping together of words into phrases reflects not only the syntactic organization of the sentence, but also the way in which word meanings are combined to give the meaning of the full sentence. Consider in this regard a sentence such as *fast cars and motorcycles are dangerous.* This sentence can mean either that there is danger in fast cars and fast motorcycles or that there is danger in fast cars and any type of motorcycle. We can use tree structures to represent these two meanings by assuming that the phrase *fast cars and motorcycles* can be analyzed in either of the two ways shown in Figure 5.13. (C marks a conjunction, a minor lexical category whose members serve to join categories of the same type.) Figure 5.13a corresponds to the interpretation in which the property expressed by the word *fast* applies to both cars and motorcycles, while Figure 5.13b represents the intepretation in which only the cars are taken to be fast.

When the same string of words can be associated with more than one tree structure, it is said to be *structurally ambiguous.* We will consider this type of ambiguity in more detail in the chapter on semantics. For the time being, the important thing to note is that tree structures provide a natural way to represent this phenomenon.

5.2 PHRASE STRUCTURE RULES

Now that we have established the existence of syntactic structures consisting of lexical and phrasal categories, our next step must be to determine the rules that allow some combinations of words but not others. As noted in the introductory chapter, there is no numerical limit on the set of possible grammatical sentences in a language. It therefore makes no sense to think that speakers simply memorize all of the syntactic structures of their language. Rather, they must have access to a system of rules that enables them to form sentences as needed. Part of this system consists of *phrase structure rules*, which specify the grouping of lexical categories into phrases. A sample set of phrase structure rules is given in 21.

The S Rule

Each arrow can be read as "branches into," "consists of," or "is rewritten as." Thus, the first phase structure rule, called "the S Rule," indicates that an S (sentence) branches into an NP and a VP (see Figure 5.14).

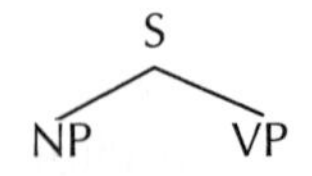

FIGURE 5.14.

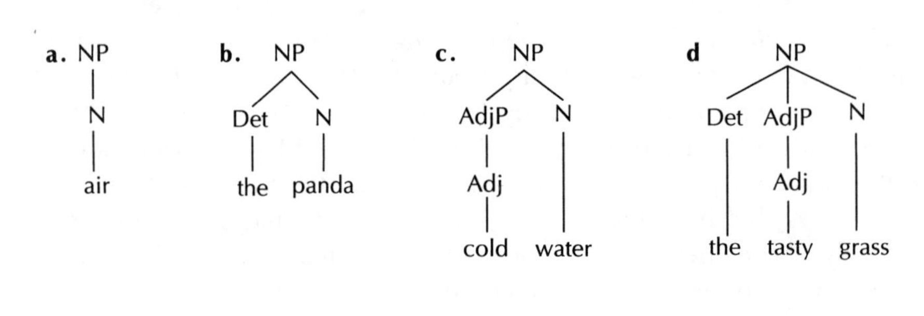

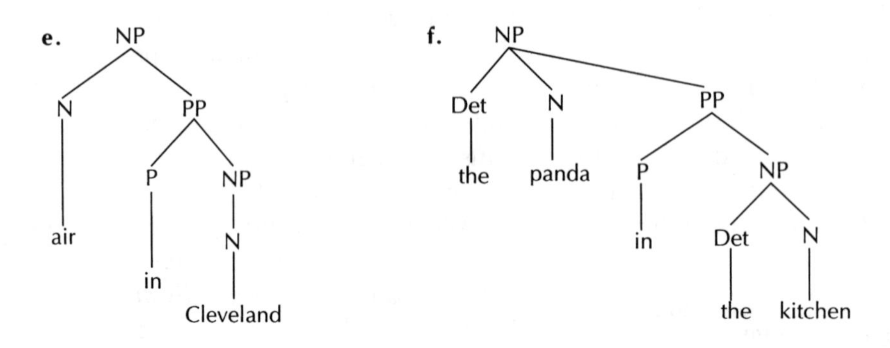

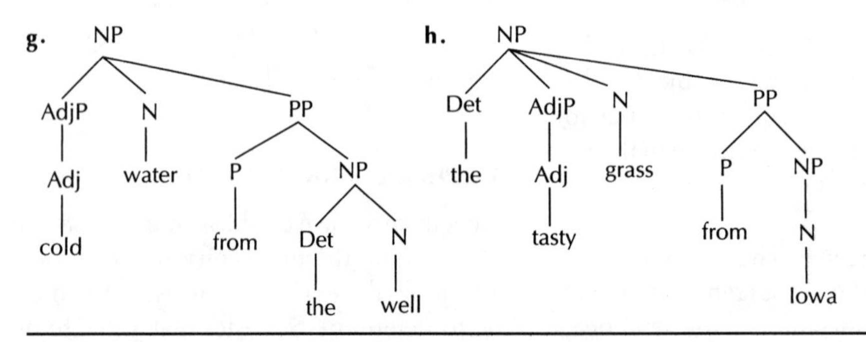

FIGURE 5.15.

21. a) S → NP VP
    b) NP → N PP
    c) VP → V (NP) (PP)
    d) PP → P NP
    e) AdjP → (Spec) Adj

The NP Rule

The NP Rule in 21b is somewhat more complicated since it indicates that NPs can optionally contain a determiner, a PP, and an adjectival phrase in addition to an obligatory noun head. (As is the custom, optional elements are enclosed in parentheses.) This gives the eight possibilities exemplified in Figure 5.15. To simplify, N′ will not be used here, and the AdjPs in these examples consist of only an adjective head.

The VP Rule

A wide range of options is also allowed by 21c, the VP Rule. These options include the verb (the head) standing alone or accompanied by an NP, a PP, or both (see Figure 5.16).

The phrase structure rules given in 21 also allow us to construct syntactic structures for entire sentences. Reconsider in this regard the syntactic structure in Figure 5.12, repeated here as Figure 5.17. In Figure 5.17, the S Rule applies first—giving NP and VP. The NP rule then permits the *determiner-noun* sequence corresponding to *the player*. The VP Rule allows the VP to branch into a verb (*lost*), an NP, and a PP. The NP Rule can then be applied, giving the *determiner-noun* sequence corresponding to *a shoe*. The PP Rule will give a preposition (*in*) and an NP. At this point, the NP Rule can be used once again to yield the *determiner-noun* sequence corresponding to *the dugout*.

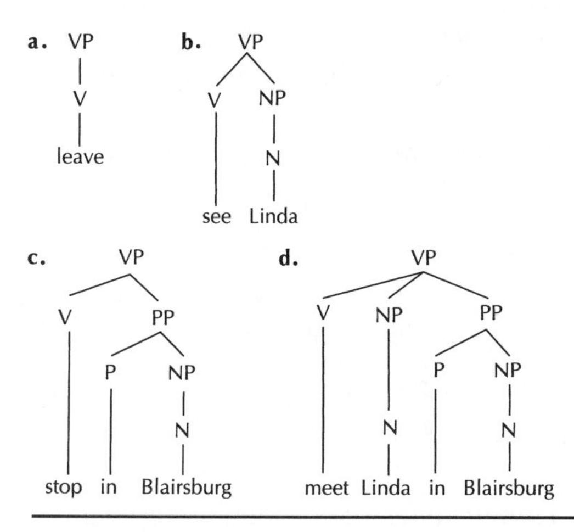

FIGURE 5.16.

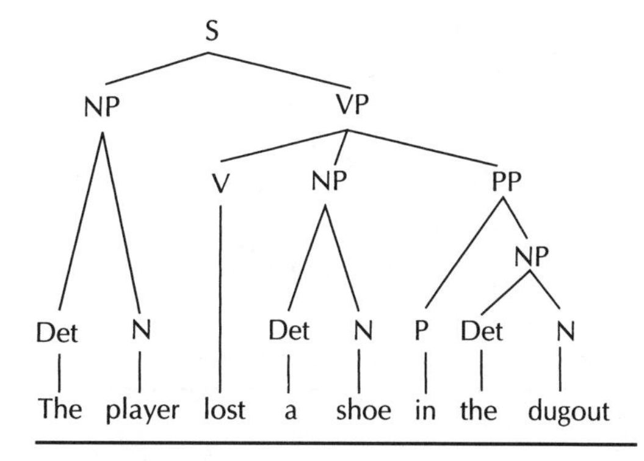

FIGURE 5.17.

Modal Auxiliaries

Now consider the following sentences.

22. a) Mosquitoes will sting.
    b) The winds can shift.
    c) This grade may impress Holly.

These sentences all include *modal auxiliary verbs* such as *will, can, may,* and *must,* which express notions like permission, possibility, obligation, and futurity. These elements are called *auxilliary* or *helping* verbs because they must always occur with a regular or *main* verb in a complete sentence. The utterance *Ships must,* for instance, is not a complete sentence of English since it has no main verb.

A second type of auxiliary verb is found in sentences such as 23.

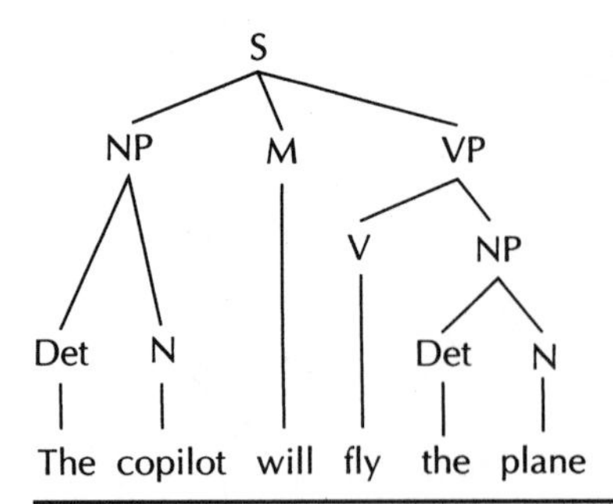

FIGURE 5.18.

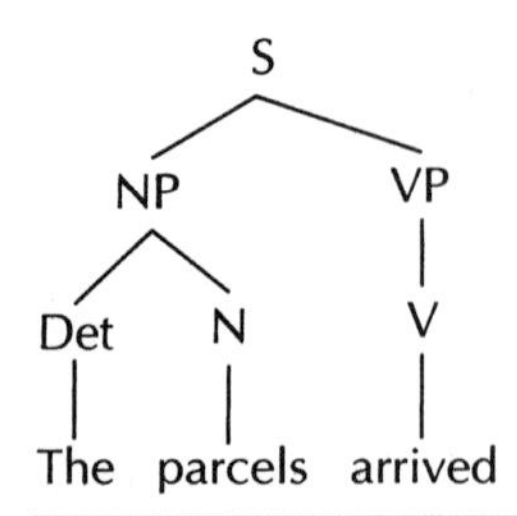

FIGURE 5.19.

23. a) The boy has done the laundry.
    b) The boy is doing the laundry.

Auxiliary *have* and *be* can be used in conjunction with a modal to create complex patterns such as the one in 24.

24. The copilot must have been flying the plane.

In order to simplify, we will focus our attention here on modal auxillaries, which are introduced by the rule in 25 and appear in structures such as Figure 5.18 (M = modal).

25. S → NP (M) VP

5.3 LEXICAL INSERTION

Having seen how phrase structure rules determine the arrangement of phrasal and lexical categories into sentences, we can now consider how individual words are inserted into syntactic structure. One obvious precondition for *lexical insertion* is a "match" between the word's syntactic category and the category of the node under which it is inserted. In Figure 5.19, for example, the determiner *The* occurs under the Det node, the noun *parcels* under the N node, and the verb *arrived* under the V node. A match between the category of the lexical item and the node under which it is inserted does not always ensure a correct result. The section that follows deals with a second equally important condition on lexical insertion.

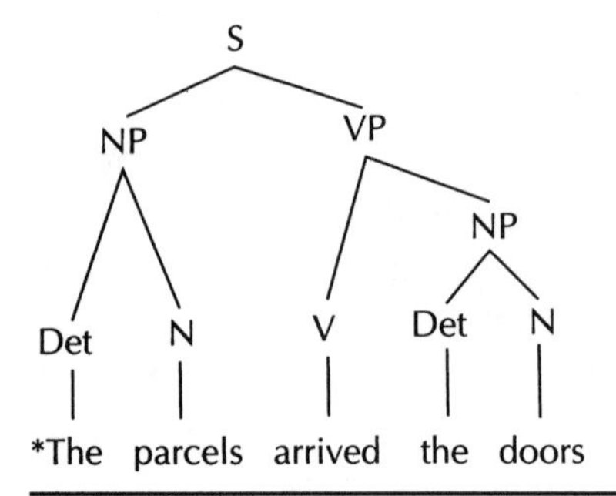

FIGURE 5.20.

Subcategorization

Lexical insertion is also sensitive to the category of other phrases in syntactic structure. As Figure 5.20 shows, not just any verb can be inserted into the V position in a tree structure. The verb *arrive* cannot take a direct object NP. That is, it cannot be inserted into a tree structure where it will have an NP as its sister. (Recall that the direct object NP is the sister of V.) In this, it differs from the verb *like*, which requires a direct object NP.

26. a) *The wrestlers like.
    b) The wrestlers like the fans.

Different again are verbs such as *study*, which can occur with or without a direct object.

27. a) The candidates must study.
    b) The candidates must study the problem.

These contrasts are captured by means of *subcategorization frames*, features that divide syntactic classes into subcategories by indicating the types of sister categories with which they can or must occur.

Verb Subcategorization. The subcategorization frame –[_NP] indicates that a verb cannot occur with a sister NP (a direct object). Such verbs are often called *intransitive.* The frame +[_NP], in contrast, indicates that the verb requires a direct object. Such verbs are called *transitive.* Verbs (such as *study*) that optionally take a direct object have the subcategorization frame +[_(NP)].

28. arrive: V, –[_NP]
    like: V, +[_NP]
    study: V, +[_(NP)]
    hit: V, +[_NP]

Verbs may also be subcategorized for a sister PP. The verb *put,* for example, requires not only a sister NP but also a sister PP.

29. a) *Trevor put.
    b) *Trevor put the glass.
    c) *Trevor put on the table.
    d) Trevor put the glass on the table.

In order to account for these facts, we will have to assume that *put* has the subcategorization frame +[_NP PP] and that it can therefore be inserted only into structures such as Figure 21 in which it will have two sisters—an NP and a PP. Verbs whose subcategorization frames make no mention of PPs are assumed to allow such elements as optional sisters.

More Ambiguity

The condition that allows PPs as optional sisters of Vs predicts more structural ambiguity of the sort discussed earlier. Consider the following sentence.

30. Curly will hit the dog with the stick.

This sentence is ambiguous: it has two meanings. The first meaning can be paraphrased by using a relative clause: *Curly will hit the dog that is carrying the stick.* Here, the PP is modifying *the dog.* In the second interpretation, Curly will use the stick as a weapon, as in *Curly will use the stick to hit the dog.* Here, we might say that the PP is modifying the verb *hit.* (The first interpretation may be called the PP modifier interpretation, and the second, the instrument interpretation.) This ambiguity is a consequence of the optionality of PP both within the VP and within the direct object NP. That is, the PP *with the stick* may be mapped into either of two positions, daughter of VP or daughter of NP, as illustrated in Figure 5.22. In each case, the resulting structure is licensed by the set of phrase structure rules.

5.4 A GENERATIVE GRAMMAR

Table 2 summarizes the phrase structure rules proposed to this point as well as the syntactic categories and subcategorization frames for some of the words used in the examples in the preceding section. Table 2 provides an illustrative fragment of a *gen-*

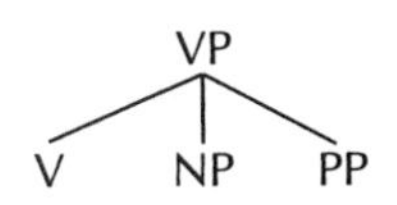

FIGURE 5.21.

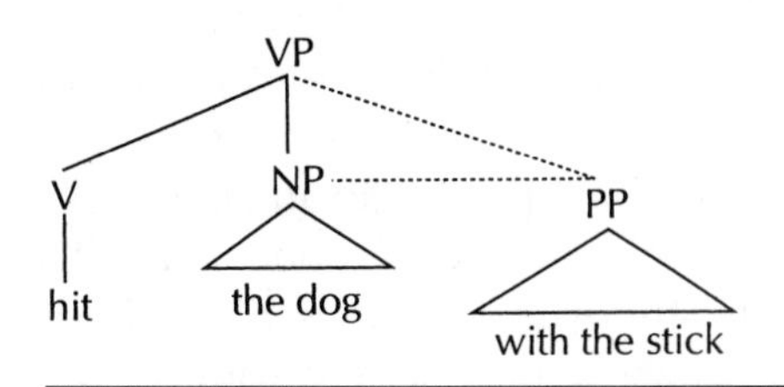

FIGURE 5.22.

TABLE 5.2. A Preliminary Generative Grammar

Rules	Lexical items	
	Examples	Syntactic categories and subcategorization frames
S → NP (M) VP	*the*	Det
NP → (Det) (AdjP) N (PP)	*in*	P
VP → V (NP) (PP)	*parcels*	N
PP → P NP	*arrive*	V, –[_ NP]
	put	V, +[_ NP PP]
	hit	V, +[_ NP]

erative grammar, a system of rules that forms or *generates* syntactic representations (tree structures) for all the grammatical sentences of a language. This approach to syntactic analysis was introduced to linguistics in the 1950s by Noam Chomsky, a linguist at the Massachusetts Institute of Technology. Since that time, many of the most influential syntactic analyses have made use of a generative grammar in one form or another. For this reason, this approach constitutes the focus of our introduction to syntax.

A major objective of current linguistic research is to construct a grammar capable of generating all the grammatical sentences of a language and no ungrammatical ones. This research involves identifying the rules that allow speakers to determine which sentences of their language are well formed and which are not.

The syntactic rules considered up to this point are very incomplete. (There has been no mention, for example, of AdvPs in the phrase structure rules.) Instead of simply adding to the list of phrase structure rules, we will turn our attention to an entirely different type of syntactic rule, one that better illustrates the type of grammar that many linguists believe is associated with human language.

5.5 TRANSFORMATIONAL RULES

Although phrase structure rules generate a very wide range of patterns, there are syntactic phenomena that they cannot describe in an entirely satisfactory way. This section presents a number of these phenomena and discusses the changes that must be made in the grammar in order to accommodate them.

Inversion in Yes-No Questions

The following structures are called *yes-no* questions because the expected response is usually *yes* or *no*.

31. a) *Will* Tiffany leave?
    b) Can Joan can scale this cliff?

Notice that the sentences in 31 have an auxiliary verb in initial position rather than after the subject NP, as in 32.

32. a) Tiffany *will* leave.
    b) Joan *can* scale this cliff.

The former structures create a problem for the S Rule (restated in 33), which allows a modal auxiliary to occur only *after* the subject NP.

33. S → NP (M) VP

What changes must be made to accommodate *yes-no* questions? One possibility is a revision to the S rule along the lines indicated in 34.

34. S → (M) NP (M) VP

Although 34 will allow a modal to occur either at the beginning of the sentence (as in 31) or after the first NP (as in 32), it can also incorrectly generate ungrammatical sentences such as 35, in which modals occur in both positions.

35. a) *Can Tiffany will leave?
    b) *Will Joan can scale this cliff?

This problem can be overcome if we retain the original (and simpler) S Rule outlined in 33 and add to the grammar an entirely new type of rule called a *transformation.* A transformation is a rule that applies to a syntactic tree to yield a new syntactic tree. In the case of *yes-no* questions, such a rule applies to the structure formed by the phrase structure rules to bring about the change stipulated in 36, where "Aux" equals any auxiliary, including modals.

36. Inversion:
    NP Aux
    1 2 ⇒ 2 1

The left side of the transformation, called the *structural description*, states the input to the rule while the right side, called the *structural change*, designates the output. Thus, 36 indicates that Inversion applies to an *NP Aux* (auxiliary verb) sequence to bring about the change indicated by the numbers in the second line.

A sentence such as *Will Alex leave?* is generated by first using the usual phrase structure rules to form the tree in Figure 23a and then applying the Inversion Rule. Since the modal *will* is a type of auxiliary verb, the Inversion Rule will convert the tree in Figure 23a into the tree in Figure 23b. What is the advantage of using the Inversion transformation to help generate *yes-no* questions? For one thing, we now avoid the ungram-

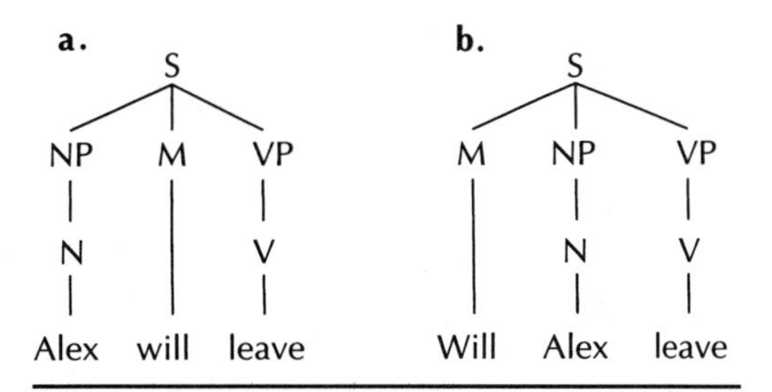

FIGURE 5.23.

matical sentences in 35. Since we can use the simple phrase structure rule in 33 to form the structure to which the Inversion Rule applies, we can be sure that there will be only one modal auxiliary verb in each S.

A second advantage of the transformational approach is that it allows us to capture the relationship between sentences such as those in 37.

37. a) Alex will leave.
    b) Will Alex leave?

Sentence 37b is the question form corresponding to 37a. This fact is captured in our analysis since both sentences are formed by the same set of phrase structure rules. The difference between them is then attributed to the fact that the Inversion transformation has applied in the question structure.

Particle Movement

English includes numerous constructions such as the following:

38. a) Chris looked up the reference.
    b) Bob threw away the wrapper.
    c) Amy put down the hamster.

In these sentences, the words, *up*, *away*, and *down* are examples of *particles*. Although many of the words in this minor lexical category can also function as prepositions, it is important to keep the two categories separate. Unlike prepositions, particles appear immediately under the VP node rather than

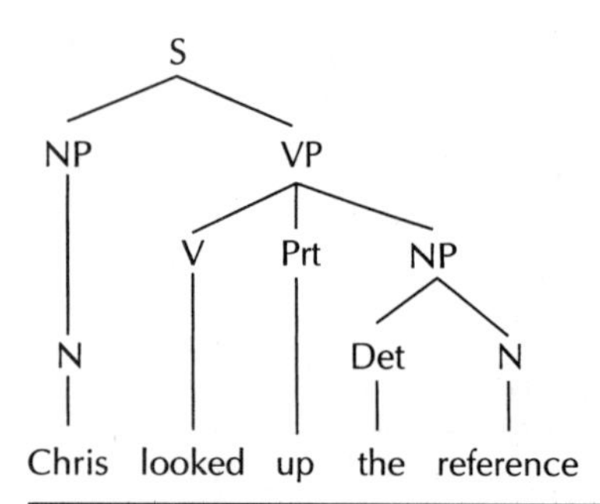

FIGURE 5.24.

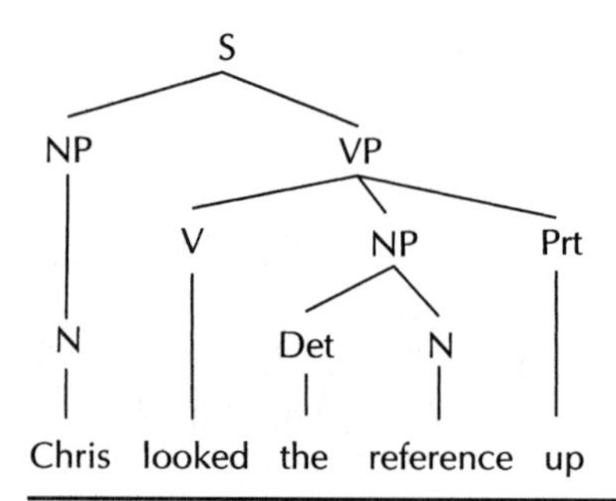

FIGURE 5.25.

a PP node. This is reflected in the revised VP Rule outlined in 39, which yields the tree structure depicted in Figure 24.

39. VP → V (Prt) (NP) (PP)

A distinctive fact about particles is that their positioning is somewhat flexible. As you can see by comparing the sentences in 40 with those in 38, the particle can occur either immediately after the verb or after the direct object NP.

40. a) Chris looked the reference up.
  b) Bob threw the wrapper away.
  c) Amy put the hamster down.

In contrast, prepositions must always occur before an NP, as stipulated in the PP Rule. Thus, we can 41a, but not 41b.

41. a) We sat near the stage.
  b) *We sat the stage near.

The flexible positioning of particles is accounted for by the following transformation, which applies optionally to the tree structure formed by the VP Rule in 39.

42. Particle Movement:
  V Prt NP
  1 2 3 ⇒ 1 3 2

Applied to Figure 24, this movement transformation will yield the structure depicted in Figure 25 by reversing the order of the particle and the direct object NP. An advantage of this analysis is that it allows the same phrase structure rule to be used in the generation of both constructions containing a particle. This provides a way of capturing the fact that the two structures are variants of the same basic pattern and differ from each other only in terms of the positioning of the particle.

Deep Structure and Surface Structure

The preceding examples show how sentences are generated with the help of two distinct rule systems—phrase structure rules, which stipulate the internal structure of phrasal categories, and transformations, which modify tree structures by reordering the elements in specific ways. Because sentences are generated in these two major steps, it is possible to identify two levels of syntactic representation. The first is called *deep structure.* It results from insertion of lexical items into the tree structure generated by the phrase structure rules. As will be shown in the chapter on semantics, deep structure plays a very central role in the interpretation of sentences. The second level of syntactic structure is called *surface structure.* It results from the application of whatever transformations are needed to yield the final syntactic form of the sentence. Thus, the deep structure for the sentence *Can chimps count?* will be Figure 26a, while the surface structure will be Figure 26b. The first structure is the product of the usual phrase structure rules, while Figure 26b is

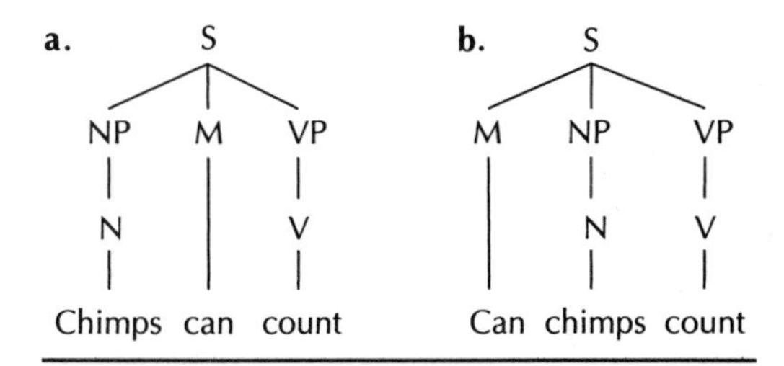

FIGURE 5.26.

formed by applying the Inversion transformation to Figure 26a.

The set of steps or rule applications that results in the formation of a sentence is called a *derivation*. In sentences where the derivation does not include any transformations, the deep structure and surface structure will look alike. Thus, the sentence *Tourists will leave*, which does not undergo any transformations, will have a surface structure (final syntactic form) identical to its deep structure (the tree produced by the phrase structure rules).

Transformations can interact with each other and with the phrase structure rules to generate a wide range of sentences. An example of this interaction is given in Figure 27.

The diagram in Figure 28 helps represent the organization of the syntactic component of the grammar as it has just been outlined. As Figure 28 shows, the grammar makes use of different syntactic operations. Some of these operations are responsible for the formation of syntactic structure, others for the insertion of lexical items, and still others for the movement of categories within syntactic structure. As we have seen, these rule systems operate in conjunction with each other to generate grammatical sentences of English. In later sections of this chapter, we will see how these rules can be modified to generate an even wider range of English sentences and how they can be further modified to account for syntactic patterns in other languages as well.

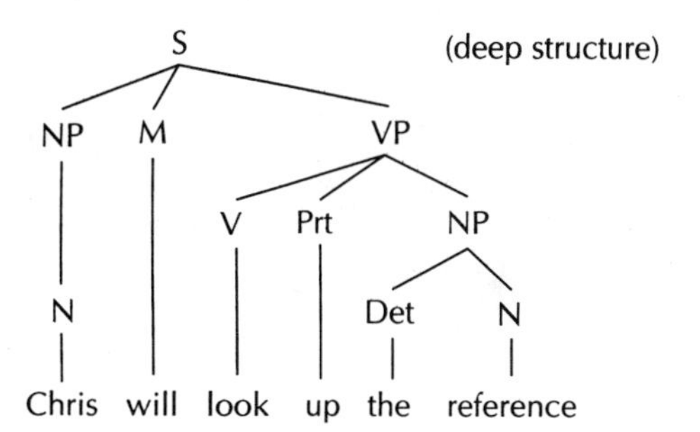

Particle Movement:

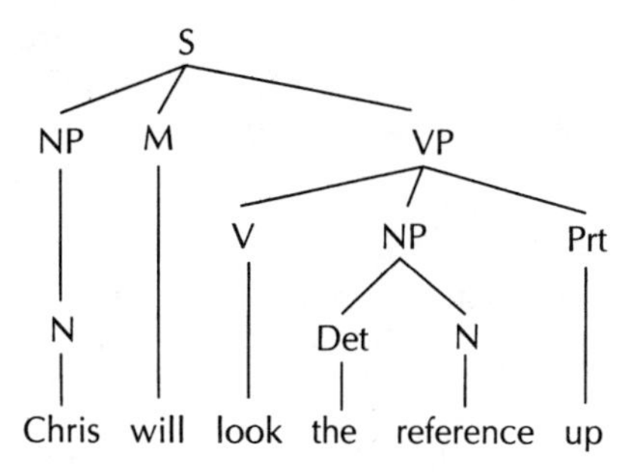

Inversion:

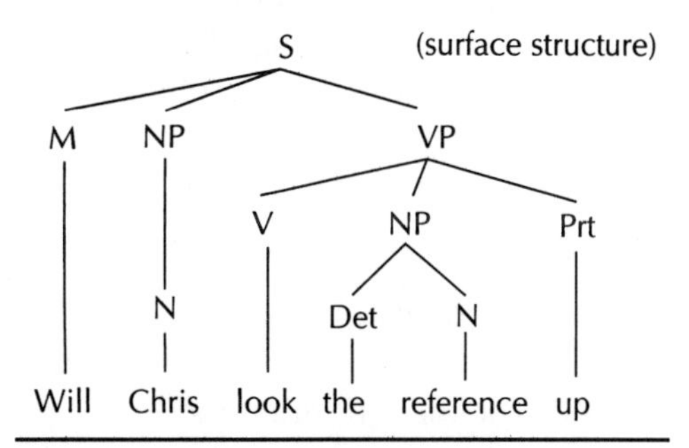

FIGURE 5.27. Interaction involving the Particle Movement and Inversion transformations.

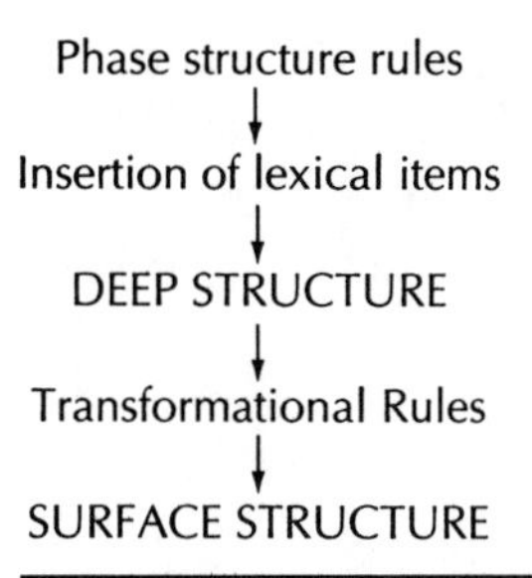

FIGURE 5.28. The syntactic component of the grammar.

Semantics: The Study of Meaning

W. O'Grady, M. Dobrovolsky, and M. Aronoff

Up to this point in the book, the emphasis has been on the form of utterances—their sound pattern, morphological structure, and syntactic composition. In order for language to fulfill its communicative function, however, utterances must also attempt to convey a meaning or message. This chapter is concerned with *semantics*, the study of meaning in human language. We will examine four major issues in this field: (1) the nature of meaning, (2) the contribution of syntactic structure to the interpretation of sentences, (3) the role of nongrammatical factors in the understanding of utterances, and (4) the possible influence of language on thought.

MEANING

Long before linguistics existed as a discipline, thinkers were speculating about the nature of meaning. For thousands of years, this question has been considered central to philosophy. More recently, it has come to be important in psychology as well. Contributions to semantics have come from a diverse group of scholars, ranging from Plato and Aristotle in ancient Greece to Bertrand Russell in the twentieth century. Our goal in this section will be to consider in a very general way what this research has revealed about the meanings of words and sentences in human language.

Word Meaning

The basic repository of meaning within the grammar is the lexicon, which provides the information about the meaning of individual words relevant to the interpretation of sentences. We know very little about the nature of this type of meaning or how it should be represented. Nonetheless, it is worthwhile to review briefly some of the better-known proposals and their attendant problems.

Referents. One well-known approach to semantics attempts to equate a word's meaning with the entities to which it refers—its *referents*. According to this theory the meaning of the word *dog* corresponds to the set of entities (dogs) that it picks out in the real world. Although not inherently implausible, this idea encounters certain serious difficulties. For one thing, there is a problem with words such as *unicorn* and *dragon*, which have no referents in the real world even though they are far from meaningless. A problem of a different sort arises with expressions such as *the Prime Minister of Great Britain* and *the leader of the Conservative Party*, both of which refer (in 1989 at least) to Margaret Thatcher. Although these two expressions may have the same referent, we would not say that they mean the same thing. No one would maintain that the phrase *Prime Minister of Great*

Source. Reprinted by permission of the publisher, from W. O'Grady, M. Dobrovolsky, and M. Aronoff, *Contemporary Linguistics*, (1989): 169–187. New York: St. Martin's Press.

TABLE 6.1. Extension versus Intension

Phrase	Extension	Intension
Prime Minister of Great Britain	Margaret Thatcher	leader of the majority party in Parliament
World Series champions (1988)	L.A. Dodgers	winners of the baseball championship
capital of California	Sacramento	city containing the state legislature

Britain could be defined as "the leader of the Conservative Party" or vice versa.

Extension and Intension. The impossibility of equating a word's meaning with its referents has led to a distinction between *extension* and *intension.* Whereas a word's extension corresponds to the set of entities that it picks out in the world, its intension corresponds to its inherent sense, the concept that it evokes. Some examples are given in Table 6.1. Thus, the extension of *woman* would be a set of real word entities (women) while its intention would involve notions like "female" and "human." Similarly, the phrase *Prime Minister of Great Britain* would have as its extension an individual ("Margaret Thatcher"), but its intension would involve the concept "leader of the majority party in Parliament." The distinction between a word's intension and its extension does not allow us to resolve the question of meaning. It simply permits us to pose it in a new way: what is the nature of a word's inherent sense of intension?

One suggestion is that word meanings (intensions) correspond to mental images. This is an obvious improvement over the referential theory since it is conceivable that one might have a mental image of a unicorn or a dragon even if there are no such entities in the real world. Unfortunately, this idea encounters serious difficulties of another sort. For one thing, it is hard to conceive of a mental image for words like *nitrogen, 522, 101, if, very,* and so on. Moreover, there seems to be no mental image for the meaning of the word *dog* that could be general enough to include Chihuahuas and Irish wolfhounds, yet still exclude foxes and wolves.

Semantic Features. Still another approach to meaning tries to equate a word's intension with an abstract concept consisting of smaller components called *semantic features.* This componential analysis is especially effective when it comes to representing similarities and differences among words with related meanings. The feature analysis in Figure 6.1 for the words *man, woman, boy,* and *girl* illustrates this. An obvious advantage of this approach is that it allows us to group entities into natural classes (much as we do in phonology). Hence, *man* and *boy* could be grouped together as [+HUMAN, +MALE], while *man* and *woman* could be put in a class defined by the features [+HUMAN, +ADULT].

Componential analysis gives its most impressive results when applied to sets of words referring to classes of entities with

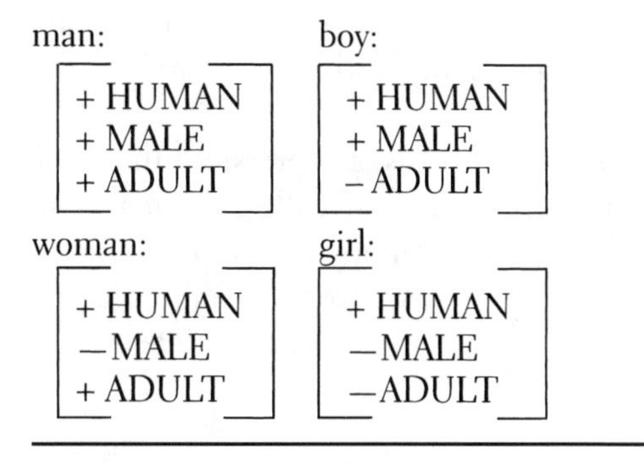

FIGURE 6.1. Semantic feature composition for *man, woman, boy, girl.*

shared properties. As illustrated above, a few simple features will allow us to distinguish among subclasses of people—men, women, boys, and girls. Unlike phonological features, however, semantic features do not seem to make up a small, well-defined class, and it is often very hard to reduce word meanings to smaller parts. Can we say, for example, that the meaning of *blue* consists of the feature [+COLOR] and something else? If so, what is that other thing? Isn't it blueness? If so, then we still have not broken the meaning of *blue* into smaller features, and we are back where we started.

In other cases, it is unclear whether semantic features really provide any insights into the nature of the meaning they are supposed to represent. What value is there, for instance, in characterizing the meaning of *dog* in terms of the feature complex [+ANIMAL, +CANINE] so long as there is no further analysis of the concept underlying the feature [CANINE]? A similar objection could be made to the use of features like [HUMAN] and [MALE] to define *man* and *woman.*

TABLE 6.2. Some English Synonyms

youth	adolescent
automobile	car
remember	recall
purchase	buy
big	large

TABLE 6.3. Some English Antonyms

dark	light
male	female
hot	cold
up	down
in	out
come	go

TABLE 6.4. Some English Polysemous Words

iron	a type of metal	an instrument (made of iron) for pressing clothes
diamond	a precious stone	a baseball field (in the shape of a diamond)
leaf	a part of a tree	a sheet of paper

TABLE 6.5. Some English Homophones

bat	a winged rodent	a piece of equipment used in baseball
bank	a commercial lending institution	a small cliff at the edge of a river
club	a social organization	a blunt weapon
pen	a writing instrument	a small cage

Semantic Relations among Words

Despite the difficulties associated with determining the precise nature of meaning, it is possible to identify a number of important universal semantic relations relevant to the analysis of word meaning. Foremost among these are the relations of synonymy, antonymy, polysemy, and homophony.

Synonymy. Words or expressions that have identical meanings are called *synonyms*. Although genuine synonymy is rare in human language, the pairs of words in Table 6.2 provide plausible examples of complete or near synonymy.

Antonymy. Words or phrases that have opposite meanings are called *antonyms*. The pairs of words in Table 6.3 provide examples of antonymy.

Polysemy and Homophony. When a word has two or more meanings that are at least vaguely related to each other, this is called *polysemy* (see Table 6.4).

Homophones are words that have a single phonetic form but two or more entirely distinct meanings (see Table 6.5). In such cases, it is assumed that there are two separate words with the same pronunciation (rather than a single word with two related meanings). Polysemy and homophony create *lexical ambiguity* in that a single word has two or more meanings. Thus, a sentence such as 1 could mean either that Liz purchased an instrument to write with or that she bought a small cage.

1. Liz bought a pen.

Of course in actual speech the context usually makes the intended meaning clear. Thus, it is improbable that anyone would perceive ambuiguity in a sentence such as 2.

2. He got a loan from the bank.

Semantic Relations Involving Sentences

Like words, sentences have meanings that can be analyzed in terms of their relation to each other. We consider three such relations here—paraphrase, entailment, and contradiction.

Paraphrase. Two sentences with identical meanings are said to be *paraphrases* of each other. The following pairs of sentences provide examples of complete or near paraphrases.

3. a) The police chased the burglar.
   b) The burglar was chased by the police.
4. a) I gave the summons to Erin.
   b) I gave Erin the summons.
5. a) It is unfortunate that the schooner lost.
   b) Unfortunately, the schooner lost.
6. a) The game will begin at 3:00 P.M.
   b) At 3:00 P.M., the game will begin.

The *a* and *b* sentences in each of the above pairs are obviously very similar in meaning. Indeed, it would be impossible for one sentence in any pair to be true without the other also being true. Thus, if it is true that the police chased the burglar, it must also be true that the burglar was chased by the police. For some linguists, the fact that two sentences must either be both true or both false is an indication that they have the same meaning. However, you may notice that there are subtle differences in emphasis between the *a* and *b* sentences in 3–6. For instance, it is natural to interpret 3a as a statement about what the police did and 3b as a statement about what happened to the burglar. Similarly, 6b seems to place more emphasis on the starting time of the game than 6a does. Some linguists feel that it would be inefficient for a language to retain two or more structures with absolutely identical meanings and that perfect paraphrases therefore do not exist.

Entailment. A relation in which the truth of one sentence necessarily implies the truth of another, as happens in examples 3–6, is called *entailment*. In the cases we have been considering, the entailment relation between the *a* and *b* sentences is mutual since the truth of either member of the pair guarantees the truth of the other. In some cases, however, entailment is asymmetrical. The following examples illustrate this.

7. a) The police wounded the burglar.
   b) The burglar is injured.
8. a) The house is red.
   b) The house is not white.

The a sentences in 7 and 8 entail the *b* sentences. If it is true that the police wounded the burglar, then it must also be true that the burglar is injured. However, the reverse does not follow since the burglar could be injured without the police having wounded him. Similarly, if it is true that the house is red, then it is also true that it cannot be white. Once again though, the reverse does not hold: even if we know that the house is not white, we cannot conclude that it must be red.

Contradiction. Sometimes, the truth of one sentence entails the falsity of another. This is the case with the examples in 9.

9. a) Charles is a bachelor.
   b) Charles is married.

If it is true that Charles is a bachelor, then it cannot be true that he is married. A relationship wherein the truth of one sentence entails the falsity of another sentence in this way is called a *contradiction.*

In this section, we have considered some of the major problems associated with the representation of word meaning as well as some basic semantic relations and contrasts involving words and sentences. Our next task must be to consider how speakers of a language are able to produce and understand meaningful utterances. Although much of the work in this area is complex, it is worthwhile to consider versions of a few representative proposals.

SYNTACTIC STRUCTURE AND INTERPRETATION

The syntactic representations (tree structures) generated by the grammar are important not only for determining the form of sentences, but also for determining their interpretation. In this section, we will consider the relevance of syntactic structure to three aspects of sentence interpretation—the representation of structural ambiguity, the assignment of thematic roles, and the interpretation of reflexive pronouns.

Structural Ambiguity

As noted in the chapter on syntax, some sentences are ambiguous because their component words can be arranged into phrases in more than one way. This is called structural ambiguity and is to be distinguished from lexical ambiguity, which is the result of homophony or polysemy.

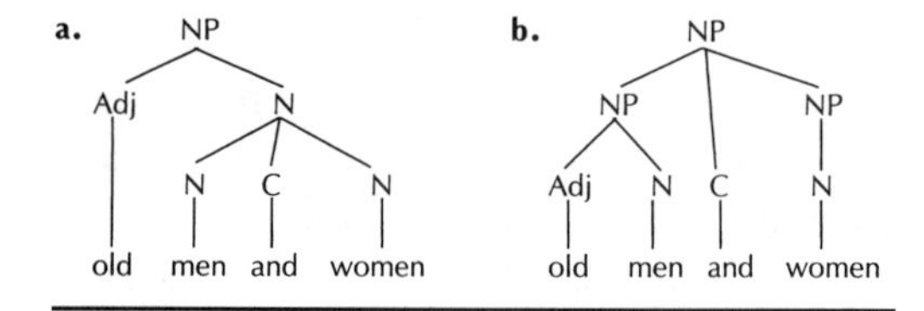

FIGURE 6.2.

Structural ambiguity is exemplified by phrases like *old men and women* where we can take old to be a property of both the men and the women or of the men alone. These two interpretations or readings can be linked to separate tree structures as Figure 6.2 shows, (C = conjunction). Figure 6.2a corresponds to the reading in which *old* modifies *men* as well as *women.* This is shown by making the adjective a sister of the category that dominates both nouns. In Figure 6.2b, on the other hand, the adjective is a sister of only the N *men,* and this structure corresponds to the reading in which "old" applies only to the men.

Another case of structural ambiguity is found in sentences such as 10.

10. Nicole saw the people with binoculars.

In one interpretation of 10, the people had binoculars when Nicole noticed them (the phrase with binoculars modifies the noun people), while in the other interpretation, Nicole saw the people by using the binoculars (the PP modifies the verb). These two readings can be represented as in Figure 6.3. In Figure 6.3a, the PP *with binoculars* combines with the N *people,* reflecting the first reading for this sentence. In Figure 6.3b, on the other hand, the PP is a sister of the verb and its direct object and is not linked in any special way to the N people.

As a final example of this type of structural ambiguity, consider the compound *French history teacher,* which can refer to a history teacher who is French or to a teacher of French history. These two readings can

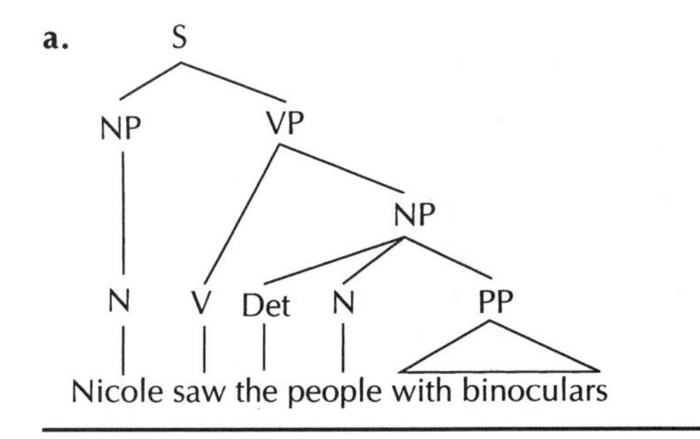

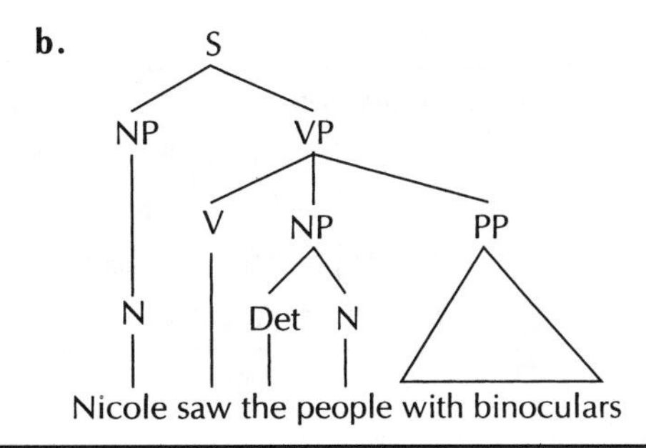

FIGURE 6.3.

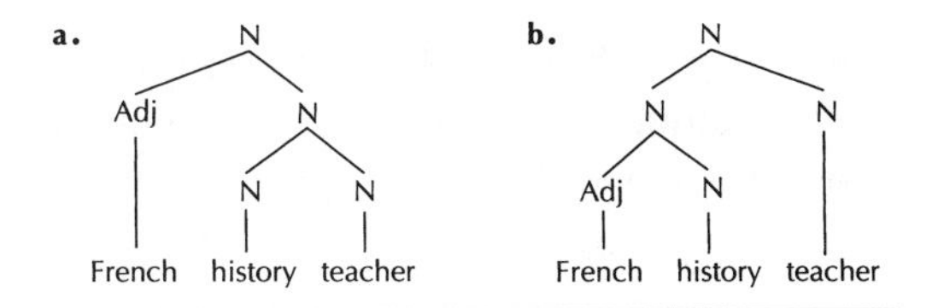

FIGURE 6.4.

be associated with the trees depicted in Figure 6.4a and 6.4b, respectively.

The three cases of structural ambiguity just outlined all have in common the fact that the two interpretations can be related to differences in the surface structure tree. Sometimes, however, ambiguity can be properly characterized only with the help of deep structure. Consider in this regard a sentence such as the following:

11. Who do you expect to play?

On one reading, 11 can be interpreted as a question about who your opponent will be (who you will play against) while on another, it asks who will be playing. Although it is difficult to see how the grouping of constituents in surface structure could reflect these different interpretations, consideration of the relevant deep structures provides the needed insight. The first reading corresponds to 12a, in which *who* appears as direct object of *play*. The second interpretation, on the other hand, is associated with the deep structure depicted in 12b, in which the *wh* word is subject of *play*. In both cases, *Wh* Movement will yield the sentence in 11. (See Section 5.7 of Chapter 5.)

12. a) You expect to play who.
    b) You expect who to play.

The fact that deep structure is needed to represent certain types of ambiguity provides interesting additional evidence for the view that there are at least two levels of syntactic structure—deep structure and surface structure.

Thematic Roles

Part of semantic interpretation involves determining the roles that the referents of NPs play in the situation described by sentences. Consider in this regard the sample sentence in 13.

13. The senator sent the lobster from Maine to Nebraska.

It would be impossible to understand this sentence if we could not identify the senator as the person who is responsible for sending something, the lobster as the thing that is sent, and so on. The term *thematic role* or *semantic role* is used to describe the part played by a particular entity in an event. In most linguistic analyses, at least the thematic roles in Table 6.6 are recognized. (These definitions have been simplified somewhat.) The notion of transfer used in the definition of theme, source, and goal is

TABLE 6.6. Thematic Roles

The senator sent the lobster from Maine to Nebraska.		
Agent:	the entity who deliberately performs an action	*the senator*
Theme:	the entity undergoing a change of state or transfer	*the lobster*
Source:	the starting point for a transfer	*Maine*
Goal:	the end point for a transfer	*Nebraska*

intended to involve not only actual physical movement, but also changes in possession, as in 14, and identity, as in 15.

14. Terry gave the skis to Mary
    agent theme goal
15. The magician changed the handkerchief
    agent theme
    into a rabbit.
    goal

Many semantic analyses recognize various other thematic roles, shown in Table 6.7, to describe the NPs in sentences such as the following:

16. The astronomer saw the comet with a new telescope at the observatory.

Thematic Role Assignment. The lexicon includes information about the type of thematic role associated with particular verbs and prepositions. The entry for the verb *send*, for example, indicates that the subject NP expresses an agent, the direct object NP a theme, and so on. (By convention, the thematic role of the subject is written to the left of the dash and that of the direct object to the right.)

17. send
    NP __ NP (from NP) (to NP)
    agent theme source goal

The lexical entries for the verbs *see* and *receive* include the following information about thematic roles.

18. *see*
    NP __NP
    experiencer stimulus
19. *receive*
    NP __ NP
    goal theme

The entry for the preposition *near* would include the following piece of information.

20. near
    __ NP
    location

The thematic role that an NP receives is determined by its position in deep structure. Consider first a sentence such as 13, repeated here as 21, whose surface structure and deep structure are identical in the relevant respects.

21. The senator sent the lobster from Maine to Nebraska.

TABLE 6.7. Some Additional Thematic Roles

The astronomer saw the comet with a new telescope at the observatory.		
Experiencer:	the entity perceiving something	*the astronomer*
Stimulus:	the entity perceived	*the comet*
Instrument:	the entity used to carry out an action	*a new telescope*
Location:	the place at which an entity or action is located	*the observatory*

Here, the order of the NPs in deep structure is such that they can be linked in one-to-one fashion with the thematic roles mentioned in the lexical entry for *send* in 17. A more interesting case involves sentences such as 22 in which the NP bearing the theme role (*what*) occurs at the beginning of the sentence rather than after the verb (the position corresponding to theme role in the lexical entry).

22. What will the senator send from Maine to Nebraska?

Fortunately, this does not present a problem since the NP *what* will occur in the right position in deep structure to receive the theme role. As 23 shows, *what* occurs in direct object position prior to *Wh* Movement.

23. The senator will send what from Maine to Nebraska.

Deep Structure and Meaning. The discovery of the relevance of deep structure to sentence interpretation had an important and lasting impact on linguistic theory, allowing formulation of the following hypothesis.

24. In sentences with the same deep structure, noun phrases will be associated with the same thematic roles.

This generalization is true not only for *wh* questions, but also for other pairs of sentences that share a deep structure. Consider the following:

25. a) Anton will throw the ball.
    b) Will Anton throw the ball?
    Anton = agent; *the ball* = theme
26. a) The boxer knocked out the champion.
    b) The boxer knocked the champion out.
    the boxer = agent; *the champion* = theme
27. a) Sandra received the book.
    b) The book was received by Sandra.
    Sandra = goal; *the book* = theme

The relevance of deep structure to the assignment of thematic roles is important for two reasons. First, it shows that syntactic structures not only represent the way in which words are organized into phrases, but also are relevant to semantic intepretation. Second, the fact that an NP's position in deep structure determines its thematic role provides additional evidence for the existence of the underlying level of syntactic structure. This, in turn, lends support to the claim that there must be at least two types of syntactic rules: phrase structure rules, which form the deep structure; and transformations, which convert it into surface structure.

The Interpretation of Reflexive Pronouns

The interpretation of *reflexive pronouns* such as *himself, herself,* or *themselves* provides another example of the relevance of syntactic structure to semantics. Reflexive pronouns are considered to be a type of NP since they occur in the positions normally reserved for this type of syntactic category. In 28, for instance, the reflexive pronoun *himself* occurs in the direct object position.

28. Jim hurt himself.

In order to interpret a reflexive pronoun, it is necessary to identify elsewhere in the sentence the NP that indicates its referent. In a sentence such as 28, the referent of the reflexive pronoun *himself* is specified by the NP *Jim*. The NP to which a pronoun looks for its interpretation is called its *antecedent*.

Consider now the following two sentences.

29. a) [S Clare showed Alice a picture of herself].
    b) [S Clare said [S Alice took a picture of herself].

Most speakers of English find that the first sentence is ambiguous in that *herself* can have either *Clare* or *Alice* as its antecedent. Thus, the picture mentioned in 29a could be of either Clare or Alice. Not so in 29b. Here, *herself* can only take *Alice* as its antecedent. The reason for this contrast stems from the following principle.

30. The Same S Requirement: A reflexive pronoun and its antecedent must occur in the same S.

In 29a, there are two NPs in the same S as the reflexive (*Alice* and *Clare*), either of which could be its antecedent according to 30. The sentence is therefore ambiguous. In 29b, in contrast, only one NP (*Alice*) occurs in the same S as the reflexive pronoun. The NP *Clare* occurs outside the embedded S in which *herself* occurs and therefore cannot serve as its antecedent. This shows that a feature of syntactic structure, the occurrence of clause boundaries, is crucial to the intepretation of sentences.

The C-Command Requirement. A somewhat more abstract feature of syntactic structure enters into the interpretation of the reflexive pronoun in sentences such as 31, which would be associated with the tree in Figure 6.5.

31. The boy's uncle admired himself.

Although there are two NPs in the same S as *himself*, only one (*the boy's uncle*) can serve as antecedent for the reflexive pronoun. Thus, the person who was admired in 31 must have been the boy's uncle, not the boy. The principle needed to ensure this interpretation makes use of the notion *c-command,* which is defined as follows.

32. The NP *x* c-commands the NP *y* if every category dominating *x* also dominates y.

A second constraint on the interpretation of reflexives is now formulated as follows.

33. The C-Command Requirement: A reflexive pronoun must be c-commanded by its antecedent.

Now consider how this principle applies to the NPs *the boy* and *the boy's uncle* in structures such as Figure 6.5. There is only one category dominating the NP *the boy's uncle*—namely S. Since this category also dominates the reflexive, NP[1] c-commands *himself* according to our definition and can therefore serve as its antecedent. As we have already seen, the sentence has this intepretation. But what of the forbidden interpretation? The NP *the boy* (NP[2]) in Figure 6.6 is dominated by two categories—S and NP[1]. Each of these categories is circled in Figure 6.6. Since only the first of these categories also dominates the reflexive, NP[2] does not c-command *himself* and can therefore not serve as its antecedent. This is the desired result.

There is much more that can and should be said about the interpretation of pronouns. A more detailed examination of

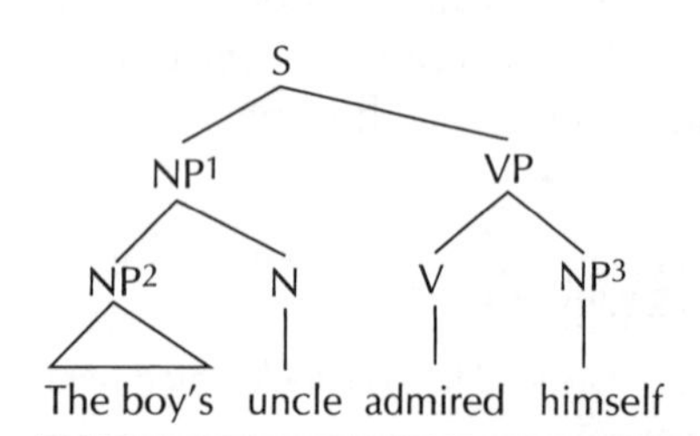

FIGURE 6.5.

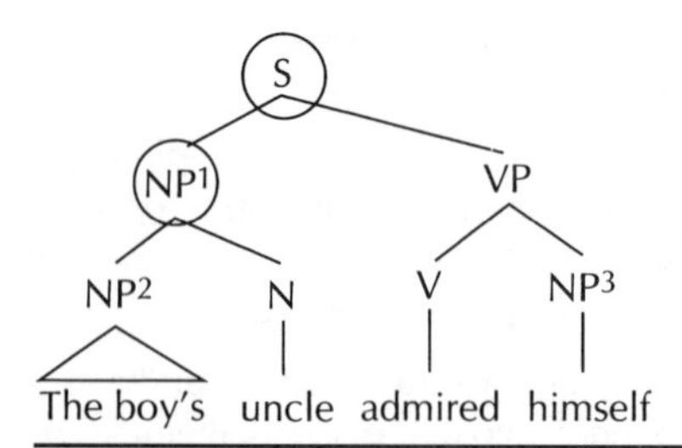

FIGURE 6.6.

this very complex phenomenon would reveal the need for even more abstract principles referring to additional properties of syntactic structure. However, the examples we have already considered suffice to illustrate the crucial point in all of this; namely, that syntactic structure plays an important role in various aspects of semantic interpretation.

OTHER FACTORS IN SENTENCE INTERPRETATION

Syntactic structure is just one of the factors entering into sentence interpretation. In order to use a language appropriately, it is also necessary to understand how the grammar interacts with other systems of knowledge and belief. Several examples of this interaction are presented in this section.

Pragmatics

A major factor in sentence interpretation involves a body of knowledge that is often called *pragmatics*. This includes the speaker's and addressee's background attitudes and beliefs, their understanding of the context in which a sentence is uttered, and their knowledge of the way in which language is used to communicate information. As an example of this, consider the following pair of sentences.

34. a) The councilors refused the marchers a parade permit because they feared violence.

    b) The councilors refused the marchers a parade permit because they advocated violence.

These two sentences have identical syntactic structures, differing only in the choice of the verb in the second clause (*feared* in the first sentence vs. *advocated* in the second). Yet the pronoun *they* is usually interpreted differently in the two sentences. Most people believe that *they* should refer to *the councilors* in 34a but to *the marchers* in 34b. These preferences seem to have nothing to do with grammatical rules. Rather, they reflect beliefs we have about different groups within our society—in particular, that councilors are more likely to fear violence than to advocate it.

The Cooperative Principle. In many cases, pragmatic knowledge is put to even subtler uses in the interpretation of sentences. Suppose, for example, that a ship's captain makes the following entry in the log: *The first mate was not drunk tonight.* Although this statement says nothing about the first mate's condition on other nights, a reader is likely to infer that he has a problem with drunkenness. This inference does not follow from the literal meaning of the sentence, but rather from the way in which language is used to communicate. Ordinarily, the sentences we use are supposed to be informative and relevant. This is part of what has been called the *Cooperative Principle* for conversation. When an utterance appears to be uninformative or irrelevant, the listener (or reader) assumes that he or she is to draw a conclusion that can restore its informativeness and relevance.

In the example we are considering, this involves taking what appears to be a relatively uninformative statement about someone (a ship's first mate is expected not to be drunk) and inferring something informative from it (namely, that the individual's not being drunk on a particular night is somehow exceptional). This conclusion follows not from the meaning or structure of the original sentence, but rather from the assumption that the captain was trying to be informative when he made the entry in the ship's log. A conclusion that is drawn on the basis of an assumption about how we communicate is called a *conversational implicature.*

Presuppositions

There are other ways in which a speaker's beliefs can be reflected in language use. A familiar example of this involves sentences such as the one in 35.

35. Have you stopped exercising regularly?

Use of the verb *stop* implies a belief on the part of the speaker that the listener has been exercising regularly. No such assumption is associated with the verb *try*, as 36 shows.

36. Have you tried exercising regularly?

The assumption or belief implied by the use of a particular word or structure is called a *presupposition*. The following two sentences provide another example of this.

37. a) Nick admitted that the team had lost.
    b) Nick said that the team had lost.

Choice of the verb *admit* in 37a indicates that the speaker is presupposing the truth of the claim that the team lost. No such presupposition is associated with choice of the verb *say* in 37b. The speaker is simply reporting Nick's statement without taking a position on its accuracy.

Still another type of presupposition is illustrated in 38.

38. a) Abraham Lincoln was assassinated in 1865.
    b) Abraham Lincoln was murdered in 1865.

Whereas use of the verb *assassinate* in 38a implies that Abraham Lincoln was a prominent political figure, no such presupposition is associated with the verb *murder*.

Speech Acts

Still another set of factors that must be taken into account in semantic analysis involves the type of act associated with the utterance of a sentence. According to one influential proposal, there are three basic speech acts: the *locutionary act*, which corresponds to the utterance of a sentence with a particular meaning, *the illocutionary act*, which reflects the intent of the speaker in uttering that sentence (to praise, to criticize, warn); and the *perlocutionary act*, which involves the effect that the speaker has on his or her addressees in uttering the sentence. Suppose, for example, that a teacher who is having trouble maintaining order in the classroom utters the sentence *I'll keep you in after class*. In uttering such a sentence, the teacher is simultaneously producing three speech acts—a locutionary act (involving utterance of a sentence with the meaning "I'll make you stay in school later than usual"), an illocutionary act (a warning), and a perlocutionary act (silencing the students).

There is no one-to-one relationship between syntactic structure and speech acts. An illocutionary act of warning, for example, could involve (1) a declarative sentence (a statement), (2) an imperative (a command), (3) a *yes-no* question, or (4) a *wh* question.

39. a) There's a bear behind you.
    b) Run!
    c) Did you know there's a bear behind you?
    d) What's that bear doing in here?

Similarly, a perlocutionary act aimed at getting someone to open the window could be expressed in a variety of ways.

40. a) I wish you'd open the window.
    b) Open the window.
    c) Could you open the window?
    d) Why don't you open the window?
    e) It's awfully hot in here.

Because of the perlocutionary act associated with these utterances, the appropriate response on the part of the listener should be to open the window. Speakers of English therefore know that 40c is not be interpreted as a simple request for information. Only as a joke would someone respond by saying *Yes, I could* and then not do anything about opening the window.

Despite the indirect relationship between sentence structure and speech acts, there is a small set of verbs whose use makes explicit the illocutionary force of a sentence. Common examples of these verbs include *promise, bet, warn,* and *agree.*

41. a) I promise that I'll be there.
    b) I bet that the Yankees will lose.
    c) I warn you that's not a good idea.
    d) I agree that you should do it.

The verbs in 41 indicate the type of illocutionary act involved in uttering the sentence—an act of promising, an act of warning, and so on. Such verbs are called *performatives* since the very act of producing them involves the performance of an illocutionary act. Thus, in saying *I promise that I'll be there,* I automatically carry out an illocutionary act of promising. Such is not the case with a sentence like *I'll be there,* which could be a simple prediction, a warning, or a threat.

When a verb is used performatively, it always has a first person subject (*I* or *we*) and occurs in the present tense. Some performative verbs are subject to an additional restriction: they can only be appropriately uttered by speakers with a certain social status or authority. Only a clergyman or a justice of the peace can appropriately utter the sentence *I pronounce you man and wife* while only a judge can properly say *I sentence you to five years in prison.*

LANGUAGE, MEANING, AND THOUGHT

As we examine the way in which words and structures are used to express meaning, it is natural to wonder about the possibility that language might play a role in shaping how we think. While it is certainly plausible to believe that language facilitates reasoning and problem solving by providing a way to represent complex thoughts, it has sometimes been proposed that linguistic systems might have a considerably more fundamental effect on cognition. Indeed, it has even been suggested that the particular language people speak shapes the way in which they think and perceive the world.

The Sapir-Whorf Hypothesis

The best-known and most influential version of this idea has come to be known as the *Sapir-Whorf Hypothesis* in honor of Edward Sapir and Benjamin Lee Whorf, the two linguists who articulated it most clearly. Sapir, for instance, wrote in 1929:

> *Human beings . . . are very much at the mercy of the particular language which has become the medium of expression for their society . . . the "real world" is to a large extent unconsciously built upon the language habits of the group.*

Several years later, Whorf expressed essentially the same sentiment when he made the following claim.

> *We dissect nature along lines laid down by our native language. The categories and types that we isolate from the world of phenomena we do not find there because they stare every observer in the face; on the contrary, the world is presented in a kaleidoscopic flux of impressions which has to be organized by our minds—this means largely by the linguistic systems in our minds.*

Two types of linguistic phenomena are commonly cited in support of the Sapir-Whorf Hypothesis: cross-linguistic differences in vocabulary, and variation in the type of grammatical contrasts a language encodes. The first type of phenomenon is exemplified by the fact that the Eskimo language has far more words for snow than does English, while Arabic has a far richer vocabulary pertaining to sand. From this, it is sometimes concluded that Eskimo and Arabic allow their speakers to make perceptual distinctions pertaining to snow and sand that English cannot.

A more plausible explanation is that language is shaped by the need to adapt to the cultural and physical environment. According to this alternate view, if a language has a large vocabulary in a particular area, it is because subtle distinctions of that type are important to its speakers. Even speakers of a language without an extensive vocabulary in that area should be able to make the relevant contrasts if they become important to them. This is presumably why skiers, for instance, are able to distinguish among many different types of snow, even though their language may not have a separate word for each. Where necessary, they can then use the resources of their language to describe these distinctions by creating expressions such as *powder snow*.

Consider now cross-linguistic differences in the expression of grammatical contrasts—the type of phenomenon on which Whorf concentrated. Whorf attempted to link the apparent lack of tense contrasts in Hopi (an Amerindian language spoken in the American Southwest) with different cultural attitudes towards time and the future. According to Whorf, time for the Hopi does not consist of the passage of countable units (like days), but rather the successive reappearance of the same entity. There is no "new day" for the Hopi, Whorf claimed, just the return of the same day. Whorf believed that this is reflected in the Hopi belief that the future is best dealt with by working on the present situation (which will return as the future).

Here again, innumerable problems arise. For one thing, Whorf was apparently mistaken in his belief that Hopi does not have tense; such a category is, in fact, found in this language. Moreover, even if there were no tense contrasts in Hopi or if they were radically different from those found in English, it is unlikely that they could be correlated with speakers' attitudes toward time. There are doubtless many individual speakers of English who share the Hopi philosophy for dealing with the future (and some Hopi speakers who do not).

The problem of Hopi tense aside, there are many grammatical phenomena that it would be absurd to correlate with the ability to make distinctions in the real world. Finnish, for instance, has no grammatical contrasts that reflect natural gender (or sex), but one would hardly conclude that the absence of a distinction between he and she impedes the ability of Finns to distinguish between males and females. Likewise, it is hard to believe that speakers of French believe that women, tents, and shirts are somehow alike even though the words for all three entities (*femmes*, *tentes*, and *chemises*) are assigned to the same gender class (feminine).

An Experiment. There have been various attempts to verify the Sapir-Whorf Hypothesis by experimental means. The most famous of these experiments was conducted in 1958. The basic idea was to determine the effect of English and Navaho on the perception of color, size, and shape. In Navaho, verbs expressing handling actions vary in form depending on the shape of the object being handled. Thus, a long flexible object (a snake) requires the verbal form *šánléh*, a long rigid object (a spear) requires the verbal form šántúh, while flat flexible material requires *šánilcóós*. Since there is no such contrast in English, it was thought that children speaking these two languages might group objects in different ways. An experiment was designed to test this.

The children participating in the experiment were presented with a pair of objects such as a piece of rope and a stick, and then shown a third object and asked to tell the experimenter which of the pair went best with the new object. It was thought that the responses of the Navaho-speaking children might reflect the classification imposed by the verb system of their language rather than similarities in size or color. However, it was found that the responses of the forty-seven white English-speaking children (from Boston) were very similar to those of the fifty-nine monolingual speakers of Navaho. Given the differences between the two languages, this is not the result predicted by the Sapir-Whorf Hypothesis.

The repeated failure of experimental attempts to uncover systematic shaping effects for language has drastically reduced the credibility of the Sapir-Whorf Hypothesis. This is not to say that languages do not represent reality in different ways. Clearly, they do. Thus, French distinguishes between knowing someone (*connaître*) and knowing something (*savoir*), a distinction that is not made in the verb system of English. On the other hand, English has an extremely fine set of contrasts involving light (*glimmer, glitter, glow, gleam,* and *glisten*) that are not found in other languages. What is in doubt is whether such differences in the linguistics description of reality reflect deeper, language-induced differences in patterns of thought or perception.

Summing Up

The study of *semantics* is concerned with a broad range of phenomena including the nature of meaning, the role of syntactic structure in the interpretation of sentences, and the effect of *pragmatics* and speaker beliefs on the understanding of utterances. Although serious problems and obstacles remain in all these areas, work in recent years has at least begun to identify the type of relations, mechanisms, and principles involved in the understanding of language. These include the notions of *extension* and *intension* in the case of word meaning, the C-Command Requirement in the case of pronoun interpretation, and *thematic role* assignment in the case of sentence interpretation.

Sources

Various positions on the nature of word meaning and on semantic relations have been outlined and discussed in many books, including those by Fodor and Kempson cited below. The Cooperative Principle is outlined and defended in Paul Grice's important article "Logic and Conversation" in *Syntax and Semantics* 3, edited by P. Cole and J. Morgan (New York: Academic Press, 1975). Speech act theory is introduced in J. Austin's classic work *How to Do Things with Words* (Oxford: Clarendon Press, 1962). The quote from Edward Sapir on language and thought comes from a passage cited in Whorf's article "The Relation of Habitual Thought and Behavior to Language" reprinted in *Language, Thought and Reality*, edited by J. Carroll (Cambridge, Mass.: MIT Press, 1956). The quote from Whorf is taken from his article "Science and Linguistics," also reprinted in *Language, Thought and Reality*. The attempt to verify the Sapir-Whorf Hypothesis experimentally is reported in an article by J. Carroll and J. Casagrande, "The Function of Language Classification in Behavior" in *Readings in Social Psychology*, edited by E. Maccoby et al. (New York: Henry Holt, 1958).

Recommended Reading

Fodor, Janet Dean 1978. *Semantics: Theories of Meaning in Generative Grammar.* Cambridge, Mass.: Harvard University Press.

Hurford, James, and Brendan Heasley. 1983. *Semantics: A Coursebook.* London: Cambridge University Press.

Kempson, Ruth. 1977. *Semantic Theory*. London: Cambridge University Press.

Lyons, John. 1977. *Semantics.* Vols. 1 and 2. London: Cambridge University Press.

McCawley, James. 1981. *Everything That Linguists Have Always Wanted to Know About Logic.* Chicago: University of Chicago Press.

File 120—Regional Variation: *The Origin of American Dialects*

M. Crabtree and J. Powers

It is obvious to most people that there is variation among languages—that, for example, English is different from Spanish which is different from Arabic which is different from Russian, and so on. It may not be so obvious, however, that each and every language exhibits internal variation (on all linguistic levels).

Within any particular language there is variation from speaker to speaker, the form of language spoken by one person being known as an *idiolect.* There is also variation from group to group. When a group of speakers of a particular language differs noticeably in its speech from another group we say they are speaking different *dialects.* A dialect, then, is simply any variety of a language, the variety being characterized by systematic differences from other varieties of the same language. These differences are in pronunciation, vocabulary, and other aspects of the grammar. Differences in pronunciation are commonly known as *accent,* but note that this represents systematic variation in the phonological component of the grammar and is more than likely accompanied by variation in the other components as well.

How do we know if two (or more) language varieties are different dialects of the same language or if in fact they are separate, distinct languages? One criterion used to distinguish dialect from language is the criterion of *mutual intelligibility;* that is, if speakers of one language variety can understand speakers of another language variety and vice versa, we say that these varieties are mutually intelligible. Suppose you are a native of Brooklyn, New York, and you go to visit some friends in Beaumont, Texas. You may notice some differences in the speech of your Beaumont friends (and they in yours), but essentially you will be able to understand each other; your variety of speech and theirs are mutually intelligible, but differ systematically, and are therefore dialects of the same language.

It is not always easy to decide if two language varieties are different dialects of the same language or different languages just on the basis of mutual intelligibility; other factors (such as cultural or historical considerations) may cloud the issue. In China, Mandarin is spoken in northern provinces and Cantonese in the southern province of Kwang Tung. Now, even though in spoken form these language varieties are not mutually intelligible, they are considered (by the speakers of these varieties themselves) to be dialects of the same language. Why? One reason is that in written form these two varieties are mutually intelligible, because they use a common writing system. The opposite situation exists in the American Southwest between Papago and Pima, two Native American languages. These two language

Source. Reprinted by permission of the publisher, from M. Crabtree and J. Powers, compilers, *Language Files: Materials for an Introduction to Language* (1991): 367–368. Columbus: Ohio State University Press.

varieties are actually mutually intelligible with less linguistic difference between them than between Standard American English and Standard British English. However, because these two tribes regard themselves as politically and culturally distinct, they consider the languages to be distinct as well.

Another complication for the criterion of mutual intelligibility can be found in a phenomenon known as a dialect continuum. This is a situation where, in a large number of contiguous dialects, each dialect is closely related to the next but the dialects at either end of the continuum (scale) are mutually unintelligible. Thus, dialect A is intelligible to dialect B which is intelligible to dialect C which is intelligible to dialect D; but D and A are not mutually intelligible. A situation such as this can be found near the border between Holland and Germany, where the dialects on either side of the national border are mutually intelligible. Because of international boundaries, however (and probably political and cultural considerations, as well), speakers of these varieties regard them as dialects of distinct languages. At what point is the line drawn? Clearly, the criterion of mutual intelligibility does not account for all the facts. Indeed, there may be no clear-cut, black-and-white answer to such a question in every case.

From the Family Tree Model in the section on historical linguistics we saw that a parent language may split and form daughter languages—e.g., Germanic split off into English, Dutch and German (among others). This type of split may occur when dialect differences become so great that the dialects are no longer mutually intelligible to the speakers of these language varieties.

A group of people speaking the same dialect is known as a *speech community*. Speech communities are defined not only by geography, but also by a number of other factors, such as age, gender, and socioeconomic class. A *regional* dialect is a dialect defined by geography.

ORIGINS OF LANGUAGE VARIATION IN THE U.S.

How did regional variation in the United States arise? Some variation can be explained in terms of early regional settlement patterns; other variation can be explained in terms of natural barriers to communication. The formation of U.S. regional dialects in part had its beginnings in England as speakers from various regions of England journeyed across the Atlantic and settled the Eastern seaboard of the U.S. Thus, from the start, settlers in any given settlement formed heterogeneous speech communities, some perhaps speaking a London dialect, others speaking a southern or northern dialect, etc. In time, because of prolonged contact and necessary communicative compromise (for example, agreeing on a southern English word for small body of water but a northern English word for a water container) the diverse dialects of a particular settlement began to coalesce into a more homogeneous speech community. Compromises would differ, however, from settlement to settlement. Thus, various dialects emerged along the Atlantic seaboard. During this time, some colonial cities such as Boston, Philadelphia and Charleston acquired prestige as a result of becoming centers of trade and culture. The dialects spoken in these cities became prestigious as well and began to exert influence on nearby settlements.

Migration westward to a large extent reflected the settlement patterns of the Atlantic states. Yankees from Western New England and Upstate New York, in moving west, fanned out, settling chiefly in the Great Lakes area; settlers from the Middle Atlantic region (primarily Pennsylvania and

Maryland) journeyed west to Ohio, West Virginia and the Mississippi Valley. Influence from the southern Atlantic colonies was felt as speakers from this area settled in the Gulf states. The lines are never clearly drawn, however, because the streams of migration often mingled. Sometimes, New Englanders and speakers from the Mid-Atlantic region would form compact communities outside their usual area of settlement—e.g., the Yankee enclave of Worthington, Ohio or the North Carolina Quaker settlement of Richmond, Indiana. Added to these patterns is the influence of the later waves of European immigrants. The spread of migration continued to the Rocky Mountain states, essentially following previously established patterns but with greater mingling and, finally, reaching the West Coast, resulting in even greater crossing of dialect lines. Moreover, the sharp increase in geographic mobility since World War II as a result of transportation technology has contributed greatly to the obscuring of dialect boundaries.

Geographic barriers have also played a role in the formation of regional dialects; that is, regional dialect boundaries often coincide with natural barriers such as rivers, mountains or swamps. For example, speakers of English east of the Alleghenies may use the word *soda* for a nonalcoholic, carbonated beverage while those west of this mountain range use *pop* instead.

File 123—Regional Variation: *Variation at Different Levels*

M. CRABTREE AND J. POWERS

While we are all aware that there is some variation in terms of pronunciation and choice of vocabulary items among dialects of the same language, we may be surprised at the extensive variation which exists at all levels of linguistic structure. This file is designed to introduce you to different types of variation that exist at each level.

PHONETIC LEVEL

A. In most American dialects [t, d, n, s, z] are produced with alveolar articulation, but some New York City dialects have dental articulation whereby the tongue tip touches the top teeth.

B. Some British and Scottish dialects of English produce a trilled "r," [r̃], while most American dialects have either a retroflex [r] or a "bunch" [ɹ].

C. Many American dialects have a mid back lax vowel which is transcribed as [ɔ]. However, this vowel is produced very differently in different dialects—some are more rounded, some less so, others are higher or lower than others (but not as high as [U] or as low as [a]).

PHONOLOGICAL LEVEL

A. Many American dialects have one vowel in *caught, dawn,* and *hawk* (something close to [ɔ] but a little lower) and another in *cot, Don, and hock* [a]; but some dialects have the same vowel in all words, and this difference in vowels is not used to distinguish between words, so that in these particular dialects *Don* and *dawn* would be homophonous.

B. In Southern England, words like *flood, but,* and cup have the vowel [ə] and words like *full, good,* and *put* have the vowel [ʊ]. In Northern English dialects, however, both sets of words have the vowel [ʊ].

C. Some Caribbean English dialects do not have the sounds [θ] or [ð]; instead the sounds [t] and [d] are substituted, respectively, e.g., *both* [bot], and *there* [dɛr].

D. Standard British English does not permit sequences of vowel-r-C or V-r-#. This is similar to Bostonian English where the sentence *Park the car* would be pronounced [pak ð əka].

E. Some Black English dialects do not permit sequences of C-r or C-l, especially in unstressed syllables, so that the word professor would be pronounced [pofɛsə].

F Northern and Southeastern British English dialects both have the phonemes [a] and [æ] in their phonemic inventories. In the Southeastern dialects, how-ever, [æ] occurs in *pat, bad* and *cap* but [a] in *path, laugh, grass,* etc., while in the North [æ] occurs in both sets of words.

G. In some Southern and Midwestern dialects of America there is no distinction between [ɪ] and [ɛ] before nasals; only [ɪ] oc-

Source. Reprinted by permission of the publisher, from M. Crabtree and J. Powers, compilers, *Language Files: Materials for an Introduction to Language* (1991): 373–374. Columbus: Ohio State University Press.

curs. So, in the words *pen* and *pin*, which are pronounced [pɛn] and [pɪn], respectively, by SAE speakers, the pronunciation is [pɪn] for both words in these dialects.

MORPHOLOGICAL LEVEL

A. Some American dialects do not mark third person singular present tense and say, for example, *he kiss, she see,* and *it jump* rather than *he kisses*, etc.
B. Some Black English dialects mark the habitual aspect on the verb, whereas SAE does not. So, for example, SAE has the same verb form for both *She is in there now* and *She is in there every Tuesday*, while the BE dialects would make a distinction, *She there now* ("zero" form) vs. *She be there every Tuesday.*
C. Some rural British dialects use the possessive morpheme only with pronouns and not with nouns: *Tom egg* for *Tom's egg; the old lady purse* for *the old lady's purse*, but *my life, his dog, etc.*
D. In parts of Northern England and Southern Wales *-s* is not just a third singular present tense marker, but a general present tense marker. These speakers say sentences like *I likes him, We goes*, etc.
E. Many dialects of English have *hisself* and *theirselves* for standard *himself* and *themselves.*
F. Appalachian English has many examples of past tense forms for various verbs which are different from other American dialects, e.g., *clum* for *climbed, et* for *ate, het* for *heated.*
G. In Appalachian English the possessive pronouns have an *-n* suffix: *yourn, hisn, hern, ourn, theirn* as in *That's hisn.*

SYNTACTIC LEVEL

A. For many Southern speakers, *done* serves not only for a form of *do* but also can be an auxiliary: *She done already told you* rather than *she has.*
B. For many Appalachian speakers *right* can be an adverb as well as an adjective, e.g., *A right good meal.*
C. In some dialects combinations of auxiliaries like *might could, might would, may can,* and *useta could* are permitted, and form a single constituent.
D. Many Appalachian and Midwestern dialects have the construction *The crops need watered* as a variant of *The crops need to be watered.*
E. Many dialects of English have the feature *multiple negation*, e.g., *Didn't nobody see it* and *Ain't nobody can touch me.*

SEMANTIC LEVEL

A. *Knock up* means "rouse from sleep by knocking" in British English, but "make pregnant" in American.
B. Words for carbonated beverages differ from place to place (*soft drink, soda, pop, soda-pop, coke, pepsi, tonic*, etc.).

Analyzing Variation in Sign Languages: Theoretical and Methodological Issues

Rob Hoopes, Mary Rose, Robert Bayley, Ceil Lucas,
Alyssa Wulf, Karen Petronio, and Steven Collins

Sociolinguistic inquiry examines the complex relationship between language and its social context. Language is much more than a means of communication; it is also a social object that both reflects and helps constitute the social context in which it is embedded. One of the ways that language accomplishes this social function is through the variable use of linguistic forms. If a language provides speakers with more than one way to say the same thing, speakers will use the variants to mark group identity, group solidarity, and social distance and also to define the social environment (Fasold 1984). Sociolinguistic theory holds that the understanding of such variation is crucial to an understanding of language itself. Unlike traditional linguistic inquiry, which might ignore or attempt to minimize the importance of linguistic variation, sociolinguistic research makes variation the primary object of inquiry, explains the variable use of a linguistic form based upon sociolinguistic factors, and reveals linguistic forms that may be in the process of change.

Sociolinguistic inquiry is especially suited to describing the differences between language varieties. By delineating the linguistic differences between two language varieties and then correlating each with the linguistic and social contexts in which they occur, the patterning of the nonstandard variety emerges. In fact, demonstrating that vernacular dialects consist of linguistic patterns just as systematic as the patterns that characterize standard varieties is one of the great contributions of sociolinguistic research (Wolfram 1993). Finally, sociolinguistic analysis of how an individual signer utilizes a particular variable can reveal the unconscious but highly complex patterning and functioning of a variable within the lect of an individual.

LINGUISTIC VARIATION

Among its other attributes, language is a social object that both reflects and helps to constitute the social structure in which it is embedded. The complex relationships among language, social structure, and the context of use compose the object of sociolinguistic inquiry. Although sociolinguists have employed a number of approaches to the study of the relationship between linguistic form and social structure, including the ethnography of speaking (e.g., Bauman and Sherzer 1974), interactional sociolinguistics (e.g., Gumperz 1982), and discourse analysis (e.g., Tannen 1984), the variationist paradigm developed by William Labov has proven to be one of the more productive.

The relationship between language and social context is most apparent in the variable use of a particular linguistic form, be it phonological, morphological, lexical, or syntactic. Since Labov's study in 1966 of variable deletion of [r] by residents of the

We are grateful to Lois Lehman-Lenderman for the sign drawings and MJ Bienvenu for serving as the sign model.

Lower East Side of New York City, sociolinguistic research has repeatedly confirmed that nonlinguistic facets of an interaction strongly influence the particular linguistic form a speaker will use at any given moment in the interaction. These include the personal, social, sociocultural, and socioeconomic characteristics of the participants, as well as the characteristics of the interaction itself (e.g., formal vs. informal). In other words, factors outside the language influence which particular linguistic forms a speaker will use. The socioeconomic factors that influence how often a variable will occur are referred to as social constraints. There may also be linguistic factors that influence how often a variable will occur, which are referred to as linguistic constraints.[1] Typically, the frequency at which a particular variant occurs is influenced by both types of constraints. For example, in his study of the phonological variable pinky extension, Hoopes (1998) found that the occurrence of pinky extension was strongly influenced by three linguistic constraints—the phonological structure of the sign, the syntactic category of the sign, and the prosodic function of the sign. But its occurrence was also influenced somewhat by the degree of social distance between the subject and her interlocutor in the interaction (i.e., a social constraint). The closer the relationship, the more likely pinky extension was to occur. Thus, the frequency of pinky extension was influenced by the linguistic and the social constraints working in concert.

The influence of contextual factors on language use was originally postulated by Labov and others, on the basis of spoken language research. It is now beyond dispute that sociolinguistic phenomena also obtain in sign language. Careful studies over the past twenty years have shown correlations between sociolinguistic factors and linguistic variables on every linguistic level. For example, Lucas and Valli (1992) demonstrated that signers code switch among varieties of ASL (along the ASL–Contact Sign–Signed English continuum) and that the particular language variety used during a given interaction is largely determined by sociolinguistic factors. Likewise, Woodward (1973, 1994) found that five morphological variables of ASL (e.g., verb reduplication and verb incorporation of negation) closely correlated with sociolinguistic factors.[2] For a thorough survey of this growing body of sociolinguistic research of sign languages, see Patrick and Metzger (1996).

DISCOVERING AND DESCRIBING VARIATION ACROSS INDIVIDUALS AND COMMUNITIES

Sociolinguistic variation in ASL has been noted since the beginning of research on the language. The *Dictionary of American Sign Language* (Stokoe, Casterline, and Croneberg 1965) reports variants for many signs, including LIE and MOTHER. Croneberg's (1965) discussion of variation in the dictionary suggests social dimensions that might be investigated for correlations with variation, including region and ethnicity. Several studies in the 1970s examined phonological variation in ASL, describing social and linguistic constraints on variation in handshape, location, and orientation of lexical signs (Battison et al. 1975; Woodward et al. 1976; Woodward and Erting 1975). These early studies of ASL variation share with studies of spoken language variation a commitment to describing patterns in a particular community's use of language, whether the community is large, as in the Deaf community of the United States, or smaller, defined in regional or social terms (Labov 1972; Milroy 1987; Lucas 1995; Rose et al. 1998). The three studies we report on here all had as their primary goal to describe systematic variation in the use of ASL within and across individuals and groups within the U.S. Deaf community.

Since the earliest studies of variation in ASL, research on variation has changed in that new quantitative and qualitative tools have been developed (Milroy 1980, 1987; Rousseau and Sankoff 1978; Rand and Sankoff 1990). At the same time, our understanding of ASL phonology, morphology, syntax, and discourse structure has deepened. It is in this environment of recent social and linguistic research that the three studies presented here took up their respective topics. In brief, the three studies are as follows:

1. Hoopes (1998) examined constraints on pinky extension in lexical ASL signs.
2. Collins and Petronio (1998) set out to discover differences in the way that deaf-blind signers use ASL, as compared to sighted users of ASL.
3. Lucas, Bayley, Valli, in collaboration with Rose, Wulf, Dudis, Sanheim, and Schatz (forthcoming) studied sociolinguistic variation in ASL, relying primarily on quantitative methods to describe phonological and morphosyntactic variation in ASL as it is used around the country and across social groups. The analysis of one variable, the sign DEAF, is summarized here; this report is a follow-up study to Lucas's earlier investigation (1995).

Certain methodological issues are common to all variation studies, and we will show how these concerns relate to the choice of informants, to the elicitation of vernacular language, and to the variables and constraints, both social and linguistic, considered in all of the studies. Next, we will discuss concerns that may be particular to studying sociolinguistic variation in sign languages. These community-particular concerns color not only the methodologies employed, but also the social constraints considered in the analyses. Finally, we will set out the methodologies of all three studies.

Defining and Sampling a Community

The first issue common to studies of variation in both signed and spoken languages concerns sampling. The goal of all variation studies is to describe the patterns of variable linguistic structure within and across language communities. Whether the study is qualitative or quantitative, participants in the study must be members of the communities whose language use is being described. Further, quantitative sociolinguistic work that seeks to reach conclusions about language use in a community as a whole must take steps to ensure that its participant group is as representative as possible of the entire community. A study of variable ASL use in the Deaf community, for example, must study the language use of deaf people who use ASL. The language community may be defined in both linguistic and social terms. If the study finds that a group of ASL users share some aspect of their language in common, (e.g., if the constraints on a particular variable affect all members of the community in the same way), then this is evidence that the group is a linguistic community (Labov 1972).

When defining the language community in social terms, variation studies have taken two main approaches. One approach is to use broad social categories like socioeconomic status and gender to draw boundaries around subgroups within a community (Labov 1966, 1972). Another is to use community-based social networks. This latter approach looks at a community in terms of the number and nature of connections among individuals in order to correlate these connections with patterns of language use (Labov 1966, 1972; Milroy 1980, 1987; Eckert 1989a). A researcher who employs either approach, however, has an explicit definition of the language community in terms of common social factors.

The three studies discussed here examined variation in language structure and use in the U.S. Deaf community (Padden and Humphries 1988; Padden 1997). The researchers in each case took steps to ensure that all participants were deaf users of ASL, and that they were all connected socially to their local Deaf communities. In the pinky extension (PE) study and in the Tactile ASL study, the participants were known to the researchers to be members of local Deaf communities. They had grown up as users of ASL, attended residential schools, and participated in social relationships with other deaf people and in Deaf organizations like Deaf clubs. For the Tactile ASL study, it was also important that participants be members of a community of deaf-blind people. Collins and Petronio defined this membership both in terms of physical blindness and in terms of language use and socialization. All fourteen participants in their study were legally blind as a result of Usher syndrome I; all of them regularly socialized with other deaf-blind adult users of Tactile ASL; and all were comfortable and experienced users of Tactile ASL. For the quantitative study of sociolinguistic variation in ASL, not all participants in the seven communities around the country were personally known to the researchers. Rather, the project relied on contact people in each area to recruit a sample that was as representative of the community as possible. This strategy was informed by the social network approach of Milroy (1987). Potential participants were approached by a contact person, a deaf individual who lived in the area, possessed a good knowledge of the local community, and was a respected member of the community. A major concern of this study was representativeness. Therefore, the researchers and contact people tried to recruit a group of participants diverse enough to match the diversity of the U.S. Deaf community. The project sampled the language of 207 women and men in seven sites: Boston, Massachusetts; Frederick, Maryland; Staunton, Virginia; New Orleans, Louisiana; Olathe, Kansas; Kansas City, Missouri; Fremont, California; and Bellingham, Washington. African-American and white women and men were represented, as were working- and middle-class signers of both races. Participants ranged in age from 13 to 93, and included signers with deaf parents as well as those with hearing parents.

Describing Natural Language Use

The second issue in variation studies concerns the type of data analyzed. Studies of sociolinguistic variation differ in a fundamental way from formal studies of abstract linguistic competence: studies of variation are committed to studying language in context (Labov 1966, 1972; Milroy 1980, 1987; Lucas 1995). Directly eliciting different variants of a sociolinguistic variable would defeat the purpose of studying how the social and linguistic environments of language use condition variation. The sociolinguistic interview, though it has been used in many studies as a way in which linguists can record conversational language use, has been recognized as not being conducive to natural speech (Milroy 1987; Schilling-Estes 1999). The ideal would be to record and study the full range of the community's styles of language use, from formal lectures given to an audience of strangers to casual daily encounters with friends and acquaintances. In reality, this is impossible. First of all, few people, if any, whether they are deaf or hearing, hang out waiting for linguists to come and record their conversations. Also, as we will discuss further below, the camcorder would get in the way.

Despite these fundamental limitations on linguists' access to natural language use, each of the three studies reported on here made methodological accommodations toward gathering conversations that were as natural as possible. The conversation types that were recorded differed on many dimensions: how well the conversational participants knew one another, the degree to which the conversations were about language itself, the length of the conversations, and the presence or absence of the researchers during the videotaping. Each of these dimensions might have provided an environment that would affect variation. For this reason, the conclusions take into account these aspects of the recorded conversations.

In the PE study, Hoopes recorded a signer during four different one- to two-hour conversations with other ASL users. The first and third conversations were with a close friend, also deaf, from the signer's residential school. The second recording was made during a conversation with a deaf graduate student from Gallaudet University, someone with whom the signer was casually acquainted. During these conversations, the deaf signer and her conversational partner were asked just to chat. The final conversation was with a hearing interpreter, a good friend of the signer. Before this conversation, the researcher suggested some topics they might discuss. During all of these conversations, the researcher was not a participant; in fact, he was absent from the room.

The Tactile ASL study relied on conversational data videotaped under two different circumstances. The first recording was made during an informal party that lasted about four hours. Eleven deaf-blind adults who regularly socialized together attended the party. The researchers videotaped their Tactile ASL conversations with one another. In the second situation, three pairs of deaf-blind adults were recorded telling stories to one another using Tactile ASL. The researchers viewed this second set of data as coming from more formally situated language use.

Lucas et al.'s study of sociolinguistic variation in ASL videotaped groups of signers during one- to two-hour data collection sessions. These sessions were divided into three parts. The first consisted of approximately one hour of free conversation among the participants, without the researchers present. In the second part, at least two participants were selected from each group and interviewed in depth by deaf researchers about their educational and linguistic backgrounds, their social networks, and their patterns of language use. The final part involved eliciting lexical variants from the participants who had been interviewed. All participants in this part of the data collection were shown the same set of thirty-three pictures and were asked to supply signs for the objects or actions represented in the pictures.

Defining Variables and Constraints

The third issue that the studies described here share with all studies of sociolinguistic variation is a concern that what is being investigated is, in fact, a sociolinguistic variable. The three studies are among the first studies of variation in ASL in about twenty years. Our hope is that we know enough now about the structure of ASL to identify what varies, to describe it, and to quantify it. The first steps in variation analysis are to define the variable and the envelope of variation. That is, decide what forms count as instances of the variable and determine that the forms that vary indeed are two ways of saying the same thing.

The three studies required, first, a consideration of what features were noticeably variable. These variables might be found at any level of linguistic structure, from phonology to discourse. For the quantitative study of sociolinguistic variation in ASL, the hope was that these variables would also correlate with both linguistic and social factors. For the qualitative study of Tactile ASL, in which a language variety is being described in detail for the first time, the goal is that the variables that are described will uniquely identify the community being studied and will be amenable to further quantitative or applied work.

An additional issue that arises early in a variation study concerns specifying the factors that may potentially influence a signer's choice of a variant. Lucas (1995), for example, investigated the potential effects of eight separate linguistic factors on the choice of a variant of DEAF. As it turned out, most of these constraints proved not to be statistically significant. However, the labor of coding for many factors was not in vain. The study demonstrated that Liddell and Johnson's (1989) hypothesis that variation in the form of DEAF is influenced primarily by the location of the preceding sign is, at best, incomplete. The present studies are at different stages in the process of identifying constraints. The Tactile ASL study, because its purpose is simply to describe the differences between visual and Tactile ASL, set out to note features that were known to be unique to tactile signing. Collins and Petronio knew that being deaf-blind is a conditioning factor for some changes in language use, but the question was, what linguistic changes take place? The investigation of pinky extension and the sociolinguistic variation in ASL study, on the other hand, needed to propose constraints, both linguistic and social, on the variables to be quantified. A central theoretical issue for variation studies is the identification of internal constraints on the variables. As Labov stated, the issue "is to discover whatever constraints may exist on the form, direction, or structural character of linguistic change" (1994, 115). Phonological constraints on the variables considered by the PE and sociolinguistic variation studies could include the segmental phonological environment or suprasegmental, or prosodic, environment. Other linguistic constraints could be morphological, syntactic, or related to discourse topic or type of discourse. The linguistic constraints considered in each of these studies will be described in more detail below.

As for social constraints, the researcher's knowledge of the community should inform what factors are considered in the model of variation within the community. The PE study was not designed to take into account social constraints other than the level of intimacy between conversational partners, as it was expressly limited to investigating the variable signing of a single individual. The Tactile ASL study suggests that if deaf-blind and sighted individuals are included in the same study of variation in ASL, then this should be taken into account, as a deaf person's vision status could affect how he or she uses the language. Sociolinguistic variation in ASL study included several social factors in its statistical analysis of variants of DEAF.

SOCIOLINGUISTIC STUDIES IN THE DEAF COMMUNITY: SOME ISSUES

Social Constraints Particular to Deaf Communities

While social constraints like gender, age, and ethnicity might be common to all studies of sociolinguistic variation, many of these need to be articulated more fully when they are put into research practice in a particular community. This is particularly true for studies of linguistic variation in

Deaf communities. Notions like socioeconomic status or even age cannot be simply borrowed whole from studies of variation in spoken language communities.[3] The differences in social constraints when applied to Deaf communities are of two types. First, there are constraints, like age, whose labels have a common application but which might have a different meaning considering the history of Deaf communities in this country. Second, there are constraints, like language background, that are unique to Deaf communities.

The first type of constraints include definitions of gender, age, regional background, and ethnicity, all of which need to be redefined when looking at Deaf communities. For deaf people, regional background, or where they grew up, may be less significant than where they attended school (especially if it was a residential school) or where their language models acquired ASL. Age as a sociolinguistic variable may have different effects on linguistic variation because of the differences in language policies in schools and classes for deaf children over this last century. Thus, while differences in the signing of older and younger people may appear to be due either to age-group differences or to natural language change such as occurs in all languages, these differences may also be the result of changes in educational policies, like the shift from oralism to Total Communication or from Total Communication to a bilingual/bicultural approach. These language policies affected not only what language was used in the classroom, but also teacher hiring practices (deaf teachers who used ASL or hearing teachers who knew no ASL). These language policies affected deaf children's access to appropriate language models, and this access may have varied across time to such an extent as to affect the kind of variation we see in ASL today.

With respect to ethnicity, demographics and oppression may work doubly against our understanding of language use in minority Deaf communities. The linguistic and social diversity in the Deaf community is just beginning to be explored by researchers (Lucas 1996; Parasnis 1997), and many questions remain about how African-American, Latin-American, or Asian-American deaf people self-identify and how they use language. Are the boundaries of these groups such that they form coherent groups whose ethnic identity is stronger than their Deaf identity? Or do the members of these groups construct a separate, minority Deaf identity? Is it reasonable to acknowledge multiple potential language influences? Is the use of a particular variant related to a person's identity as a Deaf person, or as an Anglo-American Deaf person, for example?[4] Through the social network technique of contacting potential informants, the sociolinguistic variation in ASL study uncovered one way in which ethnicity and age have intersected to create a situation of oppression multiplied. The contact people were unable to find any Black Deaf people over age 55 who were members of the middle class (that is, who had a college education and were working in professional occupations). This finding suggests that political, social, and economic factors intersect with race and ethnicity in ways that have profound effects on minority language communities like the Deaf community.

With respect to gender, several questions emerge that are also related to the minority language community status of the Deaf community. Those yet to be answered include: Is there a solidarity in language use between men and women in a language minority group because of oppression from the outside and shared experiences rooted in being Deaf? Or are usage differences as pronounced as in other communities?

The second type of differences in social constraints arises from the unique characteristics of Deaf communities. The question of the language background of signers who participate in the studies is one such characteristic. Most participants in variation studies acquired the language under study, say English or Spanish, as a native language from native-speaking parents, as well as from exposure in their everyday environment. In Deaf communities, some participants had neither of these kinds of exposure to the language at the earliest stages of their development. Even deaf parents may not be native signers. It may seem that this problem conflicts with the goal of describing use of a particular language. However, if all signers who learned ASL from people other than their parents were excluded from sociolinguistic studies, such studies would be invalidated because they would not be representative of the community. Researchers should simply take account of the language background of their participants while drawing conclusions from the data. If the analysis is qualitative, the language background of the participants should be expressly stated in the report and taken into account in the analysis. If the analysis is quantitative, the influence of language background differences on the variables being investigated may be included as a factor in the statistical model.

A related constraint is the school background of informants. Whether the signers who participated in the variation study attended a residential or mainstream school may have influenced their signing. Some questions related to this issue are: Did the signers acquire ASL at a very early age from signing adults, or did they learn it at a later age, having entered the community later? At what age did they acquire or learn ASL? What kinds of signing—SEE, Contact Signing, or ASL—did their language models use?

Collecting Data: Videotaping and the Observer's Paradox

Linguists who conduct sociolinguistic research aspire to base their conclusions on conversation that is as natural as possible. However, one aspect of the basic method required for doing careful study of natural language use impinges on this goal: A conversation being studied must be recorded, yet the fact that the conversation is being recorded makes it less likely that it will be close to the vernacular use of the language. Labov (1966, 1972) has called this problem the "Observer's Paradox." When considering sociolinguistic research in Deaf communities, this problem may be magnified. Videotaping is more intrusive than audiotaping. Equally important is the issue of anonymity. While voices on an audiotape cannot be connected to a face or a name, except by the researchers, faces on a videotape are not anonymous. The Deaf community is small, and signers may be concerned, with good reason, that what they say on videotape will be seen by others in the community and understood out of context. With videotaping, anonymity is impossible.

What We Know and What We Can Study

The limits on what we know about sign language structure pose a further consideration for studies of variation in sign languages. We have learned much about the structure of ASL in the last twenty years, since the earliest studies of variation. For example, when the first studies of variation in ASL were conducted, the phonological specifications of signs were understood to be simultaneously produced. The variables considered in the present studies, on the other hand, assume that segments of signs occur in sequence, and that what varies phonologically are either individual features of these segments or the sequence in which these segments are produced (Liddell and Johnson 1989; Lucas 1995). We need to know enough about the structure and meaning of the language to ensure that our variants have the same meaning and are simply two (or more) ways of saying the same thing. That is, we need to be able to distinguish between two forms that mean the same thing but are both part of the language and vary with respect to one another, and two forms that have different meanings and, therefore, cannot be said to be in variation. We also need to know enough about the phonological, morphological, syntactic, and discourse structures, and how they interact, in order to define carefully and clearly the environments that condition variation. In light of these concerns related to ASL structure, we are just beginning to understand what constitutes a variable in a sign language and what the possible linguistic constraints on variability are. Further, as the present studies begin to suggest, simply borrowing constraints from spoken language studies may not be sufficient to account for the variation we see in ASL (Lucas 1995).

In summary, the studies that we present here share some goals and methodological concerns with sociolinguistic research in general. They also represent three approaches to the question of variation in ASL, a question that requires attention to our understanding both of linguistic structure and of Deaf history, culture, and community.

METHODS EMPLOYED IN THE THREE STUDIES

In this section, we describe the methods used by the researchers in each of the three studies. Table 1 summarizes the goals and methodologies of these studies.

Pinky Extension: Confirming a Variable

The pinky extension (PE) study relies on data from a single individual's conversational signing to examine patterned variation in the pinky extension variable (Hoopes 1998). Sociolinguistic variables are not just variable over a community. The variation we see in ASL signing in Deaf communities does not result from one signer using one variant and one signer using another. Rather, a single speaker/signer ordinarily uses two or more variants of a single variable, even within the same conversation (Guy 1980). Signing with one's pinky extended on some signs has been anecdotally discussed as a possible phonological variable. Signs like THINK, WONDER, and TOLERATE (the latter two illustrated in Figure 1) can be signed either with the pinky (the fourth finger) closed or fully extended.

The study's goals were to determine whether pinky extension showed patterned variation that correlated with phonological, syntactic, or discourse constraints, and to consider functional explanations for these correlations. The study set out to (a) describe this potential variable as part of one individual's signing style and (b) discuss possible constraints on the individual's use of pinky extension.

The signer for the PE study was a 55-year-old Caucasian Deaf woman. She was deafened in infancy and was the only deaf member of her immediate family. She attended a residential school and Gallaudet College. She was videotaped in conversation over four separate sessions, each one to two hours long, for a total of seven hours of conversational data. Her conversational partners varied in how well she knew them (one was a long-time friend, another a recent acquaintance), and in whether they were hearing or deaf.

For the analysis, 100 occurrences of pinky extension were extracted from the videotaped data. Each of these occurrences was coded for the following linguistic and social factor groups:

TABLE 1. Summary of Goals and Methodologies of the Three Studies

GOALS AND METHODS	STUDY		
	Pinky Extension	*Tactile ASL*	*Sociolinguistic Variation in ASL*
Research questions	Is PE a sociolinguistic variable? What linguistic constraints possibly condition PE?	How does Tactile ASL differ from visual ASL in its phonology, morphology, syntax, and discourse structure?	What are the linguistic and social factors that condition use of three variants of DEAF? Which of these constraints are strongest?
Informants	1 Deaf woman, an ASL user	14 deaf-blind ASL and Tactile ASL users	207 Deaf ASL users
Videotaping procedures	4 conversations lasting 1 to 2 hours each	Conversations at a party lasting 4 hours (11 participants); Storytelling sessions (6 participants, paired)	Groups of 2 to 6 participants in three situations: Conversations in the group; Interview with the researcher; Responding to questions on lexical variants
Videotape analysis	Extracted 100 occurrences of PE. Compared timing of a subset of these occurrences with tokens of non-PE signs.	Developed specific questions about linguistic structure. Extracted examples of each type of structure from conversations. Generalized over examples to a statement about variant structure.	Watched videotapes for signers using DEAF. Glossed each occurrence of DEAF with information about constraints in a text database.
Methods of analysis	Coded each instance of PE for linguistic and social constraints. Compared percentages of PE and non-PE in different environments. Compared prosodic features. Suggested constraints that may condition PE.	Compared structures in Tactile ASL with parallel structures in visual ASL.	Coded each token for linguistic and social constraints. Entered coded tokens into VARBRUL. Used VARBRUL probabilities to find relevant and irrelevant constraints. Suggested variable linguistic rules that are part of the grammar of ASL.

- Preceding handshape,
- Following handshape,
- Sign in which PE occurs,
- Discourse topic,
- Handshape of the PE sign,
- Syntactic category of the PE sign, and
- Level of intimacy between informant and conversational partner.

A subset of these occurrences was also coded for prosodic features. This coding involved timing the duration of the tokens (occurrences) by the number of frames each lasted. These durations were averaged and compared with the duration of tokens of the same lexemes (signs) without pinky extension. The constraints investigated for this subset of tokens were the duration of the sign, whether there was a preceding or following pause, and repetition of the sign.

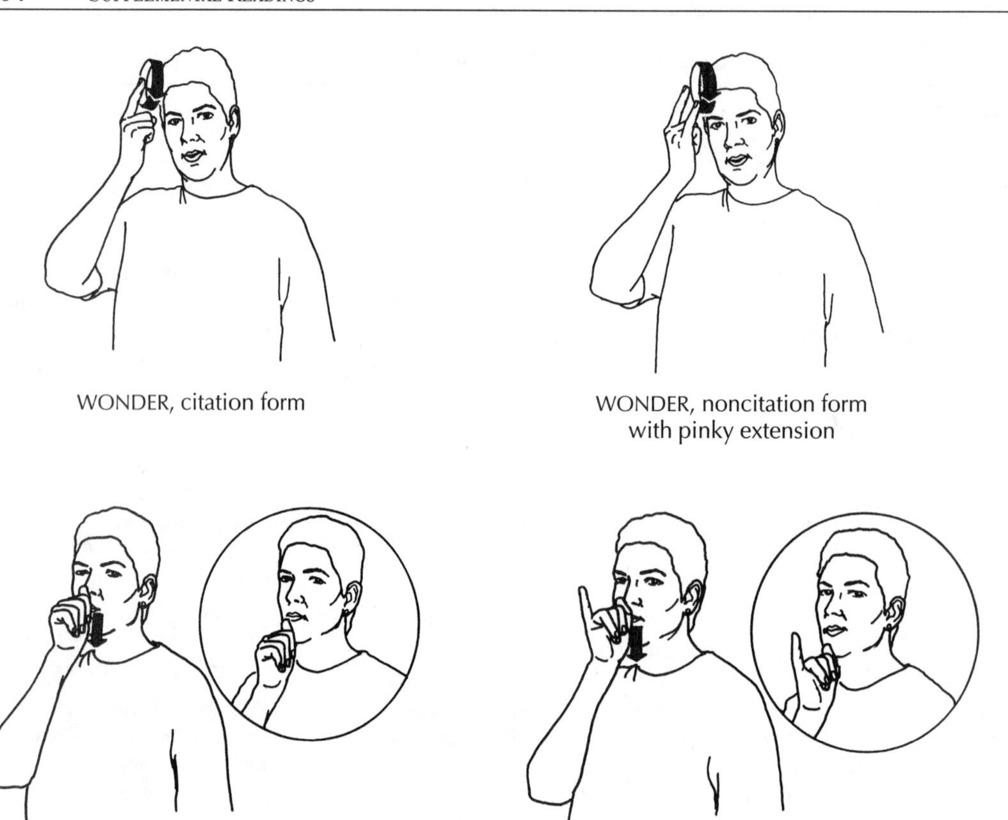

FIGURE 1. Citation and noncitation forms of WONDER and TOLERATE.

Some potential occurrences were excluded from the pool of tokens. Occurrences in fingerspelling were excluded because it was assumed that in these cases it resulted from processes other than those that could cause pinky extension in lexical signs. Also excluded were instances of lexicalized pinky extension, in which case the non-PE variant and the PE variant would not co-occur in the signing of one individual. Lastly, signs in which pinky extension did not occur over the full production of the sign were excluded.

The analysis of the full 100 tokens, not including the prosodic analysis, consisted of comparing percentages of tokens in each of the subgroupings of the constraints. In the prosodic analysis, Hoopes compared the average duration of the signs with and without pinky extension.

Tactile ASL: Identifying Variables

While the ASL of sighted deaf people has been studied for forty years, the signing of deaf-blind people is a new subject of linguistic research. The Tactile ASL study set out to describe changes in signing that occur when ASL is used in a tactile, rather than a visual, mode. The goal was to describe the particular variety of ASL used in the deaf-blind community when deaf-blind people converse with each other. Collins and Petronio (1998) considered that variation between sighted ASL and Tactile ASL could occur at any level of linguistic structure.

To collect representative samples of deaf-blind conversation, Collins and Petronio used two sets of conversational data, one more informal, one more formal. Informal data were collected at a party attended by eleven deaf-blind people. The more formal data came from another set of conversations between three pairs of deaf-blind people, all using Tactile ASL to tell stories to each other. As mentioned earlier, the fourteen signers had all been born deaf, knew and used ASL prior to becoming legally blind, became blind as a result of Usher syndrome I, and regularly socialized with deaf-blind adults who use Tactile ASL. Tactile ASL can be received with one or both hands. In order to limit the possible variation that could occur even within Tactile ASL, only one-handed conversations were included in the data set used to describe the tactile variety of ASL.

Research questions specific to each level of linguistic structure were formulated. These questions are listed in Table 2. All of these questions focus on describing differences between visual and Tactile ASL. The videotaped conversations were examined for evidence of structures or strategies that do not occur in visual ASL.

Sociolinguistic Variation in ASL: Providing Broad Quantitative Description

The goal of Lucas et al.'s study is to provide the basis for a description of phonological, morphosyntactic, and lexical variation in ASL. One of the variables, a set of three variants of the sign DEAF, is reported on here. The sign DEAF has many possible forms, but occurrences of only three of these forms were extracted from the videotapes. In citation form (+cf),[5] the sign begins just below the ear and ends near the corner of the mouth. This form is called *ear-to-chin.* A second variant begins at the corner of the mouth and moves upward to the ear. This variant was labeled the *chin-to-ear* variant. The third variant considered here, the *contact-cheek* variant, consists of the index finger tapping the lower cheek without moving up. These variants (see Figure 2) were compared using statistical programs that require many tokens as input, but which allow the researcher to investigate the effects of many potential constraints at the same time. In this section, we will first discuss the bene-

TABLE 2. Questions Addressed by the Tactile ASL Study

LEVEL OF LINGUISTIC STRUCTURE	QUESTIONS
Phonology	In Tactile ASL, the receiver's hand is placed on the signer's hand. Does this physical difference in the mode of communication result in changes in any of the sign parameters: handshape, movement, location and orientation?
Morphology	Deaf-blind people are unable to see the nonmanual adverbs and adjectives that accompany many lexical verbs and adjectives. How are these morphemes conveyed in Tactile ASL?
Syntax	Word-order in questions in visual ASL varies. What word orders occur in questions in Tactile ASL?
Discourse	The back-channel feedback given by addressees in visual ASL is inaccessible to deaf-blind people. What type of back-channeling in Tactile ASL replaces the head nods, head tilts, and facial expressions of back-channeling in visual ASL?

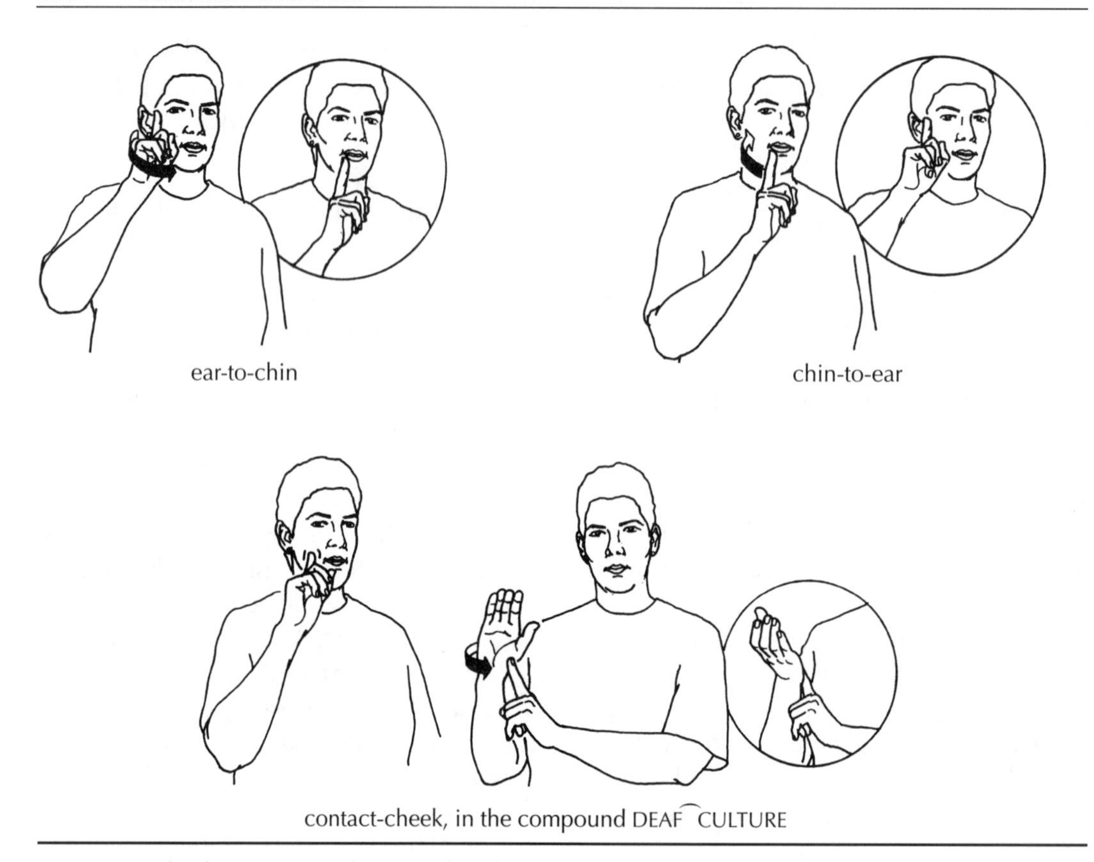

FIGURE 2. The three variants of DEAF analyzed in the sociolinguistic variation study.

fits and requirements of this kind of quantitative analysis. Then, we will describe how data were collected and how occurrences of the variants of DEAF were extracted from the videotaped data.

One of the main goals of the quantitative study of language variation is to understand linguistic phenomena and their relationship to social structure. We want to be able to understand, for example, the direction of linguistic change or the relationship between the form and the syntactic function of a class of signs. We also want to be able to test hypotheses about the relationships between different linguistic and social constraints, to compare alternative analyses, and to create models that allow us to make predictions (Guy 1993). Percentages of occurrence or nonoccurrence of particular variants cannot account for many possible simultaneous influences on variation, both linguistic and social. To accomplish the goals of the study, then, Lucas et al. needed to use statistical procedures that could model simultaneously relationships between the many contextual factors that promote or inhibit use of a particular variant. In linguistics, the program known as VARBRUL, a specialized application of logistic regression, has been used most extensively for this type of modeling because it has been deliberately designed to handle the kind of data obtained in studies of variation. It also provides heuristic tools that allow the investigator to reanalyze the data easily as hypotheses are modified.[6]

Videotaped data for this study were collected during 1994 and 1995 at the seven sites mentioned earlier. All sites have thriving com-

TABLE 3. Demographic Characteristics of Informants in the Sociolinguistic Variation in ASL Study

CHARACTERISTICS	AFRICAN-AMERICAN GROUPS		ANGLO-AMERICAN GROUPS	
Socioeconomic Status	*Middle Class*	*Working Class*	*Middle Class*	*Working Class*
Age	15–25	15–25	15–25	15–25
	26–54	26–54	26–54	26–54
	55+	55+	55+	55+

munities of ASL users. Six groups of deaf ASL signers, all white, participated in Staunton, Frederick, and Bellingham. Six white groups and five African-American groups participated in Boston, Fremont, Kansas City, Olathe, and New Orleans. In total, 207 signers participated. Their social and demographic characteristics are summarized in Table 3.

Working-class participants had no education beyond high school and were working in blue-collar jobs. Middle-class participants had completed college and were working in professional positions. The age group divisions were designed to correlate roughly with changes in the language policies in deaf education over the last ninety years. Older participants would have had purely oral instruction in schools; the middle group was in school during Total Communication; younger participants would have begun school at the beginning of the return to using ASL in the classroom.

Groups of participants were videotaped in the three parts of the data collection sessions described above: conversation, sociolinguistic interview, and lexical variation elicitation. All tokens of the three variants of DEAF, a total of 1,618 occurrences, were extracted from this videotaped database for coding for multivariate analysis with VARBRUL. Each token was entered into the statistical database along with its values for social and linguistic factors. The following social factors were coded: region, age (15–25, 26–54, 55+), gender, ethnicity (African-American, white), class (working, middle), and language background (native ASL, other). The linguistic factors coded were designed to provide a follow-up to Lucas's (1995) study, which found that the grammatical function of the sign was the most significant constraint on the form of DEAF. The coding scheme for the linguistic constraints is presented in Table 4.

Once coding was complete and the data were entered, VARBRUL estimated the factor values (or probabilities) for each contextual factor specified (e.g., the handshape of the preceding segment or the social class to

TABLE 4. Coding Scheme for Linguistic Constraints on DEAF

Grammatical function of DEAF
- noun
- adjective
- predicate adjective
- compound

Location of the preceding segment
- high (at ear or above)
- middle (between ear and chin)
- low (chin or below)
- pause

Location of the following segment
- high (at ear or above)
- middle (between ear and chin)
- low (chin or below)
- pause

Genre of text in which DEAF occurs
- conversation
- narrative

which a signer belongs). The program provided a numerical measure of the strength of each factor's influence, relative to other factors in the same group, on the occurrence of the linguistic variable under investigation. VARBRUL probability values range between 0 and 1.00. A factor value, or weight, between .50 and 1.00 indicates that the factor favors use of a variant relative to other factors in the same group. For example, in the results reported below, compounds (e.g., DEAF⁀CULTURE), with a factor value of .66, favor use of noncitation (–cf) forms. A value between 0 and .50 indicates that the factor disfavors a variant. Thus, in the same results, predicate adjectives, with a factor value of .37, disfavor use of –cf forms of DEAF. The output also includes an input probability, a measure of the overall tendency of signers to use a particular variant. In the results below, the input value for –cf forms of DEAF is .743. This value reflects the fact that –cf forms were far more common in the data than +cf forms. Of 1,618 tokens analyzed, 1,118, or 69 percent, were –cf. Finally, the program provides several measures of goodness of fit between the model and the data (see Young and Bayley 1996, 272–73).

FINDINGS

This section summarizes the more important findings of the three studies that have provided the data for our discussions of the potential contributions and methods of variationist linguistics to our understanding of sign languages. The details of the studies are available in Hoopes (1998), Collins and Petronio (1998), Lucas, Bayley, and Valli et al. (forthcoming), and Bayley, Lucas, and Rose (2000).

Pinky Extension

In contrast to the other studies, Hoopes's study (1998) analyzed the occurrence of a single phonological variable—pinky extension—in the signing of a single individual. Prior to this study, Lucas and others had observed that some signers extend their pinky during particular signs, contrary to the citation forms of these signs.

Hoopes's study sought to determine whether the occurrence of pinky extension was indeed variable and, if so, whether the frequency of occurrence correlated with any linguistic or social factors. As stated previously, a primary goal of sociolinguistic inquiry is to correlate social and economic factors (e.g., sex, age, race, education, etc.) with the frequency at which a variable occurs in a given subject's speech. To accomplish this goal, tokens must be collected from subjects in each sociolinguistic category under analysis. Why, then, would Hoopes undertake to study a single signer? The primary reason is that this was a pilot study to determine if pinky extension varied at all. Because our understanding of the structure of ASL is still emerging, it is often difficult at the outset of a sociolinguistic study to know whether the linguistic form under analysis is variable at all. In this case, it was entirely possible that the occurrence of pinky extension was subject to a categorical, as opposed to a variable, rule. Before a larger, and more expensive, study was undertaken, it was necessary to determine if pinky extension was in fact variable, and, if so, whether it could be correlated with any linguistic or social constraints.

The findings indicated that the frequency of occurrence of pinky extension upon signs did in fact vary, and that the frequency of occurrence correlated with linguistic factors (handshape and syntactic category) and the one social factor analyzed (degree of social distance). The most intriguing finding, however, was that pinky extension tended to co-occur with prosodic features of emphatic stress. Specifically, it tended to occur (a) with lexemes used repeatedly within a discourse topic, (b) before pauses, and (c) with lexemes lengthened to almost twice their usual duration. This suggests that pinky extension is itself a prosodic feature of ASL that adds emphatic stress or focus to the sign with which it co-occurs. It is quite analogous to stress in spoken language, which is indicated by a stronger signal as a result of greater articulatory effort.

It should be noted that sociolinguistic methodology was crucial to this last finding—pinky extension played a prosodic function in the lect of the subject. Prosody has largely been ignored by linguists working within either the Chomskian or the earlier structuralist framework due to the tendency of these frameworks toward categorization. Prosody tends not to be subject to categorical rules. But, as Hoopes's study shows, when one searches for factors that constrain but do not absolutely determine the occurrence of a linguistic form, the patterning of prosodic features emerge.

Tactile ASL

Space does not permit a discussion of the findings pertaining to morphology, syntax, and discourse, so here we will focus on the differences and similarities of the phonological form of signs used in visual and Tactile ASL. (For a full account of this study, see Collins and Petronio 1998). Signs were examined in terms of their handshape, location, movement, and orientation.

Early studies on visual ASL sought minimal pairs to determine the distinctive parts of signs. Minimal pairs were interpreted as providing evidence for three parameters: handshape, movement, and location. For instance, the signs DONKEY and HORSE use the same location and movement but differ in handshape; MOTHER and FATHER use the same handshape and movement but differ in location; and SICK and TO-BECOME-SICK use the same handshape and location but differ in movement. Battison (1978) later identified a fourth parameter, orientation, based on pairs such as CHILDREN and THINGS. These two signs have identical handshape, movement, and location, but they differ in the palm orientation.

Using these four parameters, Collins and Petronio examined signs to see if there were any phonological differences when the signs were used in visual ASL and Tactile ASL. They found no variation or changes in the handshape parameter. The other three parameters (movement, location, and orientation) displayed the same type of variation due to phonological assimilation that occurs in visual ASL. However, although the same forms of variation occurred in Tactile ASL, this variation was sometimes due to (a) the receiver's hand being on the signer's hand and (b) the signer and receiver being physically closer to each other than they generally are in visual ASL. The signing space used in Tactile ASL is generally smaller than that used in visual ASL because of the physical closeness of the signers. This smaller space usually results in smaller movement paths in signs. In addition, because the signer's and receiver's hands are in contact, the signing space shifts to the area where the hands are in contact; correspondingly, the location of signs articulates in neutral space and also shifts to this area. The orientation parameter showed some variation that resulted from modifications the signer made to better accommodate the receiver. One change, unique to Tactile ASL, occurred with signs that included body contact. In addition to the signer's hand moving toward the body part, the body part often moved toward the hand in Tactile ASL. This adaptation allowed the receiver to maintain more comfortable tactile contact with the signer.

The variation, adaptations, and changes that Collins and Petronio describe are examples of linguistic change that has occurred and is continuing in the U.S. deaf-blind community. In the past several years the American Association of the Deaf-Blind has expanded its membership and many state chapters have been established. The opportunity for deaf-blind people to get together and make communities has resulted in sociolinguistic changes in ASL as deaf-blind people modify it to meet their needs. From a linguistic viewpoint, Tactile ASL provides us with a unique opportunity to witness the linguistic changes ASL is experiencing as the deaf-blind community adapts the language to a tactile mode.

Sociolinguistic Variation of DEAF

Lucas et al.'s ongoing study focuses on a number of sociolinguistic variables, among them variation in the form of the sign DEAF. To examine the constraints on this variable, Lucas et al. performed multivariate analysis of 1,618 tokens using VARBRUL. The results indicated that variation in the form of DEAF is systematic and conditioned by multiple linguistic and social factors, including grammatical function, the location of the following segment, discourse genre, age, and region. The results strongly confirmed the earlier finding of Lucas (1995), which showed that the grammatical function of DEAF, rather than the features of the preceding or following sign, is the main linguistic constraint on variation. In this section, we will focus on the role of the grammatical category because the results for this factor suggest that variation in ASL operates at a much more abstract level than has previously been documented. We will also briefly review the main results of the role of signer age and geographical region.

The three variants of DEAF might logically be related to one another in a number of different ways, based on what is known about the history of ASL as well as observations of processes governing ASL compound formation (Liddell and Johnson 1986; see also Lucas, Bayley et al. forthcoming; and Bayley, Lucas, and Rose 2000, for details). The researchers in this study hypothesized that the variants were related to one another as follows: The citation or underlying form is ear-to-chin—in the first stage, this form undergoes metathesis and surfaces as chin-to-ear; in the second stage, the metathesized form undergoes deletion of the first element and surfaces as contact-cheek, a process that is especially common in compounds (e.g., DEAF⁀CULTURE). This model of the processes underlying variation in the form of DEAF necessitated two separate quantitative analyses: +cf vs. –cf, including both chin-to-ear and contact-cheek, and chin-to-ear vs. contact-cheek. Note that citation forms were eliminated from the second analysis because only forms that have undergone metathesis are eligible for deletion of the first element.

The results of both analyses for the grammatical category factor group are shown in Table 5. The table includes information on the application value, or value of the dependent variable at which the rule is said to apply; the VARBRUL weight, or factor value; the percentage of rule applications; and the number of tokens of each factor. The table also includes the input value, the overall percentage of application, and the number of tokens in each analysis.

The results of the first analysis show that compounds favor ($p = .66$) and predicate adjectives disfavor ($p = .37$) noncitation forms. Nouns and adjectives slightly favor noncitation forms as well ($p = .515$). The results of the second analysis, which excluded citation tokens, show that compounds very strongly favor the noncitation variant, contact-cheek ($p = .85$). The results also show

TABLE 5. The Influence of Grammatical Category on Choice of a Form of DEAF

FACTOR	VARBRUL WEIGHT	%	N
Analysis 1: +cf vs. –cf (application value: –cf)			
Noun, adjective	.515	71	1,063
Predicate adjective	.370	58	361
Compound	.660	81	194
Total/input	.743	69	1,618
Analysis 2: chin-to-ear vs. contact-cheek (application value: contact-cheek)			
Noun	.490	17	411
Adjective	.403	10	191
Predicate adjective	.338	12	299
Compound	.850	56	151
Total/input	.142	20	1,052

that adjectives and predicate adjectives that have undergone metathesis are unlikely to undergo deletion. Finally, as in the first analysis of citation vs. noncitation forms, the value for nouns ($p = .49$) is close to .50, which indicates that this factor has only a slight effect on signers' choice of a form of DEAF.

An obvious question arises from these results. Why should the grammatical category to which DEAF belongs have such a large effect on a signers' choices among the three variants, while other factors, such as the location of the following segment, have no significant effect? One possibility is that the grammatical constraints are a synchronic reflex of a change in progress that originates in compounds and then spreads to nouns and adjectives and finally to predicates. A change from ear-to-chin to chin-to-ear, beginning with compounds, a grammatical class that is most subject to change, is arguably a shift in the direction of greater ease of production. Such a change would conform to Kroch's (1978) model of change from below, which, at least in the case of consonants, tends to greater ease of articulation. This explanation is supported by the fact that there are a number of ASL signs that move from chin to ear in their citation form. Only two of these, however, clearly allow metathesis. They are HEAD and MOTHER⁀FATHER ("parents"). Metathesis is not allowed by other common signs with a phonological structure like DEAF, consisting of a hold, a movement, and a hold (e.g., INDIAN, HOME, YESTERDAY).[7] The fact that metathesis is not allowed by most signs whose citation form is chin to ear (that is, signs that move up), while it is allowed by DEAF, where the citation form moves down, suggests that chin to ear movement is the less marked sequence. DEAF, then, may be undergoing a change from a more marked to a less marked form that is characterized by greater ease of production.

As we have noted, in addition to identifying significant linguistic constraints on DEAF, Lucas et al. also found significant social and geographic constraints. Although social class, gender, and language background proved not to be statistically significant, both age and region were highly significant. In conducting their analyses,

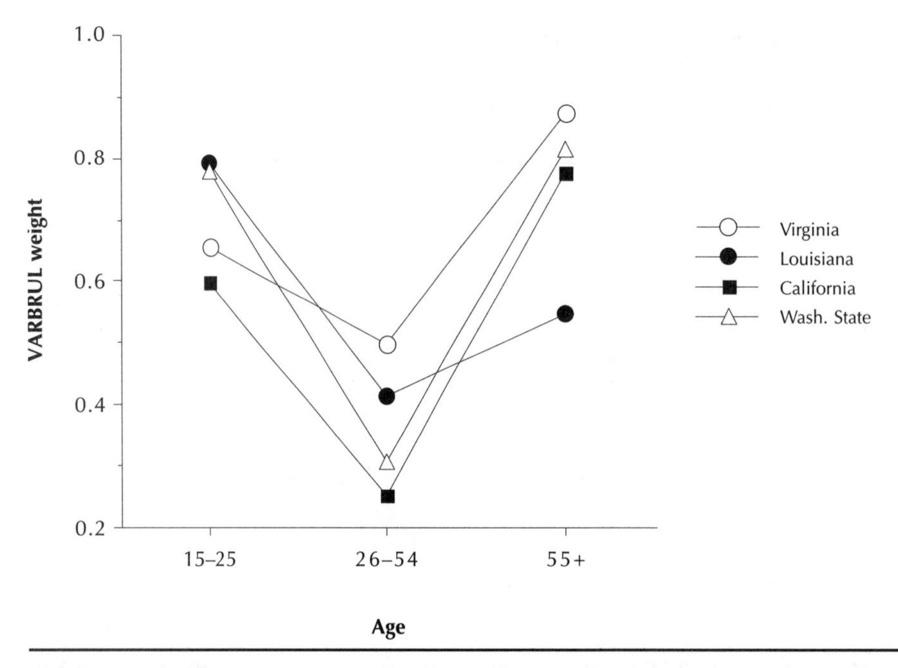

FIGURE 3. The dominant pattern of VARBRUL factor values for noncitation forms of DEAF by age and region.

Lucas et al. considered each age group within a region as a separate factor in order to investigate whether ASL was changing in the same way across the country or whether the direction of change differed from region to region. The results show interregional differences that Lucas et al. suspect are related to changes in deaf education policies in particular areas and to the complex relationships of residential schools to one another (Baynton 1996). However, in the analysis of citation vs. noncitation forms of DEAF, one dominant pattern emerged that was shared by four sites: In Virginia, Louisiana, California, and Washington state, both the youngest and the oldest signers were more likely to use noncitation forms of DEAF than signers aged 26–55. This dominant pattern is illustrated in Figure 3. Although much remains to be done, particularly in understanding the complex relationship of age and region to signers' choice of a variant of DEAF, the study demonstrates the potential contribution that variationist linguistics can make to sign language research.

CONCLUSION

The methodologies and findings from the three distinct studies described here demonstrate the range of variation in sign languages and the diversity of approaches available for studying this variation. It is hoped that continued research on a variety of languages will enhance our growing understanding of sign language variation.

NOTES

1. Preston (1996) argues that, for members of the same speech community, linguistic constraints always have a greater effect on variation than do social factors.
2. For a thorough survey of this growing body of sociolinguistic research on sign languages, see Patrick and Metzger (1996).
3. In fact, variationist studies of spoken language communities have come under considerable criti-

cism because they often rely on naive and outdated ideas of social categories such as class and gender (see, for example, Eckert 1989b; Santa Ana and Parodi 1998; and Williams 1992).

4. Issues of identity are likely to interact with other factors, and the salience of different aspects of personal identity is affected by the nature, setting, and topic of the conversational interaction. Thus, an individual may always be straight or gay, male or female, deaf or hearing, and so forth. However, not all aspects of the multiple characteristics that compose an individual's identity are always equally salient, a fact that is reflected in patterns of linguistic variation. Schilling-Estes (1999), for example, reported on an extended conversation between two university students in the South, one African-American and the other Native American. When the topic concerned their common experiences as members of ethnic minorities at a predominantly white institution, the two speakers showed very similar patterns of variation. When the topic shifted to the Civil War (during which the Native American student's tribe had supported the Confederacy), the two speakers diverged sharply. Further, the concept of dual ethnicity introduced by Broch (1987) is explored in Valli et al. (1992) in terms of language use by Deaf African-American signers, but not with specific reference to variation.
5. The citation form (+cf) is the form of a sign as it would appear in a sign language dictionary or as it might be taught in a sign language class. The noncitation form (–cf) is the form of a sign as it might occur in everyday conversation, a variant of the +cf form. Of course, citation forms occur in everyday conversation as well.
6. The statistical bases for the VARBRUL programs are set out in Sankoff (1988), and the procedures for using the software are explained in Young and Bayley (1996) and in the documentation that accompanies the programs. The present study used GoldVarb for the Macintosh (Rand and Sankoff 1990). Space does not permit a full explanation of the steps involved in a multivariate analysis with VARBRUL here. The topic is discussed in detail in the literature on the subject (e.g., Guy 1980, 1993; Rousseau and Sankoff 1978; Sankoff 1988; Young and Bayley 1996).
7. There is some question as to whether HOME permits metathesis. Liddell and Johnson (1989) claim that it does, whereas there is disagreement among Deaf informants as to whether it does.

REFERENCES

Battison, Robbin. 1978. *Lexical borrowing in American Sign Language: Phonological and morphological restructuring.* Silver Spring, Md.: Linstok Press.

Battison, Robbin, Harry Markowicz, and James Woodward. 1975. A good rule of thumb: Variable phonology in American Sign Language. In *Analyzing variation in language: Papers from the Second Colloquium on New Ways of Analyzing Variation,* ed. Ralph Fasold and Roger W. Shuy. Washington, DC: Georgetown University Press.

Bauman, Richard, and Joel Sherzer, eds. 1974. *Explorations in the ethnography of speaking.* New York: Cambridge University Press.

Bayley, Robert, Ceil Lucas, and Mary Rose. 2000. Variation in American Sign Language: The case of DEAF. *Journal of Sociolinguistics* 4(1): 81–107.

Baynton, Douglas. 1996. *Forbidden signs: American culture and the campaign against sign language.* Chicago: University of Chicago Press.

Broch, Harald. 1987. Ethnic differentiation and integration: Aspects of inter-ethnic relations at the village level on Bonerate. *Ethnic Groups* 7: 19–37.

Collins, Steven, and Karen Petronio. 1998. What happens in Tactile ASL? In *Pinky extension and eye gaze: Language use in Deaf communities,* ed. Ceil Lucas, 18–37. Sociolinguistics in Deaf Communities, vol. 4. Washington, DC: Gallaudet University Press.

Croneberg, Carl. 1965. The linguistic community. In *A dictionary of American Sign Language on linguistic principles,* by William C. Stokoe, Dorothy Casterline, and Carl Croneberg. Washington, DC: Gallaudet College Press.

Eckert, Penelope. 1989a. *Jocks and burnouts: Social categories and identity in the high school.* New York: Teachers College Press.

———. 1989b. The whole woman: Sex and gender difference in variation. *Language Variation and Change* 1: 245–68.

Fasold, Ralph. 1984. *The sociolinguistics of society.* New York: Blackwell.

Gumperz, John J., ed. 1982. *Language and social identity.* New York: Cambridge University Press.

Guy, Gregory R. 1980. Variation in the group and in the individual: The case of final stop deletion. In *Locating language in time and space,* ed. William Labov, 1–36. New York: Academic Press.

———. 1993. The quantitative analysis of linguistic variation. In *American dialect research,* ed. Dennis R. Preston, 223–24. Amsterdam: John Benjamins.

Hoopes, Rob. 1998. A preliminary examination of pinky extension: Suggestions regarding its occurrence, constraints, and function. In *Pinky extension and eye gaze: Language use in Deaf communities,* ed. Ceil Lucas, 3–17. Sociolinguistics in Deaf Communities, vol. 4. Washington, DC: Gallaudet University Press.

Kroch, Anthony. 1978. Towards a theory of social dialect variation. *Language in Society* 7: 17–36.

Labov, William. 1966. *The social stratification of English in New York City.* Washington, DC: Center for Applied Linguistics.
———. 1972. *Sociolinguistic patterns.* Philadelphia: University of Pennsylvania Press.
———. 1994. *Principles of linguistic change.* Vol. 1, *Internal factors.* Language in Society, vol. 20. Oxford: Blackwell.
Liddell, Scott, and Robert E. Johnson. 1986. American Sign Language compound formation processes, lexicalization, and phonological remnants. *Natural Language and Linguistic Theory* 4: 445–513.
———. 1989. American Sign Language: The phonological base. *Sign Language Studies* 64: 195–278.
Lucas, Ceil. 1995. Sociolinguistic variation in ASL: The case of DEAF. In *Sociolinguistics in Deaf communities,* ed. Ceil Lucas, 3–25. Washington, DC: Gallaudet University Press.
———, ed. 1996. *Multicultural aspects of sociolinguistics in Deaf communities.* Sociolinguistics in Deaf Communities, vol. 2. Washington, DC: Gallaudet University Press.
Lucas, Ceil, and Clayton Valli. 1992. *Language contact in the American Deaf community.* San Diego: Academic.
Lucas, Ceil, Robert Bayley, Mary Rose, and Alyssa Wulf. Forthcoming. Location variation in American Sign Language. *International Journal of the Sociology of Language.*
Lucas, Ceil, Robert Bayley, and Clayton Valli, in collaboration with Mary Rose, Alyssa Wulf, Paul Dudis, Laurie Sanheim, and Susan Schatz. Forthcoming. *Sociolinguistic variation in American Sign Language.* Sociolinguistics in Deaf Communities, vol. 7. Washington, DC: Gallaudet University Press.
Milroy, Lesley. 1980. *Language and social networks.* Oxford: Blackwell.
———. 1987. *Observing and analyzing natural language.* Oxford: Blackwell.
Padden, Carol. 1997. From the cultural to the bicultural: The modern Deaf community. In *Cultural and language diversity and the Deaf experience,* ed. Ila Parasnis, 79–98. Cambridge: Cambridge University Press.
Padden, Carol, and Tom Humphries. 1988. *Deaf in America: Voices from a culture.* Cambridge, Mass.: Harvard University Press.
Parasnis, Ila. 1997. On interpreting the Deaf experience within the context of cultural and language diversity. In *Cultural and language diversity and the Deaf experience,* ed. Ila Parasnis, 3–19. Cambridge: Cambridge University Press.
Patrick, Peter, and Melanie Metzger. 1996. Sociolinguistic factors in sign language research. In *Sociolinguistic variation: Data, theory, and analysis,* ed. Jennifer Arnold, Renée Blake, Brad Davidson, Scott Schwenter, and Julie Solomon, 229–40. Stanford, Calif.: Center for the Study of Language and Information.
Preston, Dennis R. 1996. Variationists' perspectives on second language acquisition. In *Second language acquisition and linguistic variation,* ed. Robert Bayley and Dennis R. Preston, 1–45. Amsterdam: John Benjamins.
Rand, David, and David Sankoff. 1990. GoldVarb: A variable rule application for the Macintosh (version 2). Montreal: Centre de recherches mathématiques, Université de Montréal.
Rose, Mary, Ceil Lucas, Robert Bayley, and Alyssa Wulf. 1998. What do variables and constraints look like in sign languages? Panel presentation at the Conference on New Ways of Analyzing Variation, October, Athens, Georgia.
Rousseau, Pascale, and David Sankoff. 1978. Advances in variable rule methodology. In *Linguistic variation: Models and methods,* ed. David Sankoff, 57–69. New York: Academic.
Sankoff, David. 1988. Variable rules. In *Sociolinguistics: An international handbook of the science of language and society,* vol. 2, ed. Ulrich Ammon, Norbert Dittmar, and Klaus J. Mattheier, 984–97. Berlin: de Gruyter.
Santa Ana, Otto A., and Claudia Parodi. 1998. Modeling the speech community: Configurations and variable types in the Mexican Spanish setting. *Language in Society* 27: 23–52.
Schilling-Estes, Natalie. 1999. In search of "natural speech": Performing the sociolinguistic interview. Paper presented at the Annual Meeting of the American Dialect Society, January, Los Angeles, California.
Stokoe, William C., Dorothy Casterline, and Carl Croneberg. 1965. *A dictionary of American Sign Language on linguistic principles.* Washington, DC: Gallaudet College Press.
Tannen, Deborah, ed. 1984. *Coherence in spoken and written discourse.* Norwood, N.J.: Ablex.
Valli, Clayton, Ruth Reed, Norman Ingram, Jr., and Ceil Lucas. 1992. Sociolinguistic issues in the Black Deaf community. In *Proceedings of the Conference on Empowerment and Black Deaf Persons,* Washington, DC: Gallaudet University College for Continuing Education.
Williams, Glyn. 1992. *Sociolinguistics: A sociological critique.* London: Routledge.
Wolfram, Walt. 1993. Teaching the grammar of vernacular English. In *Language variation in North American English: Research and teaching,* ed. A. Wayne Glowka and Donald M. Vance, 16–27. New York: Modern Language Association.
Woodward, James C. 1973. Implicational lects on the Deaf diglossic continuum. Ph.D. dissertation, Georgetown University, Washington, DC.

——. 1994. *Describing variation in American Sign Language: Implicational lects on the Deaf diglossic continuum.* Burtonsville, Md.: Linstok Press.

Woodward, James, and Carol Erting. 1975. Synchronic variation and historical change in ASL. *Language Sciences* 37: 9–12.

Woodward, James, Carol Erting, and Susanna Oliver. 1976. Facing and hand(l)ing variation in American Sign Language phonology. *Sign Language Studies* 10: 43–52.

Young, Richard, and Robert Bayley. 1996. VARBRUL analysis for second language acquisition research. In *Second language acquisition and linguistic variation,* ed. Robert Bayley and Dennis R. Preston, 253–306. Amsterdam: John Benjamins.

Sociolinguistic Aspects of the Black Deaf Community

ANTHONY J. ARAMBURO

INTRODUCTION

The black deaf community can be described as a group of individuals who live in a "hearing and color-conscious society" (Anderson 1972). They are continually striving to overcome the communication problems faced in everyday living while still having to contend with racist attitudes that govern society. They are a group of individuals that appear to be immersed in both the black and deaf cultures.

At least three issues surface as a result of this "double immersion." One issue concerns the actual reality of a black deaf community, as distinct from both the black community and the deaf community. A second issue concerns identity. That is, given the double immersion in both black and deaf cultures, the question is whether the individual's identity is primarily as a member of the black community, the deaf community, or the black deaf community. A third issue concerns communication patterns as defined in terms of differences between black signing and white signing, and in terms of sign variation and code-switching. Casual observation reveals that the signing of black deaf individuals varies as a function of the race of other participants in a conversational setting. That is, black signers sign differently with white signers than they do with other black signers.

This study investigates all of these issues and presents empirical data that permit a clearer sociolinguistic perspective than has heretofore been possible. Data relating to the issue of identity consist of the results of a survey conducted with sixty black deaf individuals. For the issue of communication patterns, data consist of videotapes made of the conversational interaction of seven dyads controlled for race, audiological status, and signing skills.

THE BLACK DEAF COMMUNITY

As defined by Hillery (1974), a community is a general social system in which a group of people live together, share common goals, and carry out certain responsibilities to each other. Loomis (1983) states that communities strive to protect the resources that will serve to inform future generations of their cultural past. Padden (1980) distinguishes between culture and community and refers to the former as a set of learned behaviors of a group of people who have their own language, values, rules for behavior, and traditions. She goes on to point out that a community cannot only have individuals who are culturally deaf but also hearing and deaf people who are not culturally deaf yet still interact with culturally deaf people and see themselves as working with them in various

Source. Reprinted by permission of the publisher, from C. Lucas, ed., *The Sociolinguistics of the Deaf Community* (1989): 103–119. San Diego: Academic Press. The references for this reading can be found in the original volume.

common concerns (Padden 1980, 92–93). Evidence for the existence of both a black community and a deaf community is presented elsewhere (e.g., Higgins 1980; Padden 1980).

The first issue here concerns the reality of the black deaf community, as distinct from both the black community and the deaf community. The contention here is that there does indeed exist a black deaf community, and that it shares the characteristics and values of both the black community and the deaf community. In addition, it has some characteristics and values that are unique. For example, members of the black deaf community share with the black community the obstacle of overcoming societal prejudices against black people. The high unemployment rate is felt more in the black community than the white community. The unemployment rate is even higher among blacks in the deaf commmunity. Indeed, underemployment is rampant in both black communities (Christiansen and Barnartt 1987). There are few black political leaders in the black community. They are nonexistent in the black deaf community. Both the black community and the black deaf community declare their black heritage, and the struggles that blacks endured in obtaining their civil rights are salient in both communities.

Features shared by the black deaf community and the deaf community are largely in the domain of communication. Their language, American Sign Language, is an important factor in the socialization process within the deaf community. Social activities such as sports events (where the teams are comprised of deaf players), deaf club activities, deaf-related conferences and meetings attract deaf individuals because all involved can identify with the mode of communication used, ASL. Stereotypes classifying the deaf as dumb, uneducated, and unable to work, to name a few, are realities both the general deaf community and the black deaf community have to overcome in a "hearing world." The black deaf individual must also overcome some additional stereotypes that society at large places on blacks. Lower-class whites have similar stereotypes placed on them.

Characteristics and values that are unique to the black deaf community can be identified by looking at patterns of social interaction, education, and use of sign language. For example, many of the clubs where the black deaf go for social purposes cater primarily to the black deaf community. This is true in most cities (Higgins 1980). There is also, in most cities, a meeting place where the white deaf go for their social activities. No law or rules laid down by the deaf community mandates this occurrence, it is simply something that happens. The separation of social meeting places is evidence of the existence of a black deaf community. The clubs where the black deaf meet are their places for disseminating key information about how they will carry out certain functions as a group. Club meetings, sports meetings, dances, card socials, and personal celebrations such as birthdays and anniversaries all happen at the club house. Information related to jobs, problems that members are faced with, new laws pertaining to the deaf is all available at the deaf club.

Not many black deaf individuals have the luxury of owning a telecommunication device for the deaf (TDD), so the telephone is not a viable means for relaying information. Members of the black deaf community do not all live in the same area of the city. For those who do live in close proximity, the club house is the most convenient place for meeting in order to discuss and pass on information. Observation of the black deaf community confirms that black deaf marry other black deaf. Judging from married couples in the black deaf community, an individual tends to marry another black deaf individual who attended the same residential school. When a black deaf individual does marry a hearing person, that hearing spouse is usually also black.

Educational patterns also provide evidence of the existence of a black deaf community. In recent years, the black and deaf communities have made significant achievements in the area of education. Blacks no longer must settle for an education that is "separate but equal" and can freely attend any school or university for which they are qualified. During the days of racial segregation, however, most elementary school programs for black deaf children were set up on campuses that accommodated an all black student population. The programs were mediocre (Hairston and Smith 1983) and in most cases, the administrative personnel had no expertise in the field of deaf education, a topic on which information was scarce. Although there were good intentions for educating this special group of students, the reality was that the tools and personnel needed to achieve the best results were not available. Teachers in black schools for the deaf were not required to have college credits or course work related to the education of deaf children. College programs that provided blacks with a degree in education offered no course work specifically geared to educating the deaf. Teachers used their knowledge and expertise in these schools to work with deaf students and provide them with a decent education. Still, the problem of communication surfaced.

Then as now, educational programs for the deaf do not require the teacher to be versed in ASL. Programs designed to teach sign language to teachers are rare. The manual alphabet was the predominant mode for teaching in many of the schools with black deaf students. Often entire lessons were fingerspelled. In many schools, sign language was not permitted in the classroom. Teachers cannot understand their students, so they insist on fingerspelling (in English) as the sole means of communication. Needless to say, the student has to have a good grasp of the English language in order to comprehend what is being taught in the classroom. In many cases, the home environment was not the ideal place for learning English. Today, black deaf children who are born to hearing parents face the same predicament of their peers in the past, namely, many hearing parents refuse to communicate with their children through sign language. Parents leave the burden of educating their child solely to the school system.

Black deaf children born to deaf parents have an advantage over their peers with hearing parents, since deaf parents communicate with their children through sign language. When these students go back to the residential schools, they bring sign language with them. This provides a means of communication other than fingerspelling. Outside the classroom, students converse using sign language. Playground activities or other nonschool-related activities permit students to develop their language and social skills. During the years that black schools were not permitted to compete with white schools in athletic activities, black students had to travel in order to compete with rival schools. During these visits, black deaf students shared their language and taught each other new signs. Upon completing school, most black deaf students chose to learn a trade in order to make their living, and it has been suggested that a correlation exists between this choice and inadequate English skills. Moreover, this choice of vocational training greatly lessened the number of black deaf students entering college (Christiansen and Barnartt 1987). The number of black deaf students entering colleges and universities today is still small. Many students, whether in the residential schools or special education programs for the hearing-impaired in local school districts, are graduating with a high school certificate and not a high school diploma. Facilities and services offered to black deaf students are becoming better, but the number of black deaf individuals possessing a doctoral degree is very low when compared to the overall deaf community.[1]

Although a certain level of achievement has been attained within the majority deaf and the majority hearing communities, black deaf individuals are still behind in terms of advancement. The black deaf person is doubly affected insofar as being labeled black, poor, and disabled amounts to simultaneous placement in two devalued worlds (Alcocer 1974). Blacks in general have made considerable gains for the black community, but members of the black deaf community have had a difficult time emulating their success. Deaf people in general did not participate in the movement to improve their civil rights until the 1970s, when they actively joined other organizations of disabled people in transforming their own special civil rights issues into the 1973 Rehabilitation Act (Boros and Stuckless 1982). The black deaf community, having missed the opportunity to gain advancement alongside the black community, must now advocate for themselves. As stated by many black deaf individuals, they have noticed no real improvements overall in the black deaf community. Deaf people, like other minorities, are subject to categorical discrimination (Schowe 1979). Being discriminated against on the basis of deafness is difficult enough to overcome, but the joint impact of handicap discrimination and ethnic discrimination compounds the hardship and increases the barriers to success.

Further evidence of the existence of a black deaf community comes from differences observed between black signing and white signing. Later in this chapter, evidence is provided of how black signing differs from white signing, mainly in the area of lexical choices.

On the whole, members of the black deaf community are aware of both their black culture and deaf culture. Much as members of the black community pass on to future generations cultural resources such as black art, black folklore, and black spirituals, members of the black deaf community pass along similar cultural resources. For example, an oral history about residential school experiences from the era when schools were segregated parallels the oral history of the black community about slavery.

BLACK OR DEAF?

As discussed earlier, black deaf individuals are immersed in both the black and deaf cultures. It appears that the black deaf individual can be part of both cultures, so a question of identity arises. That is, does a black deaf individual identify primarily with the black community or with the deaf community. In an attempt to answer this question of identity, a survey was conducted among sixty members of the black deaf community in the Washington, D.C. area. The majority of the persons who participated were high school and college students attending the Model Secondary School for the Deaf (MSSD) and Gallaudet University. Approximately one-third of the individuals interviewed lived in Washington, D.C. and surrounding areas. Twenty individuals were targeted from three age groups: eighteen to twenty-five years old, twenty-six to thirty-five years old, and thirty-six years old and above. A representative sample of ten men and ten women was targeted for each age group. Older members of the black deaf community from Washington, D.C. were sought for representation of the adult black deaf population.

In actuality, a total of thirty-three men and twenty-seven women participated in the study. The median age of the participants was 27.1 years. The age at which each respondent acquired sign language was recorded: fourteen participants (23 percent) learned sign language before age six, and forty-six participants (77 percent) learned sign language after age six. The majority of those surveyed attended a residential school, that is, fifty participants (88 percent). The remaining seven participants (12 percent) attended either public or parochial schools, or both. Four of the participants (7 percent) are children of deaf parents. The remaining fifty-six participants (93 percent) are children of hearing parents. In disclosing their competence in using ASL, fifty-five participants (92 percent) described themselves as native signers of ASL. The remaining five participants (8 percent) did not provide an assessment of their skills as native ASL signers.

The interviews were conducted with participants on a one-on-one, informal basis. A comfortable setting was agreed upon by both the interviewer and the respondent. Interviews averaged thirty minutes in duration. In the initial part of the interview, respondents were briefed about the nature of the study. These preliminaries also enabled the interviewer to gain familiarity with the communication skills of each respondent. ASL was used throughout the interview as the primary mode of communication. First, respondents were asked background questions concerning age and onset of deafness, deaf family members, and educational history. Once comfortable with the interviewing process, the respondents were next questioned about black culture and the black community in general. The questions were as follows: (1) Who are some black leaders you recognize as influential in the black community? (2) Where did you acquire your knowledge of black history? (3) Have you ever felt you were discriminated against or treated differently not because you are deaf but because you are black? (4) In terms of upward achievement, where do you see the black community headed? (5) What contribution(s) do you feel black deaf people can make in bringing about racial equality?

This session on black culture and the black community in general was followed by questions about deaf culture and the black deaf community. The questions included the following: (1) Just like we talked about a black culture, do you feel there is a deaf culture existing in the deaf community? (2) Who are some deaf leaders you identify with? (3) What is the most significant achievement obtained by deaf people? (4) When in school, were you taught deaf culture in class? (5) Did you ever feel you were discriminated against or treated differently because you are deaf?

Subsequent to the discussion of the individual topics of black culture and deaf culture, the two topics were combined in order to inquire about the participants' feelings on being black and deaf. The participants were asked to conjoin their knowledge and experiences of being black and deaf in order to comment on what they perceived to be black deaf culture. The questions leading into this discussion were the following: (1) How does black culture and the black community differ from deaf culture and the black deaf community? (2) What are advancements you notice that have been made by black deaf individuals? (3) Do you feel black deaf culture is alive and strong in the black deaf community? (4) What do you see as the most significant barrier black deaf individuals have to overcome in order to be considered equal with the black community and also with the deaf community? (5) What do you hope to contribute to the black deaf community? (6) Which do you identify with first, your black culture or your deaf culture?

RESULTS

The survey provided a general answer to the question of identity. Eight participants (13 percent) said that they identify themselves as deaf before they identify as black; the remaining fifty-two participants (87 percent) identified themselves as black first. Among those participants that identified with their deafness first, the majority have deaf parents and were educated in a residential school for the deaf. These people are more integrated into the deaf community than those who identified with their blackness first. As hypothesized, when compared to the responses of the black-identified participants, the responses of the deaf-identified participants were broader in scope with questions about deaf culture and more limited in scope with questions about black culture. This deaf-identification does not serve to preclude knowledge about black culture, but the responses of the deaf-identified do indicate much greater enthusiasm for questions related to deaf culture than to those related to black culture.

In contrast, the respondents who identified with black culture first said that they see their color as more visible than their deafness and that they want respect for their ethnicity before their deafness. One comment was typical of many of the black-identified participants: "You see I am black first. My deafness is not noticed until I speak or use my hands to communicate." Members of this group, as expected, gave more detailed answers than the deaf-identified group to questions about black culture. All were able to identify with famous black leaders such as Martin Luther King and Jesse Jackson. When asked to identify the person who invented the cotton gin or the person who discovered plasma, they were not able to produce the names. Many of the participants were babies during the time blacks fought for their civil rights, so their knowledge was not first hand. When asked where they acquired their knowledge of black history, the majority said that they did not learn about black culture in school. They were informed about their black heritage from what parents and siblings taught them in addition to what they learned on their own. Most could identify with present problems facing blacks. Many of the answers focused on racial discrimination. In response to a question about how they would achieve racial equality, these participants spoke about blacks working together. Their common goal was to see blacks and whites, both deaf and hearing, interacting on the same level.

In response to questions about deaf culture, all of the participants agreed that there is a deaf culture. When asked about prominent deaf leaders, Thomas Hopkins Gallaudet was named most frequently and nearly exclusively by a majority of the participants. No contemporary deaf leaders were identified as making a substantial contribution to the deaf community. Many of the participants, however, provided names from their school or local community when discussing who they felt made a contribution to the deaf community. On the whole, all the participants agreed that the deaf community has progressed in recent years. Areas of achievement were noted in the field of employment opportunity and education. All participants felt that they were discriminated against or treated differently because of their deafness or their blackness, or both.

Many of the participants also mentioned that they felt they were being discriminated against or treated differently by members of the deaf community, in addition to the general hearing community.[2]

In the final battery of questions, participants were asked to comment on the black deaf community. In many of the responses, participants mentioned parallels between the black community and the deaf community. Also mentioned were notable accomplishments that blacks have made since the civil rights movement began. The barrier of communication was seen as the most prevalent obstacle separating the black deaf community from the black and deaf communities. This topic of communication often surfaced in the interview segments on the black deaf community. Individuals in the black deaf community feel that their communication skills are not on the same level as hearing members of the black community. Communication is facilitated when individuals have something in common, but it is hampered when differences exist among individuals (Glenn and Glenn 1981). Members of both the black deaf community and the black community share black culture. But the members of each group lack, to a certain degree, the ability to communicate effectively with each other through either ASL or spoken English. Black deaf individuals often find themselves alienated from the dominant black culture. The lack of cross-cultural communication between members of the black deaf subculture and members of the majority black culture places both cultures at a distance. The participants who strongly identified with their black deaf culture also noted that differences exist in the ways of signing between black deaf and white deaf individuals. They mentioned too the separation of black deaf clubs and white deaf clubs as an ongoing dilemma that explains why both cultures are not totally cohesive.

The following are some not-so-flattering excerpts from the interviews. They provide an outline of what some of the participants said about the harsh realities facing members of the black deaf community.

The black community in general has more opportunities for advancement than the black deaf community.

Black deaf women have a much harder time at success than their male counterparts.

Progress within the black deaf community has seen little or no improvements within the last ten to fifteen years.

The total number of blacks seeking higher education has increased, while the number of black deaf individuals seeking higher education is still comparatively low.

The deaf community has made progress, but the black deaf community still lags behind.

Communication is important in terms of socializing skills.

Black deaf individuals' communication skills are weak when relating to the general black community.

Sign language skills are an important tool in functioning in the black deaf community.

Upward achievement is difficult for black deaf persons without sufficient role models.

We have just begun to see a focus on black culture and black history in the education setting.

Much of what black deaf people learn about black culture is through readings they do on their own or what family members teach them. We learned nothing in the schools.

A black deaf person has to identify with their blackness first because of its visibility. Deafness is invisible. You do not notice I am deaf until I begin to communicate.

Members of the black deaf community have well-developed feelings and sentiments towards each other. They behave according to well-defined norms on what is proper and improper in their black deaf culture.

Throughout the interview, the sense of identity and the feeling of belonging were apparent in the comments and behavior of the participants. To be sure, a person who is black and deaf is not automatically a member of the black deaf community. Black individuals who become deaf late in life are examples of this. They have not yet experienced the deafness aspect in the combination of what it means to be black and deaf. Many of the examples of discrimination cited by the participants were not very encouraging in terms of the comparisons made between where black deaf individuals were ten years ago and where they are today. Still, the participants expressed a commitment to positive change. Although the greater percentage of participants identified themselves as black first and deaf second, the black deaf community is nonetheless a cohesive, highly motivated culture. They demonstrate a desire for self-improvement. Prevalent in their responses is a need to educate the black deaf community. In order to find ways of improving their situation, the concerns and attitudes expressed by the participants warrant some examination and discussion.

Attitudes are commonly analyzed according to three components: affective, cognitive, and conative (McGuire 1969). The affective component refers to the subjective feeling of what is good or bad. For example, the formation of a national organization for black deaf individuals is viewed with positive feeling. In contrast, black deaf individuals who lack motivation and enthusiasm to succeed are viewed as affectively bad. The cognitive component refers to the beliefs and ideals that are attributed to members of a culture by others. Stereotypes are most frequently manifested in this component. For example, black deaf individuals are perceived by some individuals as being underachievers and lacking motivation. The conative component refers to the behavioral intentions of individuals. For example, sign language skills are looked upon by members of the black deaf community as important to effective communication. But the majority of members of the black community who have deaf relatives lack the signing skills needed to communicate with them and other members of the black deaf community. Often, individuals in the black community are shunned by members of the black deaf community for lack of productive communication skills. The attitude of discrimination, referring to the behavior adopted by members of the black community, which puts other individuals in the black community at a disadvantage, represents this conative component.

Eighty seven percent of the individuals taking part in this study stated that they identify with their black culture first. Other studies relating to deafness provide evidence of unhealthy denials of self (Stewart 1969). Stories are often told of individuals denying their deafness, claiming to belong to the hearing world. But when black deaf individuals discuss whether they identify first with the black community or with the deaf community, they state that they are not denying one or the other but rather are placing each in the proper perspective of degree of societal acceptance. An often cited reason for identifying with the black culture first is the actuality of skin color. Black deaf individuals believe that society views them as black first because of the high visibility of skin color. Deafness is an invisible handicap. Until a deaf person uses sign language or speaks in a manner unnatural to native (normal) speech, it is not immediately obvious to a viewer that the person is deaf.

COMMUNICATION PATTERNS

As discussed earlier, differences have been observed between black signing and white signing. It has also been observed casually that the signing of black deaf individuals varies as a function of the race of other participants in a conversational setting. That is, black signers sign differently with white signers than they do with other black signers. The second part of the present study collected empirical data on sign language production in black-white interaction. This data provided evidence of code-switching by black signers.

Specifically, the conversational interaction of seven dyads was videotaped. The participants in the study were two black deaf men, both native ASL users (hereafter identified as X and Y); one black hearing man, a professional working in the deaf community; one white deaf man, a native ASL user; and one white hearing man, a professional working in research on deafness. Table 1 presents the composition of the seven dyads set up among these five participants and the language used in each dyad by the participants. Each dyad was videotaped for approximately twenty minutes while the two participants, alone together in the taping room, engaged in casual conversation. The setting was kept as informal as possible. All other participants, as well as the videotaping crew, were dismissed so that the signing mode of each dyad would not be influenced by the presence of others. The general topic of conversation is the same in all dyads. ASL is the predominant mode of communication used when both participants are deaf (native ASL users). When either of the hearing participants are involved, the predominant mode of communication is ASL-like signing, as opposed to pure ASL.

Dyads 1, 2, 4, and 5 provide evidence of code-switching. Although the predominant mode of communication in these dyads is ASL-like signing, the deaf participant in each dyad often began the conversation in ASL and then switched to incorporate more English in the signing. An example of this is the initialization of ASL signs, such as the use of the *I* handshape instead of the 1 (index finger) handshape to sign "I."

Dyads 6 and 7 display sign language variation within ASL, as opposed to code-switching to ASL-like signing. ASL is used by both speakers in each dyad as their primary mode of communication. There are not any "English-like" features embodied in their conversation. Moreover, initialized signs are not used by these deaf participants in their all-deaf dyads. In contrast, the feature of initialized signs is fast apparent in dyads 1, 2, 4, and 5. Nonmanual features also are different between these two groups. Exaggerated body movements and facial expressions are not as prevalent when a deaf participant conversed with a hearing participant as compared to when both participants are deaf.

TABLE 1. Composition of Conversational Dyads and Language Used

DYAD	PARTICIPANTS	LANGUAGE
1	Black $deaf_X$–Black hearing	ASL-like signing
2	Black $deaf_Y$–Black hearing	ASL-like signing
3	Black $deaf_X$–Black $deaf_Y$	ASL
4	Black $deaf_X$–White hearing	ASL-like signing
5	Black $deaf_Y$–White hearing	ASL-like signing
6	Black $deaf_X$–White deaf	ASL
7	Black $deaf_Y$–White deaf	ASL

FIGURE 1. FLIRT, citation form.

FIGURE 2. FLIRT, the black form.

In setting up this project, it was hypothesized that the deaf participants would sign differently when paired with a hearing participant than when paired with each other. In light of this hypothesis, what takes place in dyad 3 is significant when compared to dyads 6 and 7. ASL is used in all three dyads. Yet, in dyad 3, the two black deaf participants, X and Y, use signs when paired together that they do not use when paired separately with the white deaf participant in dyads 6 and 7.

By way of explaining these differences in lexical choice, it is important to note initially that all three deaf participants had ample time to meet each other and converse about different topics before the actual process of data collection began. This time together permitted each participant to become comfortable with the other two, as well as familiar with the others' respective modes of communication. Further, analysis of the discourse in dyads 3, 6, and 7 did not reveal any discernible differences between the speakers in each dyad with respect to hesitance in signing. As opposed, then, to the social familiarity versus nonfamiliarity of coparticipants, and even participant uncertainty (hence hesitance) about particular ASL signs, the social identity of participants as black versus white appears to be sociolinguistically salient in accounting for certain lexical variation in the data. Specifically, the citation forms of FLIRT, SCHOOL, and BOSS occur in dyads 6 and 7, but black forms of these signs occur in dyad 3. (See Figures 1, 2; 3, 4; and 5, 6.) When asked about these particular forms, and other, similarly categorized forms that are not described here, the black deaf participants characterized them as older signs used by blacks, originating from the time that blacks attended segregated schools for the deaf. When questioned further about why blacks sometimes do not use these forms, one of the black deaf participants explained that the forms are not used when a black person is with "a person who is not a part of that culture."

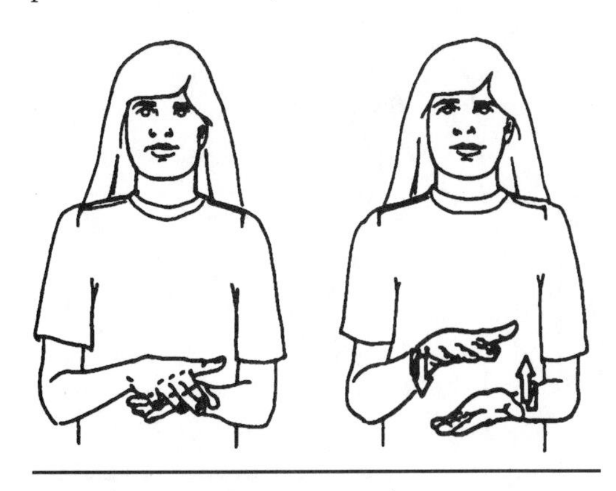

FIGURE 3. SCHOOL, citation form.

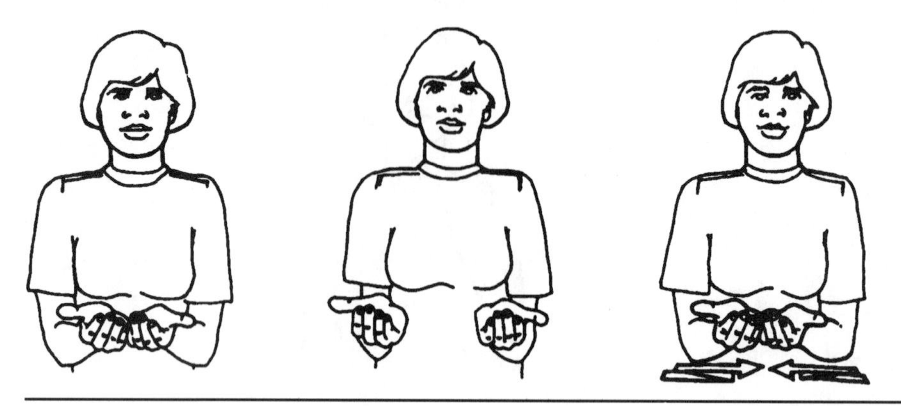

FIGURE 4. SCHOOL, black form.

The discourse in dyad 3 also differs from the discourse in dyads 6 and 7 with respect to facial expressions, body movement, and size of the signing space used by the participants. The facial expressions are exaggerated in dyad 3, and both participants use their signing space to the fullest. In contrast, these two black deaf participants, X in dyad 6 and Y in dyad 7, use less exaggerated facial expressions, fewer body movements, and a smaller signing space when conversing with the white deaf participant than when conversing with each other.

Other studies provide additional evidence of variation in ASL that is related to ethnic background (e.g., Woodward and De Santis 1977; Woodward and Erting 1975). Other findings of the present study suggest that the two sociolinguistic oppositions of deaf-hearing and black-white (i.e., variables of participant social identity) can have interlocking effects on discourse. For example, in dyad 6, the black deaf participant X is more of a passive listener when conversing with the white deaf participant than in his other conversations. Although black participant Y is far from passive in his conversation with this same white deaf participant in dyad 7, the only instances where Y interrupts his co-participant in order to speak are all in dyad 3, when he is conversing with X, the other black deaf participant.

There is a general observation in the literature that native ASL signers use a more

FIGURE 5. BOSS, citation form.

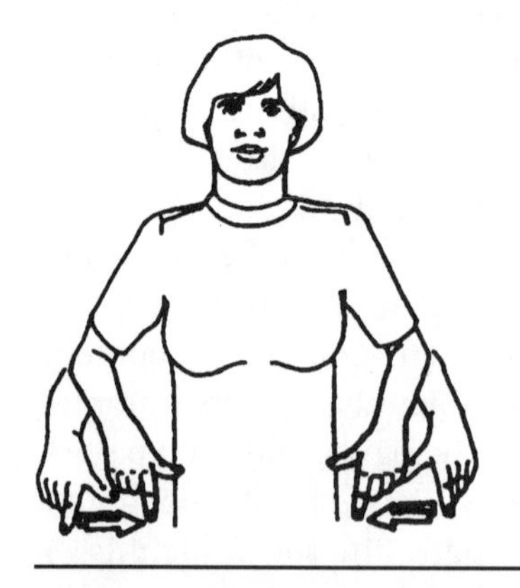

FIGURE 6. BOSS, black form.

English-like signing when conversing with hearing signers than when conversing with other deaf signers (Lucas and Valli, this volume). In dyad 1 of the present study, black deaf participant X produces a greater degree of English-like features in his signing when with the black hearing participant than occur in any other conversation in the data corpus. For example, in many instances, participant X uses an ASL sign and then "corrects" the sign with an English equivalent, such as ME TRY in ASL followed by I T-R-Y, in an effort to conform to English style. Participant X also uses more copulas in this conversation than occur in any other conversation in the corpus. Additionally, in one instance, he uses the emphatic form of WORK, which, with nonmanual features, means "working hard." He also uses the sign VERY to indicate emphasis. In contrast, when X converses with the other black deaf participant (dyad 3), copulas, as well as the initialized sign for "I," are not used at all. When these same two participants converse with the white deaf participant (dyads 6 and 7), their conversational styles include English-like features. Finally, throughout his entire conversation with the white hearing participant (dyad 5), black deaf participant Y keeps his responses short and uses almost perfect English word order. When with this same white hearing participant (dyad 4), black deaf participant X does not correct toward English as frequently as he does with the black hearing participant (dyad 1), but he still incorporates English-like features in his signing.

SUMMARY AND CONCLUSIONS

The existence of a black deaf community is in part evidenced by the survival of all-black clubs for the deaf, where members go to socialize in a setting that satisfies their communication needs. The existence of this community is reinforced by a history of segregated schooling. The lack of adequate facilities and qualified personnel needed to prepare black deaf individuals for the future is reflected not only in the high levels of unemployment and underemployment found in the black deaf community but also in the small number of black deaf individuals who enter institutions of higher learning.

In the present study, a survey was used to answer the question of which community black deaf individuals identify with first, the black community or the deaf community. The majority of the respondents identified themselves first with the black community. They believe that they are seen by others as black first, since, unlike skin color, their deafness only becomes visible when they communicate in sign language. In contrast to these respondents, the remaining respondents who identified themselves first with the deaf community are more immersed in this community than the black-identified group. That is, the deaf-identified respondents are from deaf families, grew up in residential schools for the deaf, and socialize mostly within the deaf community as adults.

The language of the black deaf community is ASL. Yet, variations of ASL occur when members of this community engage in conversations among themselves, as opposed to conversations with others who are outsiders or nonmembers of the black deaf community. Specifically, as found in the present study, black deaf individuals commonly use signs that are unknown to outsiders. These "black signs," used mostly by black deaf individuals when the schools were segregated, are used when conversing with other deaf blacks, but standard ASL signs are used when conversing with white deaf individuals. This sociolinguistic variation also evidences the existence of a black deaf community.

Overall, as an essential part of the deaf community, the black deaf community faces the challenges of securing better education, more promising employment opportunities, and social advancements similar to those already acquired by members of the black community at large. Both in drawing attention to these issues and in describing some sociolinguistic features of black deaf discourse, the overriding aim of this chapter is to stimulate further research on the black deaf community. It is hoped that future studies will increase our understanding of this particular minority group as well as other minorities within the deaf community at large.

NOTES

1. These observations come from in-depth interviews with administrators and teachers at the Southern School for the Deaf in Baton Rouge, Louisiana (closed in 1978). The interviews covered the educational situation for the black deaf in Louisiana, Mississippi, and Texas in particular.
2. This issue was raised by Dorothy Gilliam in an article in the *Washington Post* (18 April 1988), appearing a month after the Gallaudet protest. The article remarked that "it is tempting to think that within their own world, every person who is hearing impaired is totally visible, absolutely equal. But according to some black and white parents of students in Gallaudet's Model Secondary School for the Deaf, the institution over the years has sometimes displayed marked insensitivity to black students." One parent describes the racism she witnessed as "horrific, shocking." Some parents formed a Black Concerns Committee, which organized discussion groups between black and white students, and workshops on race relations. One goal of the committee is the appointment of a black deaf person as one of the deaf board members guaranteed in the student victory. A further example of the racism that exists in the deaf community was provided by a white foreign student studying at Gallaudet for one year. This student inquired about shopping at a market near the campus and was told by a white deaf university administrator that it might not be wise to shop there, because "that's where all the black people shop."

Toward a Description of Register Variation in American Sign Language

JUNE ZIMMER

INTRODUCTION

In this chapter, register variation in American Sign Language (ASL) is examined. Register variation, sometimes referred to as style variation, involves differential language use that is sensitive to situational factors. It is generally accepted that speakers use language differently in different situations, and several models have been put forward that attempt to describe the situational dynamics that control register variation. Other than several seminal studies by Ferguson, which describe features found in specific registers such as baby talk (Ferguson 1978), foreigner talk (Ferguson 1982), and sports announcer talk (Ferguson 1983), there are few empirical studies of register variation in particular languages.

Much of the discussion of register variation among deaf Americans centers on the notion of diglossia. In these models, signed English is seen as the "high" variety (used in formal situations, such as an academic conference) and ASL is seen as the "low" variety (used in more informal situations, such as casual talk among friends). Some scholars have noted special features within ASL that are sensitive to situational changes, but no truly empirical study of these differences has yet been made.

What follows is a study of register variation in ASL. The data for this study come from videotaped recordings of a native user of ASL. He was taped in three different situations: a formal lecture in an academic setting, an informal talk, and a television interview. Portions of these tapes were transcribed and compared to discover differential language use. While the findings are only preliminary, they do support the notion that language users in general, and users of ASL in particular, vary their language according to the situation of use.

SITUATIONAL VARIATION IN LANGUAGE

Halliday (1968) distinguishes register variation, which he describes as "variation according to use," from dialect variation, described as "variation according to user." Whereas dialect is seen as a function of who the speaker is in terms of social identity and determines what dialect the speaker habitually speaks, register is seen as a function of what the speaker is doing in terms of social activity, which determines how the speaker will speak in a particular situation. Some clear cases of special registers can be found in "restricted languages" (e.g., pilot radio talk or the sign language used by skin divers).

The models of language variation advanced thus far discuss register in terms of socially constituted and recognized conventions of language use. These conventions are

Source. Reprinted by permission of the publisher, from C. Lucas, ed., *The Sociolinguistics of the Deaf Community* (1989): 253–272. San Diego: Academic Press. The references for the reading can be found in the original volume.

determined by the social structures that obtain in a "speech community." Gumperz (1972, 200) describes a speech community as "any aggregate characterized by regular and frequent interaction by means of a shared body of verbal signs and set off from similar aggregates by significant differences in language use." This definition does not preclude the possibility that any individual can be a member of several different speech communities and applies readily in multilingual communities where an individual can control several different languages. It is also possible for separate speech communities to share the same "language," as illustrated by the different national varieties of English existing in many places in the world (Kachru 1983). Within one national variety, speech communities can be divided according to dialect. Speakers of a "nonstandard" dialect can control both their native dialect and the national standard. An individual speaker controls a range of language variation that can be thought of as his or her "linguistic repertoire" (Fishman 1972). The repertoire of a speaker can include separate languages and dialects, different subgroup and occupational varieties, and, within each of these, a range of variation according to register.

Culture is an important factor in determining the characteristics of a speaker's repertoire. Each culture and subculture defines the speech styles that are relevant to it (Hymes 1974). Any competent member of the community has access to the conventions operative in certain speech situations. Each speaker is also involved in a range of speech networks, and those with a more extensive system of networks control a more varied linguistic range (Fishman 1972).

MODELS OF REGISTER VARIATION

Register variation involves the relative level of formality or informality called for, and used by, a speaker in a particular situation. Joos (1968) posits a "finite" number of "styles" and proposes five in particular. The least formal level, called "intimate," is described as the level used among people who know each other very well and who interact on a regular basis. It is characterized by heavy use of ellipsis (especially of phonological segments and certain lexical items such as articles, subject pronouns, etc.) and private language, the meaning of which is known only to the interactants. The next level is dubbed "casual." This style shares many of the features of intimate style, without such a heavy reliance on private language. The third level, "consultative," is the style used in everyday conversation between speakers who are strangers or do not know each other well. It is still characterized by some ellipsis and a use of colloquial speech. But in consultative style, there is an emphasis on making speech as clear and unambiguous as possible. The fourth level Joos calls "formal." He says that the most important function of speech at this level is to impart information, and that the talk does not have a great deal of "social importance" (Joos here seems to equate "social" with interactive). The fifth level Joos calls "frozen," and he says it is characterized by language that is formulaic. This is exemplified by much of the language used in religious services and in the courtroom.

Other writers avoid talking about registers as discrete varieties. Instead, they posit the existence of contextual factors that help to determine a range of language use that will be appropriate or acceptable in any given situation. Crystal and Davey (1969) mention three categories of features that in part determine the type of utterance conventionally prescribed in a particular situation. "Province" features relate an utterance to extralinguistic factors (e.g., an occupational or professional setting in which speech takes place). "Status" features take into account the participants and their social standing vis à vis one another. "Modality" features concern the purpose(s) served by an utterance. The authors believe that these features act in combination or separately to cause speakers to follow expected conventions for the particular type of discourse in which they are involved.

The most sophisticated model for a description of register variation is proposed by Halliday (1968, 1978) and expanded upon by Gregory and Carroll (1978). Halliday also uses a three-way division to describe the characteristics of a speech situation. He calls his categories the field, the mode, and the tenor of discourse. The field includes the physical setting and the social activity that surrounds and defines a speech event. A major determining factor of field is the degree of emphasis placed on the language itself. At one extreme of this dimension are situations in which language plays a very minor role and is subordinate to the nonverbal interaction. These situations are best exemplified by work or play that involves the collaboration of participants. At the other extreme are situations in which the language itself dominates the interaction, exemplified by gossip, public lectures, and so forth. Halliday also includes subject matter in the field of discourse.

For Halliday, the mode of discourse includes the channel used (i.e., written, spoken, or signed) and involves factors such as whether speech is memorized or spontaneous and monologic or dialogic. The speech "genre" (e.g., conversation, lecture, interview) is also part of the mode. The mode can in part determine the types of cohesion used in a text. Gregory and Carroll (1978) state that certain types of texts exhibit more phonological, grammatical, and lexical cohesion than others, and that texts can also be distinguished by whether deictic processes are intra- or extralinguistic (i.e., whether the referents for pronouns and demonstratives are discourse-internal or are situationally copresent). They state that texts that rely less on shared experience tend to be more "complete" linguistically.

The tenor of discourse in Halliday's model concerns the participants and the interpersonal dynamics involved in their relationship. Halliday mentions two different types of social roles that participants can hold vis à vis one another. First-order roles are defined extralinguistically (e.g., friend, teacher, mother, etc.). Second-order roles are defined in relation to the linguistic system (e.g., questioner, informer, responder, lecturer, etc.). These factors constitute the "personal tenor" of the discourse. A discourse also has "functional tenor" (Gregory and Carroll 1978). This involves the purposes to which language is being applied. Language can be used to inform, discipline, persuade, and so forth. The functional tenor of a discourse can be more or less explicit [e.g., a salesman's choice of "hard" or "soft" sell (Gregory and Carroll 1978)]. Unlike Crystal and Davey (1969), Halliday (1978) and Gregory and Carroll (1978) do not believe that individual factors can act alone. Rather, clusters of features act on a text in aggregate fashion, although different features can have more or less importance in any particular speech situation.

All of these contextual factors serve to determine a range of language use that will be appropriate or acceptable in any given situation. Unlike Joos, Halliday and Gregory and Carroll do not believe that registers constitute totally discrete varieties (except possibly in the special registers mentioned earlier). Rather, features that are often associated with a particular register can also be found in other registers of speech. We can say that in a certain situation, a particular linguistic variable X is likely to occur, but this does not preclude the possibility that Y will occur instead. For example, in a context in which a more "formal" feature is usually found, a more "informal" feature will be used. Hudson (1980, 50) discusses the possibility that even within a sentence, individual items can be selected according to different sets of criteria. He gives as an example the sentence, "We obtained some sodium chloride." Depending on context, it may be more appropriate to say either "We got some sodium chloride" or "We obtained some salt." The word "obtained" may be selected for its level of formality, and the term "sodium chloride" may be selected because of its technical description (in scientific jargon, "salt" has a different meaning).

Register, then, is an abstract notion that is not easily definable, and any given speech event may be difficult to categorize as a variant. The concept of the appropriateness or inappropriateness of certain types of language use in particular situational contexts does, however, seem to have psychological reality for groups of speakers. This is illustrated by the ability of people to recognize certain speech styles out of context. Speakers would most likely be able to recognize differences between audiotapes of a radio announcer, a lawyer in court, and a sermon conducted in their native language (Crystal and Davey 1969). They would also probably have similar opinions about whether a particular type of speech event is appropriate or inappropriate for a particular social situation. Hymes (1974) mentions that people are often seen to use a "significant speech style" outside of the context in which it normally occurs (e.g., in reported speech, in stereotype, and in alluding to particular persons and situations). Use of certain speech styles outside of their normal contexts can involve the phenomenon of linguistic taboo, the flaunting of which can arouse strong feelings in a listener (e.g., in American society, use of "four letter words" is strongly discouraged in most situations). Furthermore, inappropriate use of register is often used in humor (Halliday 1968). Enkvist (1987) says that we spend a great deal of time observing speech of different styles and comparing these texts with each other, gaining insight into the "subvarieties" of language that we can expect in any speech situation.

MODELS OF REGISTER VARIATION IN ASL

As mentioned earlier, there has been no systematic study of the notion of register in ASL, and, until recently, most discussions of situationally conditioned sign variation assumed the existence of a "diglossic" situation. The idea of diglossia was first put forth by Ferguson (1959), after he noticed that several of the communities he was studying have separate language varieties specified for function. One variety, which he termed H (high), is used in more formal situations, whereas the other, termed L (low), is used in more colloquial situations. Fishman (1972) later expanded Ferguson's definition of diglossia to include bilingual situations, in which one language plays the H role (e.g., used for school, government) and the other plays the L role (e.g., used at home and when interacting with peers). Stokoe (1969) posits the existence of diglossia in the Deaf community. He claims that there are two very different types of signing going on in formal and colloquial interactions. Woodward and Markowicz (1975) state that Fishman's description of bilingual diglossia is more explanatory of the situation in the Deaf community, in that signed English seems to be used as the H variety and ASL as the L variety. Lee (1982), however, points out that none of these explanations adequately describes the dynamics involved. She states that both signed English and ASL show up in all of the situations differentiated by Ferguson on the basis of H and L usage. For Lee, alternate use of ASL and English is not tied to register but rather to other factors mostly determined by the characteristics of the participants involved in the interaction (most importantly, level of signing skill and attitudes about English and ASL).

Although no systematic study of register variation in ASL has been done, several authors mention speech situations that call for signing that is more or less "formal" (Baker and Cokely 1980; Kettrick 1983; Lee 1982). They state that more formal signing probably occurs at academic lectures, business meetings, banquets, and church services and that more informal signing occurs with family and friends, or at a party. Authors also list features with which these two different styles are marked. Formal ASL is said to be slower paced and to use a much larger signing space (Baker and Cokely 1980; Kettrick 1983). Formal signing is said to be more clear and more fully executed (Kettrick 1983). In casual signing, the nondominant hand can be deleted (Lee 1982). That is, formal signing tends to use two-handed variants of signs, whereas informal signing tends to use one-handed variants (Baker and Cokely 1980; Kettrick 1983). Signs that contact the forehead in formal signing can contact the cheek or be made in neutral space in casual signing (Baker and Cokely 1980; Lee 1982; Kettrick 1983; Liddell and Johnson 1985). Certain grammatical markers apparently become "more distinct" in casual signing (Kettrick 1983). These include discourse and sentence boundary markers and body shifting to indicate reported speech (as opposed to shoulder, head, or eye-gaze shifts). Nonmanual signals appear without a manual component in informal signing, but not in formal signing. These include pronominal indexing that uses eye-gaze, nonmanual adverbs (e.g., "pursed lips" that mean "very thin") (Kettrick 1983), and lexical items that have an obligatory nonmanual component, such as NOT#YET (Lee 1982). Phonological processes such as "assimilation" operate more often in casual than in formal signing (Liddell and Johnson 1985). In casual signing, a sign such as THINK, which is normally made with a 1 handshape, is made with a Y handshape with extended index finger, in anticipation of the following sign PLAY (Baker and Cokely 1980). With a sign that has a different handshape on each hand in formal signing, the nondominant hand assimilates to the dominant handshape in casual signing (Liddell and Johnson 1985).

THE PRESENT STUDY

The observations discussed here thus far are noteworthy and intuitively appealing. They are, however, based on casual observation rather than on systematic analysis of data. Until such a systematic study is conducted, no empirical conclusions can be drawn as to what register variation looks like in ASL, and what situational factors trigger the use of different linguistic forms.

The project discussed here is a very preliminary attempt at a systematic study of situational variation in ASL. The data for the analysis come from three videotapes of one Deaf native ASL signer. Tape number one consists of a lecture on the subject of linguistic attitudes among Deaf high school students. It is referred to here as "the lecture." Tape number two is a talk addressed to a small audience on the subject of being a "househusband." It is called "the informal talk." The third tape is from a television interview in which this speaker is interviewing a deaf guest. It is called "the interview."

None of these situations falls at the "casual" end on a continuum of formal to informal language, since they are all relatively planned, as opposed to spontaneous, and are each performed for an audience. The level of formality called for in each situation, however, is quite different. The most formal (and the most thoroughly planned) of the three situations is the lecture. As is the tradition at academic conferences, the speaker is presenting a paper that would later be published. Academic lectures constitute, in a way, a special genre. According to Goffman (1981), this genre is characterized by a "serious and impersonal" style.

The informal talk, although not "colloquial," is much less formal than the lecture. In this situation, the main discourse topic is an important factor to consider, along with the size of the audience being addressed. We can expect that a talk given to a small audience, about the things the speaker has experienced while taking care of his son, lends itself to a casual, conversational style, whereas a lecture at an academic conference does not. Also, while the informal talk is still somewhat planned (the speaker is using notes to remind himself of subtopics and anecdotes he wishes to relate), it is much less so than the lecture.

The interview, since it is interactive, is in some sense conversational. But because it was taped for broadcast on television, we can expect it to be much more formal than an everyday conversation among friends. The interactants are together not as friends but as performers for the television audience.

Analysis

Portions of each of these three tapes were transcribed. The transcribed portions were then analyzed to discover similarities and differences that might be linked to similarities and differences in register. Many features were found to distinguish the language used in these three speech situations. The lecture in particular is quite different from the other two tapes. Three areas that differentiate these tapes from each other are discussed here: phonological differences, morphological and lexical differences, and differences in syntax and discourse organization. A close inspection of the lecture also reveals that parts of the text are very different from each other. Therefore, intratextual register variation within the lecture is also discussed here, and three areas in which striking differences exist are described.

Phonological Differences. The lecture is most noticeably different from the other two tapes in the area of phonology. Especially obvious is a distinct difference in the use of space. The signing space used in the lecture is much larger than that used in the other two tapes. In both the informal talk and the interview, signs made in neutral space (i.e., signs in which the hand(s) does not contact the body) are usually executed within a range extending from the top of the head to the middle of the chest, and usually not beyond shoulder width. In the lecture, however, the signing space often extends considerably beyond these boundaries. In addition to being larger, signs in the lecture are also executed more slowly. Individual signs are of longer duration, and final holds are longer.

Body movements are also much more pronounced in the lecture than in the other two situations. Shifts to indicate reported speech (which usually takes the form of a dialogue between the speaker and one of his students) involve directional shifting of the entire torso. This can be contrasted with the same phenomenon in the informal talk, in which shifting to mark different speakers is done only with movements of the head. In the lecture, the signer often takes a step or two when setting up oppositions or comparisons between two or more categories of items. In the informal talk, this is once again accomplished with head movements, subtle body shifts, or hand switching, as discussed later.

A technique used extensively in the lecture and rarely in the other two tapes is that of hand-switching. Signed languages differ from spoken languages in that a signer has the use of two articulators. Thus, it is logically possible for a signer to execute two one-handed signs simultaneously, or to switch back and forth between signs made with the left hand and signs made with the right hand. The usual case is for one hand to be "dominant" and for all or most one-handed signs to be made with this hand. At times, though, a speaker will switch dominance for the length of one or more signs. Frishberg (1985) has studied hand-switching in ASL narratives and has discovered that a switch into the nondominant hand can be used for particular pragmatic or semantic purposes. She (ibid, 83) says that "the signer can manipulate the [dominance reversals] throughout [a narrative text] for the purpose of creating semantic connections or contrasts between elements within the narrative."

Hand-switching is infrequent in the interview and occurs only with pronouns and determiners. It occurs somewhat more often in the informal talk, and most of the switches also occur with pronouns and determiners. All other cases are like those described by Frishberg, that is, the switch has semantic or pragmatic significance. Consider the following examples of hand-switching from the informal talk.[1] In segment A, the speaker is relating how his son's name was created by combining his own name with that of his wife (also see Figure 1a–h).

Segment A

R ____________ L ____________
PRO.1 P-E-R-R-Y POSS.1 WIFE A-N-N
"My (name) is Perry, my wife's is Ann"

L/R ________ L/R ______ R ________
ONE-HALF MATCH P-E-R-A-N
"*Per* and *an*, make Peran"

In this example, the signer is describing a process that involves a combination of two elements. When indicating his own name and the portion of it ("Per") that occurs in the name of his son, he maintains right-hand dominance. He then switches to left-hand dominance to indicate his wife's name and the portion of it ("an") that also occurs in his son's name. It is significant that he uses both hands for the sign ONE-HALF. This sign is normally one-handed. The use of a two-handed version here helps to reinforce the idea that two elements are being combined (or "connected" in Frishberg's terms).

Hand-switching in the lecture, in contrast, is used more frequently. The following example (B) is a segment of the lecture in which hand-switching is especially pervasive. The speaker is discussing the issue of native versus nonnative signers of ASL and indicating that signers who have received the language from their parents are native ASL signers.

Segment B

R ______________________ L ______
ALL-OVER DEAF COMMUNITY POSS.3
"Throughout the deaf community"

L __ R ________ L __ R ______
DET/ PRO.1 TALK A-S-L NATIVE
L ____________
N-A-T-I-V-E DET
"There are those who are native users of ASL"

L ____ R ____ L ____
THERE MEAN THERE
"Those speakers"

R ____ L ______ R ______
MEAN POSS.3 PARENT
"the ones whose parents are deaf"

R ______________________________ L ____
A-S-L HAND-DOWN ACCEPT NATIVE A-S-L
"have received the language from them and are native users of ASL"

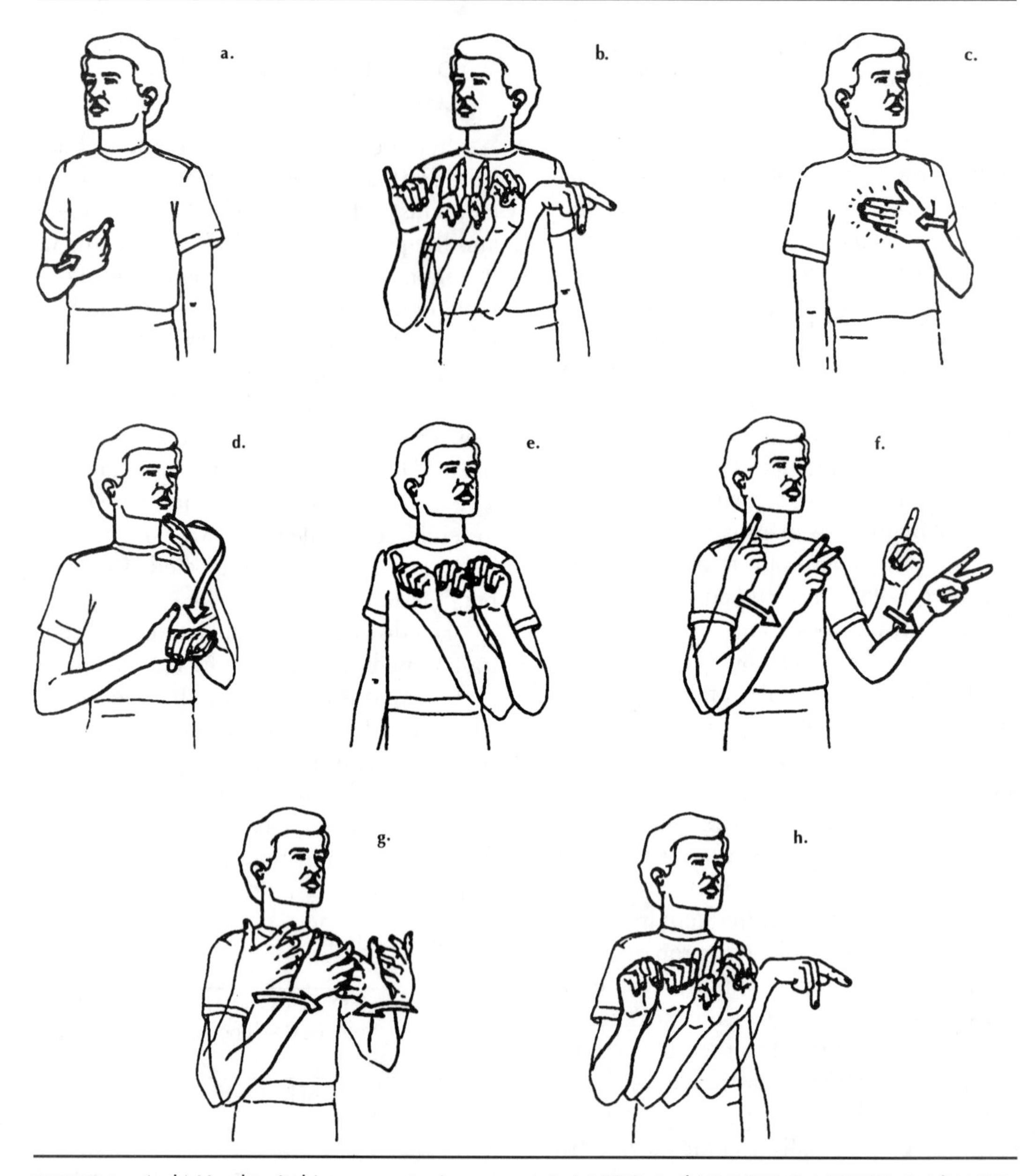

FIGURE 1. (a–h) Hand-switching sequence in segment A. (a) PRO. 1; (b) P-E-R-R-Y; (c) POSS. 1; (d) WIFE; (e) A-N-N; (f) ONE-HALF; (g) MATCH; (h) P-E-R-A-N.

In this example, there appears to be no semantic or pragmatic significance to the switching. Thus, it can only be seen as a stylistic variation occurring in this particular register of signing.

The lecture is also distinguished from the other two tapes by the relative frequency of occurrence of certain phonological processes. Liddell and Johnson (1985) describe several processes that occur in casual signing but not in formal varieties. Assimilation is a process whereby some feature of a sign (e.g., facing, orientation or handshape) assimilates to the same feature of the sign immediately preceding or following it. Handshape assimilation occurs especially often in indexical signs, for example, pointing gestures used as pronouns, locatives, and determiners (Patschke 1986). The present data were examined for handshape assimilation occurring with indexical signs. In the formal lecture, no overt evidence of assimilation was found. It should be noted, however, that this phenomenon is especially pervasive with first person pronouns, which are often hard to see clearly on a video tape. Nevertheless, some assimilation of this type occurs in the informal talk. In these instances, the *L* handshape of the first person pronoun assimilates to a following sign with a *B* handshape. In the lecture, no such assimilation was found.

Other phonological processes discussed by Liddell and Johnson (1985) are perseveration and anticipation. In each of these processes, the base handshape in a two-handed sign is in place for the length of two or more signs. With perseveration, a nondominant base handshape stays in place after the dominant hand has changed to a new sign. With anticipation, the base handshape is in place before the dominant hand begins to make the sign. In connected discourse, this means that a base handshape for one sign is in place while the dominant hand executes two or more signs. No anticipation was found in the section of the lecture analyzed, whereas it occurs fairly regularly in both the informal talk and the interview. In instances such as the following segment (C) from the informal talk. The signer is relating a discussion that he and his wife were having on a particular subject. (The overscore here indicates that the base hand for DISCUSS is in place.)

Segment C

L ______________________

R PRO.3 PRO.1 SAY DISCUSS

"She and I discussed it"

Perseveration does occur in the lecture, but it is infrequent and of short duration (usually continuing over only one extra sign or a part of a sign). In the informal talk and in the interview, it is seen much more often and it lasts longer, as in segment D, extracted from the interview (see segment D and Figure 2a–e). In this example, perseveration occurs twice within one clause. The interviewer is asking whether the interviewee's experience has been the same or different as that of others. He signs the two-handed version of SAME. The nondominant handshape for SAME perseverates through the next two signs of the dominant hand, EXPERIENCE and the fingerspelled word O-R, and then changes to the handshape for the two-handed sign DIFFERENT. This handshape then perseverates through the next one-handed sign, EXPERIENCE.

Segment D

L ______________________

R SAME EXPERIENCE O-R

L ______________________

DIFFERENT EXPERIENCE?

"Has it been the same experience or a different experience?"

Lexical and Morphological Differences. There are also striking differences at the lexical level among the three tapes, and between portions of the lecture. Certain "colloquial" lexical items appear in the informal talk and in the portions of direct speech in the lecture but do not occur in either the interview or the body of the lecture. These include: WHAT-FOR, WHAT'S-UP, EXPERT (F handshape at the chin), FINE (the version that wiggles), PEA-BRAIN, ADORE (kissing the back of the hand), BRAINY, KNOW# THAT, THAT#DET, and the sign usually glossed as SHIT. In some cases, it is not clear whether this is a matter of lexical choice or of semantics, since it is often difficult to find contexts in the lecture where these signs could

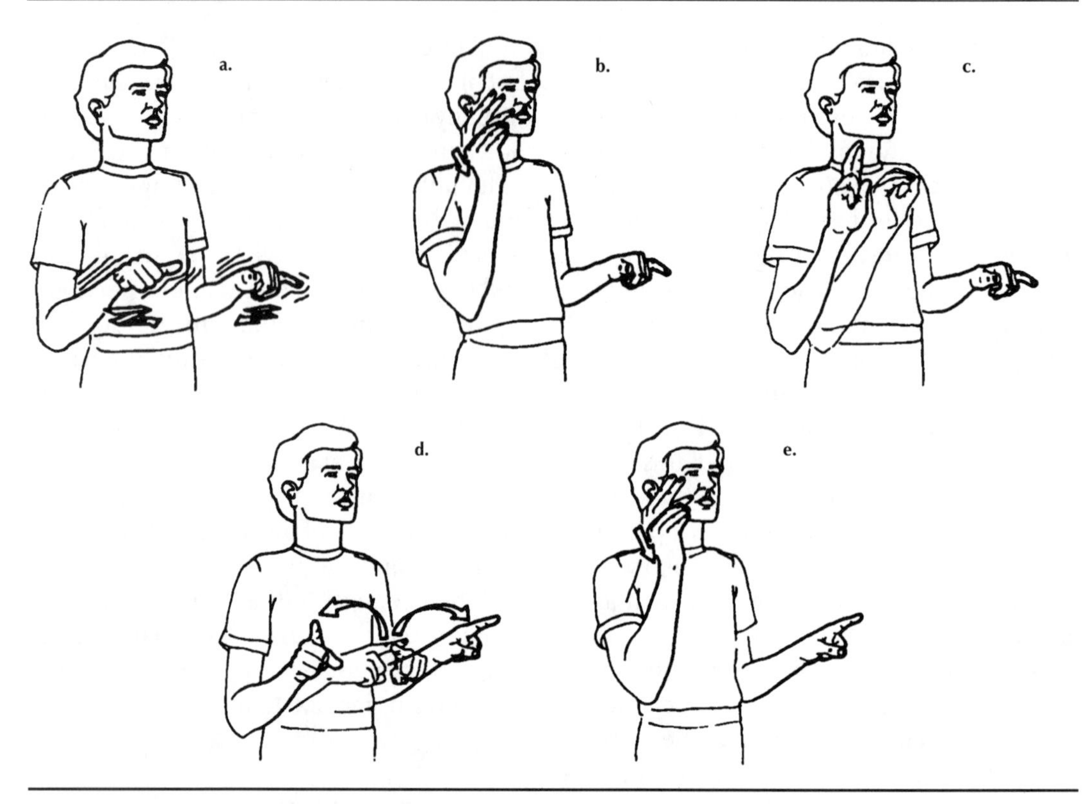

FIGURE 2. (a–e) Perseveration in segment D. (a) SAME; (b) EXPERIENCE; (c) O-R; (d) DIFFERENT; (e) EXPERIENCE.

be appropriately used. In some instances, however, these contexts can be found. An example is the sign EXPERT, which is never used in the lecture. SKILL is used in all contexts where EXPERT would be semantically appropriate.

Some signs occur only in the body of the lecture, never in the informal talk or the interview. These are: AND and THEN. AND is used much like the English word *and* to conjoin two equal elements (lexical items, clauses, etc.). In the other tapes, conjunction of elements is achieved nonlexically. THEN is used to segment ideas. In the informal talk, segmentation is usually achieved syntactically with topicalization.

A certain type of morphological inflection that often occurs in the lecture, but does not occur in either of the other tapes, is articulated by the exaggerated movement of a sign, indicating a process that is difficult or of long duration. One such example occurs with the production of the sign EQUAL (see Figure 3). The lecturer is discussing the dif-

FIGURE 3. Exaggerated movement of EQUAL.

ficulty encountered in his attempts to communicate with students on an equal basis. The sign is executed as a series of extremely large circles of the dominant hand, which eventually contacts the nondominant hand, bounces back, and contacts again. The bounce is accompanied by a jerk of the entire body. Several utterances later, the sign HEAD-TOWARD is executed in much the same manner. This same type of inflection is seen with other verbs such as AVOID and NAME.

This type of exaggerated movement may be used in the lecture in place of nonmanual signals. In the informal talk, a long and difficult process is indicated by a nonmanual signal that involves squinted eyes and spread lips. Differential uses of nonmanual signals involving facial expression are discussed more fully later.

Differences in Syntax and Discourse Organization. Differences among the three tapes are also seen at the syntactic and discourse levels. The most obvious of these is the extensive use of rhetorical questions in the lecture and their infrequent use in the other two tapes. On the other hand, the informal talk uses much more topicalization than is used in the lecture. These observations tie into formal contrasts that function at the discourse level. In the informal talk, topic marking seems to be used as a device to segment the discourse, whereas in the lecture such boundary marking is typically achieved with the lexical item NOW. Another discourse-level feature used in the lecture but not in the informal talk is the use of metaphor. This is discussed more fully in the next section.

A syntactic phenomenon that only occurs in the lecture is the use of a pointing sign with a fingerspelled word. This technique occurs with the words D-E-A-F and A-T-T-I-T-U-D-E, where each word is spelled with the dominant hand (see Figure 4). The last letter of the word is then held while the index finger of the nondominant hand points to the held letter. This occurs several times in the lecture with both of these words.

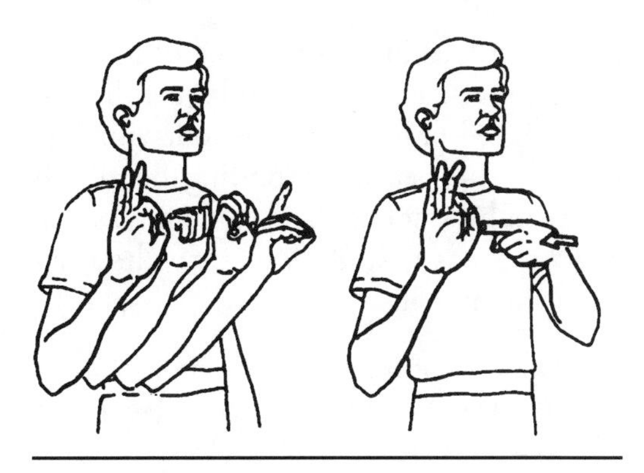

FIGURE 4. Pointing sign on final hold of D-E-A-F and A-T-T-I-T-U-D-E.

Intratextual Register Variation In an Academic Lecture. There are differences between portions of the lecture that are very striking. The intratextual register shifts between three particular portions of the text are of interest: (1) the body of the lecture, consisting of the portions that exhibit all of the features delineated earlier and in which the lecturer is giving factual information or making a point to his audience; (2) direct or so-called reported speech, consisting of the portions that exhibit features associated with a more colloquial register and in which the speaker uses a technique involving the role playing of conversations between two participants (in this case, himself and various of his high school students); and (3) metaphoric/poetic speech, consisting of the portions that exhibit features probably associated with a performance register and typically found in theater and poetry. This type of language is used during the introduction and the closing of the lecture and at various midpoints.

The sections in which direct speech is used are most clearly differentiated from the body of the lecture in the area of lexicon. Extensive use is made of colloquial lexical items (listed earlier), as in the following segment E. The speaker is reporting the speech of one of his students. The student is asking why he needs to study ASL, since he is already fluent in it.

Segment E

HEY WHAT'S-UP TAKE-UP SIGN WHAT-FOR
"Hey, why should I take sign?"

PRO.1 BRAINY EXPERT SIGN-ASL
"I'm already a great signer"

PRO.1 TAKE-UP SIGN WHAT-FOR
"Why should I take it?"

The sections of direct speech also differ somewhat from the body of the lecture at the phonological level. The shortening of the final hold makes the signs appear to flow together rather than appear separated. Signs such as PEA-BRAIN and WHAT-FOR are executed in neutral space rather than at the forehead. The signing space used in the portions of direct speech is often much smaller than that used in the body of the lecture. Phonological processes such as assimilation and perseveration still occur infrequently, but more often than in the body of the lecture.

Nongrammatical facial expression is also used differently in the main-body versus direct-speech portions of the lecture. Facial expression is minimally used in the body of the text, whereas it is used at a level that is often quite exaggerated in the portions of direct speech. A clear exemplification of meaningful nonoccurrence of facial expression in the lecture involves the use of the sign IMPORTANT. There is a nonmanual marker that is often used as an intensifier with this sign. It consists of a movement of the lips in which the signer appears to be saying "po." This nonmanual marker is not used in the body of the lecture, even when the meaning is clearly "very important." The intensified meaning is indicated, instead, by exaggeration and intensification of the movement of the sign. This absence of facial gestures in the body of the lecture happens even when the gestures have lexical significance. The only way to distinguish between the lexical items NOT-YET and LATE is by a position of the mouth and tongue. In the body of the lecture, even this facial gesture is frequently omitted.

The portions of text labeled metaphoric/poetic show less contrast with the body of the lecture than do the portions of direct speech, but they are different in some noticeable ways. Phonologically, they are very similar to the lecture. Signs in these portions are also executed in a large signing space and are fully articulated with long final holds. On the whole, phonological processes are rarely at work, the result being that the signs appear clearly signed and separated from each other. The distinctive characteristics are instead found mostly at the morphological, syntactic, and discourse levels. The portions are most clearly marked by a type of poetic line structure, in which a repetition of lexical items and syntactic patterns occurs, as in the following segment F. The signer is discussing the attitudes of deaf students about English and ASL and indicates that he has noticed changes in students' attitudes. Whereas the students originally felt positive toward MCE (manually coded English) and negative toward ASL, they now feel negative toward MCE and positive toward ASL.

Segment F

DEAF CULTURE
"The culture of the deaf"

DEAF LANGUAGE
"The language of the deaf"

POSS.3 ENGLISH
"Some use English"

POSS.3 SIGN LANGUAGE
"Some use sign language"

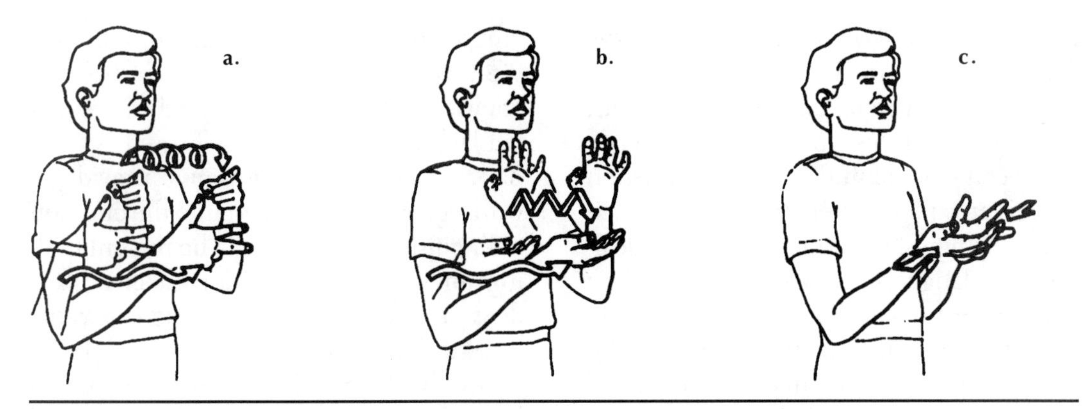

FIGURE 5. Creative morphology of signed metaphors. (a) CL: VEHICLE/HEARING; (b) BOAT/SIGN-ASL; (c) CL: BOAT-VEHICLE-MOVE-TOGETHER.

PRO.1 OBSERVE START CHANGE POSS.3 OPINION
"I've seen opinions begin to change"

BEFORE SAY NEGATIVE+++ CHANGE POSITIVE + + +
"Attitudes that were negative, have become positive"

SOME MCE POSITIVE+++ CHANGE NEGATIVE + + +
"Attitudes about MCE that were positive have become negative"

SOME ASL NEGATIVE+++ SOME STAY NEGATIVE+ + +
"Some attitudes about ASL that were negative have stayed negative"

These portions are also marked by creative use of ASL morphological systems. In the beginning of the lecture, the speaker discusses ASL metaphorically as an iceberg, which is resisting attempts to analyze it. Hearing researchers are metaphorically portrayed as a large ship, and deaf researchers as a small boat. The classifier predicate used for a moving vehicle is signed with the nondominant hand. The dominant hand executes the handshape and movements of the sign HEARING. The normal place of articulation for HEARING is at the mouth. But the sign is articulated just above the vehicle classifier. The pattern is then repeated with the signs BOAT and SIGN-ASL (see Figure 5a–c). This type of creative morphology is used only in portions of the tape that show other features of a metaphoric/poetic register.

SUMMARY

In the prior analysis, some variable features in ASL that are sensitive to changes in register have been described. These findings indicate that the notion of five discrete "styles" as posited by Joos (1968) is too simplistic. Each of the three pieces of data examined here would be classified as "formal" in his system, nevertheless they exhibit marked differences. A system such as that put forward by Halliday (1968, 1978) is much more adequate, since it posits ranges of variation that are sensitive to the interaction of many different factors present in a speech situation. However, even this view fails to capture the kinds of intratextual variation that occur within the lecture examined in this chapter. Even though the field, mode, and tenor of the discourse remain constant, the types of language used in various portions of the text differ greatly.

The present analysis is obviously only a beginning. Most of the features discussed occur at the phonological or lexical levels. A more in-depth analysis will undoubtedly uncover other variable features at the morphological, syntactic, and discourse levels.

Findings of this type have implications for several fields of study. The phenomenon of register variation is of interest to subdisciplines of linguistics, most notably those dealing with language variation and linguistic change. Features at all levels (phonological, morphological, lexical, syntactic, and discourse) seem to show marked differences owing to register variation. Therefore, any comparison of texts leading to statements about variable features that are sensitive to other sociolinguistic factors must be held suspect if register is not held constant. This is also true for studies of historical change. If an older tape of an academic lecture is compared with a newer tape in a much less formal register, there is no way to know whether the differences noted are due to change over time or to register variation.

In the area of interpretation and interpreter training, knowledge of and skill in using register variation is of the utmost importance. An interpreter's goal is to produce a target language message that is equivalent, at all levels, to the original source language message. An interpretation can be quite accurate at the level of content but still be inadequate if expressed in an inappropriate register.

In the area of second-language acquisition and the teaching of ASL, it is equally important to consider differences in register. In order to be truly fluent, a student must not only learn the correct forms and structures of the target language but also must become knowledgeable about when and where particular forms are appropriately used.

Studies of register variation provide us with a great deal of insight into the question of linguistic competence. The present findings indicate that a native speaker of ASL does truly control a range of language variation, a "repertoire" in Fishman's (1972) terms, that bears a direct and systematic relationship to a range of social situations and purposes.

Obviously, more work is needed in this area. The present study is focused on but one user of one particular language. It would be of interest to study these differences across a range of speakers and for a much broader range of situations. It would also be of interest to discover the spoken language equivalents of the manual-gestural features described here.

NOTE

1. The samples of ASL discourse presented in this chapter are transcribed in accord with the following conventions. ASL signs are indicated by English gloss-labels in small capital letters. Each signed segment is followed by a fuller English gloss, enclosed in double quotation marks. Hyphenated letters, also in small capital letters, indicate fingerspelling. In the examples of handswitching, overscoring of the line of ASL signs indicates the duration and choice of hand(s). *L* for left-hand dominant signs, *R* for right-hand dominant signs, and *L/R* for two-handed signs. + indicates that a sign is duplicated. The number of +'s indicates the number of duplications.

Features of Discourse in an American Sign Language Lecture

Cynthia B. Roy

INTRODUCTION

A videotaped talk in ASL about stickleback fish was described by users of American Sign Language (ASL) as "terrific" and "interesting." This chapter describes what kind of talk this was, explores why the talk and the speaker were received so favorably by the audience, and presents an analysis of some features of ASL discourse produced by a single speaker.

Discourse analysis in ASL is a recent development and most of the research to date concentrates on aspects of the structure of conversation and the exchange of talk in ASL (Baker 1976, 1977; Baker and Padden 1978; Wilbur and Pettito 1983). For the most part, these studies focus on macrofeatures of turn-taking, linguistic functions of nonmanual behaviors, and utterance boundaries and topic-flow. For example, Baker (1977) describes in detail devices that control turn-taking procedures in ASL dyadic conversations. Wilbur and Pettito (1983) describe the flow of discourse topics in a dyadic conversation and the devices that are used to accomplish the initiation, maintenance, and termination of topics within an ASL conversation. McIntire and Groode (1982) discuss, from their own experience, what are conversational differences in greetings, ongoing conversation, and leave-takings between Deaf and hearing interactions. Prinz and Prinz (1985) describe the acquisition of conversational behavior in the sign language of twenty-four deaf children between the ages of three and eleven.

In studying the discourse of a single speaker, Gee and Kegl (1983) give a detailed stylistic analysis of two narratives. They claim that narrative structure in ASL can be revealed via an analysis of the pause structure at each word boundary. One of the narratives, which had a known story structure, namely, "Goldilocks and the Three Bears," was analyzed in the opposite direction to see if its pause structure matched the narrative structure. Although there are other descriptions of features in ASL narratives (Baker 1983; Liddell 1980), there are no studies of the features of ASL discourse that occur in a lecture or speech.

Although brief in length, the talk described here is best labeled a lecture, for reasons explained later. Informal interviews with audience members, as well as the researcher's own experience, suggest that in a good lecture, the content is of high quality, it is well organized, and it is "interesting." Lectures are discourses with particular goals in mind, goals that are both informational and social. Although lectures tend to be monologues (as opposed to dialogues or dialogic conversation) by nature and do not require interaction in the form of talk, good

Source. Reprinted by permission of the publisher, from C. Lucas, ed., *The Sociolinguistics of the Deaf Community* (1989): 231–251. San Diego: Academic Press. The references for this reading can be found in the original volume.

lecturers are aware of the audience's needs to both follow the flow of the talk and enjoy the experience of listening.

Lectures of a scientific nature are generally expected to provide objective knowing which is created, in part, by a presentation of known facts. Lectures are thus expected to be more content-oriented than, say, conversations. Since lectures are discourses of retention, they also require the use of linguistic devices that give the listener a firm idea of how an utterance fits into the lecture process as a whole (Lebauer 1984, 42). These are the kind of linguistic elements that are not a part of the content of the lecture, per se, but do guide listeners in how to interpret the information that they are hearing. These words or phrases are cohesive, structural devices that contribute to a listener's ability to distinguish between major and minor points, old versus new information, and turns or shifts in the flow of topics. These elements contribute significantly to the gestalt of a lecture. In this chapter, the use and function of two such discourse devices found in an ASL lecture are explored.

Content and organization are necessary but not sufficient characteristics of a good lecture. Thus, in this chapter, a third criterion is also addressed, that which makes a lecture vivid and interesting. It is a sociolinguistic assumption that not only the strategies and devices typical of ordinary conversation but also the elements of good storytelling are used to create vividness and audience interest (Goffman 1981). Lecturers involve their audiences by having them participate as much as possible in the development and understanding of the information presented; this is achieved by creating the impression of immediacy and forcing the listener to make sense out of what is being said. One aim of this chapter is to examine one of the features that contributes to this involvement between the speaker, the audience, and the lecture itself.

THE LECTURE

A five-minute discourse by an ASL user on the mating habits of the stickleback fish was elicited. This user is a Deaf man in his thirties. He attended residential schools from the age of four, has hearing parents, earned a Master's degree, and was tutoring deaf college students at a technical institute in a Southwestern state. His discussions with the researcher about ASL led to a decision to make a videotape demonstrating that ASL could be used to talk about scientific subjects. Since fishing is one of his lifelong hobbies, he read about the mating habits of a particular fish in a college freshman biology book and reproduced this information on videotape, in a studio, with an audience of two people, a Deaf man and a hearing woman. He was told to picture his audience as college freshmen.

ASL speakers who have never seen this man before tell me that the lecture is fascinating and the speaker is good and clear. They also identify the language used as ASL. When asked who the potential audience is for the videotape, they say that it is young adults ranging in age from seventeen to forty.

Although the discourse is only about five minutes in duration, its structure is typical of American expectations of a lecture. As argued in this chapter, the talk is structured and organized as a lecture by two criteria: (1) the display of an ordered development of subtopics and (2) the occurrence of linguistic features that mark the transitions into those subtopics.

ANALYSIS OF THE LECTURE

The content of a lecture must be structured so as to develop the topic of the talk through subtopics and guide the listener through the relevance of each topic as it is discussed. The organizational structure of the present discourse segment reflects a naturally occurring, sequentially developed chain of related subtopics. It is generally agreed that most lectures open with an introduction and some explanation of why the speaker is talking. The introduction is then followed by the main body of the lecture and an obligatory closing. Cook (1975) calls these naturally formed segments "episodes." Episodic types include an obligatory *focal* (or introductory) episode with optional focal episodes, an obligatory *developmental* episode along with a number of optional developmental episodes, and an obligatory *closing* episode followed by optional closing episodes. These different kinds of episodes combine to form the unified piece that constitutes a lecture.

The focal episode is made up of introductory statements in which the speaker introduces the subject and generally includes his reason for talking about this subject. Developmental episodes form the body of the talk. In a talk about a fish and its mating ritual, we can expect this main body to be a sequenced account of the mating process. The obligatory closing episode reminds the listener of why the topic is being talked about, and of specific ideas that the speaker wants the listener to remember. Although the discourse about the stickleback fish is brief, when analyzed within this framework of episodes, it is a typical lecture, as American society conventionally recognizes a lecture.

There are eight episodes in the stickleback fish talk. The first two episodes form the obligatory focal episode and an optional focal episode, which together introduce the speaker and explain why he is talking. In the first episode, the speaker gives his name, the subject of his talk, and introduces the sign that he will use to refer to a particular species of fish throughout the rest of his talk. The second episode narrows the focus to the uniqueness of the mating ritual of this particular species, the stickleback fish.

The next five episodes form the obligatory developmental episode and four optional developmental episodes. These five episodes are chronologically developed and explain and describe the mating process of this fish. Each succeeding episode develops the topic of the mating process, but the focus of each of these episodes is slightly different. For example, in the first of the five episodes, the speaker explains the normal behavior of the fish and then describes the conditions under which the behavior changes and the mating ritual begins. The second episode contrasts how the males separate from the females and undergo a color change signaling the onset of the mating process. The third episode describes the nest-building activities of the male; the fourth episode explains how the male guards the nest and lures the female to the nest; the fifth and final episode relates the egg-laying process.

The final, closing episode is separate from the preceding five episodes because it is here that the speaker reminds the listeners of the purpose of the talk, that is, that this fish is the focus of scientific study because of its unusual characteristics during mating. He then describes the two characteristics that make this fish and this ritual unusual, which are that the underside of the male changes to red, and that the female swims vertically toward the male rather than horizontally. This last episode is not dependent upon real-time or chronological development. Rather, it provides the specific points the speaker wants to make in closing his talk. The following outline of the lecture reflects the sequencing of the episodes and the larger chunks of talk that they form:

Topic: The Mating Ritual of the Stickleback Fish

Episode 1 Episode 2	Focal (or introductory) episodes
Episode 3 Episode 4 Episode 5 Episode 6 Episode 7	Developmental (or main body) episodes
Episode 8	Closing episode

The analysis thus far shows that the organization of the content can be seen as a lecture format with topic development. But this is not the only assessment we can make to determine what constitutes a lecture. Lecture content is structured not only through the content of its propositions but also through textual features that reflect transition boundaries between episodes and link the episodes together. The suggestion is thus that lecturing is not static in form but is also a process whereby the speaker makes available to listeners features that show the continuity and relationship between subtopics or episodes.

Markers That Divide the Text into Episodes

Serial episodes in texts are linked together by features that can be single or phrasal lexical elements. These discrete grammatical elements serve to segment the message content into idea or informational units by marking the transition into an episode. Speakers use these markers, albeit unconsciously, to show the progression of a cumulative series of subordinate and related subtopics. The term "discourse marker" is used, following Schiffrin (1986), to talk about these elements that serve to highlight the boundaries of contiguous ideas so that hearers can appropriately interpret the continuous flow of information in discourse. In the fish lecture, episodes are closed off with markers that are identifiable on the basis of

FIGURE 1. ASL NOW.

such factors as the markers' lack of message content and the intuitions of native speakers. The category of discourse markers includes head nods and the signs OK and ANYWAY. These particular markers are not examined here. Instead, the focus is on two markers that are used to begin episodes and shift the listeners' attention to a different, yet related, subtopic: (1) the lexical sign NOW, produced simultaneously by both hands (see Figure 1) and (2) NOW-THAT, which consists of the lexical sign THAT produced on the left hand the lexical sign NOW produced on the right hand (see Figure 2).

NOW as a Discourse Marker. The sign NOW, which is consistently signed with both hands, appears eleven times in the text. This sign is generally understood as an indicator of present time in ongoing discourse, and on

FIGURE 2. ASL NOW-THAT.

some occurrences in the text, the sign functions in this way. On other occasions however, the sign functions as a discourse marker, marking a shift into a new subtopic as well as calling attention to what is coming up next in the text. To be sure, it is not always easy to discern in which of the two ways a particular token of NOW is functioning. There are, however, some distributional and formal criteria that distinguish the two uses. The discourse-marker form of NOW is a sign that occurs in an utterance-initial position and can co-occur with topic marking. This discourse-marker form of NOW occurs five times in the data corpus. Three of those occurrences exhibit no final hold in sign articulation, and the other two show only a final hold on the weak hand; the strong hand has no final hold and continues toward the next sign. Also, with some occurrences of this form, there are long pauses before the sign is articulated, and, in one instance, there is a body shift to the right.[1] The following are some examples of the discourse-marker form and function of NOW that occur in the text:[2]

> ______________t
> NOW CL: fish FISH PRO.3
> TRUE STRANGE PRO.3
> "Now, as for the fish, it is truly unique, it is"
>
> body shift
> NOW MALE WILL (point to chest)
> RED BEGIN LOOK-FOR ON
> "Now when the male changes (point to chest to red, (he) begins to search on"
>
> ______________t
> NOW MALE FISH SELF VERY JEALOUS
> "Now, as for the male fish, (he) is very jealous"

The temporal form of NOW is also a simultaneous two-hand sign that can occur in utterance-initial position but does not occur with topic marking. This form consistently displays a final hold on both hands and is not accompanied by prior pauses or body shifts:

> FISH DECIDE BEGIN NOW BREED
> "The fish decide to begin breeding now"
>
> NOW FISH LOOK-FOR WOOD THIN NARROW PIECES GREEN PLANT DIFFERENT
> "Now the fish search for sticks, thin narrow pieces, green plants, many different things"
>
> NOW ME READY FOR LOOK-FOR PRO.3 FISH PRO.3 FEMALE
> "Now I'm ready to look for it, it's a fish, it's a female"

As these examples reflect, there is variety in the formal articulation of NOW when used as a discourse marker and sameness in the formal articulation when used as a temporal marker, but this sample of language behavior is not sufficient to argue that form alone accounts for the difference in meaning or function.

How, then, can the discourse marker and the temporal marker be differentiated? Another possibility for identifying NOW as either a temporal marker or a discourse marker is to examine its meaning when influenced by discourse context (Schiffrin 1987). That is, by examining contextual factors such as the lecture in progress and the surrounding utterances, we can decide if the meaning is temporal or related to the discourse. Indeed, the distinction can even be contextually neutralized: if NOW occurs at a point of topic development that allows a temporal reading, it is not always possible on formal or distributional grounds to assign it an interpretation as either temporal or discourse-related. This particular discourse has five episodes describing biological events that must be related in chronological order. In this discourse, the real-time events of the main body episodes are matched by the speaking time relationship between the utterances themselves. Thus, the distinction between NOW meaning "present time" and NOW marking discourse can be difficult to discern.

We can examine the meaning of NOW in discourse context by substituting its occurrence with a paraphrase. If we substitute occurrences of NOW in an utterance that contains a time meaning and in an utterance that contains a discourse meaning, we can see which meaning fits the context. That is not to say that there will not be moments when NOW is ambiguous in its meaning. Consider the following examples:

t

1. NOW CL:fish FISH PRO.3 TRUE STRANGE PRO.3
   "Now, as for the fish, it is truly unique, it is"

   t

   a. *TODAY CL:fish FISH PRO.3 TRUE STRANGE PRO.3[3]
      "Today, as for the fish, it is truly unique, it is"

   t

   b. ON-TO-THE-NEXT-PART CL:fish FISH PRO.3 TRUE STRANGE PRO.3
      "On to the next part, as for the fish, it is truly unique, it is"
2. FISH DECIDE BEGIN NOW BREED
   "The fish decide to begin breeding now"
   a. FISH DECIDE BEGIN GO-AHEAD BREED
      "The fish decide to begin breeding, start ahead"
   b. *FISH DECIDE BEGIN ON-TO-THE-NEXT-PART BREED
      "The fish decide to begin breeding on to the next part"

In utterance 1a, the sign TODAY is substituted for the discourse marker NOW, and the result is an ungrammatical utterance. But in utterance 1b, ON-TO-THE-NEXT-PART is substituted for NOW, and the result is acceptable. Similarly, in sentence 2a, when the sign GO-AHEAD is substituted for the temporal marker NOW, the result is an acceptable utterance. But in sentence 2b, ON-TO-THE-NEXT-PART is substituted for NOW, and the result is unacceptable. These paraphrases are a way of confirming (or possibly rejecting) intuitions about the meaning attributed to the same lexical item, NOW.

A third and final confirmation of the existence of a temporal use of NOW and a discourse use of NOW came about by asking native speakers to view the videotape. The first step was to view the lecture in its entirety. Then the tape was viewed a second time. During this second viewing, each informant was asked to stop the tape whenever they sensed that the speaker changed or shifted to new focus. All three informants consistently stopped the tape at the junctures where the discourse form of NOW appears and indicated that the speaker was getting ready to talk about something different. Sometimes they identified NOW as signaling the shift; sometimes they identified a closing marker; and sometimes they sensed a shift that they explained by referring to the content of the text itself. Once consistent judgments were obtained about episode shifts marked by NOW, the form was further examined to ascertain the range of its distribution and function.

The Function of NOW as a Discourse Marker. The textual distribution of NOW provides a basis for ascertaining its discourse function by building on observations about its form and use. As noted earlier, the speaker's introduction consists of two episodes. In the first episode, the speaker says his name, the name of the fish, and how he will refer to the fish. The second episode explains that this fish is unusual and that scientists have been studying its mating habits for a long time. These two episodes are both introductory in nature and thus can be grouped together. NOW appears at the beginning of the first utterance of the second episode and signals a shift from the first episode to the second episode, that is, a shift to continuing and related introductory talk. It is significant that the first token of NOW co-occurs with the marking for topic:

t
NOW CL: fish FISH PRO.3 TRUE
STRANGE PRO.3
"Now, as for the fish, it is truly unique, it is"

Not only does NOW introduce the second episode, but if its meaning were that of present time (TODAY), it would be nonsense. Also, the temporal marker does not co-occur with topic marking anywhere in the text.

The following segments are the first three episodes of the text, transcribed in their entirety so that NOW as a discourse marker, and as a temporal marker, can be clearly seen in its actual contexts of use:

Episode 1

HELLO ME NAME B-O-B A-L-C-O-R-N
"Hello my name is Bob Alcorn"

ME HERE TALK-ABOUT CL-fish
"And I'm here to talk about a fish"

PRO.3 NAME S-T-I-C-K-L-E-B-A-C-K FISH
"It's called the stickleback fish"

CALL ABBREVIATE (discourse marker) OK
"Referring to it in this shortened form, so, Ok"

Episode 2

t
NOW CL:fish FISH PRO.3 TRUE STRANGE
PRO.3
"Now, as for the fish, it is truly unique, it is"

SCIENCE-AGENT UP-TIL-NOW STUDY
MANY YEARS
"Scientists have been studying it for many years"

POSS BEHAVE TRUE STRANGE HOW
BREED HOW
"Its behavior is truly unique as to how it breeds"

STUDY MANY YEAR ANYWAY
"It's been studied for many years, anyway"

Episode 3

1 hd nd
NOW-THAT PRO.3 FISH TRUE STRANGE
"Now, the one I'm talking about, (it's a fish) is truly unique"

PRO.3 ALWAYS GROUP-TRAVEL-
FORWARD
"It always travels in groups"

WITH MANY LARGE-GROUP-COME-
TOGETHER GROUP-TRAVELING-
FORWARD
"With many fish, (they) come together as a large group and swim forward"

BUT TIME FEEL SPRING CHANGE WARM
FEEL
"But there comes a time and a feeling, it's spring, there's a change and a warmness, and the fish feel it"

FISH DECIDE BEGIN NOW BREED
"The fish decide to begin breeding now"

NOW WILL BEGIN LINES-OF-FISH-
MOVING-FORWARD SEPARATE
"Now they will begin, from the lines of fish swimming forward, to separate"

NOW is not used to open the first episode nor is it used to open the third episode. NOW initially occurs at the beginning of the second part of the introduction. This is the only instance of use as a discourse marker in the first three episodes of the text. It is only in the developmental episodes that the form is again used in this capacity.

The next five episodes, as the developmental episodes, constitute the main body of the talk. This group of episodes contains the most content, has an orderly progression of events, and constitutes a straightforward exposition of the details. NOW does not occur at the shift between the introductory episodes and the developmental episodes but does occur at each utterance initial position in the four succeeding episodes within the main body. This repetitive pattern suggests that one function of NOW is to make explicit the ideational progress through these episodes by focusing attention on what the speaker is about to say in relation to what he has just said. Thus, the distribution of NOW in this particular text is a property of its function of marking shifts. That is, its repeated use between related subtopics emphasizes the forward progression of related episodes in the emerging discourse. With these markers, the speaker maintains the listener's attention to the text and the forward progress through this group of episodes.[4] The following diagram presents a recasting of the earlier-presented outline of text episodes to illustrate the distributional pattern of NOW as a discourse marker.

Episode 1 NOW Episode 2	Focal (or introductory) episodes
Episode 3 NOW Episode 4 NOW Episode 5 NOW Episode 6 NOW Episode 7	Developmental (for main body) episodes
Episode 8	Closing episode

One way in which the relationship between language and context is reflected in the structure of languages is through deixis. This term indicates a pointing or indexical property of a lexical item and is exemplified through the use of pronouns, tense, and time and place adverbs. Deixis is a way languages grammaticalize features that indicate the context of an utterance. For example, the pronoun *this* in English does not name or refer to any particular entity in all of its uses; rather, it is a place-holder for some particular entity given by the context, as in "bring me a stick about *this* big." Levinson (1983, 88) explains discourse deictics as forms serving to indicate "often in very complex ways, just how the utterance that contains them is a response to, or a continuation of, some portion of the prior discourse."

The two uses of NOW discussed here are related to its deitic meaning. Schiffrin (1987) has shown that, in English conversational data, markers which have a deictic meaning make use of such meaning. She found that in discourse use the temporal meaning is internal to the utterances in the discourse itself. In ASL the discourse marker NOW also makes use of this deictic meaning by providing a temporal index to the group of utterances of an episode within the emerging lecture. This adds to the complexity in the use of NOW. When discourse time mirrors event time, i.e., the male fish makes the nest before he protects it, then NOW not only reflects the speaker's focus on the next episode (or discourse time), but also on a new event within the description of the mating process. As Schiffrin observes, this neutralizes the distinction between a temporal use and the discourse use through the structure of the discourse. The temporal only use of NOW establishes a reference time for a content-filled utterance in relation to the real-world event sequence, such as the biological process of mating. In its use as a discourse marker, NOW makes use of the temporal sense to indicate the progression of discourse time while also indicating that the information of the next episode is one more step forward in the real-world mating process.

It remains to be seen if these observations will retain validity across longer texts with different topics. Lectures and workshop talks by native and nonnative Deaf speakers alike have been observed by the researcher, and the use of NOW as a discourse marker seems a fairly common occurrence. For example, one native speaker signed NOW as she discussed a list of qualities defining a professional, using NOW to separate the items on the list. Overall, further study is needed to substantiate the claims made here. The present analysis shows that NOW occurs and functions as a discourse marker by shifting the listener's attention to a new section of the discourse and by maintaining the progression through an episode group.

NOW-THAT as a Discourse Marker. The sign NOW-THAT occurs at the initial utterance of the episode that begins episode groups. Each time a shift is made into a group of episodes, the marker is not NOW but NOW-THAT. As explained earlier, NOW-THAT is formed by NOW on the right hand and THAT on the left hand. It is used to separate the introductory episode group from the developmental (or main body) episode group, and the developmental episode group from the closing episode. The following diagram will illustrate the distribution of NOW and NOW-THAT:

	Episode 1	Focal (or introductory) episode
NOW	Episode 2	
NOW-THAT	Episode 3	Developmental (or main body) episodes
NOW	Episode 4	
NOW	Episode 5	
NOW	Episode 6	
NOW	Episode 7	
NOW-THAT	Episode 8	Closing episode

As explained earlier, internal episodes in a group are linked by NOW. The third episode (the beginning episode of the developmental group) begins with NOW-THAT. When the speaker finishes with the final episode of the main body, the beginning of the first utterance of the closing episode is NOW-THAT.

The Form and Function of NOW-THAT. This marker occurs at the utterance-initial position. Liddell (1980) describes the forms of three tokens of THAT that had all previously been considered the same sign. One form of THAT—Liddell's (1980, 150) THATc—begins with a backward motion and ends with a hold that separates it from the other forms and means "that's the one I'm talking about." In the fish text, it is the form THATc which occurs. Both tokens of NOW-THAT co-occur with topic marking, with the articulation of NOW slightly preceding the articulation of THAT.

The first NOW-THAT occurs at the beginning of the third episode and the second NOW-THAT occurs at the beginning of the eighth episode. That is, NOW-THAT occurs at the beginning of the main body episode group, and at the beginning of the third group, the closing. The discourse context reveals an even more interesting feature: the content of the utterances at the beginning of both the third and eighth episodes co-refers with the first utterance of the second episode; that is, all three utterances are remarkably similar in form and content. These three utterances are the following:

Beginning of episode 2 (introductory group)

t
NOW CL: Fish FISH PRO.3 TRUE STRANGE PRO.3
"Now, as for the fish, it is truly unique, it is"

Beginning of the main body episodes

t hd nd
NOW-THAT PRO.3 FISH TRUE STRANGE
"Now, the one I'm talking about, it (it's a fish) is truly unique"

Beginning of the closing episode group

t
NOW-THAT SCIENCE-AGENT STUDY TRUE STRANGE
"Now, the one I'm talking about, as for the scientists, (they) have been studying it, it is truly unique"

If THAT means "that's the one I'm talking about," then there must be a segment of previous discourse that identifies "one." Antecedents do not occur only in the immediately prior discourse, nor do antecedents have to be single lexical items. They can occur further back in the discourse and constitute portions of the discourse (Halliday and Hasan 1976). In the prior three examples, the use of THAT at the beginning of the main body episodes looks back to episode 1 but also gathers in portions of episode 2. The use of THAT at the beginning of the closing episode looks back not only to the beginning of the main body episodes but also to episode 2, thus requiring the listener to keep in mind all that they have heard so far. The utterance that begins the main body episodes simultaneously looks forward with the use of NOW and looks backward at the prior episode with the use of THAT. The utterance that begins the closing episode simultaneously looks forward and backward, not only to the five episodes before but also even further back to the introduction, to remind the listener of why the speaker is talking about the fish. The repetition embedded in these NOW-THAT utterances provides evidence that this marker is pointing to prior discourse and establishing relevance to the upcoming discussion. This repetition is also typical of how lectures continually remind their audience of their main focus.

In its discourse use, THAT retains the meaning of "that's the one I'm talking about" because it refers to the fish but also makes use of its deictic property, to look backward to prior discourse. Thus, two forms, NOW-THAT, function together to mark a shift to a slightly different focus but also to remind listeners of what has gone before in the discourse.

DISCOURSE MARKERS

This analysis follows Schiffrin (1986), who has analyzed several discourse markers in English, including *now.* Her data is a large corpus of conversational interaction from Philadelphia neighborhoods in the 1970s. She points out that, on occasions, the difference between the discourse marker *now* and the adverb *now* is difficult to determine. Three ways to assess the status of *now* in English are through finding co-occurrence violations (e.g., *now then*), which is allowable for one category (discourse marker) and not the other (adverb), through discourse context, or through prosodic features. For example, the utterances "now then, what's next on the schedule?" and "now now" (as an expression of comfort) constitute co-occurrence violations for the adverbial use of *now.* Discourse context, on the other hand, can either distinguish between the categories or be ambiguous if the topic itself has a temporal sequence. For example, if a comparison is being made between "back then" and "now," *now* can be ambiguous as to whether a new topic is being introduced or *now* means something like "nowdays." Finally, Schiffrin discovered that *now* as a discourse marker receives no stress but receives intonational marking that signals "more to come."

For the discourse functions of *now,* Schiffrin explains how *now* functions on different discourse planes in conversational English. First, in comparisons and opinions, *now* shows "the speaker's progression through a discourse which contains an ordered sequence of subordinate parts" (Schiffrin 1986, 240). On another level of discourse organization, *now* marks when the speaker is shifting orientation, that is, makes explicit the stance that the speaker is taking toward what is being said. In addition, she discusses the impact of deictic meaning on the uses and functions of *now.*

In the fish text, other discourse markers are at work, such as OK, ANYWAY, and KNOW. It is obvious that a rich system of discourse markers exists in ASL and that further study will reveal some similarities to the functions of discourse markers found in spoken languages. It is also obvious that this is not the same system that exists in English, in that English has no marker known as NOW-THAT or ON-TO-THE-NEXT-PART.

CONSTRUCTED DIALOGUE IN AN ASL LECTURE

Talks that are descriptions of knowledge and that impart information are generally expected to provide a presentation of known facts, to be organized in a predictable way, and thus to be more content-oriented. The content and the structure of organization, however, do not provide a sufficient explanation as to why a speech is "good" or "interesting," since well-organized, content-filled lectures can be quite dull. There is a third criterion that makes a lecture vivid and interesting.

It is a sociolinguistic assumption that strategies and devices typical of ordinary conversation and elements of good storytelling are used to create impressions of vividness and interpersonal involvement (Chafe 1982; Labov 1972; Schiffrin 1981; Tannen 1982). One such device is reported speech. Reported speech is one of a range of features that makes a lecture vivid and involving. The use of reported speech in a lecture is a strategy that creates interest in the content and seeks to involve the audience in making sense of information.

Tannen (1986) introduces the term "constructed dialogue" to replace "reported speech," a term used when speech is represented as first-person dialogue. She argues that lines of dialogue in conversation, owing to characteristics of human memory, are probably not exactly the same as those that were actually spoken. Thus, the lines of speech are not actually reported verbatim but rather are constructed by speakers based on real people and events.

Further evidence for the notion that dialogue is constructed is based on the fact that some lines of dialogue in stories are the thoughts of the participants in the stories, or are interjected by listeners. Further support for Tannen's notion that reported speech is more appropriately termed "constructed dialogue" is found in ASL discourse. Constructed dialogue can occur between hypothetical persons or animals. It can also occur as anthropomorphically attributed speech, instances of which occur in the fish text examined here.[5] To term this hypothetical dialogue "reported speech" or "direct address" is odd, to say the least.

Lines of dialogue can also appear in lectures, as a type of discourse event. Pufahl (1984, 3) shows that constructed dialogue in a technical lecture in English about chemical compounds is "by and large different from the one found in narratives." Most of the dialogue that she examined is used to verbalize possible hearer questions or responses to information, such as "and you say, 'this looks like a mess.'" She suggests that these dialogue lines are strategies used by speakers to create interesting lectures. They serve the function of making lectures interesting or vivid.

Constructed dialogue in the present ASL lecture appears both as utterances that a fish (purportedly) is saying to other fish and as thoughts that a fish (purportedly) is thinking. One occurrence of dialogue is introduced by the speech-framing device SAY and one other occurrence is introduced by WARN. But eight instances of dialogue have no such lexical introducer. The following are examples of constructed dialogue in the fish lecture:

> THAT RED FISH WARN NOW ME READY FOR LOOK-FOR PRO.3 FISH FEMALE
> "That redness is the fish warning 'Now I'm ready to look for it, it's a fish, it's a female'"
>
> BEGIN FLIRT KNOW FISH (manual wiggle in water) FEMALE (shift to right, eye-gaze to left) FINE (with fingers wiggling)
> "(He) begins to flirt, you know, the fish 'dances' and the female (says) 'How fine!'"
>
> FISH (in holding position in front of nest) CHERISH MINE MINE PROTECT
> "The fish is guarding the nest 'I cherish this, it is mine, it is mine, and I'll protect it'"
>
> HOME PROTECT GET-AWAY GET-AWAY
> "It protects its home 'get-away, get-away'"
>
> FOLLOW SAY COME-HERE
> "(The female) will follow, (the male) says 'come here'"

The constructed dialogue in this ASL lecture is different from the dialogue found in ASL narratives. In ASL narratives, there is an exchange of dialogue between speakers, the content of the utterances is longer with more repetition than that in lectures, and there is simply more dialogue.[6] As might be expected in a scientific, content-filled talk, the dialogue in the fish lecture is brief and generally consists of only one or two manual signs accompanied by nonmanual signals. The one exception is a complete utterance spoken by the male fish. There is no actual exchange of talk between the fish. In this lecture, with or without co-occurring, signed introducers such as SAY, the dialogue is marked by ordinary ASL nonmanual markers of constructed dialogue: a difference in head orientation, whereby the head is turned and sometimes also tilted, and a change in eye-gaze.[7]

All of the dialogue in the lecture is attributed to the fish, and all of the utterances are human-like expressions of thoughts or feelings. Evidence that the dialogue can be attributed to the fish is found in (1) the use of the imperative GET-AWAY, which implies an underlying you, clearly directed toward the other fish and not the speaker or the audience and (2) the use of the possessive MINE, which is said by the male fish and not the speaker himself.[8]

Clearly there is more work to be done in describing constructed dialogue, but the purpose of this chapter is to discuss the function of dialogue in making the lecture vivid and interesting. The following example demonstrates this point: the male fish is focused on a particular female, the female notices and says FINE (with fingers wiggling). Accompanying this sign is a facial expression reminiscent of a Mae West impression, that is, repeated raising of the eyebrows. A good literal translation might be, "ooh, I like this," or "this feels good." Note that this segment of talk is not informative nor is it content-oriented. Therefore, it must be there to serve another function. Indeed, the segment appears to serve a dual purpose. One purpose is to make the talk vivid and interesting, another purpose is to create an analogous scene through which the information can be understood more completely. In effect, these are one and the same function, an interactive, communicative function.

To confirm this interpretation, deaf people ranging in age from eighteen to forty were asked to evaluate this speaker. It was a unanimous judgment that the ASL speaker was "good," and many of these speakers said that the talk itself was "clear, fascinating, and interesting."

This use of constructed dialogue, which, in turn, creates visual scenes or pictures, seems representative of a style of information noticed by the researcher in lectures by other deaf speakers and in classrooms with deaf teachers. A discourse style that makes the attempt to associate the world that is being talked about with another world, by having listeners make a lateral jump from the topic at hand to a set of terms in which the information can be seen differently, is analogical in nature. In presentations of analogies, the relationship between the two concepts is not always made explicit and is not always a "logical" one, in the Western sense of the word. That is, the fish in the talk are not really similar to a boy and a girl flirting. Rather, the listener is invited to imagine the idea of flirtatious behavior so as to understand the mating ritual of fish.

This creation of scenes through dialogue is a powerful way to present facts and involve the audience in making sense of a phenomenon. Johnstone (1986), in studying persuasive arguments in Arabic, terms these arguments, which are rich with stories and analogies, "analogic persuasion." One persuades another not through logical arguments built from facts but through the beauty and vividness of stories and analogies. Thus the use of a constructed dialogue strategy in this ASL lecture (and others) represents a type of presentation of information in ASL that might be termed an "analogic style." Since people understand and internalize information through the vividness of familiar and shared experiences, the analogic style suggests that listening to and understanding users of ASL is an exercise in cross-cultural communication, and that speakers of a visual language understand and learn about the world differently.

It must be noted, however, that analogic styles are certainly available to speakers of many languages, including English. Consequently, one cannot explain the use of these styles simply by reference to cultural determinism. Rather, the use of this style, or any other, is the result of a particular interaction, a particular context, and a particular audience, in conjunction with cultural predispositions (Johnstone 1986). That is, users of ASL might choose to use this strategy within particular interactions, whereas speakers of English, for example, might choose to use the same strategy in a different context. Thus, both might find their expectations for a particular interaction in conflict.

A FINAL POINT ABOUT NOW

Having discussed the phenomenon of constructed dialogue, the occurrence of NOW in dialogue warrants some attention. Some tokens of NOW can easily be assigned to a particular functional category on the basis of their appearance in discourse strategies. In the following ASL segments from episodes 4 and 5, NOW appears first as a discourse marker under a topic marking with FEMALE. Within the episode, it appears again in utterance-initial position, but in this instance is part of an utterance that is actually the dialogue of the fish.

Episode 4

t

NOW FEMALE WILL LINES-OF-FISH-MOVING FORWARD GROUP-SWIM-TOGETHER

"Now, as for the female, (they) will, from swimming as a school, form their own group and continue swimming"

: (intervening discourse segments)

THAT RED FISH WARN NOW ME READY FOR LOOK-FOR PRO.3 FISH PRO.3 FEMALE

"That redness is the fish warning, 'Now I'm ready to look for it, it's a fish, it's a female'"

Episode 5

bodyshift

NOW MALE WILL (point to chest)
RED BEGIN LOOK-FOR ON

"Now when the male changes (indicating the chest) to red, (he) begins to search on"

WATER-MOVING (movement) WATER (point down) GROUND LOOK-FOR GOOD ROCK (classifier) SCADS-OF FINE++

"Make movements in the water and go down to the floor looking for good rocks, small, round rocks, lots of them and (say) 'fine'"

The missing utterances between the two segments of episode 4 are about the male fish separating from the group and swimming alone while his chest area begins to turn red. After it turns red, the male fish is ready to seek a female. Thus, NOW in the second segment of episode 4 has a temporal meaning as seeking a female is the next temporal sequence in the process of mating. NOW occurs as part of the constructed dialogue of the fish.

In the next episode, there occurs a brief repetition of information from the prior episode (the male's chest turns red as a warning that he is ready to look for a mate), and the speaker uses the repetition to introduce the topic of the fish looking for the right place to build a nest. The underside of the male fish cannot turn red twice; it has already been established that the chest turns red. This kind of repetition often occurs in utterances that open new episodes. There is an expectation of a marker to introduce a new focus while reminding the listener of what he already knows. Thus, NOW in the first utterance of episode 5 marks a shift to a new point even though known information is said next. Finally, it is noteworthy that NOW as a discourse marker never appears in constructed dialogue in this text.

SUMMARY

This chapter examines a lecture produced by a user of ASL who is considered to be a good lecturer. The episodic development of the text is illustrated, and two discourse markers that contribute to the structural flow or organization of the lecture are described. The combination of episode development and discourse markers are only two of the factors that constitute this text as a lecture. In addition, constructed dialogue is discussed as a feature of lecture style in ASL that contributes to the impression of vividness in this lecture.

These findings barely scratch the surface of the complex nature of discourse in ASL. They do, however, provide ample evidence that discourse structure in ASL is a rich, undiscovered system. It is hoped that these preliminary findings stimulate further studies of discourse structure in ASL.

Schiffrin (1986) demonstrates that the analysis of discourse markers in English led to the construction of a theory of discourse coherence. As she points out, such work in other languages determines what linguistic resources are drawn upon for use as markers and how such determinations clarify discourse components and their interaction. Studying devices such as constructed dialogue and other stylistic strategies at work in all genres of discourse also builds an understanding of coherence, not only in discourse, but in the lives of the people who use a visual language. Understanding the basis of coherence in talk is understanding the intricacies of human interaction.

In addition, knowledge about how content-oriented discourse is structured in ASL will lead to questions such as how and when children learn to incorporate markers, how and when second language learners should learn these markers, and how interpreters incorporate them into the discourse flow. The answers to such questions have clear implications for communication in deaf education, second language instruction of ASL, and interpreter education. That is, in addition to being of theoretical interest, such answers have practical applications as well.

ACKNOWLEDGMENTS

I would like to thank Robert E. Johnson for originally encouraging this research, for hours spent discussing it, and for reading this chapter. I would also like to thank Scott Liddell for his insightful comments and questions, and Elizabeth Nowell for endless discussions of the data and ideas presented here. I also want to thank Bob Alcorn for a few brief minutes in time doing something that has become very important.

NOTES

1. I have closely observed two other speakers using NOW. One is a native Deaf speaker and one is a nonnative Deaf speaker. Both speakers use NOW as a discourse marker but formally articulate the sign in ways that are different from the one used by the speaker in this research. This observation calls for the study of such discourse markers across many speakers.
2. Because ASL has no written system, labels in English are used to represent signed units. The reader should be aware that these gloss-labels are problematic in that they do not allow for all the visual information that might be present to be represented nor has ASL been fully described. For ex-

ample, the label PRO.3 represents a 3rd person pronoun. But this sign has not been fully explored. Thus, at times, it represents a 3rd person pronoun but at other times seems to be working as a determiner.

The translations or full English glosses that are provided are modified literal translations. That is, they are translated as close to literal as possible, yet understandable to a speaker of English, in an attempt to represent, in English, all of the information in the ASL utterance and to show the order in which that information appears in the ASL utterance.

In addition, I translate the sign NOW in ASL as "now" in English because it is traditionally translated this way, although others could be used. The reader should keep in mind that *now* in English is spoken differently depending on its use as a temporal or discourse marker.

In the sample discourse segments presented in this chapter, the following transcription conventions are used: ASL signs are indicated by small capital gloss-labels, followed by a fuller English gloss of each segment within double quotation marks. Hyphenated single letter sequences in small capital letters indicate fingerspelling. Each + indicates one repetition of the sign immediately preceding it. Parenthetical notations provide additional description of ongoing linguistic events, for example, the occurrence of gestural deictics. Overscoring of the line of signs indicates the co-occurrence of either topic marking (t), body shift, or head nod (hd nd).

3. The articulated form of NOW in this utterance entails Movement–Hold. The articulated form of TODAY entails M M M H. Thus, these are two different lexical items.
4. I am not suggesting that NOW works alone at these shifts; undoubtedly there are a number of cues, manual and nonmanual, working together (see, for example, Baker 1976).
5. There is anecdotal evidence that this dialogue also occurs between objects and concepts.
6. These features of ASL narratives are suggested by Liddell (1980) and Baker (1983) and also based on observations of the researcher.
7. Scott Liddell directed my attention to such markers based on his work (1980).
8. I thank Ceil Lucas for pointing out this evidence to me.

Language Contact in the American Deaf Community

CEIL LUCAS AND CLAYTON VALLI

INTRODUCTION

One of the major sociolinguistic issues in the deaf community concerns the outcome of language contact. Specifically, there exists a kind of signing that results from the contact between American Sign Language (ASL) and English and exhibits features of both languages.[1] It has been claimed (Woodward 1973b; Woodward and Markowicz 1975) that this kind of signing is a pidgin and that it is the result of deaf-hearing interaction. The goal of this study is to reexamine this claim, based on a preliminary structural description of contact signing resulting from naturalistic interaction. The objectives of the study are (1) to describe the data collection methodology used to induce switching between ASL and this contact signing;[2] (2) to describe the sociolinguistic factors that sometimes correlate with the production of signing other than ASL; and (3) to describe some aspects of the morphological, syntactic, and lexical structure of the contact signing. The preliminary evidence suggests that the outcome of language contact in the American deaf community is unique, and quite different than anything that has been described to date in spoken language communities. The overall goal, then, is reexamination as a way of getting at an accurate characterization of this unique and complex phenomenon.

The first step toward understanding language contact in the deaf community involves recognizing the complexity of the contact situation with respect to not only the characteristics of participants but also the varieties of language available to those participants. For example, with participant characteristics, it is clearly not enough to simply distinguish deaf individuals from hearing individuals. Participants in a contact situation can be deaf ASL-English bilinguals who attended a residential school at an early age (entering, say, at age three or four), learned ASL as a first language from other children, and were taught some form of English, usually by hearing teachers who did not sign natively.[3] Alternatively, the participants can be deaf individuals who were mainstreamed at an early age and learned to sign relatively late, whether with ASL, signed English, or both. Or, they can be the hearing children of deaf parents, again ASL-English bilinguals who learned ASL at home natively. They can even be hearing individuals who learned ASL or some variety of signed English relatively late in life. Participants in a language contact situation

Source. Reprinted by permission of the publisher, from C. Lucas, ed., *The Sociolinguistics of the Deaf Community* (1989): 11–40. San Diego: Academic Press. The references for this reading can be found in the original volume.

Note. This reading contains the preliminary findings of the project. A full account of the project appears in C. Lucas and C. Valli. 1992. *Language contact in the American deaf community.* San Diego: Academic Press.

can also include hearing individuals who are English monolinguals and do not sign, as well as deaf ASL monolinguals with a minimal command of English in any form. Similarly, the varieties of language available to participants in a contact situation range from ASL to spoken English or signed English, and to a variety of codes for English that have been implemented in educational settings. (See Ramsey, this volume.) The participants in any given language contact situation may have been exposed to some or all of the above and may display a wide range of linguistic skills. Finally, it is crucial to understand that the participants in a language contact situation have both the vocal channel and the visual channel available, the latter including both manual and nonmanual grammatical signals. That is, the participants in a language contact situation have hands, mouth, and face available for the encoding of linguistic messages.

With spoken languages, two language communities can be in contact but there may not actually be many bilingual individuals in those communities. The linguistic outcome of language contact in that situation is different from the linguistic outcome of the interaction of bilingual individuals. In turn, the interaction of bilingual individuals who share the same native language is apt to be different from the interaction of bilinguals who have different native languages. Compare, say, two French-English Canadian bilinguals who both speak French as a first language, as opposed to two French-English Canadian bilinguals, one of whom claims French as a first language and the other of whom claims English as a first language. Code-switching can occur in both of these situations, for example, but the reasons for it and the linguistic form it takes can be quite different. And this is all in contrast, finally, with the interaction of a bilingual speaker with a monolingual speaker, whether that interaction is conducted in the second language of the bilingual (and the native language of the monolingual), or vice versa. The case of a Spanish-English bilingual interacting with a monolingual English speaker is but one example. If the bilingual's first language is Spanish and the interaction is in English, the linguistic outcome of the interaction will probably be different from any interaction in Spanish with the monolingual who is in the earliest stages of learning Spanish.

Parallels exist for all of these situations in the deaf community, and, as explained earlier, participant characteristics can vary widely between language contact situations. The following is a partial outline of possible language contact situations in the American deaf community, according to participant characteristics:

- Deaf bilinguals with hearing bilinguals
- Deaf bilinguals with deaf bilinguals
- Deaf bilinguals with hearing spoken English monolinguals
- Hearing bilinguals with deaf English signers
- Deaf bilinguals with deaf English signers
- Deaf English signers with hearing spoken English monolinguals
- Deaf English signers with hearing bilinguals
- Deaf English signers with deaf ASL monolinguals
- Deaf bilinguals with deaf ASL monolinguals
- Deaf ASL monolinguals with hearing bilinguals

ISSUES OF DEFINITION

Several issues arise from this outline. One concerns the problematic and relative concept of bilingualism. As in spoken language situations, participants in language contact situations in the deaf community display a range of competence both in ASL and in English, and in the latter, both in forms of

English-like signing and in written English. For the purposes of the present study, bilingualism is defined in demographic terms: Deaf bilinguals are individuals who not only learned ASL natively, either from their parents or at an early age from their peers in residential school settings, but also have been exposed to spoken and written English all their lives, beginning with the school system and continuing into adulthood through interaction with native English speakers. In contrast, hearing bilinguals are native English speakers who learned to sign as adults, both through formal instruction and through interaction with deaf people. Although not native ASL signers, hearing bilinguals do not use manual codes for English, either. Specific sign use in the present study will be discussed later. Again, it is crucial to recognize a range of competence in hearing bilinguals. For example, the linguistic outcome of an interaction between a hearing child of deaf parents (hence, possibly, a native user of ASL) and a deaf bilingual can be quite different from that of a deaf bilingual and a hearing bilingual who, while competent, learned ASL as an adult.

Another issue that arises concerns the distinction between deaf people and hearing people. Informal observation and anecdotal evidence suggest that this distinction is an important variable in the outcome of language contact in the American deaf community. Deaf individuals not only can sign quite differently with other deaf individuals than with hearing individuals but also can initiate an interaction in one language and radically switch when the interlocutor's ability to hear is revealed. For example, a deaf native ASL user may initiate an interaction with another individual whom he believes to be deaf or whose audiological status has not been clarified. The latter participant may well be a near-native user of ASL. Once the latter's hearing ability becomes apparent, however, it is not unusual for the deaf participant to automatically switch "away from ASL" to a more English-based form of signing. Code choice is thus sensitive to the ability versus inability of participants to hear and this distinction is carefully attended to in the present study of contact phenomena in the deaf community.

One might predict that the different contact situations outlined earlier here yield different linguistic outcomes, all of them of interest. For example, there is substantial informal observational evidence that when speaking English away from deaf individuals, hearing bilinguals occasionally code-switch into ASL and code-mix English and ASL features. Another outcome is seen, when, in interaction with hearing individuals who do not sign at all, a deaf bilingual who does not otherwise use his voice (in interaction with other deaf people or with hearing people who sign) opts to use spoken English in combination with gestures. Similarly, there is informal observational evidence that in interacting with hearing individuals who are in the early stages of learning to sign, deaf native ASL users use a form of "foreigner talk." Finally, the outcome of language contact between native signers of different sign languages (for example, ASL and Italian Sign Language) can have unique characteristics. There is anecdotal and casual observational evidence for the existence of all of the language contact situations outlined. What is clearly required at this point is carefully collected ethnographic data on videotape and descriptive analyses of these interactions.

The present study focuses on the outcome of language contact in the first situation in the outline: deaf bilinguals with hearing bilinguals. The reason for choosing this focus is that characterizations of language contact in the American deaf community have thus far been limited to the interaction between deaf people and hearing people, and this interaction contact has been characterized as producing a kind of pidgin. As stated earlier, one of the objectives of this study is to reexamine this characterization, in part by way of a preliminary description of the lexical, morphological and syntactic features of language production that result from the interaction of deaf and hearing people. There are suggestions in the literature that the outcome of the interaction of deaf bilinguals with other deaf bilinguals is sometimes a language variety other than ASL. In the present study, we collected considerable data on such interactions, a very general description of which is provided here. A detailed linguistic analysis of the deaf-deaf variety of interaction, as well as a comparison of that variety with the hearing-deaf variety, are reserved for future study.

THE OUTCOME OF LANGUAGE CONTACT

Given the variety in both participant characteristics and languages available, it is not surprising that the linguistic outcome of language contact is something that cannot be strictly described as ASL or as a signed representation of English. The issue is not that contact signing occurs, nor what label to attach to the system of signs, but rather how to characterize the system. Contact signing is characterized as "an interface between deaf signers and hearing speakers" by Fischer (1978, 314) and is labeled Pidgin Sign English (PSE) by Woodward (1972, 1973b). The linguistic characteristics of this so-called PSE are examined in three studies: Woodward (1973b), Woodward and Markowicz (1975), and Reilly and McIntire (1980). Woodward (1973b, 17) states that "Sometimes people sign something that seems to be a pidginized version of English. The syntactic order is primarily English, but inflections have been reduced in redundancy, and there is a mixture of American Sign Language and English structure." Further details are provided (Woodward 1973b, 42):

> These characteristics point up some close similarities between PSE and other pidgins. In most pidgins, articles are deleted; the copula is usually uninflected; inflections such as English plural are lost and most derivations are lost, just as they are in PSE. Perfective aspect in pidgins is often expressed through *finish* or a similar verb like *done*.

Woodward (1973b) and Woodward and Markowicz (1975) provide a description of some of the linguistic characteristics of PSE, which are summarized in Table 1.

TABLE I. Linguistic Characteristics of Pidgin Sign English (PSE)

FEATURE	ASL	SIGN ENGLISH	PSE
Articles	No	Yes	Variable: A, T-H-E (fingerspelled)
Plurality	Noun pluralization by reduplication	*-s,* etc.	Some reduplication, generally does not use marker to represent English *s* plural
Copula	No	Yes	With older signers, represented by the sign TRUE
Progressive	Verb reduplication	*-ing*	"PSE retains verb reduplication in a few heavily weighted environments, e.g., 'run', 'drive'. PSE uninflected copula or inflected forms plus a verb for Standard English be + ing. PSE, however, drops the redundant + ing" (Woodward 1973b, 41).
Perfective	FINISH		FINISH2, an allomorph of ASL FINISH

Their inventory of features includes agent-beneficiary directionality, negative incorporation, and number incorporation. They also discuss PSE phonology, specifically, handshapes, location, and movement.

Reilly and McIntire (1980, 151) define PSE as "a form of signing used by many hearing people for interacting with deaf people and thus is a commonly encountered dialect of ASL." They (1980, 152) point out that

> Although PSE has been classified as a pidgin language, it differs from most pidgins in important ways. . . . Syntactically, PSE does not appear as many other pidgins. Because it does make use of a number of English grammatical devices for creating complex sentences, it has access to a wider range of grammatical constructions than do most pidgins.

The PSE label is very widely used and the analogy with spoken language pidgin situations and language contact in general is extended to include the idea of diglossic variation along a continuum. The suggestion that Ferguson's (1959) concept of diglossia might be applicable to the deaf community was first made by Stokoe (1969). By the low (L) variety, Stokoe is referring to ASL. As he (Stokoe 1969, 23) states, "The H ('superposed' or 'high') variety is English. However, this English is a form most unfamiliar to usual linguistic scrutiny. It is not spoken but uttered in 'words' which are fingerspelled or signed." As Lee (1982, 131) points out, "The concept of a sign language 'continuum' linking the H and L varieties . . . has become quite popular. This continuum represents a scale of all the varieties of ASL and English produced by both deaf and hearing signers. These varieties imperceptibly grade into ASL on one extreme and English on the other." It is claimed that a number of varieties exist along the continuum, and it is some complex of these varieties that the label PSE is said to identify.

A notable problem with earlier descriptions concerns lack of data or problems with the data used to back up claims about the linguistic nature of the signing being described. Neither in Woodward (1973b) nor in Woodward and Markowicz (1975) is there any description of the sample that serves as the source for the list of features proposed for PSE. Woodward (personal communication, 1988) has indicated that the description of PSE was based in part on a sample from his dissertation: 140 individuals, ranging in age from thirteen to fifty-five, with 9 black signers and 131 white signers. But these data are still problematic as the basis for a description of language contact because (1) the data were elicited by a hearing researcher on a one-on-one basis with the use of a questionnaire, and were not interactional; and (2) the signers providing these data range from deaf native ASL signers to hearing nonnative signers, making it virtually impossible to separate out features of the language produced that are a function of language contact from features that are a function of second-language acquisition. For example, Woodward and Markowicz (1975, 18) claim that the ASL rule of negative incorporation can occur in PSE, but that "deaf signers use more negative incorporation than hearing signers." This may indeed be true, but it might also reflect a difference in language competence (i.e., native signers knowing and competently using a rule that nonnative signers may be in the process of learning), rather than a reflection of language contact between hearing and deaf signers.

It seems that deaf language production and hearing language production in a language contact situation are necessarily different by virtue of differences in language acquisition backgrounds. Also, the features of contact signing (PSE) cannot be described based on data that not only combine native and nonnative signers' productions but also are not interactional. Researchers are certainly aware of the need to distinguish between native and nonnative production. In fact, Lee (1982, 131) reports that

> Stokoe (personal communication) suggests that there may in fact be two PSE continua: a PSEd produced by deaf signers and a PSEh produced by hearing signers. PSEd is likely to have more ASL grammatical structures and to omit English inflections. PSEh tends to have greater English influence and rarely approaches the ASL extreme of the continuum.

The need for separation of data sources is thus recognized, but this need is not reflected in the actual descriptions of PSE that are produced. Thus, Reilly and McIntire (1980) base their description of the differences between PSE and ASL on videotapes of a children's story that was signed by four informants. Three of these informants are hearing. Three have deaf parents and two of the three hearing informants did not use sign in childhood. The instructions for different versions of the story were given either in ASL or, as Reilly and McIntire (1980, 155) describe, "in PSE and spoken English simultaneously . . . or interpreted, i.e., signed as they were being read aloud by the investigator."

Although there is an awareness of the need to control for the variable of signer skill, and even though the description of PSE is based on videotaped data, the problem of separating the consequences of language contact from the consequences of second language learning arises in Reilly and McIntire's (1980) study. In their conclusions, they (1980, 183) observe:

> It seems that there is a gradation from structures that are more obvious to the language learner (classifiers and directional verbs) to those that are more and more subtle (sustained signs and facial and other non-manual behaviors). This gradation is reflected in differential usage by different signers.

Once again, we encounter the "apples and oranges" dilemma resulting from descriptions of PSE based on the sign production of signers with different levels of competence and ages of acquisition. Furthermore, data collection in analogous spoken language situations does not typically yield naturalistic data, and, accordingly, it is not clear that the data upon which Reilly and McIntire's description of PSE is based bear any resemblance to language production in a natural language contact situation.

Clearly, any study that proposes to describe the linguistic outcome of language contact in the American deaf community should at the very least take its departure from data collected in naturalistic interactional settings that reflect actual language contact situations as closely as possible. It is fair to say that studies claiming to describe the linguistic outcome of language contact in the American deaf community to date may not reflect the actual situation, owing to either a lack of data or problematic data. In light of the problems presented by the data in research to date, the characterizations of language contact in the American deaf community—pidginization, foreigner talk, learner's grammars, diglossic continuum—warrant reexamination.

THE PRESENT STUDY

Given the enormous complexity of language contact in the American deaf community, and the problems inherent in earlier studies attempting to describe the situation, we focused on only one particular type of interaction. The major goals of the present study are (1) to provide a preliminary description of the signing of deaf bilinguals when signing with hearing bilinguals, and (2) to base that description on carefully collected data that reflect natural interaction as closely as possible. Toward this end, six dyads of informants were formed. Eleven of the twelve informants rated themselves as very skilled in ASL, and all twelve rated themselves as skilled in English. Of the twelve informants, nine were born deaf, one was born hard of hearing and is now deaf, and two were born hearing and became deaf at fifteen months of age and three years of age, respectively. Five of the twelve came from deaf families, and of the remaining seven, five attended residential schools for the deaf and learned ASL at an early age. One informant learned ASL from other deaf students in a mainstream program. Considering the family and educational background of all but one of the informants, their self-evaluations of personal language skills are accurate: They are bilinguals who learned ASL either natively from their parents or at a very early age from peers (all but one in a residential school setting). They have had exposure to and contact with English all of their lives. The data from one informant who did not learn ASL until age 21 (born deaf, hearing family) is excluded from the analysis, and, in fact, the video-tapes for this informant reveal minimal use of ASL.

The composition of each of the six dyads is shown in Table 2. The participants in dyads 1 and 2 share similar backgrounds, as do the participants in dyads 4, 5, and 6. Dyad 3 was deliberately "mixed," consisting of one individual born deaf in a deaf family and one individual born deaf in a hearing family, but both having attended residential school. In dyads 1, 3, and 6, the participants did not know each other; in dyads 2, 4, and 5, they did.

In the first part of the data collection, the videocameras were present, but at no point were the technicians visible. The sign production of the six dyads was videotaped during interaction with, first, a deaf inter-

TABLE 2. Composition of Dyads

DYAD	PARTICIPANT A	PARTICIPANT B
1	Deaf family, born deaf, residential school	Deaf family, deaf at 15 mos., public school
2	Deaf family, born deaf, deaf day school	Deaf family, born hard of hearing, now profoundly deaf, deaf day school
3	Deaf family, born deaf, residential school	Hearing family, born deaf, residential school
4	Hearing family, born deaf, residential school	Hearing family, deaf at age 3, residential school
5	Hearing family, born deaf, residential school	Hearing family, born deaf, mainstream program
6	Hearing family, deaf at age 3, residential school	Hearing family, born deaf, learned ASL at age 21, public school

viewer who signed ASL, then the dyad alone; next with a hearing interviewer who produced English-like signing and used her voice while she signed, then the dyad alone again; finally, with the deaf interviewer again. The whole interview experience began with exclusive contact with the deaf interviewer.

Each interview consisted of a discussion of several broad topics of interest to members of the deaf community. Four statements were presented and participants were asked if they agreed or disagreed, and why.[4] It was predicted that (1) the situation with the deaf researcher will induce ASL, but the relative formality of the situation and the presence of a stranger can preclude it; (2) the situation with the hearing researcher will induce a shift away from ASL to contact signing; and (3) the informants alone with each other will elicit ASL. The structure of the interviews in terms of relative formality and informality is summarized in Table 3.

This interview structure has strong parallels with Edwards' (1986) research design for a study of British Black English. Edwards' (1986, 9) major concern in that study was the improvement of methodology "so as to ensure that this corpus authentically reflects the range of individual and situational variation which exists within the black community." Edwards recognized the obvious need for the black interviewers in gaining access to vernacular speech. Edwards (1986, 17) was assured that the presence of a sympathetic, young Black interviewer, that is, a peer, would guarantee the use of the vernacular by the informants. But

> Our observation made it clear that many young black people use Patois only in in-group conversation, so that the presence of any other person, even the young black field-worker, would be enough to inhibit Patois usage The obvious solution was to create a situation in which the young people were left alone.

As in the Edwards study, participants in the present study were left alone twice and asked to continue discussing the topics introduced by the interviewers. In the first instance, the deaf interviewer was called away for "an emergency phone call." After an eight to ten minute period, the hearing interviewer arrived and explained that she would be taking the deaf interviewer's place. The interview continued and the hearing interviewer then left to check on the deaf interviewer. The dyad was again left alone until the return of the deaf interviewer for the remainder of the interview session. Following the completion of the interview, the participants were told that there had in fact been no emergency, and the reason for the deaf interviewer's departure was explained. The participants viewed portions of the tapes and discussed the purpose of the study with the researchers. All the participants were glad to be told that the "emergency" was false, but accepted it as part of the data collection procedure.

Based on a preliminary examination of the data, some important observations can be made. These observations fall into two broad categories: (1) the overall pattern of language use during the interviews, and (2) the linguistic properties of the contact signing produced by deaf native ASL sign-

TABLE 3. Interview Structure

SITUATION TYPE	FORMAL	INFORMAL
With deaf interviewer	+	
Dyad alone		+
With hearing interviewer	+	
Dyad alone		+
With deaf interviewer	+	

TABLE 4. Distribution of Language Choice, by Interview Situation and Participant

	Dyad 1 Participants		Dyad 2 Participants		Dyad 3 Participants		Dyad 4 Participants		Dyad 5 Participants		Dyad 6 Participants	
SITUATION	A	B	A	B	A	B	A	B	A	B	A	B
With deaf interviewer	ASL	CS/SE[a]	ASL	ASL/CS	ASL/CS	CS	ASL	SE	ASL	CS	ASL	CS
Dyad alone	ASL	CL	ASL	ASL	ASL/CS	ASL/CS	ASL	CS	ASL	ASL	CS	CS
With hearing interviewer	ASL	SE	ASL/CS	CS	CS	SE	ASL	CS	CS	CS	CS	CS
Dyad alone	ASL	CS	ASL	ASL	ASL/CS	ASL/CS	ASL	CS	CS/ASL	CS/ASL	CS/ASL	CS/ASL
With deaf interviewer	ASL	CS	ASL	ASL/CS	ASL/CS	ASL	ASL	CS	ASL	ASL	ASL	CS

[a]CS, Contact Signing; SE, Signed English, with voice.

ers during deaf-hearing interaction. As assessed by a deaf native ASL user, the distributional pattern of language choice during the interviews is summarized in Table 4.[5] The information in this table should be read as follows: In the first dyad, participant A uses ASL across all of the situations of interaction; A's language use here contrasts with B's, who uses contact signing and signed English with the deaf interviewer, contact signing with A, and signed English with the hearing interviewer, and so on, for all six dyads. As the distributional contrasts in Table 4 reveal, some participants start out with one kind of signing in a particular condition and then change to another kind of signing, within the same condition. Participant B in dyad 5, for example, produces contact signing with the deaf interviewer. When alone with A, B produces ASL and then produces contact signing again when the hearing interviewer appears. When the hearing interviewer leaves, and A and B are again alone, B continues to produce contact signing for a while and then produces ASL. B continues to produce ASL upon the return of the deaf interviewer and does so until the end of the interview.

In keeping with our prediction, ten of the twelve informants produce a form of signing that is other-than-ASL with the hearing interviewer—either contact signing or signed English with voice. In some cases, the informants produce ASL with the deaf interviewer and while alone with each other, as was expected. However, some unexpected results emerged. For example, three informants use ASL with the hearing interviewer, contrary to a widely held belief that deaf native signers automatically switch away from ASL in the presence of a nonnative signer. Furthermore, two of the informants (1A and 4A) use ASL consistently across all of the situations. One might predict that both of these informants come from deaf families; however, 4A is from a hearing family. Another unexpected result is the production of contact signing both with the deaf interviewer and when the informants are left alone. The deaf interviewer consistently signs ASL, and it was predicted that the informants would produce ASL in this situation and when left alone. But this is not the actual outcome. Indeed, in one case, an informant produces signed English with the deaf interviewer. These results are particularly noteworthy given another widely held belief that deaf native signers will consistently sign ASL with each other if no hearing people are present. The observations on the overall pattern of language use during the interviews can be summarized as follows:

- Some informants use contact signing or signed English with the hearing interviewer, as expected; others use ASL throughout.
- ASL is used with the hearing interviewer by some informants but not others.
- Contact signing is produced with the deaf interviewer and when the informants are alone.
- ASL is used not only by deaf informants from deaf families but also by deaf informants from hearing families.

These observations appear to challenge the traditional perspective on language contact in the American deaf community. For example, it is traditionally assumed that contact signing (known as PSE) appears in deaf-hearing interaction, mainly for the obvious reason that the hearing person might not understand ASL. On the extreme is the position that the very purpose of contact signing is to prevent hearing people from learning ASL (Woodward and Markowicz 1975, 12). More measured approaches simply describe contact signing as the product of deaf-hearing interaction. Little is said, however, about the use of contact signing in exclusively deaf settings. Although the need for comprehension might explain the occurrence of contact signing in deaf-hearing interaction, it is clearly not an issue in portions of the interviews described here, as all of the participants are native or near-native signers and, in some instances, sign ASL with each other. The choice to use contact signing with other deaf ASL natives, then, appears to be motivated by sociolinguistic factors. Two of three factors identified in the present study are the formality of the interview situation (including the presence of videotape equipment) and the participant's lack of familiarity in some cases with both the interviewer and the other informant. The videotaped data also clearly present counter-evidence to the claim that deaf people never or rarely sign ASL in the presence of hearing people, as two of the informants chose to sign ASL throughout their respective interviews. This choice may be motivated by other sociolinguistic factors, such as the desire to establish one's social identity as a bona fide member of the deaf community or cultural group, a desire that may supersede considerations of formality and lack of familiarity with one's cointerlocutor(s). Different sociolinguistic factors motivate the language choices of different individuals. This is further illustrated by the differences among informants in language choice within a given interview situation.

Figure 1 provides a more graphic summary of informant language use within the interviews. Three distinct patterns are discernible here. One pattern, as seen with dyads 1 and 4, consists of the two informants using distinctly different kinds of signing and never overlapping with each other. For example, in dyad 1, informant 1A consistently uses ASL throughout the interview, even though 1B starts out with contact signing and signed English, then moves first to contact signing, then to signed English, and then back to contact signing. Similarly, in dyad 4, informant 4A consistently uses ASL, while 4B starts out with signed English and then consistently uses contact signing. Neither 1B nor 4B ever approaches the use of ASL during the interview. The first pattern, then, is that one participant's choice of signing during the interview is consistently distinct from the co-participant's choice or choices.

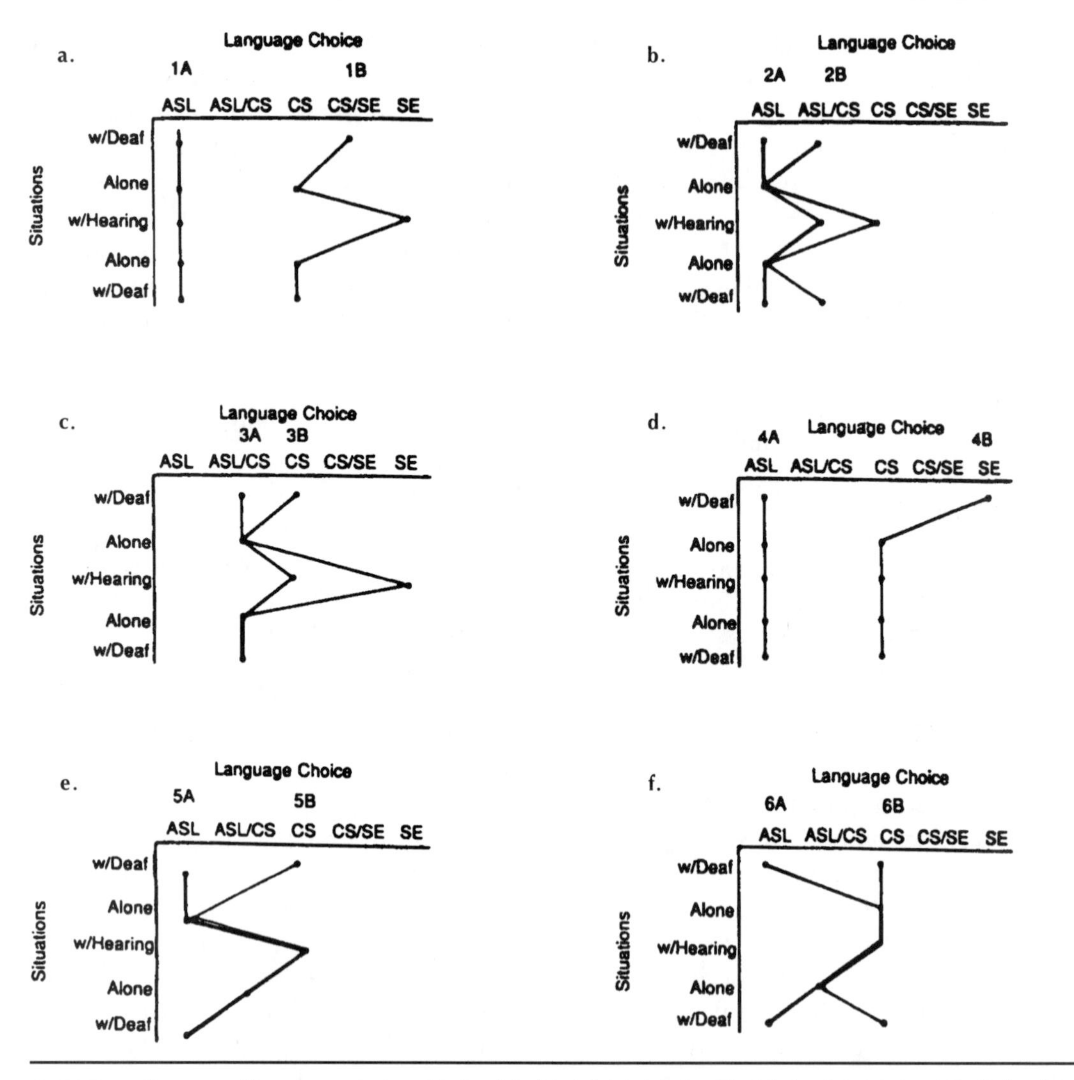

FIGURE 1. Patterns of language choice: (a) dyad 1; (b) dyad 2; (c) dyad 3; (d) dyad 4; (e) dyad 5; (f) dyad 6.

In dyads 2 and 6, we see a second pattern, where the informants use different kinds of signing during the first part of the interview with the deaf interviewer but, when left alone with each other, use the same kind of signing. In dyad 2, informant 2A continues with ASL, and 2B switches to ASL; in dyad 6, informant 6B continues with contact signing, and 6A switches to contact signing. In dyad 6, the informants use the same kind of signing and switch in the same way towards ASL when left alone and then sign quite differently with the deaf interviewer. In dyad 2, the informants do not sign in exactly the same way, but they do shift in the same direction. Also noteworthy in both dyads is the fact that despite shifting during the interview, each informant signs the same way with the deaf interviewer at the end of the interview as at the beginning.

The third pattern is seen in dyads 3 and 5, where the informants begin the interview with different kinds of signing. One informant then shifts toward the other, and then both informants either together use the same kind of signing for the remainder of the interview (dyad 5) or use the same kind of signing, then shift in the same direction, and then together use the same kind of signing again (dyad 3).

One central question is what accounts for the use of different kinds of signing by individual informants within the interviews. Switching that seems to be motivated by the presence of a hearing person can be seen in these data: seven of the twelve informants switch from ASL signing or ASL signing with some contact signing features to contact signing or signed English with voice in the presence of the hearing interviewer. Of the remaining five informants, two consistently sign ASL in all situations; the other three produce contact signing when the hearing interviewer arrives and maintain this choice for the duration of her presence. Five of the twelve informants are from deaf families, and it is important to note that four of those five are among those who switched in the presence of the hearing interviewer. Of the five informants who did not switch with the hearing interviewer, only one is from a deaf family.

Signing behavior produced in the presence of a hearing person does not explain the occurrence of contact signing with the deaf interviewer or when the informants are alone. The use of contact signing in the latter situations can be accounted for by several factors, such as the formality of the interview situation and the lack of familiarity of the informants with the deaf interviewer. Attitudes concerning the kind of signing that is appropriate in different situations have long been noticed and described. Indeed, it is this interrelationship between language attitudes and language choices that prompted Stokoe (1969) to describe the language situation in the deaf community as diglossic—that is, ASL strictly in some contexts and a more English-like signing strictly for other contexts, with no overlap. In reexamining this characterization of the language situation in the deaf community as diglossic, Lee (1982, 127) states that although "there is indeed variation [in the deaf community] . . . code-switching and style shifting rather than diglossia appear to be the norm." Three of Ferguson's (1959) nine criteria for diglossia are linguistic (lexicon, phonology, and grammar), while six are described by Lee as sociolinguistic (literary heritage, standardization, prestige, stability, acquisition, and function). As she (Lee 1982, 147) observes, "I have found none of the nine characteristics actually consistent with diglossia, at least in some parts of the linguistic community."

Even though it is not clear at this point what the roles of code-switching and style shifting are in the deaf community, it is clear from Lee's reexamination of Stokoe's (1969) work and from the present data that the language situation in the deaf community is not strictly diglossic. Clearly, some of the informants in our study see ASL as inappropriate for any part of the interview. Specifically, informants 1B and 4B never use ASL. Other informants see ASL as appropriate only when no interviewer is present. In each one of the six dyads, a shift occurs when the deaf interviewer departs and the informants are alone, and it is striking that whenever the signing of one informant shifts toward the signing of another, it is, with one exception, a shift from contact signing or signed English to or toward ASL. That is, informants 1A, 2A, 4A, 5A use ASL with the deaf interviewer at the beginning of the interview, and 1B, 2B, 3B, 4B, and 5B use contact signing or signed English. When the deaf interviewer departs, the latter informants switch to or toward ASL. The one exception is informant 6A, who uses ASL with the deaf interviewer and then switches to contact signing when left alone with 6B, who continues to use contact signing. This may have occurred because, of the twelve informants, 6B is the only one who learned ASL relatively late. 6A may have switched to contact signing in an attempt to accommodate 6B. The claim that ASL is regarded as appropriate only when the interviewers are absent is further supported by the two informants (2B and 6B) who switch away from ASL to contact signing when the deaf interviewer reappears at the end of the interview. Any attempt, however, to claim that this is evidence of diglossia is quickly thwarted by the informants who use ASL in all of the interview situations, with no apparent regard for formality, familiarity, or audiological status of the cointerlocutor(s).

The patterns seen in Figure 1 provide an illustration of Giles's (1977) theory of accommodation in linguistic behavior (also, see Valli, 1988). That accommodation can take the form of convergence, nonconvergence, or divergence. With convergence, a speaker chooses a language variety that seems to fit the needs of the cointerlocutor(s). Under some conditions, however, a speaker can diverge in order to dissociate from the cointerlocutor(s), perhaps to emphasize loyalty to his group. Nonconvergence occurs when one speaker does not move away from another but simply continues using a variety that differs from other speakers. Figure 1 provides examples of all three types of accommodation. In dyad 1, for example, participant 1B converges with or shifts toward 1A when the dyad is alone. 1B then converges with the hearing interviewer by shifting to signed English, while 1A provides an example of nonconvergence with the hearing interviewer by continuing to use ASL. In all of the dyads except 6, the B participants converge toward the A participants, which is to say, toward ASL. As mentioned earlier about dyad 6, participant A may converge toward B because B learned sign language relatively late and may not be comfortable using ASL.

A major goal of this chapter is to describe the sociolinguistic conditions that accompany the production of signing other than ASL, signing that has been labeled PSE. Contrary to claims that this kind of signing occurs in the presence of hearing people, either to aid their comprehension or to deny them access to ASL, the videotaped data in this study clearly demonstrate that contact signing is produced among deaf native ASL signers in the absence of hearing people. The sociolinguistic factors that motivate this language choice appear to include the relative formality of the interview situation and the lack of familiarity with cointerlocutors. There is clear evidence that contact signing is considered more appropriate than ASL in some situations. Furthermore, an examination of the conditions of language contact situations in the deaf community reveals that, from a sociolinguistic standpoint, these situations are not at all analogous to the sociolinguistic conditions that give rise to spoken language pidgins.

LINGUISTIC FEATURES OF CONTACT SIGNING

Another goal of this chapter is to describe some of the morphological, lexical, and syntactic features of contact signing. As explained earlier, a complete linguistic description of contact signing is planned and will be based on a corpus formed from native signer judgments of the language production on the videotapes. This linguistic description will encompass each informant's signing in all the interview situations, that is, with the deaf interviewer, with the hearing interviewer, and alone with the other informant. The present preliminary description focuses on each informant's interaction with the hearing interviewer and is

TABLE 5. Linguistic Features of Contact Signing

LEXICAL FORM	LEXICAL MEANING AND FUNCTION	MORPHOLOGICAL STRUCTURE	SYNTACTIC STRUCTURE
ASL and ASL-like lexical items, English mouthing	ASL, idiosyncratic, English	Reduced ASL and English, reduction and/or absence of nonmanual signals	Reduced English idiosyncratic constructions

based on thirty seconds of transcription per informant.[6] From this sample, Table 5 summarizes various features of contact signing.

The lexical forms found in contact signing are ASL signs. It is important to observe that these lexical forms are consistently accompanied by the mouthing of corresponding English lexical items. This mouthing is produced without voicing. Although most of the lexical forms are ASL signs with ASL meaning and function, sometimes the lexical forms have English meanings and functions. For example, the ASL sign GROW (the sign used when discussing the growth of plants, for example) is produced with the lexicalized fingerspelled sign #UP, in a discussion of the hearing children of deaf parents. Even though the sign GROW used by our informant is an ASL sign, it is not the sign typically used in ASL for talking about the growth of children. The result, then, is the use of an ASL form with a meaning not usually associated with that sign. This example is analogous to examples in the various manual codes for English, where one ASL sign is used for a wide variety of English meanings, even though separate ASL signs exist for those meanings. For example, the ASL sign RUN (as in "run down the street") is cited in these systems for the meanings of "run for president," "run a business," or "run in a stocking." The occurrence of the sign GROW with the fingerspelled #UP may be a reflection of the signer's exposure to manually coded systems for English in the educational system. And in a situation deemed appropriate for more English-like signing, evidence of those systems emerges. GROW, then, is a case of an ASL sign that is not being used with its ASL meaning. In that usage it has an English meaning. Another example in the data of ASL lexical forms with English meaning and function is the sign MEAN, which in ASL is generally used as a verb, as in

WH
WORD MEAN
"What does the word mean?"

In the data, however, this sign occurs with the meaning and function of the English noun meaning, as in the sequence WHAT MEAN OF QUOTE DEAF CULTURE "what is the meaning of 'deaf culture'"?

Both morphologically and syntactically, the contact signing examined here shows drastic reduction of both the ASL and English systems. Word order follows English patterns, as does the use of prepositional phrases, conjunctions, embedded constructions with *that*, personal pronouns, and collocations. English inflectional and derivational morphology is nonexistent, yielding a very analytic (as opposed to synthetic) picture. This extends to the mouthing of English lexical items that is a feature of contact signing. The mouthing does not include any bound English morphemes such as plural *-s*, third-person possessive *-s*, past tense *-ed*, and so forth.

Davis (this volume) draws a distinction between clear English mouthing and reduced English mouthing. The former consists of the completely silent pronunciation of a word. The latter consists of the partially

(shaking head negative) + mouthing ⟶
PRO-lst AGREE PRO-lst AGREE THAT BECAUSE PRO-lst SUPPORT DEAF INSTITUTION BECAUSE

+mouthing ⟶
PRO-center MORE ATTENTION ON SPECIFIC #OF LIFES-T-Y-L-E AND PRO-center

+mouthing ⟶
MORE GENERAL GOOD #ED DEPEND ON WHAT STATE WHICH PLACE HAVE BEST DEPEND ON

⟶ + mouthing ⟶
PEOPLE EXPERIENCE 'WELL' BACKGROUND #OF TEACHING "SO" COOPERATIVE TEAMWORK

⟶
#IS REAL MOST KEY THEIR #GOALS ETC (nodding head)

"I don't agree with that because I support deaf residential schools because they place more attention on the specifics of lifestyle and the education, in general, is better—depending on what state, which place has the best—that depends on the people's experience, on their teaching background—so, cooperative teamwork is really the key to their goals."

FIGURE 2. Contact signing. The transcription is relatively broad. The notation + mouthing indicates the mouthing without voice of English phrases or sentences that parallels the signed message. The term PRO is used for what appear to be pronominal forms. The gloss "WELL" indicates the placement of a discourse marker.

silent pronunciation of a word. For example, one signer fingerspells #ED "education" and mouths "educa-." These data contain examples of both complete and partial mouthing. Furthermore, ASL inflectional and derivational morphology are virtually absent. There is also considerable use of deictic signs, such as pronouns. Finally, the contact signing yields some examples of what can only be called idiosyncratic syntactic constructions, constructions that fit neither the ASL nor the English grammatical system. Examples include sequences such as

+ mouthing ⟶
GROW # UP OF BE DEAF,

and

+ mouthing ⟶
COOPERATIVE TEAM-WORK #IS REAL MOST KEY THEIR #GOALS.

Figure 2 provides an example of the contact signing produced by one informant in discussing whether mainstreaming is preferable to residential schools. This particular informant favors residential schools. Examples of the features of contact signing here include English word order, use of conjunctions, prepositional phrases, consistent mouthing without voice of English lexical items, idiosyncratic constructions, and the absence of determiners. Inflectional morphemes are absent except for the invented sign for English *-ing* and the fingerspelled copula, #IS. There are also examples of deictic ASL signs (e.g., pronouns), lexicalized fingerspelling (#OF, #ED), and an ASL discourse marker ("WELL"). Finally, there is the occurrence of a single spoken English word, "*so*." Recall that Woodward (1973b) and Woodward and Markowicz (1975), in their inventory of PSE features, include English word order and the absence of determiners, two of the features of the present data. However, there are many other features in these data that are not found in their inventory.

The *linguistic* outcome of contact between ASL and English is not most aptly described as a pidgin. This observation is in accord with that of Cokely (1983). In reviewing the preconditions defined by other researchers for the emergence of a pidgin (e.g., Ferguson and DeBose 1977), Cokely (1983, 11, 20) finds that the ASL-English contact situation

> can be described as one in which members of the Deaf community communicate with hearing people in a foreigner talk register of ASL, and members of the hearing community communicate with Deaf people in a foreigner talk register of English. . . . The ASL-English contact situation does not, in fact, result in the emergence of a pidgin. Although the process of pidginization may be detected in the ASL-English situation, the preconditions for the development of a pidgin language are not adequately met. Instead the variation along the ASL-English continuum of varieties or registers can be accounted for by the dynamic interplay of foreigner talk, judgments of proficiency, and learners' attempts to master the target language—whether this is ASL for hearing users or English for Deaf users.

There is one apparent difficulty with Cokely's characterization of language contact in the deaf community. Consider an analogy from spoken language contact situations. In the contact between a native speaker of Italian, for example, and a nonnative speaker, it would be quite strange to expect that the "foreigner talk" variety of Italian used by the native speaker would include any elements of the nonnative speaker's first language. More likely, the "foreigner talk" variety would simplv be a modified version of Italian. The variety of signing that the deaf native ASL signer typically uses with hearing people, however, seems to include at least some features of English and thus does not qualify strictly as "foreigner talk." This is also the case for the variety of signing that hearing people use with deaf people.

Woodward (1985, 19) describes Cokely's observations as "challenging to Woodward's (1973b) analysis of the varieties between ASL and English as a pidgin language" and contends that "by 1980, however, the notion that varieties referred to by 'PSE' as a discrete pidgin had already been abandoned." He (1985, 19) cites his own 1980 work to support this contention: "While it is true that PSE is different from pure ASL and from pure English, it is not a separate language. There is no way in the world to define where PSE begins and ends." Bochner and Albertini (1988) address the issue of PSE within the context of language acquisition and correctly observe that it is difficult to draw a clear parallel between spoken language pidgins and PSE. Although their claims are not data based, they (Bochner and Albertini 1988, 13–14) note that "a pidgin may be developing in North American schools and workplaces among users of mutually unintelligible sign systems . . . Objective and detailed descriptions of the structure and function of signing being used in these situations would clarify the picture."

To fully understand the preliminary inventory of contact signing features in these data, and to get a clearer understanding of what kind of linguistic phenomenon contact signing is, it is useful to compare it to (1) inventories of the features of English-based spoken language pidgins and (2) features of other kinds of signing such as signed English, which by its nature is English-based.

TABLE 6. Comparison of Linguistic Features among Various Systems

FEATURES	SPOKEN ENGLISH	ASL	SIGNED ENGLISH	CONTACT SIGNING	ENGLISH-BASED SPOKEN LANGUAGE PIDGINS[a]
Lexical form	English	ASL	ASL, ASL-like signs, non-ASL-like signs, spoken English	ASL and ASL-like signs, English mouthing	English, some substrate, some idiosyncratic
Lexical function	English	ASL	English	ASL, idiosyncratic, English	Usually English, some idiosyncratic
Morphology	English	ASL	Reduced English and ASL, signed repretation of bound morphemes	Reduced ASL and Enlish, reduction and/or absence of nonmanual signals	Reduced English
Syntax	English	ASL	Reduced English	Reduced English, some idiosyncratic constructions, codeswitching to ASL	Basically SVO, reduced use of pronouns and prepositions, embedding rare

[a]From Muhlhäusler (1986).

From the comparison in Table 6, we can see that the contact signing examined thus far is distinct from both English-based spoken language pidgins and from signed English. Specifically, virtually the only way in which an analogy of contact signing with spoken language pidgins may hold is with the reduction in morphology. In all other ways, contact signing and spoken language pidgins are quite different in their inventory of features. Compared to English-based pidgins, which consist of mainly English lexical items with English meanings and functions in a reduced English morphological and syntactic system, contact signing uniquely combines ASL and ASL-like lexical items in a reduced English syntactic system.

The outcome of this language contact situation appears to be a kind of code-mixing that is quite different from those described thus far for spoken languages. For example, Bokamba (1985, 4) defines code-switching as an *inter*sentential event, the embedding or mixing of words, phrases, and sentences from two codes within the same speech event and across sentence boundaries. And code-mixing is an *intra*sentential event, the embedding or mixing of various linguistic units, that is, affixes, words, phrases, and clauses from two distinct grammatical systems or subsystems within the same sentence and the same speech situation. Kachru (1978b) and Sridhar and Sridhar (1980) offer similar definitions. Central to understanding both code-switching and code-mixing in spoken languages is that even though the parts of two different codes can be switched intersententially or mixed intrasententially, the switching or mixing is sequential in nature, as opposed to being simultaneous. That is, units in spoken languages, whether phonological, morphological, or syntactic, are necessarily produced one after the other. If, in a code-mixing situation, the verb of one language is marked with an inflection from another language, this event is also sequential, that is, first the verb is produced, followed by the inflection. It is safe to say that code-mixing, for spoken languages, does not mean the consistent use of the lexical items of one language in the syntactic system of another.

There may be some parallels to code-mixing in Whinnom's (1971) description of cocoliche, the Spanish spoken by Italian immigrants in Argentina (but not spoken by Argentines). After introducing the notion of linguistic hybridization, he (1971, 97) observes:

> It is a now despised formula of "primitive" creolistics that pidgin is made up of the vocabulary of one language and the grammar of another. The observation may be faulty but it reflects a basic reality. It is, moreover, a description which fits very well certain linguistic phenomena ("secondary languages") associated with naive language learning.

At the least intense level of hybridization that he describes, Spanish lexical items (nouns, adjectives, verb radicals) are imported into an Italian morphosyntactical system without interfering with the native phonological system, a phenomenon that seems to parallel contact signing. Contact signing, however, appears to be unique in another way. In spoken language contact situations, speakers have at their disposal the phonological, morphological, syntactic, and discourse component of two or more languages, and it is possible to imagine a simultaneous mix of, say, the phonology of one language with the morphology of another, or the morphology of one with the syntax of another. It seems, however, the mixing *within* components, while possible, is necessarily sequential. That is, it seems impossible to simultaneously produce two phonological events from two different spoken languages. In the contact signing described here, however, in which a signer produces ASL lexical items on the hands and simultaneously mouths the corresponding English lexical items, the result is the simultaneous production of two separate codes. This appears to be a unique kind of code-mixing, different from what has been described for spoken language contact situations to date.[7]

The outcome of contact between ASL and English is not entirely predictable. The outcome *could* simply be a modified form of ASL, or it could be code-switching and code-mixing of the sequential type described for spoken languages. In fact, many of the instances of sequential switching observed in the present data are distinct from contact signing. An example is the following:

+ mouthing ⟶
THEY HAVE #KNOWLEDGE OF WHAT
DEAF CULTURE #IS ABOUT
+ mouthing ⟶ – mouthing
EXPOSURE TO # IT SEE (inflected)
+ mouthing ⟶
NOT IDIOTS
"They have knowledge of what deaf culture is about, exposure to it. They have seen it for a long time. They are not idiots"

In this example, the informant switches from contact signing (with mouthing of English lexical items) to an inflected form of the ASL sign SEE. This inflected form is a two-handed sign with a V handshape, produced in alternating elliptical circles away from the signer's face. It can be glossed as SEE FOR A LONG TIME. It is important to note that during the switch, the mouthing of English is interrupted and then resumed immediately following the sign.

There are also examples of simultaneous production of contact signing and ASL, such as the following:

Right hand
ONE FRIEND POINT (to 1-CL on left hand)
+ mouthing
HEARING POINT (to 1-CL)
+ mouthing ⟶
#ADOPT BY DEAF PARENT POINT (1-CL)

Left Hand:
1-CL "friend"——————
"One friend was adopted by deaf parents."

In this example, the informant starts out with ONE FRIEND and then points to a classifier predicate being produced with the left hand. (1-CL is the classifier predicate produced with a 1 handshape.) It represents the friend in question, and the use of that predicate is a feature of ASL. The left hand shaping the 1-CL stays in place while the right hand produces contact signing with mouthing of English. (#ADOPT represents fingerspelling.) That is, the left hand produces ASL, while the right hand and the mouth produce contact signing. A feature of contact signing is thus this simultaneous production of some ASL features, a phenomenon that must be distinguished from switches away from contact signing to ASL, as in the SEE example.

Contact signing is also clearly distinct from signed English, as can be seen in Table 6. Although contact signing can involve the silent mouthing of English lexical items, for example, signed English can involve spoken (voiced) English, including bound morphemes. Also, signed English can include invented, non-ASL-like signs, and bound English morphemes can be represented manually.

We observed earlier in this paper that we are reluctant at this point to call the contact signing that we have observed a *variety* or a *dialect*, that is, a discrete and consistent linguistic system. Our examination of the linguistic features of contact signing would seem to justify our reluctance. Bob Johnson (personal communication) has observed that, due to the wide variety of language skills and backgrounds and educational backgrounds that signers bring with them to language contact situations, the best way to describe the outcome of language contact in the American deaf community may be as a collection of individual grammars. Further description of our data will shed light on his observation.

SOCIOLINGUISTIC FEATURES OF CONTACT SIGNING

Sociolinguistically, the language contact situation in the deaf community also does not reflect a pidgin. It is clear that not all language contact situations result in pidginization. As Grosjean (1982, 38) succinctly summarizes this issue,

> The usual outcome of bilingualism . . . is a return to monolingualism: this may take the form of maintenance of the groups' second language and the disappearance of the first language (often referred to as mother-tongue displacement or language shift); or the evolution to a new language through processes of pidginization and creolization.

In a review of the state of the art in interlinguistics, Muysken (1984) lists third-language creation, dialect shift, foreign accent, code-switching, relexification, code-mixing, and foreigner talk as possible outcomes in a language contact situation. Further, there has been continuous and vigorous debate about the fundamental nature of pidgins and pidginization at least since Hall's pioneering work in the 1960s, with DeCamp (1971), Alleyne (1971) Whinnom (1971), Bickerton (1975, 1977, 1981, 1984), Samarin (1971), Ferguson and DeBose (1977), Todd (1974), Kay and Sankoff (1974), Rickford (1981), Sankoff (1984), and Muhlhäusler (1986). However, there is apparently a basic convergence of opinion about the unique nature of pidginization in having at its inception a very particular set of sociolinguistic circumstances. As Barbag-Stoll (1983, 24) observes,

> The fundamental condition for the occurrence of pidginization is a contact situation involving two or more different languages. This should by no means

> imply, however, that any contact of two or more languages will result in hybridization. If the source languages are closely related, the output product is more likely to be a dialect, as the prevailing process will be substitution rather than simplification. If the spread of the source language is symmetrical when it is learnt through formal means, it is likely to result in bilingualism. Whether the output is a pidgin or a standard language depends on the degree of availability of target models and the extent to which they are exposed to the learners. If the standard language models are easily accessible and if the nature of the contact situation is such that the speaker interacts mostly with native speakers of the target language, he is most likely to learn the non-pidginized version of it. However, if the target language is spoken mainly with non-native speakers and the target models are rare, the output will most probably be pidgin.

Barbag-Stoll stresses the availability of target models and the extent to which learners are exposed to them as central to the pidginization process. Hall (1962) emphasizes that the language in question is not native to any of its users. DeCamp (1971, 15) defines a pidgin as "a contact vernacular, normally not the native language of any of its speakers. It is used in trading or in any situation requiring communication between persons who do not speak each other's native language." DeCamp goes on to say that pidgins are characterized by limited vocabularies, elimination of many grammatical devices such as number and gender, and drastic reduction of redundant features. But he cautions against equating this reduction with simplification. Bickerton (1975) states that at the inception of the pidgin-creole cycle, future pidgin speakers already have established grammars of their own and, in fact, are often multilingual. They are confronted by the grammar of the superstrate language and then removed both from their own language communities and from the target superstrate language. In later work, Bickerton (1977, 49, 54) characterized pidginization as akin to

> Second-language learning with restricted input . . . We can conclude that pidginization is a process that begins by the speaker using his native tongue and relexifying first only a few key words; that, in the earliest stages, even the few superstrate words will be thoroughly rephonologized to accord with substrate sound system and phonotactics; that subsequently, more superstrate lexicon will be acquired but may still be rephonologized to varying degrees and will be, for the most part slotted into syntactic surface structures drawn from the substrate; that even substrate syntax will be partially retained, and will alternate, apparently unpredictably, with structures imported from the superstrate.

Pidginization, then, is clearly the result of a unique kind of language contact, and the key elements in understanding the pidginization process appear to be the relative access to the target model, the lack of a mutually intelligible language among interlocutors, the immediate need for communication, and the interruption of access to one's native language.

Although one result of language contact in the American Deaf community is labeled Pidgin Sign English, the sociolinguistic situation in this community does not coincide with the "classic" pidgin situation or with any of its key elements. Let us assume, for example, that English is considered the superstrate language in the deaf community. Clearly it is the native language of hearing users of contact signing. But even deaf native ASL signers, for whom English may not be a native language, have extensive exposure to and contact with English in various forms, first in educational settings and later in their adult lives through employment, interaction with hearing people, and through print and broadcast media. This exposure to and contact with English is accompanied by ongoing ASL interaction with other native signers. The result for such native ASL signers in American society is a maintained bilingualism, wrought from the many different kinds of contact situations occurring in the deaf community and dependent on the participants' characteristics.

Again, we see parallels with Whinnom's (1971) description of cocoliche. One reason for the occurrence of cocoliche is the resistance to full integration into the Spanish-speaking community. This invites speculation about a signer's choice of contact signing, for example, over strict signed English. Furthermore, because cocoliche represents a form of second-language learning, Whinnom points out that the speech of any two individual cocoliche speakers can never be even nearly identical. This has clear parallels with the diversity of educational backgrounds of individuals in the deaf community and what, as a consequence, they bring with them to a contact situation. But Whinnom also points out that with cocoliche, the pressures of formal language instruction do not contribute to language use. This represents an important difference with the deaf community, as the role of English in contact signing, owing directly to its role in the educational system, cannot be discounted. The present study describes some of the linguistic and sociolinguistic outcomes of language contact in the deaf community, and reveals the situation to be considerably more complex than earlier descriptions have indicated. One interesting and perhaps ironic fact about the linguistic outcome is the occurrence of English structural features in contact signing, features which do *not* include the invented signs that are part of the manual codes for English that have been implemented in the educational system. One part of the irony lies in the fact that there is considerable use in the educational system of these manual codes, and it would not be unreasonable to predict that elements of these codes would occur in bilingual contact situations. However, very little evidence of those codes was found in the data described here. Another part of the irony has to do with the generally negative reception that these codes have received from members of the deaf community (Baker and Cokely 1980). It should be clear from the present study that resistance to invented codes for English should not be mistaken for resistance to English per se, as the indigenous, natural signing that occurs as a result of the contact between bilinguals has many English features. Clearly the social stigma about invented systems does not preclude the occurrence of English features. The crucial difference is the difference between an invented representation of a language imposed on its users, and a naturally occurring form of language observed not only in deaf-hearing interaction, but also in the interaction of deaf native ASL users with each other.

Some final speculation about the future of language contact in the Deaf community: In this study, we have described the occurrence of contact signing in situations where ASL might be predicted, i.e., between deaf individuals who are native ASL users. We have suggested that the occurrence of "other than ASL" can be accounted for by a variety of sociolinguistic factors, including lack of familiarity between participants or formality of the situation. Clearly, the choice of "other than ASL" is being made in some situations; "other than ASL" is clearly seen as more appropriate in some situations. If this were not so, native ASL users who choose ASL in some situations would use it in situations where they now choose "other than ASL." By way of conclusion, we suggest, as have other researchers (e.g., Stokoe 1969), that the choice of "other than ASL" and the view that ASL is not appropriate for some situations are the direct results of a sociolinguistic situation in which ASL has been ignored and devalued, and in which the focus has traditionally been on the instruction and use of English. We suggest that, as ASL becomes more highly valued and becomes formally and fully recognized and used as a legitimate tool for communication in any situation, that the outcome of language contact in the American deaf community will change noticeably.

ACKNOWLEDGMENTS

We are grateful to Scott Liddell, Walt Wolfram, and Bob Johnson for providing very detailed and valuable feedback on this chapter. This research has been supported since 1986 by the Gallaudet Research Institute, and by the Office of the Provost, Gallaudet University. We gratefully acknowledge this support, and in particular, would like to recognize Dr. Michael A. Karchmer, Dean of Graduate Studies and Research. We would also like to thank our informants and judges.

NOTES

1. American Sign Language (ASL) is the visual-gestural language used by members of the deaf community in the United States. It is a natural language with an autonomous grammar that is quite distinct from the grammar of English. ASL is also quite distinct from artificially developed systems that attempt to encode English and can include the use of speech, ASL signs, and invented signs used to represent English morphemes. There are a number of such systems, which are often referred to by the generic term signed English.
2. Based on a preliminary examination of the linguistic and sociolinguistic data, we are reluctant at this point to call the contact signing that we have observed a *variety* or a *dialect*, and the absence of such labels in the present study is conscious. Further study may reveal the need for such a label.
3. At this point, evidence for the occurrence of signed or spoken English in the home, along with ASL, is largely anecdotal. For example, a Gallaudet undergraduate whose parents are deaf and who signs ASL as a first language remarked, in a class journal, "At first when I was born, my parents thought I was hearing due to a *VERY* little hearing loss. Afraid that I may have poor speech and English skills, they decided to use straight English and their voices whenever talking to me." She later remarks that her parents went back to using ASL. And another student states, "I was introduced to ASL since I'm the daughter of deaf parents and the fifth deaf generation. When SEE [Signing Exact English, a manual code for English] was emphasized in the 70s—my mama decided to learn SEE and placed me in a mainstream program where SEE was strongly used." Both of these comments imply the use of some form of English signing by native ASL signers in the home with their children. Furthermore, Woodward (1973c, 44) observes that, "it has been estimated that 10–20 percent of the deaf population has deaf parents. A tiny proportion of these parents are highly educated and have native English competence. In this tiny minority of the deaf, PSE [Pidgin Sign English, Woodward's term for the outcome of language contact in the deaf community—*editor's note*] may be learned with ASL from infancy." However, sociolinguistic and ethnographic data to support comments and observations such as these are nonexistent.
4. The four statements introduced for discussion are as follows:

    1. Someone in a public place (airport, restaurant) discovers that you're deaf and wants to help you. That is acceptable. Agree or disagree?
    2. The hearing children of deaf people are members of deaf culture. Agree or disagree?
    3. Gallaudet University should have a deaf president. Agree or disagree?
    4. Mainstreaming is better than residential schools. Agree or disagree?

5. At this stage of the study, assessment of the signing on the tapes (i.e., ASL vs. other-than-ASL vs. signed English) is based on the judgment of the researchers. ASL and other-than-ASL were judged by a deaf native signer; signed English consistently included the use of voice and hence included input from the hearing researcher. The final analysis, however, will not be limited to the judgment of the researchers. The second part of the data

collection will consist of having native signers view each tape at least twice and indicate by pushing a button when switches away from ASL or back to ASL take place. These native-signer judges will be asked to characterize the language production between the switch points, and it is this production that will form the data base for the eventual description of contact signing. The entire methodology was first designed and employed bv Robert E. Johnson, Scott Liddell, Carol Erting, and Dave Knight in a pilot project entitled "Sign Language and Variation in Context," sponsored by the Gallaudet Research Institute. The data base will eventually include the signing production of twenty individuals: twelve white and eight black. The sign production of the black informants reflects their interaction with both black and white, and hearing and deaf, interviewers.

6. These thirty seconds of data per informant were transcribed by a deaf native signer. The transcription process was as follows: after a shift to contact signing was perceived by the transcriber, thirty seconds were allowed to elapse and then the next thirty seconds were transcribed. This transcription procedure was followed for all twelve informants.
7. The situation is somewhat analogous to the one described by Gumperz and Wilson (1971, 155) as convergence, where he claims that a single syntactic surface structure is the result of the extended contact between three languages. The outcome of the ASL-English situation is different, however, in that its basic syntactic structure is English. It should be noted that in spoken language contact, there could conceivably exist a simultaneous mixing of features within a single phonological segment, and it is this kind of mixing that probably accounts for certain kinds of accents. Our data are different, however, in that we see the simultaneous production of two complete segments (as opposed to features of segments) from two distinct phonologies, each segment retaining its integrity.

Index